effective management

2e

Chuck Williams

Texas Christian University

THOMSON

SOUTH-WESTERN™

Australia · Canada · Mexico · Singapore · Spain · United Kingdom · United States

THOMSON
SOUTH-WESTERN

Effective Management: A Multimedia Approach, 2e
Chuck Williams

VP/Editorial Director:
Jack W. Calhoun

VP/Editor-in-Chief:
Dave Shaut

Sr. Publisher:
Melissa Acuña

Executive Editor:
John Szilagyi

Developmental Editor:
Jamie Gleich Bryant

Marketing Manager:
Jacquelyn Carrillo

Production Editor:
Amy McGuire

Manager of Technology, Editorial:
Vicky True

Technology Project Editor:
Kristen Meere

Web Coordinator:
Karen Schaffer

Manufacturing Coordinator:
Doug Wilke

Production House:
Pre-Press Company, Inc.

Printer:
Quebecor World Dubuque
Dubuque, Iowa

Art Director:
Michelle Kunkler

Cover and Internal Designer:
Knapke Design, Cincinnati

Cover Image:
© D. Hurst / Alamy

Photography Manager:
Deanna Ettinger

Photo Researcher:
Sam Marshall

Printed in the United States of America
2 3 4 5 08 07 06 05

SE Pkg ISBN: 0-324-25911-5
SE text ISBN: 0-324-32063-9
IE Pkg ISBN: 0-324-31402-7
IE text ISBN: 0-324-31750-6

Library of Congress Control Number:
2004112867

For more information contact:
Thomson Higher Education
5191 Natorp Boulevard
Mason, Ohio, 45040
USA
Or you can visit our Internet site at:
http://www.swlearning.com

ASIA (including India)
Thomson Learning
5 Shenton Way
#01-01 UIC Building
Singapore 068808

CANADA
Thomson Nelson
1120 Birchmount Road
Toronto, Ontario
Canada M1K 5G4

AUSTRALIA/NEW ZEALAND
Thomson Learning Australia
102 Dodds Street
Southbank, Victoria 3006
Australia

UK/EUROPE/MIDDLE EAST/AFRICA
Thomson Learning
High Holborn House
50-51 Bedford Road
London WC1R 4LR
United Kingdom

LATIN AMERICA
Thomson Learning
Seneca, 53
Colonia Polanco
11560 Mexico
D.F.Mexico

SPAIN (includes Portugal)
Thomson Paraninfo
Calle Magallanes, 25
28015 Madrid, Spain

To my parents, Robert and Mary Williams

For your love, encouragement, and support, and for demonstrating the value of education, hard work, and persistence.

To Jenny, Ben, Rebecca, and Zack

The book is done. Let's play.

FEATURES GUIDE

Personal Productivity Tip

Management Decision

Management Team Decision

BRIEF CONTENTS

CONTENTS

Preface

Different Minds Learn in Different Ways

Everyone approaches learning differently. Some learn best listening to lectures, while others learn best reading and summarizing course material on their own. Others struggle unless concepts and ideas are visually illustrated in charts, models, or graphs, while others need first-hand experience to gain understanding. Of course, many of us learn best when we combine these different approaches.

In most introductory courses with most introductory textbooks, however, student learning boils down to *one* approach to learning: (1) read the textbook; (2) take class notes during lecture; (3) participate in a bit of class discussion; (4) do a few assignments; and then (5) "cram" the night before each exam. Because nearly all introductory courses and nearly all introductory textbooks use this approach, students who ***adapt*** to this approach to learning tend to do well in all of their introductory courses. Yet, a surprisingly large percentage of college students struggle when using this "standard" approach. Consequently, many students work very hard in their introductory courses, but don't do very well. (Ask around. You'll be surprised by the number of students who have much higher grades in upper-level courses than in introductory courses.)

If you think the Second Edition of ***Effective Management: A Multimedia Approach*** is just another "introductory textbook," with just one approach to learning, think again. Instead of asking students to adapt their learning styles to one way of learning, ***Effective Management: A Multimedia Approach*** provides a variety of different learning tools to let students create and combine learning methods ***uniquely*** suited to the way in which they learn—and not the other way around. By integrating a unique organizing system in each chapter (see *Chapter Outline and Numbering System, Learning Objectives*, and *Section Reviews* below) with the most extensive multimedia learning package available, we've put together a complete teaching and learning system designed to educate students with all kinds of learning needs in all types of classroom situations. The system is flexible enough to be used in traditional classes, in completely online classes, in combinations of those two, or in independent study. In short, the Second Edition of ***Effective Management: A Multimedia Approach*** taps into multiple technologies (text, graphics, video, audio, and animation) to teach management to students with all kinds of learning styles.

Using Your Book

With today's busy schedules, very few students have the opportunity to read a chapter from beginning to end in one sitting. Likewise, today's students grew up in an electronic, interactive, visual environment (hyperlinking, emailing, Internet messaging, cell phones, text messaging, online video gaming, and music videos), so they have shorter attention spans and are oriented to multitasking. Consequently, because of their schedules and cognitive styles, today's students take anywhere from two to five study sessions to completely read a chapter. Accordingly, a chapter outline and numbering system, learning objectives, and sections reviews are used to break chapters into small, self-contained sections that can be studied separately over multiple study sessions.

Chapter Outline. Accordingly, each chapter begins with a detailed chapter outline in which each major part in the chapter is broken out into numbered sections and subsections. For example, the outline for the first part of Chapter 3, on Ethics and Social Responsibility, looks like this:

What is Ethical and Unethical Workplace Behavior?

1 Ethics and the Nature of Management Jobs
2 Workplace Deviance
3 U.S. Sentencing Commission Guidelines
3.1 Who, What, and Why?
3.2 Determining the Punishment

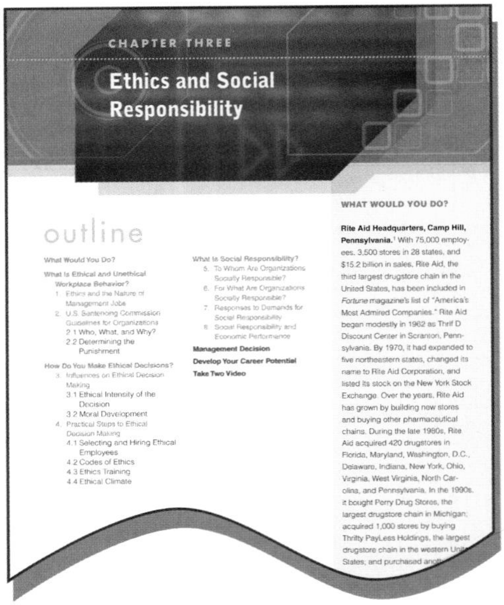
CHAPTER THREE

Ethics and Social Responsibility

outline

What Would You Do?

What Is Ethical and Unethical Workplace Behavior?
1. Ethics and the Nature of Management Jobs
2. U.S. Sentencing Commission Guidelines for Organizations
2.1 Who, What, and Why?
2.2 Determining the Punishment

How Do You Make Ethical Decisions?
3. Influences on Ethical Decision Making
3.1 Ethical Intensity of the Decision
3.2 Moral Development
4. Practical Steps to Ethical Decision Making
4.1 Selecting and Hiring Ethical Employees
4.2 Codes of Ethics
4.3 Ethics Training
4.4 Ethical Climate

What Is Social Responsibility?
5. To Whom Are Organizations Socially Responsible?
6. For What Are Organizations Socially Responsible?
7. Responses to Demands for Social Responsibility
8. Social Responsibility and Economic Performance

Management Decision

Develop Your Career Potential

Take Two Video

WHAT WOULD YOU DO?

Rite Aid Headquarters, Camp Hill, Pennsylvania.[1] With 75,000 employees, 3,500 stores in 28 states, and $15.2 billion in sales, Rite Aid, the third largest drugstore chain in the United States, has been included in *Fortune* magazine's list of "America's Most Admired Companies." Rite Aid began modestly in 1962 as Thrif D Discount Center in Scranton, Pennsylvania. By 1970, it had expanded to five northeastern states, changed its name to Rite Aid Corporation, and listed its stock on the New York Stock Exchange. Over the years, Rite Aid has grown by building new stores and buying other pharmaceutical chains. During the late 1980s, Rite Aid acquired 420 drugstores in Florida, Maryland, Washington, D.C., Delaware, Indiana, New York, Ohio, Virginia, West Virginia, North Carolina, and Pennsylvania. In the 1990s, it bought Perry Drug Stores, the largest drugstore chain in Michigan; acquired 1,000 stores by buying Thrifty PayLess Holdings, the largest drugstore chain in the western United States; and purchased anoth

Learning Objectives and Numbering System. The numbered information contained in the chapter outline is then repeated in the chapter as learning objectives (at the beginning of major parts of the chapter) and as numbered headings and subheadings (throughout the chapter) to help students remember precisely where they are in terms of the chapter outline.

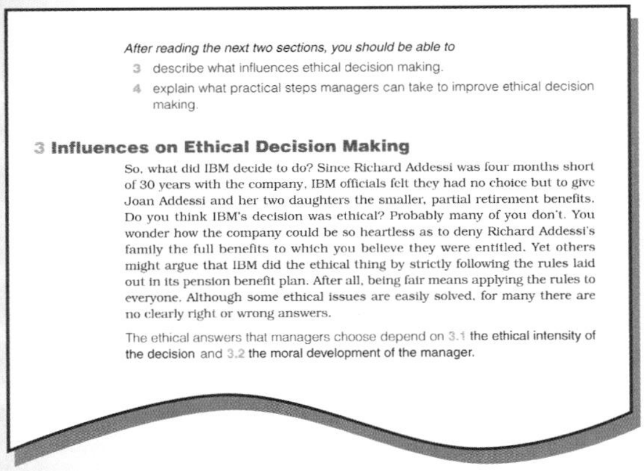
After reading the next two sections, you should be able to

3 describe what influences ethical decision making.
4 explain what practical steps managers can take to improve ethical decision making.

3 Influences on Ethical Decision Making

So, what did IBM decide to do? Since Richard Addessi was four months short of 30 years with the company, IBM officials felt they had no choice but to give Joan Addessi and her two daughters the smaller, partial retirement benefits. Do you think IBM's decision was ethical? Probably many of you don't. You wonder how the company could be so heartless as to deny Richard Addessi's family the full benefits to which you believe they were entitled. Yet others might argue that IBM did the ethical thing by strictly following the rules laid out in its pension benefit plan. After all, being fair means applying the rules to everyone. Although some ethical issues are easily solved, for many there are no clearly right or wrong answers.

The ethical answers that managers choose depend on 3.1 the ethical intensity of the decision and 3.2 the moral development of the manager.

Section Reviews. Finally, instead of a big summary at the end of the chapter, students will find a detailed review at the end of each section.

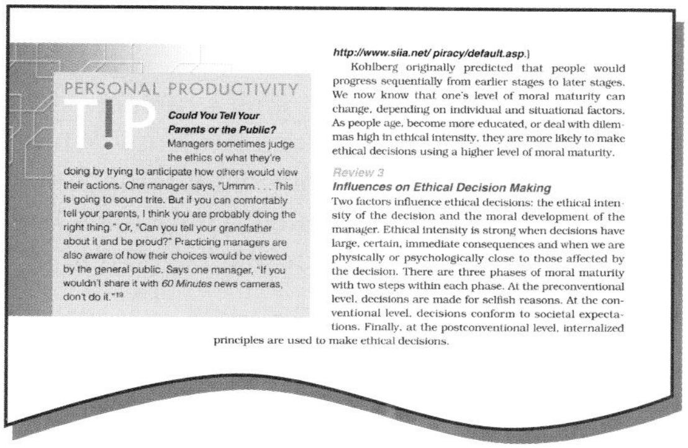
http://www.siia.net/ piracy/default.asp.)

PERSONAL PRODUCTIVITY TIP

Could You Tell Your Parents or the Public?

Managers sometimes judge the ethics of what they're doing by trying to anticipate how others would view their actions. One manager says, "Ummm . . . This is going to sound trite. But if you can comfortably tell your parents, I think you are probably doing the right thing." Or, "Can you tell your grandfather about it and be proud?" Practicing managers are also aware of how their choices would be viewed by the general public. Says one manager, "If you wouldn't share it with *60 Minutes* news cameras, don't do it."[19]

Kohlberg originally predicted that people would progress sequentially from earlier stages to later stages. We now know that one's level of moral maturity can change, depending on individual and situational factors. As people age, become more educated, or deal with dilemmas high in ethical intensity, they are more likely to make ethical decisions using a higher level of moral maturity.

Review 3

Influences on Ethical Decision Making

Two factors influence ethical decisions: the ethical intensity of the decision and the moral development of the manager. Ethical intensity is strong when decisions have large, certain, immediate consequences and when we are physically or psychologically close to those affected by the decision. There are three phases of moral maturity with two steps within each phase. At the preconventional level, decisions are made for selfish reasons. At the conventional level, decisions conform to societal expectations. Finally, at the postconventional level, internalized principles are used to make ethical decisions.

Together, the chapter outline, numbering system, learning objectives, section headings (which mark the beginning of a section), and section reviews (which mark the end of a section) allow students to break the chapter into small, self-contained sections that can be read in their entirety over multiple study sessions. This format not only makes it easier for busy students to effectively spread their studying across multiple days and times, but it also adapts textbook learning to evolving student learning styles and preferences.

Finally, all student resources and instructor resources are organized by section and subsection so that students and instructors always know where they are and what they're reviewing.

Using the Student Learning Resources That Come with Your Book

To give students access to a wide variety of learning opportunities, this book is supported by ***Effective Management Online*** (**http://em-online.swlearning.com**), the storehouse for all the student resources available with ***Effective Management,*** Second Edition. At ***EM-Online***, there are materials to help you learn by listening (audio), by reading (text), by seeing (graphics and video), by doing (learning modules and self-testing), and by combining these different approaches. Students pursuing independent study or long-distance learning can especially benefit from ***Effective Management Online*** because it helps them design a well-rounded study program to suit their particular needs.

The opening pages of each chapter list the learning resources that are available through Effective Management Online. You'll see the following icons, along with their descriptions.

"Experiencing Management," is an award-winning collection of online learning modules, created by R. Dennis Middlemist, that uses four study methods (Overview, important Terms, relevant Exercises, and illustrated Scenarios) to help students strengthen what they've learned about a variety of key topics, including ethics, strategy, communication, motivation, operations, and teams.

To help students tie this detailed learning simulation to the chapter content, a box identifies each section that has a supporting "Experiencing Management" module. You'll know there is a module for certain concepts when you see this box.

www.experiencing management.com

The ethical behaviors of managers and employees can have dramatic impacts on the way organizations are perceived by society. To learn more about ethical approaches and guidelines, visit our animated concept and activity site. Choose Ethics&Social_Responsi-bility from the "select a topic" pull-down menu, then Ethical Approaches from the "overview tab".

http://www.experiencingmanagement.com

This dynamic teaching tool engages students will all kinds of learning needs. As students work progressively through the four study methods, they are challenged to develop a deeper mastery of management concepts.

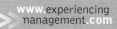

For students who learn best by listening, we have updated our audio study guide and now deliver it in streaming MP3 format. The audio study guide is similar to a condensed audio book organized by chapter. Each chapter starts with a short lecture covering the chapter material. After this review of the chapter's key topics, students listen to a presentation of an interesting management dilemma facing a well-known company. This supplemental "What Would You Do?" case is followed by its solution that tells students "What Really Happened," in other words, how the company solved (or didn't solve) its management problems. Discussing challenges at familiar companies like Ford, BMG Music, Kmart, Harley Davidson, Wal-Mart, Sun Microsystems, and Gap brings the concepts from the mini lecture to life.

Many of us are visual learners who learn better when we see things in action. This is increasingly true of today's students, who are immersed and have grown up in a highly stimulating, visually media-rich culture. ***Effective Management Online*** meets this growing need with two kinds of videos for students to review, "Biz Flix" and "Management Workplace."

People learn new material better and faster when they can relate it or connect it to something they already know or have experienced. That is why the first set of videos, "Biz Flix," presents students with scenes from well-known feature films, such as *The Bourne Identity, Mr. Baseball, The Breakfast Club, Lorenzo's Oil, Scent of a Woman, Bowfinger,* and *Casino*. Short clips from these and other films provide real-world examples of the management concepts students are learning. For example, in the *Bowfinger* clip, we learn the importance of job descriptions and structured interviews by watching Bobby Bowfinger (Steve Martin) interview Jiff Ramsey (Eddie Murphy) for the leading role in an action film, a job that also includes running errands.

The second set of videos puts management concepts in their business context by taking you directly to the "Management Workplace." These longer segments, typically 12 to 17 minutes in length, provide a more detailed look into companies like Le Meridien Hotel in Boston, Buffalo Zoo, Wahoo's Fish Taco restaurant chain in California, Student Advantage, and Timberland. For example, in the "Management Workplace" video about Timberland, you'll learn how companies are expanding their interpretation of social responsibility (beyond just recycling) by watching Timberland managers and employees prepare for the company's annual community service program, Servapalooza.

Used together, the "Biz Flix" and "Management Workplace" videos improve learning by showing students examples of management ideas or how managers are using those ideas to improve their companies. Students who have seen these ideas in action will find it easier to understand and remember them.

Effective Management Online also supports students who learn best when information is presented in a condensed format. Since many of today's students are used to receiving information in bullet-style lists, PowerPoint® slides that list the key points of each chapter are available at ***EM-Online***. Students can use these PowerPoint® slides as a prelude to a study session, as a starting point for taking notes in class, or for creating study lists for exams and quizzes.

No matter how hard we try to learn them, some topics just require additional review or instruction. Therefore, ***EM-Online*** has an "Author Insight" video for each chapter, in which author Chuck Williams addresses a frequently asked question (FAQ) from his students. "Author Insight" videos give you a one-on-one tutorial and an opportunity to see and hear Chuck explain a particular chapter concept with additional examples and in greater detail.

Nearly all students quiz themselves over course material when preparing for exams. The "Self-Test" area of ***Effective Management Online*** allows them to do this over and over. Each quiz in the "Self-Test" area of ***EM-Online*** contains approximately 50 true/false and multiple-choice questions covering all sections of the chapter. Feedback lets you know why you got the answer right (or wrong), and the section number references show you where to go in the textbook for additional review. The Self-Test area of ***EM-Online*** also provides "Exhibit Worksheets" that are based on the exhibits (i.e., charts, tables, and figures) in the book. Students who need (or want) visual reinforcement of management concepts can test their knowledge by filling in the blank "Exhibit Worksheets" and then checking their work against the actual exhibits in the text. Instructions for completion are included on each "Exhibit Worksheet." In addition, some chapters in ***EM-Online*** include a management scenario or a supplemental "What Would You Do–II?" case as part of the Self-Test area.

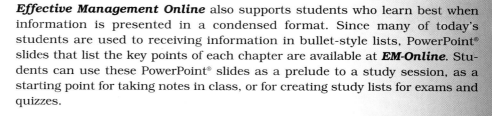

Putting it All Together

To help you see the full range of materials available in ***EM-Online*** and on the ***Effective Management*** Web site, we have put together the following grid.

effective management		CHAPTER 1	CHAPTER 2	CHAPTER 3	CHAPTER 4
EFFECTIVE MANAGEMENT ONLINE http://em-online.swlearning.com	EXPERIENCING MANAGEMENT URL	Experiencing Management modules begin in chapter 3, after you have been introduced to basic management concepts.	Experiencing Management modules begin in chapter 3	Ethics & Social Responsibility	• Planning & Strategic Processes • Organizational Control • Decision Making
	AUDIO STUDY GUIDE	Mini lecture reviews all the learning points in the chapter and concludes with a case on Ford Motor	Mini lecture reviews all the learning points in the chapter and concludes with a case on IBM	Mini lecture reviews all the learning points in the chapter and concludes with a case on BMG Records	Mini lecture reviews all the learning points in the chapter and concludes with a case on Avon
	VIDEO	Biz Flix is a scene from *8 Mile*. Management Workplace is a segment on Diversified Chemical	Biz Flix is a scene from *Backdraft*. Management Workplace is a segment on Ziba Design	Biz Flix is a scene from *Emperor's Club*. Management Workplace is a segment on Timberland	Biz Flix is a scene from *The Bourne Identity*. Management Workplace is a segment on Machado & Silvetti Associates, an architectural firm based in Boston
	PPT	12 slides with graphics provide an outline for this chapter	12 slides with graphics provide an outline for this chapter	12 slides with graphics provide an outline for this chapter	12 slides with graphics provide an outline for this chapter
	FAQ	Author Chuck Williams talks about dealing with problem subordinates	Chuck talks about the real constraints on managers	Chuck talks about why it's so hard to do the right thing	Chuck talks about the benefit of setting fewer goals and gives insight on how to avoid satisficing
	TEST	25 true/false questions, 25 multiple-choice questions, a management scenario, and 5 exhibit worksheets	25 true/false questions, 25 multiple-choice questions, a management scenario, and 3 exhibit worksheets	23 true/false questions, 22 multiple-choice questions, a management scenario, and 6 exhibit worksheets	31 true/false questions, 35 multiple-choice questions, and a "What Would You Do?" on Eli Lilly, plus 5 exhibit worksheets
BOOK WEB SITE http://williams.swlearning.com	QUIZ	Each chapter has a quiz of more than a dozen questions to help you review and test your understanding	Quiz to help you review and test your understanding	Quiz to help you review and test your understanding	Quiz to help you review and test your understanding
	NEWS	Current articles in the business and popular press available regularly on the site	Current articles in the business and popular press	Current articles in the business and popular press	Current articles in the business and popular press

effective management	CHAPTER 5	CHAPTER 6	CHAPTER 7	CHAPTER 8
EFFECTIVE MANAGEMENT ONLINE http://em-online.swlearning.com — EXPERIENCING MANAGEMENT URL	Communication	Organizational Control	International Management	Planning & Strategic Processes
AUDIO STUDY GUIDE	Mini lecture reviews all the learning points in the chapter and concludes with a case on Callaway	Mini lecture reviews all the learning points in the chapter and concludes with a case on Gap	Mini lecture reviews all the learning points in the chapter and concludes with a case on Wipro	Mini lecture reviews all the learning points in the chapter and concludes with a case on Kmart
VIDEO	Biz Flix is a scene from *Lorenzo's Oil*. Management Workplace is a segment on Cannondale	Biz Flix is a scene from *Scent of a Woman*. Management Workplace is a segment on Ping Golf	Biz Flix is a scene from *Mr. Baseball*. Management Workplace is a segment on Fallon Worldwide, a global advertising agency	Biz Flix is a scene from *Blue Crush*. Management Workplace is a segment on Caribou Coffee
PPT	12 slides with graphics provide an outline for this chapter	12 slides with graphics provide an outline for this chapter	12 slides with graphics provide an outline for this chapter	12 slides with graphics provide an outline for this chapter
FAQ	Chuck gives advice on how you can become comfortable with technology	Chuck talks about drawing the line on employee surveillance	Chuck addresses issues of thinking locally when you go global	Chuck talks about how important it is to determine what business you are in
TEST	22 true/false questions, 21 multiple-choice questions, a management scenario, and 2 exhibit worksheets	23 true/false questions, 25 multiple-choice questions, a management scenario, and 6 exhibit worksheets	22 true/false questions, 25 multiple-choice questions, a management scenario, and 1 exhibit worksheet	21 true/false questions, 21 multiple-choice questions, a management scenario, and 9 exhibit worksheets
BOOK WEB SITE http://williams.swlearning.com — QUIZ	Quiz to help you review and test your understanding	Quiz to help you review and test your understanding	Quiz to help you review and test your understanding	Quiz to help you review and test your understanding
NEWS	Current articles in the business and popular press	Current articles in the business and popular press	Current articles in the business and popular press	Current articles in the business and popular press

effective management		CHAPTER 9	CHAPTER 10	CHAPTER 11	CHAPTER 12
EFFECTIVE MANAGEMENT ONLINE http://em-online.swlearning.com	EXPERIENCING MANAGEMENT URL	Innovation & Change	Organizational Design	Teams	Human Resources
	AUDIO STUDY GUIDE	Mini lecture reviews all the learning points in the chapter and concludes with a case on Lego	Mini lecture reviews all the learning points in the chapter and concludes with a case on Oticon	Mini lecture reviews all the learning points in the chapter and concludes with a case on Harley-Davidson	Mini lecture reviews all the learning points in the chapter and concludes with a case on Wal-Mart
	VIDEO	Biz Flix is a scene from *Apollo 13*. Management Workplace is a segment on Peter Pan Bus Lines	Biz Flix is a scene from *The Paper*. Management Workplace is a segment on Student Advantage	Biz Flix is a scene from *Apollo 13* (different from Chapter 9). Management Workplace is a segment on Cannondale	Biz Flix is a scene from *Bowfinger*. Management Workplace is a segment on Gadabout Day Spa & Salon
	PPT	12 slides with graphics provide an outline for this chapter	12 slides with graphics provide an outline for this chapter	12 slides with graphics provide an outline for this chapter	12 slides with graphics provide an outline for this chapter
	FAQ	Chuck discusses how long it actually takes people to change	Chuck discusses boring jobs and why companies still create them	Chuck outlines how team charters can enhance team performance, whether for a student project or in the business world	Chuck gives you stark statistics about general mental ability in the U.S., which shows you why pre-employment tests are critical.
	TEST	22 true/false questions, 22 multiple-choice questions, a management scenario, and 7 exhibit worksheets	34 true/false questions, 22 multiple-choice questions, a management scenario, and 3 exhibit worksheets	24 true/false questions, 24 multiple-choice questions, a management scenario, and 7 exhibit worksheets	21 true/false questions, 18 multiple-choice questions, a management scenario, and 6 exhibit worksheets
BOOK WEB SITE http://williams.swlearning.com	QUIZ	Quiz to help you review and test your understanding	Quiz to help you review and test your understanding	Quiz to help you review and test your understanding	Quiz to help you review and test your understanding
	NEWS	Current articles in the business and popular press	Current articles in the business and popular press	Current articles in the business and popular press	Current articles in the business and popular press

effective management		CHAPTER 13	CHAPTER 14	CHAPTER 15	CHAPTER 16
EFFECTIVE MANAGEMENT ONLINE http://em-online.swlearning.com	EXPERIENCING MANAGEMENT URL	Operations Management	Motivation	Leadership	Communication
	AUDIO STUDY GUIDE	Mini lecture reviews all the learning points in the chapter and concludes with a case on Chrysler	Mini lecture reviews all the learning points in the chapter and concludes with a case on Sun Microsystems	Mini lecture reviews all the learning points in the chapter and concludes with a case on Unique Restaurants	Mini lecture reviews all the learning points in the chapter and concludes with a case on *Christian Science Monitor*
	VIDEO	Biz Flix is a scene from *Casino*. Management Workplace is a segment on Cannondale	Biz Flix is a scene from *For Love of the Game*. Management Workplace is a segment on Wahoo's Fish Tacos	Biz Flix is a scene from *U-571*. Management Workplace is a segment on Buffalo Zoo	Biz Flix is a scene from *Patch Adams*. Management Workplace is a segment on Le Meridien Hotel in Boston
	PPT	12 slides with graphics provide an outline for this chapter	12 slides with graphics provide an outline for this chapter	12 slides with graphics provide an outline for this chapter	12 slides with graphics provide an outline for this chapter
	FAQ	Chuck tells you how to practice service recovery and turn suddenly dissatisfied customers into satisfied customers once again	Chuck gives you suggestions on how to manage your time to meet your goals	Chuck reminds us that you don't have to be charismatic to be a good leader	Chuck talks about the importance of choosing the right medium for your message, and avoiding firing off angry emails
	TEST	22 true/false questions, 22 multiple-choice questions, a management scenario, and 3 exhibit worksheets	24 true/false questions, 25 multiple-choice questions, a management scenario, and 11 exhibit worksheets	24 true/false questions, 23 multiple-choice questions, a management scenario, and 5 exhibit worksheets	24 true/false questions, 22 multiple-choice questions, a management scenario, and 6 exhibit worksheets
BOOK WEB SITE http://williams.swlearning.com	QUIZ	Quiz to help you review and test your understanding	Quiz to help you review and test your understanding	Quiz to help you review and test your understanding	Quiz to help you review and test your understanding
	NEWS	Current articles in the business and popular press	Current articles in the business and popular press	Current articles in the business and popular press	Current articles in the business and popular press

Framework of the Text

Say "theory" to college students and they assume that you're talking about complex, arcane ideas and terms that have nothing to do with the "real world," but that need to be memorized for a test and can then be forgotten (at least until the final exam). But theories are simply good ideas. And good theories are simply good ideas that have been tested through rigorous scientific study and analysis.

Where textbooks go wrong is that they stop at theory and read like dictionaries. Or, they focus on theoretical issues related to research rather than practice. Good management theories (i.e., good ideas), however, needn't be complex, difficult to understand, or irrelevant. In fact, the late Rensis Likert, of the University of Michigan, once said that there is nothing as practical as a good theory.

So, to make sure that you're exposed to good ideas (i.e., good theories) that can provide you with practical, theory-driven advice and encourage you to put theory-driven knowledge into practice for yourself, each chapter in this book contains specific stories and examples that illustrate how managers are using management ideas in their organizations.

For example, one of the key issues in Global Management is successfully preparing employees for international assignments. In fact, the difficulty of adjusting to language, cultural, and social differences in another country is the primary reason that so many businesspersons fail in international assignments. Consequently, you'll read this passage in Chapter 7:

> *For example, while there have been recent disagreements among researchers about these numbers, it is probably safe to say that 5 to 20 percent of American expatriates sent abroad by their companies will return to the United States before they have successfully completed international assignments. Of those who do complete their international assignments, about one-third are judged by their companies to be no better than marginally effective.*

In other words, this is fairly standard, research-based information. You'll find it in most textbooks. Is it important for students to know this information? You bet! Is it likely that students will find this and the thousands of other pieces of theory and research-based facts throughout the book particularly compelling or interesting (and thus easier to learn)? Ah, there's the problem. But, what if we combined theory and research with specific, "real-world" stories and examples that illustrated good or poor use of those theories? For instance, the passage shown below is also in Chapter 7, where it follows the research-based information about the difficulty of adjusting to foreign cultures.

> *In his book Blunders in International Business, David Ricks tells the story of an American manager working in the South Pacific who, by hiring too many local workers from one native group, unknowingly upset the balance of power in the island's traditional status system. The islanders met on their own and quickly worked out a solution to the problem. After concluding their meeting at 3 A.M., they calmly went to his home to discuss their solution with him (time was not important in their culture). But, since the American didn't speak their language, and couldn't understand why they would show up in mass outside his home at 3 A.M., he called in the Marines, who were stationed nearby, to disperse what he thought was a "riot."*

After reading this passage, students have a vivid understanding of what can go wrong if people don't receive cultural and language training before traveling or moving to another country. Why does this help students learn? In this example, the first passage cites theory and research on the effectiveness of cross-cultural training, and the second brings the theory and research alive by indicating what can go wrong if you don't get that cross-cultural training.

In short, research and theory and stories and examples are important for effective learning. Therefore, this book contains hundreds of specific examples and stories to make management theories and ideas more interesting. So, to get more out of this book, read and understand the theories and theoretical ideas. Then read the stories or examples to learn how those ideas should or should not be used in practice. You'll find that both are current and up-to-date.

Text Features

Engaging Style. Chuck's compelling writing style conveys his passion for both management and teaching. The combination of theories and current stories helps students actually relate to how text topics play out in business settings.

What Would You Do? Opening vignettes set the scene by introducing business problems. Too often textbooks treat this as an opportunity for a long example of a management concept that the subsequent chapter will address. "What Would You Do?" does more than that: it creates an opportunity for students to confront the real issues that managers face before deciding on a course of action, handling a particular problem, or changing the direction of the company. Students are called upon to put themselves in the situation of the managers at companies like Home Depot, Google, McDonald's, Rite Aid, Microsoft, and IKEA.

Experiencing Management. As described above, margin icons throughout the book direct students to relevant "Experiencing Management" learning modules where appropriate. The intuitive software is built around tabs and drop-down menus and makes management concepts exciting and real.

What Really Works? Some studies show that two drinks a day increase life expectancy by decreasing your chances of having a heart attack. Other studies show that two drinks a day decrease your life expectancy. The results of both sets of studies are presented in very definitive terms, so the conflicting information confuses and frustrates ordinary people who just want to "eat right" and "live right." Managers also have trouble figuring out what works, based on the scientific research published in scholarly business journals. But thankfully, a research tool called meta-analysis, which is a study of studies, is helping management scholars understand how well their research supports management theories. The "What Really Works?" features in ***Effective Management***, Second Edition, present the results of various meta-analyses using an easy-to-understand statistic called the probability of success. Concrete study results presented in an accessible format give students the best estimate of what really works in the business world.

Doing the Right Thing. Numerous studies and well-known corporate scandals make clear that managerial ethics need some reinforcement. And, because managers set the standard for others in the workplace, unethical behavior and practices quickly spread when they don't do the right thing. Therefore, in the Second Edition, you'll find practical, useful advice to help you become a more ethical manager or businessperson by "Doing the Right Thing." A range of topics is explored throughout the book.

Personal Productivity Tips. To help students make the leap from management theory to management practice, you'll find a "Personal Productivity Tip" in each chapter. Located in the margins, "Personal Productivity Tips" are designed to give quick, practical management advice that can make an immediate difference.

Management Decision. These end-of-chapter assignments are tightly written and focus on a single management situation. Students must decide what to do and then answer several questions to explain their choices. For example, students must decide whether to mine employees' personal data to find out what might motivate them; what the company policy should be on cell phones; whether flexible work schedules are family friendly or discriminate against workers who don't have children; how to identify countries suitable for global expansion; and more.

Management Team Decision. From sports to school to work to civic involvement, working in teams is increasingly part of our experience. "Management Team Decision" exercises have been designed to give students the opportunity to work as management teams to solve various workplace dilemmas. For example, student teams will decide whether to accept sponsorship money from a company that runs counter to the corporate values; map a strategy for the United States Postal Service; brainstorm innovations for Nestlé Toll House; decide whether to implement a shopper card program at a chain of independent grocery stores; and more.

Develop Your Career Potential. "Develop Your Career Potential" assignments have one purpose: to help students develop their present and future capabilities as managers. What students learn through these assignments is not traditional "booklearning" based on memorization and regurgitation, but practical knowledge and skills that help managers perform their jobs better. Assignments include interviewing managers, dealing with the press, conducting a personal SWOT analysis, learning from failure, developing leadership skills, 360-degree feedback, and more.

Take Two Video. The textual component to the Biz Flix and Management Workplace videos prepares students for viewing. By directing students' attention to certain chapter topics before they watch the clip or segment, students are better able to connect what they are seeing with the management concepts they have been learning.

Instructor Resources

Instructor Resource CD-ROM. Key instructor ancillaries (Instructor Manual, Test Bank, and PowerPoint®) and supplemental cases are provided on an Instructor Resource CD-ROM. The Instructor Manual contains a pedagogy grid that outlines all the teaching resources you have for the chapter; class plans for lectures, group work, and videos; and teaching tips and solutions for all chapter assignments.

Each Test Bank chapter opens with a correlation grid to show the distribution of question types across learning objectives. True/false, multiple-choice, scenario, short answer, and essay questions allow instructors to test for comprehension and understanding, as well as to evaluate how well students can apply the concepts they learned in the chapter. The Test Bank contains over 2,400 questions.

A comprehensive set of PowerPoint® slides has been created for each chapter. For instructors wishing to integrate various media, we have also created a set of video PowerPoint® in which the "Biz Flix" videos are embedded in appropriate slides.

JoinIn™ on TurningPoint®. In addition to the PowerPoint® presentations described above, ***Effective Management*** offers a third, truly interactive PowerPoint® presentation through ***JoinIn***. Available on a separate CD-ROM, this unique presentation incorporates interactive audience response slides into the lecture slides for each chapter. Combined with your choice of several leading keypad systems, ***JoinIn*** enables your students to respond to multiple-choice questions, short polls, interactive exercises, and peer-review questions—all with a simple click on a hand-held device. You can take attendance, check student comprehension of difficult concepts, collect student demographics to better assess student needs, and even administer quizzes without collecting paper or grading. You can create additional interactive slides to customize your presentation to fit your particular course needs. This interactive tool is available to qualified college and university adopters. For more information, contact your Thomson representative or visit **http://turningpoint.thomsonlearningconnections.com**.

ExamView. A computerized version of the Test Bank (called ExamView) is available on your Instructor Resource CD-ROM and by special request. ExamView allows you to add or edit questions, instructions, and answers. You can create, edit, store, print, and otherwise customize all your quizzes, tests, and exams. The system is menu-driven, making it quick and easy to use.

Video. Both the "Biz Flix" and "Management Workplace" videos are available online, or on DVD. CDs containing the video clips can be made on demand using the online digitized files. The Instructor Manual includes detailed teaching notes so that you can incorporate video into your class in a meaningful way.

The Business & Company Resource Center. Put a complete business library at your fingertips with ***The Business & Company Resource Center*** (BCRC). The BCRC is a premier online business research tool that allows you to seamlessly search thousands of periodicals, journals, references, financial information, industry reports, company histories, and much more. The BCRC is a powerful and time-saving research tool for students—whether they are completing a case analysis, preparing for a presentation, creating a business plan, or writing a reaction paper. Instructors can use the BCRC like an online coursepack, quickly and easily assigning readings and research projects without the inconvenience of library reserves, permissions, and printed materials. BCRC filters out the 'junk' information students often find when searching the Internet, providing only the high quality, safe, and reliable news and information sources. Visit **http://bcrc.swlearning.com** to learn more about how this powerful electronic tool integrates a diverse collection of resources to reflect the natural research process and contact your local representative to learn how to include the Business & Company Resource Center with your text.

Acknowledgments

Let's face it, writing a textbook is a long and lonely process. It's surely the most difficult (and rewarding) project I've ever tackled. And, as I sat in front of my computer with a rough outline on the left side of my desk, a two-foot stack of journal articles on the floor, and a blank screen in front of me, it was easy at times to feel isolated. But, as I found out, a book like this doesn't get done without the help of many other talented people.

First, I'd like to thank the outstanding team of supplement authors: **Deborah Baker** (Texas Christian University), for the superb PowerPoint® slides; **Joseph Champoux** (University of New Mexico), for creating the engaging *Biz Flix* feature; **Jeff Gleich**, who revised the Instructor Manual and created the *Management Workplace* feature; and **Thomas K.** and **Betty Pritchett** (Kennesaw State University), for the outstanding Test Bank.

I'd like to thank the world-class team at Thomson South-Western for the outstanding support (and patience) they provided while I wrote this book; **John Szilagyi**, who heads the Management group at Thomson South-Western, was calm, collected, and continuously positive through the major ups and downs of this project; **Rob Bloom** and **Jacque Carrillo**, who were in charge of marketing the book, did an outstanding job of developing marketing themes and approaches; and **Amy McGuire**, who managed the production process, was consistently upbeat and positive with me when I deserved otherwise. Authors are prone to complain about their publishers. But that hasn't been my experience at all. Pure and simple, everyone at Thomson South-Western has been great to work with throughout the entire project. However, special thanks on this team goes to **Jamie Gleich Bryant**, of Bryant Editorial Development, who was my developmental editor and with whom I had the most contact while writing the book. Jamie worked with reviewers, edited the manuscript, managed the development of supplements, provided superb feedback and guidance at every stage of the book, and nudged and prodded me to write faster, make improvements, and maintain the high quality standards that were set when I began writing. Jamie's enthusiasm, professionalism, commitment, and attention to detail made me a better writer, made this a better book, and made me appreciate my good fortune to work with such an outstanding talent. Thanks, Jamie, and here's to many more editions.

I'd also like to thank the outstanding set of reviewers whose diligent and thoughtful comments helped shape the First Edition and whose rigorous feedback improved the Second Edition.

Ali Abu-Rahma
United States International University

William Acar
Kent State University

David C. Adams
Manhattanville College

Bruce R. Barringer
University of Central Florida

Gayle Baugh
University of West Florida

Katharine A. Bohley
University of Indianapolis

Michael Boyd
Owensboro Community College

Diane P. Caggiano
Fitchburg State College

Dan Cochran
Mississippi State University

Nicolette DeVille Christensen
Guilford College

Kathy Daruty
Pierce College

Jennifer Dose
University of Minnesota-Morris

Kimborough Ferrell
Spring Hill College

Charles R. Franz
University of Missouri-Columbia

Anu A. Gokhale
Illinois State University

Barry Allen Gold
Pace University

Susan C. Hanlon
University of Akron

Russell F. Hardy
New Mexico State University

David Hennessey
Mount Mercy College

Joseph Izzo
Alderson Broaddus College

Jim Jawahar
Illinois State University

Paul N. Keaton
University of Wisconsin-La Crosse

Ellen Ernst Kossek
Michigan State University

Donald R. Leavitt
Western Baptist College

Jerrold Leong
Oklahoma State University

Randy Lewis
Texas Christian University

Linda Livingstone
Baylor University

Thomas P. Loughman
Columbus State University

George Marron
Arizona State University

Lynda Martin
Oklahoma State University

David McCalman
Univeristy of Central Arkansas

Robert McGowan
University of Denver

Don Mosley
University of South Alabama

Sherry Moss
Florida International University

Stephanie Newport
Austin Peay State University

James S. O'Rourke, IV
University of Notre Dame

Rhonda S. Palladi
Georgia State University

David M. Porter, Jr.
UCLA

Robert Raspberry
Southern Methodist University

Amit Shah
Frostburg State University

Thomas Shaughnessy
Illinois Central College

James Smas
Kent State University

James O. Smith
East Carolina University

Gregory K. Stephens
Texas Christian University

Joseph Tagliaferre
Pennsylvania State University

Jennie Carter Thomas
Belmont University

James Thornton
Champlain College

Mary Jo Vaughan
Mercer University

James Whelan
Manhattan College

Finally, my family deserves the greatest thanks of all for their love, patience, and support. Writing a textbook is an enormous project with incredible stresses and pressures on authors as well as their loved ones. However, throughout this project, my wife, Jenny, was unwavering in her support of my writing. She listened patiently, encouraged me when I was discouraged, read and commented on most of what I wrote, gave me the time to write, and took wonderful care of me and our children during this long process. My children, Benjamin, Rebecca, and Zack, also deserve special thanks for their patience and for understanding why Dad was locked away at the computer for all of this time. While writing this book has been the most rewarding professional experience of my career, it pleases me to no end that my family is as excited as I am that it's done. So, to Jenny, Benjamin, Rebecca, and Zack. The book is done. Let's play.

Meet the Author Chuck Williams

Chuck Williams is an Associate Professor of Management at the M.J. Neeley School of Business at Texas Christian University, where he has also served as an Associate Dean and the Chair of the Management Department. He received his B.A. in Psychology from Valparaiso University, and specialized in the areas of Organizational Behavior, Human Resources, and Strategic Management while earning his M.B.A and Ph.D. in Business Administration from Michigan State University. Previously, he taught at Michigan State University and was on the faculty of Oklahoma State University.

His research interests include employee recruitment and turnover, performance appraisal, and employee training and goal-setting. Chuck has published research in the *Journal of Applied Psychology*, the *Academy of Management Journal*, *Human Resource Management Review*, *Personnel Psychology*, and the *Organizational Research Methods Journal*. He was a member of the *Journal of Management*'s Editorial Board, and serves as a reviewer for numerous other academic journals. He was also the webmaster for the Research Methods Division of the Academy of Management (**http://www.aom.pace.edu/rmd**). Chuck is also a co-recipient of the Society for Human Resource Management's Yoder-Heneman Research Award.

Chuck has consulted for a number of organizations: General Motors, IBM, JCPenney, Tandy Corporation, Trism Trucking, Central Bank and Trust, StuartBacon, the City of Fort Worth, the American Cancer Society, and others. He has taught in executive development programs at Oklahoma State University, The University of Oklahoma, and Texas Christian University.

Chuck teaches a number of different courses, but has been privileged to teach his favorite course, *Introduction to Management*, for nearly 20 years. His teaching philosophy is based on four principles: (1) courses should be engaging and interesting; (2) there's nothing as practical as a good theory; (3) students learn by doing; and (4) students learn when they are challenged. The undergraduate students at TCU's Neeley School of Business have named him instructor of the year. He has also been a recipient of TCU's Dean's Teaching Award.

Introduction to Management

PART ONE

PHOTOS: © TERRI MILLER; © AP TOPIC GALLERY / PR NEWS FOTO/MCDONALD'S; © TERRI MILLER

CHAPTER ONE

Management

outline

WHAT WOULD YOU DO?

Headquarters, Home Depot, Atlanta, Georgia.[1] Every year Americans spend nearly $315 billion upgrading and remodeling their homes. And 18 percent of that money is spent at Home Depot, the orange hardware and home remodeling warehouse that carries nearly everything professional contractors and home do-it-yourselfers need to do the job.

Ironically, like that old kitchen or bathroom, Home Depot itself needs extensive remodeling. In its first two decades, it was one of the most successful and fastest-growing retail chains of all time. In fact, 100 shares of Home Depot stock purchased in 1982 are worth $1.6 million today! As the company's new CEO, however, you will find it difficult to reproduce that success. When Home Depot started, its competition consisted of regional hardware store chains with small stores, high prices, and limited inventory. With its warehouse-sized stores, huge selection of products, and low prices, Home Depot quickly drove those smaller companies out of

student resources

Experiencing Management
Experiencing Management modules begin in chapter 3, after you have been introduced to basic management concepts.

Study Guide
Mini lecture reviews all the learning points in the chapter and concludes with a case on Ford Motor.

Take Two Video
Biz Flix is a scene from *8 Mile*. Management Workplace is a segment on Diversified Chemical.

PowerPoint®
12 slides with graphics provide an outline for this chapter.

Author Insights
Chuck talks about dealing with problem subordinates.

Self Test
25 true/false questions, 25 multiple-choice questions, a management scenario, and 5 exhibit worksheets

business. Today, though, it faces much tougher competition in Lowe's, which is number two in retail hardware store sales. Though Lowe's has roughly half as many stores as Home Depot, the gap is quickly narrowing. With lower costs, more attractive stores that appeal to women, a much wider selection of appliances, and more upscale products, Lowe's is increasing its market share while Home Depot's market share has begun shrinking for the very first time. Home Depot's overall sales are still increasing because it opens nearly 200 new stores per year, but it's experiencing a critical 10 percent sales drop at existing stores—what analysts call "same store sales."

In addition to declining same store sales, you've also discovered that Home Depot is a surprisingly inefficient company. You expected the company to have high tech computer systems that tracked every sale, every cost, and every item in inventory, but Home Depot has still been using pencils and clipboards to keep track of shipments. Likewise, frustrated vendors, which sold power tools, flooring, and other items to Home Depot, had to deal with nine purchasing departments instead of just one. Said one frustrated vendor, "It was like having nine different wives." And with purchasing spread across nine different departments, Home Depot had less negotiating leverage with vendors and missed out on sizable volume discounts. As a result, it paid tens of millions of dollars more than it should have for the products on its shelves. Even something as simple as evaluating store employees' performance was highly inefficient. Amazingly, over the years, various Home Depot store managers had developed 140 different performance appraisal forms, making it nearly impossible to compare employee performance from store to store.

Finally, employees say the company culture has changed for the worse since you took over, with company headquarters interfering with store managers' decisions. Employees revered founders Arthur Blank and Bernie Marcus. Marcus, who preceded you as CEO and now serves as company chairman, was much more entrepreneurial and encouraged his store managers to do what they felt was right for their stores. No wonder some long-time Home Depot employees begged the 72-year-old Marcus to return as CEO. Fortunately, Marcus hired you to replace him as CEO. And, for now, Marcus and the board of directors are firmly behind you. Of course, if you can't turn things around, you'll lose that endorsement—and your job. You order a late dinner, shut your door, and pull out your notepad. At the top of the page, you write "Back to Basics" and begin to list the key questions that you must answer if you're to turn Home Depot around: *How can I make things happen and get the results that the company and I want? What do we need to do to meet if not exceed the performance of our key competitor, Lowe's? How should we reorganize the way the company is run, that is, where decisions are made and who will do what jobs and tasks? Finally, what do I need to change to do a better job of leading, inspiring, and motivating the people at Home Depot?*

If you were the CEO of Home Depot, what would you do?

The management issues facing Home Depot are fundamental to any organization: How do we get things done, meet the competition, organize the company to be efficient and effective, and successfully lead those who work for us? Good management is basic to starting a business, growing a business, and maintaining a business once it has achieved some measure of success.

This chapter begins by defining management and discussing the functions of management. Next, we look at what managers do by examining the four kinds of managers and reviewing the various roles that managers play. Then we investigate what it takes to be a manager by reviewing management skills, what companies look for in their managers, the most serious mistakes managers make, and what it is like to make the tough transition from being a worker to being a manager. We finish this chapter by examining the competitive advantage that companies gain from good management. In other words, we end the chapter by learning how to establish a competitive advantage through people.

What Is Management?

Mistake #1. A high-level bank manager reduces a marketing manager to tears by angrily criticizing her in front of others for a mistake that wasn't hers.[2] Mistake #2. Facing hard times, Polaroid, the instant film company, files for Chapter 11 bankruptcy (which allows a company to reorganize and continue in business). It announces that it will stop paying its retirees' health-care benefits and that it will sell company assets so that it can pay its creditors. Then, astonishingly, the company asks a bankruptcy court to allow it to pay nearly *$19 million in bonuses* to encourage its top 45 managers to stay with the company![3] Ah, bad managers and bad management. Is it any wonder that companies pay management consultants nearly $150 billion a year for advice with basic management issues, like how to make things happen, how to beat the competition, how to manage large-scale projects and processes, and how to effectively lead people?[4] This textbook will help you understand some of the basic issues that management consultants help companies resolve (and it won't cost you billions of dollars).

After reading the next two sections, you should be able to

1 describe what management is.

2 explain the four functions of management.

1 Management Is . . .

Many of today's managers got their start welding on the factory floor, clearing dishes off tables, helping customers fit a suit, or wiping up a spill in aisle 3. Similarly, lots of you will start at the bottom and work your way up. There's no better way to get to know your competition, your customers, and your business. But whether you begin your career at the entry level or as a supervisor, your job is not to do the work, but to help others do their work. **Management** is getting work done through others. Pat Carrigan, a former elementary school principal who became a manager at a General Motors' car parts plant, says, "I've never made a part in my life, and I don't really have any plans to make one. That's not my job. My job is to create an environment where people who do make them can make them right, can make them right

management
getting work done through others

DOING THE RIGHT THING

At the U.S. Military Academy, there is a strict code of conduct: "A cadet will not lie, cheat or steal, nor tolerate those who do." The code is concise and unmistakable. Regrettably, there is no equivalent code for managers although there's no doubt they need one. Numerous studies and well-known corporate scandals have revealed the distressing state of managerial ethics in today's business world. Lying to stockholders about profits, cheating to win business, and stealing from companies have become all too common. And, because managers set the standard for others in the workplace, unethical behavior and practices quickly spread when they don't do the right thing. Therefore, in each chapter, you'll find practical, useful advice to help you become a more ethical manager by "Doing the Right Thing."

the first time, can make them at a competitive cost, and can do so with some sense of responsibility and pride in what they're doing. I don't have to know how to make a part to do any of those things."[5]

Pat Carrigan's description of managerial responsibilities indicates that managers also have to be concerned with efficiency and effectiveness in the work process. **Efficiency** is getting work done with a minimum of effort, expense, or waste.

By itself, efficiency is not enough to ensure success. Managers must also strive for **effectiveness**, which is accomplishing tasks that help fulfill organizational objectives, such as customer service and satisfaction. For instance, if you've ever walked into a Home Depot, the warehouse-sized hardware stores, you may have had trouble getting someone to help you.[6] To solve this problem, Home Depot started a program that makes more employees available by preventing them from running forklifts and stocking shelves between 8 A.M. and 8 P.M. Some managers even encourage Home Depot employees to wait in the "neutral zone" at the front of the store (between the cash registers and the store shelves) and to be aggressive in asking customers if they need help. The goal is to encourage orange-clad Home Depot employees to be efficient (by restocking shelves) and effective (by first helping customers).[7]

efficiency
getting work done with a minimum of effort, expense, or waste

effectiveness
accomplishing tasks that help fulfill organizational objectives

Review 1
Management Is . . .
Good management is working through others to accomplish tasks that help fulfill organizational objectives as efficiently as possible.

2 Management Functions

Traditionally, as shown in the left column of Exhibit 1.1, a manager's job has been described according to the classical functions of management: planning, controlling, organizing, and leading. **Planning** is determining organizational goals and a means for achieving them. **Controlling** is monitoring progress toward goal achievement and taking corrective action when progress isn't being made. **Organizing** is deciding where decisions will be made, who will do what jobs and tasks, and who will work for whom in the company. **Leading** is inspiring and motivating workers to work hard to achieve organizational goals.

Studies indicate that managers who perform these management functions well are better managers. The more time that chief executive officers (CEOs) spend planning, the more profitable their companies are.[8] Over a 25-year period, AT&T found that employees with better planning and decision-making skills were more likely to be promoted into management jobs, to be successful as managers, and to be promoted into upper levels of management.[9]

The evidence is clear. Managers serve their companies well when they plan, control, organize, and lead. Nevertheless, influential management authors such as Peter Drucker and Henry Mintzberg believe that the classical

planning
determining organizational goals and a means for achieving them

controlling
monitoring progress toward goal achievement and taking corrective action when needed

organizing
deciding where decisions will be made, who will do what jobs and tasks, and who will work for whom

leading
inspiring and motivating workers to work hard to achieve organizational goals

exhibit 1.1

Management Functions and Organization of the Textbook

Classical Management Functions	Updated Management Functions
	Part One: Introduction to Management
	Chapter 1, Management
	Chapter 2, Organizational Environments and Cultures
	Chapter 3, Ethics and Social Responsibility
	Part Two: Making Things Happen
Planning	Chapter 4, Planning and Decision Making
	Chapter 5, Managing Information
Controlling	Chapter 6, Control
	Part Three: Meeting the Competition
	Chapter 7, Global Management
	Chapter 8, Organizational Strategy
	Chapter 9, Innovation and Change
	Chapter 10, Designing Adaptive Organizations
	Part Four: Organizing People, Projects, and Processes
	Chapter 11, Managing Teams
Organizing	Chapter 12, Managing Human Resource Systems
	Chapter 13, Managing Service and Manufacturing Operations
	Part Five: Leading
	Chapter 14, Motivation
Leading	Chapter 15, Leadership
	Chapter 16, Managing Communication

management functions, first published by Henri Fayol in 1916, need updating.[10] Furthermore, companies with familiar names like General Electric, Dell Computer, General Motors, and Wal-Mart are facing tremendous changes and are asking—if not demanding—that managers change the way they perform these functions. According to *Fortune* magazine, these changes are embodied in the difference between "old" management and "new" management. Old-style managers think of themselves as the "manager" or the "boss." New-style managers think of themselves as sponsors, team leaders, or internal consul-

PERSONAL PRODUCTIVITY TIP

Do You Know How Efficient Your Business Is? Many managers fail to keep track of one of the most important outcomes in business: efficiency. Summit Polymers initially paid $280,000 for robots to paint and dry the dashboard vents in Toyota cars. When Toyota showed Summit how to do the same thing with $150 paint guns and much cheaper high-intensity lights, efficiency soared as Summit produced more with much less. Merck, a pharmaceutical company, improved efficiency by knocking five weeks off the time it takes to launch new products. If you want to improve your company's performance, keep close track of efficiency and productivity.[12]

tants. Old-style managers follow the chain of command (reporting to the boss, who reports to the next boss at a higher managerial level, and so on), while new-style managers work with anyone who can help them accomplish their goals. Old-style managers make decisions by themselves. New-style managers ask others to participate in decisions. Old-style managers keep proprietary company information confidential. New-style managers share that information with others. Old-style managers demand long hours. New-style managers demand results.[11]

Such changes don't make the classical managerial functions obsolete. Indeed, managers are still responsible for performing the functions of management. For example, consider this description of a new-style manager and the people she works *with* (not the people who work *for* her, which is "old" management). The managerial functions represented by each action have been inserted in brackets.

> Three years ago Ransom asked her workers at a 100-person plant in Fairfield, California, to redesign the plant's operations [*planning and organizing*]. As she watched, intervening only to answer the occasional question [*controlling*], a team of hourly workers established training programs, set work rules for absenteeism [*controlling*], and reorganized the once-traditional factory into five customer-focused business units [*organizing and leading*]. As the workers took over managerial work [*decision making, organizing, and leading*], Ransom used her increasing free time to attend to the needs of customers and suppliers [*planning and controlling*].[13]

As the terms in the brackets indicate, Ransom and the members of her work group still perform the classical management functions. They just do them differently than old-style managers.

To reconcile the "new" with the "old," this textbook is organized around four updated management functions (see the right column in Exhibit 1.1), which have evolved out of the classical functions:

- → Making things happen
- → Meeting the competition
- → Organizing people, projects, and processes
- → Leading

Note that the updated functions do not *replace* the classical functions of management; they *build* on them. For example, two of the three chapters under "Part 2: Making Things Happen" are classical management functions (planning and controlling). Furthermore, two of the four classical functions of management, organizing and leading, remain as part of the "new" management functions. Finally, a brand new management function, meeting the competition, has been added to reflect the importance of adapting and innovating to remain competitive in today's ever-changing and increasingly global marketplace.

WHAT REALLY WORKS

META-ANALYSIS

Some studies show that having two drinks a day increases life expectancy by decreasing your chances of having a heart attack. Yet other studies show that having two drinks a day shortens life expectancy. For years, we've "buttered" our morning toast with margarine instead of butter because it was supposed to be better for our health. Now, however, new studies show that the trans-fatty acids in margarine may be just as bad for our arteries as butter. Confusing scientific results like these frustrate ordinary people who want to "eat right" and "live right." They also make many people question just how useful most scientific research really is.

Managers also have trouble figuring out what works, based on the scientific research published in journals like the *Academy of Management Journal*, the *Academy of Management Review*, the *Strategic Management Journal*, the *Journal of Applied Psychology*, and *Administrative Science Quarterly*. *The Wall Street Journal* often quotes a management research article from one of these journals that says that total quality management is the best thing since sliced bread (without butter or margarine). Then, just six months later, *The Wall Street Journal* will quote a different article from the same journal that says that total quality management doesn't work. If management professors and researchers have trouble deciding what works and what doesn't, how can practicing managers know?

Thankfully, a research tool called **meta-analysis**, which is a study of studies, is helping management scholars understand how well their research supports management theories. Meta-analysis is also useful for practicing managers because it shows what works and the conditions under which management techniques may work better or worse in the "real world." Meta-analysis is based on the simple idea that if one study shows that a management technique doesn't work and another study shows that it does, an average of those results is probably the best estimate of how well that management practice works (or doesn't work). For example, medical researchers Richard Peto and Rory Collins averaged all of the different results from several hundred studies investigating the relationship between aspirin and heart attacks. Their analysis, based on more than 120,000 patients from numerous studies, showed that aspirin lowered the incidence of heart attacks by an average of 4 percent. Prior to this study, doctors prescribed aspirin as a preventive measure for only 38 percent of heart attack victims. Today, because of the meta-analysis results, doctors prescribe aspirin for 72 percent of heart attack victims.

Fortunately, you don't need a Ph.D. to understand the statistics reported in a meta-analysis. In fact, one primary advantage of meta-analysis over traditional significance tests is that you can convert meta-analysis statistics into intuitive numbers that anyone can easily understand.

Each meta-analysis reported in the "What Really Works?" sections of this textbook is accompanied by an easy-to-understand statistic called the *probability of success*. As its name suggests, the probability of success shows how often a management technique will work.

For example, meta-analyses suggest that the best predictor of a job applicant's on-the-job performance is a test of general mental ability. In other words, smarter people tend to be better workers. The average correlation (one of those often-misunderstood statistics) between scores on general mental ability tests and job performance is .60. However, very few people understand what a correlation of .60 means. What most managers want to know is how often they will hire the right person if they choose job applicants based on general mental ability test scores. Likewise, they want to know how much of a difference a cognitive ability test makes when hiring new workers. The probability of success may be high, but if the difference isn't really that large, is it worth a manager's time to have job applicants take a general mental ability test?

Well, our user-friendly statistics indicate that it's wise to have job applicants take a general mental ability test. In fact, the probability of success, shown in graphical form below, is 76 percent. This means that an employee hired on the basis of a good score on a general mental ability test stands a 76 percent chance of being a better performer than someone picked at random from the pool of all job applicants. So, chances are, you're going to be right much more often than wrong if you use a general mental ability test to make hiring decisions.[14]

General Mental Ability

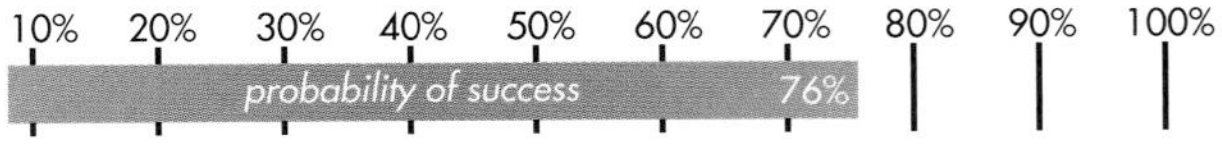

In summary, each "What Really Works?" section in this textbook is based on meta-analysis research, which provides the best scientific evidence that management professors and researchers have about what works and what doesn't work in management. We will use the easy-to-understand index known as the "probability of success" to indicate how well a management idea or strategy is likely to work in the workplace. Of course, no idea or technique works every time and in every circumstance. Nevertheless, the management ideas and strategies discussed in the "What Really Works?" sections can usually make a meaningful difference where you work. In today's competitive, fast-changing, global marketplace, few managers can afford to overlook proven management strategies like the ones discussed in "What Really Works?"

meta-analysis
a study of studies, a statistical approach that provides one of the best scientific estimates of how well management theories and practices work

Throughout this text, the major sections within each chapter are numbered using a single digit: 1, 2, 3, etc. The subsections are consecutively numbered, beginning with the major section number. For example, "2.1" marks the first subsection under the second major section. This numbering system should help you easily see the relationships among topics and follow the topic sequence. It will also help your instructor refer to specific topics during class discussion.

Now let's take a close look at each of the management functions: 2.1 making things happen; 2.2 meeting the competition; 2.3 organizing people, projects, and processes; and 2.4 leading.

2.1 Making Things Happen

For most of its existence, Gateway Computers had been a small, informally run organization. Rock music was played on the factory floor, and, reflecting its South Dakota roots, the company put its now-famous cow spots on the side of Gateway shipping boxes. But, struggling under tremendous growth, Gateway founder Ted Waitt hired Jeff Weitzen from AT&T to be Gateway's new CEO. At first, with Waitt remaining CEO and Weitzen apprenticing to replace him, Gateway thrived; sales increased by 37 percent, net income tripled, and the stock price quadrupled. However, after Waitt became chairman of the board and distanced himself from Gateway's day-to-day activities, the new CEO Weitzen began implementing changes and policies that he thought would lead to even more improvement. Although some things worked, many backfired in spectacular ways. Decision making slowed to a crawl. New policies, intended to standardize operating procedures, angered employees and lowered customer satisfaction. For example, any customer service representatives who spent more than 13 minutes on the phone with a customer lost their monthly bonus. As a result, service reps did almost anything, even lying or pretending the phone connection was bad, to get customers off the line.[15]

When Ted Waitt, pictured here, relinquished day-to-day control of Gateway, the new management team's policies and procedures not only angered employees but also reduced customer satisfaction. Waitt ultimately reclaimed control of the company and reinstated the old management team.

In his zeal to "professionalize" Gateway's management practices, new CEO Jeff Weitzen forgot that the most important management function is making things happen. To "make things happen," you must determine what you want to accomplish, plan how to achieve these goals, gather and manage the information needed to make good decisions, and control performance, so you can take corrective action if performance falls short. In his estimation, company founder Ted Waitt took corrective action when he and the board of directors fired Weitzen for his failure to make things happen at Gateway. In Chapters 4–6, you will learn more about how to make things happen.

2.2 Meeting the Competition

Before the advent of the electronic personal planner, most businesspeople used paper-based planners such as Day Timers and Filofax. Today, however, over 13 million people use Palm Pilots, made by Palm, Inc., to manage their calendars, contacts, and daily to-do lists. In fact, Palm, Inc. sold its first 1 million Palm Pilots in less than 18 months and raised $53.4 billion in the two days following its initial public offering of stock. One year after going public, however, the company's founders left to start a business to market a competing electronic personal planner with expansion slots for an MP3 player, a digital camera, and a cell phone. Combined with increased competition from industry heavyweights Microsoft, Hewlett-Packard, and Casio, Palm's market share fell rapidly from 83 percent to 63 percent.[16]

Palm's situation is not unique. With free trade agreements that promote international competition, shorter product development cycles, and barriers to entry falling in most industries, market followers will continue to topple market leaders as companies are exposed to more competition than ever in the next decade. Companies, such as Palm, Inc., that want to remain market leaders must consider the threat from international competitors, have a well-thought-out competitive strategy, be able to embrace change and foster new product and service ideas, and structure their organizations to quickly adapt to changing customers and competitors. Thus, "meeting the competition" is a critical management function in today's business world. In Chapters 7–10, you will learn some management skills for meeting the competition.

2.3 Organizing People, Projects, and Processes

When toy company Mattel acquired The Learning Company, which develops and markets games and educational software, it thought it was investing in the future of the toy industry. With a wide range of innovative and fun products, The Learning Company was poised to grow and return above-average profits for years to come. Yet, just three years after the purchase, The Learning Company was losing $1 million a day, which cost Mattel CEO Jill Barad her job. Besides out-of-control spending, a key problem was that the company was organized as seven different, autonomous work units that didn't share resources or even talk to each other. Said one manager, "We knew things were bad when we organized an executive staff meeting, and three of the unit's general managers had never met one another. And they had been working in the same complex."[17]

After establishing tight spending controls and reorganizing the seven units into three to promote resource sharing and get managers to work together, The Learning Company is again turning a profit. Mattel found out that even technology companies can't run well without considering basic people issues and work processes (how the work gets done). Therefore, our next management function is "organizing people, projects, and processes." You will learn about this management function in Chapters 11–13.

2.4 Leading

In these litigious times, managers are sued for sexual harassment, wrongful discharge, and discrimination. They are shot at, lampooned in the funny pages (*Dilbert* cartoons adorn cubicle and office walls in businesses all over the world), and, in general, not accorded the respect they once had. In periods of corporate layoffs, managers are often feared and disliked.

How is it, then, that amidst this general corporate distrust, before her death Mary Kay Ash, founder of Mary Kay cosmetics, and Herb Kelleher, founder, former CEO, and now chairman of Southwest Airlines, were not only respected but also loved by the people they led?[18] Gloria Mayfield, a former IBMer and a graduate of Harvard's MBA program, explained, "I didn't see much recognition at IBM. At Mary Kay, if you did well, you knew *for a fact* you'd get recognition. It wasn't influenced by politics." Mayfield continued, "Mary Kay called you her daughter and looked you dead in the eye. She made you feel you could do anything. She was sincerely concerned about your welfare."[19]

At Southwest Airlines, pilots pitch in at the boarding gate, ticket agents help with the luggage, and employees in general do whatever needs to be done to keep customers happy. These positive attitudes help Southwest achieve the highest productivity in the industry, flying two to three times as many passengers per employee as its competitors at a cost that is 25 to 40 percent cheaper.[20] Kelleher, a notorious jokester and storyteller, drew exceptional effort from his troops by putting people first and by making work fun. When he finished negotiating a new contract with Southwest's flight attendants, he celebrated by leading the cafeteria crowd of Southwest workers in cheers. He dressed up as Elvis, the Easter Bunny, and a boxer, complete with gloves and a silk robe, all to shape Southwest's corporate culture and win the hearts of his loyal work force.[21]

No one who has worked for an ordinary manager would ever deny the positive effects that inspirational leaders, such as Mary Kay and Herb Kelleher, brought to their companies. Thus, our last management function is "leading," which you will learn about in Chapters 14–16.

Review 2
Management Functions

Managerial jobs have traditionally been described according to the classical functions of management: planning, controlling, organizing, and leading. Although managers still perform these managerial functions, companies and the managers who run them have undergone tremendous changes in the last decade. Accordingly, this text incorporates the classical functions of management into broader, updated management functions: making things happen; meeting the competition; organizing people, projects, and processes; and leading.

What Do Managers Do?

Not all managerial jobs are the same. The demands and requirements placed on the CEO of Sony are significantly different from those placed on the manager of your local Wendy's restaurant.

After reading the next two sections, you should be able to

3 describe different kinds of managers.

4 explain the major roles and subroles that managers perform in their jobs.

3 Kinds of Managers

As shown in Exhibit 1.2, there are four kinds of managers, each with different jobs and responsibilities: 3.1 top managers, 3.2 middle managers, 3.3 first-line managers, and 3.4 team leaders.

3.1 Top Managers

top managers executives responsible for the overall direction of the organization

Top managers hold positions like chief executive officer (CEO), chief operating officer (COO), chief financial officer (CFO), and chief information officer (CIO), and are responsible for the overall direction of the organization. Top managers have the following responsibilities.[22] First, they are responsible for creating a context for change. In fact, the CEOs of Kmart, Vivendi, Lucent, Xerox, AT&T, Polaroid, and WorldCom were all fired within a year's time precisely because they had not moved fast enough to bring about significant changes in their companies. Indeed, in both Europe and the United States, nearly one-third of all CEOs are eventually fired because of their inability to successfully change their companies.[23] Creating a context for change includes forming a long-range vision or mission for the company. As one CEO said, "The CEO has to think about the future more than anyone."

Second, much more than used to be the case, top managers are responsible for developing employees' commitment to and ownership in the company's performance. For example, after losing billions of dollars following the September 11 terrorist attacks, United, U.S. Airways, Delta, and American Airlines laid off 31, 27, 23, and 21 percent of their workers, respectively.[24] By contrast, because of Southwest Airlines' commitment to its work force, not one employee was laid off.

Third, top managers are responsible for creating a positive organizational culture through language and action. Top managers impart company values, strategies, and lessons through what they do and say to others, both inside and outside the company. One CEO said, "I write memos to the board and our operating committee. I'm sure they get the impression I dash them off, but usually they've been drafted ten or twenty times. The bigger you get, the more your ability to communicate becomes important. So what I write, I write very carefully. I labor over it."[25]

Finally, top managers are responsible for monitoring their business environments. This means that top managers must closely monitor customer needs, competitors' moves, and long-term business, economic, and social trends.

3.2 Middle Managers

middle managers managers responsible for setting objectives consistent with top management's goals and for planning and implementing subunit strategies for achieving these objectives

Middle managers hold positions like plant manager, regional manager, or divisional manager. They are responsible for setting objectives consistent with top management's goals and planning and implementing subunit strategies for achieving those objectives.[26] One specific middle management responsibility is to plan and allocate resources to meet objectives. Another major responsibility is to coordinate and link groups, departments, and divisions within a company.

exhibit 1.2

Jobs and Responsibilities of Four Kinds of Managers

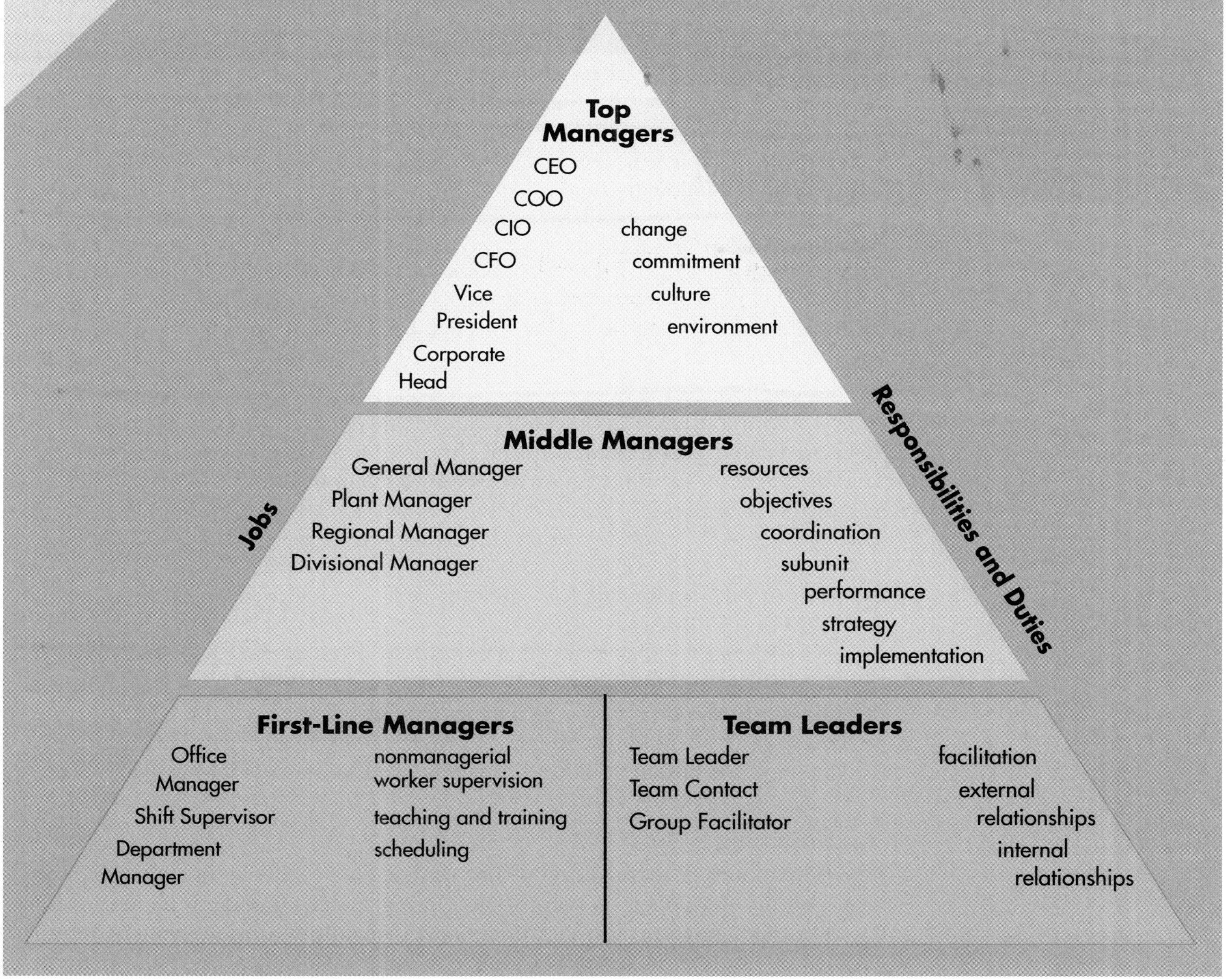

A third responsibility of middle management is to monitor and manage the performance of the subunits and individual managers who report to them. Jeremy Simon is director of engineering at Remington Associates, a small business that provides computer security services to other companies. Simon realized that productivity, which he measures by the percentage of available work hours each week that can be directly billed to clients (the higher that percentage, the better), was dropping. Each of his engineers wasted one-half day per week copying work orders, hand writing time sheets, and compiling the invoices needed to bill clients for their work. So Simon found new software that automatically completes those tasks for them. Now, each engineer has an extra four hours per week to complete billable work for clients. Not only are clients happier because their work gets done faster, but Simon is happier because his engineers' billable hours have increased from 70 percent to 82 percent per week.[27] Finally, middle managers are also responsible for implementing the changes or strategies generated by top managers.

3.3 First-Line Managers

first-line managers managers who train nonmanagerial employees and supervise their performance and who are directly responsible for producing the company's products or services

First-line managers hold positions like office manager, shift supervisor, or department manager. The primary responsibility of first-line managers is to manage the performance of entry-level employees, who are directly responsible for producing a company's goods and services. Thus, first-line managers are the only managers who don't supervise other managers. First-line managers have the following responsibilities.

First-line managers encourage, monitor, and reward the performance of their workers. For example, Jeff Dexheimer requires the waiters and waitresses he supervises at the upscale Melting Pot restaurant in St. Louis to memorize a complex menu and a 400-item wine list. To reduce turnover and keep his 65 employees motivated, Dexheimer gives out $25 nightly rewards for "best attitude" or for selling the most wine.[28]

First-line managers teach entry-level employees how to do their jobs. Because working as a telemarketing representative can be a high-stress, thankless job, most workers quit after three or four months. Since employee turnover is so high, supervisors at DialAmerica Marketing, a large telemarketing firm, are constantly training new employees. Before new employees begin their jobs, supervisors run them through intense role-plays with "angry customers." Supervisors also listen in on new representatives' phone calls to observe their performance so that the supervisor can correct their mistakes and teach them how to make sales.[29]

First-line managers also make detailed schedules and operating plans based on middle management's intermediate-range plans. In fact, in contrast to the long-term plans of top managers (three to five years out) and the intermediate plans of middle managers (6 to 18 months out), first-line managers engage in plans and actions that typically produce results within two weeks.[30]

3.4 Team Leaders

The fourth kind of manager is a team leader. This relatively new kind of management job developed as companies shifted to self-managing teams, which, by definition, have no formal supervisor. In traditional management hierarchies, first-line managers are responsible for the performance of nonmanagerial employees and have the authority to hire and fire workers, make job assignments, and control resources. Team leaders play a very different role, because in this new structure teams now perform nearly all of the functions performed by first-line managers under traditional hierarchies. Instead of directing individuals' work, **team leaders** facilitate team activities toward goal accomplishment. For example, Hewlett-Packard's ad for a team leader position says, "Job seeker must enjoy coaching, working with people, and bringing about improvement through hands-off guidance and leadership."[31] Team leaders who fail to understand this key difference often struggle in their roles. A team leader at Texas Instruments said, "I didn't buy into teams, partly because there was no clear plan on what I was supposed to do. . . . I never let the operators [team members] do any scheduling or any ordering of parts because that was mine. I figured as long as I had that, I had a job."[32]

team leaders managers responsible for facilitating team activities toward goal accomplishment

Team leaders fulfill the following responsibilities.[33] First, team leaders are responsible for facilitating team performance. This doesn't mean team leaders are responsible for team performance. They aren't. The team is. Team leaders help their team members plan and schedule work, learn to solve problems, and work effectively with each other. Management consultant Franklin Jonath says, "The idea is for the team leader to be at the service of the group. Through his or her actions, the leader should be able to show the others how to think about the work that they're doing in the context of their lives. It's a tall order, but the best teams have such leaders."[34]

Second, team leaders are responsible for managing external relationships. Team leaders act as the bridge or liaison between their teams and other teams, departments, and divisions in a company.

Third, team leaders are also responsible for internal team relationships. Getting along with others is much more important in team structures, because team members can't get work done without the help of their teammates. Jeanie Duck of the Boston Consulting Group says, "Too often, what happens is that teams get right down to work, and then some sort of conflict arises. It gets ugly and personal very fast, because everyone has been blindsided and no one knows what to do."[35] Because the entire team suffers when conflicts arise, it is critical for team leaders to know how to help team members resolve conflicts. For example, at XEL Communications, the team leader takes the fighting team members to a conference room and attempts to mediate the disagreement by hearing each side and encouraging the team members to agree to a practical solution.[36] In extreme cases at Hewlett-Packard, team leaders can dissolve the team and reassign all members to different teams.[37] Such instances are rare, however. You will learn more about teams in Chapter 11.

Review 3
Kinds of Managers

There are four different kinds of managers. Top managers are responsible for creating a context for change, developing attitudes of commitment and ownership, creating a positive organizational culture through words and actions, and monitoring their company's business environments. Middle managers are responsible for planning and allocating resources, coordinating and linking groups and departments, monitoring and managing the performance of subunits and managers, and implementing the changes or strategies generated by top managers. First-line managers are responsible for managing the performance of nonmanagerial employees, teaching direct reports how to do their jobs, and making detailed schedules and operating plans based on middle management's intermediate-range plans. Team leaders are responsible for facilitating team performance, managing external relationships, and facilitating internal team relationships.

4 Managerial Roles

So far, we have described managerial work by focusing on the functions of management (making things happen; meeting the competition; organizing people, projects, and processes; and leading), and by examining the four kinds of managerial jobs (top managers, middle managers, first-line managers, and team leaders). Although those are valid and accurate ways of categorizing managerial work, if you followed managers around as they perform their jobs, you probably would not use the terms *planning, organizing, leading,* and *controlling* to describe what they do.

In fact, that's exactly the conclusion that management researcher Henry Mintzberg came to when he followed five American CEOs around. Mintzberg spent a week "shadowing" each CEO and analyzing their mail, whom they talked to, and what they did. Mintzberg concluded that managers fulfill three major roles while performing their jobs:[38]

- interpersonal roles
- informational roles
- decisional roles

In other words, managers talk to people, gather and give information, and make decisions. Furthermore, as shown in Exhibit 1.3, these three major roles can be subdivided into 10 subroles. Let's examine each major role—4.1 interpersonal, 4.2 informational, and 4.3 decisional roles—and their 10 subroles.

4.1 Interpersonal Roles

More than anything else, management jobs are people-intensive. Estimates vary with the level of management, but most managers spend between two-thirds and four-fifths of their time in face-to-face communication with others.[39] If you're a loner, or if you consider dealing with people a "pain," then you may not be cut out for management work. In fulfilling the interpersonal role of management, managers perform three interpersonal subroles: figurehead, leader, and liaison.

figurehead role the interpersonal role managers play when they perform ceremonial duties

In the **figurehead role**, managers perform ceremonial duties like greeting company visitors, making opening remarks when a new facility opens, or representing the company at a community luncheon to support local charities. When Japanese-based Kikkoman Corporation opened its first soy sauce manufacturing plant in Europe, its CEO gave a speech pledging corporate donations to a local environmental conservation and water quality project.[40]

leader role the interpersonal role managers play when they motivate and encourage workers to accomplish organizational objectives

In the **leader role**, managers motivate and encourage workers to accomplish organizational objectives. At CDW (Computer Discount Warehouse), new CEO John Edwardson promised CDW's 2,750 workers that he would shave his head if the company met its third quarter goals. When the third quarter goals had been met, Edwardson had his head shaved to the harmonic sounds of a barbershop quartet.[41]

liaison role the interpersonal role managers play when they deal with people outside their units

In the **liaison role**, managers deal with people outside their units. Studies consistently indicate that managers spend as much time with "outsiders" as they do with their own subordinates and their own bosses.

4.2 Informational Roles

Although managers spend most of their time in face-to-face contact with others, most of that time is spent obtaining and sharing information. Indeed, Mintzberg found that the managers in his study spent 40 percent of their time giving and getting information from others. In this regard, management can be viewed as processing information, gathering information by scanning the business environment and listening to others in face-to-face conversations, and then sharing that information with people inside and outside the company. Mintzberg described three informational subroles: monitor, disseminator, and spokesperson.

monitor role the informational role managers play when they scan their environment for information

In the **monitor role**, managers scan their environment for information, actively contact others for information, and, because of their personal contacts, receive a great deal of unsolicited information. Besides receiving firsthand in-

exhibit 1.3

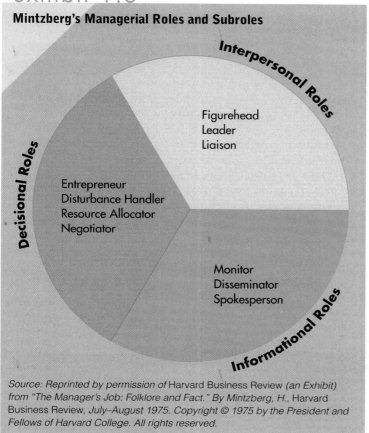

Mintzberg's Managerial Roles and Subroles

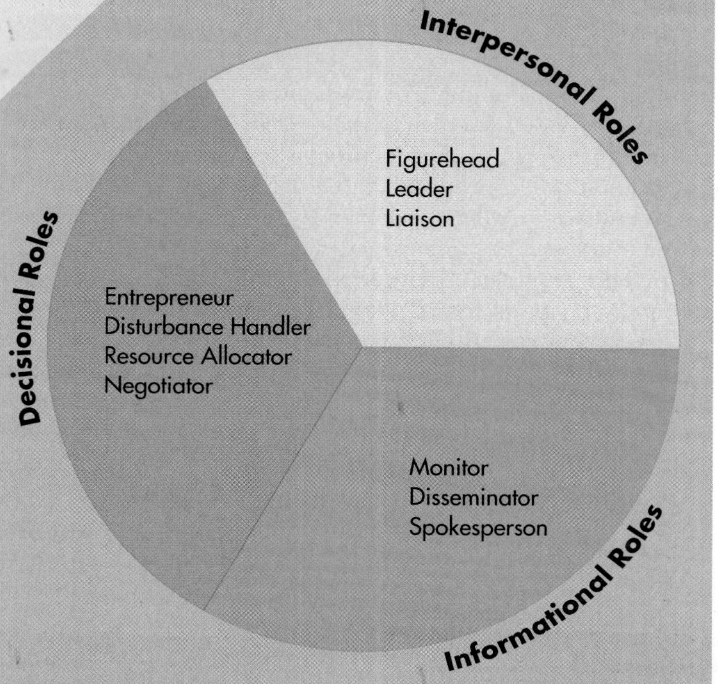

Source: Reprinted by permission of Harvard Business Review *(an Exhibit) from "The Manager's Job: Folklore and Fact." By Mintzberg, H.,* Harvard Business Review, *July–August 1975.*

formation, managers monitor their environment by reading local newspapers and *The Wall Street Journal* to keep track of customers, competitors, and technological changes that may affect their businesses. Now, managers can also take advantage of electronic monitoring and distribution services that track the news wires (Associated Press, Reuters, etc.) for stories related to their businesses. These services deliver customized electronic newspapers that include only stories on topics the managers specify.

Because of their numerous personal contacts and their access to subordinates, managers are often hubs for distribution of critical information. In the **disseminator role**, managers share the information they have collected with their subordinates and others in the company. Although there will never be a complete substitute for face-to-face dissemination of information, the primary methods of communication in large companies like Boeing and Cisco Systems are email and voice mail. Phil Condit, Boeing's CEO, sends email to 160,000 Boeing employees, sharing information with them and asking for feedback. John Chambers, Cisco's CEO, says that 90 percent of his communication with employees is through email and voice mail. Says Chambers, "If you don't have the ability to interface with customers, employees, and suppliers, you can't manage your business."[42]

disseminator role
the informational role managers play when they share information with others in their departments or companies

spokesperson role
the informational role managers play when they share information with people outside their departments or companies

In contrast to the disseminator role, in which managers distribute information to employees inside the company, in the **spokesperson role**, managers share information with people outside their departments and companies. One of the most common ways CEOs serve as spokespeople for their companies is at annual meetings with company shareholders or the board of directors. For example, at a recent Sears annual shareholder meeting, CEO Alan Lacy told investors that Sears would try to increase sales through specialty store formats, such as a 55,000-square-foot hardware store (based on Sears tools, which come with a lifetime warranty); the *Great Indoors*, which sells furniture and home decorating ideas; and *Brand Central*, which will basically offer electronic equipment and appliances.[43]

4.3 Decisional Roles

According to Mintzberg, the time managers spend obtaining and sharing information is not an end in itself. The time spent talking to and obtaining and sharing information with people inside and outside the company is useful to managers because it helps them make good decisions. According to Mintzberg, managers engage in four decisional subroles: entrepreneur, disturbance handler, resource allocator, and negotiator.

entrepreneur role
the decisional role managers play when they adapt themselves, their subordinates, and their units to incremental change

In the **entrepreneur role**, managers adapt themselves, their subordinates, and their units to incremental change.

disturbance handler role
the decisional role managers play when they respond to severe problems that demand immediate action

By contrast, in the **disturbance handler role**, managers respond to pressures and problems so severe that they demand immediate attention and action. Managers often play the role of disturbance handler when the board of a failing company hires a new CEO, who is charged with turning the company around. When *Reader's Digest*'s net income fell from $264 million to $80.6 million in one year and circulation dropped to a three-decade low of 12.5 million readers (down from 18 million), new CEO Thomas Ryder laid off 17 percent of employees, cut retirement benefits, outsourced direct marketing functions, and sold off a $100 million art collection accumulated by company founders and displayed at company headquarters. Today, new mail campaigns are developed in 13 weeks and revenues and net income have begun to rise.[44]

resource allocator role
the decisional role managers play when they decide who gets what resources

In the **resource allocator role**, managers decide who will get what resources and how many resources they get. For instance, in hopes of increasing stagnant sales and market share, former Coca-Cola CEO Doug Daft added an extra $300 million to Coke's $7.7 billion marketing budget.[45] After already cutting its costs by $240 per car, Ford announced that it wanted to cut costs by a total of $700 per car over the next three years. Accordingly, it reassigned another 200 engineers (now 1,200 in total) to achieving that goal.[46] In these instances, top managers acted as resource allocators by changing budgets (Coke) and reassigning human resources (Ford).

negotiator role
the decisional role managers play when they negotiate schedules, projects, goals, outcomes, resources, and employee raises

In the **negotiator role**, managers negotiate schedules, projects, goals, outcomes, resources, and employee raises. For example, every three years the United Auto Workers labor union renegotiates its labor contract with the "Big Three" auto companies, Ford, DaimlerChrysler, and General Motors.

Review 4

Managerial Roles

Managers perform interpersonal, informational, and decisional roles in their jobs. In fulfilling the interpersonal role, managers act as figureheads by performing ceremonial duties, as leaders by motivating and encouraging workers, and as liaisons by dealing with people outside their units. In performing their informational role, managers act as monitors by scanning their environment for information, as disseminators by sharing information with others in the company, and as spokespeople by sharing information with people outside their departments or companies. In fulfilling decisional roles, managers act as entrepreneurs by adapting their units to incremental change, as disturbance handlers by responding to larger problems that demand immediate action, as resource allocators by deciding resource recipients and amounts, and as negotiators by bargaining with others about schedules, projects, goals, outcomes, and resources.

What Does It Take to Be a Manager?

I didn't have the slightest idea what my job was. I walked in giggling and laughing because I had been promoted and had no idea what principles or style to be guided by. After the first day, I felt like I had run into a brick wall. (Sales Representative #1)

> Suddenly, I found myself saying, boy, I can't be responsible for getting all that revenue. I don't have the time. Suddenly you've got to go from [taking care of] yourself and say now I'm the manager, and what does a manager do? It takes a while thinking about it for it to really hit you . . . a manager gets things done through other people. That's a very, very hard transition to make.[47] (Sales Representative #2)

The above statements were made by two star sales representatives, who, on the basis of their superior performance, were promoted to the position of sales manager. At first they did not feel confident about their ability to do their jobs as managers. They suddenly realized that the knowledge, skills, and abilities that led to success early in their careers would not necessarily help them succeed as managers. As representatives, they were responsible only for managing their own performance. But as managers, they were now directly responsible for supervising all of the representatives in their sales territories. Furthermore, they were now directly accountable for whether those sales representatives achieved their sales goals.

If performance in nonmanagerial jobs doesn't necessarily prepare you for a managerial job, then what does it take to be a manager?

After reading the next three sections, you should be able to

5 explain what companies look for in managers.

6 discuss the top mistakes that managers make in their jobs.

7 describe the transition that employees go through when they are promoted to management.

5 What Companies Look for in Managers

Broadly speaking, when companies look for employees who would be good managers, they look for individuals who have technical skills, human skills, conceptual skills, and the motivation to manage.[48] Exhibit 1.4 shows the relative importance of these four skills to the jobs of team leaders, first-line managers, middle managers, and top managers.

technical skills the ability to apply the specialized procedures, techniques, and knowledge required to get the job done

Technical skills are the ability to apply the specialized procedures, techniques, and knowledge required to get the job done. For the sales managers described above, technical skills include the ability to find new sales prospects and close the sale.

Technical skills are most important for lower-level managers and team leaders because they supervise the workers who produce products or serve customers. Team leaders and first-line managers need technical knowledge and skills to train new employees and help employees solve problems. Technical knowledge and skills are also needed to troubleshoot problems that employees can't handle. Technical skills become less important as managers rise through the managerial ranks, but they are still important. Indeed, Bill Gates, founder and chairman of Microsoft Corporation, spends roughly 40 percent of his time dealing with technical issues related to the development of Microsoft's software products.[49]

human skill the ability to work well with others

Human skill is the ability to work well with others. Managers with people skills work effectively within groups, encourage others to express their thoughts and feelings, are sensitive to others' needs and viewpoints, and are good listeners and communicators. Human skills are equally important at all

exhibit 1.4

Relative Importance of Managerial Skills to Different Managerial Jobs

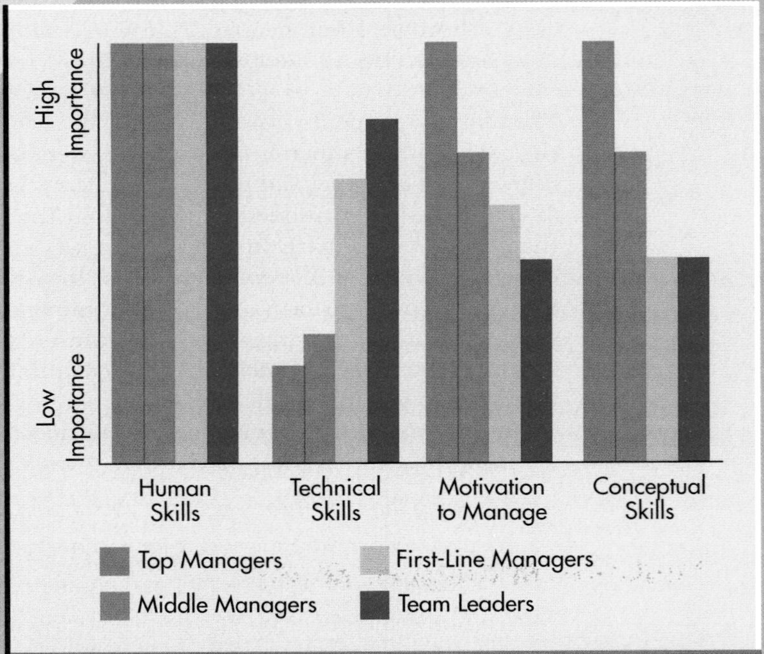

levels of management, from first-line supervisors to CEOs. However, because lower-level managers spend much of their time solving technical problems, upper-level managers may actually spend more time dealing directly with people. On average, first-line managers spend 57 percent of their time with people, but that percentage increases to 63 percent for middle managers and 78 percent for top managers.[50]

conceptual skill
the ability to see the organization as a whole, how the different parts affect each other, and how the company fits into or is affected by its environment

Conceptual skill is the ability to see the organization as whole, how the different parts of the company affect each other, and how the company fits into or is affected by its external environment, such as the local community, social and economic forces, customers, and the competition. Good managers have to be able to recognize, understand, and reconcile multiple complex problems and perspectives. In other words, managers have to be smart! In fact, intelligence makes so much difference for managerial performance that managers with above-average intelligence typically outperform managers of average intelligence by approximately 48 percent.[51] Clearly, companies need to be careful to promote smart workers into management. Conceptual skill increases in importance as managers rise through the management hierarchy.

motivation to manage
an assessment of how enthusiastic employees are about managing the work of others

Good management involves much more than intelligence, however. For example, making the department genius a manager can be disastrous if that genius lacks technical skills, human skills, or one other factor known as the motivation to manage. **Motivation to manage** is an assessment of how motivated employees are to interact with superiors, participate in competitive situations, behave assertively toward others, tell others what to do, reward good behavior and punish poor behavior, perform actions that are highly visible to others, and handle and organize administrative tasks. Managers typically have a stronger motivation to manage than their subordinates, and managers at higher levels usually have stronger motivation to manage than managers at lower levels. Furthermore, managers with stronger motivation to manage are promoted faster, are rated by their employees as better managers, and earn more money than managers with a weak motivation to manage.[52]

Review 5

What Companies Look for in Managers

Companies do not want one-dimensional managers. They want managers with a balance of skills. They want managers who know their stuff (technical skills), are equally comfortable working with blue-collar and white-collar employees (human skills), are able to assess the complexities of today's competitive marketplace and position their companies for success (conceptual skills), and want to assume positions of leadership and power (motivation to manage). Technical skills are most important for lower-level managers, human skills are equally important at all levels of management, and conceptual skills and motivation to manage increase in importance as managers rise through the managerial ranks.

6 Mistakes Managers Make

Another way to understand what it takes to be a manager is to look at the mistakes managers make. In other words, we can learn just as much from what managers shouldn't do as from what they should do. Exhibit 1.5 on the next page lists the top 10 mistakes managers make.

Several studies of U.S. and British managers have compared "arrivers," or managers who made it all the way to the top of their companies, with "derailers," managers who were successful early in their careers but were knocked off the fast track by the time they reached middle to upper levels of management.[53] The researchers found that there were only a few differences between arrivers and derailers. For the most part, both groups were talented and both groups had weaknesses. But what distinguished derailers from arrivers was that derailers possessed two or more "fatal flaws" with respect to the way that they managed people! Although arrivers were by no means perfect, they usually had no more than one fatal flaw or had found ways to minimize the effects of their flaws on the people with whom they worked.

The number one mistake made by derailers was that they were insensitive to others by virtue of their abrasive, intimidating, and bullying management style. The authors of one study described a manager who walked into his subordinate's office and interrupted a meeting by saying, "I need to see you." When the subordinate tried to explain that he was not available because he was in the middle of a meeting, the manager barked, "I don't give a damn. I said I wanted to see you now."[54] Not surprisingly, only 25 percent of derailers were rated by others as being good with people, compared to 75 percent of arrivers.

The second mistake was that derailers were often cold, aloof, or arrogant. Although this sounds like insensitivity to others, it has more to do with derailed managers being so smart, so expert in their areas of knowledge, that they treated others with contempt because they weren't experts, too.

exhibit 1.5

Top Ten Mistakes That Managers Make

1.	Insensitive to others: abrasive, intimidating, bullying style.
2.	Cold, aloof, arrogant.
3.	Betrayal of trust.
4.	Overly ambitious: thinking of next job, playing politics.
5.	Specific performance problems with the business.
6.	Overmanaging: unable to delegate or build a team.
7.	Unable to staff effectively.
8.	Unable to think strategically.
9.	Unable to adapt to boss with different style.
10.	Overdependent on advocate or mentor.

Source: M. W. McCall, Jr. & M. M. Lombardo, "What Makes a Top Executive?" Psychology Today, *February 1983, 26–31.*

The third and fourth mistakes made by the derailers, betraying a trust and being overly ambitious, reflect a lack of concern for coworkers and subordinates. Betraying a trust doesn't mean being dishonest. Instead, it means making others look bad by not doing what you said you would do when you said you would do it. That mistake, in itself, is not fatal because managers and their workers aren't machines. Tasks go undone in every company every single business day. There's always too much to do and not enough time, people, money, or resources to do it. The fatal betrayal of trust is failing to inform others when things will not be done on time. This failure to admit mistakes, quickly inform others of the mistakes, take responsibility for the mistakes, and then fix them without blaming others clearly distinguished the behavior of derailers from arrivers.

The fourth mistake, as mentioned above, was being overly political and ambitious. Managers who always have their eye on their next job rarely do more than establish superficial relationships with peers and coworkers. In their haste to gain credit for successes that would be noticed by upper management, they make the fatal mistake of treating people as though they don't matter.

The fatal mistakes of being unable to delegate, build a team, and staff effectively indicate that many derailed managers were unable to make the most basic transition to managerial work: to quit being hands-on doers and get work done through others. Two things go wrong when managers make these mistakes. First, when managers meddle in decisions that their subordinates should be making—when they can't stop being doers—they alienate the people who work for them. Second, because they are trying to do their subordinates' jobs in addition to their own, managers who fail to delegate will not have enough time to do much of anything well. For example, before Neil Rudenstine became president of Harvard University, his management style had always been to take on more and more work himself. When he became a university president and the demands on him increased, he responded by working even longer hours, usually 12 to 14 hours a day. For example, on the day before Thanksgiving, normally a quiet day on college campuses as students travel home to be with their families, Rudenstine began his day with an 8 A.M. meeting with several deans, had lunch with visiting Russian dignitaries, attended a faculty meeting, and finished his day with a dormitory dinner and reception for students. He got home at 8:30 P.M., more than 12 hours after the start of his day. Although university presidents normally put in long hours, Rudenstine made it even tougher on himself by failing to delegate work to his associates. Figuring out how to solve the shortage of parking spaces on campus and arranging to have contractors fix leaky roofs are not good uses of a university president's time. Indeed, the combination of long hours and Rudenstine's inability to delegate led to mental and physical exhaustion and a physician-mandated leave of absence from his job as Harvard University president.[55]

Review 6

Mistakes Managers Make

Another way to understand what it takes to be a manager is to look at the top mistakes managers make. Five of the most important mistakes made by managers are being abrasive and intimidating; being cold, aloof, or arrogant; betraying trust; being overly ambitious; and failing to build a team and then delegate to that team.

7 The Transition to Management: The First Year

In her book *Becoming a Manager: Master of a New Identity*, Harvard Business School professor Linda Hill followed the development of 19 people in their first year as managers. Two overall themes emerged from her study. First, becoming a manager produced a profound psychological transition that changed the way these managers viewed themselves and others. Second, the only way to really learn how to manage is to be a manager. As shown in Exhibit 1.6, the evolution of the managers' thoughts, expectations, and realities over the course of their first year in management reveals the magnitude of the changes they experienced.

Initially, the managers in Hill's study believed that their job was to exercise formal authority and to manage tasks—basically being the boss, telling others what to do, making decisions, and getting things done. One manager said, "Being the manager means running my own office, using my ideas and thoughts." Another said, "It's [the office] my baby. It's my job to make sure it works." In fact, most of the new managers were attracted to management positions because they wanted to be "in charge." Surprisingly, the new managers did not believe that their job was to manage people. The only two aspects of people management mentioned by the new managers were hiring and firing.

After six months, most of the new managers had concluded that their initial expectations about managerial work were wrong. Management wasn't being "the boss." It wasn't just about making decisions and telling others what to do. The first surprise was the fast pace and heavy workload involved in being a manager. Said one manager, "This job is much harder than you think. It is

exhibit 1.6

The Transition to Management: Initial Expectations, after Six Months, and after a Year

MANAGERS' INITIAL EXPECTATIONS	AFTER SIX MONTHS AS A MANAGER	AFTER A YEAR AS A MANAGER
• Be the boss	• Initial expectations were wrong	• No longer "doers"
• Formal authority	• Fast pace	• Communication, listening, & positive reinforcement
• Manage tasks	• Heavy workload	• Learning to adopt to and control stress
• Job is not managing people	• Job is to be problem-solver and troubleshooter for subordinates	• Job is people development

Source: L. A. Hill, Becoming a Manager: Mastery of a New Identity *(Boston, MA: Harvard Business School Press, 1992).*

40 to 50 percent more work than being a producer! Who would have ever guessed?" The pace of managerial work was startling, too. Another manager said, "You have eight or nine people looking for your time . . . coming into and out of your office all day long." A somewhat frustrated manager declared that management was "a job that never ended," "a job you couldn't get your hands around."

Informal descriptions like this are consistent with studies indicating that the average first-line manager spends no more than two minutes on a task before being interrupted by a request from a subordinate, a phone call, or an email. The pace is somewhat less hurried for top managers, who spend an average of approximately nine minutes on a task before having to switch to another. In practice, this means that supervisors may perform 30 different tasks per hour, while top managers perform seven different tasks per hour, with each task typically different from the one that preceded it. A manager described this frenetic level of activity by saying, "The only time you are in control is when you shut your door, and then I feel I am not doing the job I'm supposed to be doing, which is being with the people."

The other major surprise after six months on the job was that the managers' expectations about what they should do as managers were very different from their subordinates' expectations. Initially, the managers defined their jobs as helping their subordinates perform their jobs well. For the managers, who still defined themselves as doers rather than managers, assisting their subordinates meant going out on sales calls or handling customer complaints. One manager said, "I like going out with the rep, who may need me to lend him my credibility as manager. I like the challenge, the joy in closing. I go out with the reps and we make the call and talk about the customer; it's fun." But when the managers "assisted" in this way, their subordinates were resentful and viewed their help as interference. The subordinates wanted their managers to help them by solving problems that they couldn't solve. Once the managers realized this contradiction, they embraced their role as problem-solver and troubleshooter. Thus, they could help without interfering with their subordinates' jobs.

After a year on the job, most of the managers no longer thought of themselves as doers, but as managers. In making the transition, they finally realized that people management was the most important part of their jobs. One manager summarized the lesson that had taken him a year to learn by saying, "As many demands as managers have on their time, I think their primary responsibility is people development. Not production, but people development." Another indication of how much their views had changed was that most of the managers now regretted the rather heavy-handed approach they had used in their early attempts to manage their subordinates. "I wasn't good at managing . . . , so I was bossy like a first-grade teacher." "Now I see that I started out as a drill sergeant. I was inflexible, just a lot of how-to's." By the end of the year, most of the managers had abandoned their authoritarian approach for one based on communication, listening, and positive reinforcement. One manager explained, "Last night at five I handed out an award in the board-room just to the individual. It was the first time in his career that he had done [earned] $100,000, and I gave him a piece of glass [a small award] and said I'd heard a rumor that somebody here just crossed over $100,000 and I said congratulations, shook his hand, and walked away. It was not public in the sense that I gathered everybody around. But I knew and he did too."

Finally, after beginning their year as managers in frustration, the managers came to feel comfortable with their subordinates, with the demands of their jobs, and with their emerging managerial styles. While being managers had made them acutely aware of their limitations and their need to develop as people, it also provided them with an unexpected reward of the thrill of coaching and developing the people who worked for them. One manager said, "It gives me the best feeling to see somebody do something well after I have helped them. I get excited." Another stated, "I realize now that when I accepted the position of branch manager that it is truly an exciting vocation. It is truly awesome, even at this level; it can be terribly challenging and terribly exciting."

Review 7

The Transition to Management: The First Year

Managers often begin their jobs by using more formal authority and less people management. However, most managers find that being a manager has little to do with "bossing" their subordinates. After six months on the job, the managers were surprised at the fast pace and heavy workload and that "helping" their subordinates was viewed as interference. After a year on the job, most of the managers no longer thought of themselves as doers, but as managers who get things done through others. And, because they finally realized that people management was the most important part of their job, most of them had abandoned their authoritarian approach for one based on communication, listening, and positive reinforcement.

Why Management Matters

If you walk down the aisle of the business section in your local bookstore, you'll find hundreds of books that explain precisely what companies need to do to be successful. Unfortunately, business books tend to be faddish, changing every few years. Lately, the best-selling business books have emphasized technology, reengineering, and going global, whereas 10 years ago the hot topics were joint ventures, mergers, and management buyouts. One thing that hasn't changed, though, is the importance of good people and good management: Companies can't succeed for long without them.

After reading this section, you should be able to

8 explain how and why companies can create competitive advantage through people.

8 Competitive Advantage through People

In his books, *Competitive Advantage through People* and *The Human Equation: Building Profits by Putting People First*, Stanford University business professor Jeffrey Pfeffer contends that what separates top companies from their competitors and makes them top performers is the way they treat their work forces—in other words, management.[56] Managers in top companies use ideas like employment security, selective hiring, self-managed teams and decentralization, high pay contingent on company performance, extensive training, reduced status distinctions (between managers and employees), and extensive sharing of financial information to achieve financial performance that, on average, is 40 percent higher than that of other companies. These ideas, which are explained in detail in Exhibit 1.7, help organizations develop work forces that are smarter, better trained, more motivated, and more committed than their competitors' work forces. And, as indicated by the phenomenal growth and return on investment earned by these companies, smarter, better trained, and more committed work forces provide superior products and service to customers, who keep buying and who, by telling others about their positive experiences, bring in new customers.

Pfeffer also argues that companies that invest in their people will create long-lasting competitive advantages that are difficult for other companies to duplicate. Indeed, studies clearly demonstrate that sound management practices can produce substantial advantages in three critical areas of organizational performance: sales revenues, profits, and customer satisfaction. For example, a study of nearly 1,000 U.S. firms found that companies that use *just some* of the ideas shown in Exhibit 1.7 had $27,044 more sales per employee and $3,814 more profit per employee than companies that didn't.[57] For a 100-person company, these differences amount to $2.7 million more in sales and

exhibit 1.7

Competitive Advantage through People: Management Practices

1. **Employment Security**—Employment security is the ultimate form of commitment that companies can make to their workers. Employees can innovate and increase company productivity without fearing the loss of their jobs.
2. **Selective Hiring**—If employees are the basis for a company's competitive advantage, and those employees have employment security, then the company needs to aggressively recruit and selectively screen applicants in order to hire the most talented employees available.
3. **Self-Managed Teams and Decentralization**—Self-managed teams are responsible for their own hiring, purchasing, job assignments, and production. Self-managed teams can often produce enormous increases in productivity through increased employee commitment and creativity. Decentralization allows employees who are closest to (and most knowledgeable about) problems, production, and customers to make timely decisions. Decentralization increases employee satisfaction and commitment.
4. **High Wages Contingent on Organizational Performance**—High wages are needed to attract and retain talented workers and to indicate that the organization values its workers. Employees, like company founders, shareholders, and managers, need to share in the financial rewards when the company is successful. Why? Because employees who have a financial stake in their companies are more likely to take a long-run view of the business and think like business owners.
5. **Training and Skill Development**—Like a high-tech company that spends millions of dollars to upgrade computers or research and development labs, a company whose competitive advantage is based on its people must invest in the training and skill development of its people.
6. **Reduction of Status Differences**—These are fancy words that indicate that the company treats everyone, no matter what the job, as equal. There are no reserved parking spaces. Everyone eats in the same cafeteria and has similar benefits. The result: Much improved communication as employees focus on problems and solutions rather than how they are less valued than managers.
7. **Sharing Information**—If employees are to make decisions that are good for the long-run health and success of the company, they need to be given information about costs, finances, productivity, development times, and strategies that was previously known only by company managers.

Source: J. Pfeffer, The Human Equation: Building Profits by Putting People First *(Boston: Harvard Business School Press, 1996).*

nearly $400,000 more in annual profit! For a 1,000-person company, the difference grows to $27 million more in sales and $4 million more in annual profit!

Another study found that poorly performing companies that adopted management techniques as simple as setting expectations (setting goals, results, and schedules), coaching (informal, ongoing discussions between managers and subordinates about what is being done well and what could be done better), reviewing (annual, formal discussion about results), and rewarding (adjusting salaries and bonuses based on employee performance and results) were able to improve average return on investment from 5.1 percent to 19.7 percent and increase sales by $94,000 per employee![58] So, in addition to significantly improving the profitability of healthy companies, sound management practices can turn around failing companies.

Research also indicates that managers have an important effect on customer satisfaction. Many people find this surprising. They don't understand how managers, who are largely responsible for what goes on inside the company, can affect what goes on outside the company. They wonder how managers, who often interact with customers under negative conditions (when customers are angry or dissatisfied), can actually improve customer satisfaction. It turns out that managers influence customer satisfaction through employee satisfaction. When employees are satisfied with their jobs, their bosses, and the companies they work for, they provide much better service to customers.[59] In turn, customers are more satisfied, too.

Review 8
Competitive Advantage through People

Why does management matter? Well-managed companies are competitive because their work forces are smarter, better trained, more motivated, and more committed. Furthermore, companies that practice good management consistently have greater revenues and profits than companies that don't. Finally, good management matters because good management leads to satisfied employees who, in turn, provide better service to customers. Because employees tend to treat customers the same way that their managers treat them, good management can improve customer satisfaction.

STUDY TIP Use your textbook more like a notebook and less like a reference book. The margins are a great place for writing questions on content you don't understand, highlighting important concepts, and adding examples to help you remember the material. Writing in your book makes it a more comprehensive resource for management and a better study tool.

MANAGEMENT DECISION

PROMOTION APPREHENSION

What a joy it is to be back at work![60] After spending two weeks on vacation in Hawaii, you're ready to get back to business as usual. It seems strange, but even during your two-week stint in paradise, you couldn't stop thinking about the office and what you might be missing. While you were away, you resisted the temptation to check in, mainly to avoid sending a negative signal to your assistant, Jill, and the other employees. Jill has been with the firm for three years as an engineer and was recently promoted to the position of assistant manager because of her hard work and proven track record in the department.

Before you left, you consulted with Jill and assured her that she could "hold down the fort" while you were away. Unfortunately, as you walked through the door this morning, Jill appeared to be nervous, agitated, and lacking confidence. She expressed relief that you were back from your trip and began to discuss the happenings of the last two weeks. Many of your subordinates were also glad to see you back at work. Your secretary claimed that Jill was a tyrant while you were gone. During your absence, several impromptu decisions had to be made, and from Jill's comments, she seemed to handle them well. When one of the newer engineers was having difficulty with his project, Jill said that she would take care of it and reassigned him to a less important client. Then she told the senior engineer that "the new guy may not be able to hack it here if he's having trouble with simple stuff like that." When some of the office assistants began complaining about the number of photocopies they had to make for the drafting team, Jill decided to have the drafters do their own photocopying.

As you listen, you tell yourself that you probably wouldn't have handled the situations in the same manner, but, then, you are more experienced and have encountered similar problems throughout your 26 years as a manager with the firm. When Jill finishes briefing you, you do your best to reassure her that she performed well during your absence; however, she is still not comfortable with the decisions that she made. In fact, as Jill begins to disclose more information, she tells you that she never wants to be left in charge again. She wonders if you made a mistake by giving her the promotion and asks you to reconsider keeping her as your assistant. Even though it has been three months since Jill's promotion, you still haven't hired a full-time engineer to replace her. Jill informs you that she would be happy resuming her former job and encourages you to name a new replacement for the assistant manager position.

Questions

1. As the manager of the small engineering firm, what would you say or do to calm Jill's anxiety about her new job and help her understand why she is experiencing fear?
2. How can she work to overcome her anxiety?
3. As the manager in question, would you grant or deny Jill's request never to be left in charge again?

INTERVIEW TWO MANAGERS

Welcome to the first "Develop Your Managerial Potential" activity! These assignments have one purpose: To help you develop your present and future capabilities as a manager. What you will be learning through these assignments is not traditional "book-learning" based on memorization and regurgitation, but practical knowledge and skills that help managers perform their jobs better. Lessons from some of the assignments—for example, goal setting—can be used for immediate benefit. Other lessons will obviously take time to accomplish, but you can still benefit now by making specific plans for future improvement.

Step 1: Interview Two Practicing Managers

In her book *Becoming a Manager: Master of a New Identity*, Harvard Business School professor Linda Hill conducted extensive interviews with 19 people in their first year as managers.[61] To learn firsthand what it's like to be a manager, interview two managers that you know, asking them some of the same questions, shown below, that Hill asked her managers. Be sure to interview managers with different levels of experience. Interview one person with at least five years' experience as a manager and then interview another person with no more than two years' experience as a manager. Ask the managers these questions:

1. Briefly describe your current position and responsibilities.
2. What do your subordinates expect from you on the job?
3. What are the major stresses and challenges you face on the job?
4. What, if anything, do you dislike about the job?
5. What do you like best about your job?
6. What are the critical differences between average managers and top-performing managers?
7. Think about the skills and knowledge that you need to be effective in your job. What are they, and how did you acquire them?
8. What have been your biggest mistakes thus far? Could you have avoided them? If so, how?

Step 2: Prepare to Discuss Your Findings

Prepare to discuss your findings in class or write a report (if assigned by your instructor). What conclusions can you draw from your interview data?

BIZ FLIX 8 Mile

Jimmy "B-Rabbit" Smith, Jr. (Eminem) wants to be a successful rapper and to prove that a white man can create moving sounds. He works days at a plant run by the North Detroit Stamping Company and pursues his music at night, sometimes on the plant's grounds. The film's title refers to Detroit's northern city boundary, which divides Detroit's white and African American populations. This film gives a gritty look at Detroit's hip-hop culture in 1995 and Jimmy's desire to be accepted by it. Eminem's original songs "Lose Yourself" and "8 Mile" received Golden Globe and Academy Award nominations.

This scene is an edited composite of two brief sequences involving the stamping plant. The first half of the scene appears early in the film as part of "The Franchise" sequence. The second half appears in the last 25 minutes of the film as part of the "Papa Doc Payback" sequence. In the first part of the scene, Jimmy's car won't start so he rides the city bus to work and arrives late. The second part occurs after he is beaten by Papa Doc (Anthony Mackie) and Papa Doc's gang. Jimmy's mother (Kim Basinger) returns to their trailer and tells him she won $3,200 at bingo. The film continues to its end with Jimmy's last battle (a rapper competition).

What to Watch for and Ask Yourself

1. What is your perception of the quality of Jimmy's job and his work environment?
2. What is the quality of Jimmy's relationship with Manny, his foreman (Paul Bates)? Does it change? If it does, why?
3. How would you react to this type of work experience?

MGMT WORKPLACE Diversified Chemicals

Diversified Chemicals owns four companies that compete in the paper, packaging adhesive, and chemical supply industry. Its primary focus is on serving the automotive trade in Detroit with its superior chemical applications expertise. Since 1971, Diversified has grown from a small two-person company into a four-enterprise operation with 200 employees and $70 million in annual sales. Founders George Hill and Arnold Joseff attribute their success to their innovation-oriented approach to management. They pursue the most talented workers available and then give them the freedom to work together and unleash their collective creative powers. Instead of solving sales problems, Hill and Joseff try to solve problems for the greater good of their company, their industry, and their community.

What to Watch for and Ask Yourself

1. Describe the four functions of management at Diversified.
2. What roles do the managers at Diversified fill? Explain using only information from the video.
3. Describe how Diversified achieves a competitive advantage through people.

CHAPTER TWO

Organizational Environments and Cultures

outline

WHAT WOULD YOU DO?

McDonald's Headquarters, Oak Brook, Illinois.[1] As the CEO of McDonald's, the world's largest fast-food chain, it's not surprising that you like the food, especially your favorite, the double cheeseburger. A decade ago, customers loved McDonald's food, too, so much so that the company opened a brand new restaurant every 17 hours. Today, though, after the company posted the first quarterly loss in its history, you've ordered the closing of hundreds of unprofitable McDonald's. From record profits and store openings to today's losses and store closings, things certainly have changed since you joined the company 28 years ago.

One of the biggest changes is that McDonald's doesn't own the kids market anymore. With Happy Meals (a hamburger, cheeseburger, or chicken nuggets, with a small drink, fries, and a toy), innovative indoor playgrounds, and once popular toys like Beanie Babies, McDonald's dominated fast-food sales for children. In fact, Happy Meals account for 20 percent of McDonald's U.S.

student resources

URL
Experiencing Management
Experiencing Management modules begin in chapter 3.

GUIDE
Study Guide
Mini lecture reviews all the learning points in the chapter and concludes with a case on IBM.

VIDEO
Take Two Video
Biz Flix is a scene from *Backdraft.* Management Workplace is a segment on Ziba Design.

PPT
PowerPoint®
12 slides with graphics provide an outline for this chapter.

FAQ
Author Insights
Chuck talks about the real constraints on managers.

TEST
Self Test
25 true/false questions, 25 multiple-choice questions, a management scenario, and 3 exhibit worksheets

sales, and that's not counting sales to the adults who buy children those Happy Meals. Over the last two years, however, sales of Happy Meals have dropped 7 percent. Bill Lamar, head of McDonald's U.S. marketing, said, "We can do better with Happy Meals. We continue to be the leader, but the gap we had with our competitors is not as wide as it was a few years ago." One reason for the decline is that it's been years since McDonald's had a popular toy to give away with its Happy Meals. By contrast, sales of Burger King's similar Kids Meals have surged because it gave away toys featuring popular cartoon characters from *The Simpsons, Rugrats,* and *SpongeBob SquarePants.*

You also believe that McDonald's food isn't as good as it used to be. You suspect that food quality dropped at McDonald's U.S. restaurants when microwave ovens and different cooking procedures were introduced to speed up cooking times and customize customer orders. Hamburgers taste much better at McDonald's international restaurants, which didn't adopt these cooking techniques. Food preferences may also have changed, even among core customers, such as teenage males. For instance, 19-year-old student Froilan Landeros hasn't been to a McDonald's in years because he doesn't like the food or the décor. In his view, "Burgers and fries can go down the drain." McDonald's may also be losing business to competitors offering healthier food. Teacher Maggie Thaxton, who frequents Quizno's Subs, says, "I'm spending more money to stay healthy." It certainly didn't help that 5-foot 10-inch, 272-pound Caesar Barber, a 56-year-old maintenance worker, sued McDonald's after having two heart attacks and diabetes. Barber claimed that McDonald's fatty foods were responsible for his poor health.

With same store sales down nearly 2 percent from year to year, you've also concluded that McDonald's fast food isn't as fast as it used to be. Indeed, market researchers posing as regular customers consistently found that McDonald's restaurants met speed standards, 90 seconds per customer, only 46 percent of the time. Even worse, 30 percent of all customers had to wait more than four minutes for their meals. Also, the researchers routinely found unprofessional employees, who delivered rude, slow, inaccurate service. And, if it's not the slow service, it just might be the stores themselves. Sales are particularly weak at restaurants 15 or more years old. With their muted colors, and Formica tables and booths, these older restaurants pale in comparison to the stylish atmosphere found at newer fast-food stores, such as Starbucks and Panera Bread.

Everywhere you look, you see threats to McDonald's business. How can you deal with them and perhaps turn them into opportunities? Has McDonald's become weaker while its competitors have become stronger? If so, what can you do about it? If there has been a basic shift in people's food preferences, will McDonald's be able to effectively serve its key customers—children, families, teens, and people wanting quick, inexpensive food? **If you were the CEO of McDonald's, what would you do?**

Wherever McDonald's top managers look, they see changes and forces outside the company that threaten their ability to continue to make McDonald's a successful business. This chapter examines the internal and external forces that affect companies. We begin by explaining how the changes in external organizational environments affect companies. Next, we examine the two kinds of external organizational environments: the general environment that affects all organizations and the specific environment unique to each company. Then, we learn how managers make sense of their changing general and specific environments. The chapter finishes with a discussion of internal organizational environments by focusing on organizational culture.

External Environments

External environments are the forces and events outside a company that have the potential to influence or affect it. For instance, despite consumer objections, the German government ordered Wal-Mart's German stores (i.e., Wertkauf-Mann) to do something the company normally wouldn't do: raise prices. Although Wal-Mart managers probably anticipated that the German government would regulate store hours (under German law, stores can be open only till 8:00 P.M. on weekdays and 4:00 P.M. on Saturdays and must be closed on Sundays), they probably didn't expect that it would limit their ability to set prices.[2] Thus, even the largest companies in the world, including Wal-Mart, are influenced by events in their external environments.

external environments
all events outside a company that have the potential to influence or affect it

After reading the next four sections, you should be able to

1 discuss how changing environments affect organizations.
2 describe the four components of the general environment.
3 explain the five components of the specific environment.
4 describe the process that companies use to make sense of their changing environments.

1 Changing Environments

Let's examine the basic characteristics of changing external environments: 1.1 environmental change, 1.2 environmental complexity and resource scarcity, and 1.3 the uncertainty that environmental change, complexity, and resource scarcity can create for organizational managers.

1.1 Environmental Change

Environmental change is the rate at which a company's general and specific environments change. In **stable environments**, the rate of environmental change is slow. For instance, the liquor industry has not changed much since Prohibition was repealed in 1933. Most states use a "three-tier" system to control the sale and distribution of alcohol.[3] Breweries, wineries, and distilleries sell their products to wholesale distributors who, in turn, sell to liquor retailers who then sell to the public. In **dynamic environments**, however, the rate of environmental change is fast as in the video game industry.

environmental change
the rate at which a company's general and specific environments change

stable environment
an environment in which the rate of change is slow

dynamic environment
an environment in which the rate of change is fast

punctuated equilibrium theory a theory that holds that companies go through long, simple periods of stability (equilibrium), followed by short periods of dynamic, fundamental change (revolution), and ending with a return to stability (new equilibrium)

Although you might think that a company's external environment would be *either* stable *or* dynamic, research suggests that companies often experience both. According to **punctuated equilibrium theory**, companies go through long, simple periods of stability (equilibrium), followed by short, complex periods of dynamic, fundamental change (revolutionary periods), finishing with a return to stability (new equilibrium).[4]

Exhibit 2.1 shows one example of punctuated equilibrium—the U.S. airline industry. As depicted, the U.S. airline industry has experienced three revolutionary periods. The first occurred immediately after airline deregulation in 1978. Airlines had tremendous difficulty operating in the competitive environment created by deregulation and suffered huge losses until they were able to adjust.

Then, after experiencing record growth and profits, U.S. airlines lost billions of dollars as the industry went through dramatic changes. Key expenses, including jet fuel and employee salaries, suddenly increased, and revenues, suddenly dropped because of dramatic changes in the airlines' customer base. Leisure travelers, who wanted the cheapest flights they could get,[5] replaced business travelers, who typically pay full-priced fares, as the largest customer base. The airlines responded to these changes in their business environment by laying off 5 to 10 percent of their workers, canceling orders for new planes, and getting rid of routes that were not profitable. These changes helped profits return even stronger. The industry began to stabilize just as punctuated equilibrium theory predicts.[6]

The third revolutionary period for the U.S. airline industry began with the terrorist attacks of September 11, 2001, in which planes were used as missiles to bring down the World Trade Center towers and damage the Pentagon. The immediate effect was a 20 percent drop in scheduled flights, a 40 percent drop in passengers, and losses so large that the U.S. government approved a $15 billion bailout to keep the airlines in business. Still, after losing a combined $10 billion, the major U.S. carriers laid off over 20 percent of their total work force.[7]

exhibit 2.1

Punctuated Equilibrium: U.S. Airline Profits since 1979

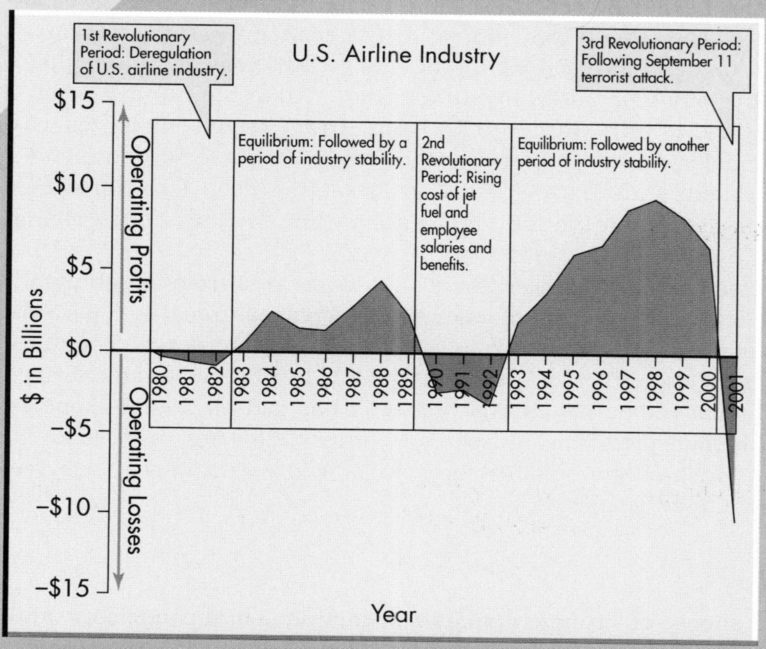

Source: "Annual Operating and Net Earnings: U.S. Scheduled Airlines—All Services," Air Transport Association, [Online] available at http://www.airlines.org/public/industry/display1.asp?nid=1034, 6 February 2003.

1.2 Environmental Complexity and Resource Scarcity

Environmental complexity is the number of external factors in the environment that affect organizations. **Simple environments** have few environmental factors, whereas **complex environments** have many environmental factors. For example, the baking industry has a relatively simple external environment: bread is baked, wrapped, and delivered fresh to stores each day much as it was

environmental complexity the number of external factors in the environment that affect organizations

simple environment an environment with few environmental factors

complex environment an environment with many environmental factors

decades ago. Likewise, although some new breads have become popular, the traditional white and wheat breads are still today's best sellers. Baking bread is a highly competitive, but simple business environment that has experienced few changes.

By contrast, in recent years, cereal companies like Kellogg's have found themselves in a more complex environment in which three significant changes have occurred. The first is that these companies now face more competition in a shrinking market.[8] Kellogg's, General Mills, and Post compete against each other, plus a dozen more private-label store brands (IGA, Good Value, etc.) and health food brands (Healthy Valley and Kashi). Furthermore, with more people eating breakfast on the run, a much smaller percentage of people eat cereal for breakfast any more.[9]

The second significant change in the cereal industry has been price cuts. For years, it cost Kellogg's only $2.50 to make a $5 box of cereal. Yet, with profits that high, private-label store brands could still make a profit of $1 per box by slashing the price to $3.50 per box of cereal.

The third significant change has been the entrance of Wal-Mart into the grocery business. Wal-Mart, much more than other national grocery chains, relies on cheaper private-label store brands like its own Sam's Choice soft drinks and Ol' Roy dog food. Consumers like these products because they cost substantially less than brand-name products. So, as Wal-Mart aggressively expanded into the grocery business and pushed its cheaper, private-label cereals, Kellogg's saw its market share drop even more. Together, these changes have made Kellogg's external environment much more complex than it used to be.[10]

resource scarcity the degree to which an organization's external environment has an abundance or scarcity of critical organizational resources

Another characteristic of external environments is resource scarcity. **Resource scarcity** is the degree to which an organization's external environment has an abundance or scarcity of critical organizational resources.

For example, from 1995 to 2000, qualified employees were scarce in many industries. The reason was simple: as the economy grew and companies expanded, demand for good job applicants greatly exceeded the supply. With the number of job openings five times greater than the number of layoffs, employers had to work harder to find and attract skilled employees, especially in technological and professional jobs.[11] To help recruit more engineers, Cisco Systems started its "Friends" program in which Cisco employees personally contacted potential job applicants within 24 hours of receiving their résumés.[12]

As I write this chapter, however, there's no longer a scarcity of job applicants. In the last two years, unemployment has increased from 4 to 6 percent as companies eliminated 1.75 million jobs.[13] This is good news for companies that have recently had difficulty attracting qualified workers. Layoffs at dot-coms and technical companies (Nortel Networks has laid off 20,000 employees), along with widespread hiring freezes in other industries, have made it much easier to find and hire qualified employees, who are no longer as scarce as they were just a few years ago.[14]

uncertainty the extent to which managers can understand or predict which environmental changes and trends will affect their businesses

1.3 Uncertainty

As Exhibit 2.2 shows, environmental change, environmental complexity, and resource scarcity affect environmental **uncertainty**, which is how well managers can understand or predict the external changes and trends affecting their businesses. Starting at the left side of the figure, environmental uncer-

exhibit 2.2

Environmental Change, Environmental Complexity, and Resource Scarcity

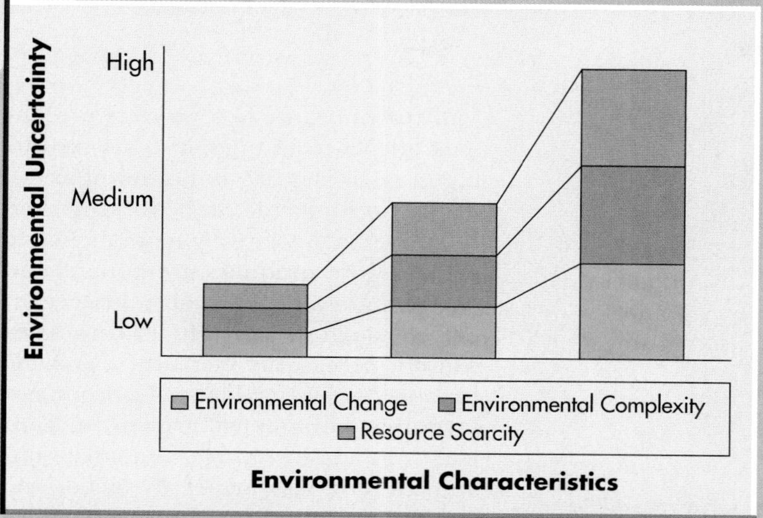

tainty is lowest when environmental change and complexity and change are at low levels and resource scarcity is small (i.e., resources are plentiful). In these environments, managers feel confident that they can understand, predict, and react to the external forces that affect their businesses. By contrast, the right side of the figure indicates that environmental uncertainty is highest when environmental change and complexity are extensive and resource scarcity is a problem. In these environments, managers may not be at all confident that they can understand, predict, and handle the external forces affecting their businesses.

Review 1

Changing Environments

Environmental change, complexity, and resource scarcity are the basic components of external environments. Environmental change is the rate at which conditions or events affecting a business change. Environmental complexity is the number of external factors in an external environment. Resource scarcity is the scarcity or abundance of resources available in the external environment. The greater the rate of environmental change, environmental complexity, and resource scarcity, the less confident managers are that they can understand, predict, and effectively react to the trends affecting their businesses. According to punctuated equilibrium theory, companies experience periods of stability followed by short periods of dynamic, fundamental change, followed by a return to periods of stability.

2 General Environment

general environment
the economic, technological, sociocultural, and political trends that indirectly affect all organizations

specific environment
the customers, competitors, suppliers, industry regulations, and advocacy groups that are unique to an industry and that directly affect how a company does business

As Exhibit 2.3 shows, two kinds of external environments influence organizations: the general environment and the specific environment. The **general environment** consists of the economy and the technological, sociocultural, and political/legal trends that indirectly affect all organizations. Changes in any sector of the general environment eventually affect most organizations. For example, when the Federal Reserve lowers its prime lending rate, most businesses benefit because banks and credit card companies often lower the interest rates they charge for loans. Consumers, who can then borrow money more cheaply, will borrow more to buy homes, cars, refrigerators, and large-screen TVs. By contrast, each organization also has a **specific environment** that is unique to that firm's industry and directly affects the way it conducts day-to-day business. The specific environment, which will be discussed in detail in Section 3 of this chapter, includes customers, competitors, suppliers, industry regulation, and advocacy groups.

exhibit 2.3

General and Specific Environments

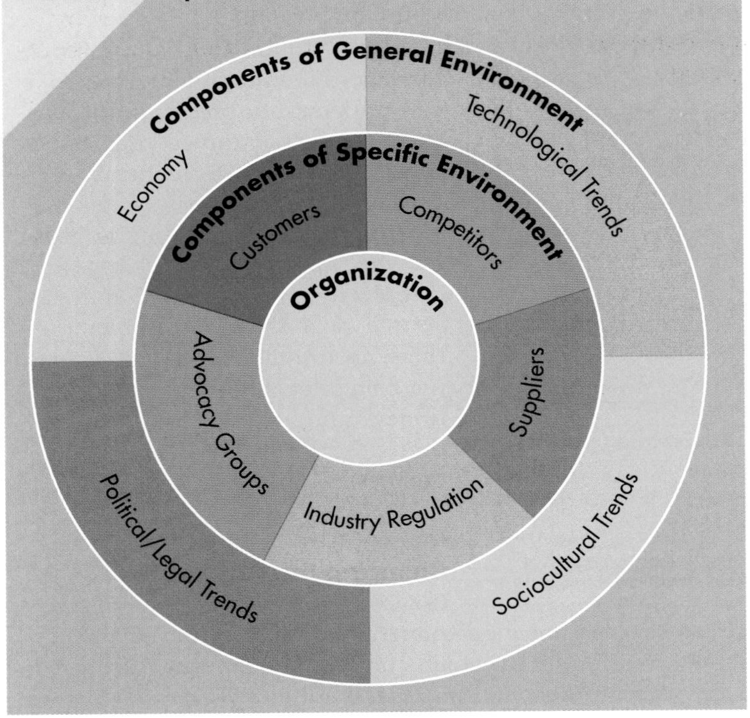

Let's take a closer look at the four components of the general environment: 2.1 the economy, and 2.2 the technological, 2.3 sociocultural, and 2.4 political/legal trends that indirectly affect all organizations.

2.1 Economy

The current state of a country's economy affects most organizations operating in it. In general, in a growing economy, more people are working and therefore have relatively more money to spend. More products are bought and sold than in a static or shrinking economy. Though an individual firm's sales will not necessarily increase, a growing economy does provide an environment favorable to business growth. In contrast, in a shrinking economy, consumers have less money to spend, and relatively fewer products are bought and sold. Thus, a shrinking economy makes growth for individual businesses more difficult.

For example, as I write this chapter, the U.S. economy is recovering from four years of economic slowdown. Growth is positive and manufacturers are reporting strong increases in incoming orders. Interest rates are low, so it costs companies and consumers little to borrow money, and there's little upward pressure on business costs (i.e., low inflation). And unemployment rates are at moderate levels. Japan's economy is still in rough shape after twelve straight years of economic recession. A *Fortune* magazine article summed up Japan's economy like this: "The yen in turn is weakening, unemployment has hit postwar highs, and the stock market is in free fall. There are fewer banks today than there were a decade ago, but they're still in trouble—and the trouble is only intensifying as the economy continues to slide."[15] In short, for more than a decade, Japanese businesses have operated in an unhealthy, shrinking economy.[16]

Of course, by the time you read this, the Japanese economy could be growing, and the U.S. economy could be shrinking into a recession (negative growth). Because the economy influences basic business decisions, such as whether to hire more employees, expand production, or take out loans to purchase equipment, managers scan their economic environments for signs of change. Unfortunately, the economic statistics that managers rely on when making these decisions are notoriously poor predictors of *future* economic activity. A manager who decides to hire 10 more employees because economic data suggest future growth could very well have to lay off those newly hired workers when the economic growth does not occur. In fact, a famous economic study found that at the beginning of a business quarter (a period of only three months), even the most accurate economic forecasters could not accurately predict whether economic activity would grow or shrink in that same quarter![17]

Because economic statistics can be poor predictors, some managers try to predict future economic activity by keeping track of business confidence. **Business confidence indices** show how confident actual managers are about future business growth. For example, the *Fortune* Business Confidence Index is a monthly survey of chief financial officers at large *Fortune* 1000 firms.[18] Another widely cited measure is the U.S. Chamber of Commerce Business Confidence Index, which asks 7,000 small business owners to express their optimism (or pessimism) about future business sales and prospects. Managers often prefer business confidence indices to economic statistics because they know that other managers make business decisions that are in line with their expectations concerning the economy's future.

business confidence indices
indices that show managers' level of confidence about future business growth

2.2 Technological Component

Technology is the knowledge, tools, and techniques used to transform input (raw materials, information, etc.) into output (products and services). For example, the knowledge of authors, editors, and artists (technology) and the use of equipment like computers and printing presses (also technology) transformed paper, ink, and glue (raw material inputs) into this book (the finished product).

Changes in technology can help companies provide better products or produce their products more efficiently. For example, advances in surgical techniques and imaging equipment have made open-heart surgery much faster and safer in recent years. While technological changes can benefit a business, they can also threaten it. For example, over the last year, with sales of blank CDs up 40 percent, and more than 180 million songs downloaded *for free* at Kazaa.com alone (the largest music file swapping Web site), it's no surprise that sales of music CDs have dropped 11 percent (following a 3 percent drop the year before).[20] Companies must embrace new technology and find effective ways to use it to improve products and services or decrease costs. If they don't, they will lose out to those that do. Chapter 9, on Organizational Change and Innovation, provides a more in-depth discussion of how technology affects a company's competitive advantage.

PERSONAL PRODUCTIVITY TIP

Computer Skills and Lifetime Earnings

People with basic computer skills earn 15 to 30 percent higher lifetime incomes than those without them. Computers are becoming an integral part of all kinds of work. What should you do to learn about computers? Subscribe to *PC Magazine, PC World,* or *Mac World.* Buy a book about Microsoft Office and then take tests to be Microsoft Office User certified (see the Microsoft Web site for more information) in Word, Excel, PowerPoint, or Access. Take more than the required computer classes for your degree. Unless you want less job security and earning power, start learning more about computers today.[19]

technology
the knowledge, tools, and techniques used to transform input into output

2.3 Sociocultural Component

The sociocultural component of the general environment refers to the demographic characteristics and general behavior, attitudes, and beliefs of people in a particular society. Sociocultural changes and trends influence organizations in two important ways.

First, changing demographic characteristics, such as the number of people with particular skills or the growth or decline in particular population segments (single or married; old or young; men or women, etc.), affect how companies run their businesses. For example, married women with children are much more likely to work today than four decades ago. In fact, between 1960 and 2000, the number of working women with children increased by 243 percent! Today, with traffic congestion creating longer commutes and both parents working longer hours, employees are much more likely to value products and services that allow them to recapture free time with their families. Companies such as CDW (Computer Discount Warehouse) in Vernon, Illinois, help their employees by providing a service that picks up their dry cleaning at their desks.[21] At First Command Financial Planning in Fort Worth, Texas, employees can borrow movies for two nights of home viewing and drop off shoes for free shining and their cars for free washing.[22]

Second, sociocultural changes in behavior, attitudes, and beliefs also affect the demand for a business's products and services. Furthermore, today's harried worker/parent can hire baby-proofing agencies (to baby-proof their homes), emergency babysitting services, bill payers, birthday party planners, kiddie taxi services, personal assistants, and personal chefs.[23] All of these services are a direct result of the need for free time, which is a result of the sociocultural changes associated with a much higher percentage of women in the workplace.

2.4 Political/Legal Component

The political/legal component of the general environment includes the legislation, regulations, and court decisions that govern and regulate business behavior. In recent years, new laws and regulations have imposed additional responsibilities on companies. Unfortunately, many managers are unaware of these new responsibilities. For example, under the 1991 Civil Rights Act, if an employee is sexually harassed by anyone at work (a supervisor, a coworker, or even a customer), the company—not just the harasser—is potentially liable for damages, attorneys' fees, and back pay.[24] Under the Family and Medical Leave Act, employees who have been on the job one year are guaranteed 12 weeks of unpaid leave per year to tend to their own illnesses or to their elderly parents, a newborn baby, or a newly adopted child. Employees are guaranteed the same job, pay, and benefits when they return to work.[25] Because of the 1990 Clean Air Act, companies located in regions with high levels of polluted air must reduce the number of employees who drive to work each day by approximately 25 percent. Companies are exploring the possibility of sponsoring car pools or renting buses and vans because the fines for noncompliance can be as high as $25,000 per day![26]

Many managers are also unaware of the potential legal risks associated with traditional managerial decisions like recruiting, hiring, and firing employees. Increasingly, businesses and managers are being sued for negligent hiring and supervision, defamation, invasion of privacy, emotional distress, fraud, and misrepresentation during employee recruitment.[27] More than 24,000 suits for wrongful termination (unfairly firing employees) are filed each year.[28] In fact, wrongful termination lawsuits have increased by 77 percent in the last decade and now account for 13 percent of all lawsuits against companies.[29] One in four employers is eventually sued for wrongful termination. Employers lose 70 percent of these cases, and on average, the former employee is awarded $500,000 or more.[30]

Not everyone agrees that companies face severe legal risks. Indeed, many believe that the government should do more to regulate and restrict business behavior and that it should be easier for average citizens to sue dishonest or negligent corporations. From a managerial perspective, the best medicine against legal risk is prevention. As a manager, it is your responsibility to educate yourself about the laws, regulations, and potential lawsuits that could affect your business. Failure to do so may put you and your company at risk of sizable penalties, fines, or legal charges.

Review 2

General Environment

The general environment consists of economic, technological, sociocultural, and political/legal events and trends that affect all organizations. Because the economy influences basic business decisions, managers often use economic statistics and business confidence indices to predict future economic activity. Changes in technology, which is used to transform input into output, can be a benefit or a threat to a business. Sociocultural trends, like changing demographic characteristics, affect how companies run their businesses. Similarly, sociocultural changes in behavior, attitudes, and beliefs affect the demand for a business's products and services. Court decisions and new federal and state laws have imposed much greater political/legal responsibilities on companies. The best way to manage legal responsibilities is to educate managers and employees about laws and regulations and potential lawsuits that could affect a business.

3 Specific Environment

Whereas general environments only influence organizations indirectly, changes in an organization's specific environment directly affect the way a company conducts its business. If customers decide to use another product, or a competitor cuts prices 10 percent, or a supplier can't deliver raw materials, or federal regulators mandate reductions in industry pollutants, or environmental groups accuse your company of selling unsafe products, the impact on your business is immediate.

Let's examine how the 3.1 **customer**, 3.2 **competitor**, 3.3 **supplier**, 3.4 **industry regulation**, and 3.5 **advocacy group components** of the specific environment affect businesses.

3.1 Customer Component

Customers purchase products and services. Companies cannot exist without customer support. Therefore, monitoring customers' changing wants and needs is critical to business success. There are two basic strategies for monitoring customers: reactive and proactive. *Reactive customer monitoring* is identifying and addressing customer trends and problems after they occur. One reactive strategy is to identify customer concerns by listening closely to customer complaints. Not only does listening to complaints help identify problems, but the way in which companies respond to complaints indicates how closely they are attending to customer concerns. For example, companies that respond quickly to customer letters of complaint are viewed much more favorably than companies that are slow to respond or never respond. In particular, studies have shown that when a company's follow-up letter thanks customers for writing, offers a sincere, specific response to the customer's complaint (i.e.,

DOING THE RIGHT THING

The Ten Commandments for Ethical Competitive Analysis

Sometimes, in their zeal to dig up information about competitors, managers and employees commit unethical or illegal acts such as digging through trash dumpsters on a competitor's property or paying a competitor's employees for information about secret designs or components. Fuld & Company, a major consulting firm in competitive intelligence, offers these "ten commandments" for ethical competitive analysis:

- Thou shalt not lie when representing thyself.
- Thou shalt observe thy company's legal guidelines as set forth by the legal department.
- Thou shalt not tape-record a conversation.
- Thou shalt not bribe.
- Thou shalt not plant eavesdropping devices.
- Thou shalt not deliberately mislead anyone in an interview.
- Thou shalt neither obtain from nor give price information to thy competitor.
- Thou shalt not swap misinformation.
- Thou shalt not steal a trade secret (or steal employees away in hopes of learning a trade secret).
- Thou shalt not knowingly press someone for information if it may jeopardize that person's job or reputation.[35]

For more information on the ethics and legality of competitive intelligence, see the Society of Competitive Intelligence Professionals (**http://www.scip.org**) and the U.S. Economic Espionage Act of 1996 (**http://www.scip.org/Library/8(3)eea.pdf**).

not a form letter, but an explanation of how the problem will be handled), and contains a small gift, coupons, or a refund to make up for the problem, customers are much more likely to purchase products or services again from that company.[31]

Proactive monitoring of customers means trying to sense events, trends, and problems before they occur (or before customers complain). For example, Cotton Inc., a trade group that encourages consumers to purchase cotton clothing ("The look, the feel of cotton . . . "), publishes a quarterly newsletter called *Lifestyle Monitor* that reports the results of ongoing research. According to Cotton Inc.'s president and CEO, the research is an "early radar detection system" for changes in consumer attitudes and behavior regarding clothing, appearance, fashion, home furnishings, and other topics.[32] Some recent research, for example, found that blue jeans are as popular as ever. Eighty-five percent of respondents disagreed with the statement, "Jeans are in my past, not in my future." The researchers also found that the average woman owns seven pairs of jeans and there's an 81 percent chance that her next pair of jeans will be some shade of blue.[33] Furthermore, when asked whether "A good-looking man looks most sexy in denim jeans and a casual shirt, or a jacket and tie or slacks and a nice sweater," 53 percent of the women said denim jeans, 25 percent said slacks and a sweater, and 20 percent said a jacket and tie.[34]

3.2 Competitor Component

Competitors are companies in the same industry that sell similar products or services to customers. General Motors, Ford, and DaimlerChrysler all compete for automobile customers. NBC, ABC, CBS, and Fox compete for TV viewers' attention. And McDonald's, Burger King, and Wendy's compete for fast-food customers' dollars. Often the difference between business success and failure comes down to whether your company is doing a better job of satisfying customer wants and needs than the competition. Consequently, companies need to keep close track of what their competitors are doing. To do this, managers perform what's called a **competitive analysis**, which is deciding who your competitors are, anticipating competitors' moves, and determining competitors' strengths and weaknesses.

competitors
companies in the same industry that sell similar products or services to customers

competitive analysis
a process for monitoring competitors that involves identifying competitors, anticipating their moves, and determining their strengths and weaknesses

Surprisingly, managers often do a poor job of identifying potential competitors; the reason is that they tend to focus on only two or three well-known competitors with similar goals and resources.[36] For example, Coke and Pepsi undoubtedly spend more time keeping track of each other than they do Dr. Pepper or Snapple. Xerox focused on its largest competitors in the copying business, Canon and Ricoh. By doing so, however, it ignored Hewlett-Packard and its inkjet printers and lost billions in sales in the small office, home office (SOHO) market. Over the last 10 years, HP's highly profitable printer division grew until it is now larger than *all* of Xerox.[37]

suppliers
companies that provide material, human, financial, and informational resources to other companies

supplier dependence
the degree to which a company relies on a supplier because of the importance of the supplier's product to the company and the difficulty of finding other sources of that product

Another mistake managers may make when analyzing the competition is to underestimate potential competitors' capabilities. When this happens, managers don't take the steps they should to continue to improve their products or services. The result can be significant decreases in both market share and profits. For example, software products like Cool Talk, Internet Phone, and Web Phone have made it possible to make very inexpensive long-distance phone calls on the Internet. The sound quality using Internet Phone is only as good as AM radio, but people are so used to poor-quality sound on their cell phones that it doesn't deter them from making Internet calls anymore.[38] Overall, Internet Phone use is still small, constituting just 3 percent of all international calls. In Japan, however, more than 12 percent of international calls are made over the Internet, and use is even greater in China.[39] It was estimated that in 2004, 40 percent of all international calls would be made over the Internet because of the much lower prices—3 to 8 cents a minute using the Internet compared to 15 cents to more than $1 a minute for a traditional call.[40] Yet, when a phone company manager was asked whether he was worried about the likes of Internet Phone, his response was "Some people will use it. But it won't really affect our business."[41]

© SUSAN VAN ETTEN

Not only is the De Beers example given in the text an example of supplier dependence (sightholders are very dependent on the giant diamond producer), it may also constitute opportunistic behavior. By forcing sightholders to take lesser quality diamonds, De Beers clearly benefits at the expense of its customers.

3.3 Supplier Component

Suppliers are companies that provide material, human, financial, and informational resources to other companies. U.S. Steel buys iron ore from suppliers to make steel products. When IBM sells a mainframe computer, it also provides support staff, engineers, and other technical consultants to the company that bought the computer. Or, when a clothing manufacturer has spent $100,000 to purchase new high-pressure "water drills" to be used to cut shirt and pants patterns to precise sizes, the water drill manufacturer will, as part of the purchase, agree to train workers on how to use the machinery.

A key factor influencing the relationship between companies and their suppliers is how dependent they are on each other.[42] **Supplier dependence** is the degree to which a company relies on a supplier because of the importance of the supplier's product to the company and the difficulty of finding other sources of that product. Supplier dependence is very strong in the diamond business, given that De Beers Consolidated Mines provides 65 percent of the wholesale diamonds in the world. Because De Beers typically offers better diamonds at cheaper prices, it has dominated the diamond industry for more than a century, controlling the supply, price, and quality of the best diamonds on the market. An example of the degree of this control is that De Beers' 125 customers, or "sightholders," as they're known in the industry, are summoned to De Beers' London office 10 times a year and given a shoebox of diamonds that they have to buy. If they refuse, they lose the opportunity to purchase any more diamonds.[43]

buyer dependence the degree to which a supplier relies on a buyer because of the importance of that buyer to the supplier and the difficulty of selling its products to other buyers

Buyer dependence is the degree to which a supplier relies on a buyer because of the importance of that buyer to the supplier and the difficulty of selling its products to other buyers. When Luxottica, an Italian eyewear company, purchased Sunglass Hut, it (the buyer) demanded immediate price cuts from its sunglasses suppliers. Oakley Sunglasses refused until Sunglass Hut stopped ordering sunglasses from Oakley altogether. Four months later, Oakley conceded, granting Luxottica most of the price cuts it wanted.[44]

opportunistic behavior a transaction in which one party in the relationship benefits at the expense of the other

relationship behavior mutually beneficial, long-term exchanges between buyers and suppliers

As Luxottica's demands indicate, a high degree of buyer or seller dependence can lead to **opportunistic behavior**, in which one party benefits at the expense of the other. Though opportunistic behavior between buyers and suppliers will never be completely eliminated, many companies believe that both buyers and suppliers can benefit by improving the buyer-supplier relationship.[45] In contrast to opportunistic behavior is **relationship behavior,** which focuses on establishing a mutually beneficial, long-term relationship between buyers and suppliers.[46]

3.4 Industry Regulation Component

industry regulation regulations and rules that govern the business practices and procedures of specific industries, businesses, and professions

Whereas the political/legal component of the general environment affects all businesses, the **industry regulation** component consists of regulations and rules that govern the practices and procedures of specific industries, businesses, and professions. For example, if your neighbor decides to make a little extra money selling homemade baked goods and sells you two apple pies, your neighbor could be fined. In most states, it is illegal to sell food from your home.

Regulatory agencies affect businesses by creating and enforcing rules and regulations to protect consumers, workers, or society as a whole. For example, the U.S. Department of Agriculture and the Food and Drug Administration regulate the safety of seafood (and meat and poultry) through the science-based Hazard Analysis and Critical Control Points (HACCP) program. Seafood processors are required to identify any hazards that could cause the fish they process to be unsafe. They must also establish critical control points to control hazards both inside and outside their fish-processing plants and then establish monitoring, corrective action, and verification procedures to certify that the fish they process is safe to consume.[47]

There are nearly 100 federal agencies and regulatory commissions that can affect nearly any kind of business. Overall, the number and cost of federal regulations has nearly tripled in the last 25 years. Today, for every $1 the federal government spends creating regulations, businesses spend $45 to comply with them.[48] Furthermore, in addition to federal regulations, businesses are also subject to state, county, and city regulations. Surveys indicate that managers rank government regulation as one of the most demanding and frustrating parts of their jobs.[49] Effective Management Online **(http://em-online.swlearning.com)** has more details on the various federal regulatory agencies and commissions, including Web sites.

3.5 Advocacy Groups

advocacy groups groups of concerned citizens who band together to try to influence the business practices of specific industries, businesses, and professions

Advocacy groups are groups of concerned citizens who band together to try to influence the business practices of specific industries, businesses, and professions. The members of a group generally share the same point of view on a particular issue. For example, environmental advocacy groups might try to get manufacturers to reduce smokestack pollution emissions. Unlike the industry regulation component of the specific environment, advocacy groups cannot force organizations to change their practices. Nevertheless, they can use a number of techniques to try to influence companies: public communications, media advocacy, and product boycotts.

public communications
an advocacy group tactic that relies on voluntary participation by the news media and the advertising industry to get an advocacy group's message out

The **public communications** approach relies on *voluntary* participation by the news media and the advertising industry to send out an advocacy group's message. For example, public service announcements for World No Tobacco Day, which is sponsored by the Campaign for Tobacco-Free Kids, the American Cancer Society, and the American Heart Association, among others, are played on radio and television stations on May 31 each year. These announcements use well-known athletes to warn against the danger of second-hand smoke.[50]

media advocacy
an advocacy group tactic of framing issues as public issues, exposing questionable, exploitative, or unethical practices, and forcing media coverage by buying media time or creating controversy that is likely to receive extensive news coverage

Media advocacy is much more aggressive than the public communications approach. A **media advocacy** approach typically involves framing issues as public issues (affecting everyone); exposing questionable, exploitative, or unethical practices; and obtaining media coverage by buying media time or creating controversy that is likely to receive extensive news coverage. PETA (People for the Ethical Treatment of Animals), which has offices worldwide, uses controversial publicity stunts and advertisements to try to change the behavior of large organizations, fashion designers, medical researchers, and anyone else it believes is hurting or mistreating animals. PETA protesters have stripped naked in front of the White House in front of a banner saying, "I'd rather go naked than wear fur." From PETA's perspective, any animal-based product is bad. Rick McCarty, director of issues management at the National Cattlemen's Beef Association, a frequent PETA target, says, "PETA thinks there is no such thing as bad media coverage. And they're very unrepentant about it."[51]

product boycott
an advocacy group tactic of protesting a company's actions by convincing consumers not to purchase its product or service

A **product boycott** is a tactic in which an advocacy group actively tries to convince consumers not to purchase a company's product or service. The advocacy group Ecopledge.com has signed up 150,000 college students online, all of whom have agreed to boycott organizations that don't respond to their demands. Ecopledge.com, which gives each company one year to make changes and then calls for a boycott, has had success in getting Staples, the office product superstore, to agree not to sell products from endangered forests and to make sure that 30 percent of the paper products it sells are recycled.[52]

Review 3

Specific Environment

The specific environment is made up of five components: customers, competitors, suppliers, industry regulators, and advocacy groups. Companies can monitor customers' needs by identifying customer problems after they occur or by anticipating problems before they occur. However, because they tend to focus on well-known competitors, managers often underestimate their competition or do a poor job of identifying future competitors. Because suppliers and buyers are very dependent on each other, that dependence sometimes leads to opportunistic behavior, in which one benefits at the expense of the other. Regulatory agencies affect businesses by creating rules and then enforcing them. Overall, the level of industry regulation has nearly tripled in the last 25 years. Advocacy groups cannot regulate organizations' practices. Nevertheless, through public communications, media advocacy, and product boycotts, they try to convince companies to change their practices.

4 Making Sense of Changing Environments

In Chapter 1, you learned that managers are responsible for making sense of their business environments. As our just-completed discussions of the general and specific environments indicate, however, making sense of business environments is not an easy task. Because external environments can be dynamic, confusing, and complex, managers use a three-step process to make sense of the changes in their external environments: 4.1 environmental scanning, 4.2 interpreting environmental factors, and 4.3 acting on threats and opportunities.

4.1 Environmental Scanning

environmental scanning searching the environment for important events or issues that might affect an organization

Environmental scanning is searching the environment for important events or issues that might affect an organization. Managers scan the environment to stay up-to-date on important factors in their industry. Managers also scan their environments to reduce uncertainty. When California began rolling blackouts to ration its limited production of electricity, businesses began looking for novel ways to shield themselves from having electricity unexpectedly turned off. Evans Keller, who raises one million turkeys on his farm in arid central California, purchased eight small generators that he can hook up to tractors to run fans and water misters to keep his turkeys cool in the event that the state turns off power in his area. Keller's appeal to the electric utility for exemption from blackout was ultimately denied.[53]

Organizational strategies also affect environmental scanning. In other words, managers pay close attention to trends and events that are directly related to their company's ability to compete in the marketplace.[54] And by keeping their eyes and ears open, managers sometimes come across important information by accident. For example, Gary Costley, an employee of Kellogg's, was pulling into the parking lot at work when he noticed a crane on the loading dock of the General Foods' Post cereal plant across the street. He could see that the crane was unloading a special machine made by a German company for manufacturing cereal. This caught his attention because Kellogg's was having trouble getting a similar machine from a French manufacturer to work. So he went to a store, purchased a camera and film, and stood across the street taking pictures. A Post employee yelled, "Hey, you can't do that." Costley responded, "I'm standing on a public street taking photos. You shouldn't unload your machines in plain sight." The pictures helped convince Kellogg's management to buy the German machines and not spend any more time or money trying to make the French machines work.[55]

Finally, environmental scanning is important because it contributes to organizational performance. Environmental scanning helps managers detect environmental changes and problems before they become organizational crises.[56] Furthermore, companies whose CEOs do more environmental scanning have higher profits.[57] CEOs in better-performing firms scan their firm's environments more frequently and scan more key factors in their environments in more depth and detail than do CEOs in poorer-performing firms.[58]

4.2 Interpreting Environmental Factors

After scanning, managers determine what environmental events and issues mean to the organization. Typically, managers view environmental events and issues as either threats or opportunities. When managers interpret environmental events as threats, they take steps to protect the company from further harm. For example, in France, the neighborhood boulangerie, boucherie, fromagerie, patisserie, and poissonnerie (bakery, butcher, cheese, pastry, and fish shops) have begun to go out of business in large numbers. Their existence is threatened by Carrefour, a grocery chain that runs huge hypermarkets that are sometimes as large as three football fields. French shoppers load up on cartloads of groceries once a week at the Carrefour to save scarce time and money. One of the best buys is France's traditional loaf of bread, the baguette, which sells for about $1 at small bakeries but goes for 40 cents at the hypermarket. So with their businesses in decline, the neighborhood shops have turned to the French government for help, asking it to limit construction of new hypermarkets. They've also asked the government to prevent Carrefour from selling products below cost, a practice that Carrefour says it doesn't use.[59]

By contrast, when managers interpret environmental events as opportunities, they will consider strategic alternatives for taking advantage of those events to improve company performance. Seeing opportunities at opposite ends of the food industry, London-based Unilever paid $2.3 billion for Slim Fast, the maker of nutritional supplements, powders, and bars that help people lose weight, and $326 million for Ben & Jerry's, known for its premium ice cream (Cherry Garcia) and emphasis on social responsibility. Unilever sees an opportunity to expand global sales of both brands.[60]

4.3 Acting on Threats and Opportunities

After scanning for information on environmental events and issues, and interpreting them as threats or opportunities, managers have to decide how to respond to these environmental factors. However, deciding what to do under conditions of uncertainty is difficult. Managers are never completely confident that they have all the information they need or that they correctly understand the information they have.

In the end, managers must complete all three steps—environmental scanning, interpreting environmental factors, and acting on threats and opportunities—to make sense of changing external environments. Environmental scanning helps managers more accurately interpret their environments and take actions that improve company performance. Through scanning, managers keep tabs on what competitors are doing, identify market trends, and stay alert to current events that affect their company's operations. Armed with the environmental information they have gathered, managers can then minimize the impact of threats and turn opportunities into increased profits.

Review 4
Making Sense of Changing Environments

Managers use a three-step process to make sense of external environments: environmental scanning, interpreting information, and acting on it. Managers scan their environments based on their organizational strategies, their need for up-to-date information, and their need to reduce uncertainty. When managers identify environmental events as threats, they take steps to protect the company from harm. When managers identify environmental events as opportunities, they formulate alternatives for taking advantage of them to improve company performance.

Internal Environments

External environments are external trends and events that have the potential to affect companies. The **internal environment** consists of the trends and events within an organization that affect the management, employees, and organizational culture. For example, consider the internal environment at SAS, the leading provider of statistical software. Unlike most software companies that expect employees to work 12- to 14-hour days, SAS offices close at 6 P.M. every evening. Employees also receive unlimited sick days each year. And to encourage employees to spend time with their families, there's an on-site day-care facility, the company cafeteria has plenty of highchairs and baby seats, and the company even has a seven-hour workday. Plus, every Wednesday, the company passes out M&M chocolate candies, plain and peanut, to all employees—a total of more than 22.5 tons of M&Ms per year. David Russo, who heads up Human Resources for SAS, says that founder and CEO Jim Goodnight's idea is that "if you hire adults and treat them like adults, then they'll behave like adults."[61]

internal environment
the events and trends inside an organization that affect management, employees, and organizational culture

Internal environments are important because they affect what people think, feel, and do at work. Given SAS's internal environment, it shouldn't surprise you to know that almost no one quits. In a typical software company the same size as SAS, 1,000 people would quit each year. At SAS, only 130 leave each year.[62] The key component in internal environments is organizational culture. More specifically, **organizational culture** is the set of key values, beliefs, and attitudes shared by organizational members.

organizational culture
the values, beliefs, and attitudes shared by organizational members

After reading the next section, you should be able to

5 explain how organizational cultures are created and how they can help companies be successful.

5 Organizational Cultures: Creation, Success, and Change

Let's take a closer look at 5.1 how organizational cultures are created and maintained, 5.2 the characteristics of successful organizational cultures, and 5.3 how companies can accomplish the difficult task of changing organizational cultures.

5.1 Creation and Maintenance of Organizational Cultures

A primary source of organizational culture is the company founder. Founders like Thomas J. Watson (IBM), Sam Walton (Wal-Mart), Bill Gates (Microsoft), and Frederick Maytag (Maytag) create organizations in their own images that they imprint with their beliefs, attitudes, and values.

Though company founders are instrumental in the creation of organizational cultures, founders retire, die, or choose to leave their companies. When the founders are gone, how are their values, attitudes, and beliefs sustained in the organizational culture? Answer: stories and heroes.

Organizational members tell **organizational stories** to make sense of organizational events and changes and to emphasize culturally consistent assumptions, decisions, and actions.[63] At Wal-Mart, stories abound about founder Sam Walton's thriftiness as he strove to make Wal-Mart the low-cost retailer that it is today.

organizational stories
stories told by organizational members to make sense of organizational events and changes and to emphasize culturally consistent assumptions, decisions, and actions

> In those days, we would go on buying trips with Sam, and we'd all stay, as much as we could, in one room or two. I remember

> one time in Chicago when we stayed eight of us to a room. And the room wasn't very big to begin with. You might say we were on a pretty restricted budget. (Gary Reinboth, one of Wal-Mart's first store managers)[64]

Today, Sam Walton's thriftiness still permeates Wal-Mart. Everyone, including top executives and the CEO, flies coach rather than business or first class. When traveling on business, it's still the norm to share rooms (though two to a room, not eight!) at inexpensive hotels like Motel 6 and Super 8 instead of more expensive Holiday Inns.[65]

organizational heroes
people celebrated for their qualities and achievements within an organization

A second way in which organizational culture is sustained is by recognizing and celebrating heroes. By definition, **organizational heroes** are organizational people admired for their qualities and achievements within the organization. The motto of the United Services Automobile Association (USAA), which provides insurance to people in the U.S. Army, Navy, Air Force, Marines, and Coast Guard, is "We know what it means to serve." Mrs. Lawless, an elderly widow of a military officer, called Stephanie Valadez, a USAA customer service representative, during an ice storm because she had no heat and couldn't get out to get the medicine she needed. Valadez immediately called the Red Cross, which helped Mrs. Lawless with her heat and her medicine. Valadez also stayed on the line for an extended time to comfort Mrs. Lawless—though her computer screen indicated that Mrs. Lawless's insurance policy had long since lapsed. Kent Williams of USAA commented, "That's what we mean when we say that customer service is a relationship, not a transaction."[66]

5.2 Successful Organizational Cultures

Preliminary research shows that organizational culture is related to organizational success. Cultures based on adaptability, involvement, a clear vision, and consistency can help companies achieve higher sales growth, return on assets, profits, quality, and employee satisfaction.[67]

Adaptability is the ability to notice and respond to changes in the organization's environment. Cultures need to reinforce important values and behaviors, but a culture becomes dysfunctional if it prevents change.

In cultures that promote higher levels of *employee involvement* in decision making, employees feel a greater sense of ownership and responsibility. For instance, some people question whether SAS's fantastic benefits create a sense of entitlement, rather than a sense of ownership and responsibility. David Russo, who heads human resources for SAS, says, "To some people, this looks like the Good Ship Lollipop, floating down a stream. It's not. It's part of a soundly designed strategy." And that strategy is to take away anything that gets in the way of people doing their work. At SAS, this strategy works. Says employee Kathy Passarella, "You're given the freedom, the flexibility, and the resources to do your job. Because you're treated well, you treat the company well. When you walk down the halls here, it's rare that you hear people talking about anything but work."[68]

company vision
a company's purpose or reason for existing

A **company's vision** is its purpose or reason for existing. In organizational cultures where there is a clear organizational vision, the organization's strategic purpose and direction are apparent to everyone in the company. And when managers are uncertain about their business environments, the vision helps guide the discussions, decisions, and behavior of the people in the company. At F. H. Faulding & Company, an Australia-based provider of health-care products and services doing business in 70 countries, the vision is "delivering innovative and valued solutions in healthcare."[69] This vision lets employees know why the company is in business (to deliver health-care solutions) and the values that really matter (innovative and valued solutions).

Specific vision statements strengthen organizational cultures by letting everyone know why the company is in business, what really matters (i.e., values), and how those values can be used to guide daily actions and behaviors.[70] Commenting on the value of Faulding's vision statement, Donna Martin, the senior vice president of human resources, says, "A vision has to be more than a set of target revenue or profit numbers to meet. It has to be elevating, inspiring, with a strong emphasis on the future. A vision has to be a compelling and crystal-clear statement about where the organization is heading."[71]

consistent organizational cultures when a company actively defines and teaches organizational values, beliefs, and attitudes

Finally, in **consistent organizational cultures**, the company actively defines and teaches organizational values, beliefs, and attitudes. Consistent organizational cultures are also called strong cultures because the core beliefs are widely shared and strongly held. The culture aboard nuclear submarines is an example of a highly consistent, extremely strong organizational culture.

5.3 Changing Organizational Cultures

As shown in Exhibit 2.4, organizational cultures exist on three levels.[72] First, on the surface level, are the reflections of an organization's culture that can be seen, heard, or observed, such as symbolic artifacts (e.g., dress codes and office layouts, and workers' and managers' behaviors). Next, just below the surface, are the values and beliefs expressed by people in the company. You can't see these, but by listening carefully to what people say and how decisions are made or explained, those values and beliefs become clear. Finally, unconsciously held assumptions and beliefs are buried deep below the surface. These are the unwritten views and rules that are so strongly held and so widely shared that they are rarely discussed or even thought about unless someone attempts to change them or unknowingly violates them. When it comes to changing cultures, it can be very difficult to change unconscious assumptions and beliefs held deep below the surface. Instead, managers should focus on the parts of the organizational culture they can control; these include observable surface-level items, such as workers' behaviors and symbolic artifacts, and expressed values and beliefs, which can be influenced through employee selection. Let's see how these can be used to change organizational cultures.

One way of changing a corporate culture is to use behavioral addition or behavioral substitution to

exhibit 2.4

Three Levels of Organizational Culture

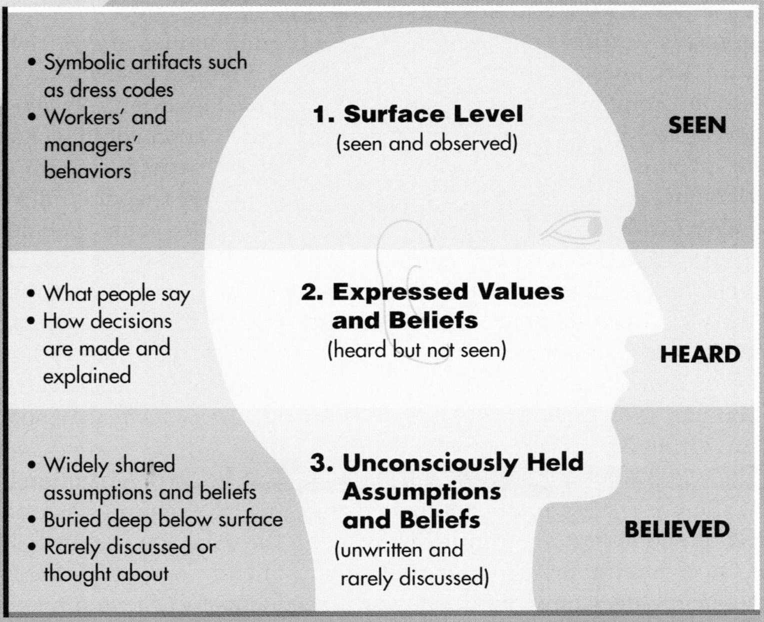

• Symbolic artifacts such as dress codes
• Workers' and managers' behaviors
1. Surface Level
(seen and observed)
SEEN
• What people say
• How decisions are made and explained
2. Expressed Values and Beliefs
(heard but not seen)
HEARD
• Widely shared assumptions and beliefs
• Buried deep below surface
• Rarely discussed or thought about
3. Unconsciously Held Assumptions and Beliefs
(unwritten and rarely discussed)
BELIEVED

behavioral addition
the process of having managers and employees perform new behaviors that are central to and symbolic of the new organizational culture that a company wants to create

behavioral substitution
the process of having managers and employees perform new behaviors central to the "new" organizational culture in place of behaviors that were central to the "old" organizational culture

visible artifacts
visible signs of an organization's culture, such as the office design and layout, company dress code, and company benefits and perks, like stock options, personal parking spaces, or the private company dining room

establish new patterns of behavior among managers and employees.[73] **Behavioral addition** is the process of having managers and employees perform a new behavior, while **behavioral substitution** is having managers and employees perform a new behavior in place of another behavior. The key in both instances is to choose behaviors that are central to and symbolic of the "old" culture you're changing and the "new" culture that you want to create. One of the key behavioral changes at Continental Airlines in the last decade is that the airline has gone from last to first in terms of on-time arrivals.[74] Under the "late-arrival culture," a flight attendant would be more worried about leaving the gate with the right number of meals on the plane than leaving on time. According to CEO Gordon Bethune, now, under the "on-time arrival culture," the flight attendant would look at the caterer and say, "Hey, don't you do this to me again." She would then close the plane's door and leave the gate on time by "finding some investment bankers in the back who will trade food for booze." According to Bethune, "That's how she gets paid. That's how behavior changes: We become collective winners and give things customers' value."[75]

Another way in which managers can begin to change corporate culture is to change the **visible artifacts** of their old culture, such as the office design and layout, company dress code, and recipients (or nonrecipients) of company benefits and perks like stock options, personal parking spaces, or the private company dining room.

Cultures can also be changed by hiring and selecting people with values and beliefs consistent with the company's desired culture. *Selection* is the process of gathering information about job applicants to decide who should be offered a job. As discussed in Chapter 12 on Human Resources, most selection instruments measure whether job applicants have the knowledge, skills, and abilities needed to succeed in their jobs. Today, however, companies are increasingly testing job applicants for their fit with the company's desired culture (i.e., values and beliefs). Management consultant Ram Charan says, "A poor job match is not only harmful to the individual but also to the company."[76] The first step in successfully hiring people who have values consistent with the desired culture is to define and describe that culture.

The second step is to ensure applicants fit with the culture by using selection tests, instruments, and exercises to measure these values and beliefs in job applicants. (See Chapter 12 for a complete review of applicant and managerial selection.) At Southwest Airlines, humor and a good attitude are two of the most important requirements in its new hires. Chairman and former CEO Herb Kelleher says, "What's important is that a customer should get off the airplane feeling: 'I didn't just get from A to B. I had one of the most pleasant experiences I ever had and I'll be back for that reason.'"[77] For instance, on one Southwest plane, Yvonne Masters jokingly introduced her fellow flight attendants as her "former husband and his new girlfriend."[78] Southwest passenger Mark Rafferty said his favorite Southwest flight attendant joke was when "They told everyone on the plane's left side, toward the terminal, to put their faces in the window and smile so our competitors can see what a full flight looks like."[79] Says Kelleher, "We draft great attitudes. If you don't have a good attitude, we don't want you, no matter how skilled you are. We can change skill level through training. We can't change attitude."[80]

Corporate cultures are very difficult to change. Consequently, there is no guarantee that any one approach—changing visible cultural artifacts, behavioral substitution, or hiring people with values consistent with a company's desired culture—will change a company's organizational culture. The best results are obtained by combining these methods. Together, these are some of the best tools managers have for changing culture because they send the clear message to managers and employees that "the accepted way of doing things" has changed.

Review 5

Organizational Cultures: Creation, Success, and Change

Organizational culture is the set of key values, beliefs, and attitudes shared by organizational members. Organizational cultures are often created by company founders and then sustained through the telling of organizational stories and the celebration of organizational heroes. Adaptable cultures that promote employee involvement, make clear the organization's strategic purpose and direction, and actively define and teach organizational values and beliefs can help companies achieve higher sales growth, return on assets, profits, quality, and employee satisfaction. Organizational cultures exist on three levels: the surface level, where cultural artifacts and behaviors can be observed; just below the surface, where values and beliefs are expressed; and deep below the surface, where unconsciously held assumptions and beliefs exist. Managers can begin to change company cultures by focusing on the top two levels and by using behavioral substitution and behavioral addition, changing visible artifacts, and selecting job applicants with values and beliefs consistent with the desired company culture.

STUDY TIP Create your own diagram of the business environment and compare it to the example in the chapter. Read a selection of business press articles and list the environmental factors at play in each of the articles. Visit Effective Management Online at **http://em-online.swlearning.com** for a wealth of review and mastery activities.

MANAGEMENT TEAM DECISION

REKINDLING THE ROMANCE WITH RETAIL

Nothing drives the world economy quite like the American consumer.[81] And until lately, Americans liked to do their consuming at the shopping mall. Americans also loved going to the mall, even if they didn't intend to shop (think mall walkers).

In the 1980s, developers transitioned from strip malls to upscale shopping malls, and your management team responded by enclosing and expanding the Kenwood Plaza, a fairly standard strip mall, and transforming it into the Kenwood Towne Centre, an upscale shopping mall similar to the King of Prussia Mall outside Philadelphia and Cherry Creek in Denver. Trendy stores looking to move into the Cincinnati, Ohio area would always land at Kenwood, a suburb 20 minutes outside downtown. The glittering, marble-floored mall wooed new and exciting tenants, lured the movie theater across the road to share part of the mall's lower level with the food court, and became *the* retail destination for shopping Cincinnatians.

Today Kenwood Towne Centre is still a primary shopping destination, but it is not *the* primary shopping destination. Trendy stores are now just as likely to end up in Norwood's Rookwood Pavilion and Rookwood Commons located in a first-ring suburb near several affluent neighborhoods. Rookwood is a lifestyle center where all storefronts are outside, but the connected retailers look like a city street. The popularity of Rookwood has significantly affected the traffic at the Towne Center.

For this exercise, your team will be researching the components of the general and specific environments of the retail development industry. Consider a mall in your area as the focus of your research. If one does not immediately come to mind, you can use the Kenwood Towne Centre example above or the better-known Hollywood and Highland Mall in Los Angeles, Woodfield Mall in a Chicago suburb, or Clearwater Mall in Pinellas County, Florida. Think critically about each component of the total environment (economic, technological, political/legal, sociocultural, customer, competition, industry regulation, suppliers, and advocacy groups).

Additional Internet resources are listed below, but if you have chosen a local mall, some trips to the mall could provide valuable information: the number of empty storefronts, the level of traffic in the mall and in the stores, the demographics of the people in the mall, and so forth. You may wish to visit a couple of competitors as well.

- **http://www.nrf.com**—*The National Retail Federation*
- **http://www.icsc.org**—The International Council of Shopping Centers
- **http://www.stores.org**—The Web site for the industry magazine *Stores*
- **http://infotrac.thomsonlearning.com**

Once the team has completed its research, get all the members together to work out the following activities and questions.

Activities and Questions

1. Each team member should present a profile of the environmental components he or she researched. Begin with the general environment, describing factors in the current general environment that affect all businesses.
2. Continue by presenting the components of the mall industry's specific environment.
3. Not all environmental factors affect all businesses equally. Next, make a list of the factors you identified in your collective research that directly affect the mall you are working on. Identify each factor as a threat, an opportunity, or a nonissue.
4. Decide as a team the seriousness of each threat and the quality of each opportunity. The team may wish to use a numerical ranking scale, such as 1 for a low threat and 5 for a severe threat, and so forth. Resolve differences of opinion by returning to your collective research.
5. What kind of changes will your management team recommend for your shopping mall? Do you simply remodel the interior? Do you try a more substantial modification to the mall's structure? Or do you bulldoze and begin anew? Explain your decision.

DEVELOP YOUR CAREER POTENTIAL

DEALING WITH THE PRESS

In this age of 24-hour cable news channels, tabloid news shows, and aggressive local and national news reporters intent on exposing corporate wrongdoing, one of the most important skills for a manager to learn is how to deal effectively with the press.[82] Test your ability to deal effectively with the press by putting yourself in the following situation. To make the situation more realistic, read the scenario and then give yourself two minutes to write a response to each question.

Hotel Customer Dies in Strange Accident

"Beep." You look at your watch. It's 4 A.M. This has been the longest night of your life. You've worked for the Hamada Jackson hotel for about a year as the late-night manager. The pay is OK, but the best part is that the job is safe, and so quiet that you can study. Your college grades have gotten much better since you started, and it looks like you'll be able to get into graduate school. But you didn't get any studying done tonight. Channel 8's news crew just left. They were monitoring the police scanner around 1:15 A.M., right after you called 911 in a panic. One of your responsibilities is to take a quick walk through the hallways a couple of times a night just to make sure everything is OK. When you made your 1 A.M. check, everything was quiet until you hit the last hallway on the west side of the hotel. As you came around the corner, you almost stepped on her. Somehow, in a freak accident, a young woman who, according to your records, had checked into the hotel at about 10:30 P.M., an hour before you came on duty, was dead on the floor. She was still soaking wet from the rain that had started that afternoon. You learned later that she had been electrocuted when she put her card-key in the lock of her metal door.

Much to your dismay, the Channel 8 news crew arrived 10 minutes after the cops and the emergency medical team. After videotaping the scene and the crews loading the body into the ambulance, they turned their attention, lights, and camera on you.

1. "Can you tell us what happened? The emergency medical team told us that the burns on her hands and the smell of smoke led them to believe that she was electrocuted in your hotel hallway. Can you tell us what happened and how someone could be electrocuted in this way?"

2. "What was the victim's name? How old was she? Where is she from? Do you know what she was doing while staying at the hotel?"

3. "The emergency medical team estimated the time of death to be between 10:30 and 11:00 P.M., which means that the body has been in the hallway for several hours. Does your hotel have a security force? Why wasn't somebody making periodic checks of the premises to make sure everything was safe? Also, does anybody on the staff have any medical training to deal with emergencies like choking or heart attacks?"

BIZ FLIX Backdraft

Two brothers follow in the footsteps of their late father, a legendary Chicago firefighter, and join the department. Stephen "Bull" McCaffrey (Kurt Russell) joins first and rises to the rank of lieutenant. Younger brother Brian (William Baldwin) joins later and becomes a member of Bull's Company 17. Sibling rivalry tarnishes their work relationships, but they continue to successfully fight Chicago fires. Add a plot element about a mysterious arsonist and you have the basis of an ordinary film. The film, however, rises above its otherwise formulaic plot thanks to great acting and amazing special effects. The intense, unprecedented special effects give the viewer an unparalleled experience of what it is like to fight a fire. Chicago firefighters applauded the realism of the fire scenes.[83]

This scene appears early in the film as part of "The First Day" sequence. Brian McCaffrey has graduated from the fire academy, and the fire department has assigned him to his brother's company. This scene shows him fighting his first real fire at a garment factory. The film continues with Company 17 fighting the fire and Brian receiving some harsh first-day lessons.

What to Watch for and Ask Yourself

1. What elements of the Chicago fire department culture does this scene show? Does the scene show any cultural artifacts or symbols? If it does, what are they?
2. Does the scene show any values that guide the firefighters' behavior?
3. What does Brian McCaffrey learn on his first day at work?

MGMT WORKPLACE Ziba Design

The best company you've never heard of is probably Ziba Design. Ziba has won more design awards per employee than any other design firm in the world. Its designs have shaped items ranging from squeegees to smoke detectors and keyboards to broom handles. Its clients include all the best companies you have heard of—Microsoft, Nike, McDonald's, Procter & Gamble, and Ford, to name just a few. The reasons for Ziba's success are many. It designs for profitability first; its employees from over 17 countries bring multiple perspectives to any problem; and its culture of perfectionism yields a scientific approach to artistic creation that satisfies aesthetic, performance, and economic demand.

What to Watch for and Ask Yourself

1. What are the key beliefs, values, and structures in Ziba's successful organizational culture?
2. Discuss Sohrab Vossoughi's role as an organizational hero in his own company.
3. How does Ziba operate in its specific environment?

CHAPTER THREE

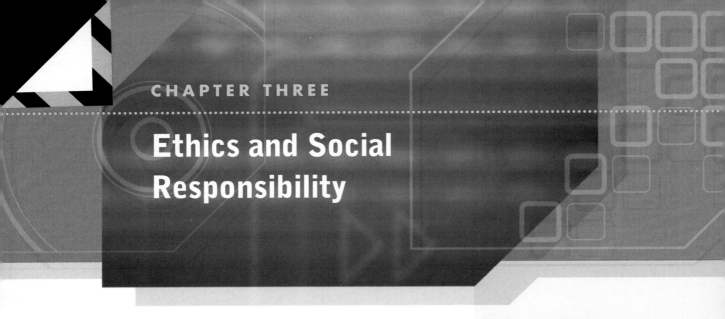

Ethics and Social Responsibility

outline

WHAT WOULD YOU DO?

Rite Aid Headquarters, Camp Hill, Pennsylvania.[1] With 75,000 employees, 3,500 stores in 28 states, and $15.2 billion in sales, Rite Aid, the third largest drugstore chain in the United States, has been included in *Fortune* magazine's list of "America's Most Admired Companies." Rite Aid began modestly in 1962 as Thrif D Discount Center in Scranton, Pennsylvania. By 1970, it had expanded to five northeastern states, changed its name to Rite Aid Corporation, and listed its stock on the New York Stock Exchange. Over the years, Rite Aid has grown by building new stores and buying other pharmaceutical chains. During the late 1980s, Rite Aid acquired 420 drugstores in Florida, Maryland, Washington, D.C., Delaware, Indiana, New York, Ohio, Virginia, West Virginia, North Carolina, and Pennsylvania. In the 1990s, it bought Perry Drug Stores, the largest drugstore chain in Michigan; acquired 1,000 stores by buying Thrifty PayLess Holdings, the largest drugstore chain in the western United States; and purchased another 332

student resources

Experiencing Management
Explore the four levels of learning by doing the simulation module on Ethics & Social Responsibility.

Study Guide
Mini lecture reviews all the learning points in the chapter and concludes with a case on BMG Records.

Take Two Video
Biz Flix is a scene from *Emperor's Club*. Management Workplace is a segment on Timberland.

PowerPoint®
12 slides with graphics provide an outline for this chapter.

Author Insights
Chuck talks about why it's hard to do the right thing.

Self Test
23 true/false questions, 22 multiple-choice questions, a management scenario, and 6 exhibit worksheets

other drugstores from Harco, Inc. and K&B, Inc. It also bought PCS Health Systems, a pharmacy benefits management company, only to sell it two years later.

Rite Aid's quick expansion has come under the leadership of your new boss, CEO and chairman Martin Grass. Approximately three years before you were hired, Martin wrested control of the company from his father, company founder Alex Grass, in a tension-filled palace coup. Roger Grass, Martin's younger brother said that Martin "told me he was going to take Dad out as chairman of the board." According to Roger, after Alex Grass picked Martin to replace him as CEO, Martin told him, "Thanks very much. You can leave."

Initially, you were thrilled to become the chief financial officer for a company with such tremendous growth and profits and a sterling reputation, but now, only months later, you are starting to worry. As you learn about the company's finances, you are finding numerous problems and mistakes. Instead of being paid out of cash flows, monthly bills have been paid from special reserve accounts that were to be accessed only when closing stores. And since Rite Aid was opening stores, not closing them, those funds should never have been touched. You have also found that millions of dollars in regular bills were recorded incorrectly to make expenses look smaller and profits look bigger. In addition, fake credits were used to indicate that $75 million worth of bills had been paid when they actually hadn't. Furthermore, you are fairly certain that public quarterly financial reports were "doctored" to improve results. Together, these mistakes or missteps or whatever they were overstated profits by hundreds of millions of dollars.

You are aware of how explosive and damaging the revelations would be if Rite Aid announced to the public, Wall Street, and the government that it had wildly overstated its earnings. Moreover, you are losing sleep over the reaction you'll get from your boss, CEO Martin Grass. In an effort to raise money to pay off hundreds of millions in acquisition-related debt, Grass has been asking the company's bankers to extend a larger line of credit. He has also been spending considerable time and effort trying to get the Securities and Exchange Commission to allow Rite Aid to approve a secondary stock offering that could raise hundreds of millions of dollars. You know that you need to discuss your findings with him, but fear that the financial pressures he faces as CEO will lead him to "shoot the messenger."

Unable to sleep, you slip out to the kitchen so that you won't disturb your wife, put on a pot of coffee, and grab a pen and paper. After two hours and three cups of coffee, you've boiled the situation down to these key questions: Should you tell your boss, CEO Martin Grass? Will you be risking your job and your retirement if you tell him? Are the consequences of not doing anything greater than the consequences of reporting these problems? In particular, who will be harmed if you don't do anything and who will be harmed if you do? If ethics means "doing the right thing," then what should you do in this situation? **If you were the chief financial officer for Rite Aid, what would you do?**

This dilemma is an example of the tough decisions that managers face about ethics and social responsibility. Unfortunately, one of the "real-world" aspects of these decisions is that no matter what you decide, someone or some group will be unhappy with the decision. Managers don't have the luxury of choosing theoretically optimal, win-win solutions that are obviously correct to everyone involved. In practice, solutions to ethics and social responsibility problems aren't optimal. Often, they are "make-do" or "do the least harm" kinds of solutions. Crystal clear rights and wrongs rarely reveal themselves to managers charged with "doing the right thing." The business world is much messier than that.

We begin this chapter by examining ethical behavior in the workplace and how the U.S. Sentencing Guidelines for Organizations make ethical behavior much more important for businesses. Second, we examine the influences on ethical decision making and review practical steps that managers can take to improve ethical decision making. We finish by considering to whom organizations are socially responsible, what organizations are socially responsible for, how they can respond to societal expectations for social responsibility, and whether social responsibility hurts or helps an organization's economic performance.

What Is Ethical and Unethical Workplace Behavior?

Ethics is the set of moral principles or values that defines right and wrong for a person or group. Unfortunately, numerous studies have consistently produced distressing results about the state of ethics in today's business world. In a nationwide survey of 2,300 workers, 75 percent indicated that they had seen unethical behavior at work, such as deceptive sales practices, unsafe working conditions, environmental breaches, and mishandling of confidential or proprietary information within the last year.[2] Furthermore, 60 percent of workers felt substantial pressure to commit unethical or illegal acts at work. And, in a study of 1,324 randomly selected workers, managers, and executives across multiple industries, 48 percent of respondents admitted to actually committing an unethical or illegal act in the past year!

ethics
the set of moral principles or values that defines right and wrong for a person or group

These studies also contained good news, however. When people are convinced that they work in an ethical work environment, they are six times more likely to stay with that company than if they believe they work in an unethical environment.[3] Furthermore, when 570 white-collar workers were asked about 28 qualities in company leaders, honesty (24 percent) and integrity/morals/ethics (16 percent) were far more important than any other qualities (caring/compassion was third at 7 percent).[4] In short, a lot of work needs to be done to make workplaces more ethical, but, and this is very important, most managers and employees want this to happen.

After reading the next two sections, you should be able to

1. discuss how the nature of management jobs creates the possibility for ethical abuses.
2. describe the U.S. Sentencing Commission Guidelines for Organizations and explain how its recommendations make ethical behavior much more important for businesses.

1 Ethics and the Nature of Management Jobs

ethical behavior behavior that conforms to a society's accepted principles of right and wrong

Ethical behavior follows accepted principles of right and wrong. By contrast, unethical management behavior, such as lying about company profits or knowingly producing an unsafe product, occurs when managers personally violate accepted principles of right and wrong or encourage others to do so. Because of the nature of their jobs, managers can be tempted to engage in unethical managerial behavior in four areas: authority and power, handling information, influencing the behavior of others, and setting goals.

The *authority and power* inherent in some management positions can tempt managers to engage in unethical practices. Since managers often control company resources, there is a risk that some managers will cross the line from legitimate use of company resources to personal use. Human resources can be misused as well. For example, unless it's in an employee's job description, using an employee to do personal chores, like picking up the manager's dry cleaning, is unethical behavior. Even worse, though, is using one's managerial authority and power for direct personal gain. Before it was known that Enron was lying about its profits, it paid out $750 million of its $975 million net income directly to company executives. Within a year, Enron had filed for bankruptcy, cheating stockholders and employees out of billions of dollars.[5]

> **www.experiencing management.com**
>
> The ethical behaviors of managers and employees can have dramatic impacts on the way organizations are perceived by society. To learn more about ethical approaches and guidelines, visit our animated concept and activity site. Choose Ethics&Social_Responsibility from the "select a topic" pull-down menu, then Ethical Approaches from the "overview tab."
> **http://www.experiencingmanagement.com**

Handling information is another area in which managers must be careful to behave ethically. Information is a key part of management work. Managers collect it, analyze it, act on it, and disseminate it. In doing so, they are expected to be truthful and, when necessary, to keep confidential information confidential. Leaking company secrets to competitors, "doctoring" the numbers, wrongfully withholding information, and lying are some of the ways managers may misuse information entrusted to them. For example, managers at Bausch & Lomb's Hong Kong division used the term "Ba dan" (literally "white sheet") to refer to the fake sales numbers they sent to company headquarters each month. To maintain Hong Kong's status as Bausch & Lomb's top international division, the managers faked the sales numbers for their Southeast Asian customers. Then, to make the fake numbers look like real sales, they would ship products (glasses and contact lenses) to a phony customer warehouse.[6] Bausch & Lomb used company auditors plus its internal security department, which was run by ex-Secret Service agents and police officers, to set up "sting" operations to catch the employees who were running the "Ba dan" scam in Hong Kong.

Managers must also be careful to engage in ethical behavior in the way they *influence the behavior of others*, especially those they supervise. Managerial work gives managers significant power to influence others. If managers tell employees to perform unethical acts (or face punishment), such as "faking the numbers to get results," then they are abusing their managerial power. This is sometimes called the "move it or lose it" syndrome. "Move it or lose it" managers tell employees, "Do it. You're paid to do it. If you can't do it, we'll find somebody who can."[7]

Setting goals is another way that managers influence the behavior of their employees. If managers set unrealistic goals, the pressure to perform and achieve those goals can influence employees to engage in unethical business behaviors, especially if they are just short of meeting their goals. After some disappointing sales numbers at WorldCom, a regional vice president threatened disciplinary action against everyone who missed their forecast. At this point, numerous sales representatives began double booking their sales (thus "doubling" their sales and their commissions) in two separate sales revenue databases (one from the MCI division and one from WorldCom) that had not yet been merged.[8]

Review 1

Ethics and the Nature of Management Jobs

Ethics is the set of moral principles or values that define right and wrong. Ethical behavior occurs when managers follow those principles and values. Because they set the standard for others in the workplace, managers can model ethical behavior by using resources for company and not personal business. Furthermore, managers can encourage ethical behavior by handling information in a confidential and honest fashion, by not using their authority to influence others to engage in unethical behavior, by not creating policies that unintentionally reward employees for unethical behavior, and by setting reasonable rather than unreasonable goals.

2 U.S. Sentencing Commission Guidelines for Organizations

A male supervisor is sexually harassing female coworkers. A sales representative offers a $10,000 kickback to persuade an indecisive customer to do business with his company. A company president secretly meets with her biggest competitor's CEO, and both agree not to compete in markets where the other has already established customers. Each of these behaviors is clearly unethical (and, in these cases, illegal, too). Historically, if management was unaware of such activities, the company could not be held responsible for an employee's unethical acts. Now, however, under the U.S. Sentencing Commission Guidelines for Organizations, companies can be prosecuted and *punished even if management didn't know about the unethical behavior.* Moreover, penalties can be substantial, with maximum fines approaching $300 million![9]

Let's examine 2.1 **to whom the guidelines apply and what they cover** and 2.2 **how, according to the guidelines, an organization can be punished for the unethical behavior of its managers and employees.**

2.1 Who, What, and Why?

Nearly all businesses, nonprofits, partnerships, labor unions, unincorporated organizations and associations, incorporated organizations, and even pension funds, trusts, and joint stock companies are covered by the guidelines. If your organization can be characterized as a business (remember, nonprofits count too), then it is subject to the guidelines.[10]

The guidelines cover offenses defined by federal laws, such as invasion of privacy, price fixing, fraud, customs violations, antitrust violations, civil rights violations, theft, money laundering, conflicts of interest, embezzlement, dealing in stolen goods, copyright infringements, extortion, and more. However, it's not enough to stay "within the law." The purpose of the guidelines is not just to punish companies *after* they or their employees break the law, but rather to encourage companies to take proactive steps that will discourage or prevent white-collar crime *before* it happens. The guidelines also give companies an incentive to cooperate with and disclose illegal activities to federal authorities.[11]

2.2 Determining the Punishment

The guidelines impose smaller fines on companies that take proactive steps to encourage ethical behavior or voluntarily disclose illegal activities to federal authorities. Essentially, the law uses a "carrot-and-stick" approach. The stick is the threat of heavy fines that can total millions of dollars. The carrot is a greatly reduced fine, but only if the company has started an effective compliance program (discussed below) to encourage ethical behavior *before* the illegal activity occurs.[12] Understanding how a company's punishment is determined can help you understand the importance of establishing a compliance program.

The first step is to compute the base fine by determining what level of offense has occurred. The level of the offense (i.e., the seriousness of the problem) varies depending on the kind of crime, the loss incurred by the victims, and how much planning went into the crime. For example, simple fraud is a level 6 offense (there are 38 levels in all). But if the victims of that fraud lost more than $5 million, that level 6 offense becomes a level 22 offense. Moreover, anything beyond minimal planning to commit the fraud results in an increase of two levels to a level 24 offense. How much difference would this make to the company? Crimes at or below level 6 incur a base fine of $5,000, whereas the base fine for level 24 is $2.1 million. So the difference is $2.095 million! The base fine for level 38, the top-level offense, is an astounding $72.5 million!

After assessing a base fine, the judge computes a culpability score, which is a way of assigning blame to the company. The culpability score can range from a minimum of 0.05 to a maximum of 4.0. The greater the corporate responsibility in conducting, encouraging, or santioning illegal or unethical activity, the higher the culpability score. A company that already has a compliance program and voluntarily reports the offense to authorities will incur a culpability score of 0.05. By contrast, a company whose management secretly plans, approves, and participates in illegal or unethical activity will receive the maximum score of 4.0.

The culpability score is critical because the total fine is computed by multiplying the base fine by the culpability score. Going back to our level 24 fraud offense, a company with a compliance program that turns itself in will be fined only $105,000 ($2,100,000 × 0.05). However, a company that secretly planned, approved, and participated in illegal activity will be fined $8.4 million ($2,100,000 × 4.0)! The difference is even greater for level 38 offenses. A "good guy" with a 0.05 culpability score is fined only $3.625 million, whereas a "bad guy" with a 4.0 culpability score is fined a whopping $290 million! These differences clearly show the importance of having a compliance program in place. Over the last decade, 1,494 companies have been charged under the U.S. Sentencing Guidelines. Seventy-six percent of those charged were fined, with the average fine exceeding $2 million. Company fines are on average 20 times larger now than before the implementation of the guidelines in 1991.[13]

Fortunately, for companies that want to avoid paying these stiff fines, the U.S. Sentencing Guidelines are clear on the seven necessary components of an effective compliance program.[14] Exhibit 3.1 lists those components.

For more information, see "An Overview of the Organizational Sentencing Guidelines" at **http://www.ussc.gov/training/corpover.PDF** and "Organization Sentencing Guidelines: Questions and Answers" at **http://www.ussc.gov/training/corpq&a.pdf**.

exhibit 3.1

Compliance Program Steps for the U.S. Sentencing Guidelines for Organizations

1. Establish standards and procedures to meet the company's business needs.
2. Put upper-level managers in charge of the compliance program.
3. Don't delegate decision-making authority to employees who are likely to act illegally or unethically.
4. Use auditing, monitoring, and other methods to encourage employees to report violations.
5. Use company publications and training to inform employees about the company's compliance standards and procedures.
6. Enforce compliance standards by fairly and consistently disciplining violators.
7. After violations occur, find appropriate ways to improve the compliance program.

Source: D. R. Dalton, M. B. Metzger, & J. W. Hill, "The 'New' U.S. Sentencing Commission Guidelines: A Wake-up Call for Corporate America," Academy of Management Executive *8 (1994): 7–16.*

Review 2

U.S. Sentencing Commission Guidelines

Under the U.S. Sentencing Commission Guidelines, companies can be prosecuted and fined up to $300 million for employees' illegal actions. Fines are computed by multiplying the base fine by a culpability score, which ranges from 0.05 to 4.0. Companies that establish compliance programs to encourage ethical behavior can reduce their culpability scores and their fines. Companies without compliance programs can face much heavier fines than companies with established compliance programs. Compliance programs must establish standards and procedures, be run by top managers, encourage hiring and promotion of honest and ethical people, encourage employees to report violations, educate employees about compliance, punish violators, and find ways to improve the program after violations occur.

How Do You Make Ethical Decisions?

On a cold morning in the midst of a winter storm, schools were closed, and most people had decided to stay home from work. Nevertheless, Richard Addessi had already showered, shaved, and dressed for the office. Addessi, whose father worked at IBM for 36 years, was just four months short of his 30-year anniversary with the company. Addessi kissed his wife Joan goodbye, but before he could get to his car, he fell dead on the garage floor of a sudden heart attack. Having begun work at IBM at the age of 18, he was just 48 years old.[15]

You're the vice president in charge of benefits at IBM. Given that he was four months short of full retirement, do you award full retirement benefits to Mr. Addessi's wife and daughters? If the answer is yes, they will receive his full retirement benefits of $1,800 a month and free lifetime medical coverage. If you say no, Mrs. Addessi and her daughters will receive only $340 a month. They will also have to pay $473 a month just to continue their current medical coverage. As the VP in charge of benefits at IBM, what would be the ethical thing to do?

After reading the next two sections, you should be able to

3 describe what influences ethical decision making.

4 explain what practical steps managers can take to improve ethical decision making.

3 Influences on Ethical Decision Making

So, what did IBM decide to do? Since Richard Addessi was four months short of 30 years with the company, IBM officials felt they had no choice but to give Joan Addessi and her two daughters the smaller, partial retirement benefits. Do you think IBM's decision was ethical? Probably many of you don't. You wonder how the company could be so heartless as to deny Richard Addessi's family the full benefits to which you believe they were entitled. Yet others might argue that IBM did the ethical thing by strictly following the rules laid out in its pension benefit plan. After all, being fair means applying the rules to everyone. Although some ethical issues are easily solved, for many there are no clearly right or wrong answers.

The ethical answers that managers choose depend on 3.1 the ethical intensity of the decision and 3.2 the moral development of the manager.

3.1 Ethical Intensity of the Decision

Managers don't treat all ethical decisions the same. The manager who has to decide whether to deny or extend full benefits to Joan Addessi and her family is going to treat that decision much more seriously than the decision of how to deal with an assistant who has been taking computer paper home for personal use. The difference between these decisions is one of **ethical intensity**, which is how concerned people are about an ethical issue. When addressing an issue of high ethical intensity, managers are more aware of the impact their decision will have on others. They are more likely to view the decision as an ethical or moral decision rather than as an economic decision. They are also more likely to worry about doing the "right thing."

ethical intensity the degree of concern people have about an ethical issue

Ethical intensity depends on six factors:[16]

- magnitude of consequences
- social consensus
- probability of effect
- temporal immediacy
- proximity of effect
- concentration of effect.

magnitude of consequences the total harm or benefit derived from an ethical decision

social consensus agreement on whether behavior is bad or good

probability of effect the chance that something will happen and then harm others

temporal immediacy the time between an act and the consequences the act produces

Magnitude of consequences is the total harm or benefit derived from an ethical decision. The more people who are harmed or the greater the harm to those people, the larger the consequences. **Social consensus** is agreement on whether behavior is bad or good. For example, most people agree that killing is wrong except in self-defense, but people strongly disagree about whether abortion or the death penalty is wrong. **Probability of effect** is the chance that something will happen and then result in harm to others.

Temporal immediacy is the time between an act and the consequences the act produces. Temporal immediacy is stronger if a manager has to lay off

proximity of effect the social, psychological, cultural, or physical distance between a decision maker and those affected by his or her decisions

concentration of effect the total harm or benefit that an act produces on the average person

workers next week as opposed to three months from now. **Proximity of effect** is the social, psychological, cultural, or physical distance of a decision maker from those affected by his or her decisions. Thus, proximity of effect is greater for the manager who works with employees who are to be laid off than it is for a manager who works where no layoffs will occur. Finally, whereas the magnitude of consequences is the total effect across all people, **concentration of effect** is how much an act affects the average person. Cheating 10 investors out of $10,000 apiece is a greater concentration of effect than cheating 100 investors out of $1,000 apiece.

Many people will likely feel IBM was wrong to deny full benefits to Joan Addessi. Why? In this situation, IBM's decision met five of the six characteristics of ethical intensity. The difference in benefits (more than $23,000 per year) was likely to have serious consequences on the family. The decision was certain to affect them and would do so immediately. We can closely identify with Joan Addessi and her daughters (as opposed to IBM's faceless, nameless corporate identity). And the decision would have a concentrated effect on the family in terms of their monthly benefits ($1,800 and free medical coverage if full benefits were awarded versus $340 a month and medical care that costs $473 per month if they weren't).

The exception, as we will discuss below, is social consensus. Not everyone will agree that IBM's decision was unethical. The judgment also depends on your level of moral development and which ethical principles you use to decide.

3.2 Moral Development

A friend of yours has given you the latest version of Microsoft Word. She stuffed the software disks in your backpack with a note saying that you should install it on your computer and get it back to her in a couple of days. You're tempted. You have papers to write, notes to take, and presentations to plan. Besides, all of your friends have the same version of Microsoft Word. They didn't pay for it either. Copying the software to your hard drive without buying your own copy clearly violates copyright laws. But no one would find out. Even if someone does, Microsoft isn't going to come after you. Microsoft goes after the big fish, companies that illegally copy and distribute software to their workers. Your computer has booted up, and you've got your mouse in one hand and the installation disk in the other. What are you going to do?[17]

preconventional level of moral development the first level of moral development in which people make decisions based on selfish reasons

conventional level of moral development the second level of moral development in which people make decisions that conform to societal expectations

postconventional level of moral development the third level of moral development in which people make decisions based on internalized principles

In part, according to Lawrence Kohlberg, your decision will be based on your level of moral development. Kohlberg identified three phases of moral development, with two stages in each phase (see Exhibit 3.2).[18] At the **preconventional level of moral development**, people decide based on selfish reasons. For example, if you are in Stage 1, the punishment and obedience stage, your primary concern will be to avoid trouble. So, you won't copy the software. Yet, in Stage 2, the instrumental exchange stage, you make decisions that advance your wants and needs. So, you copy the software.

People at the **conventional level of moral development** make decisions that conform to societal expectations. In Stage 3, the good boy, nice girl stage, you normally do what the other "good boys" and "nice girls" are doing. If everyone else is illegally copying software, you will, too. In the law and order stage, Stage 4, you do whatever the law permits, so you won't copy the software.

exhibit 3.2

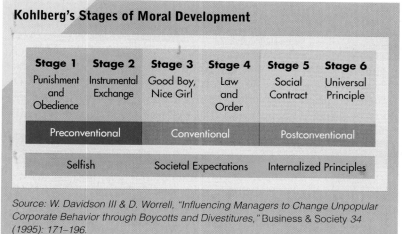

Kohlberg's Stages of Moral Development

Stage 1	Stage 2	Stage 3	Stage 4	Stage 5	Stage 6
Punishment and Obedience	Instrumental Exchange	Good Boy, Nice Girl	Law and Order	Social Contract	Universal Principle
Preconventional		Conventional		Postconventional	
Selfish		Societal Expectations		Internalized Principles	

Source: W. Davidson III & D. Worrell, "Influencing Managers to Change Unpopular Corporate Behavior through Boycotts and Divestitures," Business & Society *34 (1995): 171–196.*

People at the **postconventional level of moral development** always use internalized ethical principles to solve ethical dilemmas. In Stage 5, the social contract stage, you will refuse to copy the software because, as a whole, society is better off when the rights of others—in this case, the rights of software authors and manufacturers—are not violated. In Stage 6, the universal principle stage, you might or might not copy the software, depending on your principles of right and wrong. Moreover, you will stick to your principles even if your decision conflicts with the law (Stage 4) or what others believe is best for society (Stage 5). For example, someone with socialist or communist beliefs would probably choose to copy the software because he or she views goods and services as owned by society rather than by individuals and corporations. (For information about the dos, don'ts, and legal issues concerning software piracy, see the Software & Information Industry Association's Web site at **http://www.siia.net/ piracy/default.asp**.)

Kohlberg originally predicted that people would progress sequentially from earlier stages to later stages. We now know that one's level of moral maturity can change, depending on individual and situational factors. As people age, become more educated, or deal with dilemmas high in ethical intensity, they are more likely to make ethical decisions using a higher level of moral maturity.

PERSONAL PRODUCTIVITY TIP

Could You Tell Your Parents or the Public?

Managers sometimes judge the ethics of what they're doing by trying to anticipate how others would view their actions. One manager says, "Ummm . . . This is going to sound trite. But if you can comfortably tell your parents, I think you are probably doing the right thing." Or, "Can you tell your grandfather about it and be proud?" Practicing managers are also aware of how their choices would be viewed by the general public. Says one manager, "If you wouldn't share it with *60 Minutes* news cameras, don't do it."[19]

Review 3

Influences on Ethical Decision Making

Two factors influence ethical decisions: the ethical intensity of the decision and the moral development of the manager. Ethical intensity is strong when decisions have large, certain, immediate consequences and when we are physically or psychologically close to those affected by the decision. There are three phases of moral maturity with two steps within each phase. At the preconventional level, decisions are made for selfish reasons. At the conventional level, decisions conform to societal expectations. Finally, at the postconventional level, internalized principles are used to make ethical decisions.

4 Practical Steps to Ethical Decision Making

Managers can encourage more ethical decision making in their organizations by 4.1 carefully selecting and hiring new employees, 4.2 establishing a specific code of ethics, 4.3 training employees how to make ethical decisions, and 4.4 creating an ethical climate.

4.1 Selecting and Hiring Ethical Employees

As an employer, you can increase your chances of hiring an honest person if you give job applicants integrity tests. **Overt integrity tests** estimate employee honesty by directly asking job applicants what they think or feel about theft or about punishment of unethical behaviors.[20] For example, an employer might ask an applicant, "Do you think you would ever consider buying something from somebody if you knew the person had stolen the item?" or "Don't most people steal from their companies?" Surprisingly, because they believe that the world is basically dishonest and that dishonest behavior is normal, unethical people will usually answer yes to such questions.[21]

overt integrity test
a written test that estimates employee honesty by directly asking job applicants what they think or feel about theft or about punishment of unethical behaviors

Personality-based integrity tests indirectly estimate employee honesty by measuring psychological traits such as dependability and conscientiousness. For example, prison inmates serving time for white-collar crimes (counterfeiting, embezzlement, and fraud) scored much lower than a comparison group of middle-level managers on scales measuring reliability, dependability, honesty, conscientiousness, and abiding by rules.[22] These results show that companies can selectively hire and promote people who will be more ethical.[23] For more on integrity testing, see the "What Really Works" feature in this chapter.

www.experiencing management.com

A variety of approaches can be used to foster ethical and socially responsible behaviors. Interact with four of these approaches at our animated concept and activity site. Choose Ethics&Social_Responsibility from the "select a topic" pull-down menu, then Fostering Social Responsibility from the "overview tab."
http://www.experiencingmanagement.com

personality-based integrity test
a written test that indirectly estimates employee honesty by measuring psychological traits, such as dependability and conscientiousness

4.2 Codes of Ethics

Today, 90 percent of large corporations have an ethics code in place, 51 percent have dedicated telephone lines for reporting ethical concerns, and 30 percent have formal ethics and legal compliance offices.[24] Still, two things must happen if those codes are to encourage ethical decision making and behavior.[25] First, a company must communicate its code to others both inside and outside the company. An excellent example of a well-communicated code of ethics can be found at Nortel Networks' Internet site at **http://www.nortelnetworks.com**. With the click of a computer mouse, anyone inside or outside the company can obtain detailed information about the company's core values, specific ethical business practices, and much more.

Second, in addition to having an ethics code with general guidelines like "do unto others as you would have others do unto you," management must also develop practical ethical standards and procedures specific to the company's line of business. Visitors to Nortel's Internet site can instantly access references to 36 specific ethical standards on topics ranging from bribes and kickbacks to expense vouchers and illegal copying of software. Specific codes of ethics such as Nortel's make it much easier for employees to decide what to do when they want to do the "right thing." To see an example of an ethical code of conduct, go to Effective Management Online **(http://em-online.swlearning.com)** to read the one used by Portland General Electric.

4.3 Ethics Training

The first objective of ethics training is to develop employee awareness of ethics.[26] This means helping employees recognize which issues are ethical issues and then avoid rationalizing unethical behavior by thinking, "This isn't

WHAT REALLY WORKS

INTEGRITY TESTS

Under the 1991 U.S. Sentencing Commission Guidelines, unethical employee behavior can lead to multimillion dollar fines for corporations. Moreover, workplace deviance like stealing, fraud, and vandalism costs companies an estimated $200 billion a year. One way to reduce workplace deviance and the chances of a large fine for unethical employee behavior is to use overt and personality-based integrity tests to screen job applicants.

One hundred eighty-one studies, with a combined total of 576,460 study participants, have examined how well job performance and various kinds of workplace deviance are predicted by integrity tests. These studies show that not only can integrity tests help companies reduce workplace deviance, but they have the added bonus of helping companies hire workers who are better performers in their jobs.

Workplace Deviance (Counterproductive Behaviors)

Compared to job applicants who score poorly, there is an 82 percent chance that job applicants who score well on overt integrity tests will participate in less illegal activity, unethical behavior, drug abuse, or workplace violence.

Overt Integrity Tests & Workplace Deviance

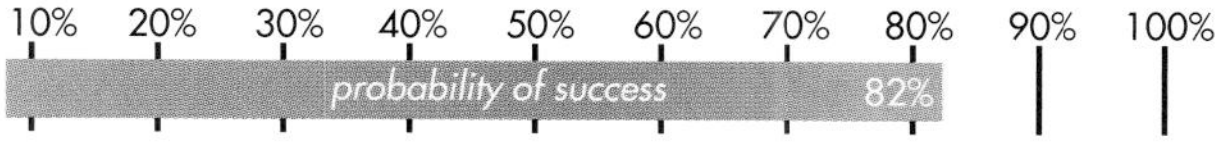

Personality-based integrity tests also do a good job of predicting who will engage in workplace deviance. Compared to job applicants who score poorly, there is a 68 percent chance that job applicants who score well on personality-based integrity tests will participate in less illegal activity, unethical behavior, excessive absences, drug abuse, or workplace violence.

Personality-Based Integrity Tests & Workplace Deviance

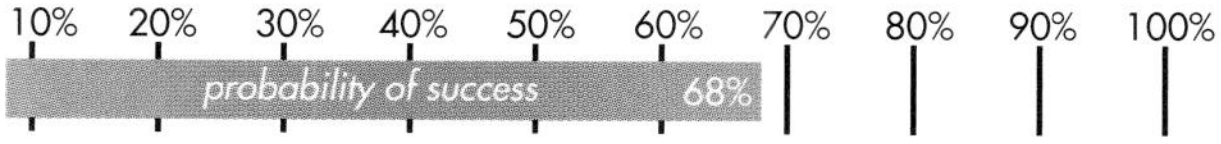

Job Performance

In addition to reducing unethical behavior and workplace deviance, integrity tests can help companies hire better performers. Compared to employees who score poorly, there is a 69 percent chance that employees who score well on overt integrity tests will be better performers.

Overt Integrity Tests & Job Performance

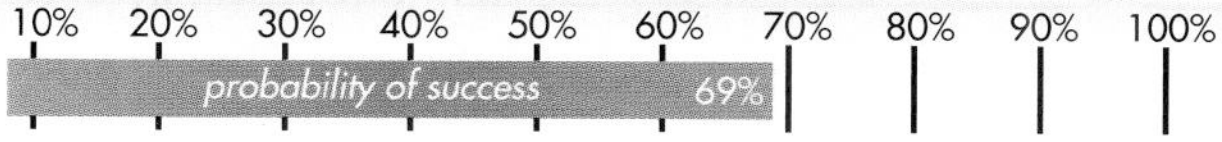

The figures are nearly identical for personality-based integrity tests. Compared to those who score poorly, there is a 70 percent chance that employees who score well on personality-based integrity tests will be better at their jobs.

Personality-Based Integrity Tests & Job Performance

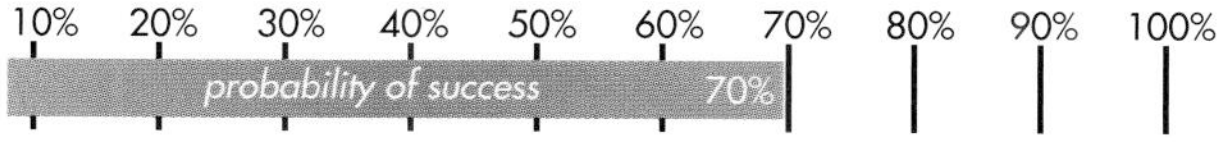

Theft

Although integrity tests can help companies decrease most kinds of workplace deviance and increase employees' job performance, they have a smaller effect on a specific kind of workplace deviance: theft. Compared to employees who score poorly, there is a 57 percent chance that employees who score well on overt integrity tests will be less likely to steal. No theft data were available to assess personality-based integrity tests.

Overt Integrity Tests & Theft

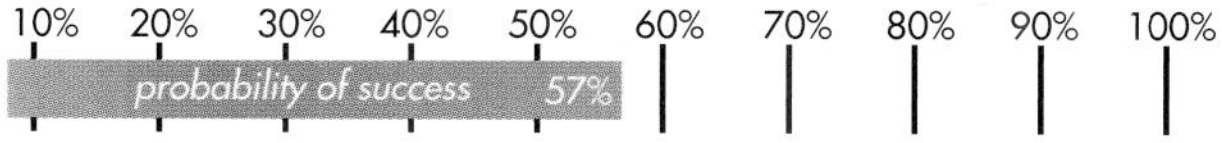

Faking and Coaching on Integrity Tests

Although overt and personality-based integrity tests do a very good job of helping companies hire people of higher integrity, it is possible to improve scores on these tests through coaching and faking. Job applicants can be coached by explaining the underlying rationale of an integrity test to them or by giving them specific directions for improving their integrity scores. Faking occurs when applicants simply try to "beat the test" or try to fake a good impression. Unfortunately for the companies that use integrity tests, both strategies work. On average, coaching can improve scores on overt integrity tests by an astounding 1.5 standard deviations and on personality-based integrity tests by a meaningful .36 standard deviations. This would be the equivalent of increasing your total SAT score by 150 and 36 points, respectively (the SAT has a mean of 500 and a standard deviation of 100). Likewise, on average, faking can improve scores on overt integrity tests by an impressive 1.02 standard deviations and on personality-based integrity tests by a meaningful .59 standard deviations. Again, this would be the equivalent of increasing your SAT score by 102 and 59 points, respectively.

Companies that want to avoid coaching and faking effects should maintain tight security over integrity tests so that applicants have little information regarding them, periodically check the validity of the tests to make sure they're accurately predicting workplace deviance and job performance, or periodically switch tests if they suspect that test security has been compromised.[27]

really illegal or immoral" or "No one will ever find out." Several companies have created board games to improve awareness of ethical issues.[28] Citigroup has a game called "The Work Ethic," in which players win or lose points depending on their answers to legal, regulatory, policy, and judgment questions. Boeing's "Ethics Challenge" game, which is similar, is available online. To play it, go to **http://active.boeing.com/** and search for "Ethics Challenge."

The second objective for ethics training programs is to achieve credibility with employees. Not surprisingly, employees can be highly suspicious of management's reasons for offering ethics training. Some companies have hurt the credibility of their ethics programs by having outside instructors and consultants conduct the classes.[29] Employees often complain that outside instructors and consultants are teaching theory that has nothing to do with their jobs and the "real world." This is why Boeing has a vice president of ethics who employs 55 people to teach Boeing's 194,000 employees the difference between right and wrong in the aerospace industry.[30] Ethics training becomes even more credible when top managers teach the initial ethics training classes to their subordinates, who in turn teach their subordinates. In time, most managers will have taken and taught the ethics classes, thereby pushing ethics training and principles throughout the entire company.[31]

The third objective of ethics training is to teach employees a practical model of ethical decision making. A basic model should help them think about the consequences their choices will have on others and consider how they will choose between different solutions. Exhibit 3.3 presents a basic model of ethical decision making.

DOING THE RIGHT THING

Using Organizational Dilemmas to Increase Ethical Awareness

When you recognize that you're facing an ethical issue, you're much more likely to choose an ethical course of action. Dealing with real-life ethical dilemmas is a good way to develop ethical awareness. Instead of waiting for life to teach you such lessons, you can use the "Dilemma Database" at the Institute for Global Ethics (**http://www.globalethics.org/**) to sensitize yourself to a variety of ethical dilemmas concerning business, education, and other aspects of life. Think about the dilemmas. Discuss them with others. Decide what you'd do. Then, read what the people in the dilemmas chose to do. You'll become much more aware of common ethical issues.[32]

4.4 Ethical Climate

In study after study, when researchers ask, "What is the most important influence on your ethical behavior at work?" the answer comes back, "My manager." The first step in establishing an ethical climate is for managers to act ethically themselves. When managers decline to accept lavish gifts from company suppliers, use the company phone, fax, and copier only for business purposes and not for personal use, and keep their promises to employees, suppliers, and customers, they encourage others to believe that ethical behavior is normal and acceptable.

exhibit 3.3

A Basic Model of Ethical Decision Making

1. **Identify the problem.** What makes it an ethical problem? Think in terms of rights, obligations, fairness, relationships, and integrity. How would you define the problem if you stood on the other side of the fence?
2. **Identify the constituents.** Who has been hurt? Who could be hurt? Who could be helped? Are they willing players, or are they victims? Can you negotiate with them?
3. **Diagnose the situation.** How did it happen in the first place? What could have prevented it? Is it going to get worse or better? Can the damage now be undone?
4. **Analyze your options.** Imagine the range of possibilities. Limit yourself to the two or three most manageable. What are the likely outcomes of each? What are the likely costs? Look to the company mission statement or code of ethics for guidance.
5. **Make your choice.** What is your intention in making this decision? How does it compare with the probable results? Can you discuss the problem with the affected parties before you act? Could you disclose without qualm your decision to your boss, the CEO, the board of directors, your family, or society as a whole?
6. **Act.** Do what you have to do. Don't be afraid to admit errors. Be as bold in confronting a problem as you were in causing it.

Source: L. A. Berger, "Train All Employees to Solve Ethical Dilemmas," Best's Review—Life-Health Insurance Edition *95 (1995): 70–80.*

A second step in establishing an ethical climate is for top management to be active in and committed to the company ethics program.[33] Top managers who consistently talk about the importance of ethics and back up that talk by participating in their companies' ethics programs send the clear message that ethics matter. Business writer Dayton Fandray says, "You can have ethics offices and officers and training programs and reporting systems, but if the CEO doesn't seem to care, it's all just a sham. It's not surprising to find that the companies that really do care about ethics make a point of including senior management in all of their ethics and compliance programs."[34]

A third step is to put in place a reporting system that encourages managers and employees to report potential ethics violations. **Whistleblowing**, that is, reporting others' ethics violations, is a difficult step for most people to take.[35] Potential whistleblowers often fear that they, and not the ethics violators, will be punished.[36] Managers who have been interviewed about whistleblowing have said, "In every organization, someone's been screwed for standing up." "If anything, I figured that by taking a strong stand I might get myself in trouble. People might look at me as a 'goody two shoes.' Someone might try to force me out."

whistleblowing
reporting others' ethics violations to management or legal authorities

Today, however, many federal and state laws protect the rights of whistleblowers (see **http://www.whistleblowers.org** for more information). In addition, some companies, including defense contractor Northrup Grumman, have made it easier to report possible violations by establishing anonymous, toll-free corporate ethics hot lines. Nortel Networks even publicizes which of its ethics hot lines don't have caller ID (so they can't identify the caller's phone number). The factor that does the most to discourage whistleblowers from reporting problems, however, is lack of company action on their complaints.[37] Thus, the final step in developing an ethical climate is for management to fairly and consistently punish those who violate the company's code of ethics.

Review 4

Practical Steps to Ethical Decision Making

Employers can increase the chances of hiring more ethical employees by administering overt integrity tests and personality-based integrity tests to all job applicants. Most large companies now have corporate codes of ethics. To affect ethical decision making, these codes must be known both inside and outside the organization. In addition to offering general rules, ethics codes must also provide specific, practical advice. Ethics training seeks to increase employees' awareness of ethical issues, make ethics a serious, credible factor in organizational decisions, and teach employees a practical model of ethical decision making. The most important factors in creating an ethical business climate are the personal examples set by company managers, involvement of management in the company ethics program, a reporting system that encourages whistleblowers to report potential ethics violations, and fair but consistent punishment of violators.

What Is Social Responsibility?

Social responsibility is a business's obligation to pursue policies, make decisions, and take actions that benefit society.[38] Unfortunately, because there are strong disagreements over to whom and for what in society organizations are responsible, it can be difficult for managers to know what is or will be perceived as socially responsible corporate behavior. For example, Procter & Gamble (P&G) no longer uses animals, such as rats and rabbits, to test the safety of cosmetics, shampoos, detergents, cleansers, and paper goods, although it continues to use animals to test the safety of new drugs and health-care products.[39] Nonetheless, P&G continues to draw protests from PETA (People for the Ethical Treatment of Animals) in the form of PETA's "Died" advertising campaign (**http://www.pginfo.net/index2.html**), which is based on P&G's best-selling laundry detergent Tide. The "Died" ad shows a woman holding a box of "Died" detergent with the words "Thousands of Animals Died for Your Laundry" on the box. PETA is encouraging a boycott of all P&G products until the company ends all forms of animal testing. In response, P&G argues that eliminating animal testing altogether would be socially irresponsible because testing is critical to producing a safe product for its customers. The company Web site states: "We have to know, for example, that a product will not cause injury if a child accidentally swallows it or gets it into their eyes."[40] Furthermore, in the event that a product liability lawsuit is filed against the company, its best legal defense would be the scientific testing it performs on rats and rabbits.[41] Finally, P&G points out that it has been vigilant in developing alternatives to animal testing. Dr. Martin Stephens, vice president for animal research issues at the U.S. Humane Society says, "P&G has perhaps done more than any other corporation to speed the development and acceptance of alternative test methods."[42]

Is P&G obligated, as PETA believes, to eliminate all animal testing? Or, by minimizing but not eliminating animal testing has P&G achieved a reasonable balance that still allows it to make sure its products are safe? In the end, are P&G's actions regarding animal testing socially responsible or irresponsible?

social responsibility
a business's obligation to pursue policies, make decisions, and take actions that benefit society

There is no single definitive understanding of social responsibility, as the dispute between P&G and PETA proves. Many argue that P&G is being socially responsible by continuing limited animal testing for health-care products to ensure the safety of future customers, including babies and children. Others, like PETA, argue that P&G is acting irresponsibly by continuing animal testing at all.

After reading the next four sections, you should be able to explain

5 to whom organizations are socially responsible.

6 for what organizations are socially responsible.

7 how organizations can choose to respond to societal demands for social responsibility.

8 whether social responsibility hurts or helps an organization's economic performance.

5 To Whom Are Organizations Socially Responsible?

There are two perspectives as to whom organizations are socially responsible: the shareholder model and the stakeholder model. According to Nobel Prize–winning economist Milton Friedman, the only social responsibility that organizations have is to satisfy their owners, that is, company shareholders. This view—called the **shareholder model**—holds that the only social responsibility that businesses have is to maximize profits. By maximizing profit, the firm maximizes shareholder wealth and satisfaction. More specifically, as profits rise, the company stock owned by shareholders generally increases in value.

shareholder model
a view of social responsibility that holds that an organization's overriding goal should be profit maximization for the benefit of shareholders

Friedman argues that it is socially irresponsible for companies to divert their time, money, and attention from maximizing profits to social causes and charitable organizations. The first problem he sees is that organizations cannot act effectively as moral agents for all company shareholders. Although shareholders are likely to agree on investment issues concerning a company, it's highly unlikely that they have common views on what social causes a company should or should not support. Rather than act as moral agents, Friedman argues that companies should maximize profits for shareholders. Shareholders can then use their time and increased wealth to contribute to the social causes, charities, or institutions they want, rather than those that companies want.

> **www.experiencing management.com**
>
> Organizations are expected to benefit in many ways beyond simply providing jobs. To learn more about social responsibilities of organizations, visit our animated concept and activity site. Choose Ethics&Social_Responsibility from the "select a topic" pull-down menu, then Social Responsibility from the "overview tab."
> **http://www.experiencingmanagement.com**

The second major problem, according to Friedman, is that the time, money, and attention diverted to social causes undermine market efficiency.[43] In competitive markets, companies compete for raw materials, talented workers, customers, and investment funds. Spending money on social causes means there is less money to purchase quality materials or to hire talented workers who can produce a valuable product at a good price. If customers find the product less desirable, sales and profits will fall. If profits fall, stock prices will decline, and the company will have difficulty attracting investment funds that could be used to fund long-term growth. In the end, Friedman argues, diverting the firm's money, time, and resources to social causes hurts customers, suppliers, employees, and shareholders.

stakeholder model
a theory of corporate responsibility that holds that management's most important responsibility, long-term survival, is achieved by satisfying the interests of multiple corporate stakeholders

stakeholders
persons or groups with a "stake" or legitimate interest in a company's actions

By contrast, under the **stakeholder model,** management's most important responsibility is long-term survival (not just maximizing profits), which is achieved by satisfying the interests of multiple corporate stakeholders (not just shareholders).[44] **Stakeholders** are persons or groups with a legitimate interest in a company.[45] Since stakeholders are interested in and affected by the organization's actions, they have a "stake" in what those actions are.

exhibit 3.4

Stakeholder Model of Corporate Social Responsibility

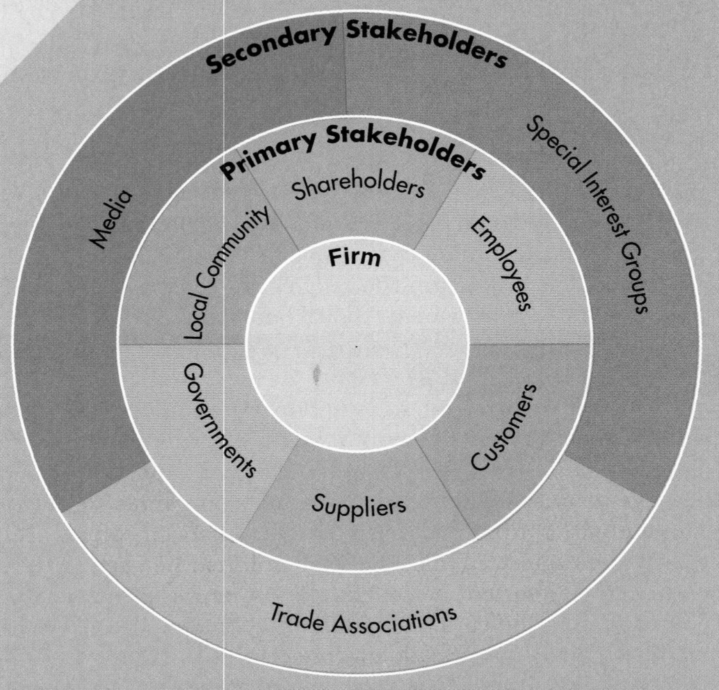

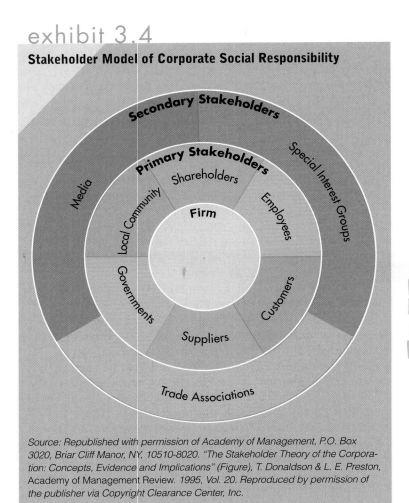

Source: Republished with permission of Academy of Management, P.O. Box 3020, Briar Cliff Manor, NY, 10510-8020. "The Stakeholder Theory of the Corporation: Concepts, Evidence and Implications" (Figure), T. Donaldson & L. E. Preston, Academy of Management Review. *1995, Vol. 20. Reproduced by permission of the publisher via Copyright Clearance Center, Inc.*

Consequently, stakeholder groups may try to influence the firm to act in their own interests. Exhibit 3.4 shows the various stakeholder groups that the organization must satisfy to assure long-term survival.

Being responsible to multiple stakeholders raises two basic questions. First, how does a company identify organizational stakeholders? Second, how does a company balance the needs of different stakeholders? Distinguishing between primary and secondary stakeholders can answer these questions.[46]

Some stakeholders are more important to the firm's survival than others. **Primary stakeholders** are groups on which the organization depends for long-term survival; they include shareholders, employees, customers, suppliers, governments, and local communities. So, when managers are struggling to balance the needs of different stakeholders, the stakeholder model suggests that the needs of primary stakeholders take precedence over the needs of secondary stakeholders. In theory, no primary stakeholder group is more or less important than another, since all are said to be critical to long-term success and survival. In practice, though, CEOs typically give somewhat higher priority to shareholders, employees, and customers than to suppliers, governments, and local communities.[47]

primary stakeholder
any group on which an organization relies for its long-term survival

secondary stakeholder
any group that can influence or be influenced by a company and can affect public perceptions about its socially responsible behavior

Addressing the concerns of primary stakeholders is important because if a stakeholder group becomes dissatisfied and terminates its relationship with the company, the company could be seriously harmed or go out of business.

Secondary stakeholders, such as the media and special interest groups, can influence or be influenced by the company. Unlike the primary stakeholders, however, they do not engage in regular transactions with the company and are not critical to its long-term survival. Consequently, meeting the needs of primary stakeholders is usually more important than meeting the needs of secondary stakeholders. Nevertheless, secondary stakeholders are still important because they can affect public perceptions and opinions about socially responsible behavior. For instance, because of a protest campaign by environmental groups, Centex and Kaufman & Broad, two of the largest homebuilders in the United States, agreed to quit buying lumber products from "old-growth" trees in endangered forests. Both companies quickly agreed to the demand after seeing hundreds of protests at Home Depot stores (which also convinced Home Depot to stop buying old-growth wood). A spokesperson for Centex said, "The action was in part motivated by the environmentalists, but also the company's own regard for the environment." Kaufman & Broad's CEO put a more

www.experiencing management.com

Different stakeholders have differing interests in the organization's social responsibilities. To interact with stakeholder issues, visit our animated concept and activity site. Choose Ethics&Social_Responsibility from the "select a topic" pull-down menu, then Responsibility to Stakeholders from the "overview tab."
http://www.experiencingmanagement.com

positive spin on the move, saying, "The world's old-growth forests are indeed threatened. This is ultimately a threat to all of us."[48]

So to whom are organizations socially responsible? Many, especially economists and financial analysts, continue to argue that organizations are responsible only to shareholders. Increasingly, however, top managers have come to believe that they and their companies must be socially responsible to their stakeholders. This view has gained adherents since the Great Depression, when General Electric first identified shareholders, employees, customers, and the general public as its stakeholders. In 1947, Johnson & Johnson listed customers, employees, managers, and shareholders as its stakeholders; and in 1950, Sears Roebuck announced that its most important stakeholders were "customers, employees, community, and stockholders."[49] Today, surveys show that as many as 80 percent of top-level managers believe that it is unethical to focus just on shareholders. Twenty-nine states have changed their laws to allow company boards of directors to consider the needs of employees, creditors, suppliers, customers, and local communities, as well as those of shareholders.[50] So, although there is not complete agreement, a majority of opinion makers would argue that companies must be socially responsible to their stakeholders.

Review 5

To Whom Are Organizations Socially Responsible?

Social responsibility is a business's obligation to benefit society. To whom are organizations socially responsible? According to the shareholder model, the only social responsibility that organizations have is to maximize shareholder wealth by maximizing company profits. According to the stakeholder model, companies must satisfy the needs and interests of multiple corporate stakeholders, not just shareholders. However, the needs of primary stakeholders, on which the organization relies for its existence, take precedence over those of secondary stakeholders.

6 For What Are Organizations Socially Responsible?

If organizations are to be socially responsible to stakeholders, for what are they to be socially responsible? As Exhibit 3.5 illustrates, companies can best benefit their stakeholders by fulfilling their economic, legal, ethical, and discretionary responsibilities.[51] Exhibit 3.5 indicates that economic and legal responsibilities play a larger part in a company's social responsibility than do ethical and discretionary responsibilities. However, the relative importance of these various responsibilities depends on society's expectations of corporate social responsibility at a particular point in time.[52] A century ago, society expected businesses to meet their economic and legal responsibilities and little else. Today, when society judges whether businesses are socially responsible, ethical and discretionary responsibilities are considerably more important than they used to be.

economic responsibility
the expectation that a company will make a profit by producing a valued product or service

Historically, **economic responsibility**, making a profit by producing a product or service valued by society, has been a business's most basic social responsibility. Organizations that don't meet their financial and economic ex-

exhibit 3.5

Social Responsibilities

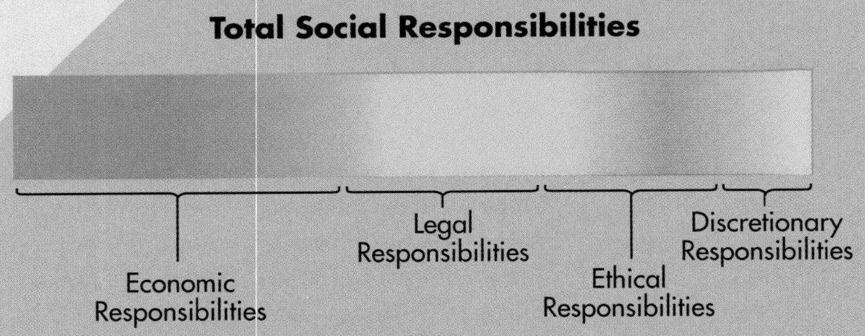

Source: Republished with permission of Academy of Management, P.O. Box 3020, Briar Cliff Manor, NY, 10510-8020. "A Three-Dimensional Conceptual Model of Corporate Performance." (Figure 3.3) A. B. Carroll, Academy of Management Review, *1979, Vol. 4. Reproduced by permission of the publisher via Copyright Clearance Center, Inc.*

pectations come under tremendous pressure. For example, company boards are very, very quick these days to fire CEOs. Typically, all it takes is two or three bad quarters in a row. William Rollnick, who became acting chairman of Mattel after the company fired CEO Jill Barad, says, "There's zero forgiveness. You screw up and you're dead."[53] Indeed, in both Europe and the United States, nearly one-third of all CEOs are fired because of their inability to successfully change their companies.[54]

legal responsibility
the expectation that a company will obey society's laws and regulations

Legal responsibility is the expectation that companies will obey society's laws and regulations as they try to meet their economic responsibilities. For example, under the 1990 Clean Air Act, the smell of fresh baked bread is now illegal because of the ethanol that is emitted when baking.[55] Although ethanol itself is nontoxic, it contributes to pollution by promoting the formation of the harmful atmospheric compound ozone. Consequently, to meet the law, large bakery plants may have to spend millions to purchase catalytic oxidizers that remove ethanol emissions.[56]

ethical responsibility
the expectation that a company will not violate accepted principles of right and wrong when conducting its business

Ethical responsibility is society's expectation that organizations will not violate accepted principles of right and wrong when conducting their business. Because different stakeholders may disagree about what is or is not ethical, meeting ethical responsibilities is more difficult than meeting economic or legal responsibilities.

discretionary responsibilities
the expectation that a company will voluntarily serve a social role beyond its economic, legal, and ethical responsibilities

Discretionary responsibilities pertain to the social roles that businesses play in society beyond their economic, legal, and ethical responsibilities. For example, dozens of companies support the fight against hunger at The Hunger Site, **http://www.thehungersite.com**. Each time someone clicks on the "donate free food" button (only one click per day per visitor), sponsors of The Hunger Site donate money to pay for food to be sent to Bosnia, Indonesia, Mozambique, or wherever people suffer from hunger. Thanks to the corporate sponsors and 206 million visitors' "clicks," almost 311 million cups (nearly 39 million pounds of food) have been distributed thus far.[57] Discretionary responsibilities such as these are voluntary. Companies are not considered unethical if they don't perform them. Today, however, corporate stakeholders expect companies to do much more than in the past to meet their discretionary responsibilities.

Review 6

For What Are Organizations Socially Responsible?

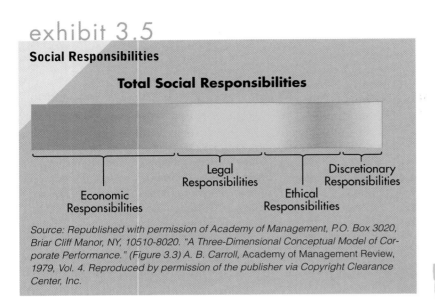

Companies can best benefit their stakeholders by fulfilling their economic, legal, ethical, and discretionary responsibilities. Being profitable, or meeting one's economic responsibility, is a business's most basic social responsibility. Legal responsibility consists of following a society's laws and regulations. Ethical responsibility means not violating accepted principles of right and wrong when doing business. Discretionary responsibilities are social responsibilities beyond basic economic, legal, and ethical responsibilities.

7 Responses to Demands for Social Responsibility

social responsiveness
the strategy chosen by a company to respond to stakeholders' economic, legal, ethical, or discretionary expectations concerning social responsibility

Social responsiveness is the strategy chosen by a company to respond to stakeholders' economic, legal, ethical, or discretionary expectations concerning social responsibility. A social responsibility problem exists whenever company actions do not meet stakeholder expectations. One model of social responsiveness, shown in Exhibit 3.6, identifies four strategies for responding to social responsibility problems: reactive, defensive, accommodative, and proactive. These strategies differ in the extent to which the company is willing to act to meet or exceed society's expectations.

reactive strategy
a social responsiveness strategy in which a company chooses to do less than society expects

defensive strategy
a social responsiveness strategy in which a company chooses to admit responsibility for a problem but to do the least required to meet societal expectations

A company using a **reactive strategy** will do less than society expects. It may deny responsibility for a problem or fight any suggestions that the company should solve a problem. By contrast, a company using a **defensive strategy** would *admit* responsibility for a problem, but would do the least required to meet societal expectations. When the sudden and unpredictable tread separation problems associated with Firestone ATX tires first became public knowledge, Firestone's response was to deny that there were problems (a reactive strategy). Not until seven months later, under intense public pressure, did Firestone recall 6.5 million of the 15-inch ATX tires. Even then, Firestone angered U.S. lawmakers by refusing to recall all the tires recommended by the National Highway Traffic Safety Administration (a defensive strategy).[58] In fact, Firestone's crisis management firm was so frustrated by the company's refusal to acknowledge the problem and act quickly to restore consumer confidence (by immediately apologizing and quickly recalling and replacing all tires) that it quit.[59]

accommodative strategy
a social responsiveness strategy in which a company chooses to accept responsibility for a problem and to do all that society expects to solve that problem

A company using an **accommodative strategy** will *accept* responsibility for a problem and take a progressive approach by doing all that could be expected to solve the problem. Finally, a company using a **proactive strategy** will *anticipate* responsibility for a problem before it occurs, do more than expected to address the problem, and lead the industry in its approach. For example, McDonald's began its McRecycle USA program to increase the use of recycled materials in its restaurants. Of course, there's nothing proactive or leading edge about a company recycling program. Lots of companies have them. In this case, however, McDonald's discovered that it could not buy the recycled materials it needed. There just weren't enough recycled materials available at the time. McDonald's innovative solution was to take out full-page advertisements in newspapers around the country to let recycling companies know that it was committed to spending $100 million

exhibit 3.6

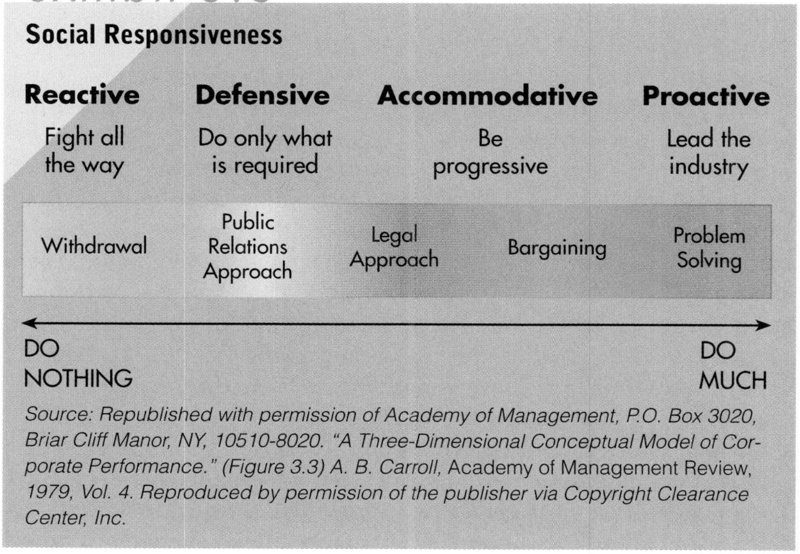

Source: Republished with permission of Academy of Management, P.O. Box 3020, Briar Cliff Manor, NY, 10510-8020. "A Three-Dimensional Conceptual Model of Corporate Performance." (Figure 3.3) A. B. Carroll, Academy of Management Review, *1979, Vol. 4. Reproduced by permission of the publisher via Copyright Clearance Center, Inc.*

proactive strategy
a social responsiveness strategy in which a company anticipates responsibility for a problem before it occurs and would do more than society expects to address the problem

a year to buy recycled products for its restaurants! The ads listed a toll-free phone number that potential suppliers could call to find out what the company needed. The ads were a phenomenal success. McDonald's now spends more than $250 million a year on recycled products for its playgrounds, floor and ceiling tiles, and paper products.[60] Indeed, since 1990, McDonald's has purchased *$3 billion* worth of recycled products for construction, equipment, and packaging.[61]

Review 7

Responses to Demands for Social Responsibility

Social responsiveness is a company's response to stakeholders' demands for socially responsible behavior. There are four social responsiveness strategies. When a company uses a reactive strategy, it denies responsibility for a problem. When it uses a defensive strategy, it takes responsibility for a problem, but does the minimum required to solve it. When a company uses an accommodative strategy, it accepts responsibility for problems and does all that society expects to solve them. Finally, when a company uses a proactive strategy, it does much more than expected to solve social responsibility problems.

8 Social Responsibility and Economic Performance

One question that managers often ask is, "Does it pay to be socially responsible?" Though understandable, asking whether social responsibility pays is a bit like asking if giving to your favorite charity will help you get a better-paying job. The obvious answer is no. There is not an inherent relationship between social responsibility and economic performance.[62] However, this doesn't stop supporters of corporate social responsibility from claiming a positive relationship. For example, one study shows that the Domini 400 Social Index, which is a stock fund consisting of 400 socially responsible companies, has outperformed the Standard and Poor's 500 (an index of 500 stocks representative of the entire economy) by nearly 5 percent. At the same time, critics have plenty of facts to support their claim that social responsibility hurts economic performance. For example, another study of 42 socially responsible mutual funds found that the socially responsible companies underperformed the Standard and Poor's 500 by 8 percent.[63]

When it comes to social responsibility and economic performance, the first reality is that being socially responsible can sometimes cost a company significantly. For example, under pressure from the federal government, cities that were threatening lawsuits, and antigun protesters, gun manufacturer Smith & Wesson announced that it would put safety locks on its guns and develop smart gun technology that allows guns to fire only for their owners. The company realized that this move could anger its key stakeholder, the gun owners who bought its products. Indeed, gun owners and the National Rifle Association (NRA), boycotted Smith & Wesson and its products. The company's former CEO Ed Shultz, who was responsible for this decision, said, "There wasn't any question there was going to be a hit [on sales and profits]. The question was how big the hit would be and for how long." Immediately, sales dropped enough to force layoffs of 125 of the 725 employees at Smith & Wesson's plant in Springfield, Missouri. So, why make this decision if you know it's going to hurt your company financially? Shultz explained, "I couldn't answer the question 'Was I doing everything I knew how to do to prevent accidents?' Would I put locks on our guns if it might save one child? The answer was yes." Harvard law professor Joseph Singer said, "Shultz may have done something that was in the best long-term interests of the company—making it seem like a corporate citizen and just doing the right thing—but since the law doesn't require others to do it, in the short run it may have hurt the company."[64]

The second reality of social responsibility and economic performance is that sometimes it does pay to be socially responsible. Seattle-based Starbucks Coffee, which markets itself as a socially responsible company, grew from 11 to more than 4,100 gourmet coffee shops worldwide. Starbucks pays its coffee shop workers much more than minimum wage, provides full health insurance coverage to anyone who works at least 20 hours a week, and gives employees with six or more months at the company the chance to participate in its stock options program. Besides taking good care of its employees, Starbucks also makes an annual six-figure charitable contribution to CARE, an international relief agency, for feeding, clothing, and educating the poor in the coffee-growing regions where it gets its coffee beans.[65] Workers from its 4,100 stores worldwide are paid to volunteer in community service programs, such as Earth Day cleanups, regional AIDS walks, and local literacy organizations. For example, Starbucks workers in the 19 New Zealand stores donate about 100 hours of volunteer work each week. Aasha Murthy, Starbucks' general manager in New Zealand, says, "Any company can write out a check to a worthy cause, send it off, and think nothing more of it, but that isn't what Starbucks is about. We've got an enormous amount of talent, energy, and passion in our business and that comes from our staff. So we decided to donate their skills. We want Starbucks New Zealand to be a successful organization, not just a profitable one, and there's more than one dimension to success. We want to reach out to the community we're part of."[66]

The third reality of social responsibility and economic performance is that while socially responsible behavior may be "the right thing to do," it does not guarantee profitability. Socially responsible companies experience the same ups and downs in economic performance that traditional businesses do. A good example is Ben & Jerry's Homemade Ice Cream. Ben & Jerry's started in 1978 when founders Ben Cohen and Jerry Greenfield sent away for a $5 course on how to make ice cream. Ben & Jerry's is as well known for its reputation as a socially responsible company as for its super premium ice cream. Ben & Jerry's donates 7.5 percent of its pretax profits to social causes supporting AIDS patients, the homeless, and the environment.[67] Moreover, customers buy Ben & Jerry's ice cream because it tastes great *and* because they want to support a socially responsible company. As Ben Cohen says, "We see ourselves as somewhat of a social service agency and somewhat of an ice cream company."[68] But, and this is a big but, despite its outstanding reputation as a socially responsible company, Ben & Jerry's consistently had financial troubles after going public (selling shares of stock to the public) a decade ago. In fact, its financial problems became so severe that Ben and Jerry sold the company to British-based Unilever. Being socially responsible may be the "right thing to do," but it doesn't guarantee business success.

In the end, if company management chooses a proactive or accommodative strategy toward social responsibility (rather than a defensive or reactive strategy), it should do so because it wants to benefit society and its corporate stakeholders, not because it expects a better financial return.

Review 8

Social Responsibility and Economic Performance

Does it pay to be socially responsible? Sometimes it costs, and sometimes it pays. Overall, there is no clear relationship between social responsibility and economic performance. Consequently, managers should not expect an economic return from socially responsible corporate activities. If your company chooses to practice a proactive or accommodative social responsibility strategy, it should do so to better society and not to improve its financial performance.

STUDY TIP Every chapter in this book contains diagrams and tables to illustrate the text material. Worksheets made from these exhibits are available on Effective Management Online **(http://em-online.swlearning.com)** to help you review. Download them, fill them in, and then check your work by comparing your worksheet to the original exhibit in the chapter.

MANAGEMENT DECISION

TO LIE OR TELL THE TRUTH?

Ethical dilemmas occur often in the workplace. Some are obvious, but others are subtle. Suppose you are the purchasing agent for a large corporation. A supplier has approached you regarding a recently submitted bid and has intimated that if you accept his bid, he will provide you and your spouse with round-trip airfare tickets to Hawaii. His company's bid is 25 percent higher than the lowest bid. Accepting his offer would clearly be unethical because it would benefit you (airline tickets for you and your spouse) and cost your company money by forcing it to pay a higher-than-necessary price for supplies. Additionally, since your company has a policy forbidding cash, gifts, and other entitlements from suppliers and vendors, you would most likely lose your job if anyone found out. Therefore, the only ethical choice is to refuse the supplier's offer and award the contract to the vendor with the best product and the best price.

Now consider a scenario that is less obvious. Assume that you have recently been hired as an entry-level manager for a small marketing agency and your supervisor, Ms. Johnson, tells you that she is running behind on an advertising proposal for a client, who will be dropping in this afternoon to discuss the proposal. She asks that you intercept the client and tell him that she was called out of town for an emergency business meeting and will contact him when she returns. Delaying the client will buy Ms. Johnson the necessary time to finalize the proposal and allow her to appear more professional when she presents it. In this dilemma, Ms. Johnson benefits by having more time to complete her assignment, but at the cost of delaying and deceiving the client. There appears to be no personal gain for you.

Questions

1. Would you do as Ms. Johnson asks, or would you refuse to cover for her? Describe what you would say to her.
2. Suppose a colleague tells you that your predecessor was fired for refusing to accommodate Ms. Johnson and her continual demands for unethical behavior/unethical responses. Would that change your decision in question 1? Why or why not?

DEVELOP YOUR CAREER POTENTIAL

It is only the farmer who faithfully plants seeds in the Spring, who reaps a harvest in the Autumn.

—B. C. Forbes, founder of *Forbes* magazine

The purpose of these assignments is to develop your present and future capabilities as a manager. Since stakeholders increasingly expect companies to do more to fulfill their discretionary responsibilities, chances are you and your company will be expected to support your community in some significant way. To begin learning about community needs and corporate social responsibility, you are assigned to visit a local charity or nonprofit organization of your choosing, perhaps a hospital, the Red Cross, Goodwill, Planned Parenthood, a soup kitchen, or a homeless shelter. Talk to the people who work or volunteer there. Gather the information you need to answer the following questions.

Questions

1. What is the organization's mission?
2. Who does the organization serve, and how does it serve them?
3. What percentage of the organization's donations is used for administrative purposes? What percentage is used to directly benefit those served by the organization? What is the ratio of volunteers to paid workers?
4. What job or task does the "typical" volunteer perform for the organization? How much time does the typical volunteer give to the organization each week? For what types of jobs does the organization need more volunteers?
5. How does the business community support the organization?
6. Why are you interested in the activities of this organization?

BIZ FLIX Emperor's Club

William Hundert (Kevin Kline), a professor at Saint Benedict's preparatory school, believes in teaching his students about living a principled life as well as teaching them his beloved classical literature. Hundert's principled ways are challenged, however, by a new student, Sedgewick Bell (Emile Hirsch). Bell's behavior during the 73rd annual Julius Caesar competition causes Hundert to suspect that Bell leads a less than principled life.

Years later Hundert is the honored guest of his former student Sedgewick Bell (Joel Gretsch) at Bell's estate. Depaak Mehta (Rahul Khanna), Bell, and Louis Masoudi (Patrick Dempsey) compete in a reenactment of the Julius Caesar competition. Bell wins the competition, but Hundert notices that Bell is wearing an earpiece. Earlier in the film Hundert had suspected that the young Bell also wore an earpiece during the competition, but Headmaster Woodbridge (Edward Herrmann) had pressed him to ignore his suspicion.

This scene appears at the end of the film. It is an edited portion of the competition reenactment. Bell announced his candidacy for the U.S. Senate just before talking to Hundert in the bathroom. He carefully desribed his commitment to specific values that he would pursue if elected.

What to Watch for and Ask Yourself

1. Does William Hundert describe a specific type of life that one should lead? If so, what are its elements?
2. Does Sedgewick Bell lead that type of life? Is he committed to any specific ethical view or theory?
3. What consequences or effects do you predict for Sedgewick Bell because of the way he chooses to live his life?

MGMT WORKPLACE Timberland

Jeff Swartz, president and CEO of The Timberland Company, a shoe and outdoor gear manufacturer, believes that performing community service is important. To date, Timberland employees have given over 200,000 hours to community service. Swartz believes that performing community service is what Timberland is about as a company and who its employees are as individuals. To support that philosophy, Timberland sponsors Servapalooza, whose 1,700 participants work on many different projects in the New England area. Recently, more than 900 Timberland employees worked at building playgrounds, refurbishing schools, and opening summer camps at 20 different locations in 13 communities.

What to Watch for and Ask Yourself

1. Does Timberland subscribe to a shareholder or a stakeholder model of social responsibility? Defend your answer.
2. What type of strategy has Timberland adopted in response to the public demand for social responsibility? Explain.
3. What, if any, benefits does the company derive from the strategy it uses to address social responsibility? How do stakeholders benefit?

Making Things Happen

PART TWO

CHAPTER FOUR

Planning and Decision Making

outline

WHAT WOULD YOU DO?

Google Headquarters, Mountain View, California.[1] "Michael Jordan and the Chicago Bulls won six National Basketball Association championships!" "No, I'm telling you for the last time, they won seven!" "Well, let's pull up Google and we'll see who's right!" With 150 million searches a day, Google.com, is the most popular search engine on the Web. Enter "meaning of life" and Google's proprietary search algorithms have to determine whether you want philosophical or religious information or Web sites about Monty Python's movie *The Meaning of Life.* Google earns money in the search business in two ways. About half of its revenues come from search-related advertising links. For instance, if you search for "hotel Rome Italy," Google returns a list of sites to help you find a hotel in Italy. In addition, along the right edge of that page (and sometimes at the very top), it also returns a list of "sponsored links" that advertisers have paid to be displayed when relevant search terms are entered. Entering "hotel Rome Italy" pulls

student resources

Experiencing Management
Simulation modules on Planning & Strategic Processes, Organizational Control, and Decision Making

Study Guide
Mini lecture reviews all the learning points in the chapter and concludes with a case on Avon.

Take Two Video
Biz Flix is from *The Bourne Identity*. Management Workplace is a segment on Machado & Silvetti.

PowerPoint®
12 slides with graphics provide an outline for this chapter.

Author Insights
Chuck talks about the benefit of setting fewer goals and gives insight on how to avoid satisficing.

Self Test
31 true/false questions, 35 multiple choice questions, a "What Would You Do?" on Eli Lilly, plus 5 exhibit worksheets

up ads for "Want a Hotel in Rome?" for Venere.com, "Hotels in Italy," for **http://www.reservationitaly.com**, and "Hotels in Italy for Less," for **http://www.gate1travel.com**. The other half of Google's revenues come from $25,000 annual licensing fees that corporations pay to use Google's search engine software to accurately search company intranets.

With the ability to search 2 billion Web pages and 400 million photographs in 74 languages, Google is today's leading Internet search site. Yet the Internet is littered with once-dominant search sites like Excite.com, Alta Vista.com, and Lycos.com that now possess extremely small market shares. And according to Chris Sherman, editor of industry newsletter *SearchDay,* "Google is not the be-all and end-all. Other search engines can do certain things better." Indeed, Google faces tough new competitors in AskJeeves.com, Teoma.com, Overture.com, and Looksmart.com, in addition to its already well-established search engine competitors, MSN.com and Yahoo.com. (At the time this was written, Google had a $7 million contract to provide searches for Yahoo.com, but Yahoo had paid $237 million to purchase Inktomi, one of Google's competitors. So, by the time you read this, Google will most likely have lost Yahoo's business.) Furthermore, since Inktomi and Alta Vista already have 2,500 and 1,000 corporate customers, respectively, Google may find it difficult to break into the already competitive corporate market.

As the head of planning and product development, it's your responsibility to make sure that customers continue to choose Google over its many competitors. Your success or lack thereof will largely determine Google's future profits and market share. But as you face this responsibility, you've got some key questions. What business will Google be in as it focuses more on earning larger profits in addition to its large market share? Will it continue to be just a search engine, or will it branch out into shopping, information, news, finance, and travel like Yahoo? Analyst Whit Andrews says that "they have to think long and hard about what they are going to excel in next—in enterprise search [search services used inside companies], as a destination site, or powering search on the Web for others [such as Yahoo]." So what is Google's planning vision for the long run, and what is its planning mission over the next five years? Next, to keep Google's share of eyeballs—Internet lingo for market share—what new products will you and your team of 50 computer science Ph.D.s need to develop to attract customers? How should you conduct your research, and how many projects should you work on at a time? Finally, given the uncertainty of high technology, and the speed with which change can affect you and your competitors, how can Google maintain flexibility so that it can quickly adapt to customers, competitors, and the marketplace? Planning usually involves commitment to goals and action steps. How can Google pursue its plans without getting locked in? **If you were in charge of planning and product development at Google, what would you do?**

Even inexperienced managers know that planning and decision making are central parts of their jobs. Figure out what the problem is. Generate potential solutions or plans. Pick the best one. Make it work. However, experienced managers know how hard it really is to make good plans and decisions. One seasoned manager said: "I think the biggest surprises are the problems. Maybe I had never seen it before. Maybe I was protected by my management when I was in sales. Maybe I had delusions of grandeur, I don't know. I just know how disillusioning and frustrating it is to be hit with problems and conflicts all day and not be able to solve them very cleanly." [2]

This chapter begins by examining the costs and benefits of planning. Next, you will learn how to make a plan that works. Then, you will look at the different kinds of plans that are used from the top to the bottom in most companies. In the second part of the chapter, we discuss the steps of rational decision making as well as its limitations. We finish the chapter by discussing how managers can use groups and group decision techniques to improve decisions.

Planning

planning
choosing a goal and developing a strategy to achieve that goal

Planning is choosing a goal and developing a method or strategy to achieve that goal. Carlos Ghosn (rhymes with stone), Nissan's CEO, stood in front of television cameras and told the world that Nissan was in "bad shape." He also announced that Nissan's goal was to be profitable within two years by following its new Revival Plan, which had taken six months to develop. Ghosn said, "I didn't have a plan in mind. I knew Nissan by the figures. I have seen many horrible situations, but if you limit yourself to the figures it's a very artificial analysis." So he put together 12 managerial teams to determine how to fix Nissan's purchasing costs, marketing strategy, excessive debt, and boring products. Since Nissan purchases 60 percent of the parts and services used to assemble its cars, Ghosn went to suppliers with this message: Costs must be cut by 20 percent over the next three years. Similarly, five factories were closed and 21,000 workers were laid off. In terms of marketing strategy and boring products, Nissan's plan was to bring 15 new cars or trucks to market within in three years. Nissan's new design director, Shiro Nakamura, who was brought in to spiff up Nissan's product line, said, "We have an incredible number of projects we are doing in a very short time. I've never experienced this kind of tough schedule." Thus far, the plan is well ahead of schedule. Nissan was profitable just over a year into the plan and enjoyed record profits in the plan's second year.[3] And while the turnaround thus far is encouraging, Ghosn still says, "What we have done today is only 5 percent. We [still] have 95 percent [of the plan] to do."[4]

After reading the next three sections, you should be able to

1. discuss the costs and benefits of planning.
2. describe how to make a plan that works.
3. discuss how companies can use plans at all management levels, from top to bottom.

1 Benefits and Pitfalls of Planning

Are you one of those naturally organized people who always makes a daily to-do list, writes everything down so you won't forget, and never misses a deadline because you keep track of everything with your handy time-management notebook or your Palm PC? Or are you one of those flexible, creative, go-with-the-flow people who dislike planning and organizing because it restricts your freedom, energy, and performance? Some people are natural planners. They love it and can only see the benefits of planning. Others dislike planning and can only see its disadvantages. It turns out that both views are correct.

Planning has advantages and disadvantages. Let's learn about 1.1 **the benefits** and 1.2 **the pitfalls of planning.**

1.1 Benefits of Planning

Planning offers several important benefits: intensified effort, persistence, direction, and creation of task strategies.[5] First, managers and employees put forth greater effort when following a plan. Take two workers. Instruct one to "do his or her best" to increase production, and instruct the other to achieve a 2 percent increase in production each month. Research shows that the one with the specific plan will work harder.[6] Second, planning leads to persistence, that is, working hard for long periods. In fact, planning encourages persistence even when there may be little chance of short-term success.[7] The third benefit of planning is direction. Plans encourage managers and employees to direct their persistent efforts *toward* activities that help accomplish their goals and *away* from activities that don't.

The fourth benefit of planning is that it encourages the development of task strategies. In other words, planning not only encourages people to work hard for extended periods and to engage in behaviors directly related to goal accomplishment, but it also encourages them to think of better ways to do their jobs.

Finally, perhaps the most compelling benefit of planning is that it has been proved to work for both companies and individuals. On average, companies with plans have larger profits and grow much faster than companies that don't.[9] The same holds true for individual managers and employees. There is no better way to improve the performance of the people who work in a company than to have them set goals and develop strategies for achieving those goals.

PERSONAL PRODUCTIVITY TIP

"Fail Forward" to Learn from Failure

Failing forward means learning something when you fail. You fail forward when you experiment by trying several different things to learn what works and what doesn't. When something fails, gather a group of people with different backgrounds to analyze what went wrong. Identify the failure as soon as possible. This gives you more time to analyze the problem and figure out how to fix it. Don't blame anyone. Be glad that someone brought the failure to your attention. Thomas Edison failed 10,000 times before inventing light bulb filaments. Abraham Lincoln lost 12 times before finally being elected to office. You can fail forward by learning from your failures, too.[8]

1.2 Planning Pitfalls

Despite the significant benefits associated with planning, planning is not a cure-all. Plans won't fix all organizational problems. In fact, many management authors and consultants believe that planning can harm companies in several ways.[10]

The first pitfall of planning is that it can impede change and prevent or slow needed adaptation. Sometimes companies become so committed to achieving the goals set forth in their plans, or on following the strategies and tactics spelled out in them, that they fail to see that their plans aren't working or that their goals need to change.

The second pitfall of planning is that it can create a false sense of certainty. Planners sometimes feel that they know exactly what the future holds for their competitors, their suppliers, and their companies. However, all plans are based on assumptions. "The price of gasoline will increase by 4 percent per year." "Exports will continue to rise." For plans to work, the assumptions on which they are based must hold true. If the assumptions turn out to be false, then plans based on them are likely to fail.

The third potential pitfall of planning is the detachment of planners. In theory, strategic planners and top-level managers are supposed to focus on the big picture and not concern themselves with the details of implementation, that is, carrying out the plan. According to management professor Henry Mintzberg, detachment leads planners to plan for things they don't understand.[11] Plans are meant to be guidelines for action, not abstract theories. Consequently, planners need to be familiar with the daily details of their businesses if they are to produce plans that can work.

Review 1
Benefits and Pitfalls of Planning

Planning is choosing a goal and developing a method to achieve that goal. Planning is one of the best ways to improve organizational and individual performance. It encourages people to work harder (intensified effort), to work hard for extended periods (persistence), to engage in behaviors directly related to goal accomplishment (directed behavior), and to think of better ways to do their jobs (task strategies). But most important, companies that plan have larger profits and faster growth than companies that don't plan. However, planning also has three potential pitfalls. Companies that are overly committed to their plans may be slow to adapt to changes in their environment. Planning is based on assumptions about the future, and when those assumptions are wrong, plans are likely to fail. Finally, planning can fail when planners are detached from the implementation of plans.

2 How to Make a Plan That Works

Planning is a double-edged sword. If done right, planning brings about tremendous increases in individual and organizational performance. At Pixar Animation Studios, the original plan was to produce one movie a year. In its first seven years, however, because of story development and technological issues, Pixar, which makes digitally animated movies, produced only four movies. But making a movie a year has been a significant long-term goal for Pixar. To achieve this goal, Pixar implemented a plan that called for three new movies in three years: *Finding Nemo*, *The Incredibles*, and one that hasn't been announced yet. If planning is done wrong, however, it can have just the opposite effect and harm individual and organizational performance.[12]

No stranger to Hollywood success, Pixar is planning to increase its output to one movie each year. With all the work that goes into a single computer-animated feature, this is a significant long-term goal for Pixar. A detailed plan is in place to help the studio achieve it.

© PHOTO EDIT

In this section, you will learn how to make a plan that works. As depicted in Exhibit 4.1, planning consists of 2.1 setting goals, 2.2 developing commitment to the goals, 2.3 developing effective action plans, 2.4 tracking progress toward goal achievement, and 2.5 maintaining flexibility in planning.

exhibit 4.1

How to Make a Plan That Works

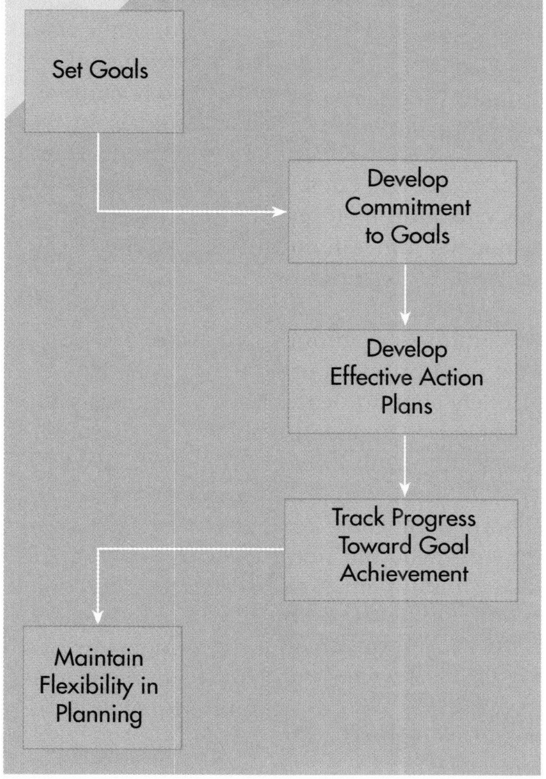

2.1 Setting Goals

Since planning involves choosing a goal and developing a method or strategy to achieve that goal, the first step in planning is to set goals. To direct behavior and increase effort, goals need to be specific and challenging.[13] For example, deciding to "increase sales this year" won't direct and energize workers as much as deciding to "increase North American sales by 4 percent in the next six months." Likewise, deciding to "drop a few pounds" won't motivate you as much as deciding to "lose 15 pounds." Specific, challenging goals provide a target for which to aim and a standard against which to measure success.

One way of writing effective goals for yourself, your job, or your company is to use the S.M.A.R.T. guidelines. **S.M.A.R.T. goals** are **S**pecific, **M**easurable, **A**ttainable, **R**ealistic, and **T**imely.[14] Let's see how a heating, ventilation, and air conditioning (HVAC) company might use S.M.A.R.T. goals in its business.

S.M.A.R.T. goals goals that are specific, measurable, attainable, realistic, and timely

The HVAC business is cyclical. It's extremely busy at the beginning of summer, when homeowners find that their air conditioning isn't working, and at the beginning of winter, when furnaces and heat pumps need repair. During these times, most HVAC companies have more business than they can handle. But at other times of year, business can be very slow. So a **s***pecific* goal would be to increase sales by 50 percent during the fall and spring, when business is slower. This goal could be **m***easured* by keeping track of the number of annual maintenance contracts sold to customers. This goal of increasing sales during the off-seasons is **a***ttainable* because maintenance contracts typically include spring tune-ups (air-conditioning systems) and fall tune-ups (furnace or heating systems). Moreover, a 50 percent increase in sales during the slow seasons is **r***ealistic*. Since customers want their furnaces and air conditioners to work the first time it gets cold (or hot) each year, they are likely to buy service contracts that ensure their equipment is in working order. Tune-up work can then be scheduled during the slow seasons, increasing sales at those times. Finally, this goal can be made **t***imely* by asking the staff to push sales of maintenance contracts before Labor Day, the traditional end of summer, when people start thinking about the cold days ahead, and in March, when winter-weary people start longing for hot days in air-conditioned comfort. The result would be more work during the slow fall and spring seasons.

2.2 Developing Commitment to Goals

Just because a company sets a goal doesn't mean that people will try to accomplish it. If workers don't care about a goal, then the goal won't encourage them to work harder or smarter. Thus, the second step in planning is to develop commitment to goals.[15]

goal commitment the determination to achieve a goal

Goal commitment is the determination to achieve a goal. Commitment to achieve a goal is not automatic. Managers and workers must choose to commit themselves to a goal. For example, Professor Edwin Locke, the foremost expert on how, why, and when goals work, told a story about an overweight

PERSONAL PRODUCTIVITY TIP

Are You an Owl or an Early Bird?

What time do you wake up on Saturday morning? Are you up and out of bed by 7:00 A.M., or are you up just in time to make it to the table for lunch? The term *morningness* describes a preference for morning activities. Studies show that morningness affects performance. Students with morning orientations get much better grades in 8:00 A.M. classes than do students with evening orientations (3.27 versus 2.78). So, to do a better job of achieving your goals, plan to do your most challenging work when you're at your peak energy levels and your routine work when your energy is low.[17]

friend who finally lost 75 pounds. Locke said that, "I asked him how he did it, knowing how hard it was for most people to lose so much weight." His friend responded, "Actually, it was quite simple. I simply decided that I *really wanted* to do it."[16] Put another way, goal commitment is really wanting to achieve a goal.

So how can managers bring about goal commitment? The most popular approach is to set goals participatively. Rather than assigning goals to workers ("Johnson, you've got 'til Tuesday of next week to redesign the flex capacitor so it gives us 10 percent more output"), managers and employees choose goals together. The goals are more likely to be realistic and attainable if employees participate in setting them.

Another technique for gaining commitment to a goal is to make the goal public. For example, college students who publicly communicated their semester grade goals ("This semester, I'm shooting for a 3.5") to significant others (usually a parent or sibling) were much more committed to achieving their grades. More importantly, students who told others about their goals earned grades that were nearly a half-grade higher than students who did not tell others about their grade goals.[18] So, one way to increase commitment to goals is to "go public" by having individuals or work units tell others about their goals.

Another way to increase goal commitment is to obtain top management's support. Top management can show support for a plan or program by providing funds, speaking publicly about the plan, or participating in the plan itself.

2.3 Developing Effective Action Plans

action plan
the specific steps, people, and resources needed to accomplish a goal

The third step in planning is to develop effective action plans. An **action plan** lists the specific steps, people, resources, and time period for accomplishing a goal. For example, for some time, at Severn Sound, one of Ontario, Canada's most popular water recreational areas, swimming and fishing had been restricted because of pollution and reduced oxygen levels in the water. Now, however, thanks to steps implemented over the last decade, the ecosystem has been restored and walleye fish, nearly once eliminated, are abundant again. Cities and towns reduced and treated storm-water runoff; farmers and local residents reduced agricultural and yard fertilizer runoff; farmers reduced animal waste runoff by erecting fences to keep livestock away from streams that fed the sound; local residents reduced human waste runoff by connecting their homes to municipal sewer systems and better maintaining their septic systems; 129,000 trees and shrubs were planted to reduce erosion; and finally, the Department of Fisheries and Oceans mapped fish habitats to determine which areas of the sound could be developed for housing without adversely affecting the sound or its fish population.[19]

2.4 Tracking Progress

proximal goals
short-term goals or subgoals

distal goals
long-term or primary goals

The fourth step in planning is to track progress toward goal achievement. There are two accepted methods of tracking progress. The first is to set proximal goals and distal goals. **Proximal goals** are short-term goals or subgoals, whereas **distal goals** are long-term or primary goals.[20] The idea behind setting proximal goals is that they may be more motivating and rewarding than waiting to achieve far-off distal goals.

The second method of tracking progress is to gather and provide performance feedback. Regular, frequent performance feedback allows workers and managers to track their progress toward goal achievement and make adjustments in effort, direction, and strategies.[21] For example, Exhibit 4.2 shows the result of providing feedback on safety behavior to the makeup and wrapping workers in a large bakery company. The company had a worker safety record that was two-and-a-half times worse than the industry average. During the baseline period, workers in the wrapping department, who measure and mix ingredients, roll the bread dough, and put it into baking pans, performed their jobs safely about 70 percent of the time. The baseline safety record for workers in the makeup department, who bag and seal baked bread and assemble, pack, and tape cardboard cartons for shipping, was a bit better at 78 percent.

exhibit 4.2

Effects of Goal-Setting, Training, and Feedback on Safe Behavior in a Bread Factory

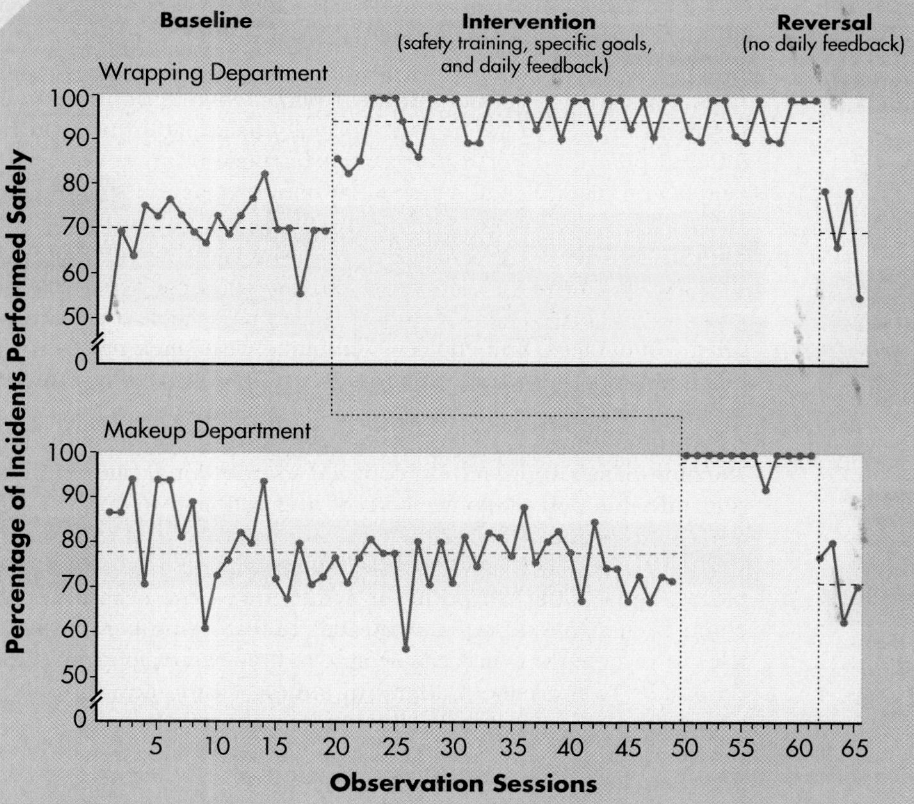

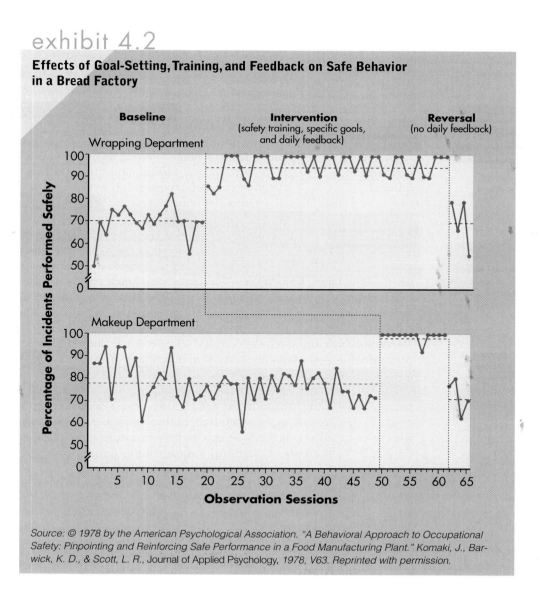

Source: © 1978 by the American Psychological Association. "A Behavioral Approach to Occupational Safety: Pinpointing and Reinforcing Safe Performance in a Food Manufacturing Plant." Komaki, J., Barwick, K. D., & Scott, L. R., Journal of Applied Psychology, *1978, V63. Reprinted with permission.*

After the company gave workers 30 minutes of safety training, set a goal of 90 percent safe behavior, and then provided daily feedback (such as a chart similar to Exhibit 4.2), performance improved dramatically. During the intervention period, the percentage of safely performed behaviors rose to an average of 95.8 percent for wrapping workers and 99.3 percent for workers in the makeup department, and never fell below 83 percent. Thus, the combination of training, a challenging goal, and feedback led to a dramatic increase in performance.

The importance of feedback alone can be seen in the reversal stage, when the company quit posting daily feedback on safe behavior. Without daily feedback, the percentage of safely performed behavior returned to baseline levels, 70.8 percent for the wrapping department and 72.3 percent for the makeup department. For planning to be effective, workers need both a specific, challenging goal and regular feedback to track their progress. Indeed, additional research indicates that the effectiveness of goal setting can be doubled by the addition of feedback.[22]

2.5 Maintaining Flexibility

Because action plans are sometimes poorly conceived and goals sometimes turn out not to be achievable, the last step in developing an effective plan is to maintain flexibility. One method of maintaining flexibility while planning is to adopt an options-based approach.[23] The goal of **options-based planning** is to keep options open by making small, simultaneous investments in many options or plans. Then, when one or a few of these plans emerge as likely winners, you invest even more in these plans while discontinuing or reducing investment in the others. In part, options-based planning is the opposite of traditional planning. For example, the purpose of an action plan is to commit people and resources to a particular course of action. In contrast, the purpose of options-based planning is to leave those commitments open by maintaining **slack resources**, that is, a cushion of resources, such as extra time, people, money, or production capacity, that can be used to address and adapt to unanticipated changes, problems, or opportunities.[24] Holding options open gives you choices, and choices, combined with slack resources, give you flexibility. Options-based planning is especially useful when uncertainty is high and you don't know how things will change or what will work in the future.

options-based planning maintaining planning flexibility by making small, simultaneous investments in many alternative plans

slack resources a cushion of extra resources that can be used with options-based planning to adapt to unanticipated changes, problems, or opportunities

Another method of maintaining flexibility while planning is to take a learning-based approach. In contrast to traditional planning, which assumes that initial action plans are correct and will lead to success, **learning-based planning** assumes that action plans need to be continually tested, changed, and improved as companies learn better ways of achieving goals.[25] For example, Knight-Ridder Corporation, which owns the second-largest newspaper chain in the United States, continues to test a number of different plans as it tries to reverse the 9 percent decline in its newspaper circulation over the last decade.[26] To increase readership among young adults, only 41 percent of whom read newspapers, Knight-Ridder newspapers have added sections with music and movie reviews and a wide listing of entertainment events. They've also switched to shorter articles, more color, and better layouts and indexes to make it easier for younger readers to find what they're looking for. So far, young adult readership hasn't budged, so four Knight-Ridder newspapers are experimenting with price cuts, slashing the cost of their papers to 25 cents on weekdays and $1 on Sundays. Since the price cuts, some papers have seen

learning-based planning learning better ways of achieving goals by continually testing, changing, and improving plans and strategies

daily and Sunday circulation increase. The company will continue to test and revise its plans until it learns how to increase readership.[27]

Review 2

How to Make a Plan That Works

There are five steps to making a plan that works: (1) Set S.M.A.R.T. goals—goals that are **S**pecific, **M**easurable, **A**ttainable, **R**ealistic, and **T**imely. (2) Develop commitment to the goal from the people who contribute to goal achievement. Managers can increase workers' goal commitment by encouraging worker participation in goal setting, making goals public, and getting top management to show their support for workers' goals. (3) Develop action plans for goal accomplishment. (4) Track progress toward goal achievement by setting both proximal and distal goals and by providing workers regular performance feedback. (5) Maintain flexibility. Keeping options open through options-based planning and seeking continuous improvement through learning-based planning help organizations maintain flexibility as they plan.

3 Planning from Top to Bottom

Planning works best when the goals and action plans at the bottom and middle of the organization support the goals and action plans at the top of the organization. In other words, planning works best when everybody pulls in the same direction. Exhibit 4.3 illustrates this planning continuity, beginning at the top with a clear definition of the company vision and ending at the bottom with the execution of operational plans. Let's see how 3.1 top managers create the organizational vision and mission, 3.2 middle managers develop tactical plans and use management by objectives to motivate employee efforts toward the overall vision and mission, and 3.3 first-level managers use operational, single-use, and standing plans to implement the tactical plans.

exhibit 4.3

Planning from Top to Bottom

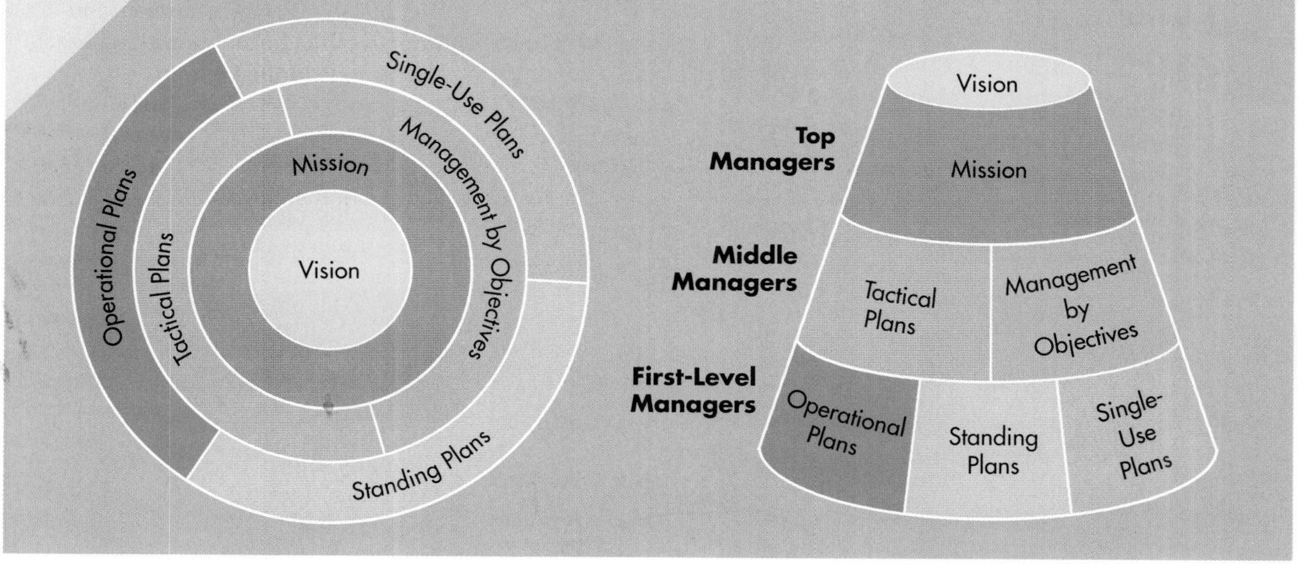

www.experiencing management.com

Planning occurs at all levels in the organization and accomplishes different purposes. Three levels of plans and specific examples of each are presented at our animated concept and activity site. Choose Planning&Strategic_Processes from the "select a topic" pull-down menu, then Types of Plans from the "overview tab."

http://www.experiencingmanagement.com

3.1 Starting at the Top

As shown in Exhibit 4.4, top management is responsible for developing long-term **strategic plans** that make clear how the company will serve customers and position itself against competitors in the next two to five years. (The strategic planning and management process is reviewed in its entirety in Chapter 8.) Strategic planning begins with the creation of an organizational vision and an organizational mission.

A **vision** is a statement of a company's purpose or reason for existing.[28] Vision statements should be brief—no more than two sentences. They should also be enduring, inspirational, clear, and consistent with widely shared company beliefs and values. For example, consider the vision statement of Merck Corporation, a leading pharmaceutical firm. Merck's vision is enduring. It is the same whether Merck uses natural or synthetic chemical compounds or whether its researchers use high-tech gene-splicing equipment or low-tech petri dishes. The vision of "innovations and solutions that improve the quality of life," "meaningful work," and "superior rate of return" stays the same. Furthermore, the vision is clear, inspirational, and consistent with Merck's company values. Other examples of organizational visions are Walt Disney Corporation's "to make people happy" and Schlage Lock Company's "to make the world more secure."[29]

strategic plans
overall company plans that clarify how the company will serve customers and position itself against competitors over the next two to five years

vision
an inspirational statement of an organization's enduring purpose

mission
a statement of a company's overall goal that unifies company-wide efforts toward its vision, stretches and challenges the organization, and possesses a finish line and a time frame

The **mission**, which flows from the vision, is a more specific goal that unifies company-wide efforts, stretches and challenges the organization, and possesses a finish line and a time frame. For example, in 1961, President John F. Kennedy established an organizational mission for NASA with this simple statement: "Achieving the goal, before this decade is out, of landing a man on the moon and returning him safely to earth."[30] NASA achieved this goal on 20 July 1969, when astronaut Neil Armstrong walked on the moon. Once a mission has been accomplished, a new one should be chosen. Again, however, the new mission must grow out of the organization's vision, which does not change significantly over time. For example, NASA's vision statement is "To improve life here, to extend life to there, to find life beyond."[31]

exhibit 4.4

Time Lines for Strategic, Tactical, and Operational Plans

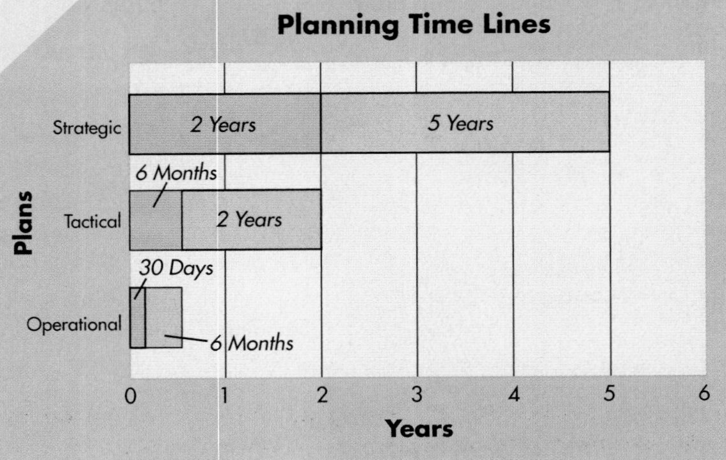

3.2 Bending in the Middle

Middle management is responsible for developing and carrying out tactical plans to accomplish the organization's mission. **Tactical plans** specify how a company will use resources, budgets, and people to accomplish specific goals within its mission. Whereas strategic plans and objectives are used to focus company efforts over the next two to five years, tactical plans and objectives are used to direct behavior, efforts, and attention over the next six months to two years. For example,

www.experiencing management.com

Management by objectives is a common planning technique. To interact with a model of this technique, visit our animated concept and activity site. Choose Planning&Strategic_Processes from the "select a topic" pull-down menu, then Management by Objectives from the "overview tab."

http://www.experiencingmanagement.com

after three years of losses, Disneyland Paris managed to earn a profit in its fourth year of operation by making specific changes in its tactical plans, which were not helping the company accomplish its mission "to make people happy." Realizing that most families wanted to spend only two or three days at the park instead of five days or longer, as the original tactical plan assumed, management redesigned Disney's special package deals (for tickets, hotel, and food). Likewise, management realized that it had miscalculated by "Europeanizing" park rides and shows. It turned out that European visitors wanted an "American experience," so Disney responded. Today, Disneyland Paris is the number one tourist destination in Europe.[32]

Management by objectives is a management technique often used to develop and carry out tactical plans. **Management by objectives**, or MBO, is a four-step process in which managers and their employees (1) discuss possible goals, (2) participatively select goals that are challenging, attainable, and consistent with the company's overall goals, (3) jointly develop tactical plans that lead to accomplishment of tactical goals and objectives, and (4) meet regularly to review progress toward accomplishment of those goals. Lee Iacocca, the CEO who brought the former Chrysler Corporation back from the verge of bankruptcy, credits MBO (though he called it a "quarterly review system") for his 30 years of extraordinary success as a manager. Iacocca said, "Over the years, I've regularly asked my key people—and I've had them ask *their* key people, and so on down the line—a few basic questions: 'What are your objectives for the next ninety days? What are your plans, your priorities, your hopes? And how do you intend to go about achieving them?'"[33]

tactical plans
plans created and implemented by middle managers that specify how the company will use resources, budgets, and people over the next six months to two years to accomplish specific goals within its mission

management by objectives (MBO)
a four-step process in which managers and employees discuss and select goals, develop tactical plans, and meet regularly to review progress toward goal accomplishment

When done right, MBO is an extremely effective method of tactical planning. Still, MBO is not without disadvantages.[34] Some MBO programs involve excessive paperwork, requiring managers to file annual statements of plans and objectives, plus quarterly or semiannual written reviews assessing goal progress. Today, however, electronic and Web-based management systems and software, such as Numetrix (**http://www.numetrix.com**), which automates the MBO process, are making it easier for managers and employees to set goals, link them to the organization's strategic direction, and continuously track and evaluate their progress.[35] Another difficulty is that managers are frequently reluctant to give employees feedback about their performance. A third disadvantage is that managers and employees sometimes have difficulty agreeing on goals. And when employees are forced to accept goals that they don't want, goal commitment and employee effort suffer. Last, because MBO focuses on quantitative, easily measured goals, employees may neglect important unmeasured parts of their jobs. In other words, if your job performance is judged only by whether you reduce costs by 3 percent or raise revenues by 5 percent, then you are unlikely to give high priority to the unmeasured, but still important parts of your job, such as mentoring new employees or sharing new knowledge and skills with coworkers.

3.3 Finishing at the Bottom

Lower-level managers are responsible for developing and carrying out **operational plans**, which are the day-to-day plans for producing or delivering the organization's products and services. Operational plans direct the behavior,

operational plans
day-to-day plans, developed and implemented by lower-level managers, for producing or delivering the organization's products and services over a 30-day to six-month period

WHAT REALLY WORKS

MANAGEMENT BY OBJECTIVES

For years, both managers and management researchers have wondered how much of a difference planning makes in terms of organizational performance or whether it really makes any difference at all. While proponents argued that planning encourages workers to work hard, to persist in their efforts, to engage in behaviors directly related to goal accomplishment, and to develop better strategies for achieving goals, opponents argued that planning impedes organizational change and adaptation, creates the illusion of managerial control, and artificially separates thinkers and doers.

Now, however, the results from 70 different organizations strongly support the effectiveness of management by objectives (i.e., short-term planning).

Management by Objectives (MBO)

Management by objectives is a process in which managers and subordinates at all levels in a company sit down together to jointly set goals, share information and discuss strategies that could lead to goal achievement, and regularly meet to review progress toward accomplishing those goals. Thus, MBO is based on goals, participation, and feedback. On average, companies that effectively use MBO will outproduce those that don't use MBO by an incredible 44.6 percent! And in companies where top management is committed to MBO, that is, where objective setting begins at the top, the average increase in performance is an even more astounding 56.5 percent. By contrast, when top management does not participate in or support MBO, the average increase in productivity drops to 6.1 percent. In all, though, there is a 97 percent chance that companies that use MBO will outperform those that don't! Thus, MBO can make a very big difference to the companies that use it.[36]

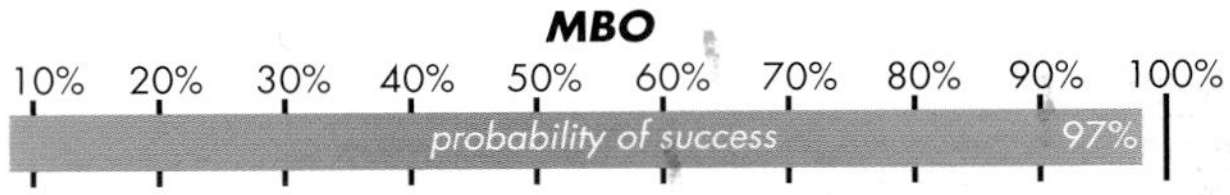

single-use plans
plans that cover unique, one-time-only events

standing plans
plans used repeatedly to handle frequently recurring event

efforts, and priorities of operative employees for periods ranging from 30 days to six months. There are three kinds of operational plans: single-use plans, standing plans, and budgets.

Single-use plans deal with unique, one-time-only events. For example, PlanetRx.com, an online health-care and pharmacy company, moved its headquarters from expensive San Francisco to low-cost Memphis, Tennessee, where 238 employees already worked at its distribution center, pharmacy, and customer-service operations. The one-time move has saved the company approximately $1.5 million a month in operating expenses.[37]

Unlike single-use plans that are created, carried out, and then never used again, **standing plans** save managers time because once the plans are created, they can be used repeatedly to handle frequently recurring events. If you encounter a problem that you've seen before, someone in your company has probably written a standing plan that explains how to address it. There are three kinds of standing plans: policies, procedures, and rules and regulations.

Policies indicate the general course of action that company managers should take in response to a particular event or situation. A well-written policy will also specify why the policy exists and what outcome the policy is intended to produce. For example, over the years, construction company Fisher Development did nearly $3 billion of work for Gap,

> **www.experiencingmanagement.com**
>
> Budgeting is a specific planning device that is also important in Control (see Chapter 6). To learn more about budgets, visit our animated concept and activity site. Choose Organizational_Control from the "select a topic" pull-down menu, then Financial and Human Controls from the "overview tab." Budgeting is presented as one type of financial control.
>
> **http://www.experiencingmanagement.com**

policy
a standing plan that indicates the general course of action that should be taken in response to a particular event or situation

procedure
a standing plan that indicates the specific steps that should be taken in response to a particular event

rules and regulations
standing plans that describe how a particular action should be performed, or what must happen or not happen in response to a particular event

budgeting
quantitative planning through which managers decide how to allocate available money to best accomplish company goals

building every Gap, Gap Kids, Baby Gap, Banana Republic, and Old Navy store in the United States. Plus, it retrofitted over 10,000 Gap stores. In fact, the relationship between Gap and Fisher Development was so close that other builders quit trying to get Gap's business. Now, however, thanks to a new policy, Gap bids out all construction work for new stores or for redoing existing stores. Gap changed its policy simply to reduce costs. A Gap spokesperson explained, "It just makes good business sense to have more than one general contractor."[38]

Procedures are more specific than policies because they indicate the series of steps that should be taken in response to a particular event. Many companies can improve procedures in the area of travel and reimbursement. At Heidrick & Struggles, an executive recruiting firm, 200 partners in 17 locations were using 35 different travel agents to make travel reservations. Consequently, Heidrick & Struggles changed its travel booking procedures, replacing the 35 travel agencies with American Express Travel Services, which not only provides American Express cards dedicated for business travel expenses, but also allows Heidrick & Struggles workers to make much cheaper hotel, car, and airline reservations by using American Express.[39]

Rules and regulations are even more specific than procedures because they specify what must happen or not happen. They describe precisely how a particular action should be performed. For instance, rules and regulations forbid many managers from writing job reference letters for employees who have worked at their firms. Companies insist on such rules because a negative reference letter may prompt a former employee to sue for defamation of character.[40]

Budgets are the third kind of operational plan. **Budgeting** is quantitative planning because it forces managers to decide how to allocate available money to best accomplish company goals. According to Jan King, author of *Business Plans to Game Plans*, "Money sends a clear message about your priorities. Budgets act as a language for communicating your goals to others." For example, Exhibit 4.5 shows the operating budget for the General Fund of Austin, Texas. With nearly half this budget dedicated to public safety (53.7 percent), it's clear that keeping the city safe is the Austin city government's most important task.

exhibit 4.5

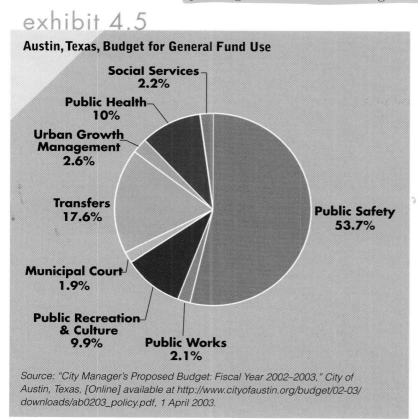

Austin, Texas, Budget for General Fund Use

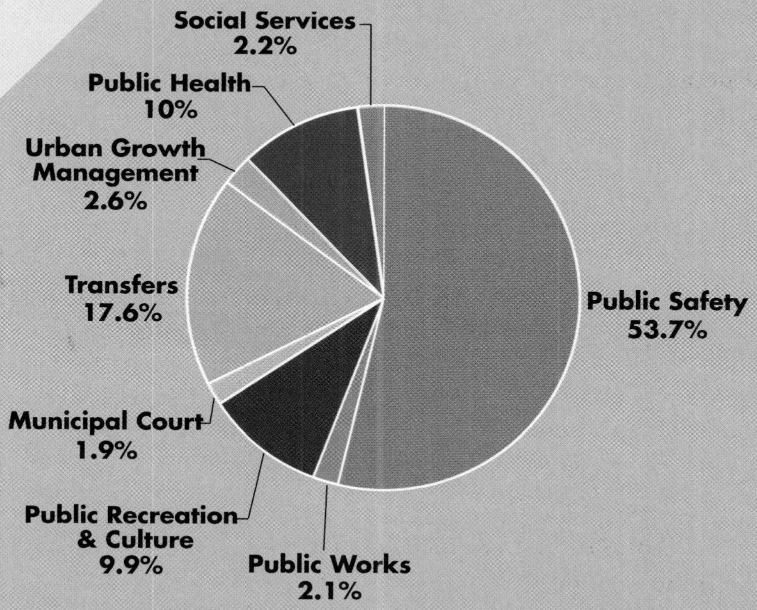

Source: "City Manager's Proposed Budget: Fiscal Year 2002–2003," City of Austin, Texas, [Online] available at http://www.cityofaustin.org/budget/02-03/downloads/ab0203_policy.pdf, 1 April 2003.

Review 3

Planning from Top to Bottom

Proper planning requires that the goals at the bottom and middle of the organization support the objectives at the top of the organization. Top management develops strategic plans that indicate how a company will serve customers and position itself against competitors over a two- to five-year period. Strategic planning starts with the creation of an organizational vision and mission. Middle managers use techniques like management by objectives to develop tactical plans that direct behavior, efforts, and priorities over the next six months to two years. Finally, lower-level managers develop operational plans that guide daily activities in producing or delivering an organization's products and services. Operational plans typically span periods ranging from 30 days to six months. There are three kinds of operational plans: single-use plans, standing plans (policies, procedures, and rules and regulations), and budgets.

What Is Rational Decision Making?

Imagine that you've been away on business. On your first day back at the office, you sort through your phone messages and find this voice mail from the boss:

> You're a computer nut, aren't you? Whaddya call yourself, an Internet geek? Well, you know more about this stuff than anyone else in the office. Here's what I need from you. You've got three weeks to get it done. I want you to prepare a presentation and write a report that details the problems we've been having with our computers. It should also summarize our current and future computer needs. Talk to everyone. Find out what they need and want. Be sure to consider upgrade options. I don't want to spend a ton of money to improve our systems, only to have them be obsolete in two years. Finally, come up with at least five plans or options for getting us where we need to be. Hey, almost forgot, you're probably going to have to do some educating here. Most of us in management don't speak "computer geek." Heck, half of the dinosaurs we've got in upper management think computers are $1,500 paperweights—don't repeat that, okay? So be sure to explain in everyday language how we can decide which plans or options are best. Have a rough draft on my desk in three weeks.

decision making
the process of choosing a solution from available alternatives

rational decision making
a systematic process of defining problems, evaluating alternatives, and choosing optimal solutions

Decision making is the process of choosing a solution from available alternatives.[41] We begin by reviewing **rational decision making**, a systematic process in which managers define problems, evaluate alternatives, and choose optimal solutions that provide maximum benefits to their organizations. When your boss delegated this "computer problem," what he really wanted from you is a rational decision. In other words, you need to define and analyze the problem and explore alternatives. Furthermore, the solution has to be "optimal," since the department is going to live with the computer equipment you recommend for the next three years.

After reading the next two sections, you should be able to

4 explain the steps and limits to rational decision making.

5 explain how group decisions and group decision-making techniques can improve decision making.

exhibit 4.6

Steps of the Rational Decision-Making Process

1 Define the Problem

2 Identify Decision Criteria

3 Weight the Criteria

4 Generate Alternative Courses of Action

5 Evaluate Each Alternative

6 Compute the Optimal Decision

4 Steps and Limits to Rational Decision Making

Exhibit 4.6 shows the six steps of the rational decision-making process. Let's learn more about each of these steps: 4.1 define the problem, 4.2 identify decision criteria, 4.3 weight the criteria, 4.4 generate alternative courses of action, 4.5 evaluate each alternative, and 4.6 compute the optimal decision. Then we'll consider 4.7 limits to rational decision making.

4.1 Define the Problem

The first step in decision making is identifying and defining the problem. A **problem** exists when there is a gap between a desired state (what managers want) and an existing state (the situation that the managers are facing). For example, despite being the largest and most popular e-tailing site on the Web with, by far, the highest customer satisfaction ratings, as of the writing of this chapter Amazon.com has never been profitable. In fact, over the last five years, Amazon has posted losses totaling more than $2.5 billion.[42]

problem
a gap between a desired state and an existing state

The existence of a gap between an existing state and a desired state is no guarantee that managers will make decisions to solve problems. Three things must occur for this to happen.[43] First, managers have to be aware of the gap. They have to know there is a problem before they can begin solving it. For example, after noticing that people were spending more money on their pets, a new dog food company created an expensive, high-quality dog food. To emphasize its quality, the dog food was sold in cans and bags with gold labels, red letters, and detailed information about its benefits and nutrients. Yet, the product did not sell very well, and the company went out of business in less than a year. Its founders didn't understand why. When they asked a manager at a competing dog food company what their biggest mistake had been, the answer was, "Simple. You didn't have a picture of a dog on the package."[44] This problem would have been easy to solve, if management had only been aware of it.

Being aware of the gap between a desired state and an existing state isn't enough to begin the decision-making process. Managers also have to be motivated to reduce the gap. For example, businesspeople have complained for years about unreasonable workplace regulation. Nevertheless, Congress was not interested in solving this "problem" until the Congressional Accountability Act subjected Congress to the same laws as private businesses. Now, like any business, Congress must give overtime pay to anyone who works more than 40 hours a week. Legislative and office assistants, all of whom used to work 60 hours a week, are now limited by law to just 40. To limit hours and overtime pay, no one is allowed to work during lunch (even if they want to).

www.experiencing management.com

There are many different models of rational decision making, but most of them contain common steps. To view an alternative decision-making model, visit our animated concept and activity site. Choose Decision_Making from the "select a topic" pull-down menu, then Decision-Making Process from the "overview tab."

http://www.experiencingmanagement.com

Computers are turned off. Phones go unanswered. Employees can't even watch C-Span while eating their sandwiches. At 6:00 P.M., office managers walk through the offices, ringing loud bells and turning off lights to force employees who want to keep working to go home. Not surprisingly, these changes have motivated many in Congress to take a second look at the unintended effects that workplace laws and regulations have on businesses.[45]

Finally, it's not enough to be aware of a problem and be motivated to solve it. Managers must also have the knowledge, skills, abilities, and resources to fix the problem.

4.2 Identify Decision Criteria

decision criteria
the standards used to guide judgments and decisions

Decision criteria are the standards used to guide judgments and decisions. Typically, the more criteria a potential solution meets, the better that solution should be.

Let's return to the employee who was given the responsibility for making a rational decision about the office computer setup. What general factors would be important when purchasing computers for the office? Reliability, price, warranty, on-site service, and compatibility with existing software, printers, and computers would all be important, wouldn't they? But you can't buy computer equipment without considering the technical details. What specific factors would you want the office computers to have? Well, with technology changing so quickly, you'll probably want to buy computers with as much capability as you can afford. At the minimum, according to *PC Magazine*, you'll probably want a 64-bit 2-gigahertz Pentium 4 or Athlon chip, with 512 megs of memory, a 40-gig hard drive, a DVD drive holding 8 gigabytes of data, a 100 megabit per second network card for high-speed Internet connections, six USB ports to connect external devices like digital cameras and zip drives, and a 17-inch monitor—all for a price of $1,300 or less![46] These general and specific factors represent the criteria that could guide the purchase of computer equipment.

4.3 Weight the Criteria

absolute comparisons
a process in which each criterion is compared to a standard or ranked on its own merits

After identifying decision criteria, the next step is deciding which criteria are more or less important. Although there are numerous mathematical models for weighting decision criteria, all require the decision maker to provide an initial ranking of the decision criteria. Some use **absolute comparisons**, in which each criterion is compared to a standard or ranked on its own merits. For example, *Consumer's Digest* uses a 12-point checklist when it rates and recommends new cars. Six points address the car's performance (starting and acceleration, fuel economy, handling and steering, shifting/transmission, ride quality, and braking), and six address the car's design (overall design, interior ergonomics, seating, accessories and amenities, cargo space, and fit and finish).[47]

Exhibit 4.7 shows the absolute weights that someone buying a car might use. Because these weights are absolute, each criterion is judged on its own importance, using a five-point scale, with "5" representing "critically important" and "1" representing "completely unimportant." In this instance, fuel economy, seating, and cargo space were rated most important, while shifting/transmission and accessories and amenities were rated least important.

relative comparisons
a process in which each decision criterion is compared directly to every other criterion

Another method uses **relative comparisons**, in which each criterion is compared directly to every other criterion.[48] For example, moving down the first column of Exhibit 4.8, we see that starting/acceleration has been rated

exhibit 4.7

Absolute Weighting of Decision Criteria for a Car Purchase

5 critically important
4 important
3 somewhat important
2 not very important
1 completely unimportant

PERFORMANCE CHARACTERISTICS					
1. starting and acceleration	1	2	3	**4**	5
2. fuel economy	1	2	3	4	**5**
3. handling and steering	1	2	**3**	4	5
4. shifting/transmission	1	**2**	3	4	5
5. ride quality	1	2	**3**	4	5
6. braking	1	2	3	**4**	5
DESIGN CHARACTERISTICS					
1. overall design	1	2	3	**4**	5
2. interior ergonomics	1	2	**3**	4	5
3. seating	1	2	3	4	**5**
4. accessories and amenities	**1**	2	3	4	5
5. cargo space	1	2	3	4	**5**
6. fit and finish	1	2	**3**	4	5

exhibit 4.8

Relative Comparison for Car Performance Characteristics

CAR PERFORMANCE CHARACTERISTICS	S/A	FE	H&S	S/T	RQ	BR
Starting/acceleration (S/A)		+1	−1	−1	−1	0
Fuel economy (FE)	−1		−1	−1	−1	−1
Handling & steering (H&S)	+1	+1		0	0	+1
Shifting/transmission (S/T)	+1	+1	0		0	0
Ride quality (RQ)	+1	+1	0	0		0
Braking (BR)	0	+1	−1	0	0	
Total Weight	+2	+5	−3	−2	−2	0

less important (−1) than fuel economy; more important (+1) than handling and steering, shifting/transmission, and ride quality; and just as important as braking (0). Total weights, which are obtained by summing the scores in each column, indicate that fuel economy and starting/acceleration are the most important factors to this car buyer, while handling and steering, shifting/transmission, and ride quality are the least important.

4.4 Generate Alternative Courses of Action

After identifying and weighting the criteria that will guide the decision-making process, the next step is to identify possible courses of action that could solve the problem. In general, at this step, the idea is to generate as many alternatives as possible. For instance, let's assume that you're trying to select a city in Europe to be the location of a major office. After meeting with your staff, you generate a list of possible alternatives: Amsterdam, the Netherlands; Barcelona or Madrid, Spain; Berlin or Frankfurt, Germany; Brussels, Belgium; London, England; Milan, Italy; Paris, France; and Zurich, Switzerland.

4.5 Evaluate Each Alternative

The next step is to systematically evaluate each alternative against each criterion. Because of the amount of information that must be collected, this step can take much longer and be much more expensive than other steps in the decision-making process. For example, in selecting a European city for your office, you could contact economic development offices in each city, systematically interview businesses or executives who operate there, retrieve and use published government data on each location, or rely on published studies such as Cushman & Wakefield Healy & Baker's *European Monitor,* which contains the results of an annual survey of more than 500 senior European executives who rate 30 European cities on 12 business-related criteria.[49]

No matter how you gather the information, once you have it, the key is to systematically use that information to evaluate each alternative against each criterion. For example, Exhibit 4.9 shows how each of the 10 cities on your staff's list fared on each of the 12 criteria (higher scores are better). Although Paris has good access to markets and very good travel to and from the city, it has a poor business climate and relatively few different languages are spoken in its business community. On the other hand, Barcelona has the lowest costs for employing staff, but weak access to markets and poor ease of travel to and from the city.

4.6 Compute the Optimal Decision

The final step in the decision-making process is to compute the optimal decision by determining each alternative's optimal value. This is done by multiplying the rating for each criterion (Step 5) by the weight for that criterion (Step 3), and then summing those scores for each alternative course of action that you generated (Step 4). For example, the 500 executives participating in Cushman & Wakefield Healy & Baker's survey of best European cities for business rated the 12 decision criteria in terms of importance as follows: qualified staff (59 percent), access to major markets (57 percent), travel to and from the city (51 percent), good telecommunications (46 percent), positive business climate (34 percent), cost of staff (32 percent), cost and value of

xhibit 4.9

iteria Ratings Used to Determine the Best Locations in Europe for a New Office

	CRITERION WEIGHTS	Amsterdam	Barcelona	Berlin	Brussels	Frankfurt	London	Madrid	Milan	Paris	Zurich
QUALIFIED STAFF	**59%**	0.32	0.22	0.33	0.38	0.65	1.39	0.24	0.34	0.84	0.23
ACCESS TO MARKETS	**57%**	0.44	0.18	0.23	0.51	0.72	1.44	0.28	0.41	1.14	0.20
TRAVEL TO/FROM CITY	**51%**	0.64	0.14	0.17	0.49	1.20	1.69	0.17	0.22	1.43	0.25
TELECOMMU-NICATIONS	**46%**	0.31	0.08	0.37	0.32	0.76	1.36	0.10	0.18	0.94	0.33
BUSINESS CLIMATE	**34%**	0.56	.037	0.30	0.35	0.19	0.65	0.40	0.20	0.24	0.36
COST OF STAFF	**32%**	0.25	0.71	0.23	0.20	0.09	0.21	0.61	0.29	0.16	0.05
COST & VALUE OF OFFICE SPACE	**30%**	0.37	0.69	0.38	0.41	0.26	0.24	0.42	0.21	0.30	0.14
AVAILABLE OFFICE SPACE	**27%**	0.34	0.41	0.52	0.38	0.45	0.60	0.46	0.26	0.40	0.18
TRAVEL WITHIN CITY	**21%**	0.35	0.48	0.45	0.31	0.39	1.17	0.30	0.21	1.13	0.43
LANGUAGES SPOKEN	**20%**	0.98	0.14	0.25	0.96	0.51	1.35	0.21	0.22	0.65	0.51
QUALITY OF LIFE	**18%**	0.31	0.99	0.27	0.28	0.14	0.43	0.54	0.33	0.71	0.41
FREEDOM FROM POLLUTION	**12%**	0.38	0.44	0.13	0.20	0.17	0.12	0.09	0.05	0.13	0.85
WEIGHTED AVERAGE (OPTIMAL SCORE)		**1.75**	**1.37**	**1.22**	**1.65**	**2.28**	**4.26**	**1.23**	**1.08**	**3.15**	**1.13**
RANKING		**4**	**6**	**8**	**5**	**3**	**1**	**7**	**10**	**2**	**9**

urce: "European Cities Monitor," Cushman & Wakefield Healy & Baker, [Online] available at http://www.frankfurt.de/sixcms_upload/media, 26 April 2003.

office space (30 percent), availability of office space (27 percent), travel within the city (21 percent), languages spoken in the business community (20 percent), quality of life (18 percent), and freedom from pollution (12 percent). Those weights are then multiplied by the ratings in each category. For example, Amsterdam's optimal value of 1.75 (i.e., weighted average) is determined by the following calculation:

$$(.59 \times .32) + (.57 \times .44) + (.51 \times .64) + (.46 \times .31) + (.34 \times .56)$$
$$+ (.32 \times .25) + (.30 \times .37) + (.27 \times .34) + (.21 \times .35) + (.20 \times .98)$$
$$+ (.18 \times .31) + (.12 \times .38) = 1.75$$

The last two rows in Exhibit 4.9 show that London clearly ranks as the best location for your company's new European office because of its large number of qualified staff, easy access to markets, outstanding ease of travel to, from, and within the city, excellent telecommunications, and top-notch business climate.

4.7 Limits to Rational Decision Making

In general, managers who diligently complete all six steps of the rational decision-making model will make better decisions than those who don't. So, when they can, managers should try to follow the steps in the rational decision-making model, especially for big decisions with long-range consequences.

It's highly doubtful, however, that rational decision making can always help managers choose *optimal* solutions that provide *maximum* benefits to their organizations. The terms *optimal* and *maximum* suggest that rational decision making leads to perfect or near-perfect decisions. Of course, for managers to make perfect decisions, they have to operate in perfect worlds with no real-world constraints. For example, in an optimal world, the manager who was given three weeks to define, analyze, and fix computer problems in the office would have followed *PC Magazine*'s advice to buy all employees the "perfect personal computer" (i.e., 2-gigahertz chip, 512 megabytes of memory, etc.). And in arriving at that decision, our manager would not have been constrained by price ("$3,000 per computer? Sure, no problem.") or time ("Need six more months to decide? Sure, take as long as you need."). Furthermore, without any constraints, our manager could identify and weight an extensive list of decision criteria, generate a complete list of possible solutions, and then test and evaluate each computer against each decision criterion. Finally, our manager would have the necessary experience and knowledge with computers to easily make sense of all these sophisticated tests and information.

Of course, it never works like that in the real world. Managers face time and money constraints. They often don't have time to make extensive lists of decision criteria. And they often don't have the resources to test all possible solutions against all possible criteria.

The rational decision-making model describes the way decisions *should* be made. In other words, decision makers wanting to make optimal decisions *should not* have to face time and costs constraints. They *should* have unlimited resources and time to generate and test all alternative solutions against all decision criteria. And they *should* be willing to recommend any decision that produces optimal benefits for the company, even if that decision would harm their own jobs or departments. Of course, very few managers actually make rational decisions the way they *should*. The way in which managers actually make decisions is more accurately described as "bounded (or limited) rationality." **Bounded rationality** means that managers try to take a rational approach to decision making, but are restricted by real-world constraints, incomplete and imperfect information, and their own limited decision-making capabilities.

bounded rationality
a decision-making process restricted in the real world by limited resources, incomplete and imperfect information, and managers' limited decision-making capabilities

maximizing
choosing the best alternative

satisficing
choosing a "good enough" alternative

In theory, fully rational decision makers **maximize** decisions by choosing the optimal solution. In practice, however, limited resources, along with attention, memory, and expertise problems, make it nearly impossible for managers to maximize decisions. Consequently, most managers don't maximize—they "satisfice." Whereas maximizing is choosing the best alternative, **satisficing** is choosing a "good enough" alternative. With 24 decision criteria, 50 alternative computers to choose from, two computer labs with hundreds of thousands of dollars of equipment, and unlimited time and money, our manager could test all alternatives against all decision criteria and choose the "perfect PC." However, our manager's limited time, money, and expertise mean that only a few alternatives will be assessed against a few decision criteria. In practice, our manager will visit two or three computer or electronic stores, read a couple of recent computer reviews, and get bids from a couple of local computer stores that sell complete computer systems at competitive prices, as well as from Dell, Gateway, IBM, and Hewlett-Packard. The decision will be complete when our manager finds a "good enough" computer that meets a few decision criteria.

Review 4
Steps and Limits to Rational Decision Making

Rational decision making is a six-step process in which managers define problems, evaluate alternatives, and compute optimal solutions. The first step is identifying and defining the problem. Problems exist where there is a gap between desired and existing states. Managers won't begin the decision-making process unless they are aware of the gap, motivated to reduce it, and possess the necessary resources to fix it. The second step is defining the decision criteria that are used when judging alternatives. In Step 3, an absolute or relative comparison process is used to rate the importance of decision criteria. Step 4 involves generating as many alternative courses of action (i.e., solutions) as possible. Potential solutions are assessed in Step 5 by systematically gathering information and evaluating each alternative against each criterion. In Step 6, criterion ratings and weights are used to compute the optimal value for each alternative course of action. Rational managers then choose the alternative with the highest optimal value.

The rational decision-making model describes how decisions should be made in an ideal world without limits. However, bounded rationality recognizes that in the real world, limited resources, incomplete and imperfect information, and managers' limited decision-making capabilities restrict managers' decision-making processes. These limitations often prevent managers from being rational decision makers.

5 Using Groups to Improve Decision Making

According to a study reported in *Fortune* magazine, 91 percent of U.S. companies use teams and groups to solve specific problems (i.e., make decisions).[50] Why do so many companies use teams and groups? Because, when done properly, group decision making can lead to much better decisions than decisions typically made by individuals. In fact, numerous studies show that groups consistently outperform individuals on complex tasks.

Let's explore the 5.1 **advantages and pitfalls of group decision making** and see how the following group decision-making methods—5.2 **structured conflict**, 5.3 **the nominal group technique**, 5.4 **the Delphi technique**, 5.5 **the stepladder technique**, and 5.6 **electronic brainstorming**—can be used to improve decision making.

5.1 Advantages and Pitfalls of Group Decision Making

Groups can do a much better job than individuals in two important steps of the decision-making process: defining the problem and generating alternative solutions. Four reasons explain why.

First, because group members usually possess different knowledge, skills, abilities, and experiences, groups are able to view problems from multiple perspectives. Being able to view problems from multiple sources, in turn, can help groups perform better on complex tasks and make better decisions than individuals.[51]

Second, groups can find and access much more information than can individuals alone. At Vignette Corporation, which makes software to help online businesses attract and keep customers, instead of being interviewed by one manager, applicants who pass the initial phone screening are interviewed by eight people with eight different areas of expertise. At end of the day, when the team meets to decide whether to make a job offer, it has eight kinds of information and eight times as much information to consider.[52]

Third, the increased knowledge and information available to groups make it easier for them to generate more alternative solutions. Studies show that generating lots of alternative solutions is a critical part of improving the quality of decisions. Fourth, if groups are involved in the decision-making process, group members will be more committed to making chosen solutions work.

groupthink a barrier to good decision making caused by pressure within the group for members to agree with each other

Although groups can do a better job of defining problems and generating alternative solutions, group decision making is subject to some pitfalls that can quickly erase these gains. One possible pitfall is groupthink. **Groupthink** occurs in highly cohesive groups when group members feel intense pressure to agree with each other so that the group can approve a proposed solution.[53] Because groupthink leads to consideration of a limited number of solutions and restricts discussion of any considered solutions, it usually results in poor decisions. Groupthink is most likely to occur under the following conditions:

- The group is insulated from others with different perspectives.
- The group leader begins by expressing a strong preference for a particular decision.
- There is no established procedure for systematically defining problems and exploring alternatives.
- Group members have similar backgrounds and experiences.[54]

NASA's decision to launch the ill-fated space shuttle *Challenger* is an example of groupthink. Despite cold weather that would normally have postponed a launch, NASA placed heavy pressure on Morton Thiokol (maker of the o-rings) and other engineering firms involved in the launch

www.experiencing management.com

There are both advantages and disadvantages to group decision making, and managers must know what action to take when group decision making is a possibility. Examine some ideas about group decision making at our animated concept and activity site. Choose Decision_Making from the "select a topic" pull-down menu, then Decision-Making Process from the "overview tab."

http://www.experiencingmanagement.com

decision to give their approval to launch. After being told twice that a launch was not recommended, NASA administrators pressured Morton Thiokol one last time for an OK. Because of the pressure and time constraints, Thiokol reversed its decision. Tragically, as Thiokol had originally feared, the o-rings failed, and the shuttle exploded, killing all aboard. Early reports seem to indicate that groupthink played a role in the loss of the space shuttle *Columbia*, too.[55]

A second potential problem with group decision making is that it takes considerable time. It takes time to reconcile schedules (so that group members can meet). Furthermore, it's a rare group that consistently holds productive task-oriented meetings to effectively work through the decision process. Some of the most common complaints about meetings (and thus decision making) are that the meeting's purpose is unclear, meeting participants are unprepared, critical people are absent or late, conversation doesn't stay focused on the problem, and no one follows up on the decisions that were made.

A third possible pitfall is that sometimes just one or two people, perhaps the boss or a strong-willed, vocal group member, dominate group discussion, restricting consideration of different problem definitions and alternative solutions. Another potential problem is that, unlike with their own decisions and actions, group members often don't feel accountable for the decisions made and actions taken by the group.

While these pitfalls can lead to poor decision making, this doesn't mean that managers should avoid using groups to make decisions. When done properly, group decision making can lead to much better decisions. The pitfalls of group decision making are not inevitable. Most of them can be overcome through good management. Let's see how structured conflict, the nominal group technique, the Delphi technique, the stepladder technique, and electronic brainstorming can help managers improve group decision making.

PERSONAL PRODUCTIVITY TIP

Want to Help? Shhhhhh, Chew Your Nails

Managers sometimes impede group decision making by beginning the process by saying what they think should be done. Because group members tend to place more importance on what their leaders say than on what other members say, the group may prematurely accept the alternatives and decision criteria laid out by the manager. So the best thing to do as a manager is to keep quiet. Do what one manager did when group members said, "Why don't you just tell us what to do so we can move on?" Her response? "I sat on my hands. Chewed on my fingernails."[57]

5.2 Structured Conflict

Most people view conflict negatively. Yet the right kind of conflict can lead to much better group decision making. **C-type conflict**, or "cognitive conflict," focuses on problem- and issue-related differences of opinion.[56] In c-type conflict, group members disagree because their different experiences and expertise lead them to view the problem and its potential solutions differently. C-type conflict is also characterized by a willingness to examine, compare, and reconcile those differences to produce the best possible solution.

By contrast, **a-type conflict**, meaning "affective conflict," refers to the emotional reactions that can occur when disagreements become personal rather than professional. A-type conflict often results in hostility, anger, resentment, distrust, cynicism, and apathy. Unlike c-type conflict, a-type conflict undermines team effectiveness by preventing teams from engaging in the activities characteristic of c-type conflict that are critical to team effectiveness. Examples of a-type conflict statements are "your idea," "our idea," "my department," "you don't know what you are talking about," or "you don't understand

c-type conflict (cognitive conflict)
disagreement that focuses on problem- and issue-related differences of opinion

a-type conflict (affective conflict)
disagreement that focuses on individuals or personal issues

our situation." Rather than focusing on issues and ideas, these statements focus on individuals.[58]

Two methods of introducing structured c-type conflict into the group decision-making process are devil's advocacy and dialectical inquiry. **Devil's advocacy** creates c-type conflict by assigning an individual or a subgroup the role of critic. The following five steps establish a devil's advocacy program:

devil's advocacy
a decision-making method in which an individual or a subgroup is assigned the role of a critic

1. Generate a potential solution.
2. Assign a devil's advocate to criticize and question the solution.
3. Present the critique of the potential solution to key decision makers.
4. Gather additional relevant information.
5. Decide whether to use, change, or not use the originally proposed solution.[59]

Dialectical inquiry creates c-type conflict by forcing decision makers to state the assumptions of a proposed solution (a thesis) and then generate a solution that is the opposite (antithesis) of the proposed solution. The following are the five steps of the dialectical inquiry process:

dialectical inquiry
a decision-making method in which decision makers state the assumptions of a proposed solution (a thesis) and generate a solution that is the opposite (antithesis) of that solution

1. Generate a potential solution.
2. Identify the assumptions underlying the potential solution.
3. Generate a conflicting counterproposal based on the opposite assumptions.
4. Have advocates of each position present their arguments and engage in a debate in front of key decision makers.
5. Decide whether to use, change, or not use the originally proposed solution.[60]

BMW uses the process of dialectical inquiry to design its cars, typically creating six internal design teams to compete against each other to design a new car. After a short time, a front-runner or leading design will emerge from one of the teams. At this point, another team is assigned to design a car that is "diametrically opposed" to the leading design (Step 3 of the dialetical inquiry method).[61]

When properly used, both the devil's advocacy and dialectical inquiry approaches introduce c-type conflict into the decision-making process. Further, contrary to the common belief that conflict is bad, studies show that these methods lead to less a-type conflict, improved decision quality, and greater acceptance of decisions once they have been made.[62] See the "What Really Works" feature on page 107 for more information on both techniques.

5.3 Nominal Group Technique

nominal group technique
a decision-making method that begins and ends by having group members quietly write down and evaluate ideas to be shared with the group

"Nominal" means "in name only." Accordingly, the **nominal group technique** received its name because it begins with "quiet time," in which group members independently write down as many problem definitions and alternative solutions as possible. In other words, the nominal group technique begins by having group members act as individuals. After the "quiet time," the group leader asks each group member to share one idea at a time with the group. As they are read aloud, ideas are posted on flipcharts or wallboards for all to see. This step continues until all ideas have been shared. In the next step, the group discusses the advantages and disadvantages of the ideas. The nominal group technique closes with a second "quiet time," in which group members independently rank the ideas presented. Group mem-

WHAT REALLY WORKS

DEVIL'S ADVOCACY, DIALECTICAL INQUIRY, AND CONSIDERING NEGATIVE CONSEQUENCES

Ninety percent of the decisions managers face are well-structured problems that recur frequently under conditions of certainty. For example, for most retailers, customers trying to get a refund on a returned item without a receipt is a well-structured problem. It happens every day (recurs frequently), and it's easy to determine if a customer has a receipt or not.

Well-structured problems are solved with programmed decisions, in which a policy, procedure, or rule clearly specifies how to solve the problem. Thus, there's no mystery about what to do when someone shows up without a receipt. You allow them to exchange the item for one of similar value, but you don't give a refund.

In some sense, programmed decisions really aren't decisions, because anyone with any experience knows what to do. There's no thought involved. What keeps managers up at night is the other 10 percent of problems. Ill-structured problems that are novel (no one's seen them before) and exist under conditions of uncertainty are solved with nonprogrammed decisions. Nonprogrammed decisions do not involve standard methods of resolution. Every time managers make a nonprogrammed decision, they have to figure out a new way of handling a new problem. That's what makes them so tough.

Both the devil's advocacy and dialectical inquiry approaches to decision making, along with a related approach, considering negative consequences, can be used to improve nonprogrammed decision making. All three work because they force decision makers to identify and criticize the assumptions underlying the nonprogrammed decisions that they hope will solve ill-structured problems.

Devil's Advocacy

There is a 58 percent chance that decision makers who use the devil's advocacy approach to criticize and question their solutions will produce better decisions than decisions based on the advice of experts.

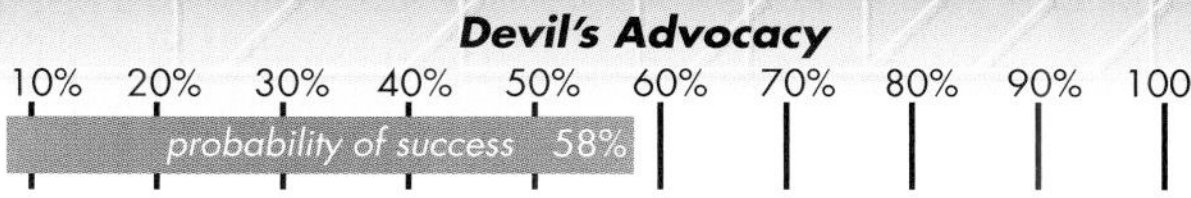

Dialectical Inquiry

There is a 55 percent chance that decision makers who use the dialectical inquiry approach to criticize and question their solutions will produce better decisions than decisions based on the advice of experts.

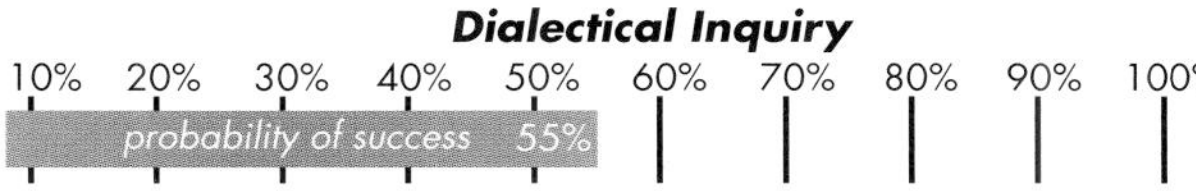

Note that each technique has been compared to decisions obtained by following experts' advice. So, while these probabilities of success, 55 percent and 58 percent, seem small, they very likely understate the effects of both techniques. In other words, the probabilities of better decisions would have been much larger if both techniques had been compared to unstructured decision-making processes.

Group Decision Making and Considering Negative Consequences

Considering negative consequences means pointing out the potential disadvantages of proposed solutions. There is an 86 percent chance that groups that consider negative consequences will produce better decisions than those that don't.[63]

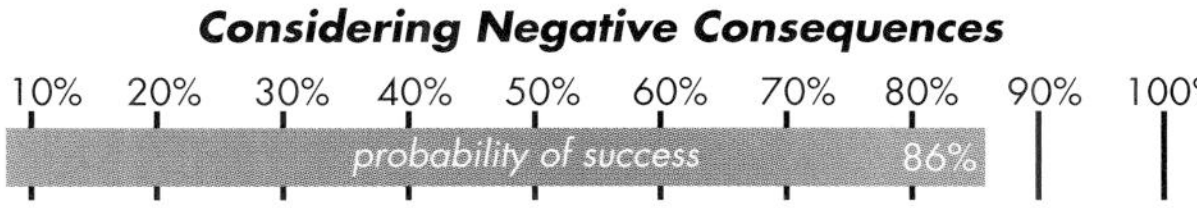

bers then read their rankings aloud, and the idea with the highest average rank is selected.[64]

The nominal group technique improves group decision making by decreasing a-type conflict. In doing so, however, it also restricts c-type conflict. Consequently, the nominal group technique typically produces poorer decisions than do the devil's advocacy and dialectical inquiry approaches. Nonetheless, more than 80 studies have found that nominal groups produce better ideas than those produced by traditional groups.[65]

5.4 Delphi Technique

Delphi technique
a decision-making method in which a panel of experts responds to questions and to each other until reaching agreement on an issue

The **Delphi technique** is a decision-making method in which the members of a panel of experts respond to questions and to each other until reaching agreement on an issue. The first step is to assemble a panel of experts. Unlike other approaches to group decision making, however, it isn't necessary to bring the panel members together in one place. Since the Delphi technique does not require the experts to leave their offices or disrupt their schedules, they are more likely to participate. For example, a colleague and I were asked to conduct a Delphi technique assessment of the "10 most important steps for small businesses." With the help of the dean of my business school and a former mayor of the city, we assembled a panel of local top-level managers and CEOs.

The second step is to create a questionnaire consisting of a series of open-ended questions for the experts. For example, we asked our panel to answer these questions: "What is the most common mistake made by small-business persons?" "Right now, what do you think is the biggest threat to the survival of most small businesses?" "If you had one piece of advice to give to the owner of a small business, what would it be?"

In Step 3, the panel members' written responses are analyzed, summarized, and fed back to the panel for reactions until the members reach agreement. In our Delphi study, it took about a month to get the panel members' written responses to the first three questions. Then we summarized their responses in a brief report (no more than two pages). We sent the summary to the panel members and asked them to explain why they agreed or disagreed with these conclusions from the first round of questions. Asking why they agreed or disagreed is important, because it helps uncover the members' unstated assumptions and beliefs. Again, this process of summarizing panel feedback and obtaining reactions to that feedback continues until panel members reach agreement. For our study, it took just one more round for panel members' views to reach a consensus. In all, it took approximately three-and-a-half months to complete our Delphi study.

The Delphi technique is not an approach that managers should use for common decisions. Because it is a time-consuming, labor-intensive, and expensive process, the Delphi technique is best reserved for important long-term issues and problems. Nonetheless, the judgments and conclusions obtained from it are typically better than those you would get from one expert.

stepladder technique
when group members are added to a group discussion one at a time (i.e., like a stepladder), the existing group members first take the time to listen to each new member's thoughts, ideas, and recommendations, and then the group, in turn, shares the ideas and suggestions that it had already considered, discusses the new and old ideas, and then makes a decision

5.5 Stepladder Technique

The stepladder technique improves group decision making by ensuring that each member's contributions are independent, and are considered and discussed by the group. As shown in Exhibit 4.10, the **stepladder technique** begins with discussion between two group members, who share their thoughts, ideas, and recommendations before jointly making a tentative decision. At each step, as other group members are added to the discussion one at a time, like a stepladder, the existing group members take the time to listen to each

exhibit 4.10

Stepladder Technique for Group Decision Making

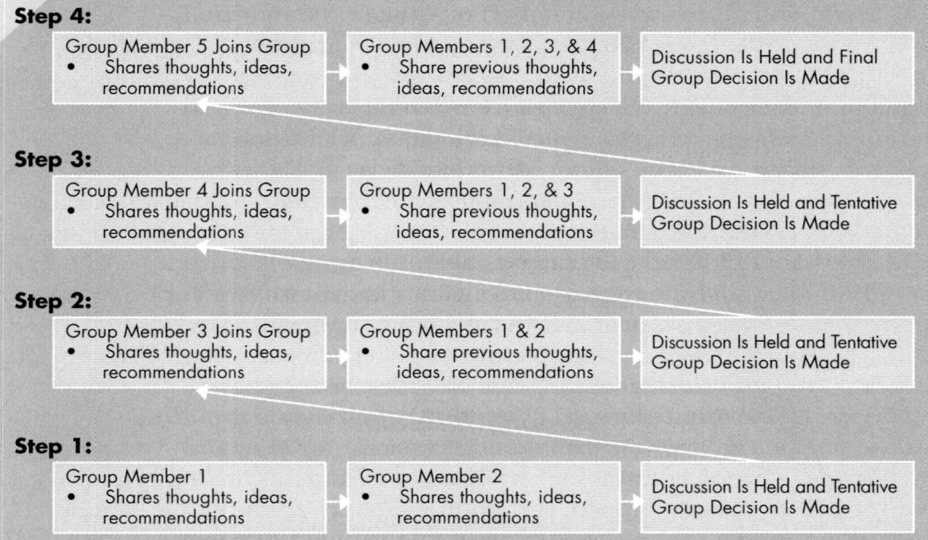

Step 4:
Group Member 5 Joins Group • Shares thoughts, ideas, recommendations
Group Members 1, 2, 3, & 4 • Share previous thoughts, ideas, recommendations
Discussion Is Held and Final Group Decision Is Made
Step 3:
Group Member 4 Joins Group • Shares thoughts, ideas, recommendations
Group Members 1, 2, & 3 • Share previous thoughts, ideas, recommendations
Discussion Is Held and Tentative Group Decision Is Made
Step 2:
Group Member 3 Joins Group • Shares thoughts, ideas, recommendations
Group Members 1 & 2 • Share previous thoughts, ideas, recommendations
Discussion Is Held and Tentative Group Decision Is Made
Step 1:
Group Member 1 • Shares thoughts, ideas, recommendations
Group Member 2 • Shares thoughts, ideas, recommendations
Discussion Is Held and Tentative Group Decision Is Made

new member's thoughts, ideas, and recommendations. The existing members then share the ideas and suggestions that they had already considered, and then the group discusses the new and old ideas and makes a tentative decision. This process (new member's ideas are heard, group shares previous ideas and suggestions, discussion is held, tentative group decision is made) continues until each group member's ideas have been discussed.

For the stepladder technique to work, group members must have enough time to consider the problem or decision on their own, to present their ideas to the group, and to thoroughly discuss all ideas and alternatives with the group at each step. Rushing through a step destroys the advantages of this technique. Also, groups must make sure that subsequent group members are completely unaware of previous discussions and suggestions. This will ensure that each member who joins the group brings truly independent thoughts and suggestions, thus greatly increasing the chances of making better decisions.

One study found that compared to traditional groups in which all group members are present for the entire discussion, groups using the stepladder technique produced significantly better decisions. Moreover, the stepladder groups performed better than the best individual member of their group 56 percent of the time, while traditional groups outperformed the best individual member of their group only 13 percent of the time.[66] Besides better performance, groups using the stepladder technique also generated more ideas and were more satisfied with the decision-making process.

5.6 Electronic Brainstorming

brainstorming
a decision-making method in which group members build on each others' ideas to generate as many alternative solutions as possible

Brainstorming, in which group members build on others' ideas, is a technique for generating a large number of alternative solutions. Brainstorming has four rules:

1. The more ideas, the better.
2. All ideas are acceptable, no matter how wild or crazy they might be.
3. Other group members' ideas should be used to come up with even more ideas.
4. Criticism or evaluation of ideas is not allowed.

electronic brainstorming
a decision-making method in which group members use computers to build on each others' ideas and generate many alternative solutions

production blocking
a disadvantage of face-to-face brainstorming in which a group member must wait to share an idea because another member is presenting an idea

evaluation apprehension
fear of what others will think of your ideas

Though brainstorming is great fun and can help managers generate a large number of alternative solutions, it does have a number of disadvantages. Fortunately, **electronic brainstorming**, in which group members use computers to communicate and generate alternative solutions, overcomes the disadvantages associated with face-to-face brainstorming.[67]

The first disadvantage that electronic brainstorming overcomes is **production blocking**, which occurs when you have an idea, but have to wait to share it because someone else is already presenting an idea to the group. During this short delay, you may forget your idea or decide that it really wasn't worth sharing. With electronic brainstorming, production blocking doesn't happen. All group members are seated at computers, so everyone can type in ideas whenever they occur. There's no "waiting your turn" to be heard by the group.

The second disadvantage that electronic brainstorming overcomes is **evaluation apprehension**, that is, being afraid of what others will think of your ideas. With electronic brainstorming, all ideas are anonymous. When you type in an idea and hit the "Enter" key to share it with the group, group members see only the idea. Furthermore, many brainstorming software programs also protect anonymity by displaying ideas in random order. So, if you laugh maniacally when you type "Cut top management's pay by 50 percent!" and then hit the "Enter" key, it won't show up immediately on everyone's screen. This makes it doubly difficult to determine which comments belong to whom.

In the typical layout for electronic brainstorming, all participants sit in front of computers around a U-shaped table. This configuration allows them to see their computer screens, each other, a large main screen, and a meeting leader or facilitator. Exhibit 4.11 shows what the typical electronic brainstorming group member will see on his or her computer screen. The first step in electronic brainstorming is to anonymously generate as many ideas as possible. It's common for groups to generate 100 ideas in a half-hour period. Step 2 is to edit the generated ideas, categorize

exhibit 4.11

What You See on the Computer during Electronic Brainstorming

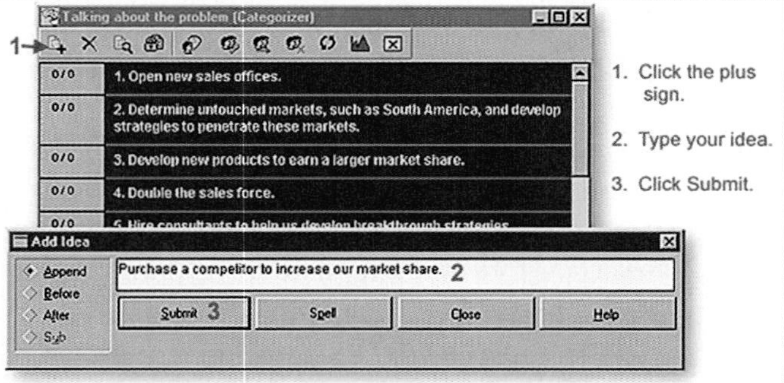

Source: Developing Consensus wth Group Systems. © 2002 GroupSystems.com.

www.experiencing management.com

Managers often emphasize creativity as an additional means of improving decision making. (Creativity is also discussed in Chapter 9.) To learn about techniques that foster creativity in decision making, visit our animated concept and activity site. Choose Decision_Making from the "select a topic" pull-down menu, then Creativity in Decision Making from the "overview tab."

http://www.experiencingmanagement.com

them, and eliminate redundancies. Step 3 is to rank-order the categorized ideas in terms of quality. Step 4, the last step, has three parts: generate a series of action steps, decide the best order for accomplishing these steps, and identify who is responsible for each step. All four steps are accomplished with computers and electronic brainstorming software.[68]

Studies show that electronic brainstorming is much more productive than face-to-face brainstorming. Four-person electronic brainstorming groups produce 25 to 50 percent more ideas than four-person regular brainstorming groups, and 12-person electronic brainstorming groups produce 200 percent more ideas than regular groups of the same size! In fact, because production blocking (i.e., waiting your turn) is not a problem for electronic brainstorming, the number and quality of ideas generally increase with group size.[69]

Even though it works much better than traditional brainstorming, electronic brainstorming has disadvantages, too. An obvious problem is the expense of computers, networks, software, and other equipment. As these costs continue to drop, however, electronic brainstorming will become cheaper.

Another problem is that the anonymity of ideas may bother people who are used to having their ideas accepted by virtue of their position (i.e., the boss). On the other hand, one CEO said, "Because the process is anonymous, the sky's the limit in terms of what you can say, and as a result it is more thought-provoking. As a CEO, you'll probably discover things you might not want to hear but need to be aware of."[70]

A third disadvantage is that outgoing individuals who are more comfortable expressing themselves verbally may find it difficult to express themselves in writing. Finally, the most obvious problem is that participants have to be able to type. Those who can't type, or who type slowly, may be easily frustrated and find themselves at a disadvantage to experienced typists. For example, one meeting facilitator was tipped off that an especially fast typist was pretending to be more than one person. Said the facilitator, "He'd type 'Oh, I agree' and then 'Ditto, ditto' or 'What a great idea,' all in quick succession, using different variations of uppercase and lowercase letters and punctuation. He tried to make it seem like a lot of people were concurring, but it was just him." Eventually, the person sitting next to him got suspicious and began watching his screen.[71]

Review 5
Using Groups to Improve Decision Making

When groups view problems from multiple perspectives, use more information, have a diversity of knowledge and experience, and become committed to solutions they help choose, they can produce better solutions than individual decision makers. However, group decisions can suffer from these disadvantages: groupthink, slowness, discussions dominated by just a few individuals, and unfelt responsibility for decisions. Group decisions work best when group members encourage c-type conflict. However, group decisions don't work as well when groups become mired in a-type conflict. The devil's advocacy and dialectical inquiry approaches improve group decisions because they bring structured c-type conflict into the decision-making process. By contrast, the nominal group technique and the Delphi technique both improve decision making by reducing a-type conflict through limited interactions between group members. The stepladder technique improves group decision making by adding each group member's independent contributions to the discussion one at a time. Finally, because it overcomes the problems of production blocking and evaluation apprehension, electronic brainstorming is a more effective method of generating alternatives than face-to-face brainstorming.

STUDY TIP Try to explain the key concepts of this chapter to a friend or family member who is not taking the class with you. This will help you identify areas where you need to review—and how much.

MANAGEMENT DECISION

CELL PHONE DILEMMA

You've just finished reading an article in *The Wall Street Journal* discussing New York State's recent ban on cell phone use while driving.[72] You agree that talking on a cell phone while driving, along with other activities such as eating or searching for a radio station, is a distraction and can increase the probability of having an accident.

As you think about the implications of the ban for individuals and companies, you realize that most of your employees use cell phones on the job, many while driving. Questions immediately pop into your head: Would your company be held liable if an employee injures or kills someone while talking on a company-issued cell phone while driving? Should you develop a policy regarding safe cell phone use while driving? As a manufacturer, your company certainly has plenty of other safety policies in place, so perhaps one for cell phones is needed. You decide to investigate the matter further before drafting a cell phone safety proposal.

In doing some basic research, you discover a case involving an investment broker who, while using a company-provided cell phone, ran a red light and killed a motorcycle rider. The family of the motorcyclist sued the broker's employer, claiming that the employer encouraged the broker to use his cell phone after hours to maintain contact with clients. Although the employer did not admit fault, it decided to avoid a jury trial by settling the suit for $500,000. Now you believe you have the ammunition needed to draft an operational plan about cell phone safety.

Questions

1. Do you need a policy, a set of procedures, or rules and regulations? Or maybe all three?
2. As the manager in question, draft the appropriate operational plan(s) for this situation.

SPONSORSHIP OR SELL-OUT?

In the world of charitable organizations, the most grueling activity must certainly be fundraising.[73] Although soliciting donations for popular causes can be easy, lesser known nonprofits, which do very important work, find it very challenging to consistently raise enough money to function for extended periods of time. Sometimes, corporate sponsorship is necessary to obtain adequate funding. The obvious plus to corporate sponsorship is the cash, and perhaps greater visibility and legitimacy in the community (depending, of course, on the reputation of the sponsor). But there are also drawbacks associated with corporate sponsorships. The community may think that the corporation is underwriting all of the charity's financial needs and that the charity no longer needs additional funding. Or potential donors might be turned off by the perception that the charity is "selling out" to corporate financial inducements.

In considering a possible sponsorship arrangement, managers of charitable organizations can find themselves faced with an ethical dilemma. Consider the following situations:

- A charity dedicated to removing drunk drivers from the highways wants to hold a recognition dinner, but it is floundering financially. A beer company offers to sponsor the event for $25,000 as part of its efforts to promote responsible drinking.
- A health-care foundation that is putting on a benefit concert to raise money to fund research on respiratory diseases signs up a popular regional band. Unable to cover the costs for the band, concert hall, decorations, and publicity, the foundation entertains an offer from operators of a new and controversial waste incineration plant, who are willing to put up $50,000 to become sponsors of the event.

These situations are all too common in the world of nonprofit fundraising, and making these decisions can often mean the continued viability of the charity or its quiet dissolution. To execute this management team decision, you will need to assemble a team of four to five students. Your management team will be working with the following scenario:

> Community Action for the Poor (CAP) is a prominent charity that has been campaigning on behalf of low-income citizens in your area for 29 years. During the 1990s, your management team was able to lift the fundraising for CAP to all-time highs. Fifteen years later, however, tight economic conditions have dried up donations. As CAP's management team is meeting to determine how and when to shut down operations, you receive a call from a local chain of check-cashing stores, FastCheck. FastCheck is a payday lending business that charges extremely high interest for the service of cashing personal checks for people who are broke. Typically, FastCheck targets people with low incomes.
>
> You put the representative from FastCheck on the speaker phone so that the entire team can hear her. She proposes that FastCheck sponsor a spring festival to raise money for CAP. FastCheck will give CAP $20,000 to organize the festival (rent tents and games, arrange concessions, etc.), and CAP will receive all of the proceeds of the festival. In return, FastCheck wants to set up a booth at the festival and have its name and logo next to CAP's on any promotional materials, such as flyers, banners, and buttons. You thank the representative and turn off the phone. Turning to your team, you say, "So, do we take the money or not?"

You will be making a decision for or against corporate sponsorship for CAP by FastCheck using the stepladder technique outlined in Section 5.5. Before beginning the exercise, review Exhibit 4.10. You may even wish to print out Worksheet 4.10 from Effective Management Online **(http://em-online.swlearning.com)** to use as a guide during the activity. When your team has arrived at a decision, answer the questions below.

Questions

1. Was the decision of the group the decision you had in mind before you began the exercise? If not, what made you change your mind?
2. What factors or arguments influenced your position the most?
3. If you have time, change teams and use the nominal group technique to make a decision for the same scenario. Compare the results of the two techniques.

DEVELOP YOUR CAREER POTENTIAL

WHAT DO YOU WANT TO BE WHEN YOU GROW UP?

What do you want to be when you grow up?[73] Still not sure? Ask around. You're not alone. Chances are, your friends and relatives aren't certain either. Sure, they may have jobs and careers, but you're likely to find that, professionally, many of them don't want to be where they are today. One reason this occurs is that people's interests change. Burnout is another reason that people change their minds about what they want to be when they grow up. And some people are unhappy with their current jobs or careers because they were never in the right one to begin with.

Getting the job and career you want is not easy. It takes time, effort, and persistence. And even though you will probably follow multiple career paths in your life, your career-planning process will be easier (and more effective!) if you take the time to develop a personal career plan.

Begin by answering the following questions. (*Hint:* Treat this seriously: If you do it effectively, this plan could guide your career decisions for the next five to seven years.)

1. Describe your strengths and weaknesses. Don't just rely on your opinions of your abilities. Ask your parents, relatives, friends, and employers what they think, too. Encourage them to be honest and then be prepared to hear some things that you may not want to hear. Remember, though, this information can help you pick the right job or career.

2. Write an advertisement for the job you want to have five years from now. Be specific. Describe the company, title, responsibilities, required education, required experience, salary, and benefits that you desire. Use employment ads in the Sunday job listings as inspiration.

3. Create a detailed plan to obtain this job. In the short term, what classes do you need to take? Do you need to change your major? Do you need a business major or minor or maybe a minor in a foreign language? What kind of summer work experience will move you closer to getting the job you want five years from now? What job do you need to get right out of college to obtain the work experience you need? Create a specific plan for each of the five years in your career plan, keeping in mind that later years are likely to change anyway. The value in planning is that it forces you to think about what you want and the steps you can take now to help achieve those goals.

4. Decide when you will monitor and evaluate the progress you're making with your plan. Career experts suggest that every six months is about right. Pick two dates and write them in your schedule. Furthermore, right now, before you forget, set five specific, challenging goals that you need to accomplish in the next six months in order to achieve your career plans.

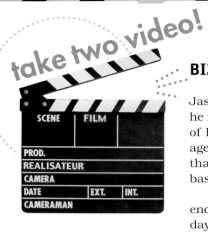

take two video!

BIZ FLIX The Bourne Identity

Jason Bourne (Matt Damon) cannot remember who he is, but others believe he is an international assassin. Bourne tries to learn his identity with the help of his new friend and lover Marie (Franka Potente). Meanwhile, while CIA agents pursue him across Europe trying to kill him, Bourne slowly discovers that he is an extremely well-trained and lethal agent. The story is loosely based on Robert Ludlum's 1981 novel.

This scene is an edited version of the "Bourne's Game" sequence near the end of the film. Jason Bourne kills the hired assassin who tried to kill him the day after Jason and Marie arrived at the home of Eamon (Tim Dutton). Eamon is Marie's friend but is a stranger to Jason. Jason uses the dead man's cell phone after returning to his apartment in Paris, France. He presses the redial button, which connects him to Conklin (Chris Cooper), the CIA manager who is looking for him. Listen carefully to Jason's conversation with Conklin.

What to Watch for and Ask Yourself

1. Does Jason Bourne describe a plan to Conklin? If he does, what are the plan's elements? What is Bourne's goal?
2. Does Bourne assess the plan's execution to determine if it conforms to his goal? If so, what does he do?
3. Was Bourne's plan successfully carried out? Why or why not? How does this scene relate to organizational strategic planning?

MGMT WORKPLACE Machado & Silvetti Associates

Machado & Silvetti Associates, an architectural firm based in Boston, specializes in designing buildings for scholastic enterprises. When the firm was awarded the contract to design a dormitory complex for one of Boston's most historic universities, project managers David Martin and Mike Yousem had to please an extremely large and diverse group of stakeholders. Besides meeting the needs of the client, Martin and Yousem had to address the concerns of the city, the historical society, and the neighborhood community, which insisted that the new structure should be compatible with existing campus architecture that was well over 100 years old. After addressing all the planning obstacles, Martin and Yousem faced difficult production decisions concerning engineering, materials, labor, budget, time lines, client satisfaction, and the demands of their upper management.

What to Watch for and Ask Yourself

1. Would rational decision-making tools apply better during the planning phase or the production phase for Martin and Yousem? Explain.
2. Which group decision-making techniques would work best during the planning stage of the project? What would work best during the production phase? Explain.
3. Under what circumstances would you use a group to make critical decisions? In what situations would you find it unnecessary?

CHAPTER FIVE

Managing Information

outline

WHAT WOULD YOU DO?

University of Illinois Medical Center, Chicago, Illinois.[1] The University of Illinois Medical Center at Chicago, which includes a 450-bed hospital, an outpatient clinic, plus eight clinics in other locations, treats over 40,000 patients in its emergency room annually. You've been its chief information officer for just over six months now, but you've encountered so many difficult problems that it seems like six years, not six months. Things are so bad that doctors and nurses hide patient charts under hospital beds after the patients are discharged so that the records won't be returned to medical records storage, a "black hole" from which they never return. And, though you've heard that doctors have terrible handwriting (they do), you never realized the significant problems that creates, such as giving the right medication at the wrong time or with the wrong dosage, giving the wrong medication, or giving a medication that reacts adversely with medication prescribed by another doctor. It's estimated that poor hand-

student resources

Experiencing Management
Explore the four levels of learning by doing the simulation module on Communication.

Study Guide
Mini lecture reviews all the learning points in the chapter and concludes with a case on Callaway.

Take Two Video
Biz Flix is a scene from *Lorenzo's Oil*. Management Workplace is a segment on Cannondale.

PowerPoint®
12 slides with graphics provide an outline for this chapter.

Author Insights
Chuck gives advice on how you can become comfortable with technology.

Self Test
22 true/false questions, 21 multiple-choice questions, a management scenario, and 2 exhibit worksheets

writing contributes to over 1 million medication errors a year in U.S. hospitals, which, in turn, lead to approximately 7,000 deaths. Such errors cost the hospital industry over $2 billion per year.

There's no doubt in your mind that the way to solve these problems is to create and use electronic medical records and something called computer physician order entry (CPOE) in which doctors record their orders, treatment, and drugs electronically. Doctors and nurses would be able to quickly access patients' medical records any time from any location. Likewise, if entered in computer systems, doctors' orders would be legible and much clearer. Indeed, because of government and corporate pressures, the hospital will eventually have to create such a system. The federal Health Insurance Portability and Accountability Act (HIPAA), which takes effect this year, requires hospitals, doctors, and insurance companies to use standardized electronic methods of recording and exchanging financial and administrative information. Moreover, the Leapfrog Group, a nonprofit organization created by 135 companies that spend $53 billion a year to provide healthcare benefits to their 31 million employees, is using its considerable purchasing power to pressure hospitals to develop and use electronic medical records. Leapfrog's Web site (**http://leapfroggroup.org**) rates hospitals on the extent to which they use information technology, such as computerized prescription order-entry systems. Worried about rising medical costs and quality of care, Leapfrog's 135 member companies will no doubt reduce the amount of business they do with hospitals that have the worst ratings. Not surprisingly, your boss has told you that the University of Illinois Medical Center must be both HIPAA and Leapfrog "compliant."

Creating electronic patient records and a CPOE from scratch won't be easy. Doctors are incredibly resistant to change, especially if they don't see how it benefits them. Therefore, your most important challenge is how to create an electronic system that doctors will use. The most advanced computerized system in the world won't work if the doctors don't buy in. But, with government and corporate pressures, you don't have a choice. You've got to develop electronic systems. Because money is tight, the system will also have to improve the practice of medicine and save the hospital money. How can you make sure it does that? Finally, given that doctors, insurance companies, corporations, the government, and health maintenance organizations will all need access to these data, how can you make sure that the data are available and easily shared among these different parties? **If you were the CIO of the University of Illinois Medical Center in Chicago, what would you do?**

exhibit 5.1

Moore's Law

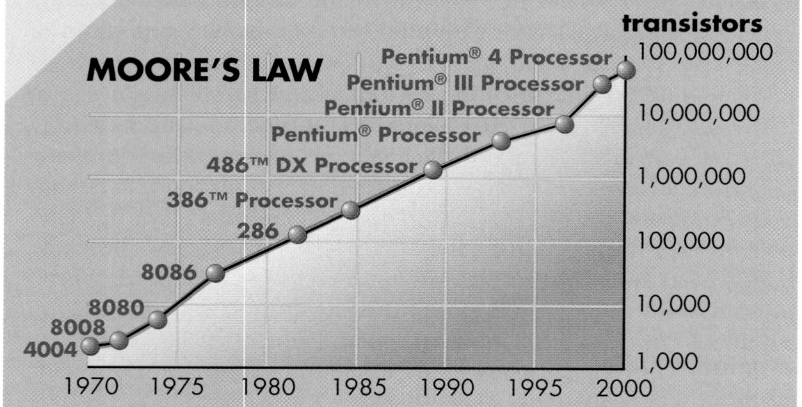

Source: "Moore's Law: Overviews," © Intel Corporation, [Online] available at http://www.intel.com/research/silicon/mooreslaw.htm, 19 August 2001. Reprinted with permission of Intel Corporation.

A generation ago, computer hardware and software had little to do with managing business information. Rather than storing information on hard drives, managers stored it in filing cabinets. Instead of uploading daily sales and inventory levels by satellite to corporate headquarters, they mailed hard-copy summaries to headquarters at the end of each month. Instead of word processing, reports were typed on an electric typewriter. Instead of spreadsheets, calculations were made on adding machines. Managers communicated by sticky notes, not email. Phone messages weren't left on voice mail; assistants and coworkers wrote them down. Workers did not use desktop or laptop computers as a daily tool to get work done; they scheduled limited access time to run batch jobs on the mainframe computer (and prayed that the batch job computer code they wrote would work—it often didn't).

Today, a generation later, computer hardware and software are an integral part of managing business information. In large part, this is due to something called **Moore's law**. Gordon Moore is one of the founders of Intel Corporation, which makes 75 percent of the integrated processors used in personal computers. In 1966, Moore predicted that every 18 months, the cost of computing would drop by 50 percent as computer-processing power doubled.[2] As Exhibit 5.1 shows, Moore was right. Every few years, computer power, as measured by the number of transistors per computer chip, *has* more than doubled. Consequently, the computer sitting in your lap or your desk is not only smaller, but also much cheaper and more powerful than the large mainframe computers used by *Fortune* 500 companies in the early 1990s. In fact, if car manufacturers had achieved the same power increases and cost decreases attained by computer manufacturers, a fully outfitted Lexus or Mercedes sedan would cost less than $1,000!

Moore's law
the prediction that every 18 months, the cost of computing will drop by 50 percent as computer-processing power doubles

We begin this chapter by explaining why information matters. In particular, you will learn the value of strategic information to companies, as well as the cost and characteristics of good information. Next, you will investigate how companies capture, process, and protect information. Finally, you'll learn how information is accessed and shared with those within and outside the company, and how knowledge and expertise (not just information or data) are shared, too.

raw data
facts and figures

Why Information Matters

Raw data are facts and figures. For example, 11, $452, 256, and 26,100 are some data that I used the day I wrote this section of the chapter. However, facts and figures aren't particularly useful unless they have meaning. For example, you probably can't guess what these four pieces of raw data represent, can you? And if you can't, these data are useless. That's why researchers make the

information
useful data that can influence people's choices and behavior

distinction between raw data and information. Whereas raw data consist of facts and figures, **information** is useful data that can influence someone's choices and behavior. So what did those four pieces of data mean to me? Well, 11 stands for channel 11, the local CBS affiliate on which I watched part of the men's PGA golf tournament; $452 is how much it would cost me to rent a minivan for a week if I go skiing over spring break; 256 is for the 256-megabyte storage card that I want to add to my digital camera (prices are low, so I'll probably buy it); and 26,100 means that it's time to get the oil changed on my car.

After reading the next section, you should be able to

1 explain the strategic importance of information.

1 Strategic Importance of Information

In today's hypercompetitive business environments, information, whether it's about real estate, product inventory, pricing, or costs, is as important as capital (i.e., money) for business success. It takes money to get businesses started, but businesses can't survive and grow without the right information. Information has strategic importance for organizations because it can be used 1.1 to obtain first-mover advantage and 1.2 to sustain a competitive advantage once it has been created.

1.1 First-Mover Advantage

first-mover advantage
the strategic advantage that companies earn by being the first to use new information technology to substantially lower costs or to make a product or service different from that of competitors

First-mover advantage is the strategic advantage that companies earn by being the first in an industry to use new information technology to substantially lower costs or to differentiate a product or service from that of competitors. For example, cable TV companies have taken a surprising lead over telephone companies in providing high-speed Internet access to people's homes. As I write this, 11 million homes have high-speed cable modems, compared to just 6.4 million that have high-speed digital subscriber lines from phone companies.[3] Cable companies invested billions to completely rewire their systems, replacing old lines with new digital lines that feed high-speed cable modems and digital TV cable channels alike (to compete with satellite TV like Dish Network or DirecTV). By contrast, the phone companies ran into unexpected technical difficulties and high expenses. Unlike cable systems, which are already able to provide high-speed Internet access in 99 percent of homes, the phone companies' systems can supply only 60 percent of households with DSL service. Indeed, Stephen Burke, executive vice president of the cable TV division of Comcast, said, "We're beating DSL 80 percent of the time in our franchise areas. Getting a cable modem for a customer is like one's first kiss. You can never go back to things as they were."[4]

In all, first-mover advantages, like those established by high-speed Internet cable companies, can be sizable. On average, first movers earn a 30 percent market share, compared to 19 percent for companies that follow.[5] Likewise, over 70 percent of market leaders started as first movers.[6]

1.2 Sustaining a Competitive Advantage

As described above, companies that use information technology to establish first-mover advantage usually have higher market shares and profits.

According to the resource-based view of information technology shown in Exhibit 5.2, companies need to address three critical issues in order to sustain

exhibit 5.2

Using Information Technology to Sustain a Competitive Advantage

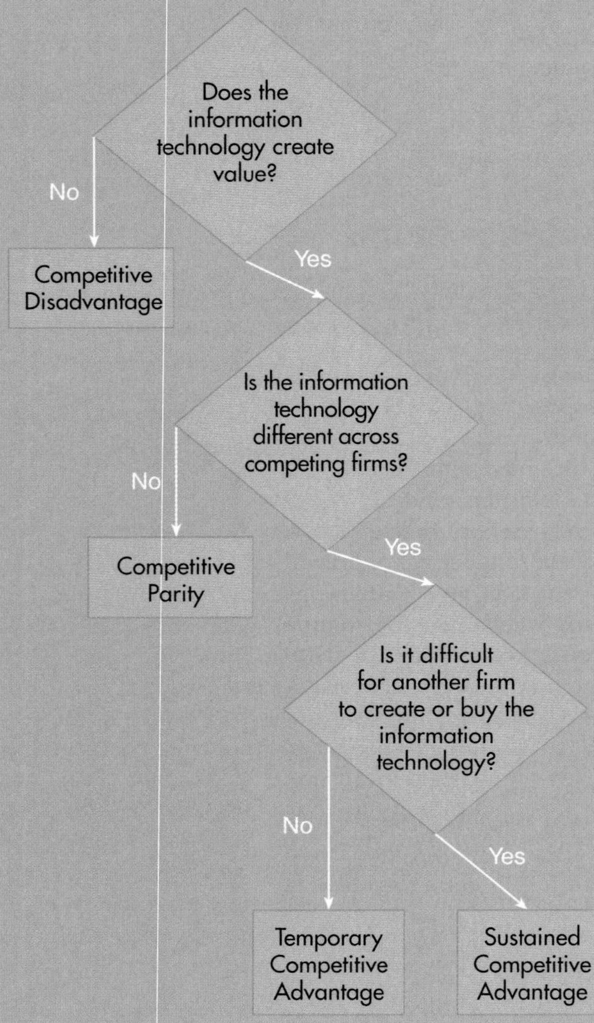

Does the information technology create value?
No
Competitive Disadvantage
Yes
Is the information technology different across competing firms?
No
Competitive Parity
Yes
Is it difficult for another firm to create or buy the information technology?
No
Yes
Temporary Competitive Advantage
Sustained Competitive Advantage

Source: Adapted from F. J. Mata, W. L. Fuerst, & J. B. Barney, "Information Technology and Sustained Competitive Advantage: A Resource-Based Analysis," MIS Quarterly 19, *no. 4, December 1995, 487–505. Reprinted by special permission by the Society for Information Management and the Management Information Systems Research Center at the University of Minnesota.*

a competitive advantage through information technology. First, does the information technology create value for the firm by lowering costs or providing a better product or service? If an information technology doesn't add value, then investing in it would put a firm at a competitive disadvantage to companies that choose information technologies that do add value.

Second, is the information technology the same or different across competing firms? If all the firms have access to the same information technology and use it in the same way, then no firm has an advantage over another (i.e., competitive parity).

Third, is it difficult for another company to create or buy the information technology used by the firm? If so, then the firm has established a sustainable competitive advantage over competitors through information technology. If not, then the competitive advantage is just temporary, and competitors should eventually be able to duplicate the advantages the leading firm has gained from information technology. You'll learn more about sustainable competitive advantage and its sources in Chapter 8.

In short, the key to sustaining a competitive advantage is not faster computers, more memory, and larger hard drives. The key is using information technology to continuously improve and support the core functions of a business. Ron Ireland, a former Wal-Mart manager, said, "Wal-Mart has always considered information technology as a competitive advantage, never as a business expense."[7] Thanks to innovative use of information technology and the largest private satellite network and database system in the world, Wal-Mart's costs are 10 percent less than its competitors' costs.[8] Wal-Mart was one of the first retailers to use computers and bar codes to track sales and inventory data and then share those data with suppliers. Today, Wal-Mart's $4 billion supplier network, Retail Link, allows vendors like Ted Haedicke of Coca-Cola to "look at how much [and what kind of] Coke [has] sold . . . and at what prices at any store in the Wal-Mart system." He went on to say that "You can't do that with any other retailer today."[9]

Companies like Wal-Mart that achieve first-mover advantage with information technology and then sustain it with continued investment create a moving target that competitors have difficulty hitting.

Review 1
Strategic Importance of Information

The first company to use new information technology to substantially lower costs or differentiate products or services often gains first-mover advantage, higher profits, and larger market share. However, creating a first-mover advantage can be difficult, expensive, and risky. According to the resource-based view of information technology, sustainable competitive advantage occurs when information technology adds value, is different across firms, and is difficult to create or acquire.

Getting and Sharing Information

In 1907, Metropolitan Life Insurance built a huge office building in New York City for its brand new, state-of-the art information technology system. What was this great breakthrough in information management? The advanced system was card files. That's right, the same card file systems that every library in America used before computers. Metropolitan Life's information "technology" consisted of 20,000 separate file drawers that sat in hundreds of file cabinets more than 15 feet tall. This filing system held 20 million insurance applications, 700,000 accounting books, and 500,000 death certificates. Metropolitan Life employed 61 workers who did nothing but sort, file, and climb ladders to pull files as needed.[10]

Less than a century later, the cost, inefficiency, and ineffectiveness of using this formerly state-of-the-art system would put an insurance company out of business within months. Today, if storms, fire, or accidents damage policyholders' property, insurance companies write checks on the spot to cover the losses. When policyholders buy a car, they call their insurance agent from the dealership to activate their insurance before driving off in their new car. And now, insurance companies are marketing their products and services to customers directly from the Internet.

From card files to Internet files in just under a century, the rate of change in information technology is spectacular. After reading the next two sections, you should be able to

2 explain the basics of capturing, processing, and protecting information.

3 describe how companies can access and share information and knowledge.

2 Capturing, Processing, and Protecting Information

When you go to your local Rite Aid pharmacy to pick up a prescription, the pharmacist reviews an electronic file that shows all of the medications you're taking. That same system automatically checks to make sure that your new prescription won't create adverse side effects by interacting with your other medications. When you pay for your prescription, Rite Aid's point-of-sale information system determines whether you've written any bad checks lately (to Rite Aid or other stores), records your payment, and then checks with the computer of the pharmaceutical company that makes your prescription drugs to see if it's time to reorder. Finally, Rite Aid protects your information to make sure that your data are readily available only to you, your physician, and your pharmacist.

In this section, you will learn about the information technologies that companies like Rite Aid use to 2.1 capture, 2.2 process, and 2.3 protect information.

2.1 Capturing Information

There are two basic methods of capturing information: manual and electronic. Manual capture of information is a labor-intensive process, which entails recording and entering data by hand into a data storage device. For example, when you applied for a driver's license, you probably recorded personal information about yourself by filling out a form. Then, after passing your driver's test, someone typed your handwritten information into the department of motor vehicles' computer database so that local and state police could access it from their patrol cars when they pulled you over for speeding. (Isn't information great?) The problem with manual capture of information is that it is slow, expensive, and often inaccurate.

Consequently, companies are relying more on electronic capture, in which data are electronically recorded and entered into electronic storage devices. Bar codes, radio frequency identification tags, and document scanners are methods of electronically capturing data. **Bar codes** represent numerical data by varying the thickness and pattern of vertical bars. The primary advantage that bar codes offer is that the data they represent can be read and recorded in an instant with a handheld or pen-type scanner. One pass of the scanner (okay, sometimes several) and "beep!" The information has been captured. Bar codes cut checkout times in half, reduce data entry errors by 75 percent, and save stores money because stockers don't have to go through the labor-intensive process of putting a price tag on each item in the store.[11]

bar code
a visual pattern that represents numerical data by varying the thickness and pattern of vertical bars

Radio frequency identification (RFID) tags contain minuscule microchips and antennas that transmit information via radio waves.[12] Unlike bar codes, which require direct scanning, RFID tags are read by turning on an RFID reader that, like a radio, tunes into a specific frequency to determine the number *and* location of products, parts, or anything else to which the RFID tags are attached. Turn on an RFID reader, and every RFID tag within the reader's range (from several hundred to several thousand feet) is accounted for. For example, Sky Chefs, the company that prepares onboard meals for the airlines, uses RFID tags to keep track of the $1,000 heavy-duty serving carts used to wheel hot meals up and down crowded airplane aisles. With airlines losing or misplacing up to 1,500 carts per month, Sky Chefs found that installing RFID readers throughout airports and attaching RFID tags to serving carts was an easy, inexpensive way to locate and recover all of its carts.[13] And with RFID readers able to process 96 RFID tags per second, it takes Sky Chefs only a couple of minutes to determine their locations.

radio frequency identification (RFID) tags
minuscule microchips that transmit information via radio waves and can be used to track the number and location of the objects into which the tags have been inserted

Because they are inexpensive and easy to use, **electronic scanners**, which convert printed text and pictures into digital images, have become an increasingly popular method of electronically capturing data. However, text that has been digitized cannot be searched or edited like the regular text in your word processing software. Therefore, companies can use **optical character**

electronic scanner
an electronic device that converts printed text and pictures into digital images

optical character recognition
software to convert digitized documents into ASCII text (American Standard Code for Information Interchange) that can be searched, read, and edited by word processing and other kinds of software

recognition software to scan and convert original or digitized documents into ASCII text (American Standard Code for Information Interchange). ASCII text can be searched, read, and edited in standard word processing, email, desktop publishing, database management, and spreadsheet software.

2.2 Processing Information

processing information
transforming raw data into meaningful information

Processing information means transforming raw data into meaningful information that can be applied to business decision making. Evaluating sales data to determine the best- and worst-selling products, examining repair records to determine product reliability, and monitoring the cost of long-distance phone calls are all examples of processing raw data into meaningful information. And, with automated, electronic capture of data, increased processing power, and cheaper and more plentiful ways to store data, managers no longer worry about getting data. Instead, they scratch their heads about how to use the overwhelming amount of data that pours into their businesses every day. Furthermore, most managers know little about statistics and have neither the time nor the inclination to learn how to use them to analyze data.

data mining
the process of discovering unknown patterns and relationships in large amounts of data

data warehouse
stores huge amounts of data that have been prepared for data mining analysis by being cleaned of errors and redundancy

One promising tool to help managers dig out from under the avalanche of data is data mining. **Data mining** is the process of discovering unknown patterns and relationships in large amounts of data.[14] Data mining works by using complex algorithms such as neural networks, rule induction, and decision trees. If you don't know what those are, that's okay. With data mining, you don't have to. Most managers only need to know that data mining looks for patterns that are already in the data but are too complex for them to spot on their own. For example, data mining helped a credit card company determine that people who fill out credit applications in pencil are much less likely to pay their credit card bills. It now scrutinizes those applications much more closely. Data mining also helped Victoria's Secret find out that it sold 20 times more size 32 bras in New York City (no one is sure why) and that ivory bras were 10 times more popular in Miami than black bras. Because of these discoveries, Victoria's Secret now customizes product inventory for each of its stores.[15]

PERSONAL PRODUCTIVITY TIP

Your Hard Drive* Will *Crash, So Buckle Up with a Backup

In theory, a hard drive will work eight hours a day for 102 years before crashing. Of course, the theory ignores power failures, computer viruses, spilled drinks, and dropped laptop computers. To protect yourself and your data, buy a tape backup drive ($200 or less). Once a day, make a backup copy of all new files. Once a month, back up your entire hard drive. Backing up data is faster and cheaper than paying a specialist $500 to $2,000 to try (no guarantees) to retrieve your data from your dead hard drive.[16]

Data mining typically splits a data set in half, finds patterns in one half, and then tests the validity of those patterns by trying to find them again in the second half of the data set. The data typically come from a **data warehouse** that stores huge amounts of data that have been prepared for data mining analysis by being cleaned of errors and redundancy. For example, Acxiom, which helps credit card companies identify potential customers, has 500 terabytes of information on over 200 million Americans in storage at its data warehouse.

supervised data mining
user tells the data mining software to look and test for specific patterns and relationships in a data set

The data in a data warehouse can then be analyzed using two kinds of data mining. **Supervised data mining** usually begins with the user telling the data mining software to look and test for specific patterns and relationships in a data set. Typically, this is done through a series of "what if?" questions or statements. For instance, a grocery store manager might instruct the data mining software to determine if coupons placed in the Sunday paper increase

unsupervised data mining user simply tells the data mining software to uncover whatever patterns and relationships it can find in a data set

or decrease sales. By contrast, with **unsupervised data mining**, the user simply tells the data mining software to uncover whatever patterns and relationships it can find in a data set. For example, Australia's Health Insurance Commission processes 300 million health insurance claims and makes $8 billion of payments each year. The commission gave IBM data tapes containing three gigabytes of information and asked the company to use its data mining software to find anything that might help cut costs. Three days later, the software had uncovered an illegal billing practice that was costing the commission millions of dollars.

association or affinity patterns when two or more database elements tend to occur together in a significant way

sequence patterns when two or more database elements occur together in a significant pattern, but one of the elements precedes the other

predictive patterns help identify database elements that are different

data clusters when three or more database elements occur together (i.e., cluster) in a significant way

Unsupervised data mining is particularly good at identifying association or affinity patterns, sequence patterns, and predictive patterns. It can also identify what data mining "techies" call data clusters.[17] **Association or affinity patterns** occur when two or more database elements tend to occur together in a significant way. Surprisingly, Osco Drugs, based in Chicago, found that beer and diapers tended to be bought together between 5 and 7 P.M. The question, of course, was "why?" The answer, on further review, was fairly straightforward: fathers, who were told by their wives to buy some diapers on their way home, decided to pick up a six-pack for themselves, too.[18]

Sequence patterns occur when two or more database elements occur together in a significant pattern, but with one of the elements preceding the other. When TWA announced a low $360 round-trip ticket between Los Angeles and San Juan, Puerto Rico, Travelocity.com, one of the largest Web travel companies used data mining to identify the customers most likely to buy the discounted ticket. A sequence pattern allowed managers to target all the customers in the area who had already used Travelocity's Web site to investigate fares to San Juan. In other words, people who had previously inquired about the fares for this route (step 1) would be more likely to buy the discounted fare (step 2) if they knew about it. Indeed, an amazing 25 percent of the 30,000 customers Travelocity notified either bought the discounted flight to Puerto Rico or another flight to the Caribbean.[19]

Predictive patterns are just the opposite of association or affinity patterns. Whereas association or affinity patterns look for database elements that seem to go together, **predictive patterns** help identify database elements that are different. On the day after Thanksgiving, typically the busiest shopping day of the year, Wal-Mart's data mining indicated that sales were unexpectedly slow for a boxed computer and printer combination that was offered at an extremely good price. Sales were slow everywhere, except one Wal-Mart store where sales greatly exceeded expectations. After noting the difference, headquarters called the store manager who said that the products were displayed in an open box that made it clear to customers that the low price was for the computer *and* the printer. Sales took off at all stores after headquarters relayed this simple message, "Open the box."[20]

One way managers can obtain usable information from mounds of data is by data mining. When Osco discovered through data mining that beer and diapers were often being purchased together, the store was able to design store displays that placed the items closer together.

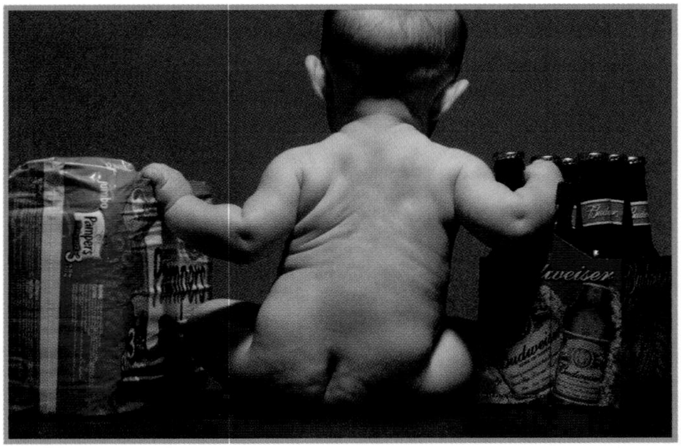

Data clusters are the last kind of pattern found by data mining. **Data clusters** occur when three or more database elements occur together (i.e., cluster) in a significant way. For example, after analyzing several years worth of repair and warranty claims, Ford might

find that, compared to cars built in its Chicago plant, the cars it builds in Atlanta (first element) are more likely to have problems with overtightened fan belts (second element) that break (third element) and result in overheated engines (fourth element), ruined radiators (fifth element), and payments for tow trucks (sixth element), which are paid for by Ford's three-year, 36,000 mile warranty.

Traditionally, data mining has been very expensive and very complex. Today, however, with services and analysis provided by companies such as Digimine.com, data mining is much more affordable and within reach of most companies' budgets. And, if it follows the path of most technologies, it will become even easier and cheaper to use in the future.

2.3 Protecting Information

protecting information
the process of ensuring that data are reliably and consistently retrievable in a usable format for authorized users, but no one else

Protecting information is the process of ensuring that data are reliably and consistently retrievable in a usable format for authorized users, but no one else. For instance, when customers purchase prescription medicine at Drugstore.com, an online drugstore and health-aid retailer, they want to be confident that their medical and credit card information is available only to them, the pharmacists at Drugstore.com, and their doctors. In fact, Drugstore.com has an extensive privacy policy (click "Privacy Policy" at **http://www.drugstore.com**) to make sure this is the case.

Companies like Drugstore.com find it necessary to protect information because of the numerous security threats to data and data security. From denial-of-service Web server attacks that can bring down some of the busiest and best-run sites on the Internet (e.g., Yahoo.com), to viruses that spread quickly and result in data loss and business disruption, to keystroke monitoring in which every mouse click and keystroke you make is unknowingly monitored, stored, and sent to unauthorized users, to password cracking software that steals supposedly secure passwords, there are many ways for people inside and outside companies to steal or destroy company data.

For more information on how to meet the threats to data and data networks, go to Effective Management Online **(http://em-online.swlearning.com).**

Some of the most important steps to secure data and data networks are authentication and authorization, firewalls, antivirus software for PCs and email servers, data encryption, and virtual private networks.[21]

authentication
making sure potential users are who they claim to be

authorization
granting authenticated users approved access to data, software, and systems

Two critical steps are required to make sure that data can be accessed by authorized users and no one else. One is **authentication**, that is, making sure users are who they claim to be.[22] The other is **authorization**, that is, granting authenticated users approved access to data, software, and systems.[23] For example, when an ATM card prompts you to enter your personal identification number (PIN), the bank is authenticating that you are you. Once you've been authenticated, you are authorized to access your funds and no one else's. Of course, as anyone who has lost a PIN or password or had one stolen knows, user authentication systems are not foolproof. In particular, users create security risks by not changing their default account passwords (such as birth dates) or by using weak passwords such as names ("Larry") or complete words ("football") that are quickly guessed by password cracker software.[24] (See the Doing the Right Thing about "Password Dos and Don'ts" to learn how to prevent this).

biometrics
identifying users by unique, measurable body features, such as fingerprint recognition or iris scanning

For these reasons, some companies are turning to biometrics for authentication. **Biometrics** involves identifying users by unique, measurable body features, such as fingerprint recognition or iris scanning.[25]

Unfortunately, stolen or cracked passwords are not the only way for hackers and electronic thieves to gain access to an organization's computer resources.

DOING THE RIGHT THING

Password Dos and Don'ts

Anyone with access to sensitive personal (personnel or medical files), customer (credit cards), or corporate data (costs) has a clear responsibility to protect those data from unauthorized access. Use the following dos and don'ts to maintain a "strong" password system and protect your data.

- Don't use any public information such as part of your name, address, or birth date to create a password.
- Don't use complete words, English or foreign, that are easily guessed by password software using "dictionary attacks."
- Use eight or more characters and include some unique characters such as !@#$ to create passwords like "cow@#boy."
- The longer the password and the more unique characters, the more difficult it is to guess.
- Remember your password and don't write it down on a sticky note attached to your computer.
- Change your password every six weeks. Better yet, specify that your computer system force all users to change their passwords this often.
- Don't reuse old passwords.

Together, these basic steps can make it much more difficult to gain unauthorized access to sensitive data.[28]

Unless special safeguards are put in place, every time corporate users are online there's literally nothing between their personal computers and the Internet (home users with high-speed DSL or cable Internet access face the same risks). Hackers can access files, run programs, and control key parts of computers if precautions aren't taken. To reduce these risks, companies use **firewalls**, hardware or software devices that sit between the computers in an internal organizational network and outside networks, such as the Internet. Firewalls filter and check incoming and outgoing data. They prevent company insiders from accessing unauthorized sites or from sending confidential company information to people outside the company. Firewalls also prevent outsiders from identifying and gaining access to company computers and data. Indeed, if a firewall is working properly, the computers behind the company firewall literally cannot be seen or accessed by outsiders.

A **virus** is a program or piece of code that, against your wishes, attaches itself to other programs on your computer and can trigger anything from a harmless flashing message to the reformatting of your hard drive to a systemwide network shutdown.[26] Today's viruses pose a much greater threat than in the past. In fact, with some viruses, just being connected to a network can infect your computer.[27] *Antivirus software for personal computers* is effective only to the extent that users of individual computers have and use up-to-date versions. With new viruses appearing all the time, users should update their antivirus software weekly. *Corporate antivirus software* automatically scans email attachments as they come across the company email server, but it also monitors and scans all file downloads across company databases and network servers. So, while antivirus software for personal computers prevents individual computers from being infected, corporate antivirus software for email servers, databases, and network servers adds another layer of protection by preventing infected files from multiplying and being sent to others.

firewall
a protective hardware or software device that sits between the computers in an internal organizational network and outside networks, such as the Internet

virus
a program or piece of code that, against your wishes, attaches itself to other programs on your computer and can trigger anything from a harmless flashing message to the reformatting of your hard drive to a systemwide network shutdown

Another way of protecting information is to encrypt sensitive data. **Data encryption** transforms data into complex, scrambled digital codes that can be unencrypted only by authorized users who possess unique decryption keys. One method of data encryption is to use products by PGP (Pretty Good Privacy) (**http://www.pgp.com**) to encrypt the files stored on personal computers or network servers and databases. This is especially important with laptop computers, which are easily stolen. And, with people increasingly gaining unauthorized access to email messages—email snooping—it's also important to encrypt sensitive email messages and file attachments.

Although firewalls can protect personal computers and network servers connected to the corporate network, people away from their offices (e.g., sales people, business travelers, telecommuters who work at home) who interact

data encryption transforms data into complex, scrambled digital codes that can be unencrypted only by authorized users who possess unique decryption keys

virtual private network (VPN) securely encrypts data sent by employees outside the company network, decrypts the data when they arrive within the company computer network, and does the same when data are sent back to employees outside the network

secure sockets layer (SSL) encryption Internet browser-based secure sockets layer (SSL) encryption provides secure off-site Web access to some data and programs

with their company networks via the Internet face a security risk. Since Internet data are not encrypted, packet sniffer software easily allows hackers to read everything sent or received, except files that have been encrypted before sending. Previously, the only practical solution was to have employees dial in to secure company phone lines for direct access to the company network. Of course, with international and long-distance phone calls, the costs quickly added up. Now, **virtual private networks** (VPNs) have solved this problem by using software to encrypt all Internet data at both ends of the transmission process. Instead of making long-distance calls, employees dial an Internet service provider, such as MSN or AOL, which provides local service all over the world. Unlike typical Internet connections in which Internet data packets are unencrypted, the VPN encrypts the data sent by employees outside the company computer network, decrypts the data when they arrive within the company network, and does the same when data are sent back to the computer outside the network.

Alternatively, many companies are now adopting Web-based **secure sockets layer (SSL) encryption** to provide secure off-site access to data and programs. If you've ever entered your credit card in a Web browser to make an online purchase, you've used SSL technology to encrypt and protect that information. SSL encryption is being used if a gold lock (Internet Explorer) or a gold key (Netscape) appears along the bottom of your Web browser. SSL encryption works the same way in the workplace. Managers and employees who aren't at the office simply connect to the Internet, open a Web browser, and then enter a user name and password to gain access to SSL encrypted data and programs. For example, the Catholic Health System of Buffalo, New York, uses an SSL system to allow radiologists to access and review medical images like x-rays from their homes. Likewise, lawyers at Sonnenschein, Nath & Rosenthal, a Chicago law firm, use the Web and their SSL encrypted system to securely access case records from anywhere in the world.[29] SSL encryption is much cheaper and more reliable than VPNs, but it typically provides only limited access to data and files. By contrast, VPN connections, though more expensive and more troublesome to use, provide complete, secure access to everything on a company's network.

Review 2
Capturing, Processing, and Protecting Information

Electronic data capture (bar codes, radio frequency identification [RFID] tags, scanners, and optical character recognition) is much faster, easier, and cheaper than manual data capture. Processing information means transforming raw data into meaningful information that can be applied to business decision making. Data mining helps managers with this transformation by discovering unknown patterns and relationships in data. Supervised data mining looks for patterns specified by managers, while unsupervised data mining looks for four general kinds of data patterns: association/affinity patterns, sequence patterns, predictive patterns, and data clusters. Protecting information ensures that data are reliably and consistently retrievable in a usable format for authorized users, but no one else. Authentication and authorization, firewalls, antivirus software for PCs and corporate email and network servers, data encryption, virtual private networks, and Web-based secure sockets layer (SSL) encryption are some of the best ways to protect information.

3 Accessing and Sharing Information and Knowledge

Today, information technologies are letting companies communicate, share, and provide data access to workers, managers, suppliers, and customers in ways that were unthinkable just a few years ago. After reading this section, you should be able to explain how companies use information technology to improve 3.1 internal access and sharing of information, 3.2 external access and sharing of information, and 3.3 the sharing of knowledge and expertise.

To learn more about the capabilities of EIS programs, go to Effective Management Online **(http://em-online.swlearning.com).**

3.1 Internal Access and Sharing

Executives, managers, and workers inside the company use three kinds of information technology to access and share information: executive information systems, intranets, and portals. An **executive information system (EIS)** uses internal and external sources of data to provide managers and executives the information they need to monitor and analyze organizational performance.[30] The goal of an EIS is to provide accurate, complete, relevant, and timely information to managers.

executive information system (EIS)
a data processing system that uses internal and external data sources to provide the information needed to monitor and analyze organizational performance

Claim service managers at AIG, an insurance company, use their EIS, which they call their "dashboard," to see how well the company is running. With just a few mouse clicks and basic commands such as *find, compare,* and *show,* the EIS displays costs, sales revenues, and other kinds of data in color-coded charts and graphs. Managers can drill down to view and compare data by region, state, time period, and kind of insurance coverage. Kevin Murray, CIO for AIG's claims service division, says, "From the perspective of an underwriter, adjuster, or upper-level executive, you can manipulate the information, juxtapose it, and change it any way you want. From a workflow perspective it saves time on both the business and IT end."[31]

intranets
private company networks that allow employees to easily access, share, and publish information using Internet software

Intranets are private company networks that allow employees to easily access, share, and publish information using Internet software. Intranet Web sites are just like external Web sites, but the firewall separating the internal company network from the Internet permits only authorized internal access.[32] With 1,000 internal Web sites and more than 2 million pages of information, Microsoft probably has one of the most advanced and most used intranets in the world, with one-third of its 30,000 employees using it every day. In fact, MSWeb, Microsoft's intranet, is so advanced, that nearly all company paperwork, forms, and paper documents have been moved onto it.[33] Indeed, a study of 323 companies in 10 different industries found that 23 percent of company intranets contained information on company benefits; 18 percent have information about savings plans, profit sharing, or company stock plans; 70 percent have information about jobs; 6 percent allow managers to conduct performance appraisals online; 24 percent are used for training; and 57 percent are used for corporate communications.[34] Intranets have exploded in popularity over the last five years. Today, more than 80 percent of companies have their own intranets.[35] Exhibit 5.3 explains the reasons for this phenomenal growth.

exhibit 5.3

Why 80 Percent of Companies Use Intranets

Intranets are inexpensive.
Intranets increase efficiencies and reduce costs.
Intranets are intuitive and easy to use (Web-based).
Intranets work across all computer systems and platforms (Web-based).
Intranets can be built on top of an existing computer network.
Intranets work with software programs that easily convert electronic documents to HTML files for intranet use.
Much of the software required to set up an intranet is either freeware (no cost) or shareware (try before you buy, usually less expensive than commercial software).

Finally, corporate portals are a hybrid of executive information systems and intranets. While an EIS provides managers and executives with the information they need to monitor and analyze organizational performance, and intranets help companies distribute and publish information and forms within the company, **corporate portals** allow company managers and employees to access customized information *and* complete specialized transactions using a Web browser.[36] For example, Maysteel, which makes components for electronics and electric utilities, created a corporate portal to allow plant managers at its six factories in Wisconsin and Ireland to track and enter information regarding parts component quality. Now, with several quick clicks via their Web browsers, each plant manager can compare costs and quality to Maysteel's other manufacturing facilities.

corporate portals
allow managers and employees to use a Web browser to gain access to customized company information and to complete specialized transactions

3.2 External Access and Sharing

Historically, companies have been unable or reluctant to let outside groups have access to corporate information. Now, however, a number of information technologies—electronic data interchange, extranets, Web services, and the Internet—are making it easier to share company data with external groups like suppliers and customers. They're also reducing costs, increasing productivity by eliminating manual information processing (70 percent of the data output from one company, like a purchase order, ends up as data input at another company, such as a sales invoice or shipping order), reducing data entry errors, improving customer service, and speeding communications. As a result, managers are scrambling to adopt these technologies.

With **electronic data interchange**, or **EDI**, two companies convert purchase and ordering information to a standardized format to enable direct electronic transmission of that information from one company's computer system to the other company's system. For example, when a Wal-Mart checkout clerk drags a CD across the checkout scanner, Wal-Mart's computerized inventory system automatically reorders another copy of that CD through the direct EDI connection that its computer has with the manufacturing and shipping computer at the company that published the CD, say, Atlantic Records. No one at Wal-Mart or Atlantic Records fills out paperwork. No one makes phone calls. There are no delays to wait to find out whether Atlantic has the CD in stock. The transaction takes place instantly and automatically because the data from both companies were translated into a standardized, shareable, compatible format.

electronic data interchange (EDI)
when two companies convert their purchase and ordering information to a standardized format to enable the direct electronic transmission of that information from one company's computer system to the other company's computer system

"Web services" are another way for companies to directly and automatically transmit purchase and ordering information from one company's computer systems to another company's computer systems. **Web services** use standardized protocols to describe and transfer data from one company in a way that those data can automatically be read, understood, transcribed, and processed by different computer systems in another company.[37] For instance, Route One is a company that was started by the financing companies of DaimlerChrysler, Ford, General Motors, and Toyota. Not surprisingly, each auto company has a different computer system with different operating systems, different programs, and different data structures. Route One is relying on Web services to connect these different computer systems to the wide variety of different databases and software used by various auto dealers, credit bureaus, banks, and other auto financing companies. Without Web services, there's no way these different companies and systems could share information.[38]

Web services
using standardized protocols to describe data from one company in such a way that those data can automatically be read, understood, transcribed, and processed by different computer systems in another company

extranet allows companies to exchange information and conduct transactions with outsiders by providing them direct, Web-based access to authorized parts of a company's intranet or information system

In EDI and Web services, the different purchasing and ordering applications in each company interact automatically without any human input. No one has to lift a finger to click a mouse, enter data, or hit the "return" key. An **extranet**, by contrast, allows companies to exchange information and conduct transactions by purposely providing outsiders with direct, Web browser–based access to authorized parts of a company's intranet or information system. Typically, user names and passwords are required to access an extranet.[39] For example, to make sure that its distribution trucks don't waste money by running half empty or make late deliveries, General Mills uses an extranet to provide Web-based access to its trucking database to 20 other companies that ship their products over similar distribution routes. When other companies are ready to ship products, they log on to General Mills' trucking database, check the availability, and then enter the shipping load, place, and pickup time. Thus, by sharing shipping capacity on its trucks, General Mills' trucks run fully loaded all the time. In several test areas, General Mills saved 7 percent on shipping costs, or nearly $2 million in the first year.[40]

Finally, similar to the way in which extranets are used to handle transactions with suppliers and distributors, companies are reducing paperwork and manual information processing by using the Internet to electronically automate transactions with customers. For example, most airlines have further automated the ticketing process by eliminating tickets altogether. Simply buy an e-ticket via the Internet and then check yourself in at the airport using an automated kiosk that prints out your boarding pass and your luggage tags. Together, Internet purchases, ticketless travel, and automated check-ins have fully automated the purchase of airline tickets. And, by eliminating the costs of recording, printing, handling, and mailing tickets, the commission that would have been paid to travel agents, and the hourly wages and benefits paid to check-in clerks, the airlines save an estimated $30 to $40 per ticket.[41]

In the long run, the goal is to link customer Internet sites with company intranets (or EDI) and extranets so that everyone—all the employees and managers within a company, and the suppliers and distributors outside the company—who is involved in providing a service or making a product for a customer is automatically notified when a purchase is made. Companies that use EDI, Web services, extranets, and the Internet to share data with customers and suppliers achieve increases in productivity 2.7 times larger than those that don't.[42]

3.3 Sharing Knowledge and Expertise

knowledge the understanding that one gains from information

At the beginning of the chapter, we distinguished between raw data, which consist of facts and figures, and information, which consists of useful data that influence someone's choices and behavior. One more important distinction needs to be made, namely, that data and information are not the same as knowledge. **Knowledge** is the understanding that one gains from information. Importantly, knowledge does not reside in information. Knowledge resides in people. That's why companies hire consultants or why family doctors refer patients to specialists. Unfortunately, it can be quite expensive to employ consultants, specialists, and experts. So companies have begun using two information technologies, decision support systems and expert systems, to capture and share the knowledge of consultants, specialists, and experts with other managers and workers.

decision support system (DSS)
an information system that helps managers to understand specific kinds of problems and potential solutions and to analyze the impact of different decision options using "what if" scenarios

Unlike an executive information system that speeds up and simplifies the acquisition of information, a **decision support system (DSS)** helps managers understand problems and potential solutions by acquiring and analyzing information with sophisticated models and tools.[43] Furthermore, unlike EIS programs that are broad in scope and permit managers to retrieve all kinds of information about a company, DSS programs are usually narrow in scope and targeted toward helping managers solve specific kinds of problems. DSS programs have been developed to help managers pick the shortest and most efficient routes for delivery trucks, select the best combination of stocks for investors, and schedule the flow of inventory through complex manufacturing facilities. It's important to understand that DSS programs don't replace managerial decision making; they improve it by furthering managers' and workers' understanding of the problems they face and the solutions that might work.

expert system
an information system that contains the specialized knowledge and decision rules used by experts and experienced decision makers so that nonexperts can draw on this knowledge base to make decisions

Expert systems are created by capturing the specialized knowledge and decision rules used by experts and experienced decision makers. They permit nonexpert employees to draw on this expert knowledge base to make decisions. Most expert systems work by using a collection of "if–then" rules to sort through information and recommend a course of action. For example, let's say that you're using your American Express card to help your spouse celebrate a promotion. After dinner and a movie, you and your spouse stroll by a travel office with a Las Vegas poster in its window. Thirty minutes later, caught up in the moment, you find yourselves at the airport ticket counter trying to purchase last-minute tickets to Vegas. But there's just one problem. American Express didn't approve your purchase. In fact, the ticket counter agent is now on the phone with an American Express customer service agent.

So what put a temporary halt to your weekend escape to Vegas? An expert system that American Express calls "Authorizer's Assistant."[44] The first "if–then" rule that prevented your purchase was the rule "*if* a purchase is much larger than the cardholder's regular spending habits, *then* deny approval of the purchase." This rule is built into American Express's transaction-processing system that handles thousands of purchase requests per second. Now that the American Express customer service agent is on the line, he or she is prompted by the Authorizer's Assistant to ask the ticket counter agent to examine your identification. You hand over your driver's license and another credit card to prove you're you. Then the ticket agent asks for your address, phone number, Social Security number, and your mother's maiden name and relays the information to American Express. Finally, your ticket purchase is approved. Why? Because you met the last series of "if–then" rules. *If* the purchaser can provide proof of identity and *if* the purchaser can provide personal information that isn't common knowledge, *then* approve the purchase.

Review 3
Accessing and Sharing Information and Knowledge

Executive information systems, intranets, and corporate portals facilitate internal sharing and access to company information and transactions. Electronic data interchange, Web services, and the Internet allow external groups, like suppliers and customers, to easily access company information. All three decrease costs by reducing or eliminating data entry, data errors, and paperwork, and by speeding up communication. Organizations use decision support systems and expert systems to capture and share specialized knowledge with nonexpert employees.

STUDY TIP Imagine you are the professor, and make up your own test for Chapter 5. What are the main topics and key concepts that students should know? If you work with a study group, exchange practice tests. Work them individually, then "grade" them collectively. This way you can discuss trouble spots and answer each other's questions.

MANAGEMENT TEAM DECISION

YOU SAVED $9.32!

The numbers are staggering: More than 12,000 U.S. supermarkets offer some kind of shopper card or customer reward program, already covering over 50 percent of the grocery market, and the trend is on the upswing.[45] Since their inception, shopper card programs have largely been confined to offering cents-off discounts to customers who join. The birth of the shopper card was a move by supermarkets to slow the intrusion of the likes of Wal-Mart and Target into the nearly $400 billion grocery industry. Supermarkets are no match for the purchasing power of big discount chains.

To keep customers from defecting to Wal-Mart Supercenter, Super Target, and Meijer, traditional supermarkets use shopper card loyalty programs to collect data on customers and their purchases. When customers sign up, they give basic demographic data: name, address, phone number, maybe even income and a credit card number. Once they start reaping the benefits of the card (i.e., discounts), the supermarket begins collecting data about how they spend money in the store, what brands are bought, how often, in what size, and so forth. By tracking customer spending habits, supermarkets have the data they need to send coupons for products a customer buys just about the time the customer is ready to buy them. Stores also know how to target their coupons. In other words, they do not send coupons for cat food to a customer who has only bought dog food in the past. Sending coupons in the mail and giving in-store discounts to shopper-card-carrying customers are the basic ways of creating customer loyalty programs.

Simple shopper card programs are expanding into areas beyond the grocery. For example, some stores work with major airlines to offer frequent-flier miles for every dollar spent at the grocery. Other stores have clubs designed around various interests: Winn Dixie has a Baby Club for new parents, a Wine Club for wine enthusiasts, and a Pet Club for animal owners. Each club produces a newsletter on the topic of interest, sends coupons and notices for in-store promotions, and some even give $10-off coupons after you have spent $200 in the store on items associated with the club (like diapers and formula for the Baby Club). One successful program allows shoppers to collect points and redeem them personally, or transfer them to a local school to buy needed supplies.

Although shopper cards enable stores to collect hoards of data, they are not without drawbacks. Many independent organizations and journalists have shown that the regular price of an item is offered to cardholders as the discounted price. If you don't have a card, you can pay 30 percent over the regular retail price of the item. Backlash against collecting consumer information is also building, as stores become more creative and assertive about collecting consumer data. (Safeway has launched computerized carts that use wireless technology to track where you are in the store and offer you discounts depending on what product you're looking at.) And people who buy more, save more, which means that lower-income shoppers will not spend enough to show up on the radar for frequent-user discounts. But perhaps the biggest drawback is the cost. Expensive computer technology is needed to automate discounting and to warehouse and sort data; special bulk mailings to residential addresses cost more than newspaper inserts; maintaining and managing extensive programs takes time and personnel. Plus, stores have typically not been able to convert their masses of data into useful information. One researcher estimates that fewer than 30 percent of stores know how to use the data they collect effectively, much less strategically. Most programs have become nothing more than electronic coupons.

Nonetheless, shopper card programs are still on an upward trend. At the very least, they help grocers analyze purchasing trends at individual stores, and with profit margins typically under 5 percent, that can mean a lot. In the world of supercenters, grocers need a tool to make intelligent decisions so that they can survive.

For this management team decision, your team will be acting as the management team of a small chain of independent supermarkets that does not yet have a shopper card program. You will decide whether to follow the rising tide and implement a shopper card program. Your team will need to consider the types of data to collect, the cost of collection (you don't need hard figures here), and the cost of converting the data to information, among other things.

Questions

1. As a team, brainstorm several ways that you can capture data about your customers. How will you turn the data you collect into useful, valuable information? (*Hint:* Information is only useful when it is accurate, complete, relevant, and timely.)

2. Since you will not be the first supermarket to implement a shopper card or loyalty program, how can you create a competitive advantage by adding one? In other words, how can you use a shopper card program to continuously improve and support the core functions of the supermarket? (Think along the lines of increasing store traffic, managing inventory, and so forth.)

3. Based on the exploratory work you have done, do you adopt a loyalty card program at your small chain of supermarkets? Explain your decision.

4. *Optional:* Using the information from Chapter 4, write a plan for implementing a shopper card/loyalty program at your supermarket network.

DEVELOP YOUR CAREER POTENTIAL

WEB PRIVACY POLICY

With the advent of the Internet and its explosive growth, the need to protect an individual's privacy has increased dramatically in recent years.[46] Many Internet Web sites require that personal information such as name, address, phone number(s), and credit card information be submitted before allowing a consumer to conduct any type of e-commerce transactions. Most Web-based companies have policies stating the extent to which this information will be used, the length of time the information will be kept, and what will happen to the information if the company folds. However, the industry has discovered that a significant number of these policies are not worth the paper they are printed on. For instance, Toysmart.com, a casualty of the dotcom bust, sought to gain approval from a bankruptcy court to auction off its database despite promising never to do so in its Web privacy policy. When dotcoms fail, the opportunity to sell customer information, possibly the only tangible asset that an Internet-based firm owns, is attractive. An example of the detrimental effects of sensitive information being publicly released occurred when pharmaceutical company Eli Lilly accidentally released the email addresses of more than 600 people currently taking Prozac, a common antidepressant medication. To combat the problems caused by the release of sensitive and confidential information, privacy advocates are pushing for more stringent legislation to protect consumers and their personal information. To appease legislators and promote self-regulation as opposed to government regulation, the Network Advertising Initiative (NAI) is proposing several recommendations for Internet-based businesses to adopt in constructing or strengthening their privacy policies. These recommendations are as follows:

1. *The word "never" should be taken literally.* If a firm promises never to sell customer information, it should abide by its promise. Additionally, this promise should survive and remain true even if the firm's assets are parceled out as a result of bankruptcy hearings.
2. *Consumers should be given a choice.* If a firm decides to sell confidential customer information, customers should be given a choice before that information is released. Although this rule is being enforced under existing legislation, the current privacy laws require customers to "opt out" if they wish that their information not be released. This places the burden on consumers to contact the retailer and indicate their wish to keep their personal information private. Privacy advocates want the rule to be changed so that consumers must "opt in," thereby placing the burden on retailers by requiring them to obtain the consumer's approval before information can be released.
3. *Companies should restrict the type of information disclosed.* If a company sells information, it should limit the information disclosed to only names and addresses, typical of the information found on most mailing lists. This would require companies to maintain separate databases: one would be for information that can be sold or disclosed, and the other would be a secure database containing more private information such as age, ethnicity, income, Social Security number, and credit information.

Exercise

As a manager charged with constructing a privacy policy for your firm, you are instructed to visit a well-known company's Web site and inspect its Web privacy policy. As you read the policy, compare it with the recommendations above. What elements of the policy could be improved, and what elements would you include in developing your own firm's Web privacy policy? Using the information presented above and another firm's Web privacy policy as a guide, draft a Web privacy policy for your firm.

take two video!

BIZ FLIX Lorenzo's Oil

This film tells the true story of young Lorenzo Odone who suffers from adrenoleukodystrophy (ALD), an incurable degenerative brain disorder. (Six actors and actresses play Lorenzo throughout the film.) Physicians and medical scientists offer little help to Lorenzo's desperate parents, Michaela (Susan Sarandon) and Augusto (Nick Nolte). They use their resources to learn about ALD to try to save their son. Director George Miller co-wrote the script, which benefited from his medical training as a physician.

Six months after Lorenzo's ALD diagnosis, his condition fails to improve with a restricted diet. Michaela and Augusto continue their research at the National Institutes of Health library in Bethesda, Maryland. Michaela finds a report of a critical Polish experiment that showed positive effects of fatty acid manipulation in rats. Convinced that a panel of experts could systematically focus on their problem, they help organize the First International ALD Symposium. This scene is an edited version of the symposium sequence that appears about midway through the film. The film continues with the Ordones' efforts to save their son.

What to Watch for and Ask Yourself

1. Do the scientists present data or information during the symposium?
2. If it is information, who transformed the data into information? Speculate about how such data become information.
3. What do you predict will be the next course of action for the Odones?

MGMT WORKPLACE Cannondale

Cannondale produces a wide variety of road racing, mountain, and recreational bicycles for both casual enthusiasts and demanding professionals. Before Mike Dower, the vice president of information technology, selected and implemented the current materials requirement planning (MRP) system, it took Cannondale months to bring a product to market. Now, with an MRP system that synchronizes design, engineering, and manufacturing and supports a company-wide network and email system, information flows more efficiently through the firm, and Cannondale can bring new products to market in a matter of weeks. In addition to shortening product-development cycles, the MRP system has helped Cannondale reduce its batch production size, increase its production flexibility, cut its market response time, and improve its inventory control.

What to Watch for and Ask Yourself

1. Explain how Cannondale's information system provides a competitive advantage. Do you think that advantage will be sustained or temporary? Explain.
2. How does management at Cannondale use its internal network and communication system to enhance productivity?

CHAPTER SIX

Control

outline

WHAT WOULD YOU DO?

Washington Mutual Bank Headquarters, Seattle, Washington.[1] Over the last decade, Washington Mutual Bank, or, as it calls itself, "WaMu," has been on an acquisition spree, purchasing 30 banks around the country for well over $100 billion. In making these acquisitions, WaMu turned itself into America's sixth largest bank, the second largest originator of home mortgages, and the largest servicer of home mortgages. If you've got a home mortgage, there's a one in eight chance that your monthly payments go to WaMU.

In growing so fast, however, WaMu has also created and acquired a number of problems for itself. For instance, though WaMu considers its friendly customer service its strength, a class-action suit has been filed alleging that financial advisers from WM Financial Services, WaMu's stock brokerage division, used their access to the bank's records to target and take advantage of elderly customers with large funds. For example, a WM Financial adviser cold-called 89-year-

student resources

URL
Experiencing Management
Explore the four levels of learning by doing the simulation module on Organizational Control.

GUIDE
Study Guide
Mini lecture reviews all the learning points in the chapter and concludes with a case on Gap.

VIDEO
Take Two Video
Biz Flix is a scene from *Scent of a Woman*. Management Workplace is a segment on Ping Golf.

PPT
PowerPoint®
12 slides with graphics provide an outline for this chapter.

FAQ
Author Insights
Chuck talks about drawing the line on employee surveillance.

TEST
Self Test
23 true/false questions, 25 multiple choice questions, a management scenario, and 6 exhibit worksheets

old Helen Wisner, a longtime WaMu bank customer, at her home and convinced her to shift $70,000 of her funds out of low-risk certificates of deposit into risky bond funds. While Wisner thought she was buying a no-risk investment from the bank, the adviser pocketed $3,000 in commissions for himself.

WaMu is also being sued for problems at Houston-based Bank United, which it bought this year. The lawsuit alleges a practice of consistently overcharging customers for late fees. While WaMu spokesperson Kevin Horn says that these are "inherited issues" and "not in line with current business practices," there's no denying that fees are a very large source of income for the bank. That's why it is critical that WaMu straighten out its fee-charging process.

Another "inherited" problem is that thousands of mortgage customers, acquired when WaMu purchased PNC Mortgage, received threatening letters from their local tax boards. Real estate taxes are typically collected as part of monthly mortgage payments and then paid to the local tax assessor, but WaMu forgot to forward those payments for 55,000 customers. WaMu quickly acknowledged this mistake and apologized to its customers. It has also paid the back taxes for all but 350 of the 55,000 accounts and reimbursed customers for any fees assessed. WaMu spokesperson Horn says, "As a company grows, problems will arise. What's important is how they solve the problem."

Nonetheless, recurring problems won't help WaMu keep costs low (a key part of its strategy), attract and keep customers, and stay ahead of its increasingly aggressive competition. For example, Chicago-based Bank One has put together a $15 million advertising campaign featuring Chicago's beloved Mike Ditka, former coach of the NFL Chicago Bears, to take business away from WaMu. In New York City, Bank of America clearly targeted WaMu with humorous TV ads, promising "higher standards," while J. P. Morgan Chase will pay new customers $100 if they've come to Chase from another bank and $200 if they've come from WaMu.

With plans to open 240 new bank branches this year and aspirations of becoming the Wal-Mart of U.S. banking (low cost and friendly service), you've got to get control of these problems. In particular, given the lawsuits, continued aggressive expansion, and the inevitable problems that come from fast growth, what do you need to do to make sure that the company's costs stay under control? And, while WaMu's customer reputation is generally good, recent problems have begun to tarnish it. So what do you need to do to continue to attract and retain bank and mortgage customers? After all, keeping customers is an important part of holding down costs. Finally, it's fairly obvious that the bank is having some problems integrating new companies into the WaMu way of doing things. There will always be some transition problems, but clearly, there's got to be a better way of bringing new customers and new banks into the WaMu system. WaMu can't totally eliminate those issues, but surely it can control them better than before. **If you were in charge at WaMu, what would you do?**

control
a regulatory process of establishing standards to achieve organizational goals, comparing actual performance against the standards, and taking corrective action, when necessary

Control is a regulatory process of establishing standards to achieve organizational goals, compare actual performance against standards, and take corrective action when necessary to restore performance to those standards.

Control is achieved when behavior and work procedures conform to standards and company goals are accomplished.[2] Control is not just an after-the-fact process, however. Preventive measures are also a form of control. In fact, we should remember that control is the last step in the first function of management, making things happen. To review, making things happen is a function of planning what you want to accomplish and deciding how to achieve those plans (Chapter 4), gathering and managing the information needed to make good decisions (Chapter 5), and controlling behavior and processes through preventive or corrective action (Chapter 6).

We begin this chapter by examining the basic control process used in organizations. Then we examine whether control is always necessary or possible (it isn't). In the third part of the chapter, we go beyond the basics to an in-depth examination of the different methods that companies use to achieve control. We finish the chapter by taking a look at the things that companies choose to control (i.e., finances, product quality, customer retention, etc.).

Basics of Control

If you wanted to control traffic speeds in your town, how would you do it? Whereas most municipalities put in speed bumps, lower speed limits, put up traffic lights, or write more speeding tickets, the city of Culemborg in the Netherlands decided to use sheep. Why sheep? One of the city council members, who had observed the driving patterns on country roads in rural England, explained, "After all, it's impossible to speed past the sheep [in the middle of the road] if you drive in the Yorkshire Dales." When animal rights groups complained, the city erected a special fence to prevent the sheep from wandering from neighborhood streets onto busier, high-speed roads where they would clearly be endangered. Apparently, Culemborg's city leaders were not familiar with the tradition of some Yorkshire locals who "accidentally" hit sheep, hoping to make off with a free supply of lamb chops.[3] The city released five or six sheep initially with the plans to increase to as many as a hundred if motorists actually slow down.

The city of Culemborg in the Netherlands devised a rather creative form of traffic control: the use of sheep in the road.

After reading the next two sections, you should be able to

1 describe the basic control process.
2 answer the question: Is control necessary or possible?

1 The Control Process

The basic control process 1.1 begins with the establishment of clear standards of performance, 1.2 involves a comparison of actual performance to desired performance, 1.3 takes corrective action, if needed, to repair performance deficiencies, 1.4 is a dynamic, cybernetic process, and 1.5 consists of three basic methods: feedback control, concurrent control, and feedforward control.

1.1 Standards

The control process begins when managers set goals, like satisfying 90 percent of customers or increasing sales by 5 percent. Companies then specify the performance standards that must be met to accomplish those goals. **Standards** are a basis of comparison for measuring the extent to which organizational performance is satisfactory or unsatisfactory. For example, many pizzerias use 30 minutes as the standard for delivery times. Since anything longer is viewed as unsatisfactory, they'll typically reduce the price if they can't deliver a hot pizza to you in 30 minutes or less.

standards
a basis of comparison when measuring the extent to which various kinds of organizational performance are satisfactory or unsatisfactory

www.experiencing management.com

Learn more about the control process and the types of management decisions that may be necessary at our animated concept and activity site. Choose Organizational_Control from the "select a topic" pull-down menu, then Control Process from the "overview tab."
http:/www.experiencingmanagement.com

So how do managers set standards? How do they decide which levels of performance are satisfactory and which are unsatisfactory? The first criterion for a good standard is that it must enable goal achievement. If you're meeting the standard, but still not achieving company goals, then the standard may have to be changed. For example, 6 percent of all retail purchases are returned each year, causing Scott Kruger of the National Retail Federation to observe, "We're seeing too many big-screen TVs coming back the day after the Super Bowl and too many prom dresses coming back the day after prom night." Consequently, retailers like Target, which used to allow customers to return or exchange goods without receipts, were losing too much money. Today, Target's new standard is no refunds or store credit without a receipt. Goods returned without a receipt can only be exchanged for a similar item.[4]

Standards can be determined by benchmarking other companies. **Benchmarking** is the process of determining how well other companies (though typically not competitors) perform business functions or tasks. In other words, benchmarking is the process of determining other companies' standards.

benchmarking
the process of identifying outstanding practices, processes, and standards in other companies and adapting them to your company

The first step in setting standards is to determine what to benchmark. Companies can benchmark anything, from cycle time (how fast) to quality (how well). The next step is to identify the companies against which to benchmark your standards. Since this can require a significant commitment on the part of the benchmarked companies, it can take time to identify them and get their agreement to be benchmarked. The last step is to collect data to determine other companies' performance standards. For example, countless companies have visited MBNA, the credit card company, to learn how to respond quickly, if not immediately, to customer requests. Indeed, visitors learn that MBNA answers its phones by the second ring 98.5 percent of the time and that it takes no more than 30 minutes to approve (or deny) customer requests for higher credit limits.[5]

1.2 Comparison to Standards

The next step in the control process is to compare actual performance to performance standards. Although this sounds straightforward, the quality of the comparison largely depends on the measurement and information systems a company uses to keep track of performance. The better the system, the easier it is for companies to track their progress and identify problems that need to be fixed. One way for retailers to verify that performance standards are being met is to use "secret shoppers." Retail stores spend $435 million a year to hire these consultants, who visit the stores pretending to be customers, to determine whether employees provide helpful customer service.

1.3 Corrective Action

The next step in the control process is to identify performance deviations, analyze those deviations, and then develop and implement programs to correct them. This is similar to the planning process discussed in Chapter 4: regular, frequent performance feedback allows workers and managers to track their performance and make adjustments in effort, direction, and strategies.

feedback control
a mechanism for gathering information about performance deficiencies after they occur

exhibit 6.1

Cybernetic Control Process

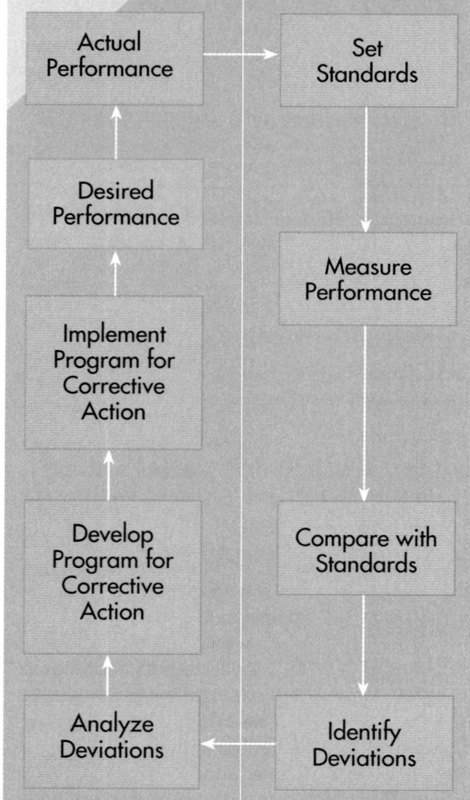

Source: H. Koontz & R. W. Bradspies, "Managing through Feedforward Control: A Future Directed View," Business Horizons, *June 1972, 25–36. Reprinted with permission from* Business Horizons, *© 1972 by the Trustees at Indiana University, Kelley School of Business.*

1.4 Dynamic, Cybernetic Process

As shown in Exhibit 6.1, control is a continuous, dynamic, cybernetic process. It begins with actual performance and measures of that performance. Managers then compare performance to the preestablished standards. If they identify deviations from standard performance, they analyze the deviations and develop corrective programs. Then implementing the programs (hopefully) achieves the desired performance. Managers must repeat the entire process again and again in an endless feedback loop (a continuous process). So control is not a one-time achievement or result. It continues over time (a dynamic process) and requires daily, weekly, and monthly attention from managers to maintain performance levels at the standard (i.e., cybernetic).

Keeping control of business expenses is an example of a continuous, dynamic, cybernetic process. Companies that don't closely monitor expenses usually find that they can quickly get out of control, even for the smallest things. For example, when Sandy Weill became the new CEO of Commercial Credit in Baltimore, everywhere he looked, he saw expenses that could be cut. When he saw stacks of "free" *Wall Street Journals* in the lobby, he proclaimed, "Cancel all subscriptions. If employees want a *Wall Street Journal*, tell them 'pay for it yourself.'"[6]

Sure, it's a cliché, but it's just as true in business as in sports: If you take your eye off the ball, you're going to strike out. Control is an ongoing, dynamic, cybernetic process.

1.5 Feedback, Concurrent, and Feedforward Control

There are three basic control methods: feedback control, concurrent control, and feedforward control.[7] **Feedback control** is a mechanism for gathering information about performance deficiencies *after* they occur. This information is then used to correct or prevent performance deficiencies. Study after study has clearly shown that feedback improves both individual and organizational performance. In most instances, any feedback is better than no feedback.

www.experiencing management.com

Learn more about the three basic control methods and their relationship to inputs, transformation, and output processes at our animated concept and activity site. Choose Organizational_Control from the "select a topic" pull-down menu, then Types of Control from the "overview tab."

http:/www.experiencingmanagement.com

If there is a downside to feedback, however, it is that it sometimes occurs too late. For example, 90 percent of the time an electrical transformer malfunctions on a neighborhood utility pole, a squirrel caused the problem. Unfortunately, electrical utilities have had little success keeping squirrels away from their equipment. In general, utilities don't find out about the problem until after a squirrel stands atop a utility pole, touches a live wire, and fries itself and the transformer, creating a huge power surge that blows out computers, televisions, and appliances in nearby homes. Power goes out in the neighborhood and customer complaints pour in with no advance warning.[8]

Concurrent control is a mechanism for gathering information about performance deficiencies *as* they occur. Thus, it is an improvement over feedback, because it attempts to eliminate or shorten the delay between performance and feedback about the performance.

concurrent control
a mechanism for gathering information about performance deficiencies as they occur, eliminating or shortening the delay between performance and feedback

feedforward control
a mechanism for monitoring performance inputs rather than outputs to prevent or minimize performance deficiencies before they occur

Feedforward control is a mechanism for gathering information about performance deficiencies before they occur. In contrast to feedback and concurrent control, which provide feedback on the basis of outcomes and results, feedforward control provides information about performance deficiencies by monitoring inputs, not outputs. Thus, feedforward seeks to prevent or minimize performance deficiencies *before* they occur. Exhibit 6.2 lists guidelines that companies can follow to get the most out of feedforward control.

exhibit 6.2

Guidelines for Using Feedforward Control

1. Thorough planning and analysis are required.
2. Careful discrimination must be applied in selecting input variables.
3. The feedforward system must be kept dynamic.
4. A model of the control system should be developed.
5. Data on input variables must be regularly collected.
6. Data on input variables must be regularly assessed.
7. Feedforward control requires action.

Source: H. Koontz & R. W. Bradspies, "Managing through Feedforward Control: A Future Directed View," Business Horizons, *June 1972, 25–36. Reprinted with permission from* Business Horizons, *© 1972 by the Trustees at Indiana University, Kelley School of Business.*

Review 1

The Control Process

The first step in the control process is to set goals and performance standards. The second is to compare actual performance to performance standards. The better a company's information and measurement systems, the easier it is to make these comparisons. The last step is to identify and correct performance deviations. However, control is a continuous, dynamic, cybernetic process, not a one-time achievement or result. Control requires frequent managerial attention. The three basic control methods are feedback control (after-the-fact performance information), concurrent control (simultaneous performance information), and feedforward control (preventive performance information).

2 Is Control Necessary or Possible?

Control is achieved when behavior and work procedures conform to standards and goals are accomplished. By contrast, **control loss** occurs when behavior and work procedures do not conform to standards.[9] Control loss usually prevents goal achievement. Mirage Resorts is one of the best-known, most profitable, and most experienced gambling companies in the world. But control loss was rampant when the company spent

control loss
a situation in which behavior and work procedures do not conform to standards

$680 million, twice the original budget, to build the state-of-the-art Beau Rivage casino and hotel in Biloxi, Mississippi. Expensive Italian marble was used throughout; the number of planned rooms quickly grew from 1,200 to 1,780; the number of restaurants grew from 4 to 13; over $1 million was spent on the 15 trees that line the drive into the casino; and $10 million was spent building a 31-boat marina—nearly $322,000 per slip—out of imported Brazilian hard woods.[10]

When control losses occur, managers need to find out what, if anything, they could have done to prevent these mistakes from occurring. In Mirage Resort's case, there was a straightforward solution: Closely monitor and check actual building expenses against planned building expenses, and then stick to them. In general, when control loss occurs, managers need to ask three questions: 2.1 Is more control necessary? 2.2 Is more control possible? and 2.3 If more control is necessary but not possible, what should we do instead?

2.1 Is More Control Necessary?

degree of dependence
the extent to which a company needs a particular resource to accomplish its goals

resources
the assets, capabilities, processes, information, and knowledge that an organization uses to improve its effectiveness and efficiency, to create and sustain competitive advantage, and to fulfill a need or solve a problem

resource flow
the extent to which companies have access to critical resources

Two factors can help managers determine whether more (or different) control is necessary: the degree of dependence and resource flows.[11] **Degree of dependence** is the extent to which a company needs a particular resource to accomplish its goals. The more important a resource is for meeting organizational standards and goals, the more necessary it is to control that resource.

Note, however, that resources are more than just raw materials. A **resource** is anything that can be used to fulfill a need or solve a problem. Thus, resources can include employee skills, space, intellectual capability, capital (dollars), specialized know-how, a cohesive corporate culture, and so forth. Basically, critical resources, whatever form they take, make it easier for managers and employees to carry out the work processes that conform to standards and lead to goal accomplishment.

The second factor that determines whether more control is necessary is resource flow. **Resource flow** is the extent to which companies have easy access to critical resources. For example, with a 23 percent market share, Tyson Foods is the largest chicken processor in the United States, providing Wal-Mart, McDonald's, and most major supermarkets and restaurant chains with 15 billion pounds of chicken each year. Unlike many of its competitors, which simply buy chickens for processing, Tyson owns the chicken from genetics to hatching, from growing and feeding the birds to factory processing, and finally to distributing the processed chicken to stores and restaurants.[12] Access to these critical resources, owning and controlling the entire production process, is the key to Tyson's low costs and high quality.

When companies have a difficult time getting the critical resources they need, they usually try to increase resource flows by creating or obtaining some form of control over them. Although Tyson Foods created, developed, and acquired the critical resources it needed to succeed in the chicken processing business, it didn't have the critical resources needed to succeed in pork and beef processing and failed when it tried to enter those businesses. So Tyson spent $4.6 billion to acquire IBP Corporation, which has the largest market share (27 percent) in U.S. beef and the second largest (19 percent) in pork. While IBP's size was important, Tyson was also gaining access to IBP's most critical resource, the ability to deliver "case-ready" beef and pork to supermarkets—the same capability that Tyson has with chicken.[13]

2.2 Is More Control Possible?

Whereas degrees of dependence and resource flow can help determine whether control is needed, the cost of control and cybernetic feasibility help determine whether control is possible. First, to determine whether more control is possible (or worthwhile), managers need to carefully assess **regulation costs**, that is, whether the costs and unintended consequences of control exceed its benefits. For example, one of the reasons that the number of U.S. pharmaceutical companies producing major vaccines has dropped significantly is that the cost of controlling legal risk (through liability insurance and in-house legal staffs) is just too high. In the 1960s, 37 U.S. companies produced 380 licensed vaccines. In 1984, 15 U.S. companies produced 88 licensed vaccines. Today, because of legal costs, just four U.S. companies produce vaccines. As a result, parents and doctors face severe shortages in 8 of the 11 recommended vaccines that prevent children from contracting diseases like diphtheria, tetanus, whooping cough, measles, mumps, rubella, and chickenpox.[14] Before choosing to implement control, managers should be confident that the benefits exceed the costs.

regulation costs
the costs associated with implementing or maintaining control

DOING THE RIGHT THING

Don't Cheat on Travel Expense Reports

Workers are often tempted to pad their travel expense reports. As one put it, "After a while you feel that they owe it to ya, so the hell with 'em. I'm going to expense it." Frank Navran of the Ethics Resource Center says that people justify this by telling themselves, "I'm not really stealing from the company—I'm just getting back what I feel I'm entitled to." However, Joel Richards, executive vice president and chief administrative officer of El Paso Corporation, says, "You learn a lot about people from their expense reports. If you can't trust an employee to be truthful on an expense report, if you can't trust them with small dollars, how can you trust them with making decisions involving millions of dollars?" So, do the right thing, don't cheat on your travel expense reports.[16]

An often-overlooked factor in determining the cost of control is the set of unintended consequences that sometimes accompany increased control. Control systems help companies, managers, and workers accomplish their goals, but at the same time that the systems help solve some problems, they can create others. Hewlett-Packard became the market leader by manufacturing high-quality, reliable computer printers. But, as competition grew and prices dropped, H-P printers grew relatively more expensive for consumers, and H-P began losing market share because it was overengineering its printers. They were too expensive because they were made too well.[15]

The second factor that helps managers determine whether control is possible is cybernetic feasibility. **Cybernetic feasibility** is the extent to which it is possible to implement each step in the control process: clear standards of performance, comparison of performance to standards, and corrective action. If one or more steps cannot be implemented, then maintaining effective control may be difficult or impossible.

cybernetic feasibility
the extent to which it is possible to implement each step in the control process

2.3 Quasi-Control: When Control Isn't Possible

If control is necessary but not possible because of costs or lack of cybernetic feasibility, then managers can use two **quasi-control** options: reducing dependence or restructuring dependence.

quasi-control
reducing dependence or restructuring dependence when control is necessary but not possible

Reducing dependence involves an explicit choice to abandon or change organizational goals by reducing dependence on critical resources. Companies are likely to choose to reduce dependence under the same conditions that they would choose control. The difference, however, is that companies

reducing dependence
abandoning or changing organizational goals to reduce dependence on critical resources

choose to reduce dependence when control is not possible, that is, when the cost is too high or cybernetic feasibility is near zero. Several years ago, because of cost concerns Boeing announced it would not build the brand new 747X, a 525-seat jet designed to compete with the new 555-seat Airbus A380.[17] Then, changing its goals from jet size to jet speed, it announced plans to build the Sonic Cruiser, a new, expensive supersonic 250-seat jet that could fly faster than the speed of sound, cutting international flight times by one-third.[18] Two years later, however, with airlines struggling financially, Boeing changed its goals again—from jet speed to jet efficiency. It abandoned the high-cost Sonic Cruiser for the new 7E7, a high-efficiency 250-seat jet that would cost 30 percent less to fly than today's passenger jets.[19]

restructuring dependence
exchanging dependence on one critical resource for dependence on another

Instead of reducing dependence when control is not possible, companies can choose to **restructure dependence**—exchange dependence on one critical resource for dependence on another. One area in which companies are exchanging resources is to substitute private planes for commercial air travel. Traveling by private plane offers a number of advantages over traveling via commercial airlines. To start, compared to last-minute business class tickets, which are much more expensive now than just a few years ago and approximately three to five times the cost of coach class tickets, corporate planes can be cheaper to fly. Tim Quinn, who owns a construction company, saw his

exhibit 6.3

Is Control Necessary or Possible?

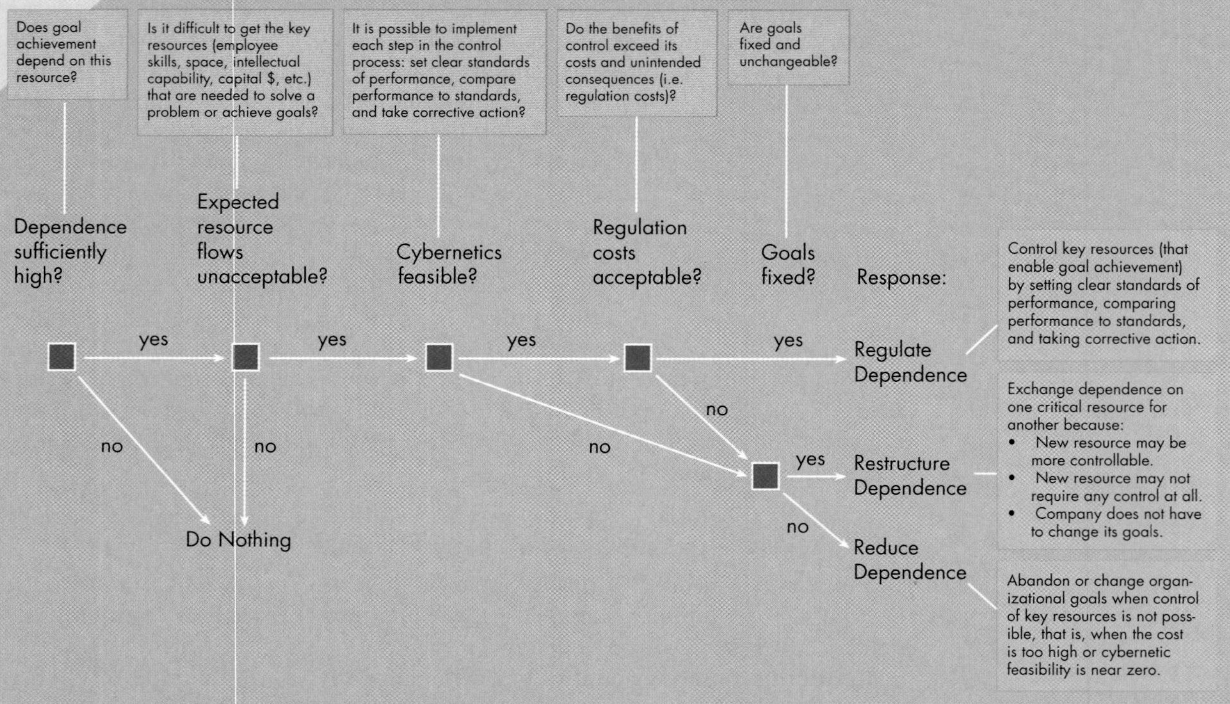

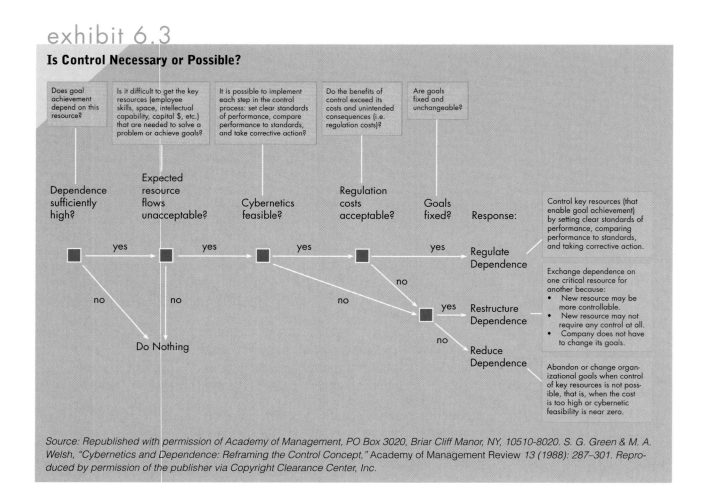

Source: Republished with permission of Academy of Management, PO Box 3020, Briar Cliff Manor, NY, 10510-8020. S. G. Green & M. A. Welsh, "Cybernetics and Dependence: Reframing the Control Concept," Academy of Management Review *13 (1988): 287–301. Reproduced by permission of the publisher via Copyright Clearance Center, Inc.*

monthly air-travel expenses drop almost in half, from $11,000 to $6,000, even after making the monthly payments for his company plane.[20] Also, while commercial airlines fly into 550 airports nationwide, smaller, private planes can fly into more than 5,500 different airports.

There are three advantages to restructuring dependence. First, like private planes, the new critical resource may be more controllable. Second, even better, the new critical resource may not require any control at all. Third, the company does not have to change its goals.

Review 2

Is Control Necessary or Possible?

Exhibit 6.3 summarizes the questions that managers should answer to determine if control is necessary or possible. First, if the degree of dependence on a critical resource is high, or if resource flows are poor, managers will want to initiate greater control over critical resources. However, if resource flows and the degree of dependence are low, managers do not need to do anything to increase control. Next, if cybernetics (i.e., the basic control process) is feasible, managers should determine if the cost of control is acceptable. If it is, then managers should choose to regulate or control the degree of dependence on critical resources. However, if cybernetics is not feasible, the next step is deciding whether goals can be changed. If goals are fixed and unchangeable, then managers should restructure their dependence on critical resources by exchanging dependence on one critical resource for dependence on another. On the other hand, if goals can be changed, then managers should reduce dependence on critical resources by abandoning or changing key goals.

How and What to Control

Have you developed a taste for gourmet coffee? With gourmet coffee seemingly everywhere, chances are you or someone in your office has. In many offices, however, the popularity of specialty coffees and coffee shops has created a problem: the long coffee break. Instead of wandering down the hall for a coffee and a chat with coworkers during a 15-minute coffee break, workers are now going to the nearest gourmet coffee shop and spending much more time on break.

The question for aspiring managers is how would you handle this situation? Should you declare coffee shops off-limits? Should you simply discuss it with employees and rely on them to exercise their own judgment? Should you closely watch for potential violators and then punish them? And then there is the question of whether long coffee breaks are something that managers should even try to control.

After reading the next two sections, you should be able to

3 discuss the various methods that managers can use to maintain control.

4 describe the behaviors, processes, and outcomes that today's managers are choosing to control their organizations.

www.experiencing management.com

Various financial and human control techniques are presented at our animated concept and activity site. Some controls are closely related to the Planning Process (see Chapter 4). Choose Organizational_Control from the "select a topic" pull-down menu, then Financial and Human Controls from the "overview tab."
http:/www.experiencingmanagement.com

3 Control Methods

Managers can use five different methods to achieve control in their organizations: 3.1 bureaucratic, 3.2 objective, 3.3 normative, 3.4 concertive, and 3.5 self-control.

3.1 Bureaucratic Control

bureaucratic control the use of hierarchical authority to influence employee behavior by rewarding or punishing employees for compliance or noncompliance with organizational policies, rules, and procedures

When most people think of managerial control, what they have in mind is bureaucratic control. **Bureaucratic control** is top-down control, in which managers try to influence employee behavior by rewarding or punishing employees for compliance or noncompliance with organizational policies, rules, and procedures. Most employees, however, would argue that bureaucratic managers emphasize punishment for noncompliance much more than rewards for compliance. For instance, when visiting the company's regional offices and managers, the president of a training company would get some toilet paper from the restrooms and aggressively ask, "What's this?" When the managers answered, "Toilet paper," he would scream that it was two-ply toilet paper that the company couldn't afford. When told of a cracked toilet seat in one of the women's restrooms, he said, "If you don't like sitting on that seat, you can stand up like I do!"[21]

Ironically, bureaucratic management and control were created to prevent just this type of managerial behavior. By encouraging managers to apply well-thought-out rules, policies, and procedures in an impartial, consistent manner to everyone in the organization, bureaucratic control is supposed to make companies more efficient, effective, and fair. Perversely, it frequently has just the opposite effect. Managers who use bureaucratic control often emphasize following the rules above all else.

Another characteristic of bureaucratically controlled companies is that due to their rule- and policy-driven decision making, they are highly resistant to change and slow to respond to customers and competitors. Even Max Weber, the German philosopher who is largely credited with popularizing bureaucratic ideals in the late nineteenth century, referred to bureaucracy as the "iron cage." He said, "Once fully established, bureaucracy is among those social structures which are the hardest to destroy."[22]

3.2 Objective Control

objective control the use of observable measures of worker behavior or outputs to assess performance and influence behavior

In many companies, bureaucratic control has evolved into **objective control**, which is the use of observable measures of employee behavior or output to assess performance and influence behavior. Whereas bureaucratic control focuses on whether policies and rules are followed, objective control focuses on the observation or measurement of worker behavior or output. For example, determining whether sales representatives filed expense reports within 30 days, as specified by company policy, is an example of bureaucratic control, while measuring whether they met their sales quotas or returned phone calls in a timely manner is an example of objective control. There are two kinds of objective control: behavior control and output control.

behavior control regulation of the behaviors and actions that workers perform on the job

Behavior control is regulating behaviors and actions that workers perform on the job. The basic assumption of behavior control is that if you do the right things (i.e., the right behaviors) every day, then those things should lead to goal achievement. Behavior control is still management-based, however, which means that managers are responsible for monitoring, rewarding, and punishing workers for exhibiting desired or undesired behaviors. When Alan

Greenberg was the CEO of Bear Stearns, a Wall Street investment company, he wrote memos to his firm's managing partners instructing them to leave word where they could be reached at all times ("All of us are entitled to eat lunch, play golf and go on vacation. But you must leave word with your secretary or associates where you can be reached at all times. Decisions have to be made and your input can be important!"). In doing so, he was enacting behavior control about the importance of always being available.[23] Greenberg also wrote pointed memos to his "troops" about not returning phone calls, the expense of overusing FedEx to mail documents, and the importance of reporting any suspicious behavior that might violate Bear Stearns' standards of honesty and integrity. All are examples of attempts to initiate behavior control.

output control
regulation of worker results or outputs through rewards and incentives

Instead of measuring what managers and workers do, **output control** measures the results of their efforts. Whereas behavior control regulates, guides, and measures how workers behave on the job, output control gives managers and workers the freedom to behave as they see fit as long as it leads to the accomplishment of prespecified, measurable results. Output control is often coupled with rewards and incentives.

Three things must occur for output control and rewards to lead to improved business results. First, output control measures must be reliable, fair, and accurate. Second, employees and managers must believe that they can produce the desired results. If they don't, then the output controls won't affect their behavior. Third, the rewards or incentives tied to outcome control measures must truly be dependent on achieving established standards of performance. When auto parts manufacturer Dana Corporation saw its sales drop 6 percent, its profits drop 44 percent, and its stock value drop by more than half, CEO Joseph Magliochetti saw his pay drop, too; his board of directors denied him a bonus and a stock grant that had been worth $1.8 million the year before. Because the company did not meet its goals for net income growth and return on investment, his pay was reduced by more than 60 percent.[24] For output control to work with rewards, the rewards must truly be at risk if performance doesn't measure up.

3.3 Normative Control

normative control
regulation of workers' behavior and decisions through widely shared organizational values and beliefs

Rather than monitoring rules, behavior, or output, another way to control what goes on in organizations is to use normative control to shape the beliefs and values of the people who work there. With **normative controls**, a company's widely shared values and beliefs guide workers' behavior and decisions. For example, at Nordstrom, a Seattle-based department store chain, one value permeates the entire work force from top to bottom: extraordinary customer service. On the first day of work at Nordstrom, trainees begin their transformation to the "Nordstrom way" by reading the employee handbook. Sounds boring, doesn't it? But Nordstrom's handbook is printed on one side of a 3-by-5-inch note card. In its entirety, it reads:

> Welcome to Nordstrom's. We're glad to have you with our company. Our Number One goal is to provide outstanding customer service. Set both your personal and professional goals high. We have great confidence in your ability to achieve them. Nordstrom Rules: Rule #1: Use your good judgment in all situations. There will be no additional rules. Please feel free to ask your department manager, store manager or division general manager any question at any time.[25]

That's it. No lengthy rules. No specifics about what behavior is or is not appropriate. Use your judgment.

Normative controls are created in two ways. First, companies that use normative controls are very careful about whom they hire. While many companies screen potential applicants on the basis of their abilities, normatively controlled companies are just as likely to screen potential applicants based on their attitudes and values. For example, before building stores in a new city, Nordstrom sends its human resource team into town to interview prospective applicants. In a few cities, the company canceled its expansion plans when it could not find enough qualified applicants who embodied the service attitudes and values that Nordstrom is known for. Nordstrom would rather give up potential sales in lucrative markets than do business using people who cannot provide Nordstrom's level of service.[26]

Second, with normative controls, managers and employees learn what they should and should not do by observing experienced employees and by listening to the stories they tell about the company. At Nordstrom, many of these stories, which employees call "heroics," have been inspired by the company motto, "Respond to Unreasonable Customer Requests!"[27] A favorite story is about a customer who just had to have a pair of burgundy Donna Karan slacks that had gone on sale, but she could not find her size. A sales associate contacted five nearby Nordstrom stores, but none had the customer's size. So rather than leave the customer dissatisfied with her shopping experience, the sales associate went to her manager for petty cash and then went across the street and paid full price for the slacks at a competitor's store. She then resold them to the customer at Nordstrom's lower sale price.[28] Obviously, Nordstrom would quickly go out of business if this were the norm. Nevertheless, this story makes clear the attitude that drives employee performance at Nordstrom in ways that rules, behavioral guidelines, or output controls could not.

3.4 Concertive Control

Whereas normative controls are based on beliefs that are strongly held and widely shared throughout a company, **concertive controls** are based on beliefs that are shaped and negotiated by work groups.[29] While normative controls are driven by strong organizational cultures, concertive controls usually arise when companies give autonomous work groups complete responsibility for task completion. **Autonomous work groups** are groups that operate without managers and are completely responsible for controlling work group processes, outputs, and behavior. These groups do their own hiring, firing, worker discipline, work schedules, materials ordering, budget making and meeting, and decision making.

concertive control
regulation of workers' behavior and decisions through work group values and beliefs

autonomous work groups
groups that operate without managers and are completely responsible for controlling work group processes, outputs, and behavior

Concertive control is not established overnight. Autonomous work groups evolve through two phases as they develop concertive control. In phase one, group members learn to work with each other, supervise each other's work, and develop the values and beliefs that will guide and control their behavior. And, because they develop these values and beliefs themselves, work group members feel strongly about following them. You will learn more about groups in Chapter 11, Managing Teams.

For example, a member of an autonomous team at ISE Electronics, a small manufacturer of electronic boards, said, "I feel bad, believe it or not. Last Friday, we missed a shipment. I feel like *I* missed the shipment since I'm the last

PERSONAL PRODUCTIVITY TIP

Learn to Say No!

Control is not just setting standards and identifying performance discrepancies. A key issue in control is deciding what to control and what to ignore. We can't do everything, and that means that sometimes we have to say no when we're asked to participate. Here are four tips for saying no.

- Listen to show interest and understanding.
- Say no immediately to avoid raising false expectations concerning your involvement.
- Explain why you can't, so the reasons for your refusal are understood.
- Offer alternatives to your participation: "I can't, but you should contact Mary Smith. Mary knows how to do this."[31]

person that sees what goes to ship. But Friday we missed the shipment by two boards and it shouldn't have been missed. But it was and I felt bad because it's me. It's a reflection on me, too, for not getting the boards out the door."[30]

The second phase in the development of concertive control is the emergence and formalization of objective rules to guide and control behavior. The beliefs and values developed in phase one usually develop into more objective rules as new members join teams. The clearer those rules, the easier it becomes for new members to figure out how and how not to behave.

Ironically, concertive control may lead to even more stress for workers to conform to expectations than bureaucratic control. Under bureaucratic control, most workers only have to worry about pleasing the boss. But with concertive control, their behavior has to satisfy the rest of their team members. For example, one team member said, "I don't have to sit there and look for the boss to be around; and if the boss is not around, I can sit there and talk to my neighbor or do what I want. Now the whole team is around me and the whole team is observing what I'm doing."[32] Plus, with concertive control, team members have a second, much more stressful role to perform—that of making sure that their team members adhere to team values and rules.

3.5 Self-Control

self-control (self-management) a control system in which managers and workers control their own behavior by setting their own goals, monitoring their own progress, and rewarding themselves for goal achievement

Self-control, also known as **self-management**, is a control system in which managers and workers control their own behavior.[33] Self-control does not result in anarchy in which everyone gets to do whatever he or she wants. In self-control or self-management, leaders and managers provide workers with clear boundaries within which they may guide and control their own goals and behaviors.[34] Leaders and managers also contribute to self-control by teaching others the skills they need to maximize and monitor their own work effectiveness. In turn, individuals who manage and lead themselves establish self-control by setting their own goals, monitoring their own progress, rewarding or punishing themselves for achieving or for not achieving their self-set goals, and constructing positive thought patterns that remind them of the importance of their goals and their ability to accomplish them.[35]

One technique for reminding yourself of your goals is daily affirmation, in which you write down or speak your goals aloud to yourself several times a day. Skeptics contend that daily affirmations are nothing more than positive thinking, but an affirmation is actually just a simple way to help control what you think about and how you spend your time. Basically, it's a technique to prevent (i.e., control) you from getting sidetracked on unimportant thoughts and activities.

Scott Adams, who illustrates the cartoon strip "Dilbert," was skeptical that affirmations would work, but he gave them a try. His first affirmations were to see the price of a company's stock rise and to impress a particular woman. Both happened. Then, when he was getting ready to take the GMAT test to get into an MBA program, every day he wrote that he wanted a score of 94. His score was 94. When he began affirming, "I will be the best cartoonist on the planet," "Dilbert" ballooned in popularity. Where it once appeared in only 100 newspapers, it now appears in more than 1,100. What's he affirming now? "I will win a Pulitzer Prize."[36] Now it's your turn; start writing, "I will get an 'A' in Management. I will get an 'A' in Management. . . ."

Review 3

Control Methods

There are five methods of control: bureaucratic, objective, normative, concertive, and self-control (self-management). Bureaucratic and objective controls are top-down, management-based, and measurement-based. Normative and concertive controls represent shared forms of control because they evolve from company-wide or team-based beliefs and values. Self-control, or self-management, is a control system in which managers turn much, but not all, control over to the individuals themselves.

exhibit 6.4

When to Use Different Methods of Control

BUREAUCRATIC CONTROL	When it is necessary to standardize operating procedures When it is necessary to establish limits
BEHAVIOR CONTROL	When it is easier to measure what workers do on the job than what they accomplish on the job When "cause-effect" relationships are clear, that is, when companies know which behaviors will lead to success and which won't When good measures of worker behavior can be created
OUTPUT CONTROL	When it is easier to measure what workers accomplish on the job than what they do on the job When good measures of worker output can be created When it is possible to set clear goals and standards for worker output When "cause-effect" relationships are unclear
NORMATIVE CONTROL	When organizational culture, values, and beliefs are strong When it is difficult to create good measures of worker behavior When it is difficult to create good measures of worker output
CONCERTIVE CONTROL	When responsibility for task accomplishment is given to autonomous work groups When management wants workers to take "ownership" of their behavior and outputs When management desires a strong form of worker-based control
SELF-CONTROL	When workers are intrinsically motivated to do their jobs well When it is difficult to create good measures of worker behavior When it is difficult to create good measures of worker output When workers have or are taught self-control and self-leadership skills

Sources: L. J. Kirsch, "The Management of Complex Tasks in Organizations: Controlling the Systems Development Process," Organization Science 7 (1996): 1–21; S. A. Snell, "Control Theory in Strategic Human Resource Management: The Mediating Effect of Administrative Information," Academy of Management Journal 35 (1992): 292–327.

Bureaucratic control is based on organizational policies, rules, and procedures. Objective controls are based on reliable measures of behavior or outputs. Normative control is based on strong corporate beliefs and careful hiring practices. Concertive control is based on the development of values, beliefs, and rules in autonomous work groups. Self-control is based on individuals' setting their own goals, monitoring themselves, and rewarding or punishing themselves with respect to goal achievement.

We end this section by noting that each of these control methods may be more or less appropriate depending on the circumstances. Examine Exhibit 6.4 to find out when each of these five control methods should be used.

4 What to Control?

In the second section of this chapter, we asked, "Is control necessary or possible?" In the third section we asked, "How should control be obtained?" In this fourth and final section, we ask the equally important question "What should managers control?" The way managers answer this question has critical implications for most businesses.

After reading this section, you should be able to explain 4.1 **the balanced scorecard approach to control and how companies can achieve balanced control of company performance by choosing to control** 4.2 **economic value added,** 4.3 **customer defections,** 4.4 **quality,** and 4.5 **waste and pollution.**

4.1 The Balanced Scorecard

balanced scorecard
measurement of organizational performance in four equally important areas: finances, customers, internal operations, and innovation and learning

In most companies, performance is measured using standard financial and accounting measures, such as return on capital, return on assets, return on investments, cash flow, net income, net margins, and so forth. The **balanced scorecard,** however, encourages managers to look beyond traditional financial measures to four different perspectives on company performance. How do customers see us (the customer perspective)? At what must we excel (the internal perspective)? Can we continue to improve and create value (the innovation and learning perspective)? How do we look to shareholders (the financial perspective)?[37]

The balanced scorecard has several advantages over traditional control processes that rely solely on financial measures. First, it forces managers at each level of the company to set specific goals and measure performance in each of the four areas. For example, Exhibit 6.5 shows that Southwest Airlines uses nine different measures in its balanced scorecard. Of those, only three, market value, seat revenue, and plane lease costs (at various rates of compounded annual growth, or CAGR), are standard financial measures of performance. But Southwest also measures its FAA (Federal Aviation Administration) on-time arrival rating and the cost of its airfares compared to competitors (customer perspective), how much time each plane spends on the ground after landing and the percentage of planes that depart on time (internal business perspective), and the percentage of its ground-crew workers, such as mechanics and luggage handlers, who own company stock and have received job training (learning perspective).

suboptimization
performance improvement in one part of an organization but only at the expense of decreased performance in another part

The second major advantage of the balanced scorecard approach to control is that it minimizes the chances of **suboptimization**, which occurs when performance improves in one area, but only at the expense of decreased performance in others. Jon Meliones, chief medical director at Duke's Children's

exhibit 6.5

Southwest Airlines' Balanced Scorecard

	OBJECTIVES	MEASURES	TARGETS	INITIATIVES
FINANCIAL	Profitability	Market Value	30% CAGR	
	Increased Revenue	Seat Revenue	20% CAGR	
	Lower Costs	Plane Lease Cost	5% CAGR	
CUSTOMER	On-Time Flights	FAA On-Time Arrival Rating	#1	Quality Management, Customer Loyalty Program
	Lowest Prices	Customer Ranking (Market Survey)	#1	
INTERNAL	Fast Ground Turnaround	Time on Ground	30 Minutes	Cycle Time Optimization Program
		On-Time Departure	90%	
LEARNING	Ground Crew Alignment with Company Goals	% Ground Crew Shareholders	Year 1: 70% Year 3: 90% Year 5: 100%	Employee Stock Option Plan
		% Ground Crew Trained		Ground Crew Training

Source: G. Anthes, "ROI Guide: Balanced Scorecard," Computer World, *[Online] available at http://www.computerworld.com/managementtopics/roi/story/0,10801,78512,00.html, 5 May 2003.*

Hospital stated, "We explained the [balanced scorecard] theory to clinicians and administrators like this. . . . if you sacrifice too much in one quadrant to satisfy another, your organization as a whole is thrown out of balance. We could, for example, cut costs to improve the financial quadrant by firing half the staff, but that would hurt quality of service, and the customer quadrant would fall out of balance. Or we could increase productivity in the internal business quadrant by assigning more patients to a nurse, but doing so would raise the likelihood of errors—an unacceptable trade-off."[38]

Let's examine some of the ways in which companies are controlling the four basic parts of the balanced scorecard: the financial perspective (budgets, cash flows, and economic value added), the customer perspective (customer defections), the internal perspective (total quality management), and the innovation and learning perspective (waste and pollution).

4.2 The Financial Perspective: Controlling Economic Value Added

The traditional approach to controlling financial performance focuses on accounting tools, such as cash flow analysis, balance sheets, income statements, financial ratios, and budgets. While no one would dispute the importance of these tools for determining the financial health of a business, accounting research also indicates that the complexity and sheer amount of information contained in these accounting tools can shut down the brain and glaze over the eyes of even the most experienced manager.[39] Sometimes, there's simply too much information to make sense of. The balanced scorecard simplifies things by focusing on one simple question when it comes to finances: How do we look to shareholders? One way to answer that question is through something called economic value added.

economic value added (EVA) the amount by which company profits (revenues minus expenses minus taxes) exceed the cost of capital in a given year

Conceptually, **economic value added (EVA)** is more than just profits. It is the amount by which profits exceed the cost of capital in a given year. It is based on the simple idea that it takes capital to run a business and that capital comes at a cost. While most people think of capital as cash, capital, once invested (i.e., spent), is more likely to be found in a business in the form of computers, manufacturing plants, employees, raw materials, and so forth. And just like the interest that a homeowner pays on a mortgage or that a college student pays on a student loan, there is a cost to that capital.

The most common costs of capital are the interest paid on long-term bank loans used to buy all those resources, the interest paid to bondholders (who lend organizations their money), and the dividends (cash payments) and growth in stock value that accrue to shareholders. EVA is positive when company profits (revenues minus expenses minus taxes) exceed the cost of capital in a given year. In other words, if a business is to truly grow, its revenues must be large enough to cover both short-term costs (annual expenses and taxes) and long-term costs (the cost of borrowing capital from bondholders and shareholders). When EVA calculations are positive, it means a company created economic value, or wealth. When EVA calculations are negative, it indicates that the company didn't make enough profit to cover the cost of capital from bondholders and shareholders, and so destroyed economic value or wealth by taking in more money than it returned.[40] If you're a bit confused, the late Roberto Goizueta, the former CEO of Coca-Cola, explained it this way: "You borrow money at a certain rate and invest it at a higher rate and pocket the difference. It is simple. It is the essence of banking."[41]

But why is EVA so important? First and most importantly, since it includes the cost of capital, it shows whether a business, division, department, profit center, or product is really paying for itself. The key is to make sure that managers and employees can see how their choices and behavior affect the company's EVA. For example, because of EVA training and information systems, factory workers at Herman Miller, a leading office furniture manufacturer, understand that using more efficient materials, such as less expensive wood-dust board instead of real wood sheeting, contributes an extra dollar of EVA from each desk the company makes.[42]

Second, because EVA can easily be determined for subsets of a company, such as divisions, regional offices, manufacturing plants, and sometimes even departments, it makes managers and workers at all levels pay much closer attention to their segment of the business. In other words, EVA motivates managers and workers to think like small business owners who must scramble to contain costs and generate enough business to meet their bills each month.

Finally, unlike many kinds of financial controls, EVA doesn't specify what should or should not be done to improve performance. Thus, it encourages managers and workers to be creative in looking for ways to improve EVA performance. For example, CSX Intermodal uses trains to transport cargo containers across the country to waiting trucks or ships. When CSX managers found that the company had an EVA of negative $70 million, they started making changes. CSX used to use four engines to pull a regularly scheduled train from New Orleans to Jacksonville at an average speed of 28 mph. However, the train usually arrived six to eight hours before it was to be unloaded. So managers made better use of their capital by using only three engines, which pulled the train at an average speed of 25 mph. The train still arrived three hours before it was scheduled to be unloaded, but with three rather than four engines, it used 25 percent less fuel.[43]

Exhibit 6.6 shows the top 10 companies in terms of EVA and market value added (MVA), as measured by the Stern Stewart Performance 1000 index. Remember that EVA is the amount by which profits exceed the cost of capital in a given year. So the more that EVA exceeds the total dollar cost of capital, the better a company has used investors' money that year. MVA is simply the cumulative EVA created by a company over time. Thus, MVA indicates how much value or wealth a company has created or destroyed in total during its existence. As indicated by the MVA figures in Exhibit 6.6, over time the top 10 companies have created considerable wealth, ranging from almost $120 billion at ExxonMobil to $339 billion at General Electric; thus, they have returned substantially more than they took in. Nevertheless, only 5 of the top 10 in MVA had positive EVAs in the most recent year, with Intel, IBM, American International Group, Pfizer, and ExxonMobil unable to cover their cost of capital.

4.3 The Customer Perspective: Controlling Customer Defections

The second aspect of organizational performance that the balanced scorecard helps managers monitor is customers. It does so by forcing managers to address the question, "How do customers see us?" Unfortunately, most companies try to answer this question through customer satisfaction surveys, but these are often misleadingly positive. Most customers are reluctant to talk about their problems because they don't know who to complain to or think that complaining will not do any good. Indeed, a study by the federal Office of

exhibit 6.6

Leading Companies by Market Value Added and Economic Value Added

MVA RANKING IN 2001	MVA RANKING IN 2002	COMPANY	MARKET VALUE ADDED ($ MILLIONS)	ECONOMIC VALUE ADDED/(LOST) ($ MILLIONS)
1	1	General Electric	$339,200	$8,285
2	3	Microsoft	325,872	2,099
3	4	Wal-Mart	221,166	2,194
4	9	Intel	169,980	(2,579)
5	7	Citigroup	155,695	2,623
6	19	IBM	146,496	(1,304)
7	15	Johnson & Johnson	138,006	2,549
8	6	American International Group	124,940	(606)
9	8	Pfizer	120,627	(3,814)
10	11	ExxonMobil	119,706	(246)

Source: R. Grizzetti, "U.S. Performance 1000," Stern Stewart & Co, [Online] available by request, http://www.sternstewart.com/index2.php, 7 May 2003.

Consumer Affairs found that 96 percent of unhappy customers never complain to anyone in the company.[44]

Another reason that customer satisfaction surveys can be misleading is that sometimes even very satisfied customers will leave to do business with competitors.

customer defections
a performance assessment in which companies identify which customers are leaving and measure the rate at which they are leaving

Rather than poring over customer satisfaction surveys from current customers, studies indicate that companies may do a better job of answering the question "How do customers see us?" by closely monitoring **customer defections**, that is, by identifying which customers are leaving the company and measuring the rate at which they are leaving. Unlike the results of customer satisfaction surveys, customer defections and retention do have a great effect on profits.

For example, very few managers realize that obtaining a new customer costs five times as much as keeping a current one. In fact, the cost of replacing old customers with new ones is so great that most companies could double their profits by increasing the rate of customer retention by just 5 to 10 percent per year.[45] And, if a company can keep a customer for life, the benefits are even larger. For Taco Bell, keeping a customer is worth $11,000 in lifetime sales. For a Cadillac dealer, the value is $332,000. For a grocery store, it can approach $200,000.[46] For an industrial manufacturer like Rolls-Royce, which manufactures IAE V2500 jet engines that cost over $2 million each, the lifetime value can approach tens of millions of dollars.

Beyond the clear benefits to the bottom line, the second reason to study customer defections is that customers who have left are much more likely than current customers to tell you what you are doing wrong. Perhaps the best way to tap into this source of good feedback is to have top-level managers from various departments talk directly to customers who have left. It's also worthwhile to have top managers talk to dissatisfied customers who are still with the company. Every day, John Chambers, CEO of Cisco Systems, listens to 15 to 20 voice mails that have been forwarded to him from dissatisfied Cisco customers. Chambers says, "Email would be more efficient, but I want to hear the emotion, I want to hear the frustration, I want to hear the caller's level of comfort with the strategy we're employing. I can't get that through email."[47]

Finally, companies that understand why customers leave can not only take steps to fix ongoing problems, but can also identify which customers are likely to leave and make changes to prevent them from leaving. For example, Citibank mails postcards to credit card holders when their credit card usage suddenly drops. The postcards say, "Call 1-800 . . . now and tell us why, and we'll make you an offer that will make your card even more valuable to you." When a customer pointed out that his Discover Card paid a cash back bonus, Citibank kept his business by offering him an identical cash back deal.[48]

4.4 The Internal Perspective: Controlling Quality

The third part of the balanced scorecard, the internal perspective, consists of the processes, decisions, and actions that managers and workers make within the organization. In contrast to the financial perspective of EVA and the outward-looking customer perspective, the internal perspective asks the question "At what must we excel?" For McDonald's, the answer would be quick, low-cost food. For America Online, the answer would be reliability—when your modem dials, the network should be up and running, and you should be able to connect without getting a busy signal. Yet no matter what area a company

value
customer perception that the product quality is excellent for the price offered

chooses, the key is to excel in that area. Consequently, the internal perspective of the balanced scorecard usually leads managers to a focus on quality.

Quality is typically defined and measured in three ways: excellence, value, and conformance to expectations.[49] When the company defines its quality goal as *excellence*, then managers must try to produce a product or service of unsurpassed performance and features. **Value** is the customer perception that the product quality is excellent for the price offered. At a higher price, for example, customers may perceive the product to be less of a value. When a company emphasizes value as its quality goal, managers must simultaneously control excellence, price, durability, or other features of a product or service that customers strongly associate with value. One company that has put value at the core of everything it does is Lands' End, the catalog company that sells quality clothing and accessories at reasonable prices. In its advertising, Lands' End says, "Value is more than price. Value is the combination of product quality, world class customer service, and a fair price."

When a company defines its quality goal as conformance to specifications, employees must base decisions and actions on whether services and products measure up to standard specifications. In contrast to excellence and value-based definitions of quality that can be somewhat ambiguous, measuring whether products and services are "in spec" is relatively easy. Furthermore, while conformance to specifications (i.e., precise tolerances for a part's weight or thickness) is usually associated with manufacturing, it can be used equally well to control quality in nonmanufacturing jobs. Exhibit 6.7 shows a quality checklist that a cook or restaurant owner would use to ensure quality when buying fresh fish.

The way in which a company defines quality affects the methods and measures that workers use to control quality. Accordingly, Exhibit 6.8 shows the advantages and disadvantages associated with the excellence, value, and conformance to specification definitions of quality.

exhibit 6.7

Conformance to Specifications Checklist for Buying Fresh Fish

QUALITY CHECKLIST FOR BUYING FRESH FISH		
FRESH WHOLE FISH	ACCEPTABLE	NOT ACCEPTABLE
Eyes	clear, bright, bulging, black pupils	dull, sunken, cloudy, gray pupils
Gills	bright red, free of slime, clear mucus	brown to grayish, thick, yellow mucus
Flesh	firm and elastic to touch, tight to the bone	soft and flabby, separating from the bone
Smell	inoffensive, slight ocean smell	ammonia, putrid smell
Skin	opalescent sheen, scales adhere tightly to skin	dull or faded color, scales missing or easily removed
Belly cavity	no viscera or blood visible, lining intact, no bone protruding	incomplete evisceration, cuts or protruding bones, off-odor

Source: "*A Closer Look: Buy It Fresh, Keep It Fresh,*" Consumer Reports Online, *[Online] available at http://www.seagrant.sunysb.edu/SeafoodTechnology/SeafoodMedia/CR02-2001/CR-SeafoodII020101.htm, 5 May 2003; Philipps, "Turn to Pros for Fish Buying Tips,"* Cincinnati Post, *2 September 2000, 3C; "How to Purchase: Buying Fish," AboutSeaFood Web site, [Online] available at http://www.aboutseafood.com/faqs/purchase1.html, 5 May 2003.*

exhibit 6.8

Advantages and Disadvantages of Different Measures of Quality

QUALITY AS EXCELLENCE	
ADVANTAGES	**DISADVANTAGES**
Promotes clear organizational vision.	Provides little practical guidance for managers.
Being/providing the "best" motivates and inspires managers and employees.	Excellence is ambiguous. What is it? Who defines it?
Appeals to customers, who "know excellence when they see it."	Difficult to measure and control.
QUALITY AS VALUE	
ADVANTAGES	**DISADVANTAGES**
Customers recognize differences in value.	Can be difficult to determine what factors influence whether a product/service is seen as having value.
Easier to measure and compare whether products/services differ in value.	Controlling the balance between excellence and cost (i.e., affordable excellence) can be difficult.
QUALITY AS CONFORMANCE TO SPECIFICATIONS	
ADVANTAGES	**DISADVANTAGES**
If specifications can be written, conformance to specifications is usually measurable.	Many products/services cannot be easily evaluated in terms of conformance to specifications.
Should lead to increased efficiency.	Promotes standardization, so may hurt performance when adapting to changes is more important.
Promotes consistency in quality.	May be less appropriate for services, which are dependent on a high degree of human contact.

Source: Republished with permission of Academy of Management, PO Box 3020, Briar Cliff Manor, NY, 10510-8020. C. A. Reeves & D. A. Bednar, "Defining Quality: Alternatives and Implications," Academy of Management Review *19 (1994): 419–445. Reproduced by permission of the publisher via Copyright Clearance Center, Inc.*

4.5 The Innovation and Learning Perspective: Controlling Waste and Pollution

The last part of the balance scorecard, the innovation and learning perspective, addresses the question "Can we continue to improve and create value?" Thus, the innovation and learning perspective is concerned with continuous improvement in ongoing products and services (discussed in Chapter 13) and relearning and redesigning the processes by which products and services are created (discussed in Chapter 9). Since these categories are discussed in more detail elsewhere in the text, this section reviews an increasingly important topic, waste and pollution minimization, which is affected by all three of these issues.

Exhibit 6.9 shows the four levels of waste minimization, from waste disposal, which produces the smallest minimization of waste, to waste prevention and reduction, which produces the greatest minimization.[50] The goals of the

exhibit 6.9

Four Levels of Waste Minimization

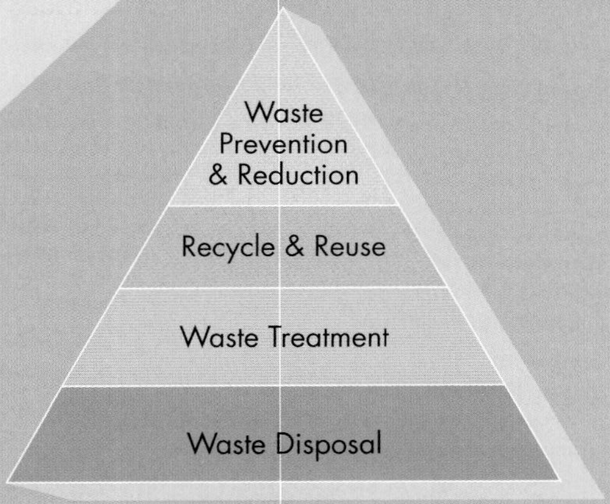

Source: D. R. May & B. L. Flannery, "Cutting Waste with Employee Involvement Teams," Business Horizons, *September-October 1995, 28–38. Reprinted with permission from* Business Horizons, *© 1995 by the Trustees at Indiana University, Kelley School of Business.*

top level, *waste prevention and reduction,* are to prevent waste and pollution before they occur, or to reduce them when they do occur. There are three strategies for waste prevention and reduction.

1. *Good housekeeping*—performing regularly scheduled preventive maintenance for offices, plants, and equipment. Quickly fixing leaky valves and making sure machines are running properly so they don't use more fuel than necessary are examples of good housekeeping.
2. *Material/product substitution*—replacing toxic or hazardous materials with less harmful materials.
3. *Process modification*—changing steps or procedures to eliminate or reduce waste.

At the second level of waste minimization, *recycle and reuse,* wastes are reduced by reusing materials as long as possible or by collecting materials for on- or off-site recycling. Sears recycles the 90 million clothes hangers used at its 860 stores each year. The hangers are collected and shipped to Sears' distribution centers where they are reused or processed for recycling. In a recent year, Sears also recycled 48,000 tons of corrugated cardboard, 1,000 tons of plastic bags and coverings, and 995,000 plastic ratchets. Over the last eight years, Sears has reduced waste by 60 percent. Now, 48 percent of its waste is recycled.[51]

At the third level of waste minimization, *waste treatment,* companies use biological, chemical, or other processes to turn potentially harmful waste into harmless compounds or useful by-products. For example, during "pickling," a process in the manufacture of steel sheets, the steel is bathed in an acid solution to clean impurities and oxides (that would rust) from its surface. Getting rid of the "pickle juice" has always been a problem. Not only is the juice an acid, but it also contains ferric chloride and other metals that prevent steel makers from dumping it into local water supplies. Fortunately, Magnetics International has found a safe, profitable way to treat the pickle juice. It sprays the juice into a 100-foot-high chamber at 1,200 degrees Fahrenheit. The iron chloride in the juice reacts with oxygen at that temperature to form pure iron oxide, which can be transformed into a useful magnetic powder. Inland Steel is now using this process to transform pickle juice into 25,000 tons of magnetic powder that can be reused in electric motors, stereo speakers, and refrigerator gaskets.[52]

The fourth and lowest level of waste minimization is *waste disposal.* Wastes that cannot be prevented, reduced, recycled, reused, or treated should be safely disposed of in processing plants or in environmentally secure landfills that prevent leakage and damage to soil and underground water supplies. Contrary to common belief, all businesses, not just manufacturing firms, have waste disposal problems. For example, Hewlett-Packard has started a unique computer disposal program that allows individual computer users to recycle PCs and electronic equipment. Prices range from $13 to $34 per item. The service is available at **http://www.hp.com/hpinfo/globalcitizenship/environment/recycle/index.html**. With three clicks and a credit card number, H-P will arrange to pick up the old PC equipment and properly dispose of it.[53] The company makes no profit from this service.

Waste disposal is becoming an increasingly important issue for many businesses, particularly computer manufacturers. At Hewlett-Packard's computer recycling operation, computer cases are sorted into bins for crushing after parts have been removed.

Review 4

What to Control?

Deciding what to control is just as important as deciding whether to control or how to control. In most companies, performance is measured using financial measures alone. However, the balanced scorecard encourages managers to measure and control company performance from four perspectives: financial, customers, internal operations, and innovation and learning. Traditionally, financial control has been achieved through cash flow analysis, balance sheets, income statements, financial ratios, and budgets. Another way to measure and control financial performance, however, is through economic value added (EVA). Unlike traditional financial measures, EVA helps managers assess whether they are performing well enough to pay the cost of the capital needed to run the business. Instead of using customer satisfaction surveys to measure performance, companies should pay attention to customer defectors, who are more likely to speak up about what the company is doing wrong. Performance of internal operations is often measured in terms of quality, which is defined in three ways: excellence, value, and conformance to expectations.[54] Minimization of waste has become an important part of innovation and learning in companies. The four levels of waste minimization are waste prevention and reduction, recycling and reuse, waste treatment, and waste disposal.

STUDY TIP The margin definitions of key terms can be a valuable study aid. Make a list of the terms and then write down the definition of each term on a separate piece of paper without consulting the margin definitions in the chapter. Cement your understanding by also writing an example if possible.

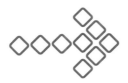

MANAGEMENT DECISION

PREVENTING PIRACY

Point, click, and pirate.[55] Software piracy, which includes the unauthorized copying, use, or distribution of software, costs the computer industry approximately $12 billion each year in lost licensing revenue. Software piracy is a problem in the United States (accounting for 27 percent of the worldwide total), but it appears to be worse in other parts of the world such as South America and Asia. According to a recent study by the Business Software Alliance (BSA), 60 percent of the computers operating in Mexico contain pirated software. Unfortunately, the numbers are just as dreary in China and elsewhere across the globe.

As the director of piracy for Microsoft, you feel that you are in a never-ending battle. To crack down on piracy in the United States, you and your staff have begun discussions aimed at coming up with solutions to the problem. Piracy occurs in both private homes and businesses, yet a recent study by the Software & Information Industry Association (SIIA) suggests that one-quarter of the piracy committed in the United States occurs in high-tech companies.

One factor leading to piracy among businesses today is expansion. Most businesses start out by purchasing legal copies of software. As they grow, however, and purchase additional computers, some businesses copy their existing software onto the new machines. Another common act of piracy involves "softloading," which occurs when a firm purchases one legal copy of software and installs it on the local area network (LAN). Once installed on the server, one copy can support hundreds of machines through a network connection.

Although the SIIA and the BSA conduct routine audits in large companies looking for violations, you and your staff want to step up efforts to identify companies engaging in piracy. Some of the computer manufacturers that you supply with software have notified you that recently the number of "naked" computer system orders has increased. A computer system is "naked" when it is ordered without any operating system software. Although a naked system might be ordered for several reasons (e.g., a company wants to use a competitor's operating software, such as Linux), you suspect that companies are beginning to pirate operating software in addition to application software. Not only does software piracy cost your company money through loss of revenue, but it is a violation of copyright law and therefore illegal.

Questions

1. What policies or plans could you implement that might help control or diminish piracy of your operating system software by U.S. businesses?
2. How vigorously will you pursue offenders once you identify them? Remember, there is a cost to control.

DEVELOP YOUR CAREER POTENTIAL

LEARNING FROM FAILURE

There is the greatest practical benefit of making a few failures early in life.

—T. H. Huxley

No one wants to fail.[56] Everyone wants to succeed. Nevertheless, some businesspeople believe that failure can have enormous value. At Microsoft, founder and CEO Bill Gates encourages his managers to hire people who have made mistakes in their jobs or careers. A Microsoft vice president said, "We look for somebody who learns, adapts, and is active in the process of learning from mistakes. We always ask, what was a major failure you had? What did you learn from it?" Another reason that failure is viewed positively is that it is often a sign of risk taking and experimentation, both of which are in short supply in many companies. John Kotter, a Harvard Business School professor says, "I can imagine a group of executives 20 years ago discussing a candidate for a top job and saying, 'This guy had a big failure when he was 32.' Everyone else would say, 'Yep, yep, that's a bad sign.' I can imagine that same group considering a candidate today and saying, 'What worries me about this guy is that he's never failed.'" Jack Matson, who teaches a class at the University of Michigan called Failure 101, says, "If you are doing something innovative, you are going to trip and fumble. So the more failing you do faster, the quicker you can get to success."

One of the most common mistakes that occurs after failure is the *attribution error*. An *attribution* is to assign blame or credit. When we succeed, we take credit for the success by owning up to our strategies, how we behaved, and how hard we worked. When we fail, however, we ignore our strategies, how we behaved, and how hard we worked (or didn't). Instead, when we fail, we assign the blame to other people, or to the circumstances, or to bad luck. In other words, the basic attribution error is that success is our fault but failure isn't. The disappointment we feel when we fail often prevents us from learning from our failures.

This means that attribution errors disrupt the control process. The three basic steps of control are to set goals and performance standards, to compare actual performance to performance standards, and to identify and correct performance deviations. When we put all of the blame on external forces rather than our own actions, we stop ourselves from identifying and correcting performance deviations.

Furthermore, by not learning from our mistakes, we make it even more likely that we will fail again.Your task in this exercise is to begin the process of learning from failure. This is not an easy thing to do. When *Fortune* magazine writer Patricia Sellers wrote an article called "So You Fail," she found most of the people she contacted reluctant to talk about their failures. She wrote,

> Compiling this story required months of pleading and letter writing to dozens of people who failed and came back. "If it weren't for the 'F' word, I'd talk," lamented one senior executive who got fired twice, reformed his know-it-all management style, and considered bragging about his current hot streak. Others cringed at hearing the word "failure" in the same breath as "your career."

Questions

1. Identify and describe a point in your life when you failed. Don't write about simple or silly mistakes. The difference between a failure and a mistake is how badly you felt afterwards. Years later, a real failure still makes you cringe when you think about it. What was the situation? What were your goals? And how did it turn out?

2. Describe your initial reaction to the failure. Were you shocked, surprised, angry, or depressed? Initially, who or what did you blame for the failure? Explain.

3. One purpose of control is to identify and correct performance deviations. With that in mind, describe three mistakes that you made that contributed to your failure. Now that you've had time to think about it, what would you have done differently to prevent these mistakes? Finally, summarize what you learned from your mistakes that will increase your chances of success the next time around.

BIZ FLIX Scent of a Woman

Young Charlie Simms (Chris O'Donnell) wants to earn extra money over Thanksgiving weekend so that he can afford the airfare to go home during Christmas break. He becomes a guide and caretaker for ill-tempered, retired Lt. Col. Frank Slade (Al Pacino) who is blind. Charlie, from Gresham, Oregon, is quiet and reserved and has had little experience with the opposite sex. He attends the exclusive Baird Preparatory School on a scholarship. His wild New York City weekend with Frank Slade bonds them forever. This film is a remake of *Profumo di Donna*, a 1974 Italian film.

This scene follows Slade's morose moments in their hotel suite after the first day and night in Manhattan. Slade wants to sleep in and perhaps even die. Charlie convinces him to venture out on this beautiful day and go for a ride. They go to a Ferrari dealership where Slade convinces salesman Freddie Bisco (Leonard Gaines) to allow a 17-year-old driver and a blind man to take the Ferrari Cabriolet T for a test drive. This scene appears in the last third of the film and defines the continued bonding of Frank Slade and Charlie Simms.

What to Watch for and Ask Yourself

1. What pattern of control do these scenes show?
2. What are the control system's elements?
3. Do these scenes show a periodic or a continuous type of performance measurement?

MGMT WORKPLACE Ping Golf, Karsten Manufacturing

Karsten Manufacturing is famous for producing Ping Golf clubs. From humble beginnings in his garage, founder Karsten Solheim built one of the most recognized manufacturing companies in the modern sports world. Ping has won its reputation by providing flawlessly customized sets of irons and woods to golfers of all skill levels. Technicians at the plant train retail sellers in fitting clubs, and Ping does all of its own mold making, steel working, and assembly. Precision and quality are built into each step of the production process and are not simply left to a final inspection. This attention to detail enables Ping to provide unparalleled customer satisfaction to clients with vastly different needs.

What to Watch for and Ask Yourself

1. Describe the control process at Ping.
2. Identify one way that Ping is using each element of the balanced scorecard.
3. Describe how Ping controls quality and minimizes customer defections.

Meeting the Competition

PART THREE

PHOTOS: © SUSAN VAN ETTEN; USED WITH PERMISSION OF INTER IKEA SYSTEMS B.V.; © JAMES GILL/THE CORNING-LEADER; © PRNEWSFOTO/WAGGENER EDSTROM

CHAPTER SEVEN

Global Management

outline

WHAT WOULD YOU DO?

Pret à Manger Headquarters, London, England.[1] You're the founder of *Pret à Manger*, which is French for "ready to eat," a London-based sandwich chain. Each *Pret à Manger* store, shining with stainless steel and typically no larger than a couple thousand square feet, features already prepared sandwiches, salads, and drinks displayed in open refrigerated coolers, a very small seating area with stools and two-person tables, and, typically, no line. Indeed, the average London customer walks in, grabs a sandwich, drink, fruit, and/or potato chips, pays, and leaves in just 90 seconds! *Pret à Manger* may be fast, but it doesn't offer "fast food." It specializes in healthy food, made fresh each morning with no additives and preservatives, and innovative sandwich offerings—a new item is added to the menu every four days. The company has been wildly successful in London over the last decade. The *London*

student resources

Experiencing Management
Explore the four levels of learning by doing the simulation module on International Management.

Study Guide
Mini lecture reviews all the learning points in the chapter and concludes with a case on Wipro.

Take Two Video
Biz Flix is a scene from *Mr. Baseball.* Management Workplace is a segment on Fallon Worldwide, a global advertising agency.

PowerPoint®
12 slides with graphics provide an outline for this chapter.

Author Insights
Chuck addresses issues of thinking locally when you go global.

Self Test
22 true/false questions, 25 multiple-choice questions, a management scenario, and 1 exhibit worksheet

Sunday Times named the company to its "Profit Track 100" list of the fastest-growing private firms in the United Kingdom, and *Fortune* magazine rated it as one of the top 10 employers in Europe.

You wonder if you could make a go of it in the States! Sure, London customers love the menu, but would fast-food-eating Americans love it, too? [Reading aloud from the menu], "Coronation Chicken Sandwich (chicken, tomato, lettuce, mango chutney, roasted almonds, and curry dressing). Do Americans even know what chutney is? I bet they don't." [Again, from the menu], "Avocado & Parmesan Sandwich (avocado, roasted pine nuts, parmesan, tomato, basil, lettuce). Well, I bet the vegetarians in the States would like that sandwich." [From the menu], "Cubano Sandwich (turkey, ham, bacon, Jarlsberg cheese, dill pickle, arugula, mustard dressing on sourdough bread). Jarlsberg cheese and arugula? Well, maybe in California." [Menu], "Asian Tuna Sandwich (tuna, cucumber, red pepper, spinach, ginger, wasabi mayo). Very few Americans know what 'wasabi' is! [Menu], "Chocolate Fudge Cake. Well, at least they'll like that!"

At this point, your company president, tired of listening to you read aloud from the menu, says, "Since World War II, America has given the world Burger King, KFC, McDonald's, and Pizza Hut. Nobody has ever gone to America, the home of fast food, with a concept that turned out to be a successful national chain."

But, if not America, where outside London and the United Kingdom could *Pret à Manger* locate its stores? Should you stick to Europe? After all, most international franchising seems to work better when you start with nearby markets. If so, does that mean Dublin, Paris, Belgium, or Amsterdam? Picking new locations in London was easy, but selecting new international locations will be a greater challenge. What's the right way to do it? Also, how should *Pret à Manger* go global? McDonald's does it with franchising, but with just 120 stores in the United Kingdom, why would anyone in the United States, Ireland, France, Belgium, the Netherlands, or anywhere else want to buy a *Pret à Manger* franchise? So far you have grown through wholly owned subsidiaries, meaning that the company owns all of the stores. But where would you get the cash for international expansion, and are you willing to bear all that risk on your own? Or should you look for a partner and consider a joint venture? But what would you have to give up in the way of control? Finally, it's taken more than a decade, but you've developed a formula that works incredibly well in London. It took you years to build relationships with the right suppliers to get the right cheese and the right seasonings. Will you be able to replicate that success abroad? Will you have to change the menu or how you prepare the food? Basically, will the things that made *Pret à Manger* a success in London make you a success elsewhere in the world? **If you were the founder of *Pret à Manger*, what would you do?**

British sandwich chain *Pret à Manger*'s struggle with international expansion is an example of the key issue in global business: How can you be sure that the way you run your business in one country is the right way to run that business in another? This chapter discusses how organizations make those decisions. We will start by examining global business in two ways: first, by exploring its impact on U.S. businesses, and then, by reviewing the basic rules and agreements that govern global trade. Next, we will examine how and when companies go global by examining the tradeoff between consistency and adaptation and by discussing how to organize a global company. Finally, we will look at how companies decide where to expand globally. Here, we will examine how to find the best business climate, how to adapt to cultural differences, and how to better prepare employees for international assignments.

What Is Global Business?

Business is the buying and selling of goods or services. Buying this textbook was a business transaction. So was selling your first car. So was getting paid for babysitting or for mowing lawns. **Global business** is the buying and selling of goods and services by people from different countries. The Timex watch on my wrist as I write this chapter was purchased at a Wal-Mart in Texas. But since it was made in the Philippines, I participated in global business when I wrote Wal-Mart a check. Wal-Mart, in turn, had already paid Timex, which had paid the company that employs the Filipino managers and workers who made my watch.

global business
the buying and selling of goods and services by people from different countries

Of course, there is more to global business than buying imported products at Wal-Mart. After reading the next two sections, you should be able to

1 describe the impact of global business on the United States.

2 discuss the trade rules and agreements that govern global trade.

1 Impact of Global Business

You are shopping at the local mall. Someone with a clipboard asks you to respond to this short questionnaire about global business. Mark your answers true or false. 1.1 "Foreigners" are buying up American companies at an astounding rate and now control a large part of our economy; 1.2 American companies are no longer competitive in the world market, especially in high-tech industries; and 1.3 if given a choice, Americans will buy American-made goods rather than foreign-made goods.

National polls show that nearly half of all Americans want to prevent foreign companies from buying U.S. companies that have developed new technologies. The polls also show that 62 percent of Americans want to protect U.S. companies from foreign competition and that more than 87 percent believe that countries, such as Japan, are ahead of the United States in exporting high-technology products. Of the respondents, 85 percent say they try to buy American-made products when they have a choice.[2] Overall, 58 to 68 percent believe that foreign trade has been bad for the U.S. economy "because cheap imports have cost wages and jobs here."[3] More specifically, when asked, "Do you think trade agreements with low-wage countries such as China and Mexico lead to higher or lower wages for Americans?" 19 percent said "higher wages," while 68 percent said "lower wages." Pollster David

Iannelli said of these results, "Americans continue to think locally as their economy expands globally. A continued us-vs.-them outlook would help explain why . . . Americans see the international economy as a threat rather than an opportunity."[4]

So, if you responded like most Americans, you probably answered "true" to each question. Yet none of the statements in our short questionnaire accurately describes the influence of global business on the United States. Let's see why.

1.1 "Foreigners" Are Buying up American Companies at an Astounding Rate and Now Control a Large Part of Our Economy

direct foreign investment
a method of investment in which a company builds a new business or buys an existing business in a foreign country

Direct foreign investment is a method of investment in which a company builds a new business or buys an existing business in a foreign country. German automaker Daimler Benz made a direct foreign investment when it purchased U.S.-based Chrysler Corporation for $38.6 billion, as did U.S.-based Procter & Gamble when it paid $4.8 billion for German hair care company Wella AG.[5]

Polls show that 64 percent of Americans believe that Asian countries engage in unfair trading practices. Moreover, 47 percent of Americans believe that European countries engage in unfair practices, too. And with large foreign companies buying American companies, such as Sony's (Japan) purchase of Columbia and Tri-Star Studios (movies) and Bertelsmann AG's (Germany) purchase of two well-known American book publishers, Bantam Doubleday and Random House, it's not surprising that newspapers periodically run stories proclaiming that the "Japanese and Germans Are Buying America."[6]

In reality, though, the headlines should read, "Foreign Invasion: The World Buys America," because companies from many other countries also own businesses in the United States. As Exhibit 7.1 shows, companies from the United Kingdom, Germany, France, the Netherlands, and Canada have the largest direct foreign investment in the United States. And Japanese companies, which popular opinion typically puts at the top of this list, rank just seventh.

exhibit 7.1

Average Direct Foreign Investment in the United States, 1994–2002

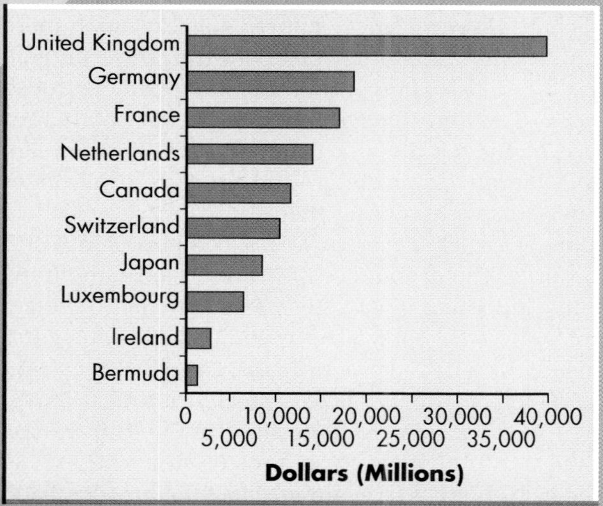

Source: International Investment Data, Bureauof Economic Analysis, [Online] available at http://www.bea.doc.gov/bea/di/di1fdibal.htm, 8 May 2003.

At the same time, direct foreign investment in the United States is just half the picture. U.S. companies also have made large direct foreign investments in countries throughout the world. As Exhibit 7.2 shows, U.S. companies have made their largest direct foreign investments in the United Kingdom, Canada, the Netherlands, Mexico, Switzerland, Japan, and Brazil. These figures clearly show that Americans have misplaced fears about direct foreign investment. Perhaps the newspaper headlines should also read, "Yankee Invasion: U.S.A. Buys the World."

Overall, direct foreign investment throughout the world is now worth $1 trillion a year![7] In fact, over the last 20 years, direct foreign investment involving the purchase or operation of businesses in another country, like Bertelsmann's buying Random House, has increased by 42 percent per year.[8] So whether foreign companies invest in the United States or U.S. companies invest abroad, direct foreign investment

exhibit 7.2

Average U.S. Direct Foreign Investment Abroad, 1994–2002

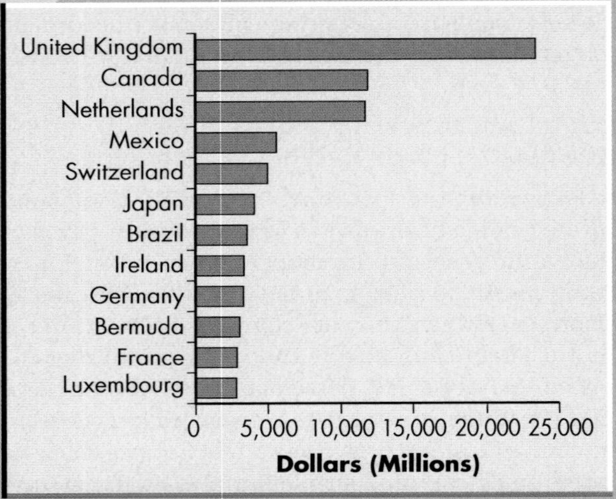

Source: International Accounts Data: U.S. Direct Investment Abroad, Bureau of Economic Analysis, [Online] available at http://www.bea.doc.gov/ bea/di/di1usdbal.htm, 8 May 2003.

is an increasingly important and common method of conducting global business.

1.2 American Companies Are No Longer Competitive in the World Market, Especially in High-Tech Industries

Nearly 90 percent of Americans consider the competitiveness of U.S. companies to be a serious problem. Yet data from the National Science Board, indicate that U.S. companies lead Japan, Germany, France, the United Kingdom, China, and South Korea in global high-technology market share.[9] The United States has a 31 percent average share of the global high-technology market, compared to 22 percent for Japan, 7 percent for Germany, and 6 percent for China. In fact, U.S. companies are market leaders in four out of the seven global high-tech industries: aircraft, scientific instruments, computers and office equipment, and pharmaceuticals. Indeed, a National Science Foundation report concluded that "U.S. producers are leading suppliers of high-technology products to the global market."[10]

So why do most Americans believe the United States is falling behind the rest of the world? It may be because U.S. companies once dominated global markets. Immediately after World War II, U.S. companies accounted for 50 percent of the **world gross national product (GNP)**.[11] World GNP is the value of all the goods and services produced annually worldwide. While U.S. companies continued to dominate world trade through the early 1960s, today U.S. companies produce approximately 30 percent of the world's GNP.[12]

world gross national product (GNP)
the value of all the goods and services produced annually worldwide

To many Americans, the drop from 50 percent to 30 percent of world GNP is proof of U.S. industrial decline. However, these figures suggest much more about economics in the rest of the world than they do about the U.S. economy. After the war, U.S. companies faced little competition. Bombing had destroyed factories throughout Japan, Europe, and Russia. In contrast, not one manufacturing plant was destroyed in the continental United States. With foreign competitors having to rebuild, literally from the ground up, is it any wonder that U.S. companies dominated the world market then?

Today, in contrast to the postwar global economy, U.S. companies face stiff competition throughout the world. The economies of France, Germany, Italy, Japan, Russia, and the United Kingdom, which the war decimated, now account for the same portion of world GNP controlled by the United States after World War II. Together, these countries, along with the United States and Canada, are part of a group of eight countries called the G8 that meet annually to discuss economic and political issues. And, because of the tremendous growth of international business over the last 25 years, the financial side of the G8 has now been expanded to the G20, meaning that 20 countries send their finance ministers and central bank governors to discuss shared financial issues.[13]

Another sign of increased competition in world markets is the *number* of multinational corporations and the location of their headquarters. **Multina-**

multinational corporation
a corporation that owns businesses in two or more countries

tional corporations are corporations that own businesses in two or more countries. In 1970, more than half of the world's 7,000 multinational corporations were headquartered in just two countries: the United States and the United Kingdom. Today, there are 63,459 multinational corporations, more than nine times as many as in 1970, and only 3,387, or 5.3 percent, are based in the United States.[14] Today, 45,404 multinationals, or 71.5 percent, are based in other developed countries, (e.g., Germany, Italy, Canada, Japan); 12,518, or 19.7 percent, of multinationals are based in developing countries; and 2,150, or 3.4 percent, are based in central and eastern Europe. So, today, multinational companies can be found by the thousands all over the world!

1.3 If Given a Choice, Americans Will Buy American-Made Goods Rather Than Foreign-Made Goods

country of manufacture
the country where a product is made and assembled

country of origin
the home country for a company, where its headquarters is located

Americans say they prefer to "buy American," but if they do, why does the demand for imported products increase year after year?[15] There are a number of potential explanations.[16] One possibility is that consumers often don't know or pay attention to the **country of manufacture** when making purchases. Stop reading for a minute. Take your shoes off. Where were they made? What about the DVD player in your house, or your computer, or your backpack? Did you find out where these products were manufactured before you purchased them? Chances are, you didn't. Many consumers don't know or care about the country of manufacture.

A second explanation for rising imports is that consumers want to buy American and think they are, but, in fact, they are unknowingly buying imported products. For example, take your Uncle Fred, who bleeds red, white, and blue. That Chrysler minivan in his driveway—he bought it because he thought it was a good "American" car. However, Chrysler assembles most of its minivans in Canada. That Honda Accord Uncle Fred's been giving you a hard time about—it was made in Marysville, Ohio. Uncle Fred has confused the country of manufacture, where the product is made, with the **country of origin**, which is the company's home country. In fact, Chrysler, which is now DaimlerChrysler, is German-owned, so Uncle Fred is confused about Chrysler's country of origin, too. Although it is true that the United States imports products from around the world, the country of origin of some may surprise you. Many Japanese auto makers have manufacturing facilities in the United States, like Honda's Marysville, Ohio, plant and Toyota's Erlanger, Kentucky, plant. These are easy mistakes to make in today's global marketplace.

A third explanation for the continued increases in sales of imports is that consumers know that many products they purchase are imported, but they just don't care, especially if they're getting significantly better quality or much lower prices. For example, Cadillac was the top luxury automobile for six decades, but in the last five years, its sales have dropped behind those of four foreign luxury auto manufacturers, Lexus, BMW, Mercedes, and Acura.[17] The same holds true for everyday items like food. Mark Sneed, president of Phillips Foods, which imports blue crab from its Asian processing factories at one-third the cost of crab caught and processed in the United States, says, "I've never once had a customer ask me if we served domestic or imported crabs, just like they never ask if we have foreign shrimp."[18] Finally, Luis de Anda, who visits one of Wal-Mart's Sam's Wholesale Clubs in Mexico once a month to purchase diapers and toilet paper in bulk for his family and friends, says, "Why should I care where they're from? With the money I save, I take my family to the movies."[19]

Review 1

Impact of Global Business

Contrary to common opinion, foreigners don't "own" a disproportionate share of U.S. assets. American companies are competitive in world markets, and consumers are less concerned with patriotism than value. In the last two decades, direct foreign investment has grown by 42 percent per year, making world markets much more competitive than they used to be. Yet despite this competition, American companies (and German companies and Japanese companies and . . .) continue to expand to meet the demands of consumer-driven world markets.

2 Trade Barriers and Agreements

Although most consumers don't especially care where the products they buy come from, national governments have traditionally preferred that consumers buy domestically made products in hopes that such purchases would increase the number of domestic businesses and workers. Indeed, governments have done much more than hope that you will buy from domestic companies. Historically, governments have actively used **trade barriers** to make it much more difficult or expensive (or sometimes impossible) for consumers to buy or consume imported goods. For example, countries throughout the world restrict the number and kind of imported television shows and movies. The French government requires that 40 percent of all TV shows be French and that at least 60 percent be European. Likewise, the European Union places a 24 percent tax on tuna imported from the Philippines and Thailand.[20] And the U.S. government places a 93 percent duty on fireworks imported from China, effectively doubling their price.[21] By establishing these restrictions and taxes, the European Union, and the French and U.S. governments are engaging in **protectionism**, which is the use of trade barriers to protect local companies and their workers from foreign competition.

trade barriers
government-imposed regulations that increase the cost and restrict the number of imported goods

protectionism
a government's use of trade barriers to shield domestic companies and their workers from foreign competition

Governments have used two general kinds of trade barriers: tariff and nontariff barriers. A **tariff** is a direct tax on imported goods. Like the U.S. government's 93 percent duty on fireworks imported from China, tariffs increase the cost of imported goods relative to that of domestic goods. For example, the U.S. import tax on trucks is 25 percent. This means that U.S. buyers will pay $25,000 for a $20,000 imported truck, with the $5,000 tariff going to the U.S. government. **Nontariff barriers** are nontax methods of increasing the cost or reducing the volume of imported goods. There are five types of nontariff barriers: quotas, voluntary export restraints, government import standards, government subsidies, and customs valuation/classification. Because there are so many different kinds of nontariff barriers, they can be an even more potent method of shielding domestic industries from foreign competition.

tariff
a direct tax on imported goods

nontariff barriers
nontax methods of increasing the cost or reducing the volume of imported goods

Quotas are specific limits on the number or volume of imported products. For example, Russia has quotas on the number of tons of beef and chicken that can be imported each year. Once the beef (315,000 tons) and chicken (1.05 million tons) quotas are reached, any more imported beef or chicken will be taxed with an additional 60 to 80 percent surcharge.[22] **Voluntary export restraints** are similar to quotas because they limit how much of a product can be imported annually. The difference is that the exporting country rather than the importing country imposes the limit. However, the "voluntary" offer to limit imports usually occurs because of the implicit threat of forced trade quotas by the importing country.

quota
a limit on the number or volume of imported products

voluntary export restraints
voluntarily imposed limits on the number or volume of products exported to a particular country

government import standard
a standard specified to protect the health and safety of citizens

In theory, **government import standards** are established to protect the health and safety of citizens. In reality, government import standards are often used to restrict or ban imported goods. For example, Japan has banned the importation of nearly all U.S. apples, which are one-third the cost of Japanese apples. Ostensibly, the ban is to prevent transmission of fire blight bacteria to Japanese apple orchards, but research conducted *jointly* by U.S. and Japanese scientists "does not support Japan's assertion that mature, symptomless apples can transmit" the fire blight bacteria.[23] In other words, the Japanese government is actually using this government import standard to protect the economic health of its apple farmers, rather than the biological health of its apple orchards.

subsidies
government loans, grants, and tax deferments given to domestic companies to protect them from foreign competition

Many nations also use **subsidies**, such as long-term, low-interest loans, cash grants, and tax deferments, to develop and protect companies in special industries. European and Japanese governments have invested billions of dollars to develop airplane manufacturers and steel companies, while the U.S. government has provided subsidies for manufacturers of computer chips. Not surprisingly, businesses complain about unfair trade practices when other companies receive government subsidies.

customs classification
a classification assigned by government officials that affects the size of a tariff and the imposition of import quotas

The last nontariff barrier is **customs classification**. As products are imported into a country, they are examined by customs agents, who must decide into which of nearly 9,000 categories they should classify a product. Classification is important because the category assigned by customs agents can greatly affect the size of the tariff and whether the item is subject to import quotas. For example, tariffs on imported leather or "nonrubber" shoes are about 8.5 percent, whereas tariffs on imported rubber shoes, such as athletic footwear or waterproof shoes, range from 20 to 67 percent.[24]

General Agreement on Tariffs and Trade (GATT)
a worldwide trade agreement that reduced and eliminated tariffs, limited government subsidies, and established protections for intellectual property

World Trade Organization (WTO)
the only international organization dealing with the global rules of trade between nations. Its main function is to ensure that trade flows as smoothly, predictably, and freely as possible

Thanks to the trade barriers described above, buying imported goods has often been much more expensive and difficult than buying domestic goods. During the 1990s, however, the regulations governing global trade were transformed. The most significant change was that 124 countries agreed to adopt the **General Agreement on Tariffs and Trade (GATT)**. Although GATT itself was replaced by the **World Trade Organization (WTO)** in 1995, the changes that it made continue to encourage international trade, for example, through tremendous decreases in tariff and nontariff barriers. GATT also put stricter limits on government subsidies and established protections for intellectual property, such as trademarks, patents, and copyrights. Finally, trade disputes between countries now are fully settled by arbitration panels from the WTO. In the past, countries could ignore arbitration panel rulings by using their veto power to cancel the decisions. Now, however, countries that are members of the WTO (every country that agreed to GATT is a member) no longer have veto power, and WTO rulings are complete and final. (For more information about GATT and the WTO, go to the WTO's Web site at **http://www.wto.org**.) Exhibit 7.3 provides a brief overview of the WTO and its functions.

regional trading zones
areas in which tariff and nontariff barriers on trade between countries are reduced or eliminated

The second major development that has reduced trade barriers has been the creation of **regional trading zones**, in which tariff and nontariff barriers are reduced or eliminated for countries within the trading zone. The largest and most important trading zones are in Europe (the Maastricht Treaty), North America (the North American Free Trade Agreement, or NAFTA), South America (the Free Trade Area of the Americas, or FTAA), and Asia (Association of Southeast Asian Nations, or ASEAN, and Asia-Pacific Economic Cooperation, or APEC). Effective Management Online contains a map that shows the extent to which free trade agreements govern global trade **(http://www.em-online.swlearning.com)**.

exhibit 7.3

World Trade Organization

FACT FILE

WORLD TRADE ORGANIZATION

Location: Geneva, Switzerland
Established: 1 January 1995
Created by: Uruguay Round negotiations (1986-94)
Membership: 146 countries (as of 4 April 2003)
Budget: 154 million Swiss francs for 2003
Secretariat staff: 550
Head: Supachai Panitchpakdi (director-general)

Functions:

- Administering WTO trade agreements
- Forum for trade negotiations
- Handling trade disputes
- Monitoring national trade policies
- Technical assistance and training for developing countries
- Cooperation with other international organizations

Source: "WTO: About the Organization," World Trade Organization, [Online] available at http://www.wto.org/english/thewto_e/thewto_e.htm, 25 September 2003.

The Maastricht Treaty of Europe transformed 12 different economies and currencies into one common economic market, called the European Union (EU), with one common currency. It also eliminated tariffs and simplified business transactions by implementing a single set of standards across Europe. (For more information about the Maastricht Treaty and the EU, go to **http://europa.eu.int/index-en.htm**. For more about Europe's common currency, the euro, see **http://www.euro.ecb.int/en.html**.)

More than any other regional trade agreement, NAFTA, the North American Free Trade Agreement, liberalizes trade between countries so that businesses can plan for one market (North America) rather than for three separate markets (the United States, Canada, and Mexico). One of NAFTA's most important achievements was to eliminate most product tariffs *and* prevent its members from increasing existing tariffs or introducing new ones. (For more information about NAFTA, see the Office of NAFTA & Inter-American Affairs at **http://www.mac.doc.gov/nafta/**.) The goal of the proposed FTAA, the Free Trade Area of the Americas, is to establish a free trade zone similar to NAFTA throughout the Western Hemisphere. If created, the FTAA would then become the largest trading zone in the world, consisting of 800 million people in 34 countries in both North and South America with a combined gross domestic product of $11 trillion![25] Leaders from each of the 34 countries have agreed to finish the FTAA negotiations by 2005. (For more information about the FTAA, see **http://www.ftaa-alca.org**. For

www.experiencing management.com

You may learn more about international trade agreements and their provisions by visiting our animated concept and activity site. Choose International_Management from the "select a topic" pull-down menu, then International Trade Agreements from the "overview tab."

http://www.experiencingmanagement.com

information about Mercosur, a South American free trade zone, see **http://www.sice.oas.org/trade/mrcsr/mrcsroc.asp**.)

ASEAN, the Association of Southeast Asian Nations, and APEC, Asia-Pacific Economic Cooperation, are the two largest and most important regional trading groups in Asia. ASEAN is a trade agreement between Brunei Darussalam, Cambodia, Indonesia, Laos, Malaysia, Myanmar, the Philippines, Singapore, Thailand, and Vietnam. Together, these countries form a market of more than 330 million people. U.S. trade with ASEAN countries is sizable, exceeding $75 billion a year.[26] (For more information about ASEAN, see **http://www.aseansec.org**.) APEC is a broader agreement between Australia, Canada, Chile, the People's Republic of China, Hong Kong (China), Japan, Korea, Mexico, New Zealand, Papua New Guinea, Peru, Russia, Taiwan, the United States and all the members of ASEAN, except Cambodia, Laos, and Myanmar.[27] APEC's 21 member countries contain 2.5 billion people, account for 47 percent of all global trade, and have a combined gross domestic product of over $19 trillion. (For more information about APEC, see **http://www.apecsec.org.sg**.)

Review 2

Trade Barriers

Tariffs and nontariff trade barriers, such as quotas, voluntary export restraints, government import standards, government subsidies, and customs classifications, have made buying foreign goods much harder or expensive than buying domestically produced products. In recent years, however, worldwide trade agreements, such as GATT, along with regional trading agreements, like the Maastricht Treaty of Europe, NAFTA, FTAA, ASEAN, and APEC, have substantially reduced tariff and nontariff barriers to international trade.

How to Go Global?

Once a company has decided that it *will* go global, it must decide *how* to go global. For example, if you decide to sell in Singapore, should you try to find a local business partner who speaks the language, knows the laws, and understands the customs and norms of Singapore's culture, or should you simply export your products from your home country? What do you do if you are also entering eastern Europe, perhaps starting in Hungary? Should you use the same approach in Hungary that you used in Singapore?

Although there is no magical formula to answer these questions, after reading the next two sections, you should be able to

3 explain why companies choose to standardize or adapt their business procedures.

4 explain the different ways that companies can organize to do business globally.

3 Consistency or Adaptation?

In this section, we return to a key issue: How can you be sure that the way you run your business in one country is the right way to run that business in another? In other words, how can you strike the right balance between global consistency and local adaptation?

DOING THE RIGHT THING

Fair and Safe Working Conditions in Foreign Factories

Requiring workers to work 15-hour days with no overtime pay, beating them for arriving late, requiring them to apply toxic materials with their bare hands—these are some of the workplace violations found in the overseas factories that make shoes, clothes, bicycles, and other goods for large American and multinational companies. The Fair Labor Association, which now inspects these factories and recommends the following workplace standards:

- Make sure there is no forced labor or child labor; no physical, sexual, psychological, or verbal abuse or harassment; and no discrimination.
- Provide a safe and healthy working environment to prevent accidents.
- Respect the right of employees to freedom of association and collective bargaining. Compensate employees fairly by paying the legally required minimum wage or the prevailing industry wage, whichever is higher.
- Provide legally required benefits. Employees should not be required to work more than 48 hours per week and 12 hours of overtime (for which they should receive additional pay), and they should have at least one day off per week.

Do the right thing. Investigate and monitor the working conditions of overseas factories where the goods sold by your company are made. Find another supplier if conditions are unjust.[29]

Global consistency means that when a multinational company has offices, manufacturing plants, and distribution facilities in different countries, it will use the same rules, guidelines, policies, and procedures to run those offices, plants, and facilities. Managers at company headquarters value global consistency because it simplifies decisions. In contrast, a company with a **local adaptation** policy modifies its standard operating procedures to adapt to differences in foreign customers, governments, and regulatory agencies. Local adaptation is typically more important to local managers who are charged with making the international business successful in their countries.

If companies lean too much toward global consistency, they run the risk of using management procedures poorly suited to particular countries' markets, cultures, and employees (i.e., a lack of local adaptation). For example, when Wal-Mart first entered Mexico, it focused too much on global consistency by filling its stores with ice skates, riding lawn mowers, fishing tackle, and clay pigeons for skeet shooting, items its American customers would want. After Mexican store managers managed to sell all of these items at heavy discounts, Wal-Mart's computerized inventory system compounded the mistake by automatically reordering all of these "sold-out" items.[28]

If companies focus too much on local adaptation, they run the risk of losing the cost efficiencies and productivity that result from using standardized rules and procedures throughout the world. Therefore, because of its vast purchasing power around the world, Wal-Mart hasn't given up completely on global consistency. In fact, the company has formed a new global sourcing team of 100 people who work together at its Bentonville, Arkansas headquarters to buy common global products like laundry detergent.[30] The risk, of course, is that the team may overlook local tastes and preferences (i.e., local adaptation). If these standard products are accepted by the locals at all of Wal-Mart's 4,000 stores around the world, however, they'll be much, much cheaper than anything Wal-Mart's competition has to offer.

global consistency
when a multinational company has offices, manufacturing plants, and distribution facilities in different countries and runs them all using the same rules, guidelines, policies, and procedures

local adaptation
when a multinational company modifies its rules, guidelines, policies, and procedures to adapt to differences in foreign customers, governments, and regulatory agencies

Review 3

Consistency or Adaptation?

Global business requires a balance between global consistency and local adaptation. Global consistency means using the same rules, guidelines, policies, and procedures in each location. Managers at company headquarters like global consistency because it simplifies decisions. Local adaptation means adapting standard procedures to differences in markets. Local managers prefer a policy of local adaptation because it gives them more control. Not all businesses need the same combinations of global consistency and local adaptation. Some thrive by emphasizing global consistency and ignoring local adaptation. Others succeed by ignoring global consistency and emphasizing local adaptation.

4 Forms for Global Business

Besides determining whether to adapt organizational policies and procedures, a company must also determine how to organize itself for successful entry into foreign markets. Historically, companies have generally followed the *phase model of globalization*, in which a company makes the transition from a domestic company to a global company in the following sequential phases: 4.1 **exporting,** 4.2 **cooperative contracts,** 4.3 **strategic alliances,** and 4.4 **wholly owned affiliates.** At each step, the company grows much larger, uses those resources to enter more global markets, is less dependent on home country sales, and is more committed in its orientation to global business. Evidence suggests, however, that some companies do not follow the phase model of globalization.[31] Some skip phases on their way to becoming more global and less domestic. Others don't follow the phase model at all. These are known as 4.5 **global new ventures.** This section reviews these forms of global business.[32]

> **www.experiencing management.com**
>
> Global business strategies and their advantages and disadvantages are graphically illustrated at our animated concept and activity site. Choose International_Management from the "select a topic" pull-down menu, then International Business Strategies from the "overview tab."
>
> **http://www.experiencingmanagement.com**

4.1 Exporting

When companies produce products in their home countries and sell those products to customers in foreign countries, they are **exporting**. Exporting as a form of global business offers many advantages. It makes the company less dependent on sales in its home market and provides a greater degree of control over research, design, and production decisions. For example, *Who Wants to Be a Millionaire?* is pretty much the same the world over. Details, such as construction of the set, the format of questions, the music, and the procedures for choosing contestants, are standardized via a 169-page guide. Consequently, there are only very small differences in the show across countries.[33]

exporting
selling domestically produced products to customers in foreign countries

Though advantageous in a number of ways, exporting also has its disadvantages. The primary disadvantage is that many exported goods are subject to tariff and nontariff barriers that can substantially increase their final cost to consumers. A second disadvantage is that transportation costs can significantly increase the price of an exported product. Another disadvantage of exporting is that companies that export depend on foreign importers for product distribution. This means that if, for example, the foreign importer makes a mistake on the paperwork that accompanies a shipment of imported goods, those goods can be returned to the foreign manufacturer at the manufacturer's expense.

4.2 Cooperative Contracts

When an organization decides to expand its business globally, but does not want to make a large financial commitment to do so, it will sign a **cooperative contract** with a foreign business owner, who pays the company a fee for the right to conduct that business in his or her country. There are two kinds of cooperative contracts: licensing and franchising.

cooperative contract
an agreement in which a foreign business owner pays a company a fee for the right to conduct that business in his or her country

licensing an agreement in which a domestic company, the licensor, receives royalty payments for allowing another company, the licensee, to produce its product, sell its service, or use its brand name in a specified foreign market

Under a **licensing** agreement, a domestic company, the *licensor*, receives royalty payments for allowing another company, the *licensee*, to produce its product, sell its service, or use its brand name in a particular foreign market. For example, brands such as Peter Paul Mounds and Almond Joy, which consumers associate with American companies, are not really American products. British company Cadbury Schweppes licenses Peter Paul Mounds and Almond Joy candy bars to Hershey Foods for U.S. production.

One of the most important advantages of licensing is that it allows companies to earn additional profits without investing more money. As foreign sales increase, the royalties paid to the licensor by the foreign licensee increase. Moreover, the licensee, not the licensor, invests in production equipment and facilities to produce the licensed product. Licensing also helps companies avoid tariff and nontariff barriers. Since the licensee manufactures the product within the foreign country, tariff and nontariff barriers don't apply. For example, Britvic Corona is licensed to bottle and distribute Pepsi-Cola within the United Kingdom. Because it bottles Pepsi in Britain, tariff and nontariff barriers do not affect the price or supply of these products.

The biggest disadvantage associated with licensing is that the licensor gives up control over the quality of the product or service sold by the foreign licensee. Unless there are specific restrictions in the licensing agreement, the licensee controls the entire business, from production, to marketing, to final sales. Many licensors include inspection clauses in their license contracts, but closely monitoring product or service quality from thousands of miles away can be difficult. An additional disadvantage is that licensees can eventually become competitors, especially when a licensing agreement includes access to important technology or proprietary business knowledge.

franchise a collection of networked firms in which the manufacturer or marketer of a product or service, the franchisor, licenses the entire business to another person or organization, the franchisee

A **franchise** is a collection of networked firms in which the manufacturer or marketer of a product or service, the *franchisor*, licenses the entire business to another person or organization, the *franchisee*. For the price of an initial franchise fee plus royalties, franchisors provide franchisees with training, help with marketing and advertising, and an exclusive right to conduct business in a particular location. Most franchise fees run between $5,000 and $35,000. McDonald's, one of the largest franchisors in the world, requires franchisees to pay an initial franchise fee of $45,000 and to invest $175,000 of their own money into a new McDonald's restaurant.[34] Since typical royalties range from 2 to 12.5 percent of gross sales, franchisors are well rewarded for the help they provide to franchisees.[35] More than 400 U.S. companies franchise their businesses to foreign franchise partners.

Overall, franchising is a fast way to enter foreign markets. Over the last 20 years, U.S. franchisors have more than doubled their global franchises for a total of more than 100,000 global franchise units! Because it gives the franchisor additional cash flows from franchisee fees and royalties, franchising can be a good strategy when a company's domestic sales have slowed. For example, fast-food franchisors are accepting very few new U.S. franchises because the U.S. market is saturated with fast-food outlets. Between Pizza Hut, Taco Bell, KFC, A&W Restaurants, and Long John Silvers, however, Yum! Brands opens nearly 1,000 new international franchise restaurants a year.[36]

Despite franchising's many advantages, franchisors face a loss of control when they sell businesses to franchisees who are thousands of miles away. Although there are exceptions, franchising success may be somewhat culture-bound. In other words, because most global franchisors begin by franchising their businesses in similar countries or regions (Canada is by far the first choice for American companies taking their first step into global franchising), and because 65 percent of franchisors make absolutely no change in their business for overseas franchisees, that success may not generalize to cultures with different lifestyles, values, preferences, and technological infrastructures.

4.3 Strategic Alliances

strategic alliance
an agreement in which companies combine key resources, costs, risk, technology, and people

joint venture
a strategic alliance in which two existing companies collaborate to form a third, independent company

Companies forming **strategic alliances** combine key resources, costs, risks, technology, and people. The most common strategic alliance is a **joint venture**, which occurs when two existing companies collaborate to form a third company. The two founding companies remain intact and unchanged, except that, together, they now own the newly created joint venture.

One of the oldest, most successful global joint ventures is Fuji-Xerox, which is a joint venture between Fuji Photo Film of Japan and Xerox Corporation, based in the United States, which makes copiers and automated office systems. More than 37 years after its creation, Fuji-Xerox employs nearly 15,000 employees and has close to $2.5 billion in revenues. Fuji-Xerox is largely responsible for copier sales in Asia, whereas Xerox is responsible for North American sales. Rank Xerox, a Xerox subsidiary, is responsible for sales in Europe.[37]

One of the advantages of global joint ventures is that, like licensing and franchising, they help companies avoid tariff and nontariff barriers to entry. Another advantage is that companies participating in a joint venture bear only part of the costs and the risks of that business. Many companies find this attractive because of the expense of entering foreign markets or developing new products. Global joint ventures can be especially advantageous to smaller local partners that link up with larger, more experienced foreign firms that can bring advanced management, resources, and business skills to the joint venture.

Global joint ventures are not without problems, though. Because companies share costs and risk with their joint venture partners, they must also share profits. At one time, sharing of profits created some tension between Fuji Color Film, Xerox, and their joint venture Fuji-Xerox. In fact, Xerox has struggled for so long that business experts joke that Fuji-Xerox, which has been highly profitable, should purchase Xerox.[38] Managing global joint ventures can also be difficult because they represent a merging of four cultures: the country and organizational cultures of the first partner, and the country and the organizational cultures of the second partner. Because of these problems, companies forming global joint ventures should carefully develop detailed contracts that specify the obligations of each party. In other words, the joint venture contract specifies how much each company will invest, what its rights and responsibilities are, and what it is entitled to if the joint venture does not work out. These steps are important, because the rate of failure for global joint ventures is estimated to be as high as 33 to 50 percent.[39]

4.4 Wholly Owned Affiliates (Build or Buy)

wholly owned affiliates
foreign offices, facilities, and manufacturing plants that are 100 percent owned by the parent company

Approximately one-third of multinational companies enter foreign markets through wholly owned affiliates. Unlike licensing, franchising, or joint ventures, **wholly owned affiliates** are 100 percent owned by the parent company. For example, Honda Motors of America in Marysville, Ohio, is 100 percent owned by Honda Motors of Japan. Ford Motor of Germany in Cologne is 100 percent owned by the Ford Motor Company in Detroit, Michigan.

The primary advantage of wholly owned businesses is that the parent company receives all of the profits and has complete control over foreign facilities. The biggest disadvantage is the expense of building new operations or buying existing businesses. While the payoff can be enormous if wholly owned affiliates succeed, the losses can be immense if they fail because the parent company assumes all of the risk. For example, Toshiba Corporation of Japan exited the DRAM computer memory chip business by selling its wholly owned memory chip subsidiary in Manassas, Virginia, to Idaho-based Micron Technology for $250 million in cash and Micron stock valued at approximately $22.5 million. Toshiba had put nearly $1.5 billion into the business, though, so it suffered a huge loss of approximately $1.23 billion on its investment.[40]

4.5 Global New Ventures

Companies used to evolve slowly from small operations selling in their home markets to large businesses selling to foreign markets. Furthermore, as companies went global, they usually followed the phase model of globalization. Recently, however, three trends have combined to allow companies to skip the phase model when going global. First, quick, reliable air travel can transport people to nearly any point in the world within one day. Second, low-cost communication technologies, such as international email, teleconferencing, phone conferencing, and the Internet, make it easier to communicate with global customers, suppliers, managers, and employees. Third, there is now a critical mass of businesspeople with extensive personal experience in all aspects of global business.[41] This combination of developments has made it possible to start companies that are global from inception. With sales, employees, and financing in different countries, **global new ventures** are new companies founded with an active global strategy.[42]

global new ventures
new companies with sales, employees, and financing in different countries that are founded with an active global strategy

Although there are several different kinds of global new ventures, all share two common factors. First, the company founders successfully develop and communicate the company's global vision. Second, rather than going global one country at a time, new global ventures bring a product or service to market in several foreign markets at the same time. For example, Bitfone Corporation provides software that allows mobile phone companies to wirelessly update the operating system in a user's mobile phone. Providing automatic, wireless updates to customers' phones helps mobile phone providers reduce costs, improve reliability, decrease problems, and provide new phone services and capabilities as they become available. With mobile phone providers and hundreds of millions of mobile phones in use on every continent but Antarctica, California-based Bitfone, which will be able to sell its software anywhere mobile phones are used, was a global company from its inception.[43]

Review 4
Forms for Global Business

The phase model of globalization says that as companies move from a domestic to a global orientation, they use these organizational forms in sequence: exporting, cooperative contracts (licensing and franchising), strategic alliances, and wholly owned affiliates. Yet not all companies follow the phase model. For example, global new ventures are global from their inception.

Where to Go Global?

Deciding where to go global is just as important as deciding how your company will go global. After reading the next three sections, you should be able to

5 explain how to find a favorable business climate.

6 discuss the importance of identifying and adapting to cultural differences.

7 explain how to successfully prepare workers for international assignments.

5 Finding the Best Business Climate

When deciding where to go global, companies try to find countries or regions with promising business climates. An attractive global business climate 5.1 positions the company for easy access to growing markets, 5.2 is an effective but cost-efficient place to build an office or manufacturing site, and 5.3 minimizes the political risk to the company.

5.1 Growing Markets

The most important factor in an attractive business climate is access to a growing market. For example, no product is known and purchased by as many people throughout the world as Coca-Cola. Yet, even Coke, which is available in over 200 countries, still has tremendous potential for further global growth. Currently, the Coca-Cola Company gets about 80 percent of its sales from its 16 largest markets.[44] The remaining 20 percent is spread across the other 200 countries in which Coke does business. Coke's former CEO said, "We have really just begun reaching out to the 95 percent of the world's population that lives outside the U.S."[45]

purchasing power
a comparison of the relative cost of a standard set of goods and services in different countries

Two factors help companies determine the growth potential of foreign markets: purchasing power and foreign competitors. **Purchasing power** is measured by comparing the relative cost of a standard set of goods and services in different countries. A Coke costs $2.30 in Tokyo. Because a Coke costs only about $1.00 in the United States, the average American would have more purchasing power than the average Japanese. Purchasing power is surprisingly strong in countries like Mexico, India, and China, which have low average levels of income. This is because basic living expenses, such as food, shelter, and transportation, are very inexpensive in those countries, so consumers still have money to spend after paying for necessities.

Consequently, countries with high and growing levels of purchasing power are good choices for companies looking for attractive global markets. Coke has found that the per capita consumption of Coca-Cola, or how many Cokes a person drinks per year, rises directly with purchasing power. For example, in eastern Europe, as countries began to embrace capitalism after the fall of communism, per capita consumption of Coke increased from 20 to 31 Cokes in just two years, and, now, more than a decade later, it is at 46 Cokes per year.[46]

The second part of assessing the growth potential of global markets is analyzing the degree of global competition, which is determined by the number and quality of companies that already compete in a foreign market. Before investing in Europe, American theme park companies sent teams to scout older theme parks across Europe. These parks featured older facilities, tame rides, and more cultural shows. So, over the last decade, a half-dozen brand new, American-style theme parks—wild rides, fireworks, cotton candy, lively song-and-dance shows, and American food—were built across Europe, and another four are under construction.[47]

5.2 Choosing an Office/Manufacturing Location

Companies do not have to establish an office or manufacturing location in each country they enter. They can license, franchise, or export to foreign markets, or they can serve a larger region from one country. Thus, the criteria for choosing an office/manufacturing location are different from the criteria for entering a foreign market.

Rather than focusing on costs alone, companies should consider both qualitative and quantitative factors. Two key qualitative factors are work force quality and company strategy. Work force quality is important because it is often difficult to find workers with the specific skills, abilities, and experience that a company needs to run its business. Work force quality is one reason that many companies doing business in Europe locate their customer call centers in the Netherlands. Workers in the Netherlands are the most linguistically gifted in Europe, with 73 percent speaking two languages, 44 percent speaking three languages, and 12 percent speaking more than three. Of course, with employees who speak several languages, call centers located in the Netherlands can handle calls from more countries and generally employ 30 to 50 percent fewer employees than those located in other parts of Europe.[48]

A company's strategy is also important when choosing a location. For example, a company pursuing a low-cost strategy may need plentiful raw materials, low-cost transportation, and low-cost labor. A company pursuing a differentiation strategy (typically a higher-priced, better product or service) may need access to high-quality materials and a highly skilled and educated work force.

In addition, quantitative factors, such as the kind of facility being built, tariff and nontariff barriers, exchange rates, and transportation and labor costs, should also be considered when choosing an office/manufacturing location.

Exhibit 7.4 shows the cities identified by *Fortune* magazine as the world's top cities for global business. This information is a good starting point if your company is trying to decide where to put an international office or manufacturing plant.

5.3 Minimizing Political Risk

When managers think about political risk in global business, they envision burning factories and riots in the streets. Although political events such as these receive dramatic and extended coverage from the media, the political risks that most companies face usually are not covered as breaking stories on FoxNews and MSNBC. Nonetheless, the negative consequences of ordinary political risk can be just as devastating to companies that fail to identify and minimize that risk.[49]

When conducting global business, companies should attempt to identify two types of political risk: political uncertainty and policy uncertainty.[50] **Political uncertainty** is associated with the risk of major changes in political regimes that can result from war, revolution, death of political leaders, social unrest, or other influential events. **Policy uncertainty** refers to the risk asso-

political uncertainty
the risk of major changes in political regimes that can result from war, revolution, death of political leaders, social unrest, or other influential events

policy uncertainty
the risk associated with changes in laws and government policies that directly affect the way foreign companies conduct business

exhibit 7.4

World's Best Cities for Business

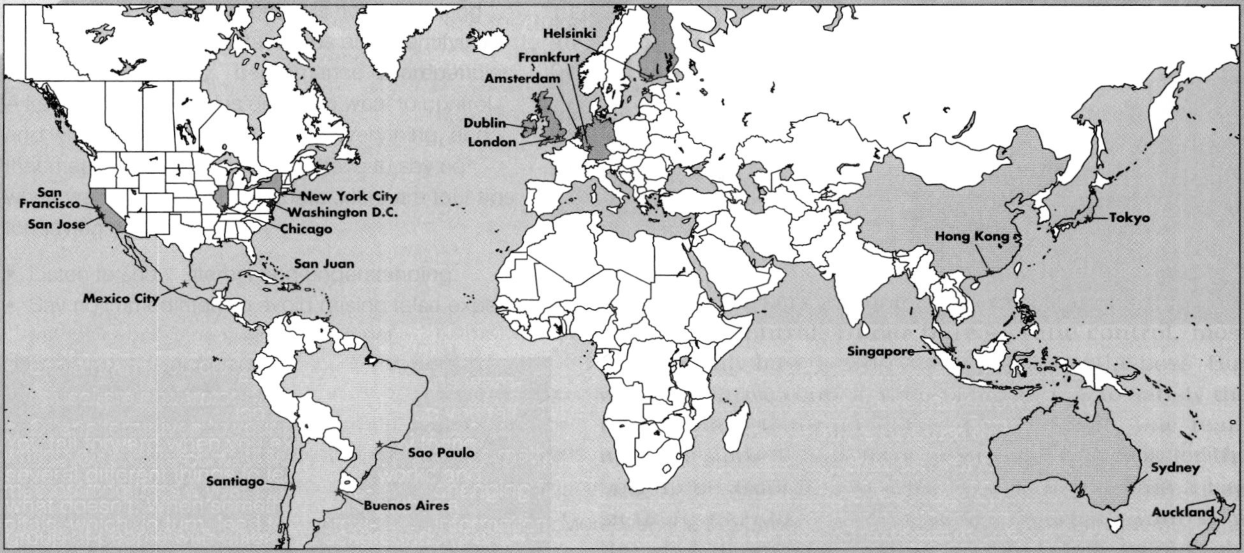

United States	Latin America	Europe	Asia Pacific
1. New York City	1. Buenos Aires	1. London	1. Hong Kong
2. San Francisco	2. San Juan	2. Frankfurt	2. Sydney
3. Chicago	3. Mexico City	3. Helsinki	3. Singapore
4. Washington D.C. area	4. Sao Paulo	4. Amsterdam	4. Auckland
5. San Jose	5. Santiago	5. Dublin	5. Tokyo

Source: M. Borden, "The Best Cities for Business: Big, Established, Monied Metropolises—With a Tech Twist—Top FORTUNE's Annual Ranking at the Turn of the Century," Fortune, *27 November 2000, 218; C. Murphy, "Winners of the World,"* Fortune, *27 November 2000, 232.*

ciated with changes in laws and government policies that directly affect the way foreign companies conduct business.

Policy uncertainty is the most common form of political risk in global business and perhaps the most frustrating. For example, most European countries have nationalized health care. So, instead of dealing with insurance providers and health maintenance organizations, pharmaceutical companies negotiate directly with European governments, which pressure them for price cuts. Reductions in prices in one European country can start a chain reaction leading to cuts in others, for example, if other countries in the European Union insist on the same low prices.[51]

Several strategies can be used to minimize or adapt to the political risk inherent to global business. An *avoidance strategy* is used when the political risks associated with a foreign country or region are viewed as too great. If firms are already invested in high-risk areas, they may divest or sell their businesses. If they have not yet invested, they will likely postpone their investment until the risk shrinks.

Control is an active strategy to prevent or reduce political risks. Firms using a control strategy lobby foreign governments or international trade agencies to change laws, regulations, or trade barriers that hurt their business in that country.

Another method for dealing with political risk is *cooperation*, which makes use of joint ventures and collaborative contracts, such as franchising and licensing. Although cooperation does not eliminate the political risk of doing business in a country, it does limit the risk associated with foreign ownership of a business. For example, a German company forming a joint venture with a Chinese company to do business in China may structure the joint venture contract so that the Chinese company owns 51 percent or more of the joint venture. Doing so qualifies the joint venture as a Chinese company and exempts it from Chinese laws that apply to foreign-owned businesses.

Review 5
Finding the Best Business Climate

The first step in deciding where to take your company global is finding an attractive business climate. Be sure to look for a growing market where consumers have strong purchasing power and foreign competitors are weak. When locating an office or manufacturing facility, consider both qualitative and quantitative factors. In assessing political risk, be sure to examine political uncertainty and policy uncertainty. If the location you choose has considerable political risk, you can avoid it, try to control the risk, or use a cooperation strategy.

6 Becoming Aware of Cultural Differences

Some of the more interesting and amusing aspects of global business are the unexpected confrontations that people have with cultural differences, "the way they do things over there." For example, American sensitivities about sexual issues are nothing compared to those in Iran's Islamic culture. All Iranian advertising must be approved by the Ministry of Islamic Guidance, whose job is to prevent anything of a sexual or Western nature from being displayed. For example, a billboard ad for women's underwear consisted of a picture of a green box with only the words "soft and delicate" written on it. Not surprisingly, no one knew what the ad was about. Despite approval by the Ministry of Islamic Guidance, billboards displaying giant red lips, which were used to advertise Goldstar televisions from South Korea, were burned down twice by Iranians who felt the ad was too sexual.[52]

national culture
the set of shared values and beliefs that affects the perceptions, decisions, and behavior of the people from a particular country

www.experiencing management.com

You may learn more about international cultures and their effect on managerial behavior by interacting with cultural concepts at our animated concept and activity site. Choose International_Management from the "select a topic" pull-down menu, then Cultural Differences from the "overview tab."

http://www.experiencingmanagement.com

National culture is the set of shared values and beliefs that affects the perceptions, decisions, and behavior of the people from a particular country. The first step in dealing with culture is to recognize that there are meaningful differences in national cultures. Geert Hofstede has spent the last 20 years studying cultural differences in 53 different countries. His research shows that there are five consistent cultural dimensions across countries: power distance, individualism, masculinity, uncertainty avoidance, and short-term versus long-term orientation.[53]

Power distance is the extent to which people in a country accept that power is distributed unequally in society and organizations. In countries where power distance is weak, such as Denmark and Sweden, employees don't like their organization or their boss to have power over them or tell

A veiled Muslim woman travels past a large billboard advertising a film that depicts the plight of a middle-class Cairo family as the parents try to come to terms with the pregnancy of their teenage daughter. The film captures the prevailing mood of contemporary urban Egypt struggling to balance tradition and modernity, religion and science.

them what to do. They want to have a say in decisions that affect them. *Individualism* is the degree to which societies believe that individuals should be self-sufficient. In individualistic societies, employees put loyalty to themselves first and loyalty to their company and work group second.

Masculinity and *femininity* capture the difference between highly assertive and highly nurturing cultures. Masculine cultures emphasize assertiveness, competition, material success, and achievement, whereas feminine cultures emphasize the importance of relationships, modesty, caring for the weak, and quality of life.

The cultural difference of *uncertainty avoidance* is the degree to which people in a country are uncomfortable with unstructured, ambiguous, unpredictable situations. In countries with strong uncertainty avoidance, like Greece and Portugal, people are aggressive, emotional, and seek security (rather than uncertainty).

Short-term/long-term orientation addresses whether cultures are oriented to the present and seek immediate gratification, or to the future and defer gratification. Not surprisingly, countries with short-term orientations are consumer driven, whereas countries with long-term orientations are savings driven.

Cultural differences affect perceptions, understanding, and behavior. Recognizing cultural differences is critical to succeeding in global business. Nevertheless, as Hofstede pointed out, descriptions of cultural differences are based on averages—the average level of uncertainty avoidance in Portugal, the average level of power distance in Argentina, and so forth. Accordingly, said Hofstede, "If you are going to spend time with a Japanese colleague, you shouldn't assume that overall cultural statements about Japanese society automatically apply to this person."[54]

After becoming aware of cultural differences, the second step is deciding how to adapt your company to those differences. Unfortunately, studies investigating the effects of cultural differences on management practice point more to difficulties than to easy solutions. One problem is that different cultures will probably perceive management policies and practices differently. For example, blue-collar workers in France and Argentina, all of whom performed the same factory jobs for the same multinational company, perceived its company-wide safety policy differently.[55] French workers perceived that safety wasn't very important to the company, but Argentine workers thought that it was. The fact that something as simple as a safety policy can be perceived differently across cultures shows just how difficult it can be to standardize management practices across different countries and cultures.

Review 6
Becoming Aware of Cultural Differences

National culture is the set of shared values and beliefs that affects the perceptions, decisions, and behavior of the people from a particular country. The first step in dealing with culture is to recognize meaningful differences, such as power distance, individualism, masculinity, uncertainty avoidance, and short-term/long-term orientation. Cultural differences should be carefully interpreted because they are based on averages, not individuals. Adapting managerial practices to cultural differences is difficult because policies and practices can be perceived differently in different cultures.

7 Preparing for an International Assignment

Around a conference table in a large U.S. office tower, three American executives sat with their new boss, Mr. Akiro Kusumoto, the newly appointed head of a Japanese firm's American subsidiary, and two of his Japanese lieutenants. The meeting was called to discuss ideas for reducing operating costs. Mr. Kusumoto began by outlining his company's aspiration for its long-term U.S. presence. He then turned to the budgetary matter. After gingerly discussing the alternatives for quite some time, a by then exasperated American blurted out: "Look, that idea is just not going to have much impact. Look at the numbers!" In the face of such bluntness, uncommon and unacceptable in Japan, Mr. Kusumoto fell silent and felt a deep longing to return east. He realized his life in this country would be filled with many such jarring encounters and lamented his posting to a land of such rudeness.[56]

expatriate
someone who lives and works outside his or her native country

Mr. Kusumoto is a Japanese **expatriate**, someone who lives and works outside his or her native country. The cultural shock that he was experiencing is common. The difficulty of adjusting to language, cultural, and social differences is the primary reason for expatriate failure in overseas assignments. For example, although there have recently been disagreements among researchers about these numbers, it is probably safe to say that 5 to 20 percent of American expatriates sent abroad by their companies will return to the United States before they have successfully completed assignments.[57] Of those who do complete their international assignments, about one-third are judged by their companies to be no better than marginally effective.[58]

Since the average cost of sending an employee on an international assignment can run between $500,000 and $3 million (depending on the length of the assignment and the employee's position), failure in those assignments can be extraordinarily expensive.[59] The chances for a successful international assignment can be increased through 7.1 language and cross-cultural training and 7.2 consideration of spouse, family, and dual-career issues.

7.1 Language and Cross-Cultural Training

Predeparture language and cross-cultural training can reduce the uncertainty that expatriates feel, the misunderstandings that take place between expatriates and natives, and the inappropriate behaviors that expatriates unknowingly commit when they travel to a foreign country. Indeed, simple things like using a phone, finding a public toilet, asking for directions, knowing how much things cost, exchanging greetings, or understanding what people want can become tremendously complex when expatriates don't know a foreign language or a country's customs and cultures. In his book *Blunders in International Business*, David Ricks tells the story of an American manager working in the South Pacific who, by hiring too many local workers from one native group, unknowingly upset the balance of power in the island's traditional status system. The islanders met on their own and quickly worked out a solution to the problem. After concluding their meeting at 3 A.M., they calmly went to his home to discuss their solution with him (time was not important in their culture). But, since the American didn't speak their language and didn't understand why they had shown up en masse outside his home at 3 A.M., he called in the Marines, who were stationed nearby, to disperse what he thought was a "riot."

Expatriates who receive predeparture language and cross-cultural training make faster adjustments to foreign cultures and perform better on their international assignments.[60] Unfortunately, only a third of the managers who go on international assignments receive any kind of predeparture training. This is somewhat surprising given the failure rates for expatriates and the high cost of those failures. It is also surprising because, with the exception of some language courses, predeparture training is not particularly expensive or difficult to provide. For example, a U.S. electronics manufacturer prepared workers for assignments in South Korea by using a combination of documentary training, cultural simulations, and field experiences. *Documentary training* focuses on identifying specific critical differences between cultures. Trainees learned that whereas U.S. subordinates normally look their boss in the eye, Korean subordinates avoid eye contact unless their boss asks them a question. Trainees also learned about other South Korean customs, such as how to greet businesspeople, how to behave toward South Korean women or elders, and how to respect privacy.

After learning specific critical differences through documentary training, the trainees participated in a *cultural simulation,* in which they practiced adapting to cultural differences. For example, the trainees engaged in a simulated cocktail party where company managers who had spent time in South Korea posed as South Korean businesspeople and their spouses. Trainees practiced South Korean greetings, introductions, and communication styles, and then received feedback on their performance.

Field simulation training, a technique made popular by the U.S. Peace Corps, places trainees in an ethnic neighborhood for three to four hours to talk to residents about cultural differences. In this instance, trainees explored a nearby South Korean neighborhood, talking to shopkeepers and people on the street about South Korean politics, family orientation, and day-to-day living practices.

PERSONAL PRODUCTIVITY TIP

Money and International Travel

Credit cards, such as Visa, MasterCard, and American Express, are accepted worldwide and offer the best exchange rates. Traveler's checks are replaceable if lost or stolen. Carry enough local currency to pay for food, transportation, and lodging your first day in a country. If you need more, you can exchange local currency at hotels, post offices, or for-profit currency exchange stores. These facilities charge 2 to 10 percent exchange fees, however, so many travelers now use automatic teller machines to withdraw cash directly from their personal bank accounts. ATMs are widely available (see the ATM locator at **http://visa.com** or **http://www.mastercard.com/cardholderservices/atm/** for the Cirrus network), and they offer exchange rates as good as credit cards.

7.2 Spouse, Family, and Dual-Career Issues

The evidence clearly shows that how well an expatriate's spouse and family adjust to the foreign culture is the most important factor in determining the success or failure of an international assignment.[61] Unfortunately, despite its importance, there has been little systematic research on what does and does not help expatriates' families successfully adapt. A number of companies, however, have found that adaptability screening and intercultural training for families can lead to more successful overseas adjustment.

WHAT REALLY WORKS

CROSS-CULTURAL TRAINING

Most expatriates will tell you that cross-cultural training helped them adjust to foreign cultures. Such anecdotal data, however, are not as convincing as systematic studies. Twenty-one studies, with a combined total of 1,611 participants, have examined whether cross-cultural training affects the self-development, perceptions, relationships, adjustment, and job performance of expatriates. Overall, they show that cross-cultural training works extremely well in most instances.

Self-Development

When you first arrive in another country, you must learn how to make decisions that you took for granted in your home country: how to get to work, how to get to the grocery, how to pay your bills, and so on. If you've generally been confident about yourself and your abilities, an overseas assignment can challenge that sense of self. However, cross-cultural training helps expatriates deal with these and other challenges. Expatriates who receive cross-cultural training are 79 percent more likely to report healthy psychological well-being and self-development than those who don't receive training.

Psychological Well-Being & Self Development

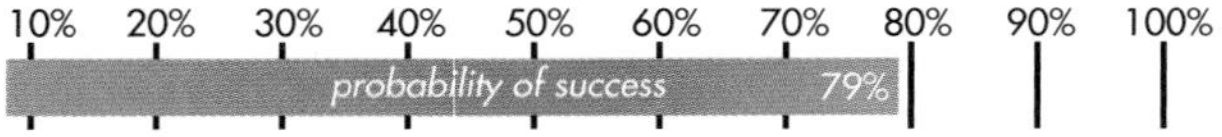

Fostering Relationships

One of the most important aspects of an overseas assignment is establishing and maintaining relationships with host nationals. If you're in Brazil, you need to make friends with Brazilians. Many expatriates, however, make the mistake of making friends only with other expatriates from their home country. In effect, they become social isolates in a foreign country. They work and live there, but as much as they can, they speak their native language, eat their native foods, and socialize with other expatriates from their home country. Cross-cultural training makes a big difference in whether expatriates establish relationships with host nationals. Expatriates who receive cross-cultural training are 74 percent more likely to establish such relationships.

Fostering Relationships with Native Citizens

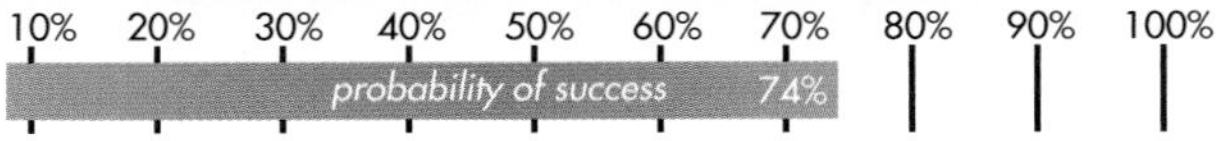

Accurate Perceptions of Culture

Another characteristic of successful expatriates is that they understand the cultural norms and practices of the host country. For example, many Americans do not understand the famous pictures of Japanese troops turning their backs to American military commanders on V-J Day, when Japan surrendered to the United States at the end of World War II. Americans viewed this as a lack of respect, when, in fact, in Japan turning one's back in this way is a sign of respect. Cross-cultural training makes a big difference in the accuracy of perceptions concerning host country norms and practices. Expatriates who receive cross-cultural training are 74 percent more likely to have accurate perceptions.

Accurate Cultural Perceptions

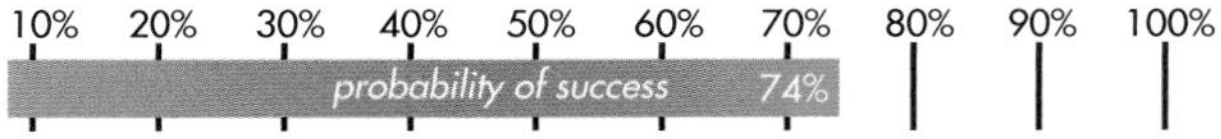

Rapid Adjustment

New employees are most likely to quit in the first six months because this initial period requires the most adjustment: learning new names, new faces, new procedures, and new information. It's tough. Of course, expatriates have a much harder time making a successful adjustment because besides learning new names, faces, procedures, and information, expatriates are learning new languages, new foods, new customs, and often new lifestyles. Expatriates who receive cross-cultural training are 74 percent more likely to make a rapid adjustment to a foreign country.

Rapid Adjustment to Foreign Cultures and Countries

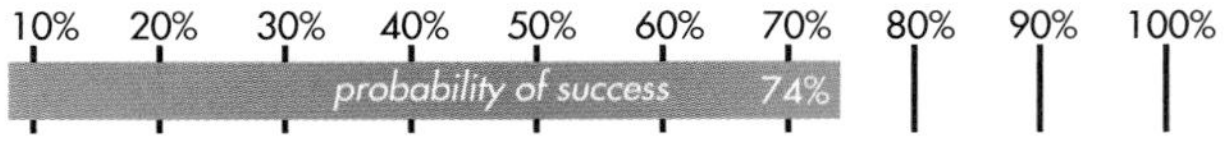

Job Performance

It's good that cross-cultural training improves self-development, fosters relationships, improves the accuracy of perceptions, and helps expatriates make rapid adjustments to foreign cultures. From an organizational standpoint, however, the ultimate test of cross-cultural training is whether it improves expatriates' job performance. The evidence shows that cross-cultural training makes a significant difference in expatriates' job performance, although the difference is not quite as big as for the other factors. Nonetheless, it is estimated that cross-cultural training for 100 managers could bring about $390,000 worth of benefits to a company, or nearly $4,000 per manager. This is an outstanding return on investment, especially when you consider the high rate of failure for expatriates. Expatriates who have received cross-cultural training are 71 percent more likely to have better on-the-job performance than those who did not receive cross-cultural training.[62]

On-the-Job Performance

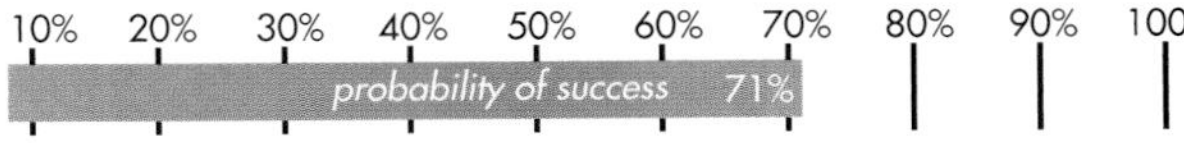

Adaptability screening is used to assess how well managers and their families are likely to adjust to foreign cultures. AMP, based in Pennsylvania, conducts extensive psychological screening on expatriates and their spouses when making international assignments. But adaptability screening does not just involve a company assessing an employee; it can also involve an employee screening international assignments for desirability. Since more employees are becoming aware of the costs of international assignments (spouses having to give up or change jobs, children having to change schools, having to learn a new language, etc.), some companies are willing to pay for a preassignment trip to enable the employee and his or her spouse to investigate the country *before* accepting the international assignment.[63]

Language and cross-cultural training is just as important for the families of expatriates as for expatriates themselves.[64] In fact, it may be more important because, unlike expatriates, whose professional jobs often shield them from the full force of a country's culture, spouses and children are fully immersed in foreign neighborhoods and schools. Households must be run, shopping must be done, and bills must be paid. Likewise, children and their parents must deal with different cultural beliefs and practices about discipline, alcohol, dating, and other issues. In addition to helping families prepare for the cultural differences they will encounter, language and cross-cultural training can help reduce uncertainty about how to act and decrease misunderstandings between expatriates, their families, and locals.

Review 7

Preparing for an International Assignment

Many expatriates return prematurely from international assignments because of poor performance. However, this is much less likely to happen if employees receive language and cross-cultural training, such as documentary training, cultural simulations, or field experiences, before going on assignment. Adjustment of expatriates' spouses and families, which is the most important determinant of success in international assignments, can be improved through adaptability screening and intercultural training.

STUDY TIP Review your class notes. Do they give you enough information? Do they give you the right information? If not, visit your campus study center to learn how to take good notes.

MANAGEMENT DECISION

ARE STARBUCKS' EXPANSION PLANS OVERCAFFEINATED?

With the seemingly ubiquitous green mermaid peeking out from around street corners across the United States, it's hard to believe that Starbucks had roughly 1,000 stores overseas before it had stores in all 50 states.[65] Although some analysts say the specialty coffee market is saturated, Starbucks thinks the company is still in the early stages of growth.

Whichever perspective you lean toward, the numbers are the same. With only 17 stores at the end of 1987, Starbucks now boasts over 7,200 stores, 15 percent of which opened in the last two years. Starbucks plans to reach 10,000 stores by 2005. International expansion is a big part of its plans: 1,257 stores are in foreign countries.

Starbucks opened its first overseas store in Toyko in 1996. Asia was chosen as the point of entry because the company decided that the European coffee market was extremely mature and wasn't going to change much over the years. The Asian market, on the other hand, was in a developmental stage. Starbucks had the opportunity to position itself as the leader of a new industry. And it did. Today, 968 of the company's 1,257 international retail outlets are in Asia.

The Pacific Rim, however, is not the only bean in the blend. Starbucks is also aggressively expanding in the Middle East, New Zealand, and Europe. The Brits have long succumbed to the charms of Starbucks, but continental Europe may be a tougher nut to crack. The first store opened there in Zurich in 2001, and new stores in Germany and Austria soon followed, with taste-sensitive Italy far down on the list. Most recently, Starbucks has entered Spain, Greece, and Mexico. The following table shows the operating regions for Starbucks international retail stores in 2003.

Still, some countries are worried and charges of cultural imperialism are being bandied about. A Chinese newspaper criticized Starbucks for operating a kiosk in Beijing's Forbidden City. The chamber of commerce in Trieste, home of one of Italy's most prominent coffee companies, formed an association of historic cafés to seek protection. "Whatever is coming from the States—Cokes, hamburgers—it always seems like an invasion," says an official of the Trieste chamber. In Seoul, Starbucks opened up shop in the Insadong area of the city, famous for Korean antiques and crafts. Even though the company's sign is in Korean—unlike the standard board in English posted throughout the world—owners of other shops in the district were upset. They posted signs of their own reading, "Starbucks' invasion of Korea's pride, Insadong." The

ASIA-PACIFIC		EUROPE/MIDDLE EAST/AFRICA		AMERICAS	
Japan	486	Saudi Arabia	29	Canada	53
China	116	United Arab Emirates	27	Hawaii	38
Taiwan	113	Germany	25	Mexico	17
South Korea	75	Kuwait	20	Puerto Rico	3
Philippines	54	Switzerland	15	Peru	1
Malaysia	37	Spain	15	Chile	1
New Zealand	35	Greece	12		
Singapore	35	Lebanon	9		
Indonesia	17	Austria	8		
		Qatar	5		
		Bahrain	4		
		Turkey	4		
		Oman	3		
TOTAL	**968**		**176**		**113**

Source: Starbucks Annual Report, 2003, 14.

French just scoff. "An American chain," laughs the barman of the Bar du Marché in Paris. "We are unique! This is Paris!"

Howard Behar, president of Starbucks International, couldn't be more pleased with the fact that his division was profitable two years ahead of schedule, and he won't even rule out Italy. "Italy didn't create coffee," Behar says. "Nobody owns coffee." It may be that nobody owns coffee, but Starbucks certainly has a lock on it—in North America and, more and more, around the world. With 7,200 stores selling $4.90 Venti Cappuccinos, that's a lot of latte.

[*Note*: This activity can also be used as a management team decision.]

Questions

1. What are the risks to Starbucks' aggressive global expansion plans?
2. What form of global business do you think best fits Starbucks' stores and products? Why?
3. Starbucks plans to open roughly 450 overseas locations this year. Should it continue expanding in countries where it already operates, or should it open stores in new countries?
4. Where did you decide Starbucks should expand? Explain your decision.

DEVELOP YOUR CAREER POTENTIAL

ARE YOU NATIONMINDED OR WORLDMINDED?

This assignment has three parts: Step 1: Complete the questionnaire shown below. Step 2: Determine your score. Step 3: Develop a plan to increase your global managerial potential.[66]

Step 1: Use the six-point rating scale to complete the questionnaire shown below.

Rating Scale

6 Strongly Agree	3 Mildly Disagree
5 Agree	2 Disagree
4 Mildly Agree	1 Strongly Disagree

___ 1. Our country should have the right to prohibit certain racial and religious groups from entering it to live.

___ 2. Immigrants should not be permitted to come into our country if they compete with our own workers.

___ 3. It would set a dangerous precedent if every person in the world had equal rights that were guaranteed by an international charter.

___ 4. All prices for exported food and manufactured goods should be set by an international trade committee.

___ 5. Our country is probably no better than many others.

___ 6. Race prejudice may be a good thing for us because it keeps many undesirable foreigners from coming into this country.

___ 7. It would be a mistake for us to encourage certain racial groups to become well educated because they might use their knowledge against us.

___ 8. We should be willing to fight for our country without questioning whether it is right or wrong.

___ 9. Foreigners are particularly obnoxious because of their religious beliefs.

___ 10. Immigration should be controlled by a global organization rather than by each country on its own.

___ 11. We ought to have a world government to guarantee the welfare of all nations irrespective of the rights of any one.

___ 12. Our country should not cooperate in any global trade agreements that attempt to better world economic conditions at our expense.

___ 13. It would be better to be a citizen of the world than of any particular country.

___ 14. Our responsibility to people of other races ought to be as great as our responsibility to people of our own race.

___ 15. A global committee on education should have full control over what is taught in all countries about history and politics.

___ 16. Our country should refuse to cooperate in a total disarmament program even if some other nations agree to it.

___ 17. It would be dangerous for our country to make international agreements with nations whose religious beliefs are antagonistic to ours.

___ 18. Any healthy individual, regardless of race or religion, should be allowed to live wherever he or she wants to in the world.

___ 19. Our country should not participate in any global organization that requires that we give up any of our national rights or freedom of action.

___ 20. If necessary, we ought to be willing to lower our standard of living to cooperate with other countries in getting an equal standard for every person in the world.

___ 21. We should strive for loyalty to our country before we can afford to consider world brotherhood.

___ 22. Some races ought to be considered naturally less intelligent than ours.

___ 23. Our schools should teach the history of the whole world rather than of our own country.

___ 24. A global police force ought to be the only group in the world allowed to have armaments.

___ 25. It would be dangerous for us to guarantee by international agreement that every person in the world should have complete religious freedom.

___ 26. Our country should permit the immigration of foreign peoples, even if it lowers our standard of living.

___ 27. All national governments ought to be abolished and replaced by one central world government.

___ 28. It would not be wise for us to agree that working conditions in all countries should be subject to international control.

___ 29. Patriotism should be a primary aim of education so that our children will believe our country is the best in the world.

___ 30. It would be a good idea if all the races were to intermarry until there was only one race in the world.

___ 31. We should teach our children to uphold the welfare of all people everywhere, even though it may be against the best interests of our own country.

___ 32. War should never be justifiable, even if it is the only way to protect our national rights and honor.

Step 2: Determine your score by entering your response to each survey item below, as follows. In blanks that say *regular score,* simply enter your response for that item. If your response was a 4, place a 4 in the *regular score* blank. In blanks that say *reverse score,* subtract your response from 6 and enter the result. So if your response was a 4, place a 2 (6 − 4 = 2) in the *reverse score* blank.

1. reverse score ___
2. reverse score ___
3. reverse score ___
4. regular score ___
5. regular score ___
6. reverse score ___
7. reverse score ___
8. reverse score ___
9. reverse score ___
10. regular score ___
11. regular score ___
12. reverse score ___
13. regular score ___
14. regular score ___
15. regular score ___
16. reverse score ___
17. reverse score ___
18. regular score ___

19. reverse score ____
20. regular score ____
21. reverse score ____
22. reverse score ____
23. regular score ____
24. regular score ____
25. reverse score ____
26. regular score ____
27. regular score ____
28. reverse score ____
29. reverse score ____
30. regular score ____
31. regular score ____
32. regular score ____

Total your scores from items 1–16 ____

Total your scores from items 17–32 ____

Add together to compute *total score* ____

Higher scores show greater worldmindedness.

Step 3: Develop a plan to increase your global managerial potential.

People don't change from being nationminded to worldminded overnight. Below you'll find the outlines of a plan to increase your worldmindedness. You need to fill in the details to make it work. This plan is based on foreign languages, living overseas, global news and television, and your openness to the different cultural experiences available right where you live!

3A. Language. How many languages do you speak fluently? If you're an average American student, you speak one language, American English. Develop a plan to become fluent in another language. Specify the courses you would need to take to become conversationally fluent. A minimum of two years is recommended. Even better is minoring in a language! What courses would you have to take to complete a minor?

3B. Living overseas. Develop a plan to study overseas. List the facts for two different overseas study programs available at your university or another university. Be sure to specify how long the program lasts, whether you would receive language training, where you would live, the activities in which you would participate, and any other important details.

3C. Global news and television. Another way to increase your worldmindedness is to increase the diversity of your news sources. Most Americans get their news from local TV and radio or from the major networks, ABC, CBS, Fox, and NBC. Luckily, you don't have to leave the country to gain access to foreign news sources. Furthermore, you don't have to speak a foreign language. Many foreign newspapers and television and radio shows are presented in English. List the foreign newspapers and television and radio shows available to you where you live. *Hint:* Check your university library, CNN, PBS, and the Internet. Be sure to indicate where you can find the newspapers, the day and time the shows are on, and whether the newspapers or TV shows are in English or a foreign language.

3D. Local cultural experiences. Many American students wrongly assume that they have to travel overseas to gain exposure to foreign cultures. Fortunately, many American cities and universities are rich in such experiences. Ethnic neighborhoods, restaurants, festivals, foreign films, and art displays, along with ethnic Americans who continue to live and celebrate their heritage, present ample opportunities to sample and learn about foreign cultures right here in our own backyards. Specify a plan of foreign restaurants, ethnic neighborhoods, and cultural events that you could attend this year.

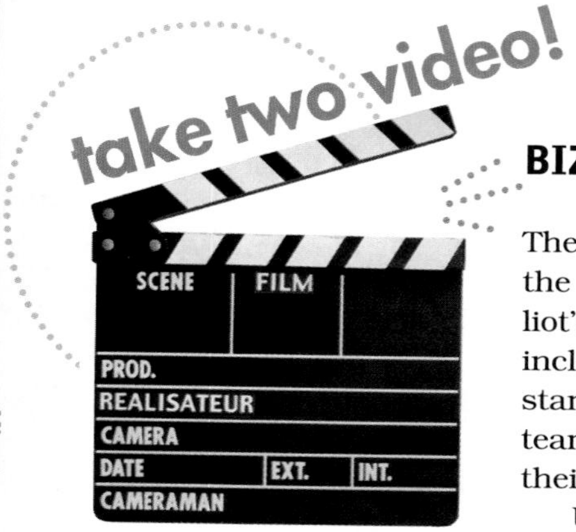

BIZ FLIX Mr. Baseball

The New York Yankees trade aging baseball player Jack Elliot (Tom Selleck) to the Chunichi Dragons, a Japanese team. This lighthearted comedy traces Elliot's bungling entry into Japanese culture where he almost loses everything including Hiroko Uchiyama (Aya Takanashi). As Elliot slowly begins to understand Japanese culture and Japanese baseball, he finally is accepted by his teammates. This film shows many examples of Japanese culture, especially their love for baseball.

Unknown to Hiroko's father, she and Jack develop an intimate relationship. Meanwhile, Jack does not know that Hiroko's father is "The Chief" (Ken Takakura), the manager of the Chunichi Dragons. This scene takes place after "The Chief" has removed Jack from a baseball game. The scene shows Jack dining with Hiroko and her grandmother (Mineko Yorozuya), grandfather (Jun Hamamura), and father.

What to Watch for and Ask Yourself

1. Does Jack Elliot behave as if he had had cross-cultural training before arriving in Japan?
2. Is he culturally sensitive or insensitive?
3. What do you propose that Jack Elliot do for the rest of his time in Japan?

MGMT WORKPLACE Fallon Worldwide

Fallon Worldwide, a small, world-class advertising firm based in Minneapolis, Minnesota, has been recognized for its creative ad campaigns and its progressive corporate culture. Before adding "Worldwide" to its name, Fallon confined its business to the United States. Its clients, however, were expanding into markets around the world, and if Fallon wanted to keep their business, it needed to develop a global presence. Fallon responded to the challenge by forging strategic relationships with several overseas firms. These relationships enabled Fallon to provide immediate global support for its clients and build a foundation for the future. Fallon communicates with its partners intensively, diligently works toward building trust, and informs its clients when a particular campaign would be better conceived within the culture of the intended target. New offices in São Paulo, Singapore, Hong Kong, and London clearly reflect the program's success.

What to Watch for and Ask Yourself

1. What kind of market-entry approach did Fallon use? Why?
2. Identify the types of risk Fallon faced when formulating its global expansion strategy and explain how it addressed them.
3. What made Fallon's global expansion initiative so successful?

CHAPTER EIGHT

Organizational Strategy

outline

WHAT WOULD YOU DO?

IKEA Design Company, Almhult, Sweden.[1] Over a lifetime of spending, the three most expensive items that consumers buy are their homes, their cars, and their furniture. Unlike the home and auto industries, which are dominated by a few large companies, the furniture industry is highly fragmented, with thousands of different manufacturers and furniture retailers, as well as huge differences in styles, costs, and preferences from country to country. There are a few well-known brands in the United States, such as Bassett and Thomasville, and some well-know furniture chains, such as Rooms-to-Go, the RoomStore, Wickes, and Ethan Allan, but consumers are just as likely to buy their furniture from major department stores, regional furniture stores, or local, family-owned furniture stores.

IKEA, the Swedish-origin furniture and home furnishings chain, has been turning problems like this into opportunities since its inception 60 years ago. IKEA was started by

student resources

Experiencing Management
Explore the four levels of learning by doing the simulation module on Planning & Strategic Processes.

Study Guide
Mini lecture reviews all the learning points in the chapter and concludes with a case on Kmart.

Take Two Video
Biz Flix is a scene from *Blue Crush.* Management Workplace is a segment on Caribou Coffee.

PowerPoint®
12 slides with graphics provide an outline for this chapter.

Author Insights
Chuck talks about how important it is to determine what business you are in.

Self Test
21 true/false questions, 21 multiple-choice questions, a management scenario, and 9 exhibit worksheets

Ingvard Kamprad and originally sold pens, wallets, watches, jewelry, and nylon stockings—whatever Kamprad could buy and then sell quickly and cheaply. After six years, IKEA started selling furniture, and with the publication of a furniture catalog a few years later, IKEA was permanently in the furniture business.

Although its strategy has always been to offer good value furniture at extremely low prices, IKEA seems to improve its business every time it runs into a tough problem. For instance, caught in a price war with its main competitor in the early 1950s, it decided to open a factory showroom so that customers could see (and touch) for themselves that quality wasn't being sacrificed as prices dropped. When its competitor and others responded by convincing local furniture suppliers not to sell to IKEA, IKEA began designing its own furniture and contracting directly with furniture manufacturers to build their designs for IKEA stores. This led to better-designed and even cheaper furniture. A few years later, an IKEA employee realized that customers might buy more furniture at one time if they could carry it home in flat packages. Of course, customers would then have to put the furniture together at home, but lower costs for shipping the flat packages from the furniture suppliers to its stores would allow IKEA to cut prices even more. The company's extremely low prices convinced millions of customers to reach for their wrenches and screwdrivers.

IKEA was willing to bet that customers in the United States, the United Kingdom, continental Europe, and Asia would do the same. But how could IKEA take what worked in its Scandinavian franchises—good value furniture at very low costs—and develop a strategy that would work on a global basis? IKEA has always been good at responding to local problems and threats, but doing so on a global basis is much more complex. It's like getting good at checkers and then being asked to master three-dimensional chess. How can IKEA systematically identify strategic global opportunities and threats while sticking to its low-cost strategy? Once those opportunities and threats are identified, what does IKEA need to be particularly good at, or even better at than its competitors? Designing its own furniture and contracting directly with manufacturers to make its furniture has worked well in Scandinavia, but what capabilities must IKEA develop to be able to do this across several continents? Working closely with 25 local furniture suppliers is one thing, but working closely with furniture suppliers in 25 different countries is another. Finally, what does IKEA need to do to make sure it doesn't fritter away its low-cost advantage as it adds franchises in other markets? As the company expands, how can its top management continue to challenge its managers and employees to stay focused and committed to IKEA's low-cost, high-value strategy?

If you were in charge at IKEA, what would you do to create and sustain a global competitive advantage?

In Chapter 4, you learned that *strategic plans* are overall company plans that clarify how a company intends to serve customers and position itself against competitors over the next two to five years. IKEA is in the process of developing new strategic plans for global expansion over the next five years, but its previous failure in Japan shows that picking the wrong strategic plan can have dire consequences. This chapter begins with an in-depth look at how managers create and use strategies to obtain a sustainable competitive advantage. Then you will learn the three steps of the strategy-making process. Next, you will learn about corporate-level strategies that help managers answer the question: What business or businesses should we be in? You will then examine the industry-level competitive strategies that help managers determine how to compete successfully within a particular line of business. The chapter finishes with a review of the firm-level strategies of direct competition.

Basics of Organizational Strategy

The first years of the twenty-first century are not working out the way Steve Case, founder and CEO of America Online (AOL), intended. AOL, the leading online company, which provides services such as email, Internet access, and chat rooms, had grown under Case's guidance from one of the smallest online service providers to the largest in less than a decade, quadrupling its customer base and achieving consistently good profits. In fact, AOL's success enabled it to buy the much larger Time Warner, which owns *Time* magazine (among others), HBO, Cinemax, CNN, and numerous providers of cable television and high-speed Internet services. Several years later, however, AOL's stock price is just one-fifth of what it was before becoming AOL Time Warner.[2] And although AOL now has 26.5 million subscribers (MSN, the Microsoft Network, and Earthlink, its two closest competitors, trail with 9 million and 5 million subscribers each), its market share among Internet service providers has actually shrunk from above 52 percent to 31.4 percent![3]

How can a company like AOL, which dominates an industry, though much less completely than before, keep its competitive advantage? What steps can AOL and other companies take to better manage the strategy-making process?

resources
the assets, capabilities, processes, information, and knowledge that an organization uses to improve its effectiveness and efficiency, to create and sustain competitive advantage, and to fulfill a need or solve a problem

After reading the next two sections, you should be able to

1 explain the components of sustainable competitive advantage and why it is important.

2 describe the steps involved in the strategy-making process.

1 Sustainable Competitive Advantage

An organization's **resources** are the assets, capabilities, processes, information, and knowledge that the organization controls. Firms use their resources to improve organizational effectiveness and efficiency. Resources are critical to organizational strategy because they can help companies create and sustain an advantage over competitors.[4]

competitive advantage
providing greater value for customers than competitors can

Organizations can achieve a **competitive advantage** by using their resources to provide greater value for customers than competitors can. For example, AOL created competitive advantage for itself and value for its customers through its simplicity. To get online with AOL, you put its software in your computer, typed "Install," and followed the directions (entered your name, credit card number, etc.) as the software automatically dialed AOL's free sign-up number.[5] In less than five minutes, you were an AOL subscriber with full online access. Though signing up for online service is commonplace today, AOL was the first company to make it easy. Furthermore, AOL's easy-to-understand menus, icons, and instructions made the process simple and intuitive, even for those who knew little about computers. AOL customer George LeMien of Bethel, Connecticut, said, "I like [AOL's] ease of use, especially how it helps guide me around the Net."[6] Other online services were more difficult to use.

sustainable competitive advantage
a competitive advantage that other companies have tried unsuccessfully to duplicate and have, for the moment, stopped trying to duplicate

The goal of most organizational strategies is to create and then sustain a competitive advantage. A competitive advantage becomes a **sustainable competitive advantage** when other companies cannot duplicate the value a firm is providing to customers. Sustainable competitive advantage is *not* the same as a long-lasting competitive advantage, though companies obviously want a competitive advantage to last a long time. Instead, a competitive advantage is *sustained* if that advantage still exists after competitors have tried unsuccessfully to duplicate the advantage and have, for the moment, stopped trying to duplicate it. It's the corporate equivalent of your competitors saying, "We give up. You win. We can't do what you do, and we're not even going to try to do it any more." As Exhibit 8.1 shows, four conditions must be met if a firm's resources are to be used to achieve a sustainable competitive advantage. The resources must be valuable, rare, imperfectly imitable, *and* nonsubstitutable.

valuable resource
a resource that allows companies to improve efficiency and effectiveness

rare resource
a resource that is not controlled or possessed by many competing firms

imperfectly imitable resource
a resource that is impossible or extremely costly or difficult for other firms to duplicate

Valuable resources allow companies to improve their efficiency and effectiveness. Unfortunately, changes in customer demand and preferences, competitors' actions, and technology can make once-valuable resources much less valuable. For sustained competitive advantage, valuable resources must also be rare resources. Think about it. How can a company sustain a competitive advantage if all of its competitors have similar resources and capabilities? Consequently, **rare resources**, resources that are not controlled or possessed by many competing firms, are necessary to sustain a competitive advantage. When AOL first created the ability to automatically charge monthly bills to customers' credit cards, none of its competitors were offering this service. Any competitive advantage gained from this was short-lived; within months, other online services and Internet providers soon had the same capability. What was initially a rare resource, the capability to bill to credit cards, had become commonplace.

exhibit 8.1

Four Requirements for Sustainable Competitive Advantage

As the previous example shows, valuable, rare resources can create temporary competitive advantage. For sustained competitive advantage, however, other firms must be unable to imitate or find substitutes for those valuable, rare resources. **Imperfectly imitable resources** are impossible or extremely costly or difficult to duplicate. For example, despite numerous attempts by competitors, AOL's ease-of-use and simplicity initially were an imperfectly imitable resource. *PC Magazine* once wrote, "AOL's graphical interface, with menus made up of single-click art icons, folders, and other documents, is a best-of-breed design. The total effect is coherent and easy to navigate. Some interface elements are even animated, adding still more visual appeal."[7] Indeed, over its first decade in the online service business, AOL's ease-of-use and intuitive design helped it displace first CompuServe and then Prodigy as the industry leader. Today, though, both MSN and Earthlink have created simple, easy-to-use software interfaces, MSN 8.0 and Earthlink Total Access, for much easier email, Web browsing, chat and messaging software, and file uploads and downloads.

nonsubstitutable resource a resource, without equivalent substitutes or replacements, that produces value or competitive advantage

Valuable, rare, imperfectly imitable resources can produce sustainable competitive advantage only if they are also **nonsubstitutable resources**, meaning that no other resources can replace them and produce similar value or competitive advantage. For example, as described above, the resource that brought AOL its strongest competitive advantage is its simplicity and ease-of-use. In the online/Internet service business, this resource has proved valuable, rare, and imperfectly imitable. AOL's service and connectivity problems (i.e., busy signals and dropped connections), however, have made customers aware that local Internet service providers (ISPs) are potential substitutes for online access. ISPs do only one thing—provide access to the Internet. Unlike AOL, they don't offer award-winning, easy-to-use software. (Typically, you have to download the software on your own.) And ISPs generally don't offer extensive, proprietary content for members.

So what do local ISPs have in the way of resources that can substitute for everything AOL has to offer? First, most ISPs have direct links to Internet sites that allow their customers to download free, simple-to-use software for email and browsing the Web, the most popular tasks on the Internet. Though it's not as easy as using AOL, most people can be up and running within minutes of activating their Internet accounts. Second, some local ISPs provide a level of customer support that is a substitute for AOL's resources. John "Zeke" Brumage, who runs Zeke's General Store Internet Services in Arizona, says, "My wife and I answer the phones 24 hours a day. It rings at the house and we call-forward to the cell phone when we're traveling."[8] In summary, AOL's resources that provide customers with simplicity and ease-of-use have been valuable, rare, and, in the past, imperfectly imitable. But, if customers decide that the Internet access provided by ISPs is an acceptable substitute, then AOL will not have a sustainable competitive advantage.

Review 1
Sustainable Competitive Advantage

Firms can use their resources to create and sustain a competitive advantage, that is, to provide greater value for customers than competitors can. A competitive advantage becomes sustainable when other companies cannot duplicate the benefits it provides and have, for now, stopped trying. To provide a sustainable competitive advantage, the firm's resources must be valuable (capable of improving efficiency and effectiveness), rare (not possessed by many competing firms), imperfectly imitable (extremely costly or difficult to duplicate), and nonsubstitutable (competitors cannot substitute other resources to produce similar value).

2 Strategy-Making Process

Companies use a *strategy-making process* to create strategies that produce sustainable competitive advantage.[9] Exhibit 8.2 displays the three steps of the strategy-making process: 2.1 **assess the need for strategic change,** 2.2 **conduct a situational analysis,** and then 2.3 **choose strategic alternatives.** Let's examine each of these steps in more detail.

exhibit 8.2

Three Steps of the Strategy-Making Process

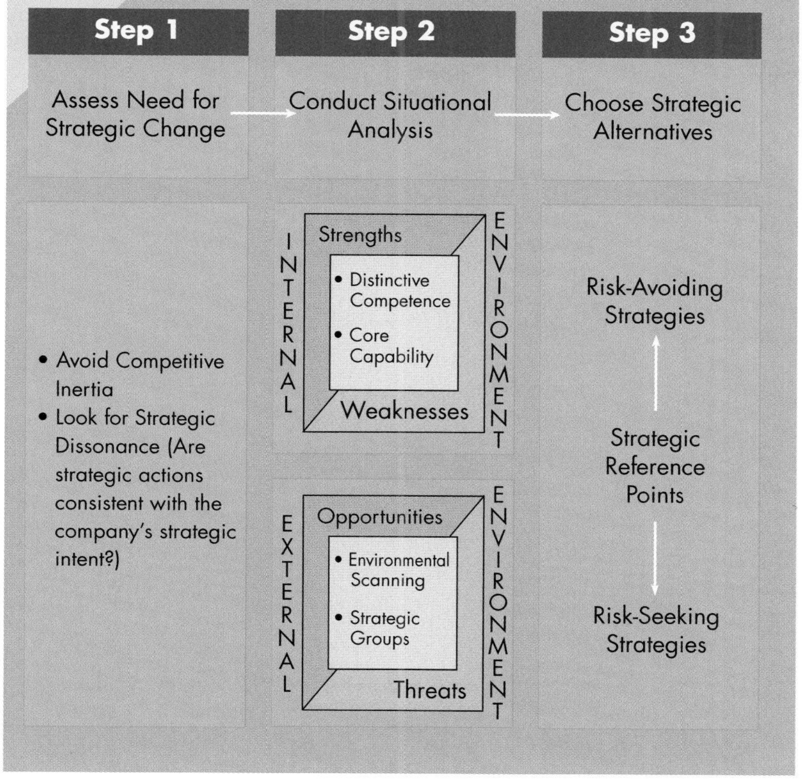

2.1 Assessing the Need for Strategic Change

The external business environment is much more turbulent than it used to be. With customers' needs constantly growing and changing, and with competitors working harder, faster, and smarter to meet those needs, the first step in strategy making is determining the need for strategic change. In other words, the company should determine whether it needs to change its strategy to sustain a competitive advantage.[10]

Determining the need for strategic change might seem easy to do, but in reality, it's not. There's a great deal of uncertainty in strategic business environments. Furthermore, top-level managers are often slow to recognize the need for strategic change, especially at successful companies that have created and sustained competitive advantages. Because they are acutely aware of the strategies that made their companies successful, they continue to rely on those strategies, even as the competition changes. In other words, success often leads to **competitive inertia**—a reluctance to change strategies or competitive practices that have been successful in the past.

competitive inertia
a reluctance to change strategies or competitive practices that have been successful in the past

For example, just a few years ago, no one in the cable TV industry believed that direct broadcast satellite (DBS) dishes would threaten their business. With huge satellite dishes costing over $1,000, why would the 70 million Americans who already had cable TV in their homes pay more than $1,500 to install an unsightly 10-foot-diameter satellite dish in their yard to get the same number of channels that they could get from their local cable company for only a $50 installation fee and $50 a month? Managers of cable TV companies laughed that "DBS" really stood for "Don't Be Stupid." But now that satellite dishes are smaller (two feet in diameter), cost less than $150, and offer 200 channels, compared to the 80 or fewer channels available on most cable systems, no one who manages a cable company is laughing anymore. Indeed, over the last seven years, DBS has increased subscribers from four million to 21 million, raising its market share from 6 percent to 23 percent.[11]

So, besides being aware of the dangers of competitive inertia, what can managers do to improve the speed and accuracy with which they determine the need for strategic change? One method is to actively look for signs of strategic dissonance. **Strategic dissonance** is a discrepancy between upper management's intended strategy and the strategy actually implemented by the lower levels of management. Upper management sets overall company strategy, but middle- and lower-level managers must carry out the strategy.

strategic dissonance
a discrepancy between upper management's intended strategy and the strategy actually implemented by lower levels of management

WHAT REALLY WORKS

STRATEGY MAKING FOR FIRMS, BIG AND SMALL

The strategy-making process (assessing the need for strategic change, conducting a situational analysis, and choosing strategic alternatives) is the method by which companies create strategies that produce sustainable competitive advantage. For years, it had been thought that strategy making was something that only large firms could do well. It was believed that small firms did not have the time, knowledge, or staff to do a good job of strategy making. However, two meta-analyses indicate that strategy making can improve the profits, sales growth, and return on investment of both big and small firms.

Strategy Making for Big Firms

There is a 72 percent chance that big companies that engage in the strategy-making process will be more profitable than big companies that don't. Not only does strategy making improve profits, but it also helps companies grow. Specifically, there is a 75 percent chance that big companies that engage in the strategy-making process will have greater sales and earnings growth than big companies that don't. Thus, in practical terms, the strategy-making process can make a significant difference in a big company's profits and growth.

Strategic Planning & Profits for Big Companies

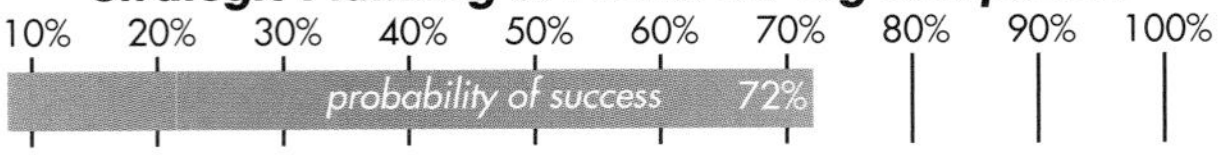

Strategic Planning & Growth for Big Companies

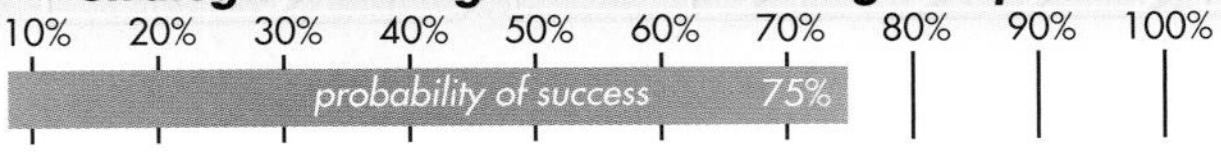

Strategy Making for Small Firms

Strategy making can also improve the performance of small firms. There is a 61 percent chance that small firms that engage in the strategy-making process will have more sales growth than small firms that don't. Likewise, there is a 62 percent chance that small firms that engage in the strategy-making process will have a larger return on investment than small companies that don't. Thus, in practical terms, the strategy-making process can make a significant difference in a small company's profits and growth, too.[12]

Strategic Planning & Sales Growth for Small Companies

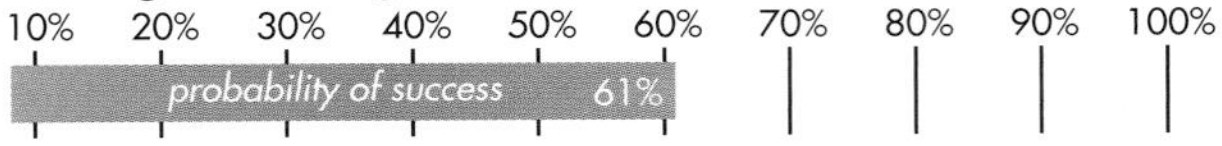

Strategic Planning & Return on Investment for Small Companies

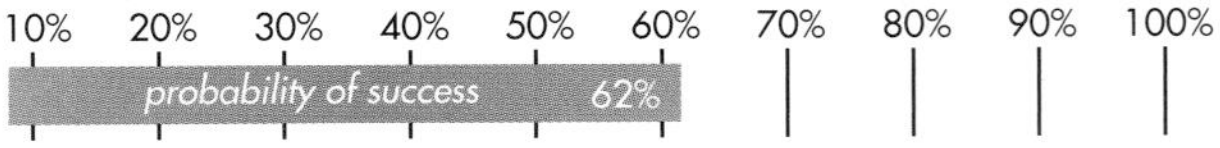

Middle- and lower-level managers are held directly responsible for meeting customers' needs and responding to competitors' actions. While strategic dissonance can indicate that these managers are not doing what they should to carry out company strategy, it can also mean that the intended strategy is out of date and needs to be changed.

Determining the need for strategic change is a difficult process, but it can be improved by actively looking for signs of strategic dissonance, a difference between the intended strategy and what managers are actually doing.

2.2 Situational Analysis

situational (SWOT) analysis
an assessment of the strengths and weaknesses in an organization's internal environment and the opportunities and threats in its external environment

A situational analysis can also help managers determine the need for strategic change. A **situational analysis**, also called a **SWOT analysis** for *strengths, weaknesses, opportunities*, and *threats*, is an assessment of the strengths and weaknesses in an organization's internal environment and the opportunities and threats in its external environment.[13] Ideally, as shown in Step 2 of Exhibit 8.2, a SWOT analysis helps a company determine how to increase internal strengths and minimize internal weaknesses while maximizing external opportunities and minimizing external threats. A basic situational analysis of Eastman Kodak, the camera, film, and photo-processing company, shows that this is not always easy to do. For nearly a century, Kodak dominated the photography business. But with five restructurings and 42,000 employees laid off over the last seven years, Kodak is clearly struggling. Unfortunately, digital photography is darkening Kodak's future even more.[14] With film-based photography, Kodak makes money selling film, cameras, developing equipment, film development chemicals, and photographic paper. But digital camera users can snap pictures and transfer them to a personal computer for viewing in just minutes. With digital photography, consumers don't need Kodak film, Kodak photographic paper, Kodak chemicals (for film labs), or Kodak film and print-developing equipment (for film labs). The opportunity for Kodak, if there is one, is that its reputation and long history in the photography business may help it sell digital cameras. Unfortunately, competition in digital photography from Canon, Sony, Olympus, Nikon, and others has been fierce. And while Kodak has done well, it's only the third largest seller of digital cameras in the United States, and the fifth largest in the world.[15]

www.experiencing management.com

Gain additional insight about situational analysis at our animated concept and activity site. Choose Planning&Strategic_Processes from the "select a topic" pull-down menu, then Strategic Situational Analysis from the "overview tab."

http://www.experiencingmanagement.com

As Kodak's experience shows, competitive advantages can erode over time if internal strengths eventually become weaknesses. Consequently, an analysis of an organization's internal environment, that is, a company's strengths and weaknesses, begins with an assessment of its distinctive competencies and core capabilities. A **distinctive competence** is something that a company can make, do, or perform better than its competitors. For example, *Consumer Reports* magazine consistently ranks Toyota cars number one in quality and reliability.[16] Likewise, for 11 of the last 12 years, *PC Magazine* readers have ranked Dell's desktop computers best in terms of service and reliability.[17]

distinctive competence
what a company can make, do, or perform better than its competitors

Whereas distinctive competencies are tangible—for example, a product or service is faster, cheaper, or better—the core capabilities that produce distinctive competencies are not. **Core capabilities** are the less visible, internal decision-making routines, problem-solving processes, and organizational cultures that determine how efficiently inputs can be turned into outputs.[18] Distinctive competencies cannot be sustained for long without superior core capabilities. Southwest Airlines' unique corporate culture is a core capability that helps it achieve its distinctive competencies in airline performance. At Southwest, employees know that company management truly values them. An example of that value occurs each year on the busiest flying day of the year, the Wednesday before Thanksgiving. On that day, CEO Jim Parker, president and chief operating officer Colleen Barrett, and other top managers show their support for Southwest's employees by helping exhausted ground crews load baggage onto planes. Southwest's employees, in turn, work even smarter, harder, and longer than most employees. Consequently, at Southwest, the corporate culture is *the* core capability that enables Southwest to create distinctive competencies in on-time performance, baggage handling, and customer satisfaction.[19]

core capabilities
the internal decision-making routines, problem-solving processes, and organizational cultures that determine how efficiently inputs can be turned into outputs

After examining internal strengths and weaknesses, the second part of a situational analysis is to look outside the company and assess the opportunities and threats in the external environment. In Chapter 2, you learned that *environmental scanning* involves searching the environment for important events or issues that might affect the organization. With environmental scanning, managers usually scan the environment to stay up-to-date on important factors in their environment, such as pricing trends and technology changes in the industry. In a situational analysis, however, managers use environmental scanning to identify specific opportunities and threats that can either improve or harm the company's ability to sustain its competitive advantage. Identification of strategic groups is one way to do this.

strategic group
a group of companies within an industry that top managers choose to compare, evaluate, and benchmark strategic threats and opportunities

Strategic groups are not "actual" groups; they are companies, usually competitors, that managers closely follow. More specifically, a **strategic group** is a group of other companies within an industry that top managers choose for comparing, evaluating, and benchmarking their company's strategic threats and opportunities.[20] Typically, managers include companies as part of their strategic group if they compete directly with those companies for customers or if those companies use strategies similar to theirs. For example, it's likely that the managers at Gannett Company, the largest U.S. newspaper publisher, assess strategic threats and opportunities by comparing themselves to a strategic group consisting of the other major newspaper companies.[21]

core firms
the central companies in a strategic group

In fact, when scanning the environment for strategic threats and opportunities, managers tend to categorize the different companies in their industries as core and secondary.[22] **Core firms** are the central companies in a strategic group. With the exception of TV stations, Knight Ridder (31 daily newspapers, including the *Detroit Free Press*, the *Philadelphia Inquirer*, and the *Miami Herald*) is the closest to Gannett and would probably be classified as the core firm in Gannett's strategic group.[23] By contrast, given Gannett's size, it's unlikely that Gannett management worries much about the *Arkansas Democrat Gazette*, with a total circulation of 177,000, mostly within Arkansas. When most managers scan their environments for strategic threats and opportunities, they do so by primarily scanning the strategic actions of core firms, not unrelated firms like the *Gazette*.

Where does the New York Times Company fit in? Over the last few years, the New York Times Company has actually become a mini-Gannett, concentrating its resources in newspapers (19 newspapers, including the *New York Times*, the *Boston Globe*, the *International Herald Tribune*) and Web sites.[24] Nonetheless, because of its small size, Gannett's managers might not classify it as a core firm.

secondary firms
the firms in a strategic group that follow related but somewhat different strategies than the core firms

Secondary firms are firms that use related but somewhat different strategies than core firms. The Tribune Company, which has a proportionate number of Web sites, slightly more TV stations than Gannett, but significantly fewer newspapers (12 newspapers, including the *Chicago Tribune*, the *Orlando Sentinel*, *Newsday*, and the *Los Angeles Times*, and a total circulation of 3.5 million), would probably be classified as a secondary firm in Gannett's strategic group.[25] Managers are aware of the potential threats and opportunities posed by secondary firms, but they spend more time assessing the threats and opportunities associated with core firms.

In short, there are two basic parts to a situational analysis. The first is to examine internal strengths and weaknesses by focusing on distinctive competencies and core capabilities. The second is to examine external opportunities and threats by focusing on environmental scanning and strategic groups.

2.3 Choosing Strategic Alternatives

After determining the need for strategic change and conducting a situational analysis, the last step in the strategy-making process is to choose strategic alternatives that will help the company create or maintain a sustainable competitive advantage. According to Strategic Reference Point Theory, managers choose between two basic alternative strategies. They can choose a conservative, *risk-avoiding strategy* that aims to protect an existing competitive advantage. Or they can choose an aggressive, *risk-seeking strategy* that aims to extend or create a sustainable competitive advantage. For example, Menards is a hardware store chain with 170 locations throughout the Midwest.[26] When hardware giant Home Depot entered the Midwest, Menards faced a basic choice: avoid risk by continuing with the strategy it had in place before Home Depot's arrival or seek risk by trying to further its competitive advantage against Home Depot, which is six times its size. Some of its competitors decided to fold. Kmart closed all of its Builder's Square hardware stores when Home Depot came to Minneapolis. Handy Andy liquidated its 74 stores when Home Depot came to the Midwest. But Menards decided to fight, spending millions to open 35 new stores at the same time that Home Depot was opening 44 of its new stores.[27]

The choice to be risk seeking or risk avoiding typically depends on whether top management views the company as falling above or below strategic reference points. **Strategic reference points** are the targets that managers use to measure whether their firm has developed the core competencies that it needs to achieve a sustainable competitive advantage. For example, if a hotel chain decides to compete by providing superior quality and service, then top management will track the success of this strategy through customer surveys or published hotel ratings, such as those provided by the prestigious *Mobil Travel Guide*. By contrast, if a hotel chain decides to compete on price, it will regularly conduct market surveys to check the prices of other hotels. The competitors' prices are the hotel managers' strategic reference points against which to compare their own pricing strategy. If competitors can consistently underprice them, then the managers need to determine whether their staff and resources have the core competencies to compete on price.

strategic reference points
the strategic targets managers use to measure whether a firm has developed the core competencies it needs to achieve a sustainable competitive advantage

As shown in Exhibit 8.3, when a company is performing above or better than its strategic reference points, top management will typically be satisfied with the company's strategy. Ironically, this satisfaction tends to make top management conservative and risk-averse. After all, since the company already has a sustainable competitive advantage, the worst thing that could happen would be to lose it. Consequently, new issues or changes in the company's external environments are viewed as threats. But, when a company is performing below or worse than its strategic reference points, top management will typically be dissatisfied with the company's strategy. In this instance, managers are much more likely to choose a daring, risk-taking strategy. After all, if the current strategy is producing substandard results, what has the company got to lose by switching to risky new strategies in the hopes that it can create a sustainable competitive advantage? Consequently, for companies in this situation, new issues or changes in external environments are viewed as opportunities for potential gain.

exhibit 8.3

Strategic Reference Points

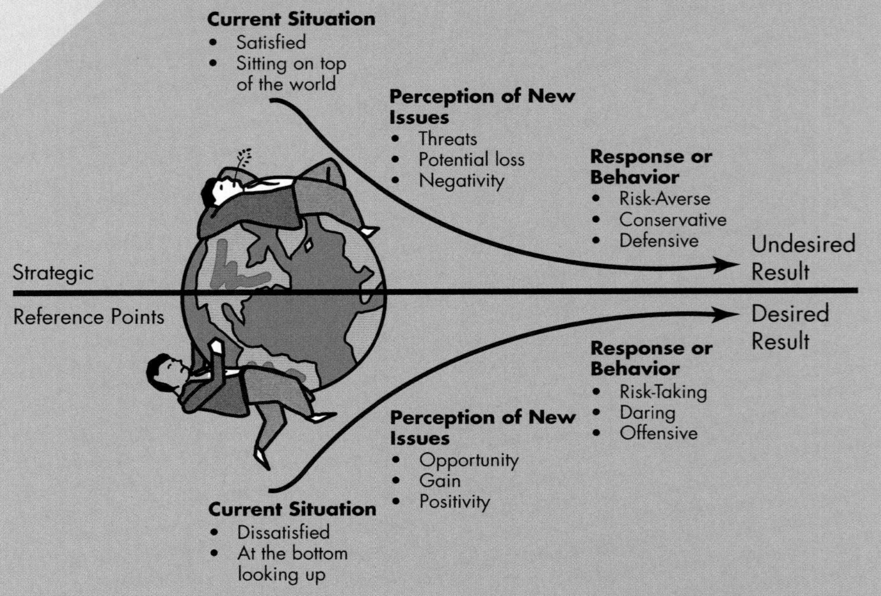

Source: A. Fiegenbaum, S. Hart, & D. Schendel, "Strategic Reference Point Theory," Strategic Management Journal *17 (1996): 219–235.*

Strategic Reference Point Theory is not deterministic, however. Managers are not predestined to choose risk-averse or risk-seeking strategies for their companies. Indeed, one of the most important elements of the theory is that managers *can* influence the strategies chosen by their company by *actively changing and adjusting* the strategic reference points they use to judge strategic performance. To illustrate, if a company has become complacent after consistently surpassing its strategic reference points, then top management can change from a risk-averse to a risk-taking orientation by raising the standards of performance (i.e., strategic reference points). Indeed, this is what happened at Menards.

Instead of being satisfied with just protecting its existing stores (a risk-averse strategy), founder John Menard changed the strategic referent points the company had been using to assess strategic performance. To encourage a daring, offensive-minded strategy that would allow the company to open nearly as many new stores as Home Depot, he determined that Menards would have to beat Home Depot on not one or two, but four strategic reference points: price, products, sales per square foot, and "friendly accessibility." Preliminary data indicate that the strategy is well on its way to succeeding. In terms of price, market research indicates that a 100-item shopping cart of goods is consistently cheaper at Menards.[28] In terms of products, Menards sells 50,000 products per store, the same as Home Depot. In terms of sales per square foot, Menards ($360 per square foot) strongly outsells Home Depot ($290 per square foot). Finally, unlike Home Depot's warehouse-like stores,

Menards' stores are built to resemble grocery stores. Shiny tiled floors, wide aisles, and easy-to-reach products all make Menards a "friendlier" place for shoppers.[29] And now with Lowe's, the second largest hardware store chain in the nation, also entering its markets, Menards has added a fifth strategic reference point, store size. Most new Menards stores will be 225,000 square feet, more than double the size of Home Depots' stores and 75,000 square feet larger than Lowe's.[30] John Caulfield, who wrote a book about Home Depot and the hardware business, said, "Menards is clearly throwing the gauntlet down at Lowe's. They're saying, 'If you come into Chicago, here is what you're going to face.'"[31]

So even when (perhaps *especially* when) companies have achieved a sustainable competitive advantage, top managers must adjust or change strategic reference points to challenge themselves and their employees to develop new core competencies for the future. In the long run, effective organizations will frequently revise their strategic reference points to better focus managers' attention on the new challenges and opportunities that occur in their ever-changing business environments.

Review 2
Strategy-Making Process

The first step in strategy making is determining whether a strategy needs to be changed in order to sustain a competitive advantage. Because uncertainty and competitive inertia make this difficult to determine, managers can improve the speed and accuracy of this step by looking for differences between top management's intended strategy and the strategy actually implemented by lower-level managers (i.e., strategic dissonance). The second step is to conduct a situational analysis that examines internal strengths and weaknesses (distinctive competencies and core capabilities), as well as external threats and opportunities (environmental scanning and strategic groups). In the third step of strategy making, Strategic Reference Point Theory suggests that when companies are performing better than their strategic reference points, top management will typically choose a risk-averse strategy. When performance is below strategic reference points, risk-seeking strategies are more likely to be chosen. Importantly, however, managers *can* influence the choice of strategic alternatives by actively changing and adjusting the strategic reference points they use to judge strategic performance.

Corporate, Industry, and Firm-Level Strategies

After years of diversifying its business, Intel has gone back to basics by refocusing on its core business of making integrated computer chips. It sold off its interactive media-services division, closed iCat, a business that managed Web sites for small businesses, and shut down a business that streamed video and audio content for other companies. CEO Craig Barrett admitted that Intel had "screwed up" by focusing too much on these other businesses. By refocusing on integrated computer chips, Barrett said, "We're prioritizing our investments—you allocate your resources into the areas of highest return. The core competency has always been integrated circuits."[32] What business are we in? How should we compete in this industry? Who are our competitors and how should we respond to them? These simple, but powerful questions are at the heart of corporate-, industry-, and firm-level strategies.

After reading the next three sections, you should be able to

3 explain the different kinds of corporate-level strategies.

4 describe the different kinds of industry-level strategies.

5 explain the components and kinds of firm-level strategies.

3 Corporate-Level Strategies

Corporate-level strategy is the overall organizational strategy that addresses the question "What business or businesses are we in or should we be in?"

Exhibit 8.4 shows the two major approaches to corporate-level strategy that companies use to decide which businesses they should be in: 3.1 portfolio strategy[33] and 3.2 grand strategies.

corporate-level strategy
the overall organizational strategy that addresses the question "What business or businesses are we in or should we be in?"

diversification
a strategy for reducing risk by buying a variety of items (stocks or, in the case of a corporation, types of businesses), so that the failure of one stock or one business does not doom the entire portfolio

portfolio strategy
a corporate-level strategy that minimizes risk by diversifying investment among various businesses or product lines

acquisition
the purchase of a company by another company

unrelated diversification
creating or acquiring companies in completely unrelated businesses

3.1 Portfolio Strategy

One of the standard strategies for stock market investors is **diversification**: buy stocks in a variety of companies in different industries. The purpose of this strategy is to reduce risk in the overall stock portfolio (i.e., the entire collection of stocks). The basic idea is simple: if you invest in 10 companies in 10 different industries, you won't lose your entire investment if one company performs poorly. Furthermore, because they're in different industries, one company's losses are likely to be offset by another company's gains. Portfolio strategy is based on these same ideas.

Portfolio strategy is a corporate-level strategy that minimizes risk by diversifying investment among various businesses or product lines. Like an investor who invests in a variety of stocks, portfolio strategy guides the strategic decisions of corporations that compete in a variety of businesses. For example, it could be used to guide the strategy of a company like 3M, which makes 50,000 products for 16 different industries. And, just as investors consider the mix of stocks in their stock portfolio when deciding which stocks to buy or sell, portfolio strategy provides the following guidelines to help managers acquire companies that fit well with the rest of their corporate portfolio and sell those that don't.

exhibit 8.4

Corporate-Level Strategies

PORTFOLIO STRATEGY	GRAND STRATEGIES
• Acquisitions, unrelated diversification, related diversification, single businesses	• Growth
• Boston Consulting Group matrix	• Stability
• Stars	• Retrenchment/recovery
• Question marks	
• Cash cows	
• Dogs	

First, the more businesses in which a corporation competes, the smaller its overall chances of failing. Think of a corporation as a stool and its businesses as the legs of the stool. The more legs or businesses added to the stool, the less likely it is to tip over. Using this analogy, portfolio strategy reduces 3M's risk of failing because the corporation's survival depends on essentially 16 different businesses. Because the emphasis is on adding "legs to the stool," managers who use portfolio strategy are often on the lookout for **acquisitions**, that is, other companies to buy.

Second, beyond adding new businesses to the corporate portfolio, portfolio strategy can reduce risk even more through **unrelated diversification**—

DOING THE RIGHT THING

Acquisition Lust: Don't Be Seduced by the "Deal"

Dennis Kozlowski, the former CEO of Tyco Corporation, was called "deal-a-month-Dennis," because he grew Tyco by doing "deals" to acquire hundreds of companies in such diverse businesses as undersea fiber-optic cable, security alarm systems, medical supplies, and valves and pipes. Why do some companies and CEOs become seduced by the "deal"? Certainly, one reason is that deals generate media coverage, make you CEO of a larger company, increase your pay (CEOs of larger companies make more money), and generate "immediate" results. But, before spending millions, if not billions, to acquire another company, don't forget that studies repeatedly show there's only a 50-50 chance that a merger or acquisition will succeed. So, before "doing the deal," ask these tough questions: Will the acquisition increase productivity, improve service, cut costs, lead to better product design, generate and sustain a competitive advantage, and, in the end, pay for itself? Do the right thing. Don't be seduced by the "deal." Merge with or acquire other companies for the right reasons.[34]

creating or acquiring companies in completely unrelated businesses. If the businesses are unrelated, then losses in one business or industry will have minimal effect on the performance of other companies in the corporate portfolio. One of the best examples of unrelated diversification is Samsung Corporation of Korea. Samsung has 7 businesses in electronics, 4 companies in machinery and heavy industries, 5 companies in chemicals, 7 companies in financial services, and 15 other companies in businesses ranging from automobiles to hotels to entertainment.[35] Because most internally grown businesses tend to be related to existing products or services, acquiring new businesses is the preferred method of unrelated diversification.

Third, investing the profits and cash flows from mature, slow-growth businesses into newer, faster-growing businesses can reduce long-term risk. The best-known portfolio strategy for guiding investment in a corporation's businesses is the Boston Consulting Group (BCG) matrix. The **BCG matrix** is a portfolio strategy that managers use to categorize their corporation's businesses by growth rate and relative market share, helping them decide how to invest corporate funds. The matrix, shown in Exhibit 8.5, separates businesses into four categories based on how fast the market is growing (high-growth or low-growth) and the size of the business's share of that market (small or large). **Stars** are companies that have a large share of a fast-growing market. To take advantage of a star's fast-growing market and its strength in that market (large share), the corporation must invest substantially in it. The investment is usually worthwhile, however, because many stars produce sizable future profits. **Question marks** are companies that have a small share of a fast-growing market. If the corporation invests in these companies, they may eventually become stars, but their relative weakness in the market (small share) makes investing in question marks more risky than investing in stars. **Cash cows** are companies that have a large share of a slow-growing market. Companies in this situation are often highly profitable, hence the name "cash cow." Finally, **dogs** are companies that have a small share of a slow-growing market. As the name "dogs" suggests, having a small share of a slow-growth market is often not profitable.

Since the idea is to redirect investment from slow-growing to fast-growing companies, the BCG matrix starts by recommending that while the substantial cash flows from cash cows last, they should be reinvested in stars (see arrow 1 in Exhibit 8.5) to help them grow even faster and obtain even more market share. Using this strategy, current profits help produce future profits. Over time, as their market growth slows, some stars may turn into cash cows (see arrow 2). Cash flows should also be directed to some question marks (see arrow 3). Though riskier than stars, question marks have great potential because of their fast-growing market. Managers must decide which question marks are most likely to turn into stars and therefore warrant further investment, and which ones are too risky and should be sold. Over time, hopefully

BCG matrix
a portfolio strategy, developed by the Boston Consulting Group, that managers use to categorize the corporation's businesses by growth rate and relative market share, helping them decide how to invest corporate funds

star
a company with a large share of a fast-growing market

question mark
a company with a small share of a fast-growing market

cash cow
a company with a large share of a slow-growing market

dog
a company with a small share of a slow-growing market

exhibit 8.5

Boston Consulting Group Matrix

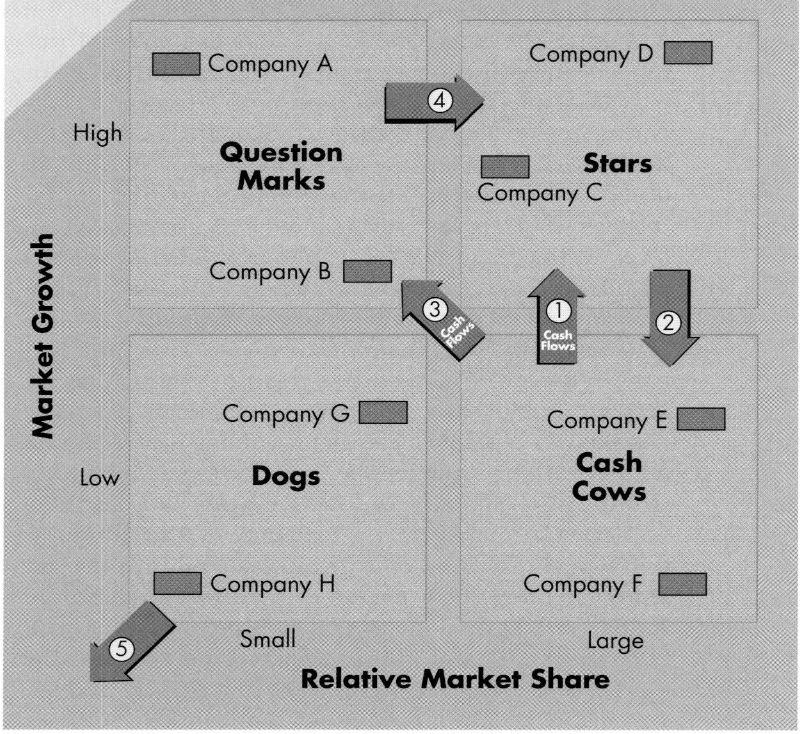

some questions marks will become stars as their small markets become large ones (see arrow 4). Finally, because dogs lose money, the corporation should "find them new owners" or "take them to the pound." In other words, dogs should either be sold to other companies or be closed down and liquidated for their assets (see arrow 5).

Although the BCG matrix and other forms of portfolio strategy are relatively popular among managers, portfolio strategy has some drawbacks. The most significant is that the evidence does not support the usefulness of acquiring unrelated businesses. As shown in Exhibit 8.6, there is a U-shaped relationship between diversification and risk. The left side of the curve shows that single businesses with no diversification are extremely risky (if the single business fails, the entire business fails). So, in part, the portfolio strategy of diversifying is correct—competing in a variety of different businesses can lower risk. However, portfolio strategy is partly wrong, too—the right side of the curve shows that conglomerates composed of completely unrelated businesses are even riskier than single, undiversified businesses.

A second set of problems with portfolio strategy has to do with the dysfunctional consequences that occur when companies are categorized as stars, cash cows, question marks, or dogs. Contrary to expectations, the BCG matrix often yields incorrect judgments about a company's future potential. This is because it relies on past performance (i.e., previous market share and previous market growth), which is a notoriously poor predictor of future company performance. For example, for the first 50 years of its existence, Krispy Kreme was a small, regional chain of doughnut shops. Sales, profits, and growth were respectable, but Krispy Kreme was clearly not a player in a highly competitive business thoroughly dominated by Dunkin' Donuts and its 1,000 U.S. stores. Believe it or not, Krispy Kreme was a "dog," according to the BCG matrix because it had a small share of a slowly growing market. In the last decade, however, Krispy Kreme has had remarkable success, quadrupling from 100 to more than 400 stores, increasing sales and profits at an annual average of over 25 percent, and becoming one of the more popular growth stocks on Wall Street.[36]

Furthermore, using the BCG matrix can also weaken the strongest performer in the corporate portfolio, the cash cow.

www.experiencing management.com

You may learn more about the BCG matrix portfolio strategy by interacting with this concept at our animated concept and activity site. Choose Planning&Strategic_Processes from the "select a topic" pull-down menu, then BCG Growth-Share Matrix from the "overview tab."

http://www.experiencingmanagement.com

exhibit 8.6

U-Shaped Relationship between Diversification and Risk

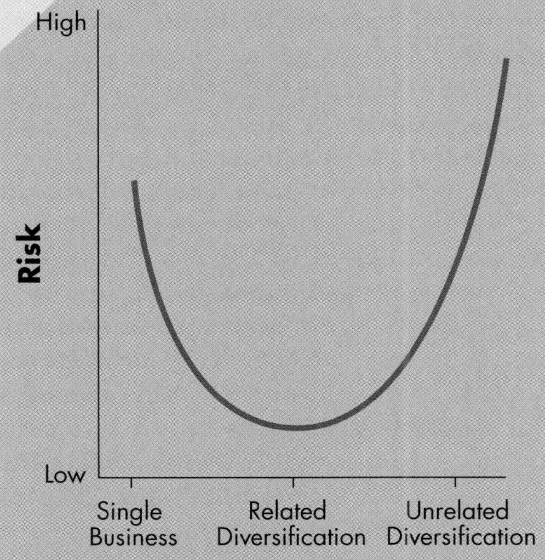

Source: Republished with permission of Academy of Management, PO Box 3020, Briar Cliff Manor, NY, 10510-8020. M. Lubatkin & P. J. Lane, "Psst . . . The Merger Mavens Still Have It Wrong!" Academy of Management Executive *10 (1996): 21–39. Reproduced with permission of the publisher via Copyright Clearance Center, Inc.*

As funds are redirected from cash cows to stars, corporate managers essentially take away the resources needed to take advantage of the cash cow's new business opportunities. As a result, the cash cow becomes less aggressive in seeking new business or in defending its present business.

So, what kind of portfolio strategy does the best job of helping managers decide which companies to buy or sell? The U-shaped curve in Exhibit 8.6 indicates that the best approach is probably **related diversification**, in which the different business units share similar products, manufacturing, marketing, technology, or cultures. The key to related diversification is to acquire or create new companies with core capabilities that complement the core capabilities of businesses already in the corporate portfolio. We began this section with the example of 3M and its 50,000 products sold in over 16 different industries. While seemingly different, most of 3M's product divisions are based in some fashion on its distinctive competencies in adhesives and tape (i.e., wet or dry sandpaper, Post-It notes, Scotchgard fabric protector, transdermal skin patches, etc.). Furthermore, all of 3M's divisions share its strong corporate culture that promotes and encourages risk taking and innovation. In sum, in contrast to a single, undiversified business or unrelated diversification, related diversification reduces risk because the different businesses can work as a team, relying on each other for needed experience, expertise, and support.

related diversification
creating or acquiring companies that share similar products, manufacturing, marketing, technology, or cultures

grand strategy
a broad corporate-level strategic plan used to achieve strategic goals and guide the strategic alternatives that managers of individual businesses or subunits may use

growth strategy
a strategy that focuses on increasing profits, revenues, market share, or the number of places in which the company does business

stability strategy
a strategy that focuses on improving the way in which the company sells the same products or services to the same customers

3.2 Grand Strategies

A **grand strategy** is a broad strategic plan used to help an organization achieve its strategic goals.[37] Grand strategies guide the strategic alternatives that managers of individual businesses or subunits may use. There are three kinds of grand strategies: growth, stability, and retrenchment/recovery.

The purpose of a **growth strategy** is to increase profits, revenues, market share, or the number of places (store, offices, locations) in which the company does business. Companies can grow in several ways. They can grow externally by merging with or acquiring other companies.

Another way to grow is internally, directly expanding the company's existing business or creating and growing new businesses. For example, over the last decade, Walgreen's, one of the largest pharmacy chains in the United States, opened approximately 100 stores a year. With baby boomers aging and the need for pharmacies to sell more prescription drugs growing rapidly, Walgreen's opened 450 new stores last year and will shoot for 500 this year. In fact, with 4,029 stores in 43 states, it hopes to add 500 stores a year and reach 7,000 Walgreen's stores within the next six years.[38]

The purpose of a **stability strategy** is to continue doing what the company has been doing, but just do it better. Consequently, companies following a stability strategy try to improve the way in which they sell the same products or services to the same customers. For example, Subaru has been making four-wheel-drive station wagons for 30 years. Recently, it has strengthened this focus by manufacturing only all-wheel-drive vehicles, like the Subaru Legacy and Outback (both come in four-door sedans or two-door coupes), which are popular in snowy and mountainous regions. Subaru's extremely loyal customers have rewarded the company with above-average annual sales increases over the last five years.[39] Companies often choose a stability strategy when their external environment doesn't change much, or after they have struggled with periods of explosive growth.

retrenchment strategy
a strategy that focuses on turning around very poor company performance by shrinking the size or scope of the business

recovery
the strategic actions taken after retrenchment to return to a growth strategy

The purpose of a **retrenchment strategy** is to turn around very poor company performance by shrinking the size or scope of the business. The first step of a typical retrenchment strategy might include making significant cost reductions; laying off employees; closing poorly performing stores, offices, or manufacturing plants; or closing or selling entire lines of products or services.[40] When Kmart filed for bankruptcy, it closed 600 stores and laid off 54,000 employees in order to increase cash flows and reduce debt.[41]

After cutting costs and reducing a business's size or scope, the second step in a retrenchment strategy is recovery. **Recovery** consists of the strategic actions that a company takes to return to a growth strategy. This two-step process of cutting and recovery is analogous to pruning roses. Prior to each growing season, roses should be cut back to two-thirds their normal size. Pruning doesn't damage the roses; it makes them stronger and more likely to produce beautiful, fragrant flowers. The retrenchment-and-recovery process is similar. Cost reductions, layoffs, and plant closings are sometimes necessary to restore companies to "good health." Recently, PeopleSoft went through this process when it laid off 10 percent of its employees. Indeed, two years later, after the layoffs and after instituting other controls, PeopleSoft was profitable and growing again.[42] When company performance drops significantly, a strategy of retrenchment and recovery may help companies return to a successful growth strategy.

Despite being one of America's leading retailers for decades, Kmart was unable to compete with rivals Wal-Mart, whose prices were lower, and Target, whose product offerings were more stylish. The end result of Kmart's bad management practices was numerous store closings, bankruptcy, and a draconian retrenchment strategy.

Review 3
Corporate-Level Strategies

Corporate-level strategies, such as portfolio strategy and grand strategies, help managers determine what businesses they should be in. Portfolio strategy focuses on lowering business risk by being in multiple, unrelated businesses and by investing the cash flows from slow-growth businesses into faster-growing businesses. One portfolio strategy, the BCG matrix, suggests that cash flows from cash cows should be reinvested in stars and in carefully chosen question marks. Dogs should be sold or liquidated. Portfolio strategy has several problems, however. Acquiring unrelated businesses actually increases risk rather than lowering it. The BCG matrix is often wrong when predicting companies' future potential (i.e., dogs, cash cows, etc.). And redirecting cash flows can seriously weaken cash cows. The most successful way to use the portfolio approach to corporate strategy is to reduce risk through related diversification.

The three kinds of grand strategies are growth, stability, and retrenchment/recovery. Companies can grow externally by merging with or acquiring other companies, or they can grow internally through direct expansion or creating new businesses. Companies choose a stability strategy—selling the same products or services to the same customers—when their external environment changes very little or after they have dealt with periods of explosive growth. Retrenchment strategy, shrinking the size or scope of a business, is used to turn around poor performance. If retrenchment works, it is often followed by a recovery strategy that focuses on growing the business again.

4 Industry-Level Strategies

industry-level strategy
a corporate strategy that addresses the question "How should we compete in this industry?"

Industry-level strategy is a corporate strategy that addresses the question "How should we compete in this industry?" Let's find out more about industry-level strategies by discussing 4.1 the five industry forces that determine overall levels of competition in an industry, 4.2 the positioning strategies, and 4.3 adaptive strategies that companies can use to achieve sustained competitive advantage and above-average profits.

4.1 Five Industry Forces

character of the rivalry
a measure of the intensity of competitive behavior between companies in an industry

threat of new entrants
a measure of the degree to which barriers to entry make it easy or difficult for new companies to get started in an industry

According to Harvard professor Michael Porter, five industry forces—character of rivalry, threat of new entrants, threat of substitute products or services, bargaining power of suppliers, and bargaining power of buyers—determine an industry's overall attractiveness and potential for long-term profitability. The stronger these forces, the less attractive the industry becomes to corporate investors because it is more difficult for companies to be profitable. Porter's industry forces are illustrated in Exhibit 8.7. Let's examine how these industry forces are bringing changes to several kinds of industries.

Character of the rivalry is a measure of the intensity of competitive behavior between companies in an industry. Is the competition among firms aggressive and cutthroat, or do competitors focus more on serving customers than on attacking each other? Both industry attractiveness and profitability decrease when rivalry is cutthroat. For example, selling cars is a highly competitive business. Pick up a local newspaper on Friday, Saturday, or Sunday morning, and you'll find dozens of pages of car advertising. In fact, competition is so intense that if it weren't for used-car sales, repair work, and replacement parts, many auto dealers would actually lose money.

The **threat of new entrants** is a measure of the degree to which barriers to entry make it easy or difficult for new companies to get started in an industry. If it is easy for new companies to enter the industry, then competition will increase and prices and profits will fall. However, if there are sufficient barriers to entry, such as large capital requirements to buy

exhibit 8.7

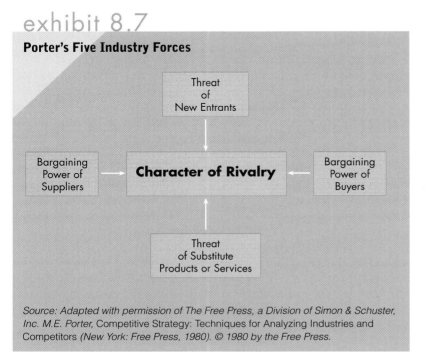

Porter's Five Industry Forces

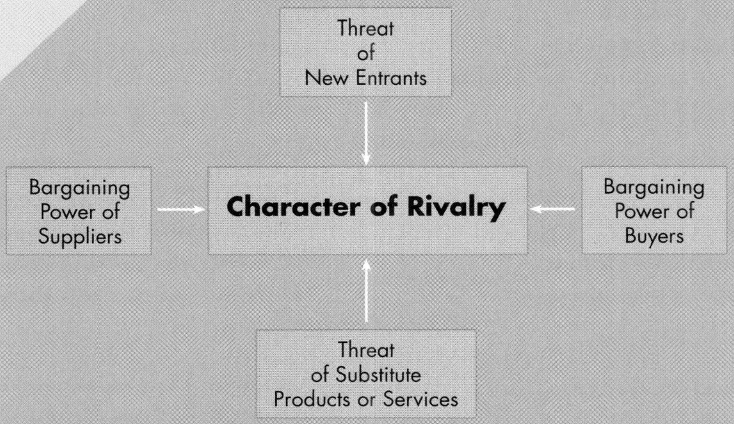

Source: Adapted with permission of The Free Press, a Division of Simon & Schuster, Inc. M.E. Porter, Competitive Strategy: Techniques for Analyzing Industries and Competitors *(New York: Free Press, 1980). © 1980 by the Free Press.*

expensive equipment or plant facilities or the need for specialized knowledge, then competition will be weaker, and prices and profits will generally be higher.

threat of substitute products or services
a measure of the ease with which customers can find substitutes for an industry's products or services

The **threat of substitute products or services** is a measure of the ease with which customers can find substitutes for an industry's products or services. If customers can easily find substitute products or services, the competition will be greater and profits will be lower. If there are few or no substitutes, competition will be weaker and profits will be higher. Generic medicines are some of the best-known examples of substitute products. Under U.S. patent law, a company that develops a drug has exclusive rights to produce and market that drug for 20 years. During this time, if the drug sells well, prices and profits are generally high. After 20 years, however, the patent will expire, and any pharmaceutical company can manufacture and sell the same drug. When this happens, drug prices drop substantially, and the company that developed the drug typically sees its revenues drop sharply. For example, Prozac, a medication that fights depression, cost $30 a pill and returned $2.7 billion in sales revenues to Eli Lilly & Co. the last year it was under patent. In contrast, fluoxetine, a generic version of Prozac made by Merck-Medco that became available the day the patent for Prozac expired, costs only $5 per pill.[43]

bargaining power of suppliers
a measure of the influence that suppliers of parts, materials, and services to firms in an industry have on the prices of these inputs

bargaining power of buyers
a measure of the influence that customers have on a firm's prices

Bargaining power of suppliers is a measure of the influence that suppliers of parts, materials, and services to firms in an industry have on the prices of these inputs. If an industry has numerous suppliers from whom to buy parts, materials, and services, companies will be able to bargain with suppliers to keep prices low. On the other hand, if there are few suppliers, or if a company is dependent on a supplier with specialized skills and knowledge, then suppliers will have the bargaining power to dictate price levels. In contrast, **bargaining power of buyers** is a measure of the influence that customers have on the firm's prices. If a company is dependent on just a few high-volume buyers, those buyers will typically have enough bargaining power to dictate prices. By contrast, if a company sells a popular product or service to multiple buyers, then the company has more power to set prices.

4.2 Positioning Strategies

After analyzing industry forces, the next step in industry-level strategy is to protect your company from the negative effects of industry-wide competition and to create a sustainable competitive advantage. According to Michael Porter, there are three positioning strategies: cost leadership, differentiation, and focus.

cost leadership
the positioning strategy of producing a product or service of acceptable quality at consistently lower production costs than competitors can, so that the firm can offer the product or service at the lowest price in the industry

Cost leadership means producing a product or service of acceptable quality at consistently lower production costs than competitors, so that the firm can offer the product or service at the lowest price in the industry. Cost leadership protects companies from industry forces by deterring new entrants, who will have to match low costs and prices. Cost leadership also forces down the prices of substitute products and services, attracts bargain-seeking buyers, and increases bargaining power with suppliers, who have to keep their prices low if they want to do business with the cost leader. For example, although it sells the occasional $106,000 diamond ring or $11,000 Lalique crystal vase, thousands of $3,000 42-inch plasma televisions, and too many cases of $90 Dom Perignon champagne to count, Costco, the second largest warehouse chain (behind Sam's), has a simple strategy—ultra low costs. At Costco, nothing, not even the $106,000 diamond ring, is marked up more than 14 percent over the wholesale price. By contrast, low-priced Wal-Mart uses an average 33 percent markup. "This is not a tricky business. We just try to sell high-quality merchandise at a cost lower than everybody else," says Costco's CEO Jim Sinegal who, to keep overhead costs low, still answers his own phone and eats lunch at the same desk he had when starting the company two decades ago.[44]

differentiation
the positioning strategy of providing a product or service that is sufficiently different from competitors' offerings that customers are willing to pay a premium price for it

Differentiation means making your product or service sufficiently different from competitors' offerings so that customers are willing to pay a premium price for the extra value or performance that it provides. Differentiation protects companies from industry forces by reducing the threat of substitute products. It also protects companies by making it easier to retain customers and more difficult for new entrants trying to attract new customers.

focus strategy
the positioning strategy of using cost leadership or differentiation to produce a specialized product or service for a limited, specially targeted group of customers in a particular geographic region or market segment

With a **focus strategy**, a company uses either cost leadership or differentiation to produce a specialized product or service for a limited, specially targeted group of customers in a particular geographic region or market segment. Focus strategies typically work in market niches that competitors have overlooked or have difficulty serving. An example of a focus strategy is the Container Store, which sells products to reorganize and rebuild your closets, sort out your kitchen drawers and cabinets, or add shelves, hooks, and storage anywhere in your home, office, or dorm room.

4.3 Adaptive Strategies

Adaptive strategies are another set of industry-level strategies. While the aim of positioning strategies is to minimize the effects of industry competition and build a sustainable competitive advantage, the purpose of adaptive strategies is to choose an industry-level strategy that is best suited to changes in the organization's external environment. There are four kinds of adaptive strategies: defenders, prospectors, analyzers, and reactors.[45]

defenders
an adaptive strategy aimed at defending strategic positions by seeking moderate, steady growth and by offering a limited range of high-quality products and services to a well-defined set of customers

Defenders seek moderate, steady growth by offering a limited range of products and services to a well-defined set of customers. In other words, defenders aggressively "defend" their current strategic position by doing the best job they can to hold on to customers in a particular market segment.

prospectors
an adaptive strategy that seeks fast growth by searching for new market opportunities, encouraging risk taking, and being the first to bring innovative new products to market

Prospectors seek fast growth by searching for new market opportunities, encouraging risk taking, and being the first to bring innovative new products to market. Prospectors are analogous to gold miners who "prospect" for gold nuggets (i.e., new products) in hopes that the nuggets will lead them to a mine that has a rich deposit of gold (i.e., fast growth). 3M has long been known for its innovative products, particularly in the areas of adhesives. Since 1904, it has invented sandpaper; masking, cellophane, electrical, and scotch tapes; the first commercially available audio and video tapes; and its most famous invention, Post-It notes. Lately, 3M has invented a film that increases the brightness of LCD displays on laptop computers, developed a digital system for construction companies to detect underground telecommunication, gas, water, sewer, or electrical lines without digging, and created a pheromone spray that, by preventing harmful insects from mating, will protect apple, walnut, tomato, cranberry, and grape crops.[46]

analyzers
an adaptive strategy that seeks to minimize risk and maximize profits by following or imitating the proven successes of prospectors

Analyzers are a blend of the defender and prospector strategies. Analyzers seek moderate, steady growth *and* limited opportunities for fast growth. Analyzers are rarely first to market with new products or services. Instead, they try to simultaneously minimize risk and maximize profits by following or imitating the proven successes of prospectors. India-based Ranbaxy Laboratories follows an analyzer strategy by making low-priced generic copies of already popular patented drugs, such as GlaxoSmithKline's antibiotic Ceftin and Eli

Lilly & Co.'s Ceclor. And, with $80 billion of patented drugs losing their patent protection in the next four years, Ranbaxy plans to file applications with the U.S. Food and Drug Administration to make 20 more generic drugs.[47]

reactors
an adaptive strategy of not following a consistent strategy, but instead reacting to changes in the external environment after they occur

Finally, unlike defenders, prospectors, or analyzers, **reactors** do not follow a consistent strategy. Rather than anticipating and preparing for external opportunities and threats, reactors tend to "react" to changes in their external environment after they occur. Not surprisingly, reactors tend to be poorer performers than defenders, prospectors, or analyzers.

Review 4
Industry-Level Strategies

Industry-level strategies focus on how companies choose to compete in their industry. Five industry forces determine an industry's overall attractiveness to corporate investors and potential for long-term profitability. Together, a high level of new entrants, substitute products or services, bargaining power of suppliers, bargaining power of buyers, and rivalry between competitors combine to increase competition and decrease profits. Three positioning strategies can help companies protect themselves from the negative effects of industry-wide competition. Under a cost leadership strategy, firms try to keep production costs low so that they can sell products at prices lower than competitors'. Differentiation is a strategy aimed at making a product or service sufficiently different from competitors' that it can command a premium price. Using a focus strategy, firms seek to produce a specialized product or service for a limited, specially targeted group of customers. The four adaptive strategies help companies adapt to changes in the external environment. Defenders want to "defend" their current strategic positions. Prospectors look for new market opportunities by bringing innovative new products to market. Analyzers minimize risk by following the proven successes of prospectors. Reactors do not follow a consistent strategy, but instead react to changes in their external environment after they occur.

5 Firm-Level Strategies

Sony brings out its PlayStation2 video game console; Microsoft counters with its Xbox. SprintPCS drops prices and increases monthly cell phone minutes; Verizon strikes back with better reception and even lower prices and more minutes. FedEx, the overnight delivery company, decides to begin delivering much larger goods, the sweet spot in UPS's business, so UPS retaliates by moving aggressively into overnight delivery of smaller packages. Starbucks Coffee opens a store, and nearby locally run coffeehouses respond by improving service, increasing portions, and holding the line on prices. Attack and respond, respond and attack. **Firm-level strategy** addresses the question "How should we compete against a particular firm?"

firm-level strategy
a corporate strategy that addresses the question "How should we compete against a particular firm?"

Let's find out more about the firm-level strategies (i.e., direct competition between companies) by reading about 5.1 the basics of direct competition and 5.2 the strategic moves involved in direct competition between companies.

5.1 Direct Competition

While Porter's five industry forces indicate the overall level of competition in an industry, most companies do not compete directly with all the firms in their industry. For example, McDonald's and Red Lobster are both in the restaurant business, but no one would characterize them as competitors. McDonald's offers low-cost, convenient fast food in a "seat yourself" restaurant, while Red Lobster offers mid-priced, sit-down seafood dinners complete with servers and a bar.

Instead of "competing" with the industry, most firms compete directly with just a few companies. **Direct competition** is the rivalry between two companies offering similar products and services that acknowledge each other as rivals and take offensive and defensive positions as they act and react to each other's strategic actions.[48] Two factors determine the extent to which firms will be in direct competition with each other: market commonality and resource similarity. **Market commonality** is the degree to which two companies have overlapping products, services, or customers in multiple markets. The more markets in which there is product, service, or customer overlap, the more intense the direct competition between the two companies. **Resource similarity** is the extent to which a competitor has similar amounts and kinds of resources, that is, similar assets, capabilities, processes, information, and knowledge used to create and sustain an advantage over competitors. From a competitive standpoint, resource similarity means that your direct competitors can probably match the strategic actions that your company takes.

direct competition
the rivalry between two companies that offer similar products and services, acknowledge each other as rivals, and act and react to each other's strategic actions

market commonality
the degree to which two companies have overlapping products, services, or customers in multiple markets

resource similarity
the extent to which a competitor has similar amounts and kinds of resources

Exhibit 8.8 shows how market commonality and resource similarity interact to determine when and where companies are in direct competition.[49] The overlapping area in each quadrant (between the triangle and the rectangle, or between the differently colored rectangles) depicts market commonality. The larger the overlap, the greater the market commonality. Shapes depict resource similarity, with rectangles representing one set of competitive resources and triangles representing another. Quadrant I shows two companies in direct competition because they have similar resources at their disposal and a high degree of market commonality. This reflects the fact that they try to sell similar products and services to similar customers. McDonald's and Burger King would clearly fit here as direct competitors.

In Quadrant II, the overlapping parts of the triangle and rectangle show two companies going after similar customers with some similar products or services, but doing so with different competitive resources. McDonald's and Wendy's restaurants would fit here. Wendy's is after the same lunchtime and dinner crowds that McDonald's is. Nevertheless, it is less of a direct competitor to McDonald's than Burger King is, because Wendy's hamburgers, fries, shakes, and salads are more expensive. For example, Wendy's Garden Sensation salads (using fancy lettuce varieties, grape tomatoes, mandarin oranges,

exhibit 8.8

A Framework of Direct Competition

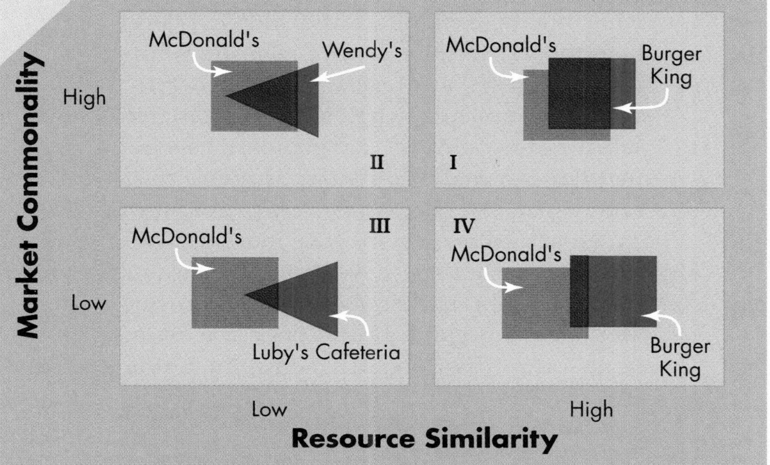

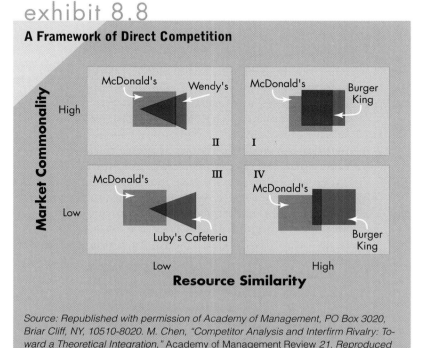

Source: Republished with permission of Academy of Management, PO Box 3020, Briar Cliff, NY, 10510-8020. M. Chen, "Competitor Analysis and Interfirm Rivalry: Toward a Theoretical Integration," Academy of Management Review *21. Reproduced by permission of the publisher via Copyright Clearance Center, Inc.*

etc.) bring in new customers who would have eaten at more expensive casual dining restaurants like Applebee's.[50]

In Quadrant III, the very small overlap shows two companies with different competitive resources and little market commonality. McDonald's and Luby's cafeteria fit here. Although both are in the fast-food business, there's almost no overlap in terms of products and customers. For example, Luby's sells baked chicken, turkey, roasts, meat loaf, and vegetables, none of which are available at McDonald's. Furthermore, Luby's customers aren't likely to eat at McDonald's. In fact, Luby's is not really competing with other fast-food restaurants, but with eating at home.[51]

Finally, in Quadrant IV, the small overlap between the two rectangles shows two companies competing with similar resources but with little market commonality. Surprisingly, McDonald's and Burger King fit here, too. The major difference from Quadrant I is that Quadrant IV represents direct competition between McDonald's and Burger King in Japan, not the United States. Both sell burgers and fries in Japan (i.e., similar products). Unlike the U.S. market, however, market commonality is low because of Burger King's small size and because few Japanese fast-food customers have ever heard of it. As Jun Fujita, an assistant manager at a Tokyo McDonald's, said, "We don't see them as a threat at all. Who has ever heard of Burger King?"[52] Unfortunately for Burger King, that statement turned out to be prophetic: after suffering substantial losses, it ended up selling all but a small handful of its restaurants in Japan.[53] This example also illustrates the point that even between direct competitors, competition in each market (i.e., geographic regions, particular products or services, etc.) is unique. Furthermore, direct competitors have different strengths and weaknesses in different markets. So, while Burger King and McDonald's are fierce competitors in the United States, McDonald's, with 3,892 stores, is clearly dominant in Japan.

attack
a competitive move designed to reduce a rival's market share or profits

response
a competitive countermove, prompted by a rival's attack, to defend or improve a company's market share or profit

PERSONAL PRODUCTIVITY T!P

Competitive Intelligence: Shopping the Competition

One of the best ways to keep abreast of the need for strategic change is to "shop the competition." Every time the Wal-Mart CEO visits a local Wal-Mart store, he also visits the nearby Kmart or Target store. When FedEx wants to benchmark its delivery services against the competition, it has FedEx employees, posing as customers, mail identical packages with identical destinations at FedEx *and* UPS offices. Likewise, when Burger King wants to study the efficiency of its drive-through windows, it sends researchers through the drive-through windows at McDonald's and Wendy's, as well as at its own restaurants. Curious about what your competitors are up to? Go shopping.[56]

5.2 Strategic Moves of Direct Competition

While corporate-level strategies help managers decide what business to be in and industry-level strategies help them determine how to compete within an industry, firm-level strategies help managers determine when, where, and what strategic actions should be taken against a direct competitor. Firms in direct competition can make two basic strategic moves: attacks and responses.

An **attack** is a competitive move designed to reduce a rival's market share or profits. For example, hoping to increase its market share at Burger King's expense, McDonald's began a brutal price war by putting eight items on a new $1 value menu, including two sandwiches, the Big'n Tasty quarter pounder and the McChicken sandwich, that usually sold for $1.99.[54] Sales of those sandwiches doubled within weeks. The attack worked very well at first, as Robert Doughty, a Burger King spokesperson complained, "They've created a senseless price war. That has put a lot of competitive pressure on us and others, too."[55] By contrast, a **response** is a countermove, prompted by a rival's at-

exhibit 8.9

Likelihood of Attacks and Responses in Direct Competition

Competitor Analysis	Interfirm Rivalry: Action and Response
Strong Market Commonality	Less Likelihood of an Attack
Weak Market Commonality	Greater Likelihood of an Attack
High Resource Similarity	Greater Likelihood of a Response
Low Resource Similarity	Less Likelihood of a Response

Source: M. Chen, "Competitor Analysis and Interfirm Rivalry: Toward a Theoretical Integration," Academy of Management Review *21 (1996): 100–134.Strategy Making for Firms, Big and Small.*

tack, that is designed to defend or improve a company's market share or profit. Not surprisingly, Burger King swung back at McDonald's, selling 11 menu items for 99 cents, including its popular double cheeseburgers.

Exhibit 8.9 shows that market commonality and resource similarity determine the likelihood of an attack or response, that is, whether a company is likely to attack a direct competitor or to strike back with a strong response when attacked. When market commonality is strong and companies have overlapping products, services, or customers in multiple markets, there is less motivation to attack and more motivation to respond to an attack. The reason for this is straightforward: when firms are direct competitors in a large number of markets, they have a great deal at stake. So, when McDonald's launched an aggressive price war with its value menu, Burger King had no choice but to respond by cutting its own prices.

Whereas market commonality affects the likelihood of an attack or a response to an attack, resource similarity largely affects response capability, that is, how quickly and forcefully a company can respond to an attack. When resource similarity is strong, the responding firm will generally be able to match the strategic moves of the attacking firm. Consequently, firms are less likely to attack firms with similar levels of resources, because they're unlikely to gain any sustained advantage when the responding firm strikes back. On the other hand, if one firm is substantially stronger than another (i.e., low resource similarity), then a competitive attack is more likely to produce sustained competitive advantage. With over 30,000 stores to Burger King's 11,000 stores and much more in the way of financial resources, McDonald's launched a price war hoping to inflict serious financial damage on Burger King while suffering minimal financial damage to itself. This strategy worked to some extent. Although Burger King sold 11 menu items for 99 cents, it wasn't willing or able to cut the price of its best-selling Whopper sandwiches to 99 cents (from $1.99). Basically admitting that it couldn't afford to match McDonald's price cuts on more expensive sandwiches, a Burger King spokesperson insisted, "McDonald's can't sell those sandwiches at $1 without losing money. It isn't sustainable." Thanks to its much larger financial resources, McDonald's had the funds to outlast Burger King in the price war. As often happens, though, the price war ended up hurting both companies' profits.[57] McDonald's ended the price war when it became clear that lower prices didn't help it draw more customers to its restaurants.

In general, the greater the number of moves (i.e., attacks) a company initiates against direct competitors, and the greater a firm's tendency to respond when attacked, the better its performance. More specifically, attackers and early responders (companies that are quick to launch a retaliatory attack) tend to gain market share and profits at the expense of late responders. This is not to suggest that a "full-attack" strategy always works best. In fact, attacks can provoke harsh retaliatory responses. Consequently, when deciding when, where, and what strategic actions to take against a direct competitor, managers should always consider the possibility of retaliation.

Review 5
Firm-Level Strategies

Firm-level strategies are concerned with direct competition between firms. Market commonality and resource similarity determine whether firms are in direct competition and thus likely to attack each other or respond to each other's attacks. In general, the more markets in which there is product, service, or customer overlap, and the greater the resource similarity between two firms, the more intense the direct competition between them. When firms are direct competitors in a large number of markets, attacks are less likely, because responding firms are highly motivated to quickly and forcefully defend their profits and market share. By contrast, resource similarity affects response capability, meaning how quickly and forcefully a company responds to an attack. When resource similarity is strong, attacks are much less likely to produce a sustained advantage, because the responding firm is capable of striking back with equal force.

Market entries and exits are the most important kinds of attacks and responses. Entering a new market is a clear offensive signal, while exiting a market is a clear signal that a company is retreating. Market entry is perhaps the most forceful attack or response, because it sends the clear signal that the company is committed to gaining or defending market share and profits at a direct competitor's expense. In general, attackers and early responders gain market share and profits at the expense of late responders. Attacks must be carefully planned and carried out, however, because they can provoke harsh retaliatory responses.

STUDY TIP Fresh examples of management topics can be found everyday in the business press. Pick up a copy of *The Wall Street Journal* and read several articles. List the strategy issues facing the companies you read about.

MANAGEMENT TEAM DECISION

WE DELIVER FOR YOU

When the United States Postal Service (USPS) closed its books in December 2002, for the first time in history, its loss decreased from the previous year.[58] Not only was the loss of $676 million much less than predicted, but it came during a year when revenue increased $819 million. With total annual revenue of $66.7 billion, the USPS is more than twice the size of UPS and three times the size of FedEx. The USPS has 750,000 employees to help it deliver mail to every address in the United States, six days a week. With so much revenue and so many employees, why isn't the Postal Service more competitive?

Over the same period, the USPS's volume of mail (and packages) dropped by 4.6 billion pieces. Standard and First Class mail dropped 4 billion pieces, a testament to the pervasiveness of email and fax. The drops in Priority and Express Mail, however, were more precipitous at 10.7 and 11.7 percent, respectively. Priority and Express mail are losing out to internal competition—the less expensive Parcel Post—and they are also losing market share to their commercial competitors, FedEx, UPS, and Airborne.

Despite its declining volumes, Express Mail makes money for the Postal Service. Priced at $14, an Express mail letter costs $6 to deliver, adding about $8 to the bottom line, or about $600 million annually. The cost of delivering that letter is declining because the USPS no longer flies a dedicated fleet of aircraft to support the product. In fact, it has enlisted the assistance of FedEx to provide Priority mail with some much needed stability. Lacking the sophisticated technology that is prevalent at its competitors, the USPS is benefiting from FedEx's technology, which enables the USPS to track every container and every piece, something the USPS couldn't do on its own. FedEx's system of quality control has been an eye-opener for USPS executives, who are considering increasing the amount of international mail and ground mail shipped on FedEx's network.

But why can't the Postal Service be successful on its own? That's exactly what the Presidential Commission for the Overhaul of the USPS wants to find out. Since 1971, the Postal Service has been governed by the Postal Reform Act, which transformed the government agency into a government entity run more like a business. But even that legislation is fair game for change by the nine members of the newly formed commission, who include several business leaders such as Michael Eskew, the chairman and CEO of rival UPS, and James Johnson, former chairman of Fannie Mae.

For this Management Team Decision, you will need to form a team of four to five members and assume the role of the Presidential Commission for the Overhaul of the USPS.

Questions

1. Clearly, there is a great need for strategic change at the USPS. As the Presidential Commission, conduct a situational analysis for the USPS. What are its internal strengths (i.e., core competencies) and weaknesses? What strategic opportunities and threats does it face?

2. The job of the commission is to figure out what the Postal Service should get into, what it should not be in, and its future role. In other words, "How should the USPS compete in its industry?" Sketch the industry using Porter's five industry forces. Based on your sketch of the industry, determine a positioning and an adaptive strategy for the USPS.

3. Will the strategy your commission has created be sufficient to create a sustainable competitive advantage for the Postal Service? Why or why not? If not, then what is the goal of the strategy?

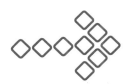

DEVELOP YOUR CAREER POTENTIAL

AN INDIVIDUAL SWOT ANALYSIS

In order to maintain and sustain a competitive advantage, companies continue to analyze their overall strategy in light of their current situation.[59] In doing so, a SWOT analysis is often used. The SWOT analysis focuses on the strengths and weaknesses evident in the firm's internal environment and the opportunities and threats present in the firm's external environment. One way to gain experience in conducting a SWOT analysis is to perform one on yourself—in other words, conduct a personal SWOT analysis.

Assume you have just completed your college education and are ready to apply for a job as a manager of a small to medium-sized facility. Perform a personal SWOT analysis to determine if your current situation matches your overall strategy. Identifying your strengths will most likely be the easiest step in the analysis. They will most likely be the skills, abilities, experience, and knowledge that help differentiate you from your competitors. Take care to be realistic and honest in analyzing your strengths and weaknesses.

One way of identifying both strengths and weaknesses is to look at previous job evaluation comments and talk to former and present employers and coworkers. Their comments will typically focus on objective strengths and weaknesses that you exhibit or exhibited while on the job. You may also gather information about your strengths and weaknesses by analyzing your personal interests and learning more about your personality type. Most college placement offices have software to help students identify their interests and personality types and then match that information to certain career paths. This type of assessment can help ensure that you do not choose a career path that is incongruent with your personality and interests.

Probably the hardest portion of the personal SWOT analysis will be the identification of your weaknesses. As humans, we are often reluctant to focus on our deficiencies; nonetheless, being aware of potential weaknesses can help us reduce them or improve upon them. Since you are preparing for a career in management, you should research what skills, abilities, knowledge, and experience are needed to be a successful manager. Comparing your personal strengths to those needed as a manager can help you identify potential weaknesses. Once you identify weaknesses, develop a plan to overcome them. Remember that most annual evaluations will include both strengths and weaknesses, so don't forget to include this valuable piece of information in your analysis.

Opportunities can be chosen by looking at various employment possibilities for entry-level managers at this particular point in time. In this part of the analysis, it helps to match your personal strengths with opportunities. For example, if you have experience in manufacturing, you may choose to initially apply only to manufacturing-type businesses.

The last step of the analysis involves identifying potential threats. Threats are barriers that can prevent you from obtaining your goals. Threats may include events such as an economic recession that reduces the number of job openings for entry-level managers. By knowing what the barriers are and by assembling proactive plans to help deal with them, you can reduce the possibility of your strategy becoming ineffective.

Focusing on a personal SWOT analysis can be a practical way to prepare for an actual company analysis, and it also allows you to learn more about yourself and your long-term plans.

Questions

1. In light of the SWOT analysis, what plans might you propose for yourself that will help you maximize your strengths, exploit your opportunities, and minimize your weaknesses and threats? Write three S.M.A.R.T. goals (remember Chapter 4) that will help you implement your plans.
2. How might this assignment prepare you for both your academic and your professional career?

take two video!

BIZ FLIX Blue Crush

Anne Marie Chadwick (Kate Bosworth) and her friends Eden (Michelle Rodriguez) and Lena (Sanoe Lake) work as hotel maids to support their commitment to surfing the magnificent waves of Hawaii's North Shore. They live in a simple beach shack where Anne Marie also cares for her sister Penny (Mika Boorem). Anne Marie trains daily to compete in the Pipe Masters surf competition. She also must fight off nagging fears from a nearly fatal surfing accident. Professional quarterback Matt Tollman (Matthew Davis) asks her to teach him to surf, and their romance soon presents another distraction for Anne Marie. *Blue Crush* is easy to watch and features some extraordinary surfing sequences including many with professional surfers.

This scene comes from the "No Fear" sequence near the end of the film. Anne Marie was thrown from her board during her first ride, almost re-creating her earlier accident. The judges gave her a score of 4.6, enough to move her into this second round. She now competes against top surfer Keala Kennelly (herself). Anne Marie has not yet had a scoring ride in this round. Kennelly has more points than Anne Marie but encourages and coaches her to catch a wave and have no fear. This section of the scene follows Kennelly's efforts to encourage Anne Marie to successfully ride "The Pipe."

What to Watch for and Ask Yourself

1. Describe the level of risk in Anne Marie's strategy.
2. What level of competitive advantage does Anne Marie have?
3. What parallels do you see between Anne Marie's involvement in the competition and a modern manager's experience in the competitive business environment? Perform a SWOT analysis for Anne Marie.

MGMT WORKPLACE Caribou Coffee

Caribou Coffee buys, roasts, and serves premium blend coffee in its growing chain of retail stores. Founded in Minnesota, Caribou has built upon quality ratings consistently higher than those of Starbucks to gradually expand into potentially more lucrative markets such as Chicago, Atlanta, and Washington, D.C. CEO Don Dempsey stresses that entering new markets is a tricky business and that the firm needs to consider several factors when doing so. Using its move into Washington, D.C., as an example, Dempsey explains how Caribou analyzed the size of the market, its quality, and the possibility that it could serve as a platform for entering additional proximate markets.

What to Watch for and Ask Yourself

1. According to the Boston Consulting Group matrix, what category best fits Caribou Coffee? Do you agree with Don Dempsey's expansion strategy?
2. Describe Caribou's strategic approach to direct competition. Is Caribou an attacker, a responder, or both? Explain.
3. Assess Caribou's entrepreneurial orientation.

CHAPTER NINE

Innovation and Change

outline

WHAT WOULD YOU DO?

Sullivan Park Research & Development Campus, Corning, Incorporated, Erwin, New York.[1] Corning, Incorporated research and development lab was founded in 1908 and soon developed a new signal lantern for communicating on railroads. Made of special glass, Corning's area of expertise, the lantern wouldn't shatter even if it was hot on the inside (from the bright light) and cold on the outside (from ice).

Since then, innovation has been the key to Corning's strategy of continuous renewal. Corning made some of the first light bulbs for Thomas Edison and then invented machines that could make light bulbs by the thousands. Corning created a way to make color TV tubes out of glass, thoroughly dominating that industry. And it invented and used machines to make all of the thermometer glass produced in the United States. But Corning doesn't make light bulbs, color TV tubes, or thermometer glass any more. Corning usually invents

student resources

Experiencing Management
Explore the four levels of learning by doing the simulation module on Innovation & Change.

Study Guide
Mini lecture reviews all the learning points in the chapter and concludes with a case on Lego.

Take Two Video
Biz Flix is a scene from *Apollo 13*. Management Workplace is a segment on Peter Pan Bus Lines.

PowerPoint®
12 slides with graphics provide an outline for this chapter.

Author Insights
Chuck discusses how long it actually takes people to change.

Self Test
22 true/false questions, 22 multiple-choice questions, a management scenario, and 7 exhibit worksheets

something, comes up with a way to mass-produce it, goes into that business, dominating it at first, and then gets out of the business when other companies bring down prices by copying what it does. At that point, Corning reinvents itself by turning to the next set of innovations coming out of its R&D labs at Sullivan Park.

As the new director of glass and glass ceramics (Corning's specialty) at Sullivan Park, it's your job to make sure that this creative, "let's keep innovating" atmosphere continues. You "supervise," and you use that word loosely, 25 Ph.D.s and 20 technicians and support personnel. Their job is to invent new kinds of glass and improve the performance of optical fiber used in telecommunications networks. You're responsible for their performance and success, but many are extremely independent and difficult to manage. Your first responsibility, however, is keeping your researchers happy; after all, you depend on their creativity. But your second responsibility is making sure that Corning gets a payback on the $2 million per day it spends on R&D. Somehow, you've got to find the right balance between allowing freedom, promoting creativity, and controlling costs and schedules.

But beyond this, you and your researchers are faced with the difficult responsibility of deciding which ideas deserve their time and Corning's dollars. The choices you make are critical. Guess right, and profits and market share rise. Guess wrong, and losses pile up and people lose their jobs. For example, Corning's latest cash cow product is optical fiber, which accounts for 40 percent of its total revenues. But, with the telecommunications bust almost as bad as the dotcom bust, it may not make sense to spend millions more on optical fiber research. On the other hand, if you de-emphasize research on optical fibers, you may lose ground to your competitors in the future. Management is counting on you and your researchers to come up with a series of blockbuster innovations to revive sales and profits.

You've been in this business long enough to know that technological innovation is both competence enhancing and competence destroying. Companies that bet on the wrong or old technology often struggle, while companies that bet on the right technology usually prosper. But how do you decide which technologies and ideas are the best bets? Well, you've got difficult decisions to make. To start, what should you do to continue to encourage creativity and innovation among your researchers? Next, should you shoot for incremental improvements in existing technologies or new, transformational ideas that are quantum improvements over today's technology? This choice will affect the way you manage your group. Finally, what's the best way of deciding which ideas deserve your researchers' time and Corning's dollars? No matter what you choose, your responsibility is to turn out ideas or technologies that can be turned into products or services that give Corning a sustainable competitive advantage. **With Corning's prospects for growth on your shoulders, what would you do?**

organizational innovation
the successful implementation of creative ideas in organizations

creativity
the production of novel and useful ideas

organizational change
a difference in the form, quality, or condition of an organization over time

We begin this chapter by reviewing the issues associated with organizational innovation. **Organizational innovation**, the problem facing Corning, is the successful implementation of creative ideas in an organization.[2] **Creativity**, which is a form of organizational innovation, is the production of novel and useful ideas.[3] In the first part of this chapter, you will learn why innovation matters and how to manage innovation to create and sustain a competitive advantage.

In the second half of this chapter, you will learn about organizational change. **Organizational change** is a difference in the form, quality, or condition of an organization over time.[4] For example, for most people, the name "Olivetti" brings to mind typewriters, the product that first made Olivetti famous internationally. Over the years, however, Olivetti moved away from typewriters to become a technology company. In fact, the Olivetti M20 was one of the very first personal computers. Then, Olivetti changed again, selling its computer division, and refocusing on telecommunications to become the sixth largest provider of fixed and mobile phone services in the world (and the largest in Italy).[5] In each instance, from typewriters to computers and then from computers to telecommunications, Olivetti changed significantly in form, quality, and condition. In the second half of this chapter, you will learn the ways in which companies can manage changes like these.

Organizational Innovation

Do you remember when you were a child and first saw a blimp floating overhead? It moved slowly, was visible for miles, and held your attention as it got closer, passed overhead, and then floated away. The same characteristics that make blimps fascinating to kids also make them great for advertising (i.e., slow, visible, hold attention). Company names are clearly displayed on the side of blimps at sporting events attended by thousands and seen by millions on TV. Blimps are so commonplace that major sporting events such as the Super Bowl would seem incomplete without overhead camera shots from the blimp.

Today, however, the "Lightship," an innovative blimp made by the American Blimp Company, is revolutionizing the blimp business and the advertising revenues that go with it. Lightships are much smaller and cheaper, so it takes only 14 people to staff the ground and flight crews at a cost of $200,000 per month, rather than 24 people at a cost of $300,000 per month for a typical blimp. But the most important advantage is that Lightships are lighted from the inside. So, when it gets dark, the company name and logo on the side of the blimp are still visible! Since most sporting events take place at night, this is critical to maximizing the size of their TV audience.[6]

Organizational innovation, like American Blimp's new Lightships, is the successful implementation of creative ideas in an organization.[7]

After reading the next two sections on organizational innovation, you should be able to

1. explain why innovation matters to companies.
2. discuss the different methods that managers can use to effectively manage innovation in their organizations.

1 Why Innovation Matters

We can only guess what changes technological innovations will bring in the next 20 years. Maybe we'll be listening to compact chips rather than compact discs. Maybe cars won't need tune-ups. Maybe we'll use the Internet to have cookies delivered hot to our homes like pizza. And maybe TVs will be voice-activated, so it won't matter if you lose the remote (just don't lose your voice). Who knows? The only thing we do know about the next 20 years is that innovation will continue to change our lives.

Let's begin our discussion of innovation by learning about 1.1 technology cycles and 1.2 innovation streams.

1.1 Technology Cycles

technology cycle
a cycle that begins with the "birth" of a new technology and ends when that technology reaches its limits and is replaced by a newer, substantially better technology

In Chapter 2, you learned that *technology* is the knowledge, tools, and techniques used to transform inputs (raw materials, information, etc.) into outputs (products and services). A **technology cycle** begins with the "birth" of a new technology and ends when that technology reaches its limits and "dies" as it is replaced by a newer, substantially better technology.[8] For example, technology cycles occurred when air conditioning supplanted fans, when Henry Ford's Model T replaced horse-drawn carriages, when planes replaced trains as a means of cross-country travel, when vaccines that prevented diseases replaced medicines designed to treat them, and when battery-powered wristwatches replaced mechanically powered, stem-wound wristwatches.

S-curve pattern of innovation
a pattern of technological innovation characterized by slow initial progress, then rapid progress, and then again by slow progress as a technology matures and reaches its limits

From Gutenberg's invention of the printing press in the 1400s to the rapid advance of the Internet, studies of hundreds of technological innovations have shown that nearly all technology cycles follow the typical **S-curve pattern of innovation** shown in Exhibit 9.1.[9] Early in a technology cycle, there is still much to learn and progress is slow, as depicted by point A on the S-curve. The flat slope indicates that increased effort (i.e., money, research and development) brings only small improvements in technological performance. Intel's technology cycles have followed this pattern. Intel spends billions to develop new computer chips and to build new production facilities to produce them. Intel has found that the technology cycle for its integrated circuits (that power personal computers) is about three years. In each three-year cycle, Intel introduces a new chip, improves the chip by making it a little bit faster each year, and then replaces that chip at the end of the cycle with a brand new chip that is substantially faster than the old chip. At first, though, the billions Intel spends typically produce only small improvements in performance. For instance, as shown in Exhibit 9.2, Intel's first 60 megahertz (MHz) Pentium processors ran at a speed of 51 based on the iComp Index.[10] (The iComp Index is a benchmark test for measuring relative computer speed. For example, a computer with an iComp score of 200 is twice as fast as a computer with an iComp score of 100.) Yet, six months later, Intel's new 75 MHz Pentium was only slightly faster, with an iComp speed of 67.

Fortunately, as the technology matures, researchers figure out how to get better performance from the new

exhibit 9.1

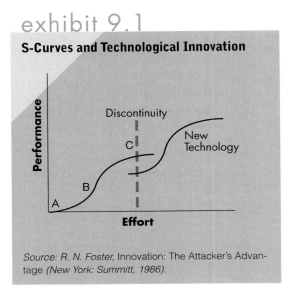

S-Curves and Technological Innovation

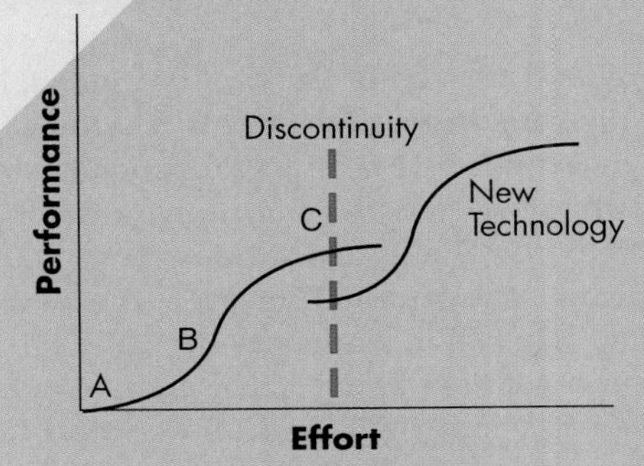

Source: R. N. Foster, Innovation: The Attacker's Advantage *(New York: Summitt, 1986).*

exhibit 9.2

iComp Index 2.0 Comparing the Relative Performance of Different Intel Microprocessors

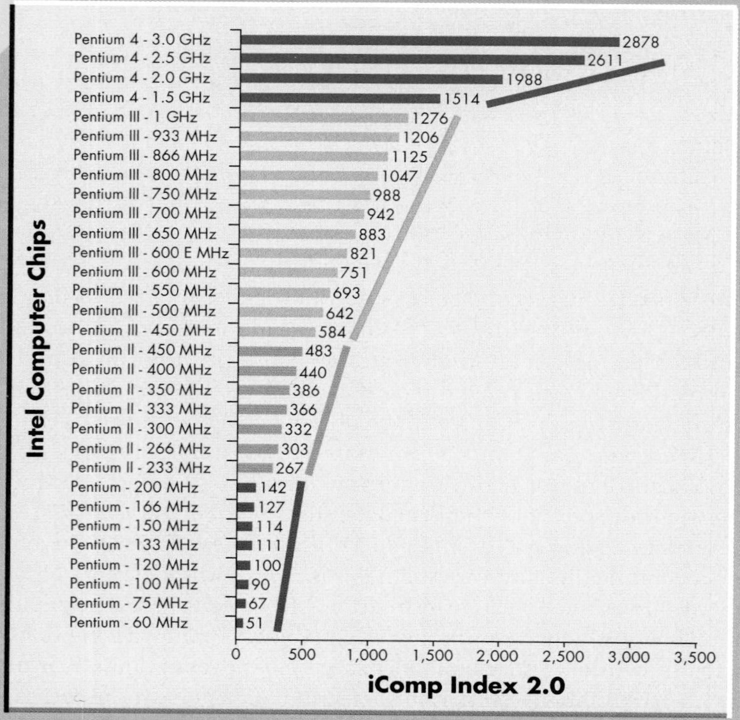

Source: "Intel iComp (Full List)," Ideas International, [Online] available at http://www.ideasinternational.com/benchmark/intel/icomp.html, 16 May 2002; "Benchmark Resources: iComp Index3.0," Intel, [Online] available at http://developer.intel.com/procs/perf/icomp/index.htm, 13 October 2001. "PC CPU Benchmarks, News, Prices and Reviews," CPU Scorecard, *[Online] available at http:///www.cpuscorecard.com, 16 May 2003.*

technology. This is represented by point B of the S-curve in Exhibit 9.1. The steeper slope indicates that small amounts of effort will result in significant increases in performance. Again, Intel's technology cycles have followed this pattern. In fact, after six months to a year with a new chip design, Intel's engineering and production people typically figure out how to make the new chips much faster than they were initially. For example, as shown in Exhibit 9.2, Intel soon rolled out 100 MHz, 120 MHz, 133 MHz, 150 MHz, and 166 MHz Pentium chips that were 76 percent, 117 percent, 124 percent, 149 percent, and 178 percent faster than the original 60 MHz speed.

At point C, the flat slope again indicates that further efforts to develop this particular technology will result in only small increases in performance. More importantly, however, point C indicates that the performance limits of that particular technology are being reached. In other words, additional significant improvements in performance are highly unlikely. For example, Exhibit 9.2 shows that with iComp speeds of 127 and 142, Intel's 166 MHz and 200 MHz Pentiums were 2.49 and 2.78 times faster than its original 60 MHz Pentiums. Yet, despite these impressive gains in performance, Intel was unable to make its Pentium chips run any faster, because the basic Pentium design had reached its limits.

After a technology has reached its limits at the top of the S-curve, significant improvements in performance usually come from radical new designs or new performance-enhancing materials. In Exhibit 9.1, that new technology is represented by the second S-curve. The changeover or discontinuity between the new and old technologies is represented by the dotted line. At first, the new and old technologies will likely coexist. Eventually, however, the new technology will replace the old technology. When that happens, the old technology cycle will be complete, and a new one will have started. The changeover between Intel's Pentium processors, the old technology, and its Pentium II processors, the new technology (these chips used significantly different technologies despite their similar names), took approximately one year. Exhibit 9.2 shows this changeover or discontinuity between the two technologies. With an iComp speed of 267, the first Pentium II (233 MHz) was 88 percent faster than the last and fastest 200 MHz Pentium processor. And because their design and performance were significantly different (and faster) from Pentium II chips, Intel's Pentium III chips represented the beginning of yet another S-curve technology cycle in integrated circuits. This can be seen by the fact that a 450 MHz Pentium III processor was 21 percent faster than a 450 MHz Pentium II chip. Over time, improving existing technology (tweaking the performance of the current technology cycle), combined with replacing old technology with new technology cycles (i.e., the Pentium 4 replacing the Pentium III replacing the Pentium II replacing the Pentium), has increased the speed of Pentium computer processors by a factor of 56 in just 15 years and all computer processors by a factor of 300!

While the evolution of Intel's Pentium chips has been used to illustrate the idea of S-curves and technology cycles, it's important to note that technology cycles and technological innovation don't necessarily mean "high technology." Remember, *technology* is simply the knowledge, tools, and techniques used to transform inputs (raw materials, information, etc.) into outputs (products and services). So a technology cycle occurs whenever there are major advances or changes in the *knowledge*, *tools*, and *techniques* of a field or discipline. For example, one of the most important technology cycles in the history of civilization occurred in 1859, when 1,300 miles of central sewer line were constructed throughout London to carry human waste to the sea more than 11 miles away. This extensive sewer system replaced the widespread practice of directly dumping raw sewage into streets, where people walked through it and where it drained into public wells that supplied drinking water. Though the relationship wasn't known at the time, preventing waste runoff from contaminating water supplies stopped the spread of cholera that had killed millions of people for centuries in cities throughout the world.[11] Safe water supplies immediately translated into better health and longer life expectancies. Indeed, the water you drink today is safe thanks to this "technology" breakthrough. So, when you think about technology cycles, don't automatically think "high technology." Instead, broaden your perspective by considering advances or changes in knowledge, tools, and techniques.

1.2 Innovation Streams

In Chapter 8, you learned that organizations can create *competitive advantage* for themselves if they have a *distinctive competence* that allows them to make, do, or perform something better than their competitors. Furthermore, a competitive advantage becomes sustainable if other companies cannot duplicate the benefits obtained from that distinctive competence. Technological innovation, however, makes it possible not only to duplicate the benefits obtained from a company's distinctive advantage, but also to quickly turn a company's competitive advantage into a competitive disadvantage.

Companies that want to sustain a competitive advantage must understand and protect themselves from the strategic threats of innovation. Over the long run, the best way to do that is for a company to create a stream of its own innovative ideas and products year after year. Consequently, we define **innovation streams** as patterns of innovation over time that can create sustainable competitive advantage.[12] Exhibit 9.3 shows a typical innovation consisting of a series of technology cycles. Recall that technological cycles begin with a new technology and end when that technology is replaced by a newer, substantially better technology. The innovation stream in Exhibit 9.3 shows three such technology cycles.

innovation streams
patterns of innovation over time that can create sustainable competitive advantage

exhibit 9.3

Innovation Streams: Technology Cycles over Time

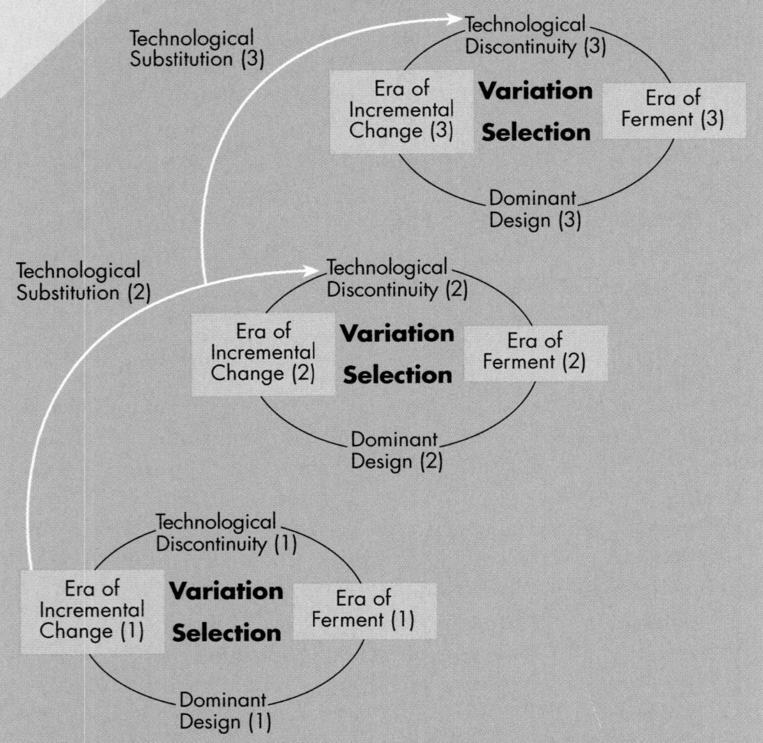

Source: M. L. Tushman, P. C. Anderson, & C. O'Reilly, "Technology Cycles, Innovation Streams, and Ambidextrous Organizations," in Managing Strategic Innovation and Change, *ed. M. L. Tushman & P. Anderson (1997), 3–23. © 1997 by Oxford University Press, Inc. Used by permission of Oxford University Press, Inc.*

An innovation stream begins with a **technological discontinuity**, in which a scientific advance or a unique combination of existing technologies creates a significant breakthrough in performance or function. For example, coronary bypass surgery, which is a common treatment for heart attacks, has saved millions of lives, but because of the intrusive nature of the surgery—an incision is made from the belly button to the middle of the chest, the breast bone is sawed through, and then a metal ratchet is used to spread the rib cage open—it takes anywhere from three to six months to recover from the operation. Now, thanks to miniature lights, cameras, and surgical tools, surgeons can do bypass operations by making several small, key-sized holes in the chest. So little trauma is associated with this new technique that people can be back at work or on the golf course three to four days after the surgery.[13]

Technological discontinuities are followed by an **era of ferment**, characterized by technological substitution and design competition. **Technological substitution** occurs when customers purchase new technologies to replace older technologies. For example, when the telegraph was invented, people used it instead of the Pony Express for cross-country communication. In fact, the Pony Express went out of business almost immediately after the completion of the transcontinental telegraph, which linked telegraph systems from coast to coast.[14]

An era of ferment is also characterized by **design competition**, in which the old technology and several different new technologies compete to establish a new technological standard or dominant design. Because of large investments in old technology, and because the new and old technologies are often incompatible with each other, companies and consumers are reluctant to switch to a different technology during design competition. Also, during design competition, the changeover from older to newer technologies is often slowed by the fact that the older technology usually improves significantly in response to the competitive threat from the new technologies.

An era of ferment is followed by the emergence of a **dominant design**, which becomes the accepted market standard for technology.[15] Dominant designs emerge in several ways. One is critical mass, meaning that a particular technology can become the dominant design simply because most people use it. For example, the QWERTY keyboard (look at the top left line of letters on a

technological discontinuity
a scientific advance or unique combination of existing technologies that creates a significant breakthrough in performance or function

era of ferment
the phase of a technology cycle characterized by technological substitution and design competition

technological substitution
the purchase of new technologies to replace older ones

design competition
competition between old and new technologies to establish a new technological standard or dominant design

dominant design
a new technological design or process that becomes the accepted market standard

keyboard) became the dominant design for typewriters, because it slowed typists who, by typing too fast, caused mechanical typewriter keys to jam. Ironically, though computers can easily be switched to the DVORAK keyboard layout, which doubles typing speed and cuts typing errors by half, QWERTY lives on as the standard keyboard. Thus, the best technology doesn't always become the dominant design.

Another way in which dominant designs emerge is through independent standards bodies. For example, the International Telecommunication Union is an independent organization that establishes standards for the communications industry. Various standards are proposed, discussed, negotiated, and changed until the members of the ITU reach agreement on a final set of standards that communication industries (i.e., Internet, telephony, satellites, radio, 3G mobile phones, etc.) will follow worldwide.[16] The ITU will choose an official standard from several competing standards.

Yet, no matter how it happens, the emergence of a dominant design is a key event in an innovation stream. First, the emergence of a dominant design indicates that there are winners and losers. Technological innovation is both competence enhancing and competence destroying. Companies that bet on the wrong design or on the old technology often struggle, while companies that bet on the now-dominant design usually prosper. In fact, more companies are likely to go out of business in an era of ferment than in an economic recession or slowdown. Second, the emergence of a dominant design signals a change away from design experimentation and competition to **incremental change**, a phase in which companies innovate by lowering the cost and improving the functioning and performance of the dominant design. For example, during a technology cycle, manufacturing efficiencies enable Intel to cut the cost of its chips by half to two-thirds, while doubling or tripling their speed. This focus on improving the dominant design continues until the next technological discontinuity occurs.

incremental change
the phase of a technology cycle in which companies innovate by lowering costs and improving the functioning and performance of the dominant technological design

Review 1

Why Innovation Matters

Technology cycles typically follow an S-curve pattern of innovation. Early in the cycle, technological progress is slow and improvements in technological performance are small. As a technology matures, however, performance improves quickly. Finally, small improvements occur as the limits of a technology are reached. At this point, significant improvements in performance must come from new technologies. The best way to protect a competitive advantage is to create a stream of innovative ideas and products. Innovation streams begin with technological discontinuities that create significant breakthroughs in performance or function. Technological discontinuities are followed by an era of ferment, in which customers purchase new technologies (technological substitution) and companies compete to establish the new dominant design (design competition). Dominant designs emerge because of critical mass, because they solve a practical problem, or because of the negotiations of independent standards bodies. Because technological innovation is both competence enhancing and competence destroying, companies that bet on the wrong design often struggle, while companies that bet on the eventual dominant design usually prosper. Emergence of a dominant design leads to a focus on incremental change, lowering costs and making small, but steady, improvements in the dominant design. This focus continues until the next technological discontinuity occurs.

2 Managing Innovation

The previous discussion of technology cycles and innovation streams showed that managers must be equally good at managing innovation in two very different circumstances. First, during eras of ferment, companies must find a way to anticipate and survive the technological discontinuities that can suddenly transform industry leaders into losers and industry unknowns into powerhouses. Companies that can't manage innovation following technological discontinuities risk quick organizational decline and dissolution. Second, after a new dominant design emerges following an era of ferment, companies must manage the very different process of incremental improvement and innovation. Companies that can't manage incremental innovation slowly deteriorate as they fall farther behind industry leaders.

www.experiencing management.com

Managers must encourage and manage innovation or their organizations may become obsolete. To learn about fostering innovation, visit our animated concept and activity site. Choose Innovation&Change from the "select a topic" pull-down menu, then Fostering Innovation from the "overview tab."

http://www.experiencingmanagement.com

Unfortunately, what works well when managing innovation after technological discontinuities doesn't work well when managing innovation during periods of incremental change (and vice versa). Consequently, to successfully manage innovation streams, companies need to be good at three things: 2.1 managing sources of innovation, 2.2 managing innovation during discontinuous change, and 2.3 managing innovation during incremental change.

2.1 Managing Sources of Innovation

Innovation comes from great ideas. So a starting point for managing innovation is to manage the sources of innovation, that is, where new ideas come from. One place that new ideas originate is with brilliant inventors. For example, do you know who invented the telephone, the light bulb, a way to collect and store electricity, air conditioning, radio, television, automobiles, the jet engine, computers, and the Internet? Respectively, these innovations were created by Alexander Graham Bell, Thomas Edison, Pieter van Musschenbroek, Willis Carrier, Guglielmo Marconi, John Baird and Philo T. Farnsworth, Gottlieb Daimler and Wilhelm Maybach, Sir Frank Whittle, Charles Babbage, and Vint Cerf and Robert Kahn. These innovators and their innovations forever changed the course of modern life. Only a few companies, however, have the likes of an Edison, Marconi, or Graham Bell working for them. Given that great thinkers and inventors are in short supply, what might companies do to ensure a steady flow of good ideas?

PERSONAL PRODUCTIVITY T!P

Cultivate Your Most Demanding Customer

Once something is successful, it can be difficult to change. One way to battle complacency is to cultivate demanding customers, who always want more. PPG Industries shoots dead chickens at 850 mph into aircraft windshields to simulate the impact of birds hitting an airplane. Boeing and Airbus won't buy from PPG unless its windshields withstand these tests. PPG also tests antitheft glass for automobiles by seeing how many hits a glass window layered with special plastic can take until it breaks. Luxury automakers that purchase from PPG asked it to develop this new product. So, to force yourself to keep changing, cultivate a demanding customer![17]

Well, when we say that innovation begins with great ideas, we're really saying that innovation begins with creativity. *Creativity* is the production of novel and useful ideas.[18] While companies can't command creativity from employees ("You *will* be more creative!"), they can jump-start innovation by building **creative work environments**, in which workers perceive that creative thoughts and ideas are welcomed and valued. As Exhibit 9.4 shows, creative work environments have six components that encourage creativity: challenging work, organizational encouragement, supervisory encouragement,

creative work environments workplace cultures in which workers perceive that new ideas are welcomed, valued, and encouraged

exhibit 9.4

Components of Creative Work Environments

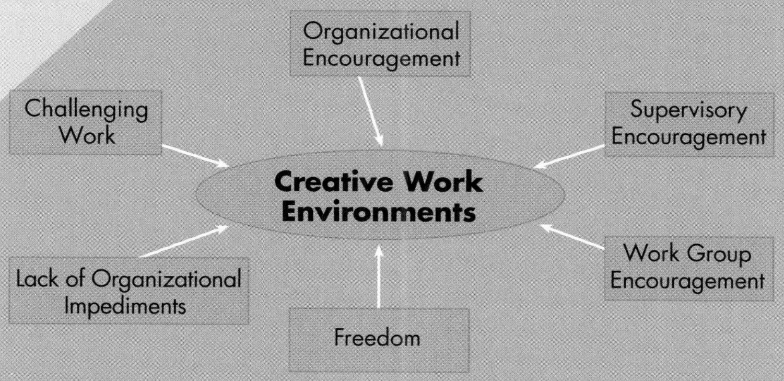

Source: T. M. Amabile, R. Conti, H. Coon, J. Lazenby, & M. Herron, "Assessing the Work Environment for Creativity," Academy of Management Journal *39 (1996): 1154–1184.*

work group encouragement, freedom, and a lack of organizational impediments.[19]

Work is *challenging* when it requires hard work, demands attention and focus, and is perceived as important to others in the organization. Researcher Mihaly Csikszentmihalyi (pronounced ME-high-ee CHICK-sent-me-high-ee) said that challenging work promotes creativity because it creates a rewarding psychological experience known as "flow." **Flow** is a psychological state of effortlessness, in which you become completely absorbed in what you're doing and time seems to fly. (You begin work, become absorbed in it, and then suddenly realize that several hours have passed.) When flow occurs, who you are and what you're doing become one. Csikszentmihalyi first encountered flow when studying artists, but he also found that chess players, rock climbers, dancers, surgeons, and athletes regularly experience flow, too.[20] A key part of creating flow experiences, and thus creative work environments, is to achieve a balance between skills and task challenge. When workers can do more than is required of them, they become bored, and when their skills aren't sufficient to accomplish a task, they become anxious. When skills and task challenge are balanced, however, flow and creativity can occur.

flow
a psychological state of effortlessness, in which you become completely absorbed in what you're doing and time seems to pass quickly

A creative work environment requires three kinds of encouragement: organizational, supervisory, and work group encouragement. *Organizational encouragement* of creativity occurs when management encourages risk taking and new ideas, supports and fairly evaluates new ideas, rewards and recognizes creativity, and encourages the sharing of new ideas throughout different parts of the company.

Supervisory encouragement of creativity occurs when supervisors provide clear goals, encourage open interaction with subordinates, and actively support development teams' work and ideas. *Work group encouragement* occurs when work group members have diverse experience, education, and backgrounds; when there is a mutual openness to ideas; when there is positive, constructive challenge to ideas; and when there is shared commitment to ideas. See Chapter 11, "Managing Teams," for further discussion of the importance of these ideas.

Freedom means having autonomy over one's day-to-day work and a sense of ownership and control over one's ideas. Numerous studies have indicated that creative ideas thrive under conditions of freedom. To foster

DOING THE RIGHT THING

Give Credit, Don't Take It

You came up with a great idea and ran it by your boss, who loved it. Next thing you know, the office is buzzing about this "great new idea." But instead of giving you the credit, your boss took the credit and shamelessly sold the idea as his own. Not only is stealing others' ideas wrong, but nothing kills a creative work environment faster than not giving people credit for their ideas. So, if you're the boss, no matter who comes up with "the" idea, give them credit. Spread the recognition and acknowledgment around so that their coworkers and your boss's boss know about your employees' great ideas. Do the right thing. Give credit where it's due. You'll be rewarded with more great ideas.[21]

COURTESY OF SPORTIME, LLC

Companies can avoid internal impediments to creativity by looking outside the organization. Customers are an important source of innovation. Sportime International followed a customer idea and created Hands-On basketballs for children who need help learning how to shoot.

creativity, companies may also have to remove some impediments to creativity from their work environments. Internal conflict and power struggles, rigid management structures, and a conservative bias toward the status quo can all discourage creativity. They create the perception that others in the organization will decide which ideas are acceptable and deserve support. One way in which many companies avoid a conservative, anti-innovation bias is to ask their customers for ideas. After all, if customers are enthusiastic about new ideas, it's harder to discount them. For example, Sportime International sold a million Hands-On basketballs with color-coded markings that show kids where to place their hands for better shooting accuracy. The idea was suggested by nine-year-old Chris Haas, who has made $35,000 in royalties thus far from the suggestion. Spinmaster started selling its Proshops line of simple, unassembled skateboards and bicycles that kids could put together themselves with interchangeable parts. The idea came from its "kids' advisory board." The unassembled Proshops products and bikes far outsell its already assembled products.[22]

2.2 Managing Innovation during Discontinuous Change

A study of 72 product-development projects (i.e., innovation) in 36 computer companies across the United States, Europe, and Asia found that companies that succeeded in periods of discontinuous change (in which a technological discontinuity created a significant breakthrough in performance or function) typically followed an experiential approach to innovation.[23] **The experiential approach to innovation** assumes that innovation is occurring within a highly uncertain environment and that the key to fast product innovation is to use intuition, flexible options, and hands-on experience to reduce uncertainty and accelerate learning and understanding. The experiential approach to innovation has five parts: design iterations, testing, milestones, multifunctional teams, and powerful leaders.[24]

experiential approach to innovation
an approach to innovation that assumes a highly uncertain environment and uses intuition, flexible options, and hands-on experience to reduce uncertainty and accelerate learning and understanding

design iteration
a cycle of repetition in which a company tests a prototype of a new product or service, improves on that design, and then builds and tests the improved prototype

testing
systematic comparison of different product designs or design iterations

An "iteration" is a repetition. So a **design iteration** is a cycle of repetition in which a company tests a prototype of a new product or service, improves on the design, and then builds and tests the improved product or service prototype. A product prototype is a full-scale working model that is being tested for design, function, and reliability. **Testing** is a systematic comparison of different product designs or design iterations. Companies that want to create a new dominant design following a technological discontinuity quickly build, test, improve, and retest a series of different product prototypes. For example, when the Orion division of Thermedics Detection Company was designing the handle of a surgical laser tool used in cosmetic surgery, its goal was to design a comfortable, functional tool for cosmetic surgeons to use. But since it was impossible to bring busy cosmetic surgeons to the company for product testing, it sent product prototypes to the surgeons and then conducted conference calls with several surgeons at a time to gather their feedback. In the first round of feedback, all the surgeons complained that the tool was too big to be comfortable in their hands for any length of time. After each feedback session, changes were made, and new prototypes were sent to the surgeons for additional feedback. According to product engineer Sam Millen, thanks to testing numerous design iterations, "We finished the working prototype phase in just seven weeks [rather than the usual 18 weeks] and well under budget."[25]

By trying a number of very different designs, or by making successive improvements and changes in the same design, frequent design iterations reduce uncertainty and improve understanding. Simply put, the more prototypes you build, the more likely you are to learn what works and what doesn't. Plus, building a number of prototypes also means that designers and engineers are less likely to "fall in love" with a particular prototype. Instead, they'll be more concerned with improving the product or technology as much as they can. Testing speeds up and improves the innovation process, too. When two very different design prototypes are tested against each other, or the new design iteration is tested against the previous iteration, product design strengths and weaknesses quickly become apparent. Likewise, testing uncovers errors early in the design process when they are easiest to correct. Finally, testing accelerates learning and understanding by forcing engineers and product designers to examine hard data about product performance. When there's hard evidence that prototypes are testing well, the confidence of the design team grows. Also, personal conflict between design team members is less likely when testing focuses on hard measurements and facts rather than personal hunches and preferences.

milestones
formal project review points used to assess progress and performance

Milestones are formal project review points used to assess progress and performance. For example, a company that has put itself on a 12-month schedule to complete a project might schedule milestones at the 3-month, 6-month, and 9-month points on the schedule. By making people regularly assess what they're doing, how well they're performing, and whether they need to take corrective action, milestones provide structure to the general chaos that follows technological discontinuities. Milestones also shorten the innovation process by creating a sense of urgency that keeps everyone on task. For example, when Florida Power & Light was building its first nuclear power facility, the company's construction manager passed out 2,000 desk calendars to company employees, construction contractors, vendors, and suppliers, so that everyone involved in the project was aware of the construction time line. Contractors that regularly missed deadlines were replaced.[26] Finally, milestones are beneficial for innovation, because meeting regular milestones builds momentum by giving people a sense of accomplishment.

multifunctional teams
work teams composed of people from different departments

Multifunctional teams are work teams composed of people from different departments. Multifunctional teams accelerate learning and understanding by mixing and integrating technical, marketing, and manufacturing activities. By involving all key departments in development from the start, multifunctional teams speed innovation through early identification of new ideas or problems that would typically not have been generated or addressed until much later. Kellogg's, the cereal company, isn't known as a particularly innovative company. After all, its best-selling cereal, Frosted Flakes, was created 50 years ago. Furthermore, after creating its top-selling breakfast food, Pop Tarts, Kellogg's took nearly three decades to come up with another new kind of breakfast food, NutriGrain cereal bars. Today, however, the company is using multifunctional design teams composed of market researchers, food technologists, engineers, and cooks to develop new cereals and breakfast foods. Each design team is located between a restaurant-quality kitchen to come up with new food ideas and a minimanufacturing line that is used to run test batches. Thus far, the approach seems to be working. In their first month, Kellogg's multifunctional teams came up with 65 new product ideas and 94 new ways to package existing products. Two of the best new ideas are the popular Raisin Bran Crunch, with thick flakes that don't get soggy in milk, and Rice Krispie Treats, which is a cereal version of the marshmallow squares made in millions of home kitchens (melted marshmallows over Rice Krispies, baked in the oven).[27]

Powerful leaders provide the vision, discipline, and motivation to keep the innovation process focused, on time, and on target. Powerful leaders are able to get resources when they are needed, are typically more experienced, have high status in the company, and are held directly responsible for product success or failure. On average, powerful leaders can get innovation-related projects done nine months faster than leaders with little power or influence.

2.3 Managing Innovation during Incremental Change

As you just read, the experiential approach is used to manage innovation in highly uncertain environments during periods of discontinuous change. In contrast, the compression approach is used to manage innovation in more certain environments during periods of incremental change. And whereas the goals of the experiential approach are significant improvements in performance and the establishment of a *new* dominant technology design, the goals of the compression approach are lower costs and incremental improvements in the performance and function of the *existing* technological design. Finally, the general strategies in each approach are different, too. With the experiential approach, the general strategy is to build something new, different, and substantially better. Since there's so much uncertainty—no one knows which technology will become the market leader—companies adopt a winner-take-all approach by trying to create the market-leading, dominant design. With the compression approach, the general strategy is to compress the time and steps needed to bring about small, consistent improvements in performance and functionality. Because a dominant technology design already exists, the general strategy is to continue improving the existing technology as rapidly as possible.

compression approach to innovation
an approach to innovation that assumes that incremental innovation can be planned using a series of steps, and that compressing those steps can speed innovation

In short, a **compression approach to innovation** assumes that innovation is a predictable process, that incremental innovation can be planned using a series of steps, and that compressing the time it takes to complete those steps can speed up innovation. The compression approach to innovation has five parts: planning, supplier involvement, shortening the time of individual steps, overlapping steps, and multifunctional teams.[28]

In Chapter 4, *planning* was defined as choosing a goal and a method or strategy to achieve that goal. When *planning for incremental innovation*, the goal is to squeeze or compress development time as much as possible, and the general strategy is to create a series of planned steps to accomplish that goal. Planning for incremental innovation helps avoid unnecessary steps. Plus, planning allows developers to sequence steps in the right order to avoid wasted time and shorten the delays between steps. Planning also reduces misunderstandings and decreases coordination problems regarding when and how things are to be done.

generational change change based on incremental improvements to a dominant technological design such that the improved technology is fully backward compatible with the older technology

Most planning for incremental innovation is based on the idea of generational change. **Generational change** occurs when incremental improvements are made to a dominant technological design such that the improved version of the technology is fully backward compatible with the older version.[29] So, unlike technological discontinuities that result in the replacement of older technologies, generational change allows the old and newer versions of the same technological design to coexist in the marketplace. For example, Sony used the idea of generational change to extend the life of its Sony Walkman products. After inventing the Walkman tape player, Sony introduced 250 different kinds of Walkmans over the next decade while making only a few significant changes in the basic Walkman. In fact, 85 percent of the new models simply represented small improvements (i.e., generational change) based on a four-point plan that Sony developed. First, make the Walkmans smaller. Second, make them cheaper. Third, when possible, add small improvements. For example, the first Walkman only played audio tapes, but subsequent Walkmans added AM/FM stereo radio, auto reverse, Dolby sound, water resistance, TV audio band, digital tuning, and enhanced bass. Finally, make minor cosmetic changes in the Walkman's color and appearance. Together, these generational changes have helped Sony maintain above-average profits and a 50 percent share of this market.[30] Furthermore, Sony has used the same generational approach in designing and selling its Walkman CD players, varying colors and adding MP3-playing capability and skip-protection.

Because the compression approach assumes that innovation can follow a series of preplanned steps, one of the ways to shorten development time is *supplier involvement*. Delegating some of the preplanned steps in the innovation process to outside suppliers reduces the amount of work that internal development teams must do. Plus, suppliers provide an alternative source of ideas and expertise that can lead to better designs. In general, the earlier suppliers are involved, the quicker they catch and prevent future problems, such as unrealistic designs or mismatched product specifications.

Another way to shorten development time is simply to *shorten the time of individual steps* in the innovation process. One of the most common ways to do that is through computer-aided design (CAD). CAD speeds up the design process by allowing designers and engineers to make and test design changes using computer models rather than physically testing expensive automobile prototypes. CAD also speeds innovation by making it easy to see how design changes affect engineering, purchasing, and production. Karenann Terrell, director of e-business strategy, explains how DaimlerChrysler's CAD system, FastCar, works: "FastCar takes a virtual CAD/CAM design and teams it with all the other information that we already have on hand about the part or vehicle. So, no longer do we change a part and then ask: 'How much do those new components cost? What are the quality implications?' As we make changes, all that information is integrated into the new designs."[31]

In a sequential design process, each step must be completed before the next step begins. But sometimes multiple development steps can be performed at the same time. *Overlapping steps* shorten the development process by reducing the delays or waiting time between steps. By using overlapping rather than sequential steps, most car companies have reduced the time it takes to develop a brand new car from five years to three years. However, they still develop new models sequentially. First, they design and build, say, a four-door sedan. Then, after perfecting the design and manufacture of the sedan, two or three years later they introduce the two-door coupe. A couple of years after that, they introduce the station wagon version of the same model. Toyota, however, takes the notion of overlapping steps even further by developing all three versions (four-door sedan, two-door coupe, and station wagon) simultaneously. By overlapping model development, Toyota cut its total development time for all three models in half! This helped Toyota bring 18 new or redesigned cars to market in just two years. And its new Picnic and Corolla Spacio models went into production just 14½ months after designs were approved, well under the three years it normally takes to develop a new car.[32] Today, however, Toyota has squeezed development time even more, cutting the time between initial design and production to just 8 months in some cases![33]

Review 2

Managing Innovation

To successfully manage innovation streams, companies must manage the sources of innovation and learn to manage innovation during both discontinuous and incremental change. Since innovation begins with creativity, companies can manage the sources of innovation by supporting a creative work environment in which creative thoughts and ideas are welcomed, valued, and encouraged. Creative work environments provide challenging work; offer organizational, supervisory, and work group encouragement; allow significant freedom; and remove organizational impediments to creativity.

Go to Effective Management Online for a quick comparison of the experiential and compression approaches to managing innovation (http://em-online.swlearning.com).

Companies that succeed in periods of discontinuous change typically follow an experiential approach to innovation. The experiential approach assumes that intuition, flexible options, and hands-on experience can reduce uncertainty and accelerate learning and understanding. This approach involves frequent design iterations, frequent testing, regular milestones, creation of multifunctional teams, and use of powerful leaders to guide the innovation process.

A compression approach to innovation works best during periods of incremental change. This approach assumes that innovation can be planned using a series of steps and that compressing the time it takes to complete those steps can speed up innovation. The five parts to the compression approach are planning (generational change), supplier involvement, shortening the time of individual steps (computer-aided design), overlapping steps, and multifunctional teams.

Organizational Change

The idea was simple. Build a series of music superstores and watch the customers and profits pour in. For a while, it worked. Sales at MARS Music grew from $49 million to $340 million in just five years as the company built 50 new stores. But, while MARS set records for sales, it also lost $100 million during the same period. When MARS when out of business, founder Mark Bergelman blamed the poor economy and tight capital markets. Chief operating officer Ray Miller was more blunt, saying, "Our stores were too big."[34] Bergelman, who successfully founded Office Depot, made sure that each MARS Music store covered 35,000 square feet with $2.5 million in inventory and a staff of 40. But, at that size, the breakeven point for each store was $10 million in sales per year. By contrast, the stores of Guitar Centers, Mars' leading competitor, were half as large at 17,000 square feet and had a much lower breakeven point. When MARS Music went out of business, investors lost $190 million, music equipment suppliers lost $35 million, landlords who had financed $1.8 million in improvements at each store location lost $50 million, and 2,400 people lost their jobs.

The company's collapse wasn't a surprise. MARS Music and everyone else in the industry knew it was hemorrhaging cash. Yet MARS Music was unable to change its business to stop the bleeding. That inability to change, to figure out ways to bring in more customers and to be more efficient, eventually led to its demise.

After reading the next section on organizational change, you should be able to

3 discuss the different methods that managers can use to better manage change as it occurs.

3 Managing Change

According to social psychologist Kurt Lewin, change is a function of the forces that promote change and the opposing forces that slow or resist change.[47] **Change forces** lead to differences in the form, quality, or condition of an organization over time. By contrast, **resistance forces** support the status quo, that is, the existing state of conditions in organizations.

change forces
forces that produce differences in the form, quality, or condition of an organization over time

resistance forces
forces that support the existing state of conditions in organizations

With great views, fine service, and good food, Atwaters, located on top of the 30-story U.S. Bancorp tower in Portland, Oregon, "wanted to be the best restaurant in town and didn't care how much it cost." Under new manager Stephen Earnhart, however, Atwaters' new goal was to be the best restaurant in town *and* make a profit. To attract younger customers, waiters replaced their tuxedos with more casual white aprons and ties. Instead of a team of waiters at each table (waiters, back waiters, and maître d's), service was personalized by having each waiter take responsibility for particular tables in the dining room. When it was slow in the bar, bartenders were asked to help out in the dining room. When it was slow in the dining room, waiters were asked to help out in the bar. Within weeks, employees began to complain. "That's not my job." "That's not what I was hired for." "You're asking me to do more, but you're not paying me for it." As employee dissatisfaction with the changes grew stronger, food began disappearing from the kitchen. Bartenders gave away drinks. The reservation book vanished on busy nights. Stephen Gagnon, a former Atwaters bartender, summed things up, saying, "Employee morale went to hell with all the changes."[35]

resistance to change
opposition to change resulting from self-interest, misunderstanding and distrust, or a general intolerance for change

Resistance to change, like that shown by Atwaters' employees, is caused by self-interest, misunderstanding and distrust, and a general intolerance for change.[36] People resist change out of *self-interest* because they fear that change will cost or deprive them of something they value. For example, resistance might stem from a fear that the changes will result in a loss of pay, power, responsibility, or even perhaps one's job. People also resist change because of *misunderstanding and distrust;* they don't understand the change or the reasons for it, or they distrust the people, typically management, behind the change. Resistance isn't always visible at first, however. In fact, some of the strongest resisters may initially support the changes in public, nodding and smiling their agreement, but then ignore the changes in private and do their jobs as they always have.

www.experiencing management.com

Attempts to unfreeze old behaviors are often met with resistance for a variety of reasons. Learn more about reasons for resistance at our animated concept and activity site. Choose Innovation&Change from the "select a topic" pull-down menu, then Resistance to Change from the "overview tab."

http://www.experiencingmanagement.com

Management consultant Michael Hammer calls this deadly form of resistance the "Kiss of Yes."[37]

Resistance may also come from a generally low tolerance for change. Some people are simply less capable of handling change than others. People with a *low tolerance for change* feel threatened by the uncertainty associated with change and worry that they won't be able to learn the new skills and behaviors needed to successfully negotiate change in their companies.

Because resistance to change is inevitable, successful change efforts require careful management. In this section you will learn about 3.1 managing resistance to change, 3.2 different change tools and techniques, and 3.3 what *not* to do when leading organizational change.

3.1 Managing Resistance to Change

unfreezing getting the people affected by change to believe that change is needed

change intervention the process used to get workers and managers to change their behavior and work practices

refreezing supporting and reinforcing new changes so they "stick"

According to Kurt Lewin, managing organizational change is a basic process of unfreezing, change intervention, and refreezing. **Unfreezing** is getting the people affected by change to believe that change is needed. During the **change intervention** itself, workers and managers change their behavior and work practices. **Refreezing** is supporting and reinforcing the new changes so that they "stick."

Resistance to change, as shown by Atwaters' employees, is an example of frozen behavior. Given the choice between changing and not changing, most people would rather not change. Because resistance to change is natural and inevitable, managers need to unfreeze resistance to change to create successful change programs. The following methods can be used to manage resistance to change: education and communication, participation, negotiation, top management support, and coercion.[38]

When resistance to change is based on insufficient, incorrect, or misleading information, managers should *educate* employees about the need for change and *communicate* change-related information to them. Managers must also supply the information and funding or other support employees need to make changes. For example, resistance to change can be particularly strong when one company buys another company. Jeff Boyd, who worked for a large Canadian company, described the first meeting between the people in his department (the company that was acquired) and the people in the same department from the acquiring company: "It wasn't a friendly meeting. It wasn't hostile or anything like that, but everybody was on their guard a little bit. Right now, everybody's wondering if they'll be able to get along with the other employees, because there's a big difference in both companies' cultures and in the way both companies operate." Boyd concluded, "There's a lot of tension down at the employee level. We're still being kept in the dark about certain things. Everything seems to be up in the air right now."[39]

> **www.experiencing management.com**
>
> A common model of change involves unfreezing old methods, changing and refreezing the new methods. To learn more about this management model of change, visit our animated concept and activity site. Choose Innovation&Change from the "select a topic" pull-down menu then Managing Change from the "overview tab."
>
> **http://www.experiencingmanagement.com**

Another way to reduce resistance to change is to have those affected by the change *participate in planning and implementing the change process*. Employees who participate have a better understanding of the change and the need for it. Furthermore, employee concerns about change can be addressed as they occur if employees participate in the planning and implementation process. For example, when Avis, the car rental company, became an employee-owned company, hundreds of significant changes were made in the way it was run. This degree of change would be difficult for any company. But Avis has handled it by creating more than 150 employee-participation groups. On the first Thursday of every month, these groups meet to discuss specific problems and find ways to increase company productivity. Because other Avis employees elect the people who attend as representatives, there is typically little resistance to the changes and recommendations made by the groups.[40]

coercion using formal power and authority to force others to change

Employees are also less likely to resist change if they are allowed *to discuss and agree on who will do what* after change occurs. Resistance to change also decreases when change efforts receive *significant managerial support*. Top managers must do more than talk about the importance of change, though. They must provide the training, resources, and autonomy needed to make change happen.

Finally, use of formal power and authority to force others to change is called **coercion**. Because of the intense negative reactions it can create (i.e., fear, stress, resentment, sabotage of company products), coercion should be used only when a crisis exists or when all other attempts to reduce resistance to change have failed.

Exhibit 9.5 summarizes some additional suggestions for what managers can do when employees resist change.

exhibit 9.5

What to Do When Employees Resist Change

UNFREEZING	
• Share reasons.	Share the reasons for change with employees.
• Empathize.	Be empathetic to the difficulties that change will create for managers and employees.
• Communicate.	Communicate the details simply, clearly, extensively, orally, and in writing.
CHANGE	
• Benefits.	Explain the benefits, "what's in it for them."
• Champion.	Identify a highly respected manager to manage the change effort.
• Input.	Allow the people who will be affected by change to express their needs and offer their input.
• Timing.	Don't begin change at a bad time, for example, during the busiest part of the year or month.
• Security.	If possible, maintain employees' job security to minimize fear of change.
• Training.	Offer training to ensure that employees are both confident and competent to handle new requirements.
• Pace.	Change at a manageable pace. Don't rush.

Source: G. J. Iskat & J. Liebowitz, "What to Do When Employees Resist Change," Supervision, *1 August 1996.*

3.2 Change Tools and Techniques

Imagine that your boss came to you and said, "All right, genius, you wanted it. You're in charge of turning around the division." How would you start? Where would you begin? How would you encourage change-resistant managers to change? What would you do to include others in the change process? How would you get the change process off to a quick start? Finally, what long-term approach would you use to promote long-term effectiveness and performance? Results-driven change, the General Electric workout, transition management teams, and organizational development are different change tools and techniques that can be used to address these issues.

One of the reasons that organizational change efforts fail is that they are activity oriented, meaning that they focus primarily on changing company procedures, management philosophy, or employee behavior. Typically, there is much buildup and preparation as consultants are brought in, presentations are made, books are read, and employees and managers are trained. There's a tremendous emphasis on "doing things the new way." But, for all the focus on activities, on "doing," there's almost no focus on results, on seeing if all this activity has actually made a difference.

results-driven change change created quickly by focusing on the measurement and improvement of results

By contrast, **results-driven change** supplants the emphasis on activity with a laser-like focus on quickly measuring and improving results.[41] For example, at Monarch Marking Systems, quality-assurance engineer Steve Schneider guided the company's results-driven change process by first identifying everything in Monarch's factory that could be measured easily. He found 162 measures in all.[42] He further emphasized the importance of quick results by declaring that problem-solving teams had only 30 days to solve a particular problem. He encouraged workers to get to it, saying, "It's a project, not a process."

Another advantage of results-driven change is that managers introduce changes in procedures, philosophy, or behavior only if they are likely to improve measured performance. In other words, managers actually test to see if changes make a difference. Consistent with this approach, Schneider announced that Monarch's problem-solving teams could make any permanent changes they wanted, as long as those changes improved one of the 162 different measures of performance.

General Electric workout a three-day meeting in which managers and employees from different levels and parts of an organization quickly generate and act on solutions to specific business problems

A third advantage of results-driven change is that quick, visible improvements motivate employees to continue to make additional changes to improve measured performance. For example, one team at Monarch used cross-training to reduce the number of job categories from 120 to 32. Another, encouraged by the success of 90 other problem-solving teams, trained machine operators how to enter production data directly into the computer on the factory floor, eliminating the 7,600 hours of staff work that it used to take to enter those data from paper records. Consequently, unlike most change efforts, the quick successes associated with results-driven change were particularly effective at reducing resistance to change. Exhibit 9.6 describes the basic steps of results-driven change.

exhibit 9.6

Results-Driven Change Programs

1. Management should create measurable, short-term goals to improve performance.
2. Management should use action steps only if they are likely to improve measured performance.
3. Management should stress the importance of immediate improvements.
4. Consultants and staffers should help managers and employees achieve quick improvements in performance.
5. Managers and employees should test action steps to see if they actually yield improvements. Action steps that don't should be discarded.
6. It takes few resources to get results-driven change started.

Source: R. H. Schaffer & H. A. Thomson, J. D, "Successful Change Programs Begin with Results," Harvard Business Review on Change *(Boston: Harvard Business School Press, 1998), 189–213.*

The **General Electric workout** is a special kind of results-driven change. It is a three-day meeting that brings together managers and employees from different levels and parts of an organization to quickly generate and act on solutions to specific business problems.[43] On the first morning of a workout, the boss discusses the agenda and targets specific business problems that the group is to try to solve. Then, the boss leaves, and an outside facilitator breaks the group, typically 30 to 40 people, into five or six teams and helps them spend the next day and a half discussing and debating solutions. On day three, in what GE calls a "town meeting," the teams present specific solutions to their boss, who has been gone since day one. As each team's spokesperson makes specific suggestions, the boss has only three options: agree on the spot, say no, or ask for more information so that a decision can be made by a specific, agreed-on date. GE boss Amand Lauzon sweated his way through a town meeting. To encourage him to say yes, his workers set up the meeting room so that Lauzon couldn't make eye contact with his boss. He said, "I was wringing wet within half an hour. They had 108 proposals, I had about a minute to say yes or no to each one, and I couldn't make eye contact with my boss without turning around, which would show everyone in the room that I was chicken."[44] In the end, Lauzon agreed to all but eight suggestions. Furthermore, once those decisions were made, no one at GE was allowed to overrule them.

While the GE workout clearly speeds up change, it may also fragment change, if different managers approve different suggestions in different town meetings across a company. By contrast, a transition management team provides a way to coordinate change throughout an organization. A **transition management team** (TMT) is a team of 8 to 12 people whose full-time job is to manage and coordinate a company's change process.[45] One member of the TMT is assigned the task of anticipating and managing the emotions and behaviors related to resistance to change. Despite their importance, many companies overlook the impact that emotions and resistant behaviors can have on the change process. TMTs report to the CEO every day, decide which change projects are approved and funded, select and evaluate the people in charge of different change projects, and make sure that different change projects complement one another. Microsoft relied on a TMT to implement its .Net strategy, in which major parts of its Windows operating system and its Office software programs were redesigned to work seamlessly through the Internet. Microsoft's TMT consisted of a close-knit group of upper-level managers who advised founder Bill Gates on Microsoft's key strategies and products.

transition management team (TMT)
a team of 8 to 12 people whose full-time job is to completely manage and coordinate a company's change process

organizational development
a philosophy and collection of planned change interventions designed to improve an organization's long-term health and performance

It is also important to say what a TMT is not. A TMT is not an extra layer of management further separating upper management from lower managers and employees. Indeed, at Microsoft, nearly all the members of the TMT already headed key divisions or departments, so their participation on the TMT did not create another layer of management. A TMT is not a steering committee that creates plans for others to carry out. Instead, the members of the TMT are fully involved with making change happen on a daily basis. Furthermore, it's not the TMT's job to determine how and why the company will change. That responsibility belongs to the CEO and upper management. Finally, a TMT is not permanent. Once the company has successfully changed, the TMT is disbanded. Exhibit 9.7 lists the primary responsibilities of TMTs.

Organizational development is a philosophy and collection of planned

exhibit 9.7

Primary Responsibilities of Transition Management Teams

1. Establish a context for change and provide guidance.
2. Stimulate conversation.
3. Provide appropriate resources.
4. Coordinate and align projects.
5. Ensure congruence of messages, activities, policies, and behaviors.
6. Provide opportunities for joint creation.
7. Anticipate, identify, and address people problems.
8. Prepare the critical mass.

Source: J. D. Duck, "Managing Change: The Art of Balancing," Harvard Business Review on Change *(Boston: Harvard Business School Press, 1998), 55–81.*

change agent
the person formally in charge of guiding a change effort

change interventions designed to improve an organization's long-term health and performance. Organizational development takes a long-range approach to change; assumes that top management support is necessary for change to succeed; creates change by educating workers and managers to change ideas, beliefs, and behaviors so that problems can be solved in new ways; and emphasizes employee participation in diagnosing, solving, and evaluating problems.[46] As shown in Exhibit 9.8, organizational development interventions begin with recognition of a problem. Then, the company designates a **change agent** to be formally in charge of guiding the change effort. This person can be someone from the company or a professional consultant. The change agent clarifies the problem, gathers information, works with decision makers to create and implement an action plan, helps to evaluate the plan's effectiveness, implements the plan throughout the company, and then leaves (if from outside the company) only after making sure the change intervention will continue to work.

For example, Hajime Oba is a change agent and one of the key reasons that Toyota cars are tops in quality and reliability. Oba's job is to work closely with Toyota suppliers, showing them how to increase quality and decrease costs. For example, Michigan Summit Polymers installed a $280,000 paint system with robots and a paint oven to bake paint onto the dashboard vents that went into Toyota cars, but Oba showed that a $12 hair dryer did the job better and faster (3 minutes versus 90 minutes for the robots and paint oven). Because of Oba's demonstration, Summit replaced the robots with simple but effective $150 spray guns and the paint oven with intense light bulbs. Overall, Oba has helped Summit cut its defects to less than 60 parts per million, down from 3,000 parts per million five years ago.[47] Oba's efforts as a change agent have significantly improved the quality of parts at Toyota's suppliers. That, in turn,

exhibit 9.8

General Steps for Organizational Development Interventions

1. Entry	A problem is discovered and the need for change becomes apparent. A search begins for someone to deal with the problem and facilitate change.
2. Startup	A change agent enters the picture and works to clarify the problem and gain commitment to a change effort. A search begins for someone to deal with the problem and facilitate change.
3. Assessment & Feedback	The change agent gathers information about the problem and provides feedback about it to decision makers and those affected by it.
4. Action Planning	The change agent works with decision makers to develop an action plan.
5. Intervention	The action plan, or organizational development intervention, is carried out.
6. Evaluation	The change agent helps decision makers assess the effectiveness of the intervention.
7. Adoption	Organizational members accept ownership and responsibility for the change, which is then carried out through the entire organization.
8. Separation	The change agent leaves the organization after first ensuring that the change intervention will continue to work.

Source: W. J. Rothwell, R. Sullivan, & G. M. McLean, Practicing Organizational Development: A Guide for Consultants *(San Diego: Pfeiffer & Co., 1995).*

has helped put Toyota at the top of quality rankings issued by J. D. Power and Associates and *Consumer Reports* magazine.[48]

Organizational development interventions are aimed at changing large systems, small groups, or people.[49] More specifically, the purpose of *large system interventions* is to change the character and performance of an organization, business unit, or department. The purpose of a *small group intervention* is to assess how a group functions and help it work more effectively toward the accomplishment of its goals. The purpose of a *person-focused intervention* is to help people become aware of their attitudes and behaviors and acquire new skills and knowledge to increase interpersonal effectiveness. Exhibit 9.9 describes the most frequently used organizational development interventions for large systems, small groups, and people. For additional information about changing systems, groups, and people, see the "What Really Works" feature.

organizational decline
a large decrease in organizational performance that occurs when companies don't anticipate, recognize, neutralize, or adapt to the internal or external pressures that threaten their survival

Organizational decline occurs when companies don't anticipate, recognize, neutralize, or adapt to the internal or external pressures that threaten their survival.[50] In other words, decline occurs when organizations don't recognize the need for change. Companies can pull themselves out of organizational decline by making necessary changes. But if needed change does not occur, a company in decline will ultimately be dissolved through bankruptcy proceedings and sales of assets.

3.3 What *Not* to Do When Leading Change

So far, you've learned about the basic change process (unfreezing, change, refreezing), managing resistance to change, the four kinds of change tools and techniques to promote change (results-driven change, the GE workout,

exhibit 9.9

Different Kinds of Organizational Development Interventions

LARGE SYSTEM INTERVENTIONS	
Sociotechnical Systems	An intervention designed to improve how well employees use and adjust to the work technology used in an organization.
Survey Feedback	An intervention that uses surveys to collect information from organizational members, reports the results of that survey to organizational members, and then uses those results to develop action plans for improvement.
SMALL GROUP INTERVENTIONS	
Team Building	An intervention designed to increase the cohesion and cooperation of work group members.
Unit Goal Setting	An intervention designed to help a work group establish short- and long-term goals.
PERSON-FOCUSED INTERVENTIONS	
Counseling/Coaching	An intervention designed so that a formal helper or coach listens to managers or employees and advises them how to deal with work or interpersonal problems.
Training	An intervention designed to provide individuals with the knowledge, skills, or attitudes they need to become more effective at their jobs.

Source: W. J. Rothwell, R. Sullivan, & G. M. McLean, Practicing Organizational Development: A Guide for Consultants *(San Diego: Pfeiffer & Co., 1995).*

exhibit 9.10

Errors Managers Make When Leading Change

UNFREEZING
1. Not establishing a great enough sense of urgency.
2. Not creating a powerful enough guiding coalition.
CHANGE
3. Lacking a vision.
4. Undercommunicating the vision by a factor of 10.
5. Not removing obstacles to the new vision.
6. Not systematically planning for and creating short-term wins.
REFREEZING
7. Declaring victory too soon.
8. Not anchoring changes in the corporation's culture.

Source: J. P. Kotter, "Leading Change: Why Transformation Efforts Fail," Harvard Business Review *73, no. 2 (March–April 1995): 59.*

transition management teams, and organizational development). However, John Kotter of the Harvard Business School argues that knowing what *not* to do is just as important as knowing what to do when it comes to achieving successful organizational change.[51]

Exhibit 9.10 shows the most common errors that managers make when they lead change. The first two errors occur during the unfreezing phase, when managers try to get the people affected by change to believe that change is really needed. The first and potentially most serious error is *not establishing a great enough sense of urgency*. Indeed, Kotter estimates that more than half of all change efforts fail because the people affected are not convinced that change is necessary. People will feel a greater sense of urgency about change if a leader in the company makes a public, candid assessment of the company's problems and weaknesses. For example, Continental Airlines CEO Gordon Bethune said, "We had a crappy product, and we were trying to discount ourselves into profitability. Nobody wants to eat a crummy pizza, no matter if it's 99 cents."[52] Plus, by sharing extensive (and depressing) financial information with Continental's workers, Bethune made it clear that the company was truly at risk of going bankrupt. And, because employees knew that no airline had ever recovered after declaring bankruptcy, resistance to change evaporated at Continental as employees concluded that accepting change was the only reasonable option.[53]

The second mistake that occurs in the unfreezing process is *not creating a powerful enough coalition*. Change often starts with one or two people, but to build enough momentum to change an entire department, division, or company, change has to be supported by a critical and growing group of people. Besides top management, Kotter recommends that key employees, managers, board members, customers, and even union leaders be members of a *core change coalition*, which guides and supports organizational change. Furthermore, it's important to strengthen this group's resolve by periodically bringing its members together for off-site retreats.

www.experiencing management.com

Four general approaches for overcoming resistance to change and their advantages and disadvantages are presented at our animated concept and activity site. Choose Innovation&Change from the "select a topic" pull-down menu, then Overcoming Resistance from the "overview tab."

http://www.experiencingmanagement.com

The next four errors that managers make occur during the change phase, when a change intervention is used to try to get workers and managers to change their behavior and work practices.

Lacking a vision for change is a significant error at this point. As you learned in Chapter 4, a *vision* is a statement of a company's purpose or reason for existing. A vision for change makes clear where a company or department is headed and why the change is occurring. Change efforts that lack vision tend to be confused, chaotic, and contradic-

WHAT REALLY WORKS

CHANGE THE WORK SETTING OR CHANGE THE PEOPLE? DO BOTH!

Let's assume that you believe that your company needs to change. Congratulations! Just recognizing the need for change puts you ahead of 80 percent of the companies in your industry. But now that you've recognized the need for change, how do you make change happen? Should you focus on changing the work setting or the behavior of the people who work in that setting? It's a classic chicken or egg type of question. Which would you do?

A recent meta-analysis based on 52 studies and a combined total of 29,611 study participants indicated that it's probably best to do both!

Changing the Work Setting

An organizational work setting has four parts: organizing arrangements (control and reward systems, organizational structure), social factors (people, culture, patterns of interaction), technology (how inputs are transformed into outputs), and the physical setting (the actual physical space in which people work). Overall, there is a 55 percent chance that organizational change efforts will successfully bring changes to a company's work setting. Although the odds are 55–45 in your favor, this is a much lower probability of success than you've seen with the management techniques discussed in other chapters. This simply reflects how strong resistance to change is in most companies.

Probability of Success

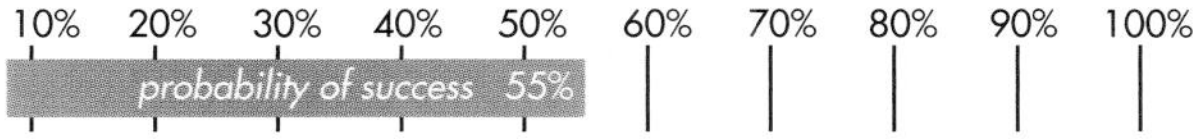

Changing the People

Changing people means changing individual work behavior. The idea is powerful. Change the decisions people make. Change the activities they perform. Change the information they share with others. And change the initiatives they take on their own. Change these individual behaviors and collectively you change the entire company. Overall, there is a 57 percent chance that organizational change efforts will successfully change people's individual work behavior. If you're wondering why the odds aren't higher, consider how difficult it is to change personal behavior. It's incredibly difficult to quit smoking, change your diet, or maintain a daily exercise program. Not surprisingly, changing personal behavior at work is also difficult. Thus, viewed in this context, a 57 percent chance of success is a notable achievement.

Probability of Success

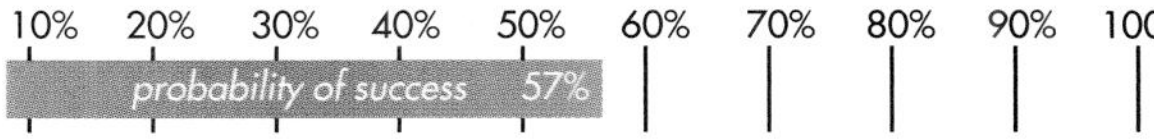

Changing Individual Behavior and Organizational Performance

The point of changing individual behavior is to improve organizational performance (i.e., higher profits, market share, and productivity, and lower costs). Overall, there is a 76 percent chance that changes in individual behavior will produce changes in organizational outcomes. So, if you want to improve your company's profits, market share, or productivity, focus on changing the way that your people behave at work.[54]

Probability of Success

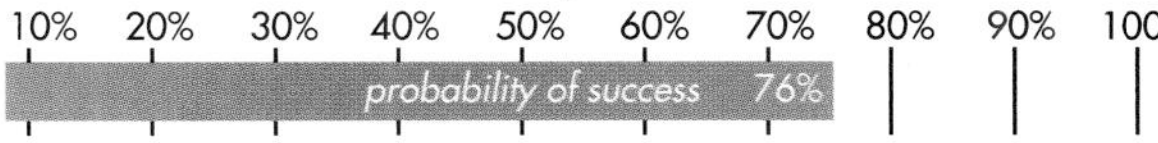

tory. By contrast, change efforts guided by visions are clear and easy to understand and can be effectively explained in five minutes or less. At Continental Airlines, the initial change vision was simple: "getting passengers where they were supposed to be on time."[55] With this clear-cut vision focusing managers and workers, Continental now ranks third in on-time arrivals and in baggage handling.[56] Previously, it had ranked tenth on both.[57] These improved results also explain why Continental has ranked first or second in the J. D. Power airline customer satisfaction ratings over the last five years.

Undercommunicating the vision by a factor of 10 is another mistake in the change phase. According to Kotter, companies mistakenly hold just one meeting to announce the vision. Or, if the new vision receives heavy emphasis in executive speeches or company newsletters, senior management then undercuts the vision by behaving in ways contrary to it. Successful communication of the vision requires that top managers link everything the company does to the new vision and that they "walk the talk" by behaving in ways consistent with the vision.

Furthermore, even companies that begin change with a clear vision sometimes make the mistake of *not removing obstacles to the new vision*. They leave formidable barriers to change in place by failing to redesign jobs, pay plans, and technology to support the new way of doing things. One way Continental removed obstacles to its new vision was by completely rewriting its employee policy manual. CEO Bethune said, "And we don't call it a manual anymore; we call it guidelines. The new guidelines are supposed to help employees solve problems—give them a sense of where the boundaries are when they run into trouble. But in the general pursuit of their jobs, we want them to use their heads and use their resources." In short, "if you find yourself in the middle of something complicated, something unusual, something that just doesn't fit, then use your head and make the best decision you can."[58]

As with results-driven change, another error in the change phase is *not systematically planning for and creating short-term wins*. Most people don't have the discipline and patience to wait two years to see if the new change effort works. Change is threatening and uncomfortable, so for people to continue to support it, they need to see an immediate payoff. Kotter recommends that managers create short-term wins by actively picking people and projects that are likely to work extremely well early in the change process. The short-term wins at Continental came in the form of $65 checks. Bethune told managers and employees that every employee would get a check for $65 each month that Continental finished in the top five in on-time arrivals (as rated by the Department of Transportation). The first time that Continental made it into the top five, it sent out $2.5 million worth of $65 checks to its employees. In all, Continental has spent more than $100 million for on-time bonuses to reward and remind its employees that getting customers to their travel destinations on time is one of the most important things it does.[59]

The last two errors that managers make occur during the refreezing phase, when attempts are made to support and reinforce changes so they "stick." *Declaring victory too soon* is a tempting mistake in the refreezing phase. Managers typically declare victory right after the first large-scale success in the change process. But this stops change efforts dead in their tracks. With success declared, supporters of the change process stop pushing to make change happen. After all, why "push" when success has been achieved? Rather than declaring victory, managers should use the momentum from short-term wins to push for even bigger or faster changes. This maintains urgency and prevents change supporters from slacking off before the changes are frozen into the company's culture. For example, Continental maintained urgency by raising the requirements for monthly, on-time bonuses. Now, instead of the top five, Continental had to finish in the top three in on-time arrivals. When it raised the bar, however, it also raised the reward, increasing the on-time bonus from $65 to $100.[60]

The last mistake that managers make is *not anchoring changes in the corporation's culture*. An *organization's culture* is the set of key values, beliefs, and attitudes shared by organizational members that determines the "accepted way of doing things" in a company. As you learned in Chapter 2, cultures are extremely difficult and slow to change. Kotter said that two things help anchor changes in a corporation's culture. The first is directly showing people that the changes have actually improved performance. At Continental, this was easily demonstrated by the company's improved rankings for on-time arrival and baggage handling. The second is to make sure that the people who get promoted fit the new culture. If they don't, it's a clear sign that the changes were only temporary.

When did CEO Gordon Bethune know that the changes he was seeking were anchored in Continental's culture? He was getting on a Continental flight at the last minute, as the gate agent was scrambling to get the plane out of the gate on time. Bethune, whose back was to the agent, heard him say, " Excuse me, sir, you'll have to sit down. The plane has to leave." The flight attendant became upset and said to the agent, "Do you know who that is? That's Mr. Bethune!" The agent responded, "That's very nice, but we gotta go. Tell him to sit down." Bethune said that this "is how Continental Airlines stays on time—and how it has changed for the better."[61]

Review 3
Managing Change

The basic change process is unfreezing, change, and refreezing. Resistance to change, which stems from self-interest, misunderstanding and distrust, and a general intolerance for change, can be managed through education and communication, participation, negotiation, coercion, and top management support.

Managers can use a number of change techniques. Results-driven change and the GE workout reduce resistance to change by getting change efforts off to a fast start. Transition management teams, which manage a company's change process, coordinate change efforts throughout an organization. Organizational development is a collection of planned change interventions (large system, small group, person-focused), guided by a change agent, that are designed to improve an organization's long-term health and performance. Finally, knowing what *not* to do is as important as knowing what to do to achieve successful change. Managers should avoid these errors when leading change: not establishing urgency, not creating a guiding coalition, lacking a vision, undercommunicating the vision, not removing obstacles to the vision, not creating short-term wins, declaring victory too soon, and not anchoring changes in the corporation's culture.

STUDY TIP On a separate sheet, write the titles of the exhibits in this chapter. Then, with your book closed, try to reproduce the diagrams exactly as they are in the text. Write a short description of what each diagram depicts, then open your book to check your work.

MANAGEMENT TEAM DECISION

TOLL HOUSE—STRENGTHENING A CHIPPED BRAND

Ever since 1930, when Ruth Wakefield, proprietor of the Toll House Inn, in Whitman, Massachusetts, assumed chunks of a Nestlé Semi-Sweet Chocolate Bar would melt evenly in the batter of her Butter Drop Do cookies, chocolate chip cookies have been a staple of the American diet.[62] Wakefield's failed experiment for chocolate cookies soon became famous, and in 1939, Nestlé introduced the tiny morsels we know today.

Seventy-some years later, however, Nestlé is no longer a simple chocolate manufacturer, and Toll House is not the only chocolate chip cookie on the block. With Wakefield's recipe on every bag, anyone can bake what most people consider the best chocolate chip cookies around, but a cook who saves the recipe can use a competitor's chips, like Hershey or Ghirardelli. To make matters worse, not many people make cookies from scratch anymore except during the holidays. In a way, Nestlé has lost some control over the Toll House brand.

Nestlé's FoodServices Division hopes to combat this brand weakness with Vision 2010, a 10-year strategic growth plan designed to grow a company already valued at $800 million. The Nestlé Baking Group (NBG), the division responsible for Toll House, might have the toughest time contributing to the company's growth goals. In an attempt to bolster its sales and reach, the NBG worked on making cookie baking more convenient. The result was the innovation of break-and-bake refrigerated dough. Pillsbury soon followed with its own version, and now Pillsbury and Toll House are fierce competitors in refrigerated dough. But Toll House also faces competition from products other than refrigerated dough. The NBG also competes with companies like Kellogg that make snacks you can eat on the run (like the new break-apart Pop Tarts and prepackaged Rice Krispie Treats). Prepackaged snack food is everywhere, and now even break-and-bake dough seems less convenient than it did when the NBG invented it.

For this Management Team Decision, you will need to put together a team of four to five students to represent the management team of the Nestlé Baking Group. For question 3, refer to the discussion of brainstorming on page 110 in Chapter 4 (Planning and Decision Making).

Questions

1. Consider the above scenario. As a team, plot Toll House products and innovations on the diagram of technology cycles represented by Exhibit 9.3. Reach consensus on any disagreements before continuing.
2. Does the Nestlé Baking Group need to take an experiential or compression approach to managing innovation? Decide as a group, based on your work from question 1 and what you read in the scenario.
3. Your decision from question 2 will determine how you approach this last activity. No matter what you decided—either experiential or compression—your team will now brainstorm as many ideas as you can with the goal of getting Toll House out of the break-and-bake rut. Your decision from question 2, however, will frame *how* you brainstorm, whether you are looking for a breakthrough or for a slew of incremental changes. You may wish to consider new flavors, new packaging, new distribution channels—anything that can help the NBG reach its Vision 2010 goal of increased sales and stronger branding.

A PERSONAL FORCE FIELD ANALYSIS

In the "What Really Works" section of this chapter, you learned that when people change their behavior in the workplace, there is a 76 percent chance that organizational profits, market share, and productivity can be improved. However, you also learned that organization-wide change efforts have only a 57 percent chance of successfully changing people's work behavior. In other words, changing people's behavior works great for company improvement. The hard part is getting them to change their behavior. This "Develop Your Career Potential" assignment reviews how you can use a personal force field analysis to change your behavior at work.

At the beginning of this chapter, you learned that organizational change is a function of change forces and resistance forces. Change forces lead to differences in the form, quality, or condition of an organization over time. Resistance forces support the status quo, that is, the existing state of conditions in organizations.

Listing resistance and change forces is also a useful way to conduct a personal force field analysis. The first step of a personal force field analysis is to clearly describe how or what behavior you intend to change. For example, if you're always late with your expense reports, you might write, "I will turn in my expense reports within three days of returning from a business trip." In Chapter 4, you learned that to be effective, goals need to be S.M.A.R.T.: specific, measurable, attainable, realistic, and timely. Descriptions of the behaviors you intend to change should follow the S.M.A.R.T. guidelines, too.

The second step of a personal force field analysis is to list and describe resistance forces, that is, the reasons it is difficult for you to change your behavior. Since resistance to change is caused by self-interest, misunderstanding and distrust, and a general intolerance for change, be sure to assess whether these factors are making it difficult for you to change your behavior.

The final step of a personal force field analysis is to list the change forces, that is, the reasons prompting you to consider changing your behavior. At this step, it can be useful to separate your reasons by category, such as personal or organizational benefits, or personal or organizational consequences (i.e., the negative consequences associated with not changing your behavior). For example, turning in your expense report on time gets you your money faster, a personal benefit; helps the organization stay current with its expenses, an organizational benefit; and helps you avoid getting yelled at by your boss for being late with the expense report, which is a personal negative consequence.

Now use these steps to conduct a personal force field analysis.

Questions

1. Clearly describe how or what behavior you intend to change. Be sure your description is S.M.A.R.T.: specific, measurable, attainable, realistic, and timely.
2. List and describe the resistance forces that make it difficult for you to change this behavior. Do these reasons have anything to do with
   - *Self-interest?* Will the change cost or deprive you of something you value?
   - *Misunderstanding and distrust?* Do you not understand the change or the reasons for it? Do you distrust the people behind the change? In other words, is someone other than yourself pressuring you to make this change?
   - *A general intolerance for change?* Are you simply less capable of handling change than others? Are you worried that you won't be able to learn the new skills and behaviors needed to successfully negotiate this behavior change?
3. List and describe the change forces that are leading you to consider changing your behavior. Separate your reasons into personal or organizational benefits, or personal or organizational consequences (i.e., the negative consequences associated with not changing your behavior).

take two video!

BIZ FLIX Apollo 13

This film dramatically portrays the Apollo 13 mission to the moon that almost ended in disaster. Only innovative problem solving and decision making amid massive ambiguity saved the crew. Almost any scene dramatically makes this point. Flight Director Gene Kranz wrote a book describing the mission and the actions that prevented disaster.

A zero gravity simulator, a KC-135 four-engine jet aircraft (NASA's "Vomit Comet"), helped create the film's realistic weightless scenes. These scenes required 600 parabolic loops over 10 days of filming.[63] See the Take Two exercise in Chapter 11 for a discussion of another scene from *Apollo 13*.

This scene is a composite built from portions of the "Carbon Dioxide Problem" sequence, which occurs a little after the midway point of the film, and parts of the "With Every Breath ..." sequence, which appears about seven minutes later. The scene's first part follows the nearly complete shutdown of the Apollo 13 module to save battery power. Mission Control has detected rising carbon dioxide levels in the module, which could kill the astronauts if NASA engineers on the ground cannot solve the problem. The film continues with the Apollo 13 crew building a carbon dioxide filter designed by the engineers.

What to Watch for and Ask Yourself

1. What is the problem in this scene?
2. What are the engineers' options for solving the problem?
3. Does this scene show innovation and innovative behavior? If so, in what form?

MGMT WORKPLACE Peter Pan Bus Lines

Following the terrorist attacks on September 11, 2001, almost every business in the travel industry was forced to reevaluate its approach to security. Like other firms in the business, Peter Pan Bus Lines knew that it had to upgrade its security to ensure the safety of its employees and customers or risk going out of business. To adapt to the post-9/11 environment, safety directors Chris Crean and James Stiles upgraded the company's customer interaction, internal operation, and training processes. Managing the change process was key, as was obtaining organizational buy-in to the new programs. After writing a new safety manual, Crean and Stiles conducted seminars, briefings, and training sessions to educate employees and familiarize them with the new procedures.

What to Watch for and Ask Yourself

1. Why was innovation so important to Peter Pan Bus Lines? Did the company have any other alternatives?
2. Was the change in the travel industry after 9/11 a discontinuous change or an incremental change? Explain your answer.
3. What change tool(s) or technique(s) did Crean and Stiles use to address their situation? Discuss how they dealt with resistance to change and how they enforced their plan for implementing necessary changes at the firm.

CHAPTER TEN

Designing Adaptive Organizations

outline

WHAT WOULD YOU DO?

Microsoft Headquarters, Redmond, Washington.[1] You've worked for and with chairman and chief software architect Bill Gates since 1981. You went to Harvard together and have served him and Microsoft by performing nearly every important management job in the company. You've been best friends for over two decades, but ever since you replaced him as CEO six months ago, you seem to have been at each other's throats. Even though you were Microsoft's president for the previous two years, both you and Gates have had trouble adjusting to your new roles. Gates, who has been involved in nearly every key decision in Microsoft's history, is having trouble letting go. Several meetings have even turned into public shouting matches. In one meeting, Gates approved a budget increase for a project. You then denied the increase, shouting a retort at Gates.

Unfortunately, the struggle between you and Gates is emblematic of one of the key problems in the

student resources

URL — Explore the four levels of learning by doing the simulation module on Organizational Design.

GUIDE — Mini lecture reviews all the learning points in the chapter and concludes with a case on Oticon.

VIDEO — Biz Flix is a scene from *The Paper*. Management Workplace is a segment on Student Advantage.

PPT — 12 slides with graphics provide an outline for this chapter.

FAQ — Chuck discusses boring jobs and why companies still create them.

TEST — 24 true/false questions, 22 multiple-choice questions, a management scenario, and 3 exhibit worksheets

company: though it employs 50,000 people in 74 different countries, Microsoft is still run like a startup company in someone's garage. In other words, even managers with two decades of high-tech experience have to run everything by you and Gates. This has been a very difficult habit for you to break, especially since you're a self-admitted control freak who obsesses about each aspect of Microsoft's business, sometimes knowing a division's numbers and details better than the divisional managers who report to you. For instance, when you became president four years ago, you also took on responsibility for Microsoft's online businesses. Last year, as CEO, when the head of your wireless division quit, you took up the job and ran the division for nine months, despite your pressing responsibilities as CEO. A former Microsoft executive said this about you (and you know it's true): "He'll have to learn to delegate. He wants to, but he's not wired that way."

But Microsoft had grown so big and complex that you could no longer keep track of all its "moving parts." To deal with this complexity, you reorganized the company around customer groups, figuring that it would be easier for managers and software developers to specialize and make decisions for one kind of customer at a time (home, organizational, software developers, etc.). But software is too interconnected to work that way. Expertise and knowledge need to be shared so that databases, email, spreadsheets, Web browsers, and operating systems can work together. Organizing around customers spread too many important decisions across too many places in Microsoft, which was the opposite of what you intended.

Since becoming CEO, you've spent a lot of time thinking about the difference between good companies and truly great companies. From a management standpoint, you see Microsoft as a very good company with lots of room for improvement. Indeed, no one would argue that Microsoft isn't doing well. Last year's profits were a very healthy $9 billion on revenues of $28 billion, bringing the company's cash reserves to $38 billion. Few companies in the *Fortune* 100 could top that. But cash isn't going to help you solve your transition struggles with Bill Gates. What can you do, what can he do, or what can you do together to make the transition from him as CEO to you as CEO easier? How can he become more comfortable "delegating" his old job to you? Similarly, if Gates needs to "let go," so do you. How do you, a certified control freak, give your managers decentralized authority that not only allows, but encourages them to make their own decisions and—feel confident doing so? Finally, what organizational structure best suits Microsoft at this point? Organizing around the customer didn't work, even though you thought it would. In retrospect, you now feel that Microsoft needs an organizational structure that balances the clear need for accountability (after all, budgets and deadlines have to be met) with the autonomy that Microsoft's seasoned managers need to make good, quick decisions in their divisions and departments. **If you were the new CEO of Microsoft, what would you do?**

No one builds a house without first looking at the design. Put a window there. Take out a wall here. Soon you've got the design you want. Only then do you start building. These days, the design of a company is just as important as the design of a house. As Microsoft's case shows, even the most successful companies are affected if they don't have the right design.

organizational structure
the vertical and horizontal configuration of departments, authority, and jobs within a company

This chapter begins by reviewing the traditional organizational structure approach to organizational design. **Organizational structure** is the vertical and horizontal configuration of departments, authority, and jobs within a company. For example, Exhibit 10.1 shows Microsoft's organizational chart. From

exhibit 10.1

Microsoft Corporation's Organizational Chart

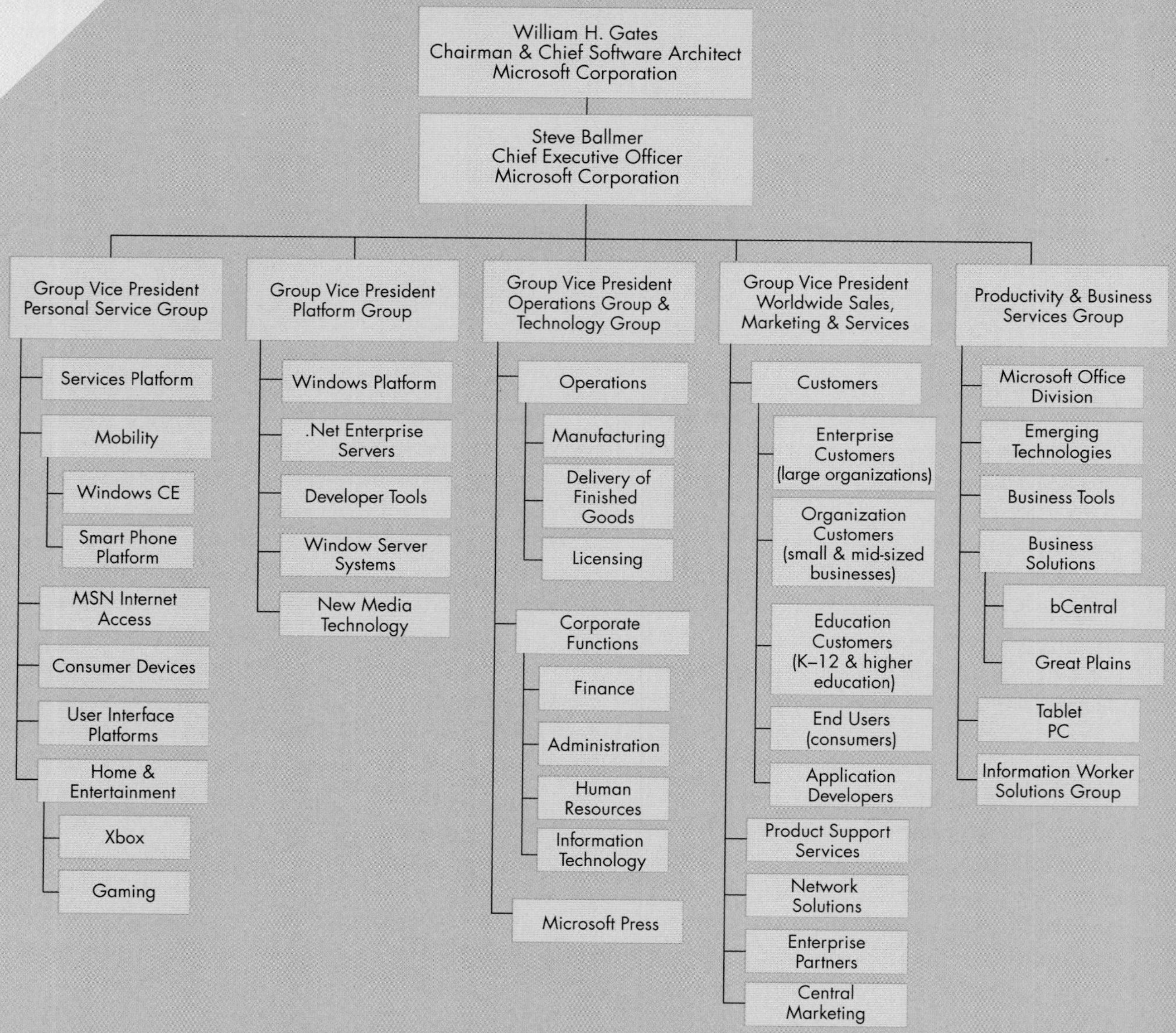

Source: "Microsoft Corporate Profile and Organizational Structure Overview," Microsoft, [Online] available at http://www.microsoft.com/presspass/corpprofile.com, 21 May 2003; "Presspass: Information for Journalists," Microsoft, [Online] available at http://www.microsoft.com/msft/default.mspx, 21 May 2003.

this chart, you can see the vertical dimensions of the company—who reports to whom, the number of management levels, who has authority over what, and so forth. Founder Bill Gates is the chairman and chief software architect. In this role, Gates focuses on Microsoft's product and technology strategies. As you learned in the opening case, he has left the running of the company to CEO Steve Ballmer, who reports directly to him.[2] Five group vice presidents report directly to Ballmer. In turn, each group vice president oversees a number of divisions. For instance, the group vice president of the Personal Services Group works with managers and employees to make it easier for consumers and businesses to stay connected when away from the office (via the Mobility and MSN Internet Access Divisions), to deliver software as a service on a variety of devices (via the Services Platform and User Interface Platforms Divisions), and to have fun (via Microsoft's game and Xbox gaming machine).

organizational process the collection of activities that transform inputs into outputs that customers value

The organizational chart also displays Microsoft's horizontal dimensions—who does what jobs, the number of different departments, and so forth. For instance, in addition to the Personal Services Group, Microsoft has groups in Platforms (where software such as Windows XP is written); Operations & Technology (manufacturing, delivery, and corporate functions); Worldwide Sales, Marketing & Services (for all customers, application developers, and product support services); and Productivity & Business Services (responsible for Microsoft Office software, as well as emerging technologies, business tools, business solutions, Tablet PCs, and information worker solutions). In the first half of the chapter, you will learn about the traditional vertical and horizontal approaches to organizational structure, including departmentalization, organizational authority, and job design.

exhibit 10.2

Process View of Microsoft's Organization

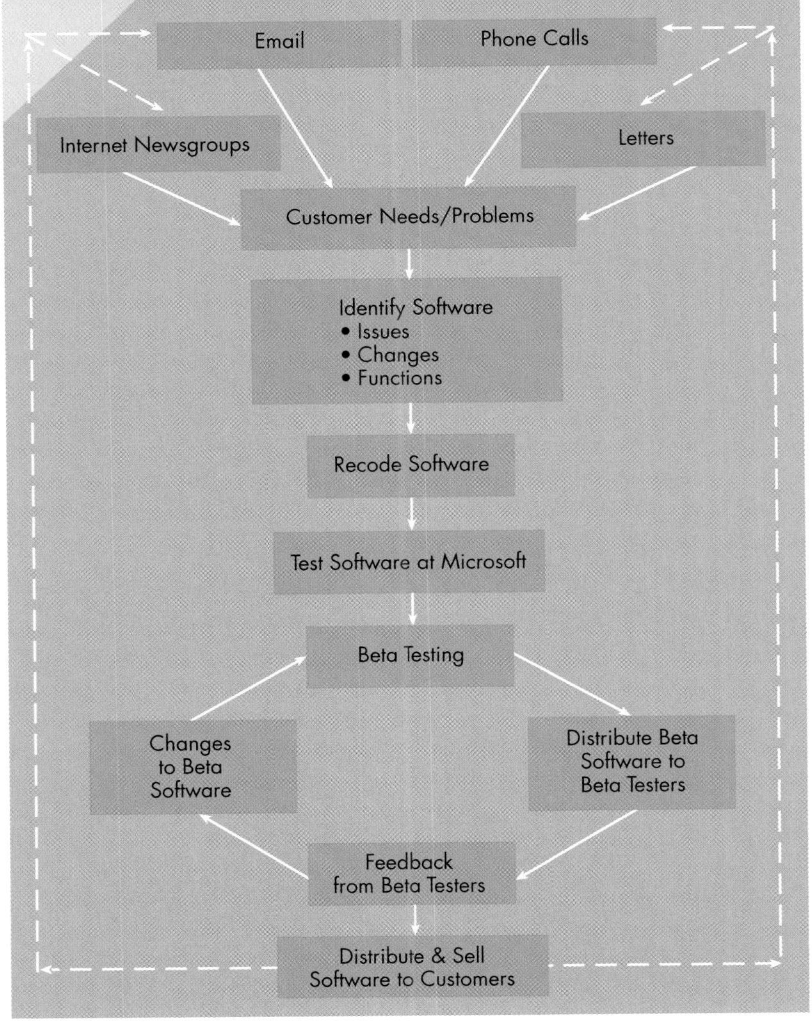

In the second half of the chapter, you will learn how contemporary organizations are becoming more adaptive by redesigning their internal and external processes. An **organizational process** is the collection of activities that transform inputs into outputs that customers value.[3] For example, Exhibit 10.2 shows the basic internal and external processes that Microsoft uses to write computer software. The process starts when Microsoft gets feedback from customers through Internet newsgroups, email, phone calls, or letters. This information helps Microsoft understand customers' needs and problems and identify important software issues and needed changes and functions. Microsoft then rewrites the software, testing it internally at the company and then externally through its beta-testing process. In beta testing, early versions of software are distributed to beta testers (i.e., customers who volunteer or are selected by Microsoft), who give the company extensive feedback, which is then used to make improvements. The beta-testing process may take as long as a year and involve thousands of customers. After "final" corrections are made to the software, the company distributes and sells it to customers, who start the process again by giving Microsoft more feedback.

This process view of Microsoft, which focuses on how things get done, is very different from the hierarchical view of Microsoft (go back to Microsoft's organizational chart in Exhibit 10.1), which focuses on accountability, responsibility, and positions within the chain of command. In the second half of the chapter, you will learn how companies are using reengineering, empowerment, and behavior informality to redesign their internal organizational processes. The chapter ends with a discussion about the ways in which companies are redesigning their external processes, that is, how they are changing to improve their interactions with those outside the company. In that discussion, you will explore the basics of modular and virtual organizations.

Designing Organizational Structures

With 405 Borders bookstores and 775 Waldenbooks stores in the United States, 37 "Books etc." stores in the United Kingdom, and 32,000 employees, Borders is one of the largest sellers of books in the world.[4] Nevertheless, in hopes of improving sales growth, Borders is replacing its division structure with a product structure. Formerly, each retail division (Borders, Waldenbooks, and Borders.com) had its own purchasing, accounting, merchandising, and marketing departments. In the new product structure, each product category (books, children's, multimedia, gifts and stationery, periodicals, café, and calendars) will have its own purchasing, accounting, merchandising, and marketing departments. Borders' CEO expressed hope that the product structure would improve the company's ability to track the various product lines and to "specifically address consumer needs in these categories."[5]

Why would a large company like Borders, with 32,000 employees and $3.4 billion in annual revenues, completely restructure its organizational design? What does it expect to gain from this change?

After reading the next three sections, you'll have a better understanding of the importance of organizational structure because you should be able to

1 describe the departmentalization approach to organizational structure.
2 explain organizational authority.
3 discuss the different methods for job design.

1 Departmentalization

departmentalization subdividing work and workers into separate organizational units responsible for completing particular tasks

Traditionally, organizational structures have been based on some form of departmentalization. **Departmentalization** is a method of subdividing work and workers into separate organizational units that take responsibility for completing particular tasks.[6] For example, the Sony Corporation has separate departments or divisions for electronics, music, movies, computer games and game consoles, and theaters.[7] Likewise, Bayer, a German-based company, has

www.experiencing management.com

You may learn more about departmentalization approaches and their advantages and disadvantages by interacting with this concept at our animated concept and activity site. Choose Organizational_Design from the "select a topic" pull-down menu, then Departmentalization from the "overview tab."

http://www.experiencingmanagement.com

separate departments or divisions for health care, agriculture, polymers, and chemicals.[8]

Traditionally, organizational structures have been created by departmentalizing work according to five methods: 1.1 functional, 1.2 product, 1.3 customer, 1.4 geographic, and 1.5 matrix.

1.1 Functional Departmentalization

The most common organizational structure is functional departmentalization. Companies tend to use this structure when they are small or just starting out. **Functional departmentalization** organizes work and workers into separate units responsible for particular business functions or areas of expertise. For example, a common set of functions would consist of accounting, sales, marketing, production, and human resources departments.

functional departmentalization
organizing work and workers into separate units responsible for particular business functions or areas of expertise

Not all functionally departmentalized companies have the same functions, however. For example, Exhibit 10.3 shows functional structures for an insurance company and an advertising agency. The light-colored boxes indicate that both companies have sales, accounting, human resources, and information systems departments. The darker boxes are different for each company. As would be expected, the insurance company has separate departments for life, auto, home, and health insurance. By contrast, the advertising agency has departments for artwork, creative work, print advertising, and radio advertising. So the kind of functional departments in a functional structure depends, in part, on the business or industry a company is in.

exhibit 10.3

Functional Departmentalization

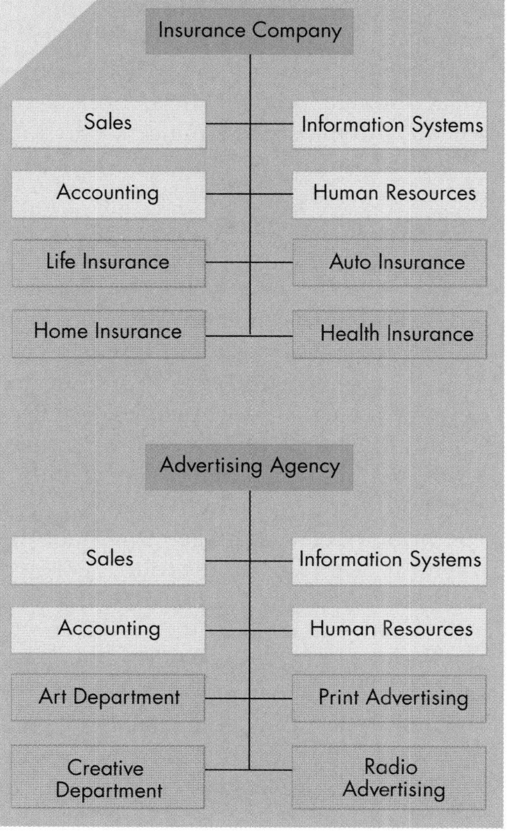

Functional departmentalization has some advantages. First, it allows work to be done by highly qualified specialists. While the accountants in the accounting department take responsibility for producing accurate revenue and expense figures, the engineers in research and development can focus their efforts on designing a product that is reliable and simple to manufacture. Second, it lowers costs by reducing duplication. When the engineers in research and development come up with that fantastic new product, they don't have to worry about creating an aggressive advertising campaign to sell it. That task belongs to the advertising experts and sales representatives in marketing. Third, with everyone in the same department having similar work experience or training, communication and coordination are less problematic for departmental managers.

At the same time, functional departmentalization has a number of disadvantages, too. To start, cross-department coordination can be difficult. Managers and employees are often more interested in doing what's right for their function than in doing what's right for the entire organization. A good example is the traditional conflict between marketing and manufacturing. Marketing typically pushes for spending more money to make more products with more accessories and capabilities to meet customer needs. By contrast, manufacturing pushes for fewer products with simpler designs so that manufacturing facilities can ship finished products on time and keep costs within expense budgets. As companies grow, functional departmentalization may also lead to slower decision making and produce managers and workers with narrow experience and expertise.

1.2 Product Departmentalization

product departmentalization organizing work and workers into separate units responsible for producing particular products or services

Product departmentalization organizes work and workers into separate units responsible for producing particular products or services. Exhibit 10.4 shows the product departmentalization structure used by the General Electric Company. GE is organized along 13 different product lines: aircraft engines, consumer products, commercial finance, transportation systems, consumer finance, specialty materials, medical systems, NBC, insurance, power systems, plastics, equipment management, and industrial products and systems.

exhibit 10.4

Product Departmentalization: General Electric Company

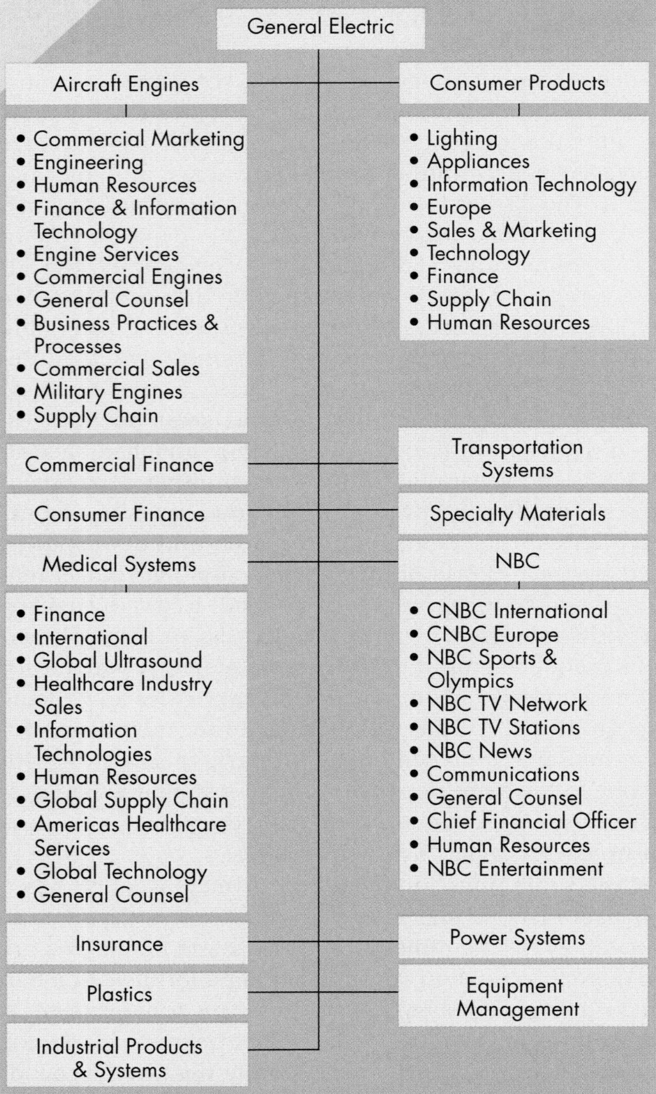

Source: General Electric Annual Report 2002, [Online] available at http://www.ge. com/files/usa/en/ar2002/ge_ar2002_full_book.pdf, 21 May 2003.

One of the advantages of product departmentalization is that, like functional departmentalization, it allows managers and workers to specialize in one area of expertise. Unlike the narrow expertise and experiences in functional departmentalization, however, managers and workers develop a broader set of experiences and expertise related to an entire product line. Likewise, product departmentalization makes it easier for top managers to assess work-unit performance. For example, because of their clear separation, it is a relatively straightforward process for GE's top managers to evaluate the performance of their 13 different product divisions. For instance, GE's Commercial Finance product division outperformed GE's Aircraft Engines division. Both had similar revenues, $11.41 billion for Aircraft Engines and $10.27 billion for Commercial Finance, but Commercial Finance had a profit of $3.19 billion compared to just $2.06 billion for Aircraft Engines.[9] Finally, decision making should be faster because managers and workers are responsible for the entire product line rather than for separate functional departments, and thus there are fewer conflicts (compared to functional departmentalization).

The primary disadvantage of product departmentalization is duplication. For example, you can see in Exhibit 10.4 that the Aircraft Engines and Consumer Products divisions both have human resources, finance, and supply chain departments. Likewise, the Medical Systems and NBC divisions both have finance and general counsel departments. Duplication like this often results in higher costs.

A second disadvantage is that it can be difficult to achieve coordination across the different product departments. For example, GE would probably have difficulty standardizing its policies and procedures in product departments as different as the Consumer Products (light bulbs, lighting products, and appliances) and Commercial Finance (growth capital, revolving lines of credit, cash flow programs, and asset financing programs) divisions.

1.3 Customer Departmentalization

customer departmentalization organizing work and workers into separate units responsible for particular kinds of customers

Customer departmentalization organizes work and workers into separate units responsible for particular kinds of customers. For example, Exhibit 10.5 shows that American Express is organized into departments that cater to consumers (Cards, Travel & Entertainment, Financial Advisors, and Banking) and businesspeople (Corporate Card Services and Merchant Services).[10]

The primary advantage of customer departmentalization is that it focuses the organization on customer needs rather than on products or business functions. Furthermore, creating separate departments to serve specific kinds of customers allows companies to specialize and adapt their products and services to customer needs and problems.

The primary disadvantage of customer departmentalization is that, like product departmentalization, it leads to duplication of resources. Furthermore, as with product departmentalization, it can be difficult to achieve coordination across different customer departments. Finally, the emphasis on meeting customers' needs may lead workers to make decisions that please customers but hurt the business.

1.4 Geographic Departmentalization

geographic departmentalization organizing work and workers into separate units responsible for doing business in particular geographic areas

Geographic departmentalization organizes work and workers into separate units responsible for doing business in particular geographic areas. For example, Exhibit 10.6 on page 261 shows the geographic departmentalization used by Coca-Cola Enterprises (CCE), the largest bottler and distributor of Coca-Cola products in the world. (The Coca-Cola Company develops and advertises soft drinks. CCE, which is a separate company with its own stock, buys the soft drink concentrate from the Coca-Cola Company, combines it with other ingredients, and then distributes the final product in cans, bottles, or fountain containers.) As shown in Exhibit 10.6, CCE has two regional groups: North America and Europe. As the table shows, each of these regions would be a sizable company by itself. For example, the European Group alone serves a population of 143 million people in Great Britain, France, Luxembourg, and the Netherlands; sells one billion cases of soft drinks a year; employs 10,000 people; runs 31 bottling facilities; and has a customer base that drinks an average of 173 soft drinks per year per person.

The primary advantage of geographic departmentalization is that it helps companies respond to the demands of different markets. This can be especially important when the company sells in different countries. For example, CCE's geographic divisions sell products suited to the taste preferences in different countries. CCE bottles and distributes the following products in Europe but not in the United States: Aquarius, Bonaqua, Burn, Canada Dry, Coca-Cola light (which is somewhat different from Diet Coke), Cresta flavors, Five Alive, Kia-Ora, Kinley, Lilt, Malvern, and Oasis.[11] Another advantage is that geographic departmentalization can reduce costs by locating unique organizational resources closer to customers. For instance, it is much cheaper for CCE

exhibit 10.5

Customer Departmentalization: American Express Corporation

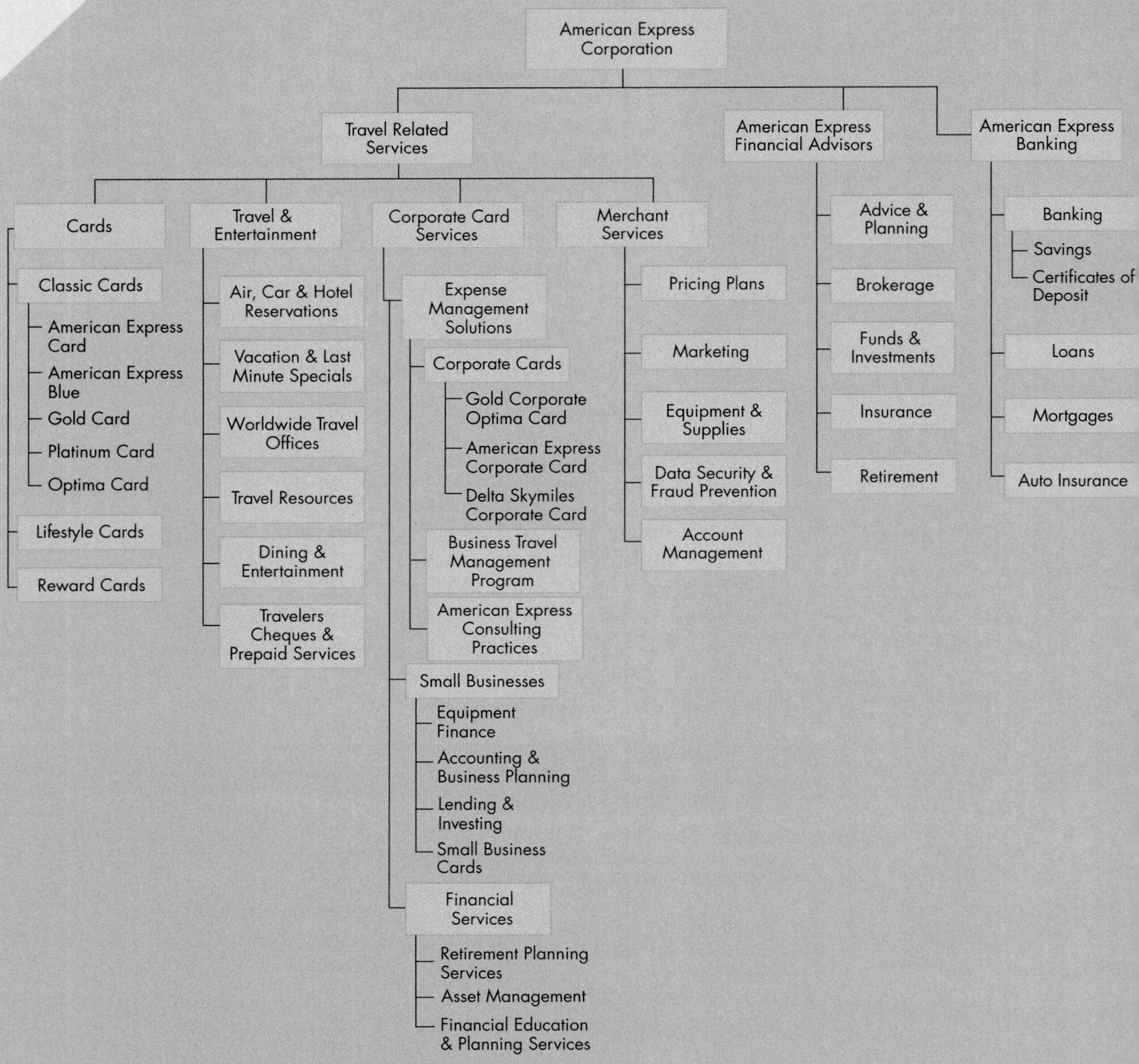

Source: "02 Annual Report," American Express, [Online] available at http://www.onlineproxy.com/amex/2003/ar/, 22 May 2003.

exhibit 10.6

Geographic Departmentalization: Coca-Cola Enterprises

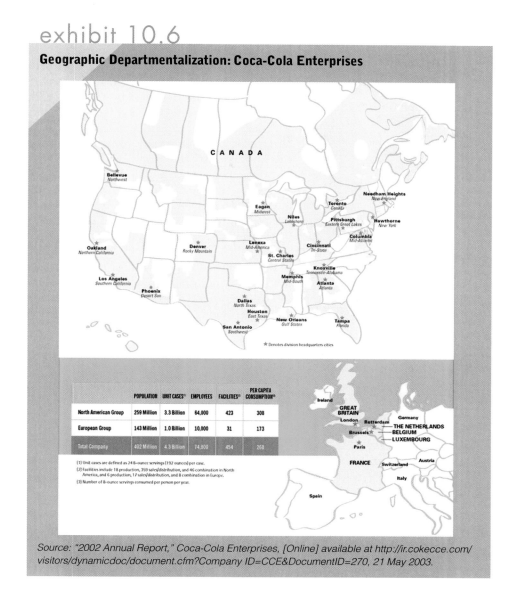

	POPULATION	UNIT CASES[1]	EMPLOYEES	FACILITIES[2]	PER CAPITA CONSUMPTION[3]
North American Group	259 Million	3.3 Billion	64,000	423	308
European Group	143 Million	1.0 Billion	10,000	31	173
Total Company	402 Million	4.3 Billion	74,000	454	260

(1) Unit cases are defined as 24 8-ounce servings (192 ounces) per case.

(2) Facilities include 18 production, 359 sales/distribution, and 46 combination in North America, and 6 production, 17 sales/distribution, and 8 combination in Europe.

(3) Number of 8-ounce servings consumed per person per year.

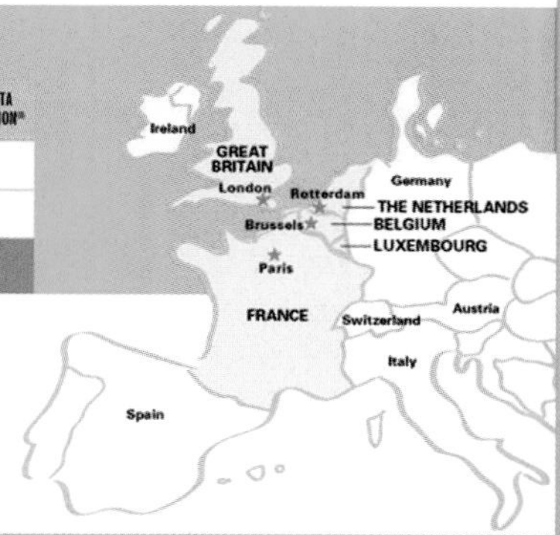

Source: "2002 Annual Report," Coca-Cola Enterprises, [Online] available at http://ir.cokecce.com/visitors/dynamicdoc/document.cfm?Company ID=CCE&DocumentID=270, 21 May 2003.

to build bottling plants in Belgium than to bottle Coke in England and then transport it across the English Channel to Belgium.

The primary disadvantage of geographic departmentalization is that it can lead to duplication of resources. For example, while it may be necessary to adapt products and marketing to different geographic locations, it's doubtful that CCE needs significantly different inventory tracking systems from location to location. Also, even more than with the other forms of departmentalization, it can be difficult to coordinate departments that are literally thousands of miles from each other and whose managers have very limited contact with each other.

1.5 Matrix Departmentalization

matrix departmentalization a hybrid organizational structure in which two or more forms of departmentalization, most often product and functional, are used together

Matrix departmentalization is a hybrid structure in which two or more forms of departmentalization are used together. The most common matrix combines product and functional forms of departmentalization. Exhibit 10.7 shows the matrix structure used by CitiGroup International, which accounts for all of CitiGroup's corporate and consumer banking outside North America (where CitiGroup uses a product structure). Across the top of Exhibit 10.7, you can see that the company uses a geographic/customer structure. The company's 99 country managers, who are responsible for CitiGroup business in a particular country, report to CEOs for Corporate or Consumer Business in their region (Western Europe; Latin America; Central & Eastern Europe, Middle East, Africa; or Asia). Down the left side of the figure, however, notice that the company is using a product structure for global consumers, global corporate and investment banking, global investment management, and Smith Barney.

The boxes in the figure represent the matrix structure, created by the combination of the geographic/customer and product structures. For example, in the global investment management business in Asia, country managers in China, Japan, South Korea, etc., are responsible for developing CitiGroup's

exhibit 10.7

Matrix Departmentalization: CitiGroup International

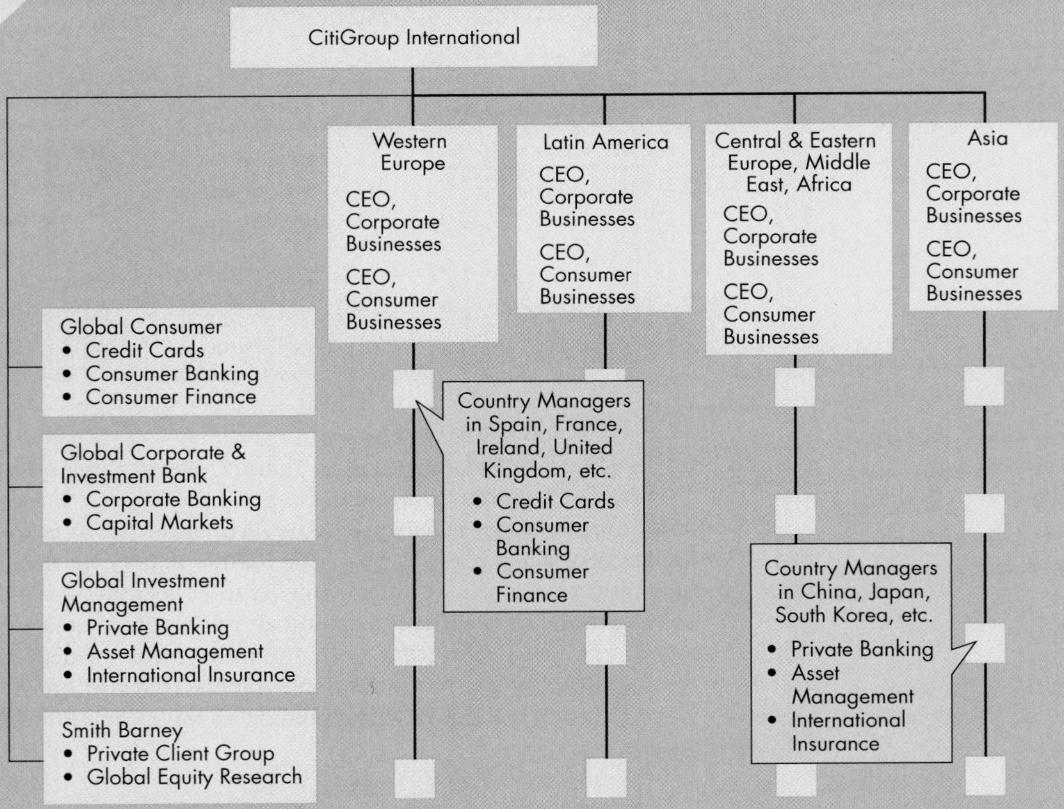

Source: "Annual Report 2002," CitiGroup, [Online] available at http://www.citigroup.com/citigroup/fin/data/ar021c.pdf, 22 May 2003.

private banking, asset management, and international insurance businesses in those countries.

Several things distinguish matrix departmentalization from the other traditional forms of departmentalization.[12] First, most employees report to two bosses, one from each core part of the matrix. For example, in Exhibit 10.7, the French country manager responsible for credit cards, consumer banking, and consumer finance would report to the CEO for Consumer Businesses in Western Europe and the Group Vice President for all Global Consumer business. Second, by virtue of their hybrid design, matrix structures lead to much more cross-functional interaction than other forms of departmentalization. In fact, while matrix workers are typically members of only one functional department (based on their work experience and expertise), they are also commonly members of several ongoing project groups. Third, because of the high level of cross-functional interaction, matrix departmentalization requires significant coordination between managers in the different parts of the matrix. In particular, managers have the complex job of tracking and managing the multiple project and functional demands on employees' time.

The primary advantage of matrix departmentalization is that it allows companies to efficiently manage large, complex tasks like researching, developing, and marketing pharmaceuticals or carrying out complex global businesses such as CitiGroup International. Efficiency comes from avoiding duplication. For example, rather than having an entire marketing function for each project, the company simply assigns and reassigns workers from the marketing department as they are needed at various stages of product completion. More specifically, an employee from a department may simultaneously be part of five different ongoing projects, but may be actively completing work on only a few projects at a time.

Another advantage is the ability to carry out large, complex tasks. Because of the ability to quickly pull in expert help from all the functional areas of the company, matrix project managers have a much more diverse set of expertise and experience at their disposal than do managers in the other forms of departmentalization.

The primary disadvantage of matrix departmentalization is the high level of coordination required to manage the complexity involved with running large, ongoing projects at various levels of completion. Matrix structures are notorious for confusion and conflict between project bosses in different parts of the matrix. Disagreements or misunderstandings about schedules, budgets, available resources, and the availability of employees with particular functional expertise are common. Another disadvantage is that matrix structures require much more management skill than the other forms of departmentalization.

Because of these problems, many matrix structures evolve from a **simple matrix**, in which managers in different parts of the matrix negotiate conflicts and resources directly, to a **complex matrix**, in which specialized matrix managers and departments are added to the organizational structure. In a complex matrix, managers from different parts of the matrix might report to the same matrix manager, who helps them sort out conflicts and problems.

simple matrix
a form of matrix departmentalization in which project and functional managers negotiate conflicts and resources

complex matrix
a form of matrix departmentalization in which project and functional managers report to matrix managers, who help them sort out conflicts and problems

Review 1
Departmentalization

There are five traditional departmental structures: functional, product, customer, geographic, and matrix. Functional departmentalization is based on the different business functions or expertise used to run a business. Product departmentalization is organized according to the different products or services a company sells. Customer departmentalization focuses its divisions on the different kinds of customers a company has. Geographic departmentalization is based on the different geographic areas or markets in which the company does business. Matrix departmentalization is a hybrid form that combines two or more forms of departmentalization, the most common being the product and functional forms. There is no "best" departmental structure. Each structure has advantages and disadvantages.

2 Organizational Authority

authority
the right to give commands, take action, and make decisions to achieve organizational objectives

The second part of traditional organizational structures is authority. **Authority** is the right to give commands, take action, and make decisions to achieve organizational objectives.[13] Traditionally, organizational authority has been characterized by the following dimensions: 2.1 chain of command, 2.2 line versus staff authority, 2.3 delegation of authority, and 2.4 degree of centralization.

2.1 Chain of Command

chain of command
the vertical line of authority that clarifies who reports to whom throughout the organization

unity of command
a management principle that workers should report to just one boss

Turn back a few pages to Microsoft's organizational chart in Exhibit 10.1. If you place your finger on any position in the chart, say, the Director of Human Resources (under Corporate Functions in the Operations & Technology Group), you can trace a line upward to the company CEO, Steve Ballmer. This line, which vertically connects every job in the company to higher levels of management, represents the chain of command. The **chain of command** is the vertical line of authority that clarifies who reports to whom throughout the organization. People higher in the chain of command have the right, *if they so choose*, to give commands, take action, and make decisions concerning activities occurring anywhere below them in the chain. In the following discussion about delegation and decentralization, you will learn that managers don't always choose to exercise their authority directly.[14]

One of the key assumptions underlying the chain of command is **unity of command**, which means that workers should report to just one boss.[15] In practical terms, this means that only one person can be in charge at a time. Matrix organizations, in which employees have two bosses, or two headquarters, automatically violate this principle. This is one of the primary reasons that matrix organizations are difficult to manage. The purpose of unity of command is to prevent the confusion that might arise when an employee receives conflicting commands from two different bosses. For example, if someone walks into an emergency room describing symptoms similar to a heart attack, the first person in charge, most likely a nurse, makes the initial assessment, assigns the patient to a treatment room, and gets the necessary doctors, nurses, and equipment to begin evaluation and treatment. Then the emergency room physician, who is higher than the nurse in the chain of command, takes charge and begins the process of determining whether the patient is really having a heart attack by conducting an examination, ordering tests, and taking the patient's medical history. If the physician calls in a cardiologist for consultation, the cardiologist becomes the person in charge and makes the final treatment decision. Despite the number of people involved in the process, it's clear who is in charge at each point, because the emergency room follows the principle of unity of command.

www.experiencing management.com

Learn more about principles of coordination at our animated concept and activity site. Choose Organizational_Design from the "select a topic" pull-down menu, then Principles of Coordination from the "overview tab."

http://www.experiencingmanagement.com

2.2 Line versus Staff Authority

line authority
the right to command immediate subordinates in the chain of command

staff authority
the right to advise, but not command, others who are not subordinates in the chain of command

line function
an activity that contributes directly to creating or selling the company's products

staff function
an activity that does not contribute directly to creating or selling the company's products, but instead supports line activities

A second dimension of authority is the distinction between line and staff authority. **Line authority** is the right to command immediate subordinates in the chain of command. For example, in the Microsoft organizational chart in Exhibit 10.1, CEO Steve Ballmer has line authority over the manager of the Personal Services Group. Ballmer can issue orders to that group vice president and expect them to be carried out.

Staff authority is the right to advise but not command others who are not subordinates in the chain of command. For example, at Microsoft, a manager in human resources might advise the vice president of the Personal Services Group in making a hiring decision but cannot order him or her to hire a certain applicant.

The terms *line* and *staff* are also used to describe different functions within the organization. A **line function** is an activity that contributes directly to creating or selling the company's products. So, for example, activities that take place within the manufacturing and marketing departments would be considered line functions. A **staff function** does not contribute directly to creating or selling the company's products, but instead supports line activities. Typical staff functions within an organization are accounting, human resources, and legal services. For example, marketing managers might consult with the legal staff to make sure the wording of a particular advertisement is legal.

www.experiencing management.com

Delegation affects the authority, responsibility, and accountability of employees. Learn how these three concepts are related at our animated concept and activity site. Choose Organizational_Design from the "select a topic" pull-down menu, then Delegation from the "overview tab."

http://www.experiencingmanagement.com

2.3 Delegation of Authority

delegation of authority
the assignment of direct authority and responsibility to a subordinate to complete tasks for which the manager is normally responsible

Managers can exercise their authority directly by completing the tasks themselves, or they can choose to pass on some of their authority to subordinates. **Delegation of authority** is the assignment of direct authority and responsibility to a subordinate to complete tasks for which the manager is normally responsible.

When a manager delegates work, three transfers occur, as illustrated in Exhibit 10.8. First, the manager transfers full responsibility for the assignment to the subordinate. Many managers find giving up full responsibility somewhat difficult

Second, delegation transfers to the subordinate full authority over the budget, resources, and personnel needed to do the job. To do the job effectively, subordinates must have the same tools and information at their disposal that managers had when they were responsible for the same task. In other words, for delegation to work, delegated authority must be commensurate with delegated responsibility.

The third transfer that occurs with delegation is the transfer of accountability. The subordinate now has the authority and responsibility to do the job and is then accountable for getting the job done. In other words, managers give subordinates their managerial authority and responsibility in exchange for results. *Forbes* magazine columnist John Rutledge calls delegation "MBB," Managing by Belly Button. He says, "The belly button is the person whose belly you point your finger at when you want to know how the work is proceeding, i.e., the person who will actually be accountable for each step. . . . The belly button is not a scapegoat—a person to blame later when things go wrong. He or she is the person who makes sure that things go right."[16] Exhibit 10.9 gives some tips on how to be an effective delegator.

exhibit 10.8

Delegation: Responsibility, Authority, and Accountability

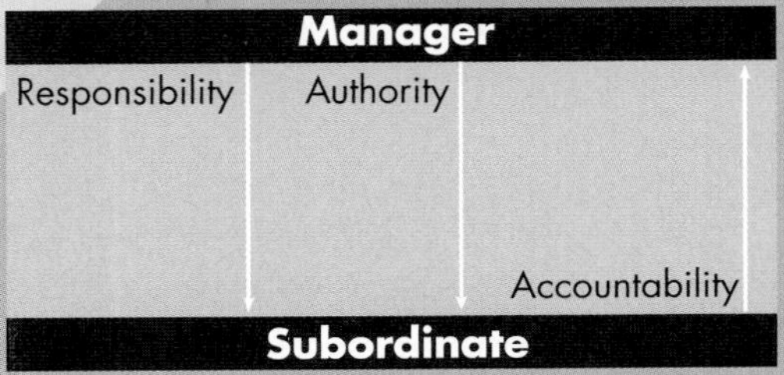

Source: C. D. Pringle, D. F. Jennings, and J. G. Longenecker, Managing Organizations: Functions and Behaviors *© 1990. Adapted by permission of Pearson Education, Inc., Upper Saddle River, NJ.*

exhibit 10.9

How to Be a More Effective Delegator

1. Trust your staff to do a good job. Recognize that others have the talent and ability to complete projects.
2. Avoid seeking perfection. Establish a standard of quality and provide a time frame for reaching it.
3. Give effective job instructions. Make sure employees have enough information to complete the job successfully.
4. Know your true interests. Delegation is difficult for some people who actually prefer doing the work themselves rather than managing it.
5. Follow up on progress. Build in checkpoints to help identify potential problems.
6. Praise the efforts of your staff.
7. Don't wait to the last minute to delegate. Avoid crisis management by routinely delegating work.
8. Ask questions, expect answers, and assist employees to help them complete the work assignments as expected.
9. Provide the resources you would expect if you were doing an assignment yourself.
10. Delegate to the lowest possible level to make the best possible use of organizational resources, energy, and knowledge.

Source: S. B. Wilson, "Are You an Effective Delegator?" Female Executive, *1 November 1994, 19.*

2.4 Degree of Centralization

centralization of authority
the location of most authority at the upper levels of the organization

If you've ever called a company's 1-800 number with a complaint or a special request and been told by the customer service representative, "I'll have to ask my manager," or "I'm not authorized to do that," you already know that centralization of authority exists in that company. **Centralization of authority** is the location of most authority at the upper levels of the organization. In a centralized organization, managers make most decisions, even the relatively small ones. That's why the customer service representative you called couldn't make a decision without first asking the manager.

decentralization
the location of a significant amount of authority in the lower levels of the organization

If you are lucky, however, you may have talked to a customer service representative at another company who said, "I can take care of that for you right now." In other words, the person was able to handle your problem without any input from or consultation with company management. **Decentralization** is the location of a significant amount of authority in the lower levels of the organization. An organization is decentralized if it has a high degree of delegation at all levels. In a decentralized organization, workers closest to problems are authorized to make the decisions necessary to solve the problems on their own.

www.experiencing management.com

The basic structure of an organization is affected by centralizing or decentralizing authority. Gain additional insight regarding this at our animated concept and activity site. Choose Organizational_Design from the "select a topic" pull-down menu, then Decentralization from the "overview tab."

http://www.experiencingmanagement.com

Decentralization has a number of advantages. It develops employee capabilities throughout the company and leads to faster decision making and more satisfied customers and employees. Furthermore, a study of 1,000 large companies found that companies with a high degree of decentralization outperformed those with a low degree of decentralization in terms of return on assets (6.9 percent versus 4.7 percent), return on investment (14.6 percent versus 9 percent), return on equity (22.8 percent versus 16.6 percent), and return on sales (10.3 percent versus 6.3 percent). Ironically, however, the same study found that few large companies are actually decentralized. Specifically, only 31 percent of employees in these 1,000 companies were responsible for recommending improvements to management. Overall, just 10 percent of employees received the training and information needed to support a truly decentralized approach to management.[17]

standardization
solving problems by consistently applying the same rules, procedures, and processes

With results like these, the key question is no longer whether companies should decentralize, but where they should decentralize. One rule of thumb is to stay centralized where standardization is important and to decentralize where standardization is unimportant. **Standardization** is solving problems by consistently applying the same rules, procedures, and processes.

Review 2
Organizational Authority

Organizational authority is determined by the chain of command, line versus staff authority, delegation, and the degree of centralization in a company. The chain of command vertically connects every job in the company to higher levels of management and makes clear who reports to whom. Managers have line authority to command employees below them in the chain of command, but have only staff or advisory authority over employees not below them in the chain of command. Managers delegate authority by transferring to subordinates the authority and responsibility needed to do a task; in exchange, subordinates become accountable for task completion. In centralized companies, most authority to make decisions lies with managers in the upper levels of the company. In decentralized companies, much of the authority is delegated to the workers closest to problems, who can then make the decisions necessary for solving the problems themselves. Centralization works best for tasks that require standardized decision making. When standardization isn't important, decentralization can lead to faster decisions, greater employee and customer satisfaction, and significantly better financial performance.

3 Job Design

Imagine that McDonald's decided to pay $50,000 a year to its drive-through window cashiers. That's $50,000 for saying, "Welcome to McDonald's. May I have your order please?" Would you take the job? Sure you would. Work a couple of years. Make a hundred grand. Why not? Let's assume, however, that to get this outrageous salary, you have to be a full-time McDonald's drive-through window cashier for the next 10 years. Would you still take the job? Just imagine, 40 to 60 times an hour, you repeat the same basic process:

1. "Welcome to McDonald's. May I have your order please?"
2. Listen to the order. Repeat it for accuracy. State the total cost. "Please drive to the second window."
3. Take the money. Make change.
4. Give customers drinks, straws, and napkins.
5. Give customers food.
6. "Thank you for coming to McDonald's."

Could you stand to do the same simple tasks an average of 50 times per hour, 400 times per day, 2,000 times per week, or 8,000 times per month? Few can. Fast-food workers rarely stay on the job more than six months. Indeed, McDonald's and other fast-food restaurants have well over 100 percent employee turnover each year.[18]

job design
the number, kind, and variety of tasks that individual workers perform in doing their jobs

In this next section, you will learn about **job design**—the number, kind, and variety of tasks that individual workers perform in doing their jobs. You will learn 3.1 why companies continue to use specialized jobs like the McDonald's drive-through job, 3.2 how job rotation, job enlargement, job enrichment, and 3.3 the job characteristics model are being used to overcome the problems associated with job specialization.

3.1 Job Specialization

job specialization
a job composed of a small part of a larger task or process

Job specialization occurs when a job is composed of a small part of a larger task or process. Specialized jobs are characterized by simple, easy-to-learn steps, low variety, and high repetition, like the McDonald's drive-through window job described above. One of the clear disadvantages of specialized jobs is that, being so easy to learn, they quickly become boring. This, in turn, can lead to low job satisfaction and high absenteeism and employee turnover, all of which are very costly to organizations.

Why, then, do companies continue to create and use specialized jobs? The primary reason is that specialized jobs are very economical. Once a job has been specialized, it takes little time to learn and master. Consequently, when experienced workers quit or are absent, the company can replace them with new employees and lose little productivity. For example, the pictures of the food on McDonald's cash registers make it easy for McDonald's trainees to quickly learn to take orders. Likewise, to simplify and speed operations, the drink dispensers behind the counter are set to automatically fill drink cups, while the worker goes to get your fries. At McDonald's, every task has been simplified in this way. Because the work is designed to be simple, wages can remain low, since it isn't necessary to pay high salaries to attract highly experienced, educated, or trained workers.

3.2 Job Rotation, Enlargement, and Enrichment

Because of the efficiency of specialized jobs, companies are often reluctant to eliminate them. Consequently, job redesign efforts have focused on modifying jobs to keep the benefits of specialized jobs, while reducing their obvious costs and disadvantages. Three methods—job rotation, job enlargement, and job enrichment—have been used to try to improve specialized jobs.[19]

In factory work or even some office jobs, many workers perform the same task all day long. For example, if you attach side mirrors in an auto factory, you probably complete this task 45 to 60 times an hour. If you work as the cashier at a grocery store, you check out a different customer every two to three minutes.

job rotation
periodically moving workers from one specialized job to another to give them more variety and the opportunity to use different skills

Job rotation attempts to overcome the disadvantages of job specialization by periodically moving workers from one specialized job to another to give them more variety and the opportunity to use different skills. For example, the "mirror attacher" in the automobile plant might attach mirrors in the first half of the day's work shift and then install bumpers during the second half. Because employees simply switch from one specialized job to another, job rotation allows companies to retain the economic benefits of specialized work. At the same time, the greater variety of tasks makes the work less boring and more satisfying for workers.

job enlargement
increasing the number of different tasks that a worker performs within one particular job

Another way to counter the disadvantages of specialization is to enlarge the job. **Job enlargement** is increasing the number of different tasks that a worker performs within one particular job. So, instead of having to perform just one task, workers with enlarged jobs are given several tasks to perform. For example, an enlarged "mirror attacher" job might include attaching the mirror, checking to see that the mirror's power adjustment controls work, and then cleaning the mirror's surface. Though job enlargement increases variety, many workers report feeling more stress when their jobs are enlarged. Consequently, many workers view enlarged jobs as simply "more work," especially if they are not given additional time to complete the additional tasks.

job enrichment
increasing the number of tasks in a particular job and giving workers the authority and control to make meaningful decisions about their work

Job enrichment attempts to overcome the deficiencies in specialized work by increasing the number of tasks *and* by giving workers the authority and control to make meaningful decisions about their work.[20] At AES, an independent power company that sells electricity to public utilities and steam (for power) to industrial organizations, workers have been given an extraordinary level of authority and control. For example, with his hands still blackened after unloading coal from a barge, employee Jeff Hatch calls a broker to determine which Treasury bills the company should buy to maximize the short-term return on its available cash. Hatch asks his broker, "What kind of rate can you give me for $10 million at 30 days?" When the broker tells him, "6.09 percent," he responds, "But I just got a 6.13 percent quote from Chase."[21] Indeed, at AES, ordinary plant technicians are given budgets worth several million dollars and are trusted to purchase everything from mops to gas turbines.

3.3 Job Characteristics Model

job characteristics model (JCM)
an approach to job redesign that seeks to formulate jobs in ways that motivate workers and lead to positive work outcomes

internal motivation
motivation that comes from the job itself rather than from outside rewards

In contrast to job rotation, job enlargement, and job enrichment, which focus on providing variety in job tasks, the **job characteristics model (JCM)** is an approach to job redesign that seeks to formulate jobs in ways that motivate workers and lead to positive work outcomes.[22] As shown in Exhibit 10.10, the primary goal of the model is to create jobs that result in positive personal and work outcomes such as internal work motivation, satisfaction with one's job, and work effectiveness. Of these, the central concern of the JCM is internal motivation. **Internal motivation** is motivation that comes from the job itself rather than from outside rewards, such as a raise or praise from the boss. If workers feel that performing the job well is itself rewarding, then the job has internal motivation. Statements such as "I get a nice sense of accomplishment" or "I feel good about myself and what I'm producing" are examples of internal motivation.

Moving to the left in Exhibit 10.10, you can see that the JCM specifies three critical psychological states that must occur for work to be internally motivating. First, workers must *experience the work as meaningful*; that is, they must view their job as being important. Second, they must *experience responsibility for work outcomes*—they must feel personally responsible for the work being done well. Third, workers must have *knowledge of results*; that is, they must know how well they are performing their jobs. All three critical psychological states must occur for work to be internally motivating.

For example, let's return to our grocery store cashier. Cashiers usually have knowledge of results. When you're slow, your checkout line grows long. If you make a mistake, customers point it out. Likewise, cashiers experience responsibility for work outcomes. At the end of the day, the register is totaled and the money is counted. If the money in the till is less than what's recorded in the register, most stores make the cashier pay the difference. Nonetheless, despite knowing results and experiencing responsibility for work outcomes, most grocery store cashiers (at least where I shop) aren't internally motivated, because they don't experience the work as meaningful. With scanners, it takes little skill to learn or do the job. Anyone can do it. In addition, cashiers have few decisions to make, and the job is highly repetitive.

Of course, this raises the question: What kinds of jobs produce the three critical psychological states? Again, moving to the left in Exhibit 10.10, the JCM specifies that the three critical psychological states arise from jobs that are strong on five core job characteristics: skill variety, task identity, task significance, autonomy, and feedback. **Skill variety** is the number of different activities performed in a job. **Task identity** is the degree to which a job requires completion of a whole and identifiable piece of work, from beginning to end. **Task significance** is the degree to which a job is perceived to have a substantial impact on others inside or outside the organization. **Autonomy** is the degree to which a job gives workers the discretion, freedom, and inde-

skill variety
the number of different activities performed in a job

task identity
the degree to which a job requires, from beginning to end, the completion of a whole and identifiable piece of work

task significance
the degree to which a job is perceived to have a substantial impact on others inside or outside the organization

autonomy
the degree to which a job gives workers the discretion, freedom, and independence to decide how and when to accomplish the job

exhibit 10.10

Job Characteristics Model

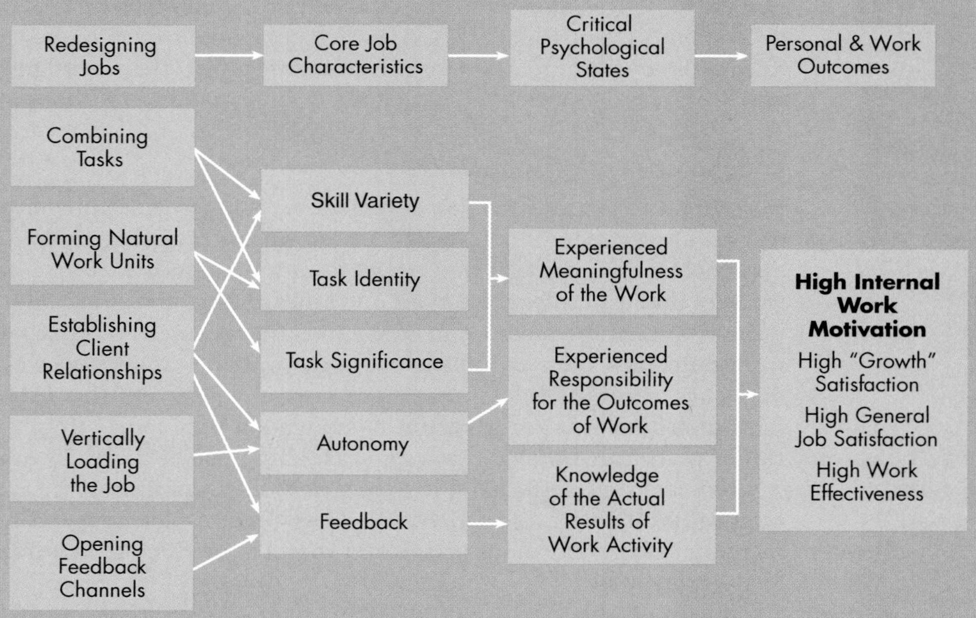

Source: J. R. Hackman and G. R. Oldham, Work Redesign *(Reading, MA: Addison-Wesley, 1980). Reprinted by permission of Addison-Wesley Longman.*

feedback
the amount of information the job provides to workers about their work performance

pendence to decide how and when to accomplish the work. Finally, **feedback** is the amount of information the job provides to workers about their work performance.

To illustrate how the core job characteristics work together, let's use them to more thoroughly assess why the McDonald's drive-through window job is not particularly satisfying or motivating. To start, skill variety is low. Except for the size of an order or special requests (no onions), the process is the same for each customer. At best, task identity is moderate. Although you take the order, handle the money, and deliver the food, others are responsible for a larger part of the process, preparing the food. Task identity will be even lower if the McDonald's has two drive-through windows because each drive-through window worker will have an even more specialized task. The first is limited to taking the order and making change, while the second just delivers the food. Task significance, the impact you have on others, is probably low. Autonomy is also very low. McDonald's has strict rules about dress, cleanliness, and procedures. But the job does provide immediate feedback, such as positive and negative customer comments, car horns honking, the amount of time it takes to process orders, and the number of cars in the drive-through. With the exception of feedback, the low levels of the core job characteristics show why the drive-through window job is not internally motivating for many workers.

What can managers do when jobs aren't internally motivating? The far left column of Exhibit 10.10 lists five job redesign techniques that managers can use to strengthen a job's core characteristics. *Combining tasks* increases skill variety and task identity by joining separate, specialized tasks into larger work modules. Work can be formed into *natural work units* by arranging tasks according to logical or meaningful groups. Forming natural work units increases task identity and task significance. *Establishing client relationships* increases skill variety, autonomy, and feedback by giving employees direct contact with clients and customers.

One important element of the JCM is establishing client relationships. UPS drivers are the face of UPS to many people in the United States (and around the world). In fact, these positive relationships were the focus of a recent television ad campaign, which depicted drivers interacting with their clients on a business level ("Will that be all?") as well as on a personal level ("Happy Birthday, Dan!").

Vertical loading means pushing some managerial authority down to workers. And the last job redesign technique offered by the model, *opening feedback channels*, means finding additional ways to give employees direct, frequent feedback about their job performance. For additional information on the JCM, see this chapter's "What Really Works" feature.

Review 3
Job Design

Companies use specialized jobs because they are economical and easy to learn and don't require highly paid workers. However, specialized jobs aren't motivating or particularly satisfying for employees. Companies have used job rotation, job enlargement, job enrichment, and the job characteristics model to make specialized jobs more interesting and motivating. With job rotation, workers move from one specialized job to another. Job enlargement simply increases the number of different tasks within a particular job. Job enrichment increases the number of tasks in a job and gives workers authority and control over their work. The goal of the job characteristics model is to make jobs intrinsically motivating. For this to happen, jobs must be strong on five core job characteristics (skill variety,

WHAT REALLY WORKS

THE JOB CHARACTERISTICS MODEL: MAKING JOBS MORE INTERESTING AND MOTIVATING

Think of the worst job you ever had. Was it factory work where you repeated the same task every few minutes? Was it an office job requiring a lot of meaningless paperwork? Or was it a job so specialized that it took no effort or thinking whatsoever to do?

The job characteristics model reviewed in this chapter suggests that workers will be more motivated or satisfied with their work if their jobs have greater task identity, task significance, skill variety, autonomy, and feedback. Eighty-four studies, with a combined total of 22,472 study participants, indicated that, on average, these core job characteristics make jobs more satisfying for most workers. In addition, jobs rich with the five core job characteristics are especially satisfying for workers who possess an individual characteristic called *growth need strength*. Read on to see how well the JCM really increases job satisfaction and reduces workplace absenteeism.

Job Satisfaction

There is a 66 percent chance that workers will be more satisfied with their work when their jobs have task identity, the chance to complete an entire job from beginning to end, than when they don't.

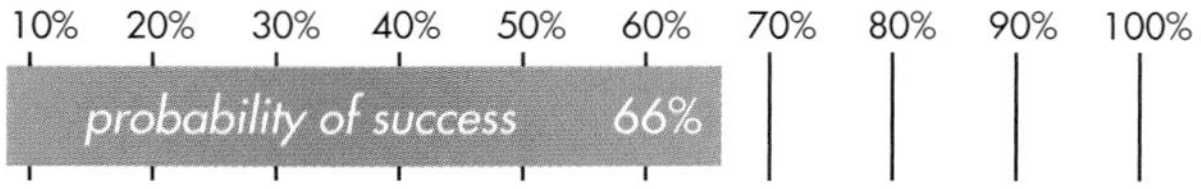

On average, there is a 69 percent chance that workers will be more satisfied with their work when their jobs have task significance, meaning a substantial impact on others, than when they don't.

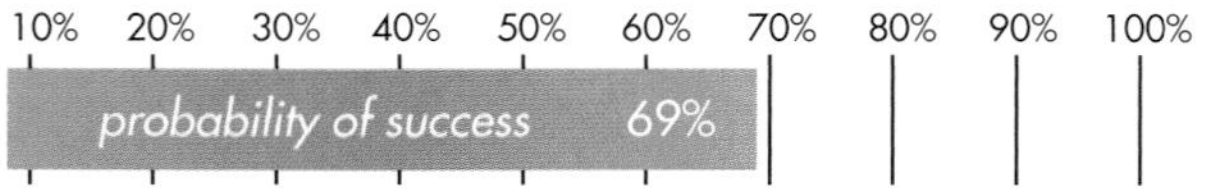

On average, there is a 70 percent chance that workers will be more satisfied with their work when their jobs have skill variety, meaning a variety of different activities, skills, and talents, than when they don't.

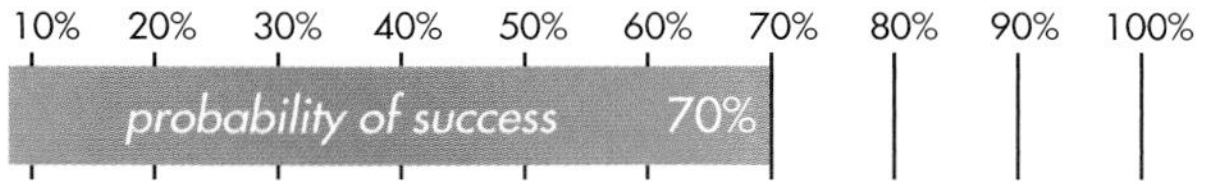

On average, there is a 73 percent chance that workers will be more satisfied with their work when their jobs have autonomy, meaning the discretion to decide how and when to accomplish the work, than when they don't.

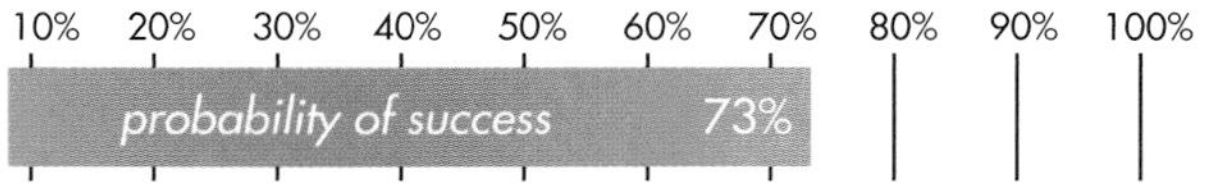

On average, there is a 70 percent chance that workers will be more satisfied with their work when their jobs provide feedback, meaning information about their work performance, than when they don't.

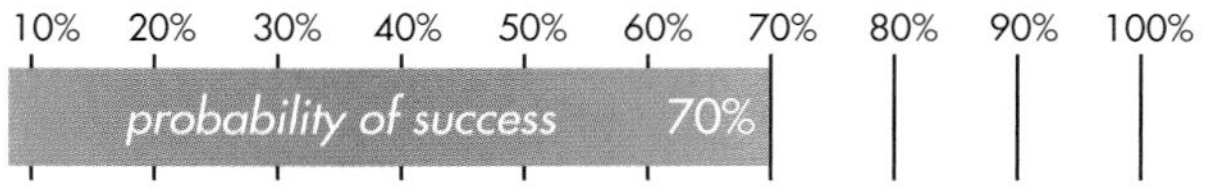

The statistics presented above indicate that, on average, the JCM has, at worst, a 66 percent chance of improving workers' job satisfaction. In all, this is impressive evidence that the model works. In general, you can expect these results when redesigning jobs based on the model.

We can be more accurate about the effects of the JCM, however, if we split workers into two groups: those with high growth need strength and those with low growth need strength. *Growth need strength* is the need or desire to achieve personal growth and development through one's job. Workers high in growth need strength respond well to jobs designed according to the JCM, because they enjoy work that challenges them and allows them to learn new skills and knowledge. In fact, there is an 84 percent chance that workers with high growth need strength will be more satisfied with their work when their jobs are redesigned according to the JCM.

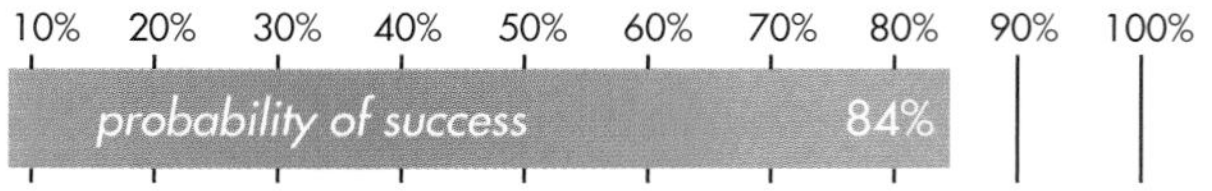

By comparison, because they aren't as interested in being challenged or learning new things at work, there is only a 69 percent chance that workers low in growth need strength will be satisfied with jobs that have been redesigned according to the principles of the JCM. This is still a favorable percentage, but it is weaker than the 84 percent chance of job satisfaction that occurs for workers high in growth need strength.

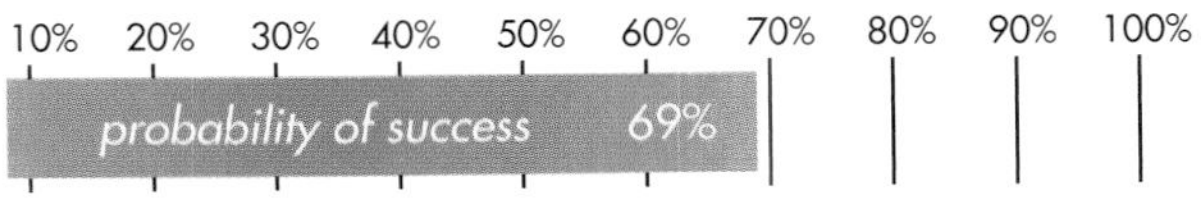

Workplace Absenteeism

Although not shown in the job characteristics model displayed in Exhibit 10.10, workplace absenteeism is an important personal or work outcome affected by a job's core job characteristics. In general, the "richer" your job is with task identity, task significance, skill variety, autonomy, and feedback, the more likely you are to show up for work every day.

Workers are 63 percent more likely to attend work when their jobs have task identity than when they don't.

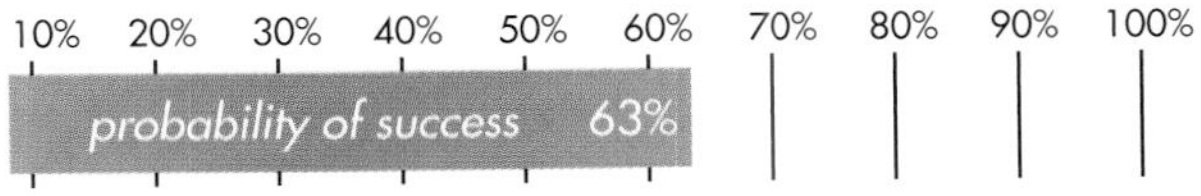

Workers are 68 percent more likely to attend work when their jobs have task significance than when they don't.

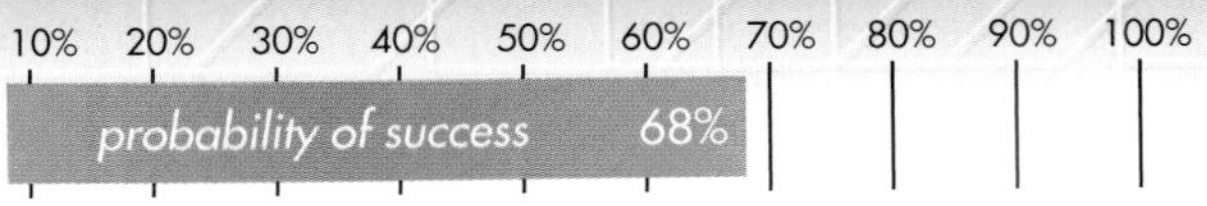

Workers are 72 percent more likely to attend work when their jobs have skill variety than when they don't.

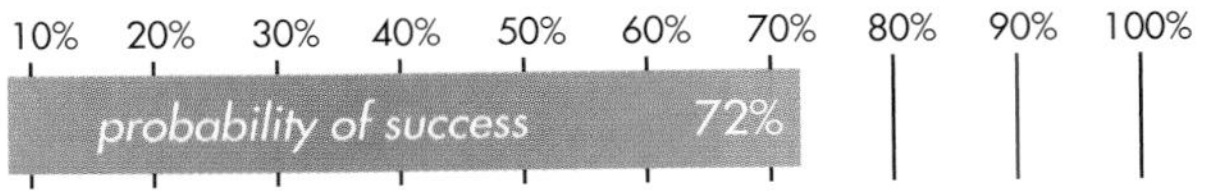

Workers are 74 percent more likely to attend work when their jobs have autonomy than when they don't.

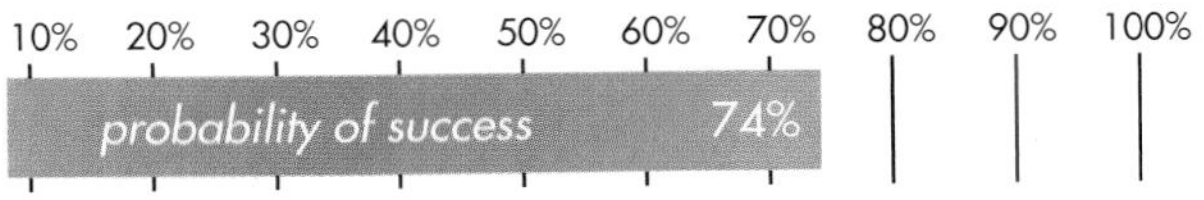

Workers are 72 percent more likely to attend work when their jobs provide feedback than when they don't.[23]

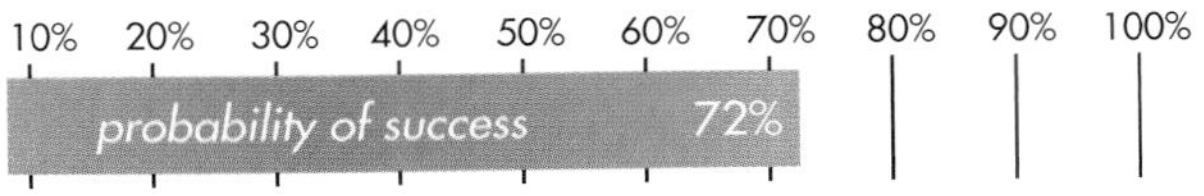

task identity, task significance, autonomy, and feedback), and workers must experience three critical psychological states (knowledge of results, responsibility for work outcomes, and meaningful work). If jobs aren't internally motivating, they can be redesigned by combining tasks, forming natural work units, establishing client relationships, vertical loading, and opening feedback channels.

Designing Organizational Processes

Over 40 years ago, Tom Burns and G. M. Stalker described how two kinds of organizational designs, mechanistic and organic, are appropriate for different kinds of organizational environments.[24] **Mechanistic organizations** are characterized by specialized jobs and responsibilities, precisely defined, unchanging roles, and a rigid chain of command based on centralized authority and vertical communication. This type of organization works best in stable, unchanging business environments. By contrast, **organic organizations** are characterized by broadly defined jobs and responsibility, loosely defined, frequently changing roles, and decentralized authority and horizontal communication based on task knowledge. This type of organization works best in dynamic, changing business environments.

mechanistic organization
an organization characterized by specialized jobs and responsibilities, precisely defined, unchanging roles, and a rigid chain of command based on centralized authority and vertical communication

The organizational design techniques described in the first half of this chapter, departmentalization, authority, and job design, are better suited for mechanistic organizations and the stable business environments that were more prevalent before 1980. In contrast, the organizational design techniques discussed here in the second part of the chapter are more appropriate for or-

organic organization
an organization characterized by broadly defined jobs and responsibility, loosely defined, frequently changing roles, and decentralized authority and horizontal communication based on task knowledge

ganic organizations and the increasingly dynamic environments in which today's businesses compete.

The key difference between these approaches is that whereas mechanistic organizational designs focus on organizational structure, organic organizational designs are concerned with organizational process, the collection of activities that transform inputs into outputs valued by customers. After reading the next two sections, you should be able to

4 explain the methods that companies are using to redesign internal organizational processes (i.e., intraorganizational processes).

5 describe the methods that companies are using to redesign external organizational processes (i.e., interorganizational processes).

4 Intraorganizational Processes

intraorganizational process
the collection of activities that take place within an organization to transform inputs into outputs that customers value

An **intraorganizational process** is the collection of activities that take place within an organization to transform inputs into outputs that customers value. The steps involved in an automobile insurance claim are a good example of an intraorganizational process:

1. Document the loss (i.e., the accident).
2. Assign an appraiser to determine the dollar amount of damage.
3. Make an appointment to inspect the vehicle.
4. Inspect the vehicle.
5. Write an appraisal and get the repair shop to agree to the damage estimate.
6. Pay for the repair work.
7. Return the repaired car to the customer.

Let's take a look at how companies are using 4.1 reengineering, 4.2 empowerment, and 4.3 behavioral informality to redesign internal organizational processes like these.

4.1 Reengineering

reengineering
fundamental rethinking and radical redesign of business processes to achieve dramatic improvements in critical measures of performance, such as cost, quality, service, and speed

In their best-selling book *Reengineering the Corporation*, Michael Hammer and James Champy defined **reengineering** as "the *fundamental* rethinking and *radical* redesign of business *processes* to achieve *dramatic* improvements in critical, contemporary measures of performance, such as cost, quality, service and speed."[25] Hammer and Champy further explained the four key words shown in italics in this definition. The first key word is *fundamental*. When reengineering organizational designs, managers must ask themselves, "Why do we do what we do?" and "Why do we do it the way we do?" The usual answer is, "Because that's the way we've always done it." The second key word is *radical*. Reengineering is about significant change, about starting over by throwing out the old ways of getting work done. The third key word is *processes*. Hammer and Champy noted that "most business people are not process oriented; they are focused on tasks, on jobs, on people, on structures, but not on processes." The fourth key word is *dramatic*. Reengineering is about achieving "quantum" improvements in company performance.

An example from IBM Credit's operation illustrates how work can be reengineered.[26] IBM Credit loans businesses money to buy IBM computers. Previously, the loan process began when an IBM salesperson called to obtain

task interdependence
the extent to which collective action is required to complete an entire piece of work

pooled interdependence
work completed by having each job or department independently contribute to the whole

credit approval for a customer's purchase. Then the loan application bounced around five departments over six days before being approved or denied. Of course, this delay cost IBM business. Some customers got their loans elsewhere. Others, frustrated by the wait, simply canceled their orders.

Finally, two IBM managers decided to walk a loan straight through to each of the five departments involved in the process. At each step, they asked the workers to stop what they were doing and immediately process their loan application. They were shocked by what they found. From start to finish, the entire process took just 90 minutes! It turned out that the average time of six days occurred because of delays in handing off the work from one department to another. The solution: IBM redesigned the process so that one person, not five in five separate departments, handled the entire loan approval process without any handoffs. The results were "dramatic." Reengineering the credit process reduced approval time from six days to four hours and allowed IBM Credit to increase the number of loans it handled by a factor of 100!

exhibit 10.11

Reengineering and Task Interdependence

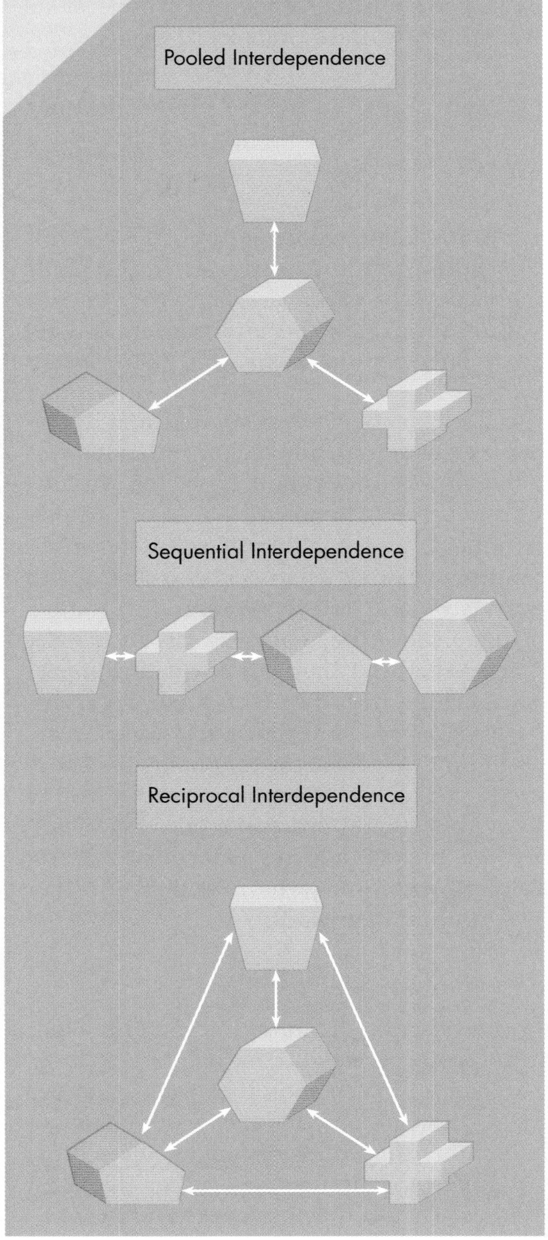

Reengineering changes an organization's orientation from vertical to horizontal. Instead of "taking orders" from upper management, lower- and middle-level managers and workers "take orders" from a customer who is at the beginning and end of each process. Instead of running independent functional departments, managers and workers in different departments take ownership of cross-functional processes. Instead of simplifying work so that it becomes increasingly specialized, reengineering complicates work by giving workers increased autonomy and responsibility for complete processes.

In essence, reengineering changes work by changing **task interdependence**, the extent to which collective action is required to complete an entire piece of work. As shown in Exhibit 10.11, there are three kinds of task interdependence.[27] In **pooled interdependence**, each job or department independently contributes to the whole. In **sequential interdependence**, work must be performed in succession, as one group's or job's outputs become the inputs for the next group or job. Finally, in **reciprocal interdependence**, different jobs or groups work together in a back-and-forth manner to complete the process. By reducing the handoffs between different jobs or groups, reengineering decreases sequential interdependence. Likewise, reengineering decreases pooled interdependence by redesigning work so that formerly independent jobs or departments now work together to complete processes. Finally, reengineering increases reciprocal interdependence by making groups or individuals responsible for larger, more complete processes in which several steps may be accomplished at the same time.

As an organizational design tool, reengineering promises big rewards, but it has also come under severe criticism. The most serious complaint is that because it

sequential interdependence work completed in succession, with one group's or job's outputs becoming the inputs for the next group or job

reciprocal interdependence work completed by different jobs or groups working together in a back-and-forth manner

allows a few workers to do the work formerly done by many, reengineering is simply a corporate code word for cost cutting and worker layoffs.[28] Likewise, for that reason, detractors claim that reengineering hurts morale and performance. For example, despite reducing ordering times from three weeks to three days, Levi Strauss ended an $850 million reengineering project because of the fear and turmoil it created in the company's work force. One of the low points occurred when Levi management, encouraged by its reengineering consultants, told 4,000 workers that they would have to "reapply for their jobs" as the company shifted from its traditional vertical structure to a process-based form of organizing. Thomas Kasten, Levi's vice president for reengineering and customer service, said, "We felt the pressure building up [over reengineering efforts], and we were worried about the business."[29] Today, even reengineering gurus Hammer and Champy admit that roughly 70 percent of all reengineering projects fail because of the effects on people in the workplace. Says Hammer, "I wasn't smart enough about that [the people issues]. I was reflecting my engineering background and was insufficiently appreciative of the human dimension. I've learned [now] that's critical."[30]

empowering workers permanently passing decision-making authority and responsibility from managers to workers by giving them the information and resources they need to make and carry out good decisions

empowerment feelings of intrinsic motivation, in which workers perceive their work to have impact and meaning and perceive themselves to be competent and capable of self-determination

4.2 Empowerment

Another way of redesigning interorganizational processes is through empowerment. **Empowering workers** means permanently passing decision-making authority and responsibility from managers to workers. For workers to be fully empowered, however, companies must give them the information and resources they need to make and carry out good decisions, and then reward them for taking individual initiative.[31]

When workers are given the proper information and resources and are allowed to make good decisions, they experience strong feelings of empowerment. **Empowerment** is a feeling of intrinsic motivation, in which workers perceive their work to have meaning and perceive themselves to be competent, having an impact, and capable of self-determination.[32] Work has meaning when it is consistent with personal standards and beliefs. Workers feel competent when they believe they can perform an activity with skill. The belief that they are having an impact comes from a feeling that they can affect work outcomes. A feeling of self-determination arises from workers' belief that they have the autonomy to choose how best to do their work. Empowerment can lead to changes in organizational processes because meaning, competence, impact, and self-determination produce empowered employees who take active, rather than passive, roles in their work.

PERSONAL PRODUCTIVITY TIP

Dress for Success the Casual Way

Dressing for success used to be easy. Conservative suits, shirts, blouses, and ties were the norm. Now, with the popularity of casual dress, many workers are unsure what to wear to work. In general, women should not wear denim, leggings, sneakers, tank tops, plunging necklines, or short skirts. Men should not wear jeans, shorts, T-shirts, gym shoes, or sandals. In general, women can wear flat shoes, blazers, and linen slacks or full-skirted dresses. Men can wear pleated pants (e.g., Dockers) with a polo or dress shirt. To be safe, though, always check with coworkers and read your company's casual dress policy.[33]

4.3 Behavioral Informality

How would you describe the atmosphere in the office where you last worked? Was it a formal, by-the-book, follow-the-rules, address-each-other-by-last-names atmosphere? Or was it more informal, with an emphasis on results rather than rules, casual business dress rather than suits, and first names rather than last names and titles? Or was it somewhere in between?

behavioral informality
a workplace atmosphere characterized by spontaneity, casualness, and interpersonal familiarity

behavioral formality
a workplace atmosphere characterized by routine and regimen, specific rules about how to behave, and impersonal detachment

Behavioral informality (or formality) is a third influence on intraorganizational processes. **Behavioral informality** refers to workplace situations characterized by spontaneity, casualness, and interpersonal familiarity. By contrast, **behavioral formality** refers to workplace situations characterized by routine and regimen, specific rules about how to behave, and impersonal detachment.

Two main factors affecting behavioral formality are casual dress codes and office space layout. Casual dress policies and open office systems are two of the most popular methods for increasing behavioral informality. In fact, a survey conducted by the Society for Human Resource Management indicates that casual dress policies (no suits, ties, jackets, dresses, or formal clothing required) are extremely popular.[34] Contrary to news stories that say suits are back (sales of suits and sports coats actually fell 13.3 percent last year), today 86 percent of companies have some form of casual dress code compared to 63 percent 5 years ago and 24 percent 10 years ago.[35] Similarly, 42 percent of all companies permit casual dress at least one day a week compared to 17 percent five years ago. Moreover, 33 percent of companies permit casual dress every day of the week, up from 20 percent five years ago. Amazingly, even staid, stuffy IBM, known as "Big Blue" in part for the dark blue suits and white shirts traditionally worn by its employees, has gone business casual. So has AT&T. Burke Stinson, an AT&T spokesperson, says, "Brainpower is more important than appearance, and brainpower is what makes you productive, not a gray flannel suit."[36] Many managers seem to agree. In fact, 85 percent of human resources directors believe that casual dress can improve office morale, and 79 percent say that employees are very satisfied with casual dress codes.[37] Moreover, nearly two-thirds of them believe that casual dress policies are an important tool for attracting qualified employees in tight labor markets. Michael Losey, president of the Society for Human Resource Management, concludes that "for the majority of corporations and industries, allowing casual dress can have clear advantages at virtually no cost."[38]

While casual dress increases behavioral informality by having managers and workers at all levels dress in a more relaxed manner, open office systems increase behavioral informality by significantly increasing the level of communication and interaction among employees. By definition, **open office systems** try to increase interaction by removing physical barriers that separate workers. One characteristic of open office systems is that they have much more shared space than private space. **Shared spaces** are areas used by and open to all employees. Cubicles with low-to-the-ground partitions (used by 75 percent of office workers), offices with no doors or with glass walls, collections of comfortable furniture that encourage people to congregate, and common areas with tables and chairs that encourage people to meet, work, or eat together are examples of

DOING THE RIGHT THING

Don't Scavenge That Office If Somebody Is Still in It

It's like road kill in the animal kingdom. As soon as the word gets out that someone is leaving the company, the remaining coworkers start scheming to scavenge the office leftovers—chairs, computer monitors, filing cabinets, and even staplers. Mary Wong, president of a human resources consulting company, says, "This issue is practically everywhere . . . , professionals—anyone you and I would normally consider to be very adult—turn into children" over the prospect of picking an empty office clean of its "goodies." Sometimes, however, and this is where it gets disrespectful, office scavengers move in before the employee, who's often been laid off, has left. Ethics consultant Steve Lawler tells the story of a laid-off manager who, just hours after hearing the bad news, was already getting requests for the expensive Herman Miller Aeron chair in which he was still sitting. Office scavenging is a strange and predictable aspect of office life. It happens everywhere. But, if you're going to scavenge, and you probably will, do the right thing by maintaining the dignity of departing coworkers: wait till the office is empty before you strike.[39]

open office systems
offices in which the physical barriers that separate workers have been removed in order to increase communication and interaction

shared spaces
spaces used by and open to all employees

private spaces
spaces used by and open to just one employee

shared space.[40] In contrast, **private spaces**, such as private offices with doors, are used by and open to just one employee.

The advantage of an open office with extensive shared space is that it dramatically increases the amount of unplanned, spontaneous, and chance communication between employees.[41] People are much more likely to plan meetings and work together when numerous "collaboration spaces" with conference tables, white boards, and computers are readily available. With no office walls, inviting common areas, and different departments mixed together in large open spaces, spontaneous communication occurs more often. Also, open office systems increase chance communication by making it much more likely that people from different departments or areas will run into each other. When Alcoa moved its headquarters from a 31-story building with traditional offices to a 6-story building with open offices, glass-walled conference rooms, family-style kitchens on each floor, and escalators instead of elevators, the transformation was dramatic. Then-CEO Paul O'Neill said, "I'd run into three people in the elevator [in the old building] and that's how many people I saw each day—except for those I had scheduled appointments with." But in the new open office design, he says, "I take the escalator down and I see 50 people or 50 people can see me."[42]

Not everyone is enthusiastic about open offices, however. Indeed, because there is so much shared space and so little private space, companies with open systems have to take a number of steps to give employees privacy when they need to concentrate on individual work. One step is simply to use taller cubicles. Another approach is to install white noise machines to prevent voices and other noises from disrupting others.[43] Yet another approach is to make conference rooms available. In contrast to traditional offices, where such rooms are used for meetings, many employees in open systems reserve conference rooms when they need private time to work. Advertising agency GSD&M built 43 conference rooms of varying sizes to give its workers privacy when they needed it. Since most of its employees use laptop computers, they simply unplug from their cubicles and plug back in after reaching the conference room. Account director Nancy Ryan uses a small conference room as much as eight times per day to make phone calls, write, or have private conversations with employees or clients.[44]

Review 4
Intraorganizational Processes

Today, companies are using reengineering, empowerment, and behavioral informality to change their intraorganizational processes. Through fundamental rethinking and radical redesign of business processes, reengineering changes an organization's orientation from vertical to horizontal. Reengineering changes work processes by decreasing sequential and pooled interdependence and by increasing reciprocal interdependence. Reengineering promises dramatic increases in productivity and customer satisfaction, but has been criticized as simply an excuse to cut costs and lay off workers. Empowering workers means taking decision-making authority and responsibility from managers and giving it to workers. Empowered workers develop feelings of competence and self-determination and believe their work to have meaning and impact. Workplaces characterized by behavioral informality are spontaneous and casual. Formal workplaces are characterized by routine and specific rules about how to behave. Casual dress policies and open office systems are two of the most popular methods for increasing behavioral informality.

5 Interorganizational Processes

interorganizational process a collection of activities that take place among companies to transform inputs into outputs that customers value

An **interorganizational process** is a collection of activities that occur *among companies* to transform inputs into outputs that customers value. In other words, many companies work together to create a product or service that keeps customers happy. For example, when you purchase a Benetton sweater at the mall, you're not just buying from Benetton. A network of small companies supplies Benetton's factories. While Benetton performs weaving, cutting, dyeing, and quality control, another network of small companies provides labor for production tasks, such as tailoring, finishing, and ironing. A worldwide network of retail sales agents selects the Benetton designs that they feel will sell best in their local markets. In turn, those agents supply Benetton products to retailers who sell them to consumers. Although this network design originated in Italy, it is repeated throughout the world. For example, Benetton Hungary coordinates the network of production companies in Hungary, Ukraine, the Czech Republic, Poland, Moldova, Bulgaria, and Romania.[45]

In this section, you'll explore interorganizational processes by learning about 5.1 modular organizations and 5.2 virtual organizations.[46]

5.1 Modular Organizations

modular organization an organization that outsources noncore business activities to outside companies, suppliers, specialists, or consultants

Except for the core business activities that they can perform better, faster, and cheaper than others, **modular organizations** outsource all remaining business activities to outside companies, suppliers, specialists, or consultants. The term "modular" is used because the business activities purchased from outside companies can be added and dropped as needed, much like adding pieces to a three-dimensional puzzle. Exhibit 10.12 depicts a modular organization in which the company has chosen to keep training, human resources, sales, research and development, information technology, product design, customer service, and manufacturing as core business activities, but, it has outsourced the noncore activities of product distribution, Web page design, advertising, payroll, accounting, and packaging.

exhibit 10.12

Modular Organization

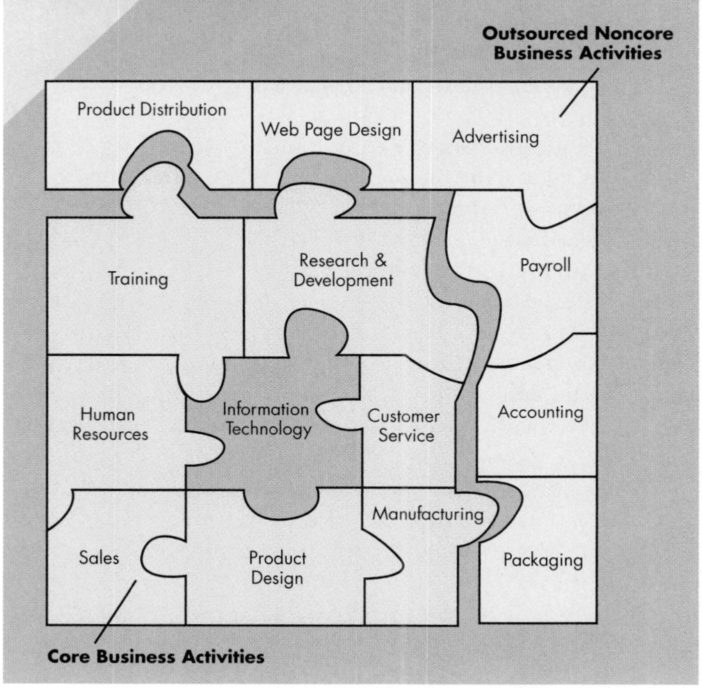

Modular organizations have several advantages. First, because modular organizations pay for outsourced labor, expertise, or manufacturing capabilities only when needed, they can cost significantly less to run than traditional organizations. When you buy a laptop computer from Dell, Gateway, Hewlett-Packard, or Apple, the chances are very good that you're really buying a Quanta, a laptop made by Taiwan-based Quanta Computer, the world's largest laptop manufacturer. H-P's worldwide supply-chain director Jim Burns says that outsourcing to Quanta "saved our business. It was the biggest turnaround in H-P's history."[47]

Modular organizations have disadvantages, too. The primary disadvantage is the loss of control that occurs when key business activities are outsourced to other companies. Also, companies may reduce their competitive advantage in two ways if they mistakenly outsource a core business activity. First, competitive and technological change may produce a situation in which the noncore business activities a company has outsourced suddenly become the basis for competitive advantage. Second, related to that point, companies to which work is outsourced can sometimes become competitors.

5.2 Virtual Organizations

virtual organization an organization that is part of a network in which many companies share skills, costs, capabilities, markets, and customers to collectively solve customer problems or provide specific products or services

In contrast to modular organizations in which the interorganizational process revolves around a central company, a **virtual organization** is part of a network in which many companies share skills, costs, capabilities, markets, and customers with each other. Exhibit 10.13 shows a virtual organization in which, for "today," the parts of a virtual company consist of product design, purchasing, manufacturing, advertising, and information technology. However, unlike modular organizations, in which outside organizations are tightly linked to one central company, virtual organizations work with some companies in the network alliance, but not with all. So, whereas a puzzle with various pieces is a fitting metaphor for a modular organization, a potluck dinner is an appropriate metaphor for a virtual organization. All participants bring their finest food dish, but only eat what they want.

Another difference is that the working relationships between modular organizations and outside companies tend to be more stable and longer lasting than the shorter, often temporary relationships found among the virtual companies in a network alliance. Thus, the composition of a virtual organization is always changing. The combination of network partners that a virtual corporation has at any one time simply depends on the expertise needed to solve a particular problem or provide a specific product or service. This is why the businessperson in the network organization shown in Exhibit 10.13 is saying, "Today, I'll have . . ." Tomorrow, the business could want something completely different. In this sense, the term "virtual organization" means the organization that exists "at the moment." For example, 19 small companies in Pennsylvania have formed a network of virtual organizations that they call the "Agile Web."[48] Together, the companies have expertise in product development and design, machining, metal fabrication, diecasting, plastic-injection molding, finishing and coating, and the design and manufacture of electronic components. Tony Nickel, who coordinates business opportunities for the 19 Web members, says, "We do have multiple machine shops and multiple sheet-metal shops. If only one is needed, I make the decision based on the nature of the [customer's] request and the areas of specialization of the member firms." He adds, "We've already had one occasion where, while negotiating with a customer, we discovered that we really didn't have the right Web member for a particular part—so we changed members."[49]

exhibit 10.13

Network Organization

Virtual organizations have a number of advantages. They let companies share costs. And, because members can quickly combine their efforts to meet customers' needs, they are fast and flexible. For example, Tony Nickel of the Agile Web says, "Where we think we really can have rapid response is when a customer wants help in the design and building of an assembly or system. Then I can bring members of the Web to the table—or to the customer's facility—right away; the next day, if required. We are able to assemble a team from the Web within 24 hours if that is what the customer wants."[50] Finally, because each member of the network alliance is the "best" at what it does, in theory, virtual organizations should provide better products and services in all respects.

As with modular organizations, a disadvantage of virtual organizations is that once work has been outsourced, it can be difficult to control the quality of work done by network partners. The greatest disadvantage, however, is that it requires tremendous managerial skills to make a network of independent organizations work well together, especially since their relationships tend to be shorter and based on a single task or project. Virtual organizations are using two methods to solve this problem. The first is to use a *broker*, like Tony Nickel. In traditional, hierarchical organizations, managers plan, organize, and control. But, with the horizontal, interorganizational processes that characterize virtual organizations, the job of a broker is to create and assemble the knowledge, skills, and resources from different companies for outside parties, such as customers.[51] The second way to make networks of virtual organizations more manageable is to use a *virtual organization agreement* that, somewhat like a contract, specifies the schedules, responsibilities, costs, payouts and liabilities for participating organizations.[52]

Review 5
Interorganizational Processes

Organizations are using modular and virtual organizations to change interorganizational processes. Because modular organizations outsource all noncore activities to other businesses, they are less expensive to run than traditional companies. However, modular organizations require extremely close relationships with suppliers, may result in a loss of control, and could create new competitors if the wrong business activities are outsourced. Virtual organizations participate in a network in which they share skills, costs, capabilities, markets, and customers. As customer problems, products, or services change, the combination of virtual organizations that work together changes. Virtual organizations reduce costs, respond quickly, and, if they can successfully coordinate their efforts, can produce outstanding products and service.

STUDY TIP Take advantage of all the review opportunities on Effective Management Online at **http://em-online.swlearning.com**. Write up a list of questions you have about concepts you don't understand and visit your professor or TA during office hours.

MANAGEMENT TEAM DECISION

PLUSH MANAGEMENT PERKS: PARTAKING OR PRUNING?

"They do, too!" "*They do not!*" "You don't know what you're talking about." "*See, it's attitudes like yours that prove my point!*"

Ah, nothing like hearing your two top executives argue during lunch to raise your blood pressure.[53] You knew that Sam, the VP of Sales, was going to get mad when Catherine, the VP of Human Resources, suggested getting rid of executive perks (the private dining room, company cars, first-class air travel, etc.). It took Sam 25 years to become a vice president, and understandably, he doesn't want to see his perks and rewards reduced. You didn't think it was possible for someone to get that mad that fast, though. Given the way Sam's face instantly turned beet red when Catherine suggested that the reserved parking spaces be eliminated, it's a good thing she caught him between bites or he might have choked on his shrimp salad.

Well, with executive perks topping the agenda for the annual executive retreat next weekend, Sam and Catherine's argument has given you something to think about. Is Catherine right? Should all executive perks be eliminated? Or is Sam right? Should the executive perks be left alone? After all, even Catherine got defensive when Sam asked her how happy she'd be if the company closed its on-site day care. When she responded, "They wouldn't dare do that," Sam barked, "That's exactly the way I feel about your recommendations!"

Well, you need to get your thoughts sorted out. A good place to start is with the list of executive perks currently being offered by the company:

- company cars
- reserved parking spaces
- company cellular phones
- personal financial counseling
- personal liability insurance
- executive dining room
- first-class air travel
- free travel for a spouse on extended business trips
- signing bonuses
- stock options
- country club memberships
- large, expensively furnished private offices
- home security systems
- home computer/office equipment

For this exercise, assemble a five-person management team and use the stepladder group decision-making technique described in Chapter 4. At each point in the stepladder, discuss all three questions and come to a consensus on each before adding the next group member.

Questions

1. Of the perks listed above, choose three that your managers are most likely to desire. In other words, which three executive perks would your managers scream the most about if you took them away? Explain your reasoning for each of your three choices.
2. Of the perks listed above, which three probably create the most resentment among your nonmanagerial work force? In other words, which three executive perks anger your workers the most? Explain your reasoning for each of your three choices.
3. Which of the following options is likely to benefit the company most in the long run?
   a. Eliminate all executive perks.
   b. Retain all executive perks.
   c. Selectively eliminate perks.

   Explain the reasoning behind your choice. If you choose option (c), specify the perks you kept and explain why you kept them.

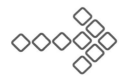

"WORK" IN SOMEONE ELSE'S SHOES

Why is learning to see things from someone else's perspective one of the most difficult things to do in today's workplace? Sometimes, the inability to see things as others see them has to do with the people involved. Inexperience, ignorance, and selfishness can all play a role. In most organizations, however, the inability to see things from someone else's perspective results from the jobs themselves, not the people who do them. Because jobs limit who we talk to, what we talk about, what we think about, and what we care about at work, it should not be a surprise that people who perform different jobs have very different views about each other and the workplace.

For example, at Southwest Airlines the pilots who fly the planes and the ground crews who unload, load, and refuel them had little appreciation for each other. The ground crews felt that the pilots treated them like second-class citizens. The pilots couldn't understand why the ground crews weren't doing more to get their planes out of the gates and in the air as fast as possible. To improve understanding and help them see things from each other's perspective, Southwest created a program called the "Cutting Edge," in which the captains and ground crews learned a lot about each other's jobs. For example, the pilots brought the ground crews into their cockpits and showed them the detailed processes they were required to follow to get planes ready for departure. The pilots, on the other hand, gained appreciation and understanding by actually working as members of Southwest's ground crews. After several days of demanding ground crew work, Southwest pilot Captain Mark Boyter said:

> I remember one time when I was working the ramp [as a member of a ground crew] in Los Angeles. I was dead tired. I had flown that morning and had a couple of legs in, so I got out of my uniform and jumped into my ramp clothes. That afternoon was very hot. It was in the 80s—I can't imagine how they do it on a 120-degree day in Phoenix. I was tired and hungry and hadn't had a break. Then I saw this pilot sitting up there in the cockpit eating his frozen yogurt. I said to myself, "Man, I'd like to be up there now." Then I caught myself. I'm up there every day. Now, I know that pilot has been up since 3:00 in the morning. I know that he's been flying an airplane since 6:00 A.M. I know it's 3:00 in the afternoon and he hasn't had a chance to get off and have a meal yet today. I know all that, and yet, the yogurt still looks really good to me. Then I thought, "How can a ramp agent [on the ground crew] in Los Angeles who works his butt off for two or three years, working double shifts two or three times a week, understand this? It hit me that there's a big gap in understanding here."[54]

The misunderstandings between Southwest's pilots and ground crews are not unique. All organizations experience them. Nurses and doctors, teachers and students, and managers and employees all have difficulty seeing things from each other's perspective. As Southwest's Cutting Edge program shows, however, you can minimize differences and build understanding by "working" in someone else's shoes.

Questions

1. Describe the job-related differences or tensions where you work. Who is involved? What jobs do they do? Explain why the job-related differences or tensions exist.
2. Since the best way to see things from someone else's perspective is to "work" in his or her shoes, see if you can spend a day, a morning, or even two hours performing one of these jobs. If that's not possible, spend some time carefully observing the jobs and then interview several people who perform them. Describe your boss's reaction to this request. Was he or she supportive? Why or why not?
3. Answer the following questions after you have worked the job or conducted your interviews. What most surprised you about this job? What was easiest? What was hardest? Explain. Now that you've had the chance to see things as others see them, what do you think would happen, good or bad, from letting other people in your organization work in someone else's shoes? Explain.

take two video!

BIZ FLIX The Paper

This engaging film shows the ethical dilemmas and stress of producing the *New York Sun*, a daily metropolitan newspaper. Metro Editor Henry Hackett (Michael Keaton) races against the clock to publish a story about a major police scandal that could send two young African American men to jail. He is in constant conflict with Managing Editor Alicia Clark (Glenn Close) who is more concerned about controlling the budget than about running accurate stories. Hackett is also under constant pressure from his wife Marty (Marisa Tomei), who is pregnant with their first child. While Hackett tries to get his story, Marty urges him to take a less demanding job at *The Sentinel*.

This scene is an edited version of the "The Managing Editor" sequence, which occurs early in *The Paper*. It shows a staff meeting that takes place the day after the *Sun* missed a story about a murder and other shootings with racial overtones. Instead, the *Sun* ran a front-page story about parking problems. At the meeting, Senior Editor Bernie White (Robert Duvall) discusses his preferences in front-page stories.

What to Watch for and Ask Yourself

1. Senior Editor Bernie White wants to reach a specific goal with the next edition of the *New York Sun*. What is this goal?
2. What method of departmentalization best describes the organizational structure at the *Sun:* functional, product, customer, geographic, or matrix? Explain your choice.
3. Is the organizational structure of the *Sun* appropriate for reaching White's goal? Why or why not?

MGMT WORKPLACE Student Advantage

Student Advantage is an innovative finance company that offers specialty debit cards to college and university students. The company partners with retail and service firms that wish to promote discounted products to the highly attractive 18- to 25-year-old market. Based in Boston, Student Advantage has rapidly grown from a small entrepreneurial firm to a 400-employee powerhouse. Though CEO Ray Sozzi welcomes the growth as a reflection of his venture's success, he is aware that it poses many organizational challenges. Sozzi wants to maintain the energy and transparency of a fledgling entrepreneurial venture while adding the structure, rigor, and process control befitting a highly professional organization.

What to Watch for and Ask Yourself

1. What is the organizational structure at Student Advantage? Describe the organizational process and explain how it is influenced by structure.
2. Why is empowerment an effective tool for the managers at Student Advantage?
3. How do the different dimensions of organizational authority work together at Student Advantage? Is this approach to organizational authority effective?

Organizing People, Projects, and Processes

PART FOUR

CHAPTER ELEVEN

Managing Teams

outline

WHAT WOULD YOU DO?

Cessna Headquarters, Wichita, Kansas.[1] The words "Cessna Skyhawk" have special meaning for anyone who has ever wanted to learn to fly. More people have learned to fly in a Cessna Skyhawk than in any other plane in aviation history. In fact, the Skyhawk with its 36-foot wingspan, 140 mph cruising speed, and room for two adults and their luggage is the best-selling plane of all time. Since 1911, Cessna has been a storied name in aviation. Cessna built gliders for the army in World War II, introduced the Skyhawk in 1956, produced the first turbocharged and cabin-pressurized single-engine planes in the 1960s, delivered its first business jet in the 1970s, and topped $1 billion in sales in the 1980s. Then in the 1990s, as the aviation industry experienced one of its worst downturns ever, Cessna nearly went out of business. Sales of general aviation aircraft for the entire industry, which had reached 17,000 planes per year, hit rock bottom at 928 planes in 2001. During the same period, sales of

student resources

URL
Explore the four levels of learning by doing the simulation module on Teams.

GUIDE
Mini lecture reviews all the learning points in the chapter and concludes with a case on Harley-Davidson.

VIDEO
Biz Flix is a scene from *Apollo 13* (different from chapter 9). Management Workplace is a segment on Cannondale.

PPT
12 slides with graphics provide an outline for this chapter.

FAQ
Chuck outlines how team charters can enhance team performance, whether for a student project or in the business world.

TEST
24 true/false questions, 24 multiple-choice questions, a management scenario, and 7 exhibit worksheets

Cessna's piston-engine planes, like the Skyhawk, dropped from 8,000 planes per year to just 600. Cessna laid off 75 percent of the employees at its piston-engine plane factories and, eventually, stopped making piston-engine planes altogether. Now, however, positive changes in the external environment have prompted Cessna to start building its legendary Skyhawks again.

This is where you come in. You have been with the company nearly 20 years and have just been made the vice president of Cessna's "new" single-engine business. It's your job to rebuild this part of the business from scratch. Pilots tend to remain loyal to the kind of airplane on which they learned to fly, so if you can rebuild Cessna's single-engine business today, pilots who learn to fly on today's Skyhawks will still be buying and flying Cessna jets 20 years from now.

One of the advantages of starting over completely is that you get to design the entire production facility—everything from its location, to the new workers, to the suppliers. For instance, Cessna does most of its production in Wichita, Kansas (the aviation center of the United States), and you've located the new single-engine plane factory about 100 miles outside Wichita. Furthermore, instead of using a standard production line where each worker does just one task, you have tentatively decided to use teams to assemble the planes.

You're aware that switching to teams may strike some people as radical, particularly at conservative Cessna where, as one of your fellow managers admitted, "we probably got into a mode of doing things for the future based on how we'd always done things in the past." But the more you think about it, the more you believe you've made the right decision.

You expect to see several benefits from a team-based approach: increased customer satisfaction from improved product quality; faster, more efficient production; and higher employee job satisfaction. A few things worry you, however. Despite all of their promise, teams and teamwork are also prone to significant disadvantages: they're expensive to implement, they require significant training, and they work only about a third of the time they're used. So, despite their promise, you can't ignore the reality that using teams would be quite risky for Cessna.

Still, you can't help thinking that teams could pay off and that there might be ways for you to minimize the risk of failure. For example, since the plant will be in a new location, you get to start with a brand new work force. What kinds of people should you hire for teamwork? What kinds of skills and experience will they need to succeed in a team environment? How much authority and responsibility should you give them? Should they be limited to just advising management, or should they be totally responsible for quality, costs, and productivity?

Finally, are there other places where you might use teams besides the assembly line? How could teams contribute to the success of Cessna's "new" single-engine plane manufacturing facility in other ways?

If you were in charge of Cessna's "new" single-engine factory, what would you do?

A growing number of organizations are significantly improving their effectiveness by establishing work teams. In fact, 91 percent of U.S. companies use teams and groups of one kind or another to solve specific problems.[2] Nonetheless, as Exhibit 11.1 shows, with the exception of Procter & Gamble, which began using teams in 1962, many companies did not establish work teams until the mid to late 1980s. Many of the companies shown in Exhibit 11.1 were early adopters; most companies have only been using teams for 15 to 20 years, if that long. In other words, teams are a relatively new phenomenon in companies, and there's still much for organizations to learn about managing them.

work team
a small number of people with complementary skills who hold themselves mutually accountable for pursuing a common purpose, achieving performance goals, and improving interdependent work processes

We begin this chapter by reviewing the advantages and disadvantages of teams and exploring when companies should use them instead of more traditional approaches. Next, we discuss the different types of work teams and the characteristics common to all teams. The chapter ends by focusing on the practical steps to managing teams—team goals and priorities and organizing, training, and compensating teams.

Why Work Teams?

Work teams consist of a small number of people with complementary skills who hold themselves mutually accountable for pursuing a common purpose, achieving performance goals, and improving interdependent work processes.[3] By this definition, computer programmers working on separate projects in the same department of a company would not be considered a team. To be a team, the programmers would have to be interdependent and share responsibility and accountability for the quality and amount of computer code they produced.[4]

exhibit 11.1

When Selected Companies First Began Using Work Teams

Boeing	1987
Caterpillar	1986
Champion International	1985
Cummins Engine	1973
Digital Equipment	1982
Ford	1982
General Electric	1985
LTV Steel	1985
Procter & Gamble	1962

Source: J. Hoerr, "The Payoff from Teamwork—The Gains in Quality Are Substantial—So Why Isn't It Spreading Faster?" BusinessWeek, *10 July 1989, 56.*

Julia Garcia is a member of a work team in a Frito-Lay snack plant in Lubbock, Texas. Before teams were established at the plant, Garcia and her coworkers never paid any attention to the quality and cost data posted on company bulletin boards and rarely concerned themselves with ways to improve the plant's operation. Today, however, Garcia and her teammates receive weekly updates on costs, quality, and performance and take as much responsibility for quality standards and performance as company management does. When products don't meet Frito-Lay's quality standards, Garcia and her teammates reject them. When machines are shut down for maintenance and too many workers are sitting around with nothing to do, Garcia and her teammates keep costs down by deciding who should be sent home until the machines are working.

Since the move to teams, the number of managers at the Frito-Lay plant has dropped from 38 to 13, while the number of hourly workers (i.e., team members) has increased by 20 percent to more than 220. More importantly, the teams have produced double-digit reductions in costs and such huge improvements in quality that the plant is now ranked sixth out of 48 plants by Frito management, up from the bottom 20 where it was previously ranked. Furthermore, Garcia and her coworkers are thriving in the team atmosphere. She says, "It kind of frightened me at first. I thought, 'I'm not going to be able to decide anything.' [But now] I really enjoy [the team approach] because it gives me a sense of pride. I know my work and what we need to do. . . . It's more fun. It used to be it was just the 'same-ol–same-ol,' [but] now there are more things happening."[5]

The success that Julia Garcia and Frito-Lay experienced with teams is not uncommon. In many industries, teams are growing in importance because they help organizations respond to specific problems and challenges. For Frito-Lay, the challenges were to increase product quality and lower costs. For a service business, like a restaurant or an airline, the challenge may be to increase customer satisfaction or employee motivation. Though work teams are not the answer for every situation or organization, if the right teams are used properly and in the right settings, teams can dramatically improve company performance over more traditional management approaches and instill a sense of vitality in the workplace that is otherwise difficult to achieve.

After reading the next two sections, you should be able to

1 explain the good and bad of using teams.

2 recognize and understand the different kinds of teams.

1 The Good and Bad of Using Teams

Let's begin our discussion of teams by learning about 1.1 the advantages of teams, 1.2 the disadvantages of teams, and 1.3 when to use and not use teams.

1.1 The Advantages of Teams

Companies are making greater use of teams because teams have been shown to increase customer satisfaction, product and service quality, speed and efficiency in product development, and employee job satisfaction.[6]

Teams help businesses increase *customer satisfaction* in several ways. One way is to create work teams that are trained to meet the needs of specific customer groups. When Eastman Kodak reengineered its customer service center, it created specific teams to field calls from the general public (based on the geographic location of the caller), scientific users, and corporate users. Under this system, customers are immediately directed to the team trained to meet their needs. Within a year, the work teams doubled the rate at which Kodak solved customer problems on the first phone call.[7]

Businesses also create problem-solving teams and employee involvement teams to study ways to improve overall customer satisfaction and make recommendations for improvements. Teams like these typically meet on a weekly or monthly basis. Every day at the Longaberger Company, 2,500 skilled weavers make over 40,000 high-quality baskets (which sell for $30 to $260). But when productivity began to drop, management turned to an employee involvement group to solve the problem. After studying 40 basket makers for three weeks, the team came up with a solution that makes sure the different kinds of wood veneers used to make different baskets go to the right weavers (who were often stuck with the wrong materials). Before the new system, workers ran out of the proper materials 53 times per day. But with the new system, that happens only nine times per day. And, because the new system has also cut scrap (i.e., leftover, unusable materials) by 75 percent, the company is saving $3 million per year.[8]

Teams also help firms improve *product and service quality* in several ways.[9] In contrast to traditional organizational structures where management is responsible for organizational outcomes and performance, teams take direct responsibility for the quality of the products and service they produce. And making teams directly responsible for service and production quality pays off. A survey by *Industry Week* indicates that 42 percent of the companies that use teams report revenues of more than $250,000 per employee, compared to only 25 percent of the companies that don't use teams.[10]

As you learned in Chapter 9, companies that are slow to innovate or integrate new features and technologies into their products are at a competitive disadvantage. Therefore, a third reason that teams are increasingly popular is that they can increase *speed and efficiency when designing and manufacturing products.*[11] Traditional product design proceeds sequentially, meaning that one department, such as engineering or manufacturing, has to finish its work on the design before the next department, such as marketing, can start. Unfortunately, this is not only slow, but it also encourages departments to work in isolation from one another.[12] Teams of employees from the different functional areas in a firm (i.e., engineering, manufacturing, and marketing) work on various aspects of the project at the same time. Because each of the different functional areas is involved in the design process from the start, the company can avoid most of the delays and frustration associated with sequential development. Industrial Light & Magic (ILM), founded by George Lucas, the originator and producer of *Star Wars*, has won 19 Academy Awards for visual effects and technical achievement. ILM uses overlapping development phases to quickly produce specialized, computer effects for movies. Teams of artists and animators work simultaneously on different scenes, such as the opening and closing of a movie, to speed up production. Visual-effects producer Jacqui Lopez says, "When we get down to the wire, our artists need every second they can get in front of their computers."[13] Oftentimes, she says, "Being late is not an option. The publicity is already locked in, and the studios have schedules to keep. We can't be late."[14] And ILM has *never* been late. Indeed, whether the movie is *Terminator 3* or *Harry Potter*, when film studios and directors fall behind, they regularly come to ILM to avoid missing deadlines.

Another reason for using teams is that teamwork often leads to increased *job satisfaction.*[15] One reason that teamwork can be more satisfying than traditional work is that it gives workers a chance to improve their skills. This is often accomplished through **cross training**, in which team members are taught how to do all or most of the jobs performed by the other team members. A second reason that teamwork is satisfying is that work teams often receive proprietary business information that is available only to managers at most companies. For example, at Whole Foods, the supermarket chain that sells groceries and health foods, team members are given full access to their store's financial information and everyone's salaries, including the store manager and the CEO.[16] Each day, next to the time clock, Whole Foods employees can see the previous day's sales for each team, as well as the sales on the same day from the previous year. Each week, team members can examine the same information, broken down by team, for all of the Whole Foods stores in their region. And each month, store managers review information on profitability, including sales, product costs, wages, and operating profits, with each team in the store. Since team members decide how much to spend, what to order, what things should cost, and how many team members should work each day, this information is critical to making teams work at Whole Foods.[17]

cross training
training team members to do all or most of the jobs performed by the other team members

Team members also gain job satisfaction from unique leadership responsibilities that would typically not be available in traditional organizations. For example, at Colgate-Palmolive, work teams are responsible for determining their own work assignments, scheduling overtime, scheduling vacations, performing preventive equipment maintenance, and assuring quality control. For each work team, the position of team leader rotates, giving different team members the opportunity to build leadership skills.[18] Furthermore, rotating leadership among team members can lead to more participation and cooperation in team decision making and improved team performance.[19]

Finally, teams share many of the advantages of group decision making discussed in Chapter 4. For instance, because team members possess different knowledge, skills, abilities, and experiences, a team is able to view problems from multiple perspectives. This diversity of viewpoints increases the odds that team decisions will solve the underlying causes of problems rather than simply address the symptoms. The increased knowledge and information available to teams also make it easier for them to generate more alternative solutions, which is a critical part of improving the quality of decisions. Because team members are involved in decision-making processes, they are also likely to be more committed to making those decisions work. In short, teams can do a much better job than individuals in two important steps of the decision-making process: defining the problem and generating alternative solutions.

1.2 The Disadvantages of Teams

Although teams can significantly increase customer satisfaction, product and service quality, speed and efficiency in product development, and employee job satisfaction, using teams does not guarantee these positive outcomes. In fact, if you've ever participated in team projects in your classes, you're probably already aware of some of the problems inherent in work teams. Despite all of their promise, teams and teamwork are also prone to these significant disadvantages: initially high turnover, social loafing, and the problems associated with group decision making.

The first disadvantage of work teams is *initially high turnover*. Teams aren't for everyone, and some workers balk at the responsibility, effort, and learning required in team settings. When General Electric's Salisbury plant switched to teams, the turnover rate jumped from near zero to 14 percent.[20] People may quit because they object to the way team members closely scrutinize each other's job performance, particularly when teams are small. Randy Savage, who works for Eaton Corporation, a manufacturer of car and truck parts, said, "They say there are no bosses here, but if you screw up, you find one pretty fast." Beverly Reynolds, who quit Eaton's team-based system after nine months, said her coworkers "weren't standing watching me, but from afar, they were watching me." And even though her teammates were willing to help her improve her job performance, she concluded, "As it turns out, it just wasn't for me at all."[21]

Social loafing is another disadvantage of work teams. **Social loafing** occurs when workers withhold their efforts and fail to perform their share of the work. A nineteenth-century German scientist named Ringleman first documented social loafing when he found that one person pulling on a rope alone exerted an average of 63 kilograms of force on the rope. In groups of three, the average force dropped to 53 kilograms. In groups of eight, the average dropped to just 31 kilograms. Ringleman concluded that

social loafing
behavior in which team members withhold their efforts and fail to perform their share of the work

www.experiencing management.com

Cement your understanding of the social loafing concept by interacting with the concept and related materials at our animated concept and activity site. Choose Teams from the " select a topic" pull-down menu, then Social Loafing from the "overview tab."

http://www.experiencingmanagement.com

DOING THE RIGHT THING

Don't Be a Team Slacker—Do Your Share. Given the amount of teamwork required in business classes, most of you have encountered slackers in student groups. Perhaps you've even "slacked" yourself from time to time. But, from an ethical perspective, slacking is clearly wrong. In reality, it's no different than cheating on an exam. When you slack, you're relying on others to do your work. You benefit without putting forth effort. And "your" team's project, paper, or presentation hasn't benefited from your contributions. In fact, it's very likely that your slacking may have significantly hurt "your" team's performance. Furthermore, in the real world, the consequences of team slacking, such as lost sales, poorer decisions, lower-quality service or products, or poorer productivity, are much larger. So, do the right thing. Whether it's in class or in business, don't be a slacker. Don't cheat your teammates. Pull your share of the "rope."

the larger the team, the smaller the individual effort. In fact, social loafing is more likely to occur in larger groups where it can be difficult to identify and monitor the efforts of individual team members.[22] In other words, social loafers count on being able to blend into the background, where their lack of effort isn't easily spotted. Because of team-based class projects, most students already know about social loafers or "slackers," who contribute poor, little, or no work whatsoever. Not surprisingly, research with 250 student teams showed that the most talented students are typically the least satisfied with teamwork because of having to carry "slackers" and having to do a disproportionate share of their team's work.[23]

How prevalent is social loafing on teams? One study found that when team activities were not mandatory, only 25 percent of manufacturing workers volunteered to join problem-solving teams, 70 percent were quiet, passive supporters (i.e., not putting forth effort), and 5 percent were actively opposed to these activities.[24] Another study found that on management teams, 56 percent of the managers, or more than half, withheld their effort in one way or another. Exhibit 11.2 lists the factors that encourage people to withhold effort in teams.

Finally, teams share many of the *disadvantages of group decision making* discussed in Chapter 4, such as groupthink. In *groupthink*, members of highly cohesive groups feel intense pressure not to disagree with each other so that the group can approve a proposed solution. Because groupthink restricts discussion and leads to consideration of a limited number of alternative solutions, it usually results in poor decisions. Also, team decision making takes considerable time, and team meetings can often be unproductive and inefficient. Another possible pitfall is that sometimes just one or two people dominate team discussions, restricting consideration of different problem definitions and alternative solutions. Last, team members may not feel accountable for the decisions and actions taken by the "team."

1.3 When to Use Teams

As the two previous subsections made clear, teams have significant advantages *and* disadvantages. Therefore, the question is not whether to use teams, but when and where to use teams for maximum benefit and minimum cost. As Doug Johnson, associate director at the Center for the Study of Work Teams, put it, "Teams are a means to an end, not an end in themselves. You have to ask yourself questions first. Does the work require interdependence? Will the team philosophy fit company strategy? Will management make a long-term commitment to this process?"[25] Exhibit 11.3 provides some additional guidelines on when to use or not use teams.[26]

First, teams should be used when there is a clear, engaging reason or purpose for using them. Too many companies use teams because they're popular or because the companies assume that teams can fix all problems. Teams are much more likely to succeed if they know why they exist and what they are

exhibit 11.2

Factors That Encourage People to Withhold Effort in Teams

1. *The presence of someone with expertise.* Team members will withhold effort when another team member is highly qualified to make a decision or comment on an issue.
2. *The presentation of a compelling argument.* Team members will withhold effort if the arguments for a course of action are very persuasive or similar to their own thinking.
3. *Lacking confidence in one's ability to contribute.* Team members will withhold effort if they are unsure about their ability to contribute to discussions, activities, or decisions. This is especially so for high-profile decisions.
4. *An unimportant or meaningless decision.* Team members will withhold effort by mentally withdrawing or adopting a "who cares" attitude if decisions don't affect them or their units, or if they don't see a connection between their efforts and their team's successes or failures.
5. *A dysfunctional decision-making climate.* Team members will withhold effort if other team members are frustrated or indifferent or if a team is floundering or disorganized.

Source: P. W. Mulvey, J. F. Veiga, & P. M. Elsass, "When Teammates Raise a White Flag," Academy of Management Executive *10, no. 1 (1996): 40–49.*

supposed to accomplish, and more likely to fail if they don't. For example, because headquarters did not stress the importance of cost savings, the platform teams that develop new cars at DaimlerChrysler didn't communicate with one another about the possibility of using identical parts on different cars to cut costs and increase efficiency. As a result, five different platform teams chose three different kinds of corrosion protection for a simple piece of steel used in all automobile bumpers. The resulting cost was $1 or $2 higher for each part. Multiply that by 3 million cars a year, and Chrysler's costs increased by $3 million to $6 million because it wasn't made clear to the teams that cost savings were one of their objectives.[27]

Second, teams should be used when the job can't be done unless people work together. This typically means that teams are required when tasks are complex, require multiple perspectives, or require repeated interaction with others to complete. If tasks are simple and don't require multiple perspectives or repeated interaction with others, however, teams should not be used. For instance, production levels dropped by 23 percent when Levi Strauss introduced teams in its factories. Levi's mistake was assuming that teams were appropriate for garment work, where workers perform single, specialized tasks, like sewing zippers or belt

exhibit 11.3

When to Use or Not Use Teams

USE TEAMS WHEN . . .	DON'T USE TEAMS WHEN . . .
there is a clear, engaging reason or purpose.	there isn't a clear, engaging reason or purpose.
the job can't be done unless people work together.	the job can be done by people working independently.
rewards can be provided for teamwork and team performance.	rewards are provided for individual effort and performance.
ample resources are available.	the necessary resources are not available.
teams will have clear authority to manage and change how work gets done.	management will continue to monitor and influence how work gets done.

Source: R. Wageman, "Critical Success Factors for Creating Superb Self-Managing Teams," Organizational Dynamics *26, no. 1 (1997): 49–61.*

loops. Because this kind of work does not require interaction with others, Levi's unwittingly pitted the faster workers against the slower workers on each team. Arguments, infighting, insults, and threats were common between faster workers and the slower workers who held back team performance. One seamstress even had to physically restrain an angry coworker who was about to throw a chair at a faster worker who constantly nagged her about her slow pace.[28]

Third, teams should be used when rewards can be provided for teamwork and team performance. Team rewards that depend on team performance rather than individual performance are the key to rewarding team behaviors and efforts. You'll read more about team rewards later in the chapter, but for now it's enough to know that if the level of rewards (individual versus team) is not matched to the level of performance (individual versus team), groups won't work. As discussed above, this was the case with Levi's, where a team structure was superimposed on individual jobs that didn't require interaction between workers. After the switch to teams, faster workers placed tremendous pressure on slower workers to increase their production speed. And since pay was determined by team performance, top individual performers saw their pay drop by several dollars an hour, while slower workers saw their pay increase by several dollars an hour—all while overall productivity dropped in the plant.[29]

Fourth, teams should be used when ample resources are available. The resources that teams need include training (discussed later in the chapter), sufficient time and a place or method to work together, job-specific tools, and consistent information and feedback concerning team work processes and job performance. At Levi's, team members complained that there were few resources, such as training, to support the transition from independent, individual-based work to team-based work. They also complained about not being given enough time to learn how to run the new machines to which they were assigned on the team system.

Sometimes, teams lack resources because of management resistance. Managers who have been in charge are often reluctant to help teams or turn over resources to them. At Levi's, when team members asked supervisors for assistance, a common reaction was "Y'all are empowered; y'all decide."[30]

Finally, teams should be used when they have clear authority to manage and change how the work gets done. This means that teams—not managers—decide what problem to tackle next, when to schedule time for maintenance or training, or how to solve customer problems. Research clearly shows that teams with the authority to manage their own work strongly outperform teams that don't.[31] Unfortunately, managers can undermine teams' authority by closely monitoring their work, asking teams to change their decisions, or directly ignoring or overruling team decisions. Jeffrey Pfeffer, a Stanford professor and management consultant/author, says, "The fact is, the people doing the work know better how to do it. Get the managers out of the way and you will do better."[32]

Review 1

The Good and Bad of Using Teams

In many industries, teams are growing in importance because they help organizations respond to specific problems and challenges. Teams have been shown to increase customer satisfaction (specific customer teams), product and service quality (direct responsibility), speed and efficiency in product development (overlapping development phases), and employee job satisfaction (cross training, unique opportunities, and leadership responsibilities). While teams can produce significant improvements in these areas, using teams does not guarantee these positive outcomes. Teams and teamwork have the disadvantages of initially high turnover and social loafing (especially in large groups). Teams also share many of the advantages (multiple perspectives, generation of more alternatives, and more commitment) and disadvantages (groupthink, time, poorly run meetings, domination by a few team members, and weak accountability) of group decision making. Finally, teams should be used for a clear purpose, when the work requires that people work together, when rewards can be provided for both teamwork and team performance, when ample resources can be provided, and when teams can be given clear authority over their work.

2 Kinds of Teams

Companies use different kinds of teams for different purposes. For example, Merck, a leading pharmaceutical firm, found that it was taking much too long to bring new drugs to market following final Food and Drug Administration approval. Merck now has teams of marketing, manufacturing, and research people who are responsible for speeding up this process. Wendy Dixon, a marketing vice president who managed the launch of Vioxx, a new painkiller, said, "We carved four to five weeks off the normal product launch process."[33] Likewise, at Maytag's Cleveland, Tennessee manufacturing plant, which makes gas and electric stoves, the use of teams has helped cut production costs by $7 million and reduce inventory by $10 million.[34]

www.experiencing management.com

You may learn more about types of teams and their relationship to the organization by interacting with team concepts at our animated concept and activity site. Choose Teams from the "select a topic" pull-down menu, then Types of Teams from the "overview tab."

http://www.experiencingmanagement.com

Let's continue our discussion of teams by learning about the different kinds of teams that companies like Merck and Maytag use to make themselves more competitive. We look first at 2.1 how teams differ in terms of autonomy, which is the key dimension that makes one team different from another, and then at 2.2 some special kinds of teams.

2.1 Autonomy, the Key Dimension

Teams can be classified in a number of ways, such as permanent or temporary, or functional or cross-functional. However, studies indicate that the amount of autonomy possessed by a team is the key dimension that makes teams different from each another.[35] *Autonomy* is the degree to which workers have the discretion, freedom, and independence to decide how and when to accomplish their jobs.

Exhibit 11.4 displays an autonomy continuum that shows how five kinds of teams differ in terms of autonomy. Moving left to right across the top of the exhibit, traditional work groups and employee involvement groups have the least autonomy, semi-autonomous work groups have more autonomy, and, finally, self-managing teams and self-designing teams have the most autonomy. Moving from bottom to top along the left side of the exhibit, note that the number of responsibilities given to each kind of team increases directly with its autonomy. Let's review each of these teams and their autonomy and responsibilities in more detail.

exhibit 11.4

Team Autonomy Continuum

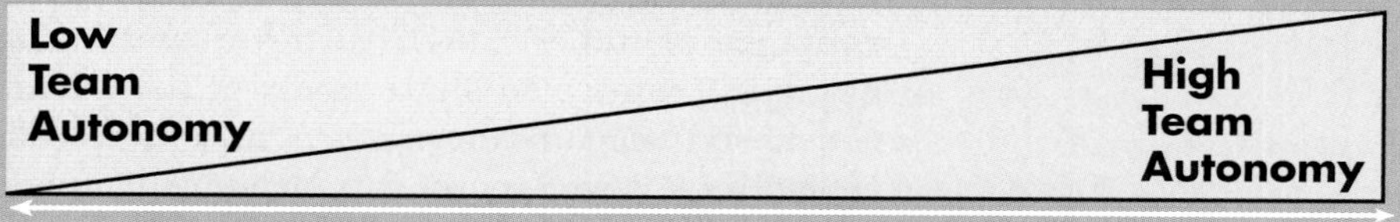

RESPONSIBILITIES	TRADITIONAL WORK GROUPS	EMPLOYEE INVOLVEMENT GROUPS	SEMI-AUTONOMOUS WORK GROUPS	SELF-MANAGING TEAMS	SELF-DESIGNING TEAMS
CONTROL DESIGN					
Team					✔
Tasks					✔
Membership					✔
ALL PRODUCTION/SERVICE TASKS					
Make Decisions				✔	✔
Solve Problems				✔	✔
MAJOR PRODUCTION/SERVICE TASKS					
Make Decisions			✔	✔	✔
Solve Problems			✔	✔	✔
Information			✔	✔	✔
Give Advice/Make Suggestions		✔	✔	✔	✔
Execute Task	✔	✔	✔	✔	✔

Sources: R. D. Banker, J. M. Field, R. G. Schroeder, & K. K. Sinha, "Impact of Work Teams on Manufacturing Performance: A Longitudinal Field Study," Academy of Management Journal *39 (1996): 867–890; J. R. Hackman, "The Psychology of Self-Management in Organizations," in* Psychology and Work: Productivity, Change, and Employment, *ed. M. S. Pallak & R. Perlof (Washington, D.C.: American Psychological Association), 85–136.*

traditional work group
a group composed of two or more people who work together to achieve a shared goal

employee involvement team
a team that provides advice or makes suggestions to management concerning specific issues

The smallest amount of autonomy is found in **traditional work groups**, where two or more people work together to achieve a shared goal. In these groups, workers do not have direct responsibility or control over their work, but are responsible for doing the work or "executing the task." Workers report to managers, who are responsible for their performance and have the authority to hire and fire them, make job assignments, and control resources.

Employee involvement teams, which have somewhat more autonomy, meet on company time on a weekly or monthly basis to provide advice or make suggestions to management concerning specific issues, such as plant safety, customer relations, or product quality.[36] Though they offer advice and suggestions, they do not have the authority to make decisions. Membership on these teams is often voluntary, but members may be selected because of their expertise. The idea behind employee involvement teams is that the people closest to the problem or situation are best able to recommend solutions.

semi-autonomous work group a group that has the authority to make decisions and solve problems related to the major tasks of producing a product or service

Semi-autonomous work groups not only provide advice and suggestions to management, but also have the authority to make decisions and solve problems related to the major tasks required to produce a product or service. Semi-autonomous groups regularly receive information about budgets, work quality and performance, and competitors' products. Furthermore, members of semi-autonomous work groups are typically cross-trained in a number of different skills and tasks. In short, semi-autonomous work groups give employees the autonomy to make decisions that are typically made by supervisors and managers. That authority is not complete, however. Managers still play a role, though much reduced compared to traditional work groups, in supporting the work of semi-autonomous work groups.

self-managing team a team that manages and controls all of the major tasks of producing a product or service

Self-managing teams are different from semi-autonomous work groups in that team members manage and control *all* of the major tasks *directly related* to production of a product or service without first getting approval from management. This includes managing and controlling the acquisition of materials, making a product or providing a service, and ensuring timely delivery. At the Crown Cork aluminum can factory in Sugarland, Texas, "The teams make and implement decisions regarding production, product quality, training, attendance, safety, maintenance, and certain types of discipline. The teams can stop production lines without management approval, stop delivery of cans that do not meet quality standards, decide which workers should receive training, decide whether to grant leave requests, and investigate and correct safety problems."[37]

self-designing team a team that has the characteristics of self-managing teams but also controls team design, work tasks, and team membership

Self-designing teams have all the characteristics of self-managing teams, but they can also control and change the design of the teams themselves, the tasks they do and how and when they do them, and who belongs on the teams. At the GE Aerospace Engines manufacturing plant in Durham, North Carolina, which makes jet engines, all workers have email addresses, access to the Internet, their own voicemail boxes, business cards, and their own desks, all of which are extremely uncommon for factory workers. Team member Duane Williams said, "We had to come up with a schedule. We had the chance to order tools, tool carts, and so on. We had to figure out the *flow of the assembly line* [emphasis added] that makes the engine. We were put on councils for every part of the business." Williams went on to say, "I was never valued that much as an employee in my life. I had never been at the point where I couldn't wait to get to work. Here, I couldn't wait to get to work every day."[38]

2.2 Special Kinds of Teams

Companies are also increasingly using several other kinds of teams that can't easily be categorized in terms of autonomy: cross-functional teams, virtual teams, and project teams. Depending on how these teams are designed, they can be either low- or high-autonomy teams.

cross-functional team a team composed of employees from different functional areas of the organization

Cross-functional teams are intentionally composed of employees from different functional areas of the organization.[39] Because their members have different functional backgrounds, education, and experience, cross-functional teams usually attack problems from multiple perspectives and generate more ideas and alternative solutions, all of which are especially important when trying to innovate or do creative problem solving.[40] Cross-functional teams can

© WAYNE R. BELENDUKE/GETTY IMAGES/STONE

Telecommunications and information technology allow geographically dispersed virtual teams to work together to accomplish organizational tasks.

be used almost anywhere in an organization and are often used in conjunction with matrix and product organizational structures (see Chapter 10). They can also be used either with part-time or temporary team assignments or with full-time, long-term teams.

Virtual teams are groups of geographically and/or organizationally dispersed coworkers who use a combination of telecommunications and information technologies to accomplish an organizational task.[41] In other words, members of virtual teams rarely meet face-to-face. The idea of virtual teams is relatively new and has been made possible by advances in communications and technology, such as email, the World Wide Web, and videoconferencing. Virtual teams can be nearly any kind of team discussed in this chapter. Virtual teams are often (but not necessarily) temporary teams that are set up to accomplish a specific task.[42] Because the team members don't meet in a physical location, one of the unique qualities of virtual teams is that it is much easier to include other key stakeholders, such as suppliers and customers. The development of the Boeing 777 was largely a virtual team effort. Boeing developed the 777 through the combined efforts of 238 design teams in locations around the world including Japan and several U.S. cities. The teams, which included representatives from airlines that had purchased the 777 and suppliers who provided key expertise and parts, worked on the 777 in each location and communicated via a network of 1,700 individual computer systems.[43]

virtual team
a team composed of geographically and/or organizationally dispersed coworkers who use telecommunication and information technologies to accomplish an organizational task

The principal advantage of virtual teams is that they are very flexible. Employees can work with each other, regardless of physical location, time zone, or organizational affiliation.[44] Plus, virtual teams have certain efficiency advantages over traditional team structures. Because the teammates do not meet face-to-face, typically a virtual team requires a smaller time commitment than a traditional team does. Moreover, employees can fulfill the responsibilities of their virtual team membership from the comfort of their own offices, without the travel time or downtime typically required for face-to-face meetings.[45]

A drawback of virtual teams is that the team members must learn to express themselves in new contexts.[46] For example, the give-and-take that naturally occurs in face-to-face meetings is more difficult to achieve through videoconferencing or other methods of virtual teaming. In addition, several studies have shown that physical proximity enhances information processing.[48] Therefore, some companies bring virtual team members together on a regular basis. Exhibit 11.5 provides a number of tips for successfully managing virtual teams.

PERSONAL PRODUCTIVITY T!P

A Picture Is Worth a Thousand Words

As companies make greater use of teams, it has become increasingly common for teammates to work in separate locations. For example, insurance companies have teams with agents in the field and claims processors in the central offices. In virtual teams like these, sometimes teammates never meet. One way for geographically separated teammates to increase team cohesion is to exchange photos and display the photos in their work areas. So, if you have teammates you've never met, swap photos. It will help you feel more like part of a team.[47]

exhibit 11.5

Tips for Managing Successful Virtual Teams

- Select people who are self-starters and strong communicators.
- Keep the team focused by establishing clear, specific goals and by explaining the consequences and importance of meeting these goals.
- Provide frequent feedback so that team members can measure their progress.
- Keep team interactions upbeat and action-oriented by expressing appreciation for good work and completed tasks.
- "Personalize" the virtual team by periodically bringing team members together and by encouraging team members to share information with each other about their personal lives.
- Improve communication through increased telephone calls, emails, and Internet messaging and videoconference sessions.
- Periodically ask team members how well the team is working and what can be done to improve performance.

Sources: C. Solomon, "Managing Virtual Teams," Workforce *80 (June 2001), 60; W. F. Cascio, "Managing a Virtual Workplace,"* Academy of Management Executive *14 (2000): 81–90.*

Project teams are created to complete specific, one-time projects or tasks within a limited time.[49] Project teams are often used to develop new products, significantly improve existing products, roll out new information systems, or build new factories or offices. The project team is typically led by a project manager, who has the overall responsibility for planning, staffing, and managing the team, which usually includes employees from different functional areas. One advantage of project teams is that drawing employees from different functional areas can reduce or eliminate communication barriers. In turn, as long as team members feel free to express their ideas, thoughts, and concerns, free-flowing communication encourages cooperation among separate departments and typically speeds up the design process.[50] For example, GE Global eXchange Services used a cross-functional team to design its Web site so that it would have the same simple, intuitive-looking feel in English, French, Spanish, German, and Italian. The success of this Web site across all of these languages and cultures can be attributed to the fact that the development team came from all areas of the business and from all across the globe.[51]

project team
a team created to complete specific, one-time projects or tasks within a limited time

Another advantage of project teams is their flexibility. When projects are finished, project team members either move on to the next project or return to their functional units. For example, publication of this book required designers, editors, page makeup artists, and Web designers, among others. When the task was finished, these people applied their skills to other textbook projects. Because of this flexibility, project teams are often used with the matrix organizational designs discussed in Chapter 10.

Review 2

Kinds of Teams

Companies use different kinds of teams to make themselves more competitive. Autonomy is the key dimension that makes teams different. Traditional work groups (which execute tasks) and employee involvement groups (which make suggestions) have the lowest levels of autonomy. Semi-autonomous work groups (which control major, direct tasks) have more autonomy, while self-managing teams (which control all direct tasks) and self-designing teams (which control membership and how tasks are done) have the highest levels of autonomy. Cross-functional, virtual, and project teams are common, but are not easily categorized in terms of autonomy. Cross-functional teams combine employees from different functional areas to help teams attack problems from multiple perspectives and generate more ideas and solutions. Virtual teams use telecommunications and information technologies to bring coworkers "together," regardless of physical location or time zone. Virtual teams reduce travel and work time, but communication may suffer since team members don't work face-to-face. Finally, project teams are used for specific, one-time projects or tasks that must be completed within a limited time. Project teams reduce communication barriers and promote flexibility; teams and team members are reassigned to their department or new projects as old projects are completed.

Managing Work Teams

"Why did I ever let you talk me into teams? They're nothing but trouble."[52] Lots of managers have this reaction after making the move to teams. Many don't realize that this reaction is normal, both for them and for workers. In fact, such a reaction is characteristic of the *storming* stage of team development (discussed in Section 3.5). Managers who are familiar with these stages and with the other important characteristics of teams will be better prepared to manage the predictable changes that occur when companies make the switch to team-based structures.

After reading the next two sections, you should be able to

3 understand the general characteristics of work teams.

4 explain how to enhance work team effectiveness.

3 Work Team Characteristics

Understanding the characteristics of work teams is essential for making teams an effective part of an organization. Therefore, in this section you'll learn about 3.1 team norms, 3.2 team cohesiveness, 3.3 team size, 3.4 team conflict, and 3.5 the stages of team development.

3.1 Team Norms

norms
informally agreed-on standards that regulate team behavior

Over time, teams develop **norms**, informally agreed-on standards that regulate team behavior.[53] Norms are valuable because they let team members know what is expected of them. At Nucor Steel, work groups expect their members to get to work on time. To reinforce this norm, anyone who is late to work cannot receive the team bonus for that day (assuming the team is productive). If the worker is more than 30 minutes late, he or she cannot receive the team bonus for the entire week. At Nucor losing a bonus matters because work group bonuses can easily double the size of a worker's take-home pay.[54]

Studies indicate that norms are one of the most powerful influences on work behavior. Team norms are often associated with positive outcomes, such as stronger organizational commitment, more trust in management, and stronger job and organizational satisfaction.[55] In general, effective work teams develop norms about the quality and timeliness of job performance, absenteeism, safety, and honest expression of ideas and opinions. The power of norms also comes from the fact that they regulate the everyday behaviors that allow teams to function effectively.

Norms can also influence team behavior in negative ways. For example, most people would agree that damaging organizational property; saying or doing something to hurt someone at work; intentionally doing one's work badly, incorrectly, or slowly; griping about coworkers; deliberately bending or breaking rules; or doing something to harm the company or boss are negative be-

WHAT REALLY WORKS

COHESION AND TEAM PERFORMANCE

Have you ever worked in a really cohesive group where everyone really liked and enjoyed each other and was glad to be part of the group? It's great. By contrast, have you ever worked in a group where everyone really disliked each other and was unhappy to be a part of the group? It's terrible. Anyone who has had either of these experiences can appreciate how important group cohesion is and the effect it can have on team performance. Indeed, 46 studies based on 1,279 groups confirm that cohesion does matter.

Team Performance

On average, there is a 66 percent chance that cohesive teams will outperform less cohesive teams.

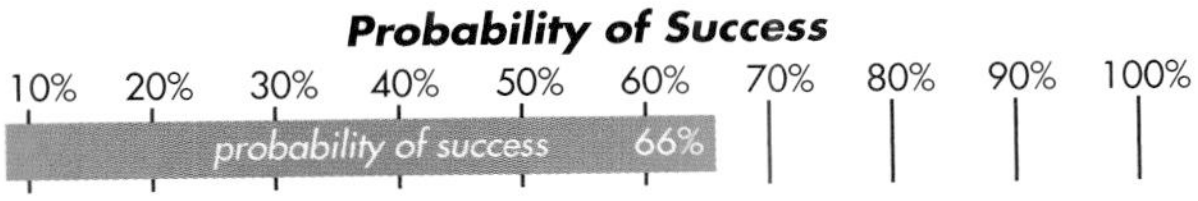

Team Performance with Interdependent Tasks

Teams work best for interdependent tasks that require people to work together to get the job done. When teams perform interdependent tasks, there is a 73 percent chance that cohesive teams will outperform less cohesive teams.

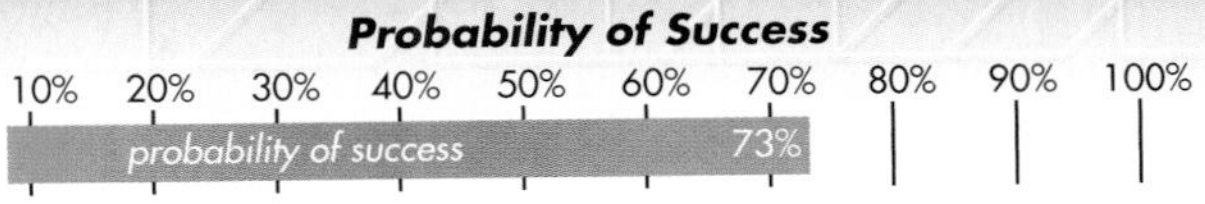

Team Performance with Independent Tasks

Teams generally are not suited for independent tasks that people can accomplish by themselves. When teams perform independent tasks, there is a only a 60 percent chance that cohesive teams will outperform less cohesive teams.

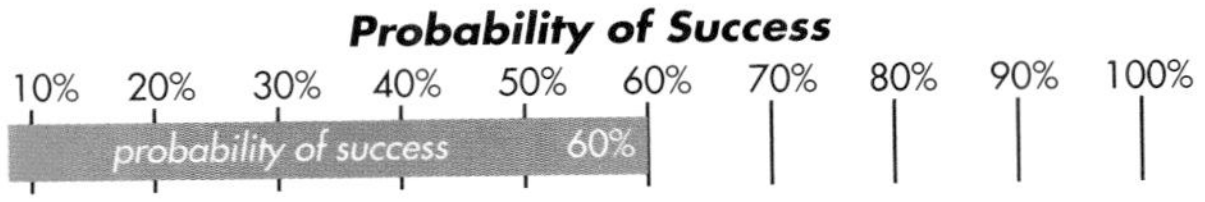

Some caution is warranted in interpreting these results. For example, there is always the possibility that a team could become so cohesive that its team goals become more important than organizational goals. Also, teams sometimes unite around negative goals and norms that are harmful rather than helpful to organizations. Nonetheless, there is also room for even more optimism about cohesive teams. Teams that are cohesive *and* committed to the goals they are asked to achieve should have an even higher probability of success than the numbers shown here.[56]

haviors. Nonetheless, a study of workers from 34 teams in 20 different organizations found that teams with negative norms strongly influenced their team members to engage in these negative behaviors. In fact, the longer individuals were members of a team with negative norms and the more frequently they interacted with their teammates, the more likely they were to perform negative behaviors. Since team norms typically develop early in the life of a team, these results indicate how important it is for teams to establish positive norms from the outset.[57]

3.2 Team Cohesiveness

cohesiveness
the extent to which team members are attracted to a team and motivated to remain in it

Cohesiveness is another important characteristic of work teams. **Cohesiveness** is the extent to which team members are attracted to a team and motivated to remain in it.[58]

The level of cohesiveness in a group is important for several reasons. To start, cohesive groups have a better chance of retaining their members. As a result, cohesive groups typically experience lower turnover.[59] In addition, team cohesiveness promotes cooperative behavior, generosity, and a willingness on the part of team members to assist each other.[60] When team cohesiveness is high, team members are more motivated to contribute to the team, because they want to gain the approval of other team members. As a result of these reasons and others, studies have clearly established that cohesive teams consistently perform better.[61] Furthermore, cohesive teams quickly achieve high levels of performance. By contrast, teams low in cohesion take much longer to reach the same levels of performance.[62]

What can be done to promote team cohesiveness? First, make sure that all team members are present at team meetings and activities. Team cohesiveness suffers when members are allowed to withdraw from the team and miss team meetings and events.[63] Second, create additional opportunities for teammates to work together by rearranging work schedules and creating common workspaces. When task interdependence is high and team members have lots of chances to work together, team cohesiveness tends to increase.[64] Third, engaging in nonwork activities as a team can help build cohesion. At Cambridge Technology Partners, where teams put in extraordinarily long hours coding computer software, the software teams maintained cohesion by doing "fun stuff" together. Team leader Tammy Urban said, "We went on team outings at least once a week. We'd play darts, shoot pool. Teams work best when you get to know each other outside of work—what people's interests are, who they are. Personal connections go a long way when you're developing complex applications in our kind of time frames."[65]

3.3 Team Size

There appears to be a curvilinear relationship between team size and performance. In other words, very small or very large teams may not perform as well as moderately sized teams. For most teams, the right size is somewhere between six and nine members.[66] This size is conducive to high team cohesion, which has a positive effect on team performance, as discussed above. A team of this size is small enough for the team members to get to know each other and for each member to have an opportunity to contribute in a meaningful way to the success of the team. At the same time, the team is also large enough to take advantage of team members' diverse skills, knowledge, and perspectives. It is also easier to instill a sense of responsibility and mutual accountability in teams of this size.[67]

By contrast, when teams get too large, team members find it difficult to get to know one another, and the team may splinter into smaller subgroups. When this occurs, subgroups sometimes argue and disagree, weakening overall team cohesion. As teams grow, there is also a greater chance of *minority domination,* where just a few team members dominate team discussions. Even if minority domination doesn't occur, larger groups may not have time for all team members to share their input. And when team members feel that their contributions are unimportant or not needed, the result is less involvement, effort, and accountability to the team.[68] Large teams also face logistical problems, such as finding an appropriate time or place to meet. Finally, the incidence of social loafing, discussed earlier in the chapter, is much higher in large teams.

Just as team performance can suffer when a team is too large, it can also be negatively affected when a team is too small. Teams with just a few people may lack the diversity of skills and knowledge found in larger teams. Also, teams that are too small are unlikely to gain the advantages of team decision making (i.e., multiple perspectives, generating more ideas and alternative solutions, and stronger commitment) found in larger teams.

What signs indicate that a team's size needs to be changed? If decisions are taking too long, if the team has difficulty making decisions or taking action, if a few members dominate the team, or if the commitment or efforts of team members are weak, chances are the team is too big. In contrast, if a team is having difficulty coming up with ideas or generating solutions, or if the team does not have the expertise to address a specific problem, chances are the team is too small.

3.4 Team Conflict

Conflict and disagreement are inevitable in most teams. But this shouldn't surprise anyone. From time to time, people who work together are going to disagree about what and how things get done. What causes conflict in teams? Although almost anything can lead to conflict—casual remarks that unintentionally offend a team member or fighting over scarce resources—the primary cause of team conflict is disagreement over team goals and priorities.[69] Other common causes of team conflict include disagreements over task-related issues, interpersonal incompatibilities, and simple fatigue.

Though most people view conflict negatively, the key to dealing with team conflict is not avoiding it, but making sure that the team experiences the right kind of conflict. In Chapter 4, you learned about *c-type conflict*, or *cognitive conflict*, which focuses on problem-related differences of opinion; and *a-type conflict*, or *affective conflict*, which refers to the emotional reactions that can occur when disagreements become personal rather than professional.[70] Cognitive conflict is strongly associated with improvements in team performance, whereas affective conflict is strongly associated with decreases in team performance.[71] Why does this happen? With cognitive conflict, team members disagree because their different experiences and expertise lead them to different views of the problem and solutions. Indeed, managers who participated on teams that emphasized cognitive conflict described their teammates as "smart," "team players," and "best in the business." They described their teams as "open," "fun," and "productive." One manager summed up the positive attitude that team members had about cognitive conflict by saying, "We scream a lot, then laugh, and then resolve the issue."[72] Thus, cognitive conflict is also characterized by a willingness to examine, compare, and reconcile differences to produce the best possible solution.

By contrast, affective conflict often results in hostility, anger, resentment, distrust, cynicism, and apathy. Managers who participated on teams that emphasized affective conflict described their teammates as "manipulative," "secretive," "burned out," and "political."[73] Not surprisingly, affective conflict can make people uncomfortable and cause them to withdraw and decrease their commitment to a team.[74] Affective conflict also lowers the satisfaction of team members, may lead to personal hostility between coworkers, and can decrease team cohesiveness.[75] So, unlike cognitive conflict, affective conflict undermines team performance by preventing teams from engaging in the kinds of activities that are critical to team effectiveness.

So, what can managers do to manage team conflict? First, managers need to realize that emphasizing cognitive conflict alone won't be enough. Studies show that cognitive and affective conflicts often occur together in the same

exhibit 11.6

How Teams Can Have a Good Fight

1. Work with more, rather than less, information.
2. Develop multiple alternatives to enrich debate.
3. Establish common goals.
4. Inject humor into the workplace.
5. Maintain a balance of power.
6. Resolve issues without forcing a consensus.

Source: K. M. Eisenhardt, J. L. Kahwajy, & L. J. Bourgeois III, "How Management Teams Can Have a Good Fight," Harvard Business Review *75, no. 4 (July-August 1997): 77–87.*

teams! Therefore, sincere attempts to reach agreement on a difficult issue can quickly deteriorate from cognitive to affective conflict if the discussion turns personal and tempers and emotions flare. So, while cognitive conflict is clearly the better approach to take, efforts to engage in cognitive conflict should be approached with caution.

Can teams disagree and still get along? Fortunately, they can. In an attempt to study this issue, researchers examined team conflict in 12 high-tech companies. In four of the companies, work teams used cognitive conflict to address work problems but did so in a way that minimized the occurrence of affective conflict. Exhibit 11.6 shows the steps these teams took to be able to have a "good fight."[76]

3.5 Stages of Team Development

As teams develop and grow, they pass through four stages of development. As shown in Exhibit 11.7, those stages are forming, storming, norming, and performing.[77] Although not every team passes through each of these stages, teams that do tend to be better performers.[78] This holds true even for teams composed of seasoned executives. After a period of time, however, if a team is not managed well, its performance may start to deteriorate as the team begins a process of decline and progresses through the stages of de-norming, de-storming, and de-forming.[79]

forming
the first stage of team development in which team members meet each other, form initial impressions, and begin to establish team norms

storming
the second stage of team development, characterized by conflict and disagreement, in which team members disagree over what the team should do and how it should do it

Forming is the initial stage of team development. This is the getting-acquainted stage, when team members first meet each other, form initial impressions, and try to get a sense of what it will be like to be part of the team. Some of the first team norms will be established during this stage, as team members begin to find out what behaviors will and won't be accepted by the team. During this stage, team leaders should allow time for team members to get to know each other, set early ground rules, and begin to set up a preliminary team structure.

Conflicts and disagreements often characterize the second stage of team development, **storming**. As team members begin working together, different personalities and work styles may clash. Team members become more assertive at this stage and more willing to state opinions. This is also the stage when team members jockey for position and try to establish a favorable role for themselves on the team. In addition, team members are likely to disagree about what the group should do and how it should do it. Team performance is still relatively low, given that team cohesion is weak and team members are still reluctant to support each other. Since teams that get stuck in the storming stage are almost always ineffective, it is important for team leaders to focus the team on team goals and on improving team performance. Team members need to be particularly patient and tolerant with each other in this stage.

During **norming**, the third stage of team development, team members begin to settle into their roles as team members. Positive team norms will have developed by this stage, and teammates should know what to expect from each other.

www.experiencing management.com

Reinforce your understanding of the stages of team development by interacting with this concept at our animated concept and activity site. Choose Teams from the "select a topic" pull-down menu, then Stages of Development from the "overview tab."

http://www.experiencingmanagement.com

exhibit 11.7

Stages of Team Development

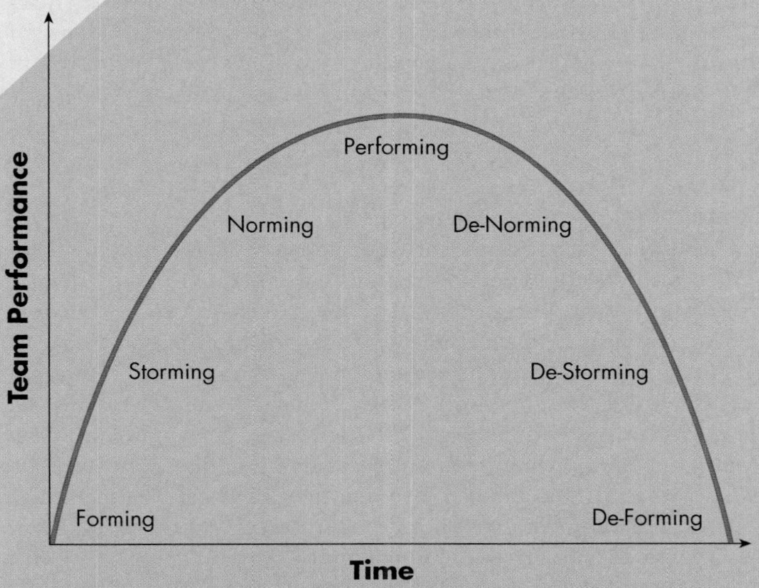

Sources: J. F. McGrew, J. G. Bilotta, & J. M. Deeney, "Software Team Formation and Decay: Extending the Standard Model for Small Groups," Small Group Research *30, no. 2 (1999): 209–234; B. W. Tuckman, "Development Sequence in Small Groups,"* Psychological Bulletin *63, no. 6 (1965): 384–399.*

Petty differences should have been resolved, friendships will have developed, and group cohesion will be relatively strong. At this point, team members will have accepted team goals, be operating as a unit, and, as indicated by the increase in performance, be working together effectively. This stage can be very short and is often characterized by someone in the team saying, "I think things are finally coming together." Note, however, that teams may also cycle back and forth between storming and norming several times before finally settling into norming.

In the last stage of team development, **performing**, performance improves because the team has finally matured into an effective, fully functioning team. At this point, members should be fully committed to the team and think of themselves as "members of a team" and not just "employees." Team members often become intensely loyal to one another at this stage and feel mutual accountability for team successes and failures. Trivial disagreements, which can take time and energy away from the work of the team, should be rare. At this stage, teams get a lot of work done, and it is fun to be a team member.

The team should not become complacent, however, because without effective management, its performance may begin to decline as the team passes through the stages of de-norming, de-storming, and de-forming.[80] Indeed, John Puckett, manufacturing vice president for circuit board maker XEL Communications, says, "The books all say you start in this state of chaos and march through these various stages, and you end up in this state of ultimate self-direction, where everything is going just great. They never tell you it can go back in the other direction, sometimes just as quickly."[81]

In **de-norming**, which is a reversal of the norming stage, team performance begins to decline as the size, scope, goal, or members of the team change. With new members joining the group, older members may become defensive as established ways of doing things are questioned and challenged. Expression of ideas and opinions becomes less open. New members change team norms by actively rejecting or passively neglecting previously established team roles and behaviors.

In **de-storming**, which is a reversal of the storming phase, the team's comfort level decreases. Team cohesion weakens as more group members resist conforming to team norms and quit participating in team activities. Angry emotions flare as the group explodes in conflict and moves into the final stage of de-forming.

In **de-forming**, which is a reversal of the forming stage, team members position themselves to gain control of pieces of the team. Team members begin to

norming
the third stage of team development, in which team members begin to settle into their roles, group cohesion grows, and positive team norms develop

performing
the fourth and final stage of team development, in which performance improves because the team has matured into an effective, fully functioning team

de-norming
a reversal of the norming stage, in which team performance begins to decline as the size, scope, goal, or members of the team change

de-storming
a reversal of the storming phase, in which the team's comfort level decreases, team cohesion weakens, and angry emotions and conflict may flare

de-forming a reversal of the forming stage, in which team members position themselves to control pieces of the team, avoid each other, and isolate themselves from team leaders

avoid each other and isolate themselves from team leaders. Team performance rapidly declines as the team quits caring about even minimal requirements of team performance.

If teams are actively managed, decline is not inevitable. However, managers need to recognize that the forces at work in the de-norming, de-storming, and de-forming stages represent a powerful, disruptive, and real threat to teams that have finally made it to the performing stage. Getting to the performing stage is half the battle. Staying there is the second half.

Review 3
Work Team Characteristics

The most important characteristics of work teams are team norms, cohesiveness, size, conflict, and development. Norms let team members know what is expected of them and can influence team behavior in positive and negative ways. Positive team norms are associated with organizational commitment, trust, and job satisfaction. Team cohesiveness helps teams retain members, promotes cooperative behavior, increases motivation, and facilitates team performance. Attending team meetings and activities, creating opportunities to work together, and engaging in nonwork activities can increase cohesiveness. Team size has a curvilinear relationship with team performance: very small or very large teams do not perform as well as moderately sized teams of six to nine members. Teams of this size are cohesive and small enough for team members to get to know each other and contribute in a meaningful way, but are large enough to take advantage of team members' diverse skills, knowledge, and perspectives. Conflict and disagreement are inevitable in most teams. The key to dealing with team conflict is to maximize cognitive conflict, which focuses on issue-related differences, and minimize affective conflict, the emotional reactions that occur when disagreements become personal rather than professional. As teams develop and grow, they pass through four stages of development: forming, storming, norming, and performing. After a period of time, however, if a team is not managed well, its performance may decline as the team regresses through the stages of de-norming, de-storming, and de-forming.

4 Enhancing Work Team Effectiveness

Making teams work is a challenging and difficult process. Nonetheless, companies can increase the likelihood that teams will succeed by carefully managing 4.1 the setting of team goals and priorities, 4.2 how work team members are selected, 4.3 trained, and 4.4 compensated.[82]

4.1 Setting Team Goals and Priorities

In Chapter 4, you learned that specific, measurable, attainable, realistic, and timely (i.e., S.M.A.R.T.) goals are one of the most effective means for improving individual job performance. Fortunately, team goals also improve team performance. In fact, team goals lead to much higher team performance 93 percent of the time.[83] For example, Nucor Steel sets specific, challenging *hourly* goals for each of its production teams, which consist of first-line supervisors and production and maintenance workers. The average in the steel industry is 10 tons of steel per hour. Nucor production teams have an hourly goal of 8 tons per hour, but get a 5 percent bonus for *every* ton over 8 tons they produce.

With no limit on the bonuses they can receive, Nucor's production teams produce an average of 35 to 40 tons of steel per hour![84]

Why is setting specific, challenging team goals so critical to team success? One reason is that increasing a team's performance is inherently more complex than just increasing one individual's job performance. For instance, consider that for any team there are likely to be at least four different kinds of goals: each member's goal for the team, each member's goal for himself or herself on the team, the team's goal for each member, and the team's goal for itself.[85] In other words, without a specific, challenging goal for the team itself (the last of the four goals listed), these other goals may encourage team members to head off in 12 different directions at once. Consequently, setting a specific, challenging goal *for the team* clarifies team priorities by providing a clear focus and purpose.

Specific, challenging team goals also regulate how hard team members work. In particular, challenging team goals greatly reduce the incidence of social loafing. When faced with difficult goals, team members necessarily expect everyone to contribute. Consequently, they are much more likely to notice and complain if a teammate isn't doing his or her share. In fact, when teammates know each other well, when team goals are specific, when team communication is good, and when teams are rewarded for team performance (discussed below), there is only a one in 16 chance that teammates will be social loafers.[86]

What can companies and teams do to ensure that team goals lead to superior team performance? One increasingly popular approach is to give teams stretch goals. *Stretch goals* are extremely ambitious goals that workers don't know how to reach.[87] The purpose of stretch goals is to achieve extraordinary improvements in performance by forcing managers and workers to throw away old, comfortable solutions and adopt radical, never-used-before solutions.

Four things must occur for stretch goals to effectively motivate teams.[88] First, teams must have a high degree of autonomy or control over how they achieve their goals. Second, teams must be empowered with control resources, such as budgets, workspaces, computers, or whatever they need to do their jobs. Steve Kerr, Goldman Sachs' chief learning officer, says, "We have a moral obligation to try to give people the tools to meet tough goals. I think it's totally wrong if you don't give employees the tools to succeed, then punish them when they fail."[89] Third, teams need structural accommodation. **Structural accommodation** means giving teams the ability to change organizational structures, policies, and practices if doing so helps them meet their stretch goals. And finally, teams need bureaucratic immunity. **Bureaucratic immunity** means that teams no longer have to go through the frustratingly slow process of multilevel reviews and sign-offs to get management approval before making changes. Once granted bureaucratic immunity, teams are immune from the influence of various organizational groups and are accountable only to top management. Therefore, teams can act quickly and even experiment with little fear of failure. Climate Engineering Corporation gave its self-directed work teams bureaucratic immunity so they could have more control over their work and provide better service to customers. Although others in the company strongly resisted, President Eric Bindner told each repair service team (which services heating and air-conditioning systems) that they were free to schedule regular maintenance, day-to-day jobs and repairs, and emergency nighttime and weekend repairs, as well as their own vacation time. They were also given complete control over recruiting new team members and structuring and running each team.[90]

structural accommodation
the ability to change organizational structures, policies, and practices in order to meet stretch goals

bureaucratic immunity
the ability to make changes without first getting approval from managers or other parts of an organization

4.2 Selecting People for Teamwork

University of Southern California professor Edward Lawler says, "People are very naive about how easy it is to create a team. Teams are the Ferraris of work design. They're high performance but high maintenance and expensive."[91] It's almost impossible to have an effective work team without carefully selecting people who are suited for teamwork or for working on a particular team. A focus on teamwork (individualism-collectivism), team level, and team diversity can help companies choose the right team members.[92]

Are you more comfortable working alone or with others? If you strongly prefer to work alone, you may not be well suited for teamwork. Indeed, studies show that job satisfaction is higher in teams when team members prefer working with others.[93] An indirect way to measure someone's *preference for teamwork* is to assess the person's degree of individualism or collectivism. **Individualism-collectivism** is the degree to which a person believes that people should be self-sufficient and that loyalty to one's self is more important than loyalty to one's team or company.[94] *Individualists*, who put their welfare and interests first, generally prefer independent tasks in which they work alone. In contrast, *collectivists*, who put group or team interests ahead of self-interests, generally prefer interdependent tasks in which they work with others. Collectivists would also rather cooperate than compete and are fearful of disappointing team members or of being ostracized from teams. Given these differences, it makes sense to select team members who are collectivists rather than individualists. Indeed, many companies use individualism-collectivism as an initial screening device for team members. If team diversity is desired, however, individualists may be appropriate, as discussed below. To determine your preference for teamwork, take the Team Player Inventory shown in Exhibit 11.8.

individualism-collectivism
the degree to which a person believes that people should be self-sufficient and that loyalty to one's self is more important than loyalty to team or company

Team level is the average level of ability, experience, personality, or any other factor on a team. For example, a high level of team experience means that a team has particularly experienced team members. This does not mean that every member of the team has considerable experience, but that enough team members do to significantly raise the average level of experience on the team. Team level is used to guide selection of teammates when teams need a particular set of skills or capabilities to do their jobs well. For example, at GE's Aerospace Engines manufacturing plant in Durham, North Carolina, everyone hired had to have an FAA-certified mechanic's license. Following that, all applicants were tested in 11 different areas, only one of which involved those technical skills. Keith McKee, who works at the plant, said, "You have to be above the bar in all 11 of the areas: helping skills, team skills, communication skills, diversity, flexibility, coaching ability, work ethic, and so forth. Even if just one thing out of the 11 knocks you down, you don't come to work here."[95]

team level
the average level of ability, experience, personality, or any other factor on a team

Whereas team level represents the average level or capability on a team, **team diversity** represents the variances or differences in ability, experience, personality, or any other factor on a team.[96] For example, teams with strong team diversity on job experience have a mix of team members, ranging from seasoned veterans to people with three or four years of experience to rookies with little or no experience. Team diversity is used to guide selection of teammates when teams are asked to complete a wide range of different tasks or when tasks are particularly complex.

team diversity
the variances or differences in ability, experience, personality, or any other factor on a team

And not only is it important to put the right team together in terms of individualism-collectivism, team level, and team diversity, it's also important

exhibit 11.8

The Team Player Inventory

	STRONGLY DISAGREE				STRONGLY AGREE
1. I enjoy working on team/group projects.	1	2	3	4	5
2. Team /group project work easily allows others to not "pull their weight."	1	2	3	4	5
3. Work that is done as a team/group is better than the work done individually.	1	2	3	4	5
4. I do my best work alone rather than in a team/group.	1	2	3	4	5
5. Team/group work is overrated in terms of the actual results produced.	1	2	3	4	5
6. Working in a team/group gets me to think more creatively.	1	2	3	4	5
7. Team/groups are used too often, when individual work would be more effective.	1	2	3	4	5
8. My own work is enhanced when I am in a team/group situation.	1	2	3	4	5
9. My experiences working in team/group situations have been primarily negative.	1	2	3	4	5
10. More solutions/ideas are generated when working in a team/group situation than when working alone.	1	2	3	4	5

Reverse score items 2, 4, 5, 7, and 9. Then add the scores for items 1 to 10. Higher scores indicate a preference for teamwork, while lower total scores indicate a preference for individual work.

Source: T.J.B. Kline, "The Team Player Inventory: Reliability and Validity of a Measure of Predisposition Toward Organizational Team-Working Environments," Journal for Specialists in Group Work *24, no. 1 (1999): 102–112.*

to keep the team together as long as practically possible. Interesting research by the National Transportation Safety Board shows that 73 percent of the serious mistakes made by jet cockpit crews are made the very first day that a crew flies together as a team and that 44 percent of serious mistake occur on their very first flight together (pilot teams fly two to three flights per day). Moreover, research has shown that fatigued pilot crews who have worked together before make significantly fewer errors than rested crews who have never worked together.[97] Their experience working together helps them overcome their fatigue and outperform new teams that have not worked together before. So, once you've created effective teams, keep them together as long as possible.

4.3 Team Training

After selecting the right people for teamwork, you need to train them. And, for teams to be successful, they need significant training, particularly in interpersonal skills, decision making and problem solving, conflict resolution, and technical training. Team leaders need training, too.

Organizations that create work teams *often underestimate the amount of training* required to make teams effective. This mistake occurs frequently in successful organizations, where managers assume that if employees can work effectively on their own, they can work effectively in teams. In reality, companies that successfully use teams provide thousands of hours of training to make sure that teams work.

interpersonal skills
skills, such as listening, communicating, questioning, and providing feedback, that enable people to have effective working relationships with others

Most commonly members of work teams receive training in interpersonal skills. **Interpersonal skills**, such as listening, communicating, questioning, and providing feedback, enable people to have effective working relationships with others. When Super Sack, a maker of heavy-duty plastic bags for the food and pharmaceutical industries, first used teams, it failed. David Kellenberger, Super Sack's vice president of manufacturing, said, "One of our greatest mistakes at the beginning was our failure to recognize how important training was. You need to make a huge commitment of time and resources for training people in communication, goal-setting, and general team-building skills to make a successful transition [to teams]."[98]

Because of their autonomy and responsibility, many companies give teams training in *decision-making and problem-solving skills* to help them do a better job of cutting costs and improving quality and customer service. Many organizations also teach teams *conflict resolution skills.* Coldwater Machine Company formed teams but waited several months to provide conflict resolution training. Ken Meyer, Coldwater's coordinator of work groups, explained why: "People are starting to encounter differences right now, so we're starting conflict resolution training. We think work group members will appreciate the training more now that they're in particular situations and see the relevance."[99]

exhibit 11.9

Top 10 Problems Reported by Team Leaders

1. Confusion about their new roles and about what they should be doing differently.
2. Feeling they've lost control.
3. Not knowing what it means to coach or empower.
4. Having personal doubts about whether the team concept will really work.
5. Uncertainty about how to deal with employees' doubts about the team concept.
6. Confusion about when a team is ready for more responsibility.
7. Confusion about how to share responsibility and accountability with the team.
8. Concern about promotional opportunities, especially about whether the "team leader" title carries any prestige.
9. Uncertainty about the strategic aspects of the leader's role as teams mature.
10. Not knowing where to turn for help with team problems, since few, if any, of their organization's leaders have led teams.

Source: B. Filipczak, M. Hequet, C. Lee, M. Picard, & D. Stamps, "More Trouble with Teams," Training, *Octobert 1996, 21.*

Firms must also provide team members with the *technical training* they need to do their jobs, particularly if they are expected to perform all of the different jobs on the team (i.e., cross training). Before teams were created at Milwaukee Mutual Insurance, separate employees performed the tasks of rating, underwriting, and processing insurance policies. After extensive cross training, however, each team member can now do all three jobs.[100] Cross training is less appropriate for teams of highly skilled workers. For instance, it is unlikely that a group of engineers, computer programmers, and systems analysts would be cross-trained for each other's jobs.

Finally, companies need to provide *training for team leaders,* who often feel unprepared for their new duties. Exhibit 11.9 shows the top 10 problems reported by new team leaders. These range from confusion about their new roles as team leaders (compared to their old jobs as managers or employees) to not knowing where to go for help when their teams have problems. The solution is extensive training for team leaders.

4.4 Team Compensation and Recognition

Compensating teams correctly is very difficult. For instance, one survey found that only 37 percent of companies were satisfied with their team compensation plans and even fewer, just 10 percent, reported being "very positive."[101] One of the problems, according to Monty Mohrman of the Center for Effective Organizations, is that "there is a very strong set of beliefs in most organizations that people should be paid for how well they do. So when people first get put into team-based organizations, they really balk at being paid for how well the team does. It sounds illogical to them. It sounds like their individuality and their sense of self-worth are being threatened."[102] Consequently, companies need to carefully choose a team compensation plan and then fully explain how teams will be rewarded. One basic requirement for team compensation to work is that the level of rewards (individual versus team) must match the level of performance (individual versus team).

There are three methods of compensating employees for team participation and accomplishments, skill-based pay, gainsharing, and nonfinancial rewards. **Skill-based pay** programs pay employees for learning additional skills or knowledge.[103] These programs encourage employees to acquire the additional skills they will need to perform multiple jobs within a team. For example, at XEL Communications, the number of skills each employee has mastered determines his or her individual pay. An employee who takes a class and on-the-job training in advanced soldering (XEL makes circuit boards) will earn 30 cents more per hour. Passing a written test or satisfactorily performing a skill or job for a supervisor or trainer certifies mastery of new skills and results in increased pay.

skill-based pay
a compensation system that pays employees for learning additional skills or knowledge

In **gainsharing** programs, companies share the financial value of performance gains, such as productivity, cost savings, or quality, with their workers.[104] Over the last 25 years, the U.S. Postal Service (USPS) has lost $9 billion. Recently, however, a gainsharing program for its 84,000 supervisors produced annual savings of $497 million for the USPS and average annual gainsharing payments of $3,100 for each supervisor. Thanks to cost-saving suggestions, improved productivity, and better management, on-time delivery of first class mail increased by 10 percent, the number of workdays lost to injury dropped significantly, and, most impressively of all, the USPS had five straight years of positive net income. Nonetheless, Congress killed the USPS gainsharing program by passing a law prohibiting payment of any gainsharing savings to employees any year the USPS lost money (which it has done the last few years).[105]

gainsharing
a compensation system in which companies share the financial value of performance gains, such as productivity, cost savings, or quality, with their workers

Nonfinancial rewards are another way to reward teams for their performance. These rewards, which can range from vacation trips to T-shirts, plaques, and coffee mugs, are especially effective when coupled with management recognition, such as awards, certificates, and praise.[106] Nonfinancial awards tend to be most effective when teams or team-based interventions, such as total quality management (see Chapter 13), are first introduced.[107]

Which team compensation plan should your company use? In general, skill-based pay is most effective for self-managing and self-directing teams performing complex tasks. In these situations, the more each team member knows and can do, the better the whole team performs. By contrast, gainsharing works best in relatively stable environments where employees can focus on improving the productivity, cost savings, or quality of their current work system.

Finally, given the level of dissatisfaction with most team compensation systems, what compensation plans would today's managers like to use with the teams in their companies? Forty percent of managers would directly link merit pay increases to team performance, but allow adjustments within teams for differences in individual performance. By contrast, 13.7 percent would link merit-based increases directly to team performance, but would give each team member an equal share of the team's merit-based reward. Nineteen percent would use gainsharing plans based on quality, delivery, productivity, or cost reduction and then provide equal payouts to all teams and team members. Another 14.5 percent would also use gainsharing, but they would vary the team gainsharing award, depending on how much money the team saved the company. Payouts would still be equally distributed within teams. Finally, 12.2 percent of managers would opt for plantwide profit-sharing plans tied to overall company or division performance.[108] In this case, there would be no payout distinctions between or within teams.

Review 4
Enhancing Work Team Performance

Companies can make teams more effective by setting team goals and managing how team members are selected, trained, and compensated. Team goals provide a clear focus and purpose, reduce the incidence of social loafing, and lead to higher team performance 93 percent of the time. Extremely difficult stretch goals can be used to motivate teams as long as teams have autonomy, control over resources, structural accommodation, and bureaucratic immunity. Not everyone is suited for teamwork. When selecting team members, companies should select people who have a preference for teamwork (individualism-collectivism) and should consider the importance of team level (average ability on a team) and team diversity (different abilities on a team). Organizations that successfully use teams provide thousands of hours of training to make sure that teams work. The most common types of team training are for interpersonal skills, decision-making and problem-solving skills, conflict resolution, technical training to help team members learn multiple jobs (i.e., cross training), and training for team leaders. There are three methods of compensating employees for team participation and accomplishments: skill-based pay, gainsharing, and nonfinancial rewards.

STUDY TIP Make up a crossword puzzle using the key terms in this chapter. Writing the clues will help you remember the definition and the context of each concept. Make photocopies for exam time and for your study group.

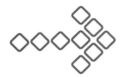

FOSTERING TEAM SPIRIT

What would you do to build a sense of camaraderie among your team members? Walk across a bed of nails together? Hot coals? What about putting together a circus complete with trapeze and high wire, or a rodeo with mechanical bulls and cattle branding? Although farfetched, these are some of the tamest of the odd feats companies are asking employees to perform (beyond sitting in a corporate training facility for two days), all in the name of teamwork.[109]

EMC, Burger King, Genentech, Adobe Systems, Pepsi, Goodyear, and Hewlett-Packard have all sent employees to some pretty wacky (and pretty fun) team-building camps. Burger King enrolls employees in a fire-walking seminar; they also march across a bed of nails and smash their hands against inch-thick boards. Adobe and Genentech have sponsored work team circuses, and Pepsi, Goodyear, and H-P have sent employees to Mid-Ohio Speedway for seminars in race-car driving. If these exercises are too tame, Teambuildinginc.com offers team beekeeping and honey gathering, rattlesnake hunts, skydiving, bull riding, and paint-ball wars. If you crave a more intensely realistic experience, you can sign up your team for simulated hostage negotiations or to do a space shuttle launch simulation at NASA. Stylish teams can stomp grapes and make Merlot. If you really need something outlandish, try Barbie Heroism. In this exercise designed by a consulting company called Total Rebound, four employees use cranks and pulleys to operate a toy helicopter in an effort to rescue a school of floating Barbies from deadly plastic sharks.

Although these exercises vary widely in their effectiveness, companies are still shelling out big bucks for team coaching, proving that they see teamwork as an essential part of the management toolkit. Though some employees might balk at the rattlesnake hunt or the beekeeping exercise, it's probably not too difficult to rally the troops around the race-car driving or NASA seminars.

As a team, answer questions 1 and 2 on the team activities described above. Then read the scenario about a company that wants to organize its sales staff into teams, and answer questions 3, 4, and 5.

Questions

1. Do the activities described above qualify as team training? Why or why not?
2. Based on the limited descriptions given, try to rank the activities mentioned above according to how well you think they (a) teach teamwork skills and (b) foster team spirit. Your two lists may not be the same. Explain your rankings. Are some activities more appropriate for certain kinds of teams, for example, circus activities for cross-functional teams or making Merlot for self-managing teams?

Scenario

Now imagine that your group is a management consulting team. Your client is Landscape Forms, a manufacturer of upscale commercial public space furniture (think designer outdoor tables, park benches, and waste cans). Top managers at Landscape Forms want to reorganize the company's sales staff into teams, and they are asking for your advice. Currently, 15 sales representatives each cover a separate geographic territory, and each rep is paid a base salary and a commission on the sales he or she closes. The company is headquartered in Michigan, but its reps live across the United States (each in his or her territory). Reps are responsible not only for generating sales, but also for completing sales proposals, negotiating sales contracts, and expanding dealership and distribution networks throughout their territory. In essence, each sales rep for Landscape Forms fully manages the business functions in his or her own territory, but no sales rep manages any subordinates.

3. What kind of team would you recommend for Landscape Forms' sales staff? Why?
4. Although the sales reps know each other from national sales meetings, they have never worked together as a team. What kind of training would you recommend for the newly formed sales teams at Landscape Forms? Would you suggest one of the activities discussed in the first part of this exercise? Why or why not?
5. As a management team, present your recommendations to the board of Landscape Forms (i.e., the rest of your class).

A QUICK CHECK OF YOUR TEAM SKILLS

To be part of an effective team, you have to be a good team member.[110] Sometimes, however, it's hard to objectively judge our contributions in a team or group effort. Think about one of your most important team experiences. Were you an effective team member? Take the following test to find out. After you take the test, answer the questions below to begin thinking about how you can improve.

Instructions:

Step 1: Answer the following questions the way that you think other members of your team would if they were describing your actions.

Step 2: Total your score for each section. Then transfer all totals to the "A Quick Check of My Team Skills" section at the conclusion of the exercise.

Scale: 1 = Almost never
2 = Seldom
3 = Sometimes
4 = Usually
5 = Almost always

I. Honor team values and agreements.

As a team member, I | **Your score:**

a. show appreciation for other team members' ideas. ________
b. help other team members cope with change. ________
c. encourage others to use their strengths. ________
d. help the team develop a productive relationship with other teams. ________
e. willingly assume a leadership role when needed. ________

Total: ________

II. Promote team development.

As a team member, I | **Your score:**

a. volunteer for all types of tasks, including the hard ones. ________
b. help orient and train new team members. ________
c. help organize and run effective meetings. ________
d. help examine how we are doing as a team and make any necessary changes in the way we work together. ________
e. help identify milestones and mini-successes to celebrate. ________

Total: ________

III. Help make team decisions.

As a team member, I | **Your score:**

a. analyze what a decision entails. ________
b. ensure that the team selects and includes the appropriate people in the decision process. ________
c. clearly state my concerns. ________
d. search for common ground when team members have different views. ________
e. actively support the team's decisions. ________

Total: ________

IV. Coordinate and carry out team tasks.

As a team member, I — **Your score:**

a. help identify the information, skills, and resources necessary to accomplish team tasks. ________
b. help formulate and agree on a plan to meet performance goals. ________
c. stay abreast of what is happening in other parts of the organization and bring that information to the team. ________
d. find innovative ways to meet the needs of the team and of others in the organization. ________
e. maintain a win-win outlook in all dealings with other teams. ________

Total: ________

V. Handle difficult issues with the team.

As a team member, I — **Your score:**

a. bring team issues and problems to the team's attention. ________
b. encourage others on the team to state their views. ________
c. help build trust among team members by speaking openly about the team's problems. ________
d. give specific, constructive, and timely feedback to others. ________
e. admit when I've made a mistake. ________

Total: ________

A Quick Check of My Team Skills

Category	**Total Score**
Honor team values and agreements.	________
Promote team development.	________
Help make team decisions.	________
Coordinate and carry out team tasks.	________
Handle difficult issues with the team.	________

Interpreting Scores

- A score of 20 or above in any activity indicates an area of strength.
- A score of 20 or below in any activity indicates an area that needs more attention.

Questions to Ask Yourself

Looking at your scores, what areas are strengths? How can you maintain these strengths? What areas are weaknesses? What steps can you take to turn these areas into strengths?

take two video!

BIZ FLIX Apollo 13

This film re-creates the heroic efforts of astronaut Jim Lovell (Tom Hanks), his crew, NASA, and Mission Control to return the damaged Apollo spacecraft to earth. Examples of both problem solving and decision making occur in almost every scene. See the Take Two exercise in Chapter 9 for more information about this film and a discussion of another scene.

This scene takes place during day 5 of the mission about two-thrids of the way through the film. Early in Apollo 13's mission Jack Swigert (Kevin Bacon) stirred the oxygen tanks at the request of Mission Control. After this procedure, an explosion occurred, causing unknown damage to the command module. Before the scene takes place, the damage has forced the crew to move into the LEM (Lunar Exploration Module), which becomes their lifeboat for return to earth.

What to Watch for and Ask Yourself

1. What triggers the conflict in this scene?
2. Is this intergroup conflict or intragroup conflict? What effects can such conflict have on the group dynamics on board Apollo 13?
3. Does mission commander Jim Lovell successfully manage the group dynamics to return the group to a normal state?

MGMT WORKPLACE Cannondale

Bicycle maker Cannondale produces and sells a wide variety of road racing, mountain, and recreational bikes. When deciding which revisions to apply to the next iteration of its Jekyll brand mountain bike, managers at Cannondale assembled a horizontal special-purpose team to tackle the problem. The team includes design, marketing, engineering, and research and development personnel. When the team members meet, they have physical examples of the bicycle frames, components from the existing version of the bike, and prototypes of components that are proposed for the next version. The collaborative approach at Cannondale ultimately yields improved decision making with respect to customer needs, production efficiency, and design and cost constraints.

What to Watch for and Ask Yourself

1. What kind of team did Cannondale assemble to manage the Jekyll revision? Explain.
2. Describe the level of autonomy on the Jekyll revision team. Use specific examples to support your answer.

CHAPTER TWELVE

Managing Human Resource Systems

outline

WHAT WOULD YOU DO?

Electronic Arts Headquarters, Redwood City, California.[1] You're a world-class footballer (i.e., a soccer player), a forward who blasts by a defender with a speed dribble on the right side of the goal. Suddenly, you "cross," passing the ball to your left as your center trails in behind you. Expecting a shot on goal, your defender leaves you to help pick up the center. As soon as that happens, you break for the goal. The center takes four steps to the left, taking the defenders with him. But then, with the defenders closing in, he stops and turns, splitting the defenders with a touch pass that puts the ball two steps ahead of you as you angle in from the right. In a microsecond, you take those two steps and blast the ball, bending it in a topspin arc into the upper left-hand corner of the net over the outstretched hands of the best goalie in the world. Well, at least the best *computer* goalie in the world in Electronic Arts' sports game, FIFA

student resources

URL Explore the four levels of learning by doing the simulation module on Human Resources.

GUIDE Mini lecture reviews all the learning points in the chapter and concludes with a case on Wal-Mart.

VIDEO Biz Flix is a scene from *Bowfinger*. Management Workplace is a segment on Gadabout Day Spa & Salon.

PPT 12 slides with graphics provide an outline for this chapter.

FAQ Chuck gives you stark statistics about general mental ability in the United States, which shows you why pre-employment tests are critical.

TEST 21 true/false questions, 18 multiple-choice questions, a management scenario, and 6 exhibit worksheets

Soccer, which has generated over $1 billion in sales since its release seven years ago.

With $10 billion in annual revenues, videogames are the largest and fastest-growing sector of the entertainment industry, generating more money than all of Hollywood's film box-office sales combined. Electronic Arts (EA) is the leading videogame publisher in the world.

Like Hollywood, EA's success depends on finding, developing, and keeping talent. Unfortunately, there's not enough to go around. But, as senior vice president of human resources, it's your job to make sure that scarce game industry talent (programmers, designers, and marketers) signs with EA and not with Oracle, Informix, Microsoft, or Sega. But, it's not just a matter of "putting butts in the seats," as your boss crudely puts it. With the average EA game taking 12 to 36 months to create and $5 million to $10 million to develop, you can't risk hiring inexperienced people low on the learning curve. Plus, you've got to hire people who are both creative and disciplined: creative enough to develop realistic graphics, captivating story lines, and innovative game capabilities, but disciplined enough to meet budgets and very strict deadlines and still produce efficient, reliable, bug-free code. Bing Gordon, EA's chief creative officer, puts it this way, "In Hollywood, if you succeed one out of three times, you're doing okay. In this industry, that's not enough." EA president and COO John Riccitiello agrees, saying "Every time we ship a game, we're as nervous as someone who's on Broadway for the first time. Every time we do it."

With plans to hire 600 new people, 300 in EA's new Los Angeles office alone (in the heart of Hollywood), you've got plenty of work to do, so you need to put together your human resources plan. First, how do you build a pipeline of talent? In other words, given the competition for talent in the industry, how do you recruit a large pool of talented coders and game developers from which to choose? Second, how do you create a pool of talented applicants for managerial positions? Assessment centers are great, but they're useful for determining whether your *existing* employees would make good managers. Unfortunately, with so many techies on the payroll, there's not a lot of in-house managerial talent with which to work. How can you create an external recruiting system that enables you to consistently find and attract the top management talent that EA needs to expand? Finally, all that recruitment won't do any good if EA isn't a great place to work. If people leave after a year or two, then you've recruited a lot of talent only to watch it walk out the door to work, most likely, for a competitor. So what does EA need to do to make sure that the talented people you recruit will stay with the company? **If you were the senior vice president of human resources at Electronic Arts, what would you do?**

human resource management (HRM) the process of finding, developing, and keeping the right people to form a qualified work force

The experience of Electronic Arts indicates that **human resource management (HRM)**, the process of finding, developing, and keeping the right people to form a qualified work force, remains one of the most difficult and important of all management tasks. Accordingly, this chapter begins by reviewing basic human resource legislation. Next, we explore how companies use recruiting and selection techniques to attract and hire qualified employees to fulfill those needs. The third part of the chapter reviews how training and performance appraisal can develop the knowledge, skills, and abilities of the work force. The chapter concludes with a review of compensation and employee separation, that is, how companies can keep their best workers through effective compensation practices and how they can manage the separation process when employees leave the organization.

Understanding Human Resource Legislation

Understanding how employment legislation affects businesses is a critical first step in human resource planning and management. This is because there are employment laws that govern each stage of the human resource process, from how employees are recruited and selected, to how employees are terminated, and nearly every stage in between.

After reading the next section, you should be able to

1 explain how different employment laws affect human resource practice.

1 Employment Legislation

Since their inception, Hooters restaurants have hired only female servers. Moreover, consistent with the company's marketing theme, the servers wear short nylon shorts and cutoff T-shirts that show their midriffs. The Equal Employment Opportunity Commission (EEOC) began an investigation of Hooters when a Chicago man filed a gender-based discrimination charge. The man alleged that he had applied for a server's job at a Hooters restaurant and was rejected because of his gender. The dispute between Hooters and the EEOC quickly gained national attention. One sarcastic letter to the EEOC printed in *Fortune* magazine read as follows:

> Dear EEOC:
>
> Hi! I just wanted to thank you for investigating those Hooters restaurants, where the waitresses wear those shorty shorts and midriffy T-shirts. I think it's a great idea that you have decided to make Hooters hire men as—how do you say it?—waitpersons. Gee, I never knew so many men wanted to be waitpersons at Hooters. No reason to let them sue on their own either. You're right, the government needs to take the lead on this one.[2]

This letter characterized public sentiment at the time. With a backlog of 100,000 job discrimination cases, many wondered why the EEOC didn't have better things to do with its scarce resources.

www.experiencing management.com

Learn more about employment laws and how they affect human resource practice at our animated concept and activity site. Choose Human_Resources from the "select a topic" pull-down menu, then Equal Employment Opportunity (EEO) from the "overview tab."

http://www.experiencingmanagement.com

This photo epitomizes how ludicrous the public thought the EEOC's suit againt Hooters was. Despite a favorable ruling, Hooters was still required to create more support jobs that would be open to men. A group of men calling themselves "Hooter Guys" dressed like the female employees of the popular restaurant as part of their entry in the Boulder Kinetic Sculpture Challenge.

Three years after the initial complaint, the EEOC ruled that Hooters had violated antidiscrimination laws. The EEOC offered Hooters a settlement that would have required the company to pay $22 million to the EEOC for distribution to male victims of the "Hooters Girl" hiring policy, establish a scholarship fund to enhance opportunities or education for men, and provide sensitivity training to teach Hooters' employees how to be more sensitive to men's needs. Hooters responded with a $1 million publicity campaign, chastising the EEOC for its investigation. Billboards featuring "Vince," a male dressed in a Hooters Girl uniform and blond wig sprang up all over the country. Hooters customers were given postcards to send complaints to the EEOC. Of course, Hooters paid the postage. As a result of the publicity campaign, restaurant sales increased by 10 percent. Soon thereafter, the EEOC announced that it would not pursue discriminatory hiring charges against Hooters. Nonetheless, the company still ended up paying $3.75 million to settle a class-action suit brought by seven men who claimed that their inability to get a job at Hooters violated federal law.[3] The settlement allowed Hooters to maintain its women-only policy for server jobs, but required the company to create additional support jobs, such as hosts and bartenders, that would also be open to men.

As the Hooters example illustrates, the human resource planning process occurs in a very complicated legal environment. Let's explore employment legislation by reviewing 1.1 the major federal employment laws that affect human resource practice, 1.2 how the concept of adverse impact is related to employment discrimination, and 1.3 the laws regarding sexual harassment in the workplace.

1.1 Federal Employment Laws

Exhibit 12.1 lists the major federal employment laws and their Web sites, where you can find more detailed information. The general effect of this body of law, which is still evolving through court decisions, is that employers may not discriminate in employment decisions on the basis of gender, age, religion, color, national origin, race, or disability. The intent is to make these factors irrelevant in employment decisions. Stated another way, employment decisions should be based on factors that are "job related," "reasonably necessary," or a "business necessity" for successful job performance. The only time that gender, age, religion, and the like can be used to make employment decisions is when they are considered a bona fide occupational qualification.[4] Title VII of the 1964 Civil Rights Act says that it is not unlawful to hire and employ someone on the basis of gender, religion, or national origin when there is a **bona fide occupational qualification (BFOQ)** that is "reasonably necessary to the normal operation of that particular business." For example, a Baptist church hiring a new minister can reasonably specify that being a Baptist rather than a Catholic or Presbyterian is a BFOQ for Baptist ministers. However, it's unlikely that the church could specify race or national origin as a BFOQ. In general, the courts and the EEOC take a hard look when a business claims that gender, age, religion, color, national origin, race, or disability is a BFOQ. For instance,

bona fide occupational qualification (BFOQ) an exception in employment law that permits gender, age, religion, and the like to be used when making employment decisions, but only if they are "reasonably necessary to the normal operation of that particular business." BFOQs are strictly monitored by the Equal Employment Opportunity Commission.

exhibit 12.1

Summary of Major Federal Employment Laws

• Equal Pay Act of 1963	(http://www.eeoc.gov/policy/epa.html)	Prohibits unequal pay for males and females doing substantially similar work.
• Civil Rights Act of 1964	(http://www.eeoc.gov/policy/vii.html)	Prohibits discrimination on the basis of race, color, religion, gender, or national origin.
• Age Discrimination in Employment Act of 1967	(http://www.eeoc.gov/policy/adea.html)	Prohibits discrimination in employment decisions against persons age 40 and over.
• Pregnancy Discrimination Act of 1978	(http://www.eeoc.gov/facts/fs-preg.html)	Prohibits discrimination in employment against pregnant women.
• Americans with Disabilities Act of 1990	(http://www.eeoc.gov/policy/ada.html)	Prohibits discrimination on the basis of physical or mental disabilities.
• Civil Rights Act of 1991	(http://www.eeoc.gov/policy/cra91.html)	Strengthened the provisions of the Civil Rights Act of 1964 by providing for jury trials and punitive damages.
• Family and Medical Leave Act of 1993	(http://www.dol.gov/esa/whd/fmla/index.htm)	Permits workers to take up to 12 weeks of unpaid leave for pregnancy and/or birth of a new child, adoption or foster care of a new child, illness of an immediate family member, or personal medical leave.

the EEOC disagreed with Hooters' claim that it was "in the business of providing vicarious sexual recreation" and that "female sexuality is a bona fide occupational qualification."[5]

It is important to understand, however, that these laws apply to the entire HRM process and not just to selection decisions (i.e., hiring and promotion). Thus, these laws also cover all training and development activities, performance appraisals, terminations, and compensation decisions.

Except for the Department of Labor (**http://www.dol.gov**), which administers the Family and Medical Leave Act, all of these laws are administered by the EEOC (**http://www.eeoc.gov**). Employers who use gender, age, race, or religion to make employment-related decisions when those factors are unrelated to an applicant's or employee's ability to perform a job may face charges of discrimination from employee lawsuits or the EEOC. For example, five women sued Met Life, a large insurance company, accusing it of gender discrimination in hiring, pay, and promotions. The lawyer representing the women said that only 25 percent of the company's 6,000 sales representatives were women, that only 7 percent of branch managers and managing directors were women, and that there were no female vice presidents at the highest levels of sales management. Likewise, Ford Motor Company settled a lawsuit after being sued for age discrimination when it switched to a new employee evaluation system in which 10 percent of workers received A grades, 80 percent received

B's, and 10 percent received C's. If you received a C, you wouldn't get a pay raise or a bonus. If you got a C two years in a row, you were to be demoted or asked to leave the company. The lawyer representing the workers who sued Ford said, "We believe the new evaluation system was deliberately designed to reduce Ford's work force based on age."[6]

In addition to the laws presented in Exhibit 12.1, there are two other important sets of federal laws: labor laws and laws and regulations governing safety standards. Labor laws regulate the interaction between management and labor unions that represent groups of employees. These laws guarantee employees the right to form and join unions of their own choosing. For more information about labor laws, see the National Labor Relations Board at **http://www.nlrb.gov**. The Occupational Safety and Health Act (OSHA) requires that employers provide employees with a workplace that is "free from recognized hazards that are causing or are likely to cause death or serious physical harm." OSHA sets safety and health standards for employers and conducts inspections to determine whether those standards are being met. Employers who do not meet OSHA standards may be fined.[7] For example, OSHA fined Rocky Mountain Steel Mills (a division of Oregon Steel Mills) $1.1 million for having elevated platforms without guardrails and $487,000 for having electricians use the wrong kind of gloves. The second fine, which was prompted by two employees' deaths, was reduced to $300,000 after the company agreed to spend another $150,000 on safety improvements.[8] On a subsequent inspection, however, OSHA investigators found 22 repeat violations that had not been corrected, 74 new safety violations, and 11 new health violations.[9] For more information about OSHA, see **http://www.osha.gov**.

1.2 Adverse Impact and Employment Discrimination

The EEOC has investigatory, enforcement, and informational responsibilities. Therefore, it investigates charges of discrimination, enforces the employment discrimination laws in federal court, and publishes guidelines that organizations can use to ensure they are in compliance with the law. One of the most important guidelines jointly issued by the EEOC, the Department of Labor, the U.S. Justice Department, and the federal Office of Personnel Management is the *Uniform Guidelines on Employee Selection Procedures*, which can be read in their entirety at **http://www.access.gpo.gov/nara/cfr/waisidx_02/41cfr60-3_02.html**. These guidelines define two important criteria, disparate treatment and adverse impact, that are used in deciding whether companies have participated in discriminatory hiring and promotion practices.

disparate treatment
intentional discrimination that occurs when people are purposely not given the same hiring, promotion, or membership opportunities because of their race, gender, age, ethnic group, national origin, or religious beliefs

Discrimination means treating people differently. **Disparate treatment**, which is intentional discrimination, occurs when people, because of their race, gender, ethnic group, national origin, religious beliefs, and so forth, are intentionally not given the same hiring, promotion, or membership opportunities as other employees, despite being qualified.[10] For example, Coca-Cola paid $192.5 million to settle a class-action disparate treatment lawsuit in which it was accused of purposely not giving African American employees equal opportunities in pay, promotions, and performance reviews.[11] Likewise, Rent-A-Center paid $12.3 million to settle a class-action disparate treatment lawsuit in which it was accused of not providing fair hiring and promotion opportunities to 4,600 female employees and job applicants.[12]

Legally, a key element of discrimination lawsuits is establishing motive, meaning that the employer intended to discriminate. If no motive can be established, then a claim of disparate treatment may actually be a case of

adverse impact
unintentional discrimination in which there is a substantially different rate of selection in hiring, promotion, or other employment decisions that works to the disadvantage of members of a particular race, gender, age, ethnicity, or protected group

four-fifths (or 80 percent) rule
a rule of thumb used by the courts and the EEOC to determine whether there is evidence of adverse impact. A violation of this rule occurs when the selection rate for a protected group is less than 80 percent or four-fifths of the selection rate for a nonprotected group.

adverse impact. **Adverse impact**, which is unintentional discrimination, is a substantially different rate of selection in hiring, promotion, or other employment decisions that works to the disadvantage of members of a particular race, gender, or ethnic group. The courts and federal agencies use the **four-fifths (or 80 percent) rule** to determine if adverse impact has occurred. Adverse impact occurs if the selection rate for a protected group of people is less than four-fifths (or 80 percent) of the selection rate for a nonprotected group (usually white males). So, if 100 white applicants and 100 black applicants apply for entry-level jobs, and 60 white applicants are hired ($60/100 = 60\%$), but only 20 black applicants are hired ($20/100 = 20\%$), adverse impact has occurred ($0.20/0.60 = 0.33$). The criterion for the four-fifths rule in this situation is 0.48 ($0.60 \times 0.80 = 0.48$). Since 0.33 is less than 0.48, the four-fifths rule has been violated.

Violation of the four-fifths rule is not an automatic indication of discrimination, however. If an employer can demonstrate that a selection procedure or test is valid, meaning that the test accurately predicts job performance or that the test is job related because it assesses applicants on specific tasks actually used in the job, then the organization may continue to use the test. If validity cannot be established, however, then a violation of the four-fifths rule may likely result in a lawsuit brought by employees, job applicants, or the EEOC itself.

1.3 Sexual Harassment

sexual harassment
a form of discrimination in which unwelcome sexual advances, requests for sexual favors, or other verbal or physical conduct of a sexual nature occurs while performing one's job

quid pro quo sexual harassment
a form of sexual harassment in which employment outcomes, such as hiring, promotion, or simply keeping one's job, depend on whether an individual submits to sexual harassment

hostile work environment
a form of sexual harassment in which unwelcome and demeaning sexually related behavior creates an intimidating and offensive work environment

According to the EEOC, **sexual harassment** is a form of discrimination in which unwelcome sexual advances, requests for sexual favors, or other verbal or physical conduct of a sexual nature occurs. From a legal perspective, there are two kinds of sexual harassment, quid pro quo and hostile work environment.[13]

Quid pro quo sexual harassment occurs when employment outcomes, such as hiring, promotion, or simply keeping one's job, depend on whether an individual submits to being sexually harassed. For example, in a quid pro quo sexual harassment lawsuit against Prudential Insurance, a female employee alleged that her boss repeatedly propositioned her for sexual favors and that when she refused, he said that "she would not amount to anything in this business without his help."[14] By contrast, a **hostile work environment** occurs when unwelcome and demeaning sexually related behavior creates an intimidating, hostile, and offensive work environment. For example, a hostile work environment occurred at Sears, where a manager would ask his female subordinates to step into his office to look at close-up photos of women's breasts and bottoms that he had taken while on vacation at a beach.[15] As another example, the same Prudential manager who allegedly engaged in quid pro quo harassment was also alleged to have made inappropriate sexual comments about women in front of female workers, to have allowed the display of pornographic material on company computers, and to have permitted the posting of a sign saying, "Sexual harassment will not be tolerated, it will be graded."[16]

What common mistakes do managers make when it comes to sexual harassment laws?[17] First, many assume that the victim and harasser must be of the opposite sex. According to the courts, they do not. Sexual harassment can also occur between people of the same sex. Second, it is assumed that sexual harassment can occur only between coworkers or between supervisors and subordinates. Not so. Sexual harassers can also include agents of employers, such as consultants, and can even include nonemployees. The key is not employee status but whether the harassment takes place while company business is being conducted. Third, it is often assumed that only people who have themselves been harassed can file complaints or lawsuits. In fact, especially in hostile work environments, anyone affected by offensive conduct can file a complaint or lawsuit.

Finally, what should companies do to make sure that sexual harassment laws are followed and not violated?[18] First, respond immediately when sexual harassment is reported. A quick response encourages victims of sexual harassment to report problems to management rather than to lawyers or the EEOC. Furthermore, a quick and fair investigation may serve as a deterrent to future harassment. A lawyer for the EEOC said, "Worse than having no sexual harassment policy is a policy that is not followed. It's merely window dressing. You wind up with destroyed morale when people who come forward are ignored, ridiculed, retaliated against, or nothing happens to the harasser."[19] Next, take the time to write a clear, understandable sexual harassment policy that is strongly worded, gives specific examples of what constitutes sexual harassment, spells outs sanctions and punishments, and is widely publicized within the company. This lets potential harassers and victims know what will not be tolerated and how the firm will deal with harassment should it occur.

Next, establish clear reporting procedures that indicate how, where, and to whom incidents of sexual harassment can be reported. The best procedures ensure that a complaint will receive quick response, that impartial parties will handle the complaint, and that the privacy of the accused and accuser will be protected. At Du Pont, AT&T, Avon, and Texas Industries, employees can call a confidential hotline 24 hours a day, 365 days a year.[20]

Finally, managers should also be aware that most states and many cities or local governments have their own employment-related laws and enforcement agencies. So compliance with federal law is often not enough. In fact, organizations can be in full compliance with federal law and at the same time be violating state or local sexual harassment laws.

Review 1
Employment Legislation

Human resource management is subject to the following major federal employment laws: Equal Pay Act, Civil Rights Acts of 1964 and 1991, Age Discrimination in Employment Act, Pregnancy Discrimination Act, Americans with Disabilities Act, and Family and Medical Leave Act. Human resource management is also subject to review by these federal agencies: Equal Employment Opportunity Commission, Department of Labor, Occupational Safety and Health Administration, and National Labor Relations Board. In general, these laws indicate that gender, age, religion, color, national origin, race, disability, and pregnancy may not be considered in employment decisions unless these factors reasonably qualify as BFOQs. Two important criteria, disparate treatment (intentional discrimination) and adverse impact (unintentional discrimination), are used to decide whether companies have wrongly discriminated against someone. While motive is a key part of determining disparate treatment, the courts and federal enforcement agencies use the four-fifths rule to determine if adverse impact has occurred. The two kinds of sexual harassment are quid pro quo and hostile work environment. Managers often wrongly assume that the victim and harasser must be of the opposite sex, that sexual harassment can only occur between coworkers or between supervisors and their employees, and that only people who have themselves been harassed can file complaints or lawsuits. To make sure that sexual harassment laws are followed, companies should respond immediately when harassment is reported; write a clear, understandable sexual harassment policy; establish clear reporting procedures; and be aware of and follow city and state laws concerning sexual harassment.

Finding Qualified Workers

Ironically, despite record sales, Technical Materials, which sells electroplating and metal-bonding processes to car manufacturers and high-tech industries, could not find enough qualified employees to work in its factories. Its pool of prospective employees was so weak that the number of applicants who failed its drug test had increased from one in 25 to one in six. Company president Al Lubrano made numerous strong job offers, added more pay and benefits to those offers when applicants asked for more, and still couldn't hire anybody. Finally, Lubrano said, "When it got ridiculous, we walked away."[21] Likewise, the nursing shortage is so severe in some areas that Mary Viney, director of patient care services, found herself in Manila, trying to encourage Filipino nurses to work for her hospital in Austin, Texas. In Texas, says Viney, "it's a day-to-day, shift-to-shift challenge to get enough nurses."[22]

As these examples illustrate, finding qualified workers can be an increasingly difficult task. Finding qualified applicants is just the first step, however. Deciding which applicants to hire is the second. CEO John Chambers of Cisco Systems, the leading designer and manufacturer of the high-tech equipment that serves as the backbone of the Internet, says, "Cisco has an overall goal of getting the top 10 to 15 percent of people in our industry. Our philosophy is very simple—if you get the best people in the industry to fit into your culture and you motivate them properly, then you're going to be an industry leader."[23]

After reading the next two sections, you should be able to

2 explain how companies use recruiting to find qualified job applicants.

3 describe the selection techniques and procedures that companies use when deciding which applicants should receive job offers.

2 Recruiting

recruiting
the process of developing a pool of qualified job applicants

Recruiting is the process of developing a pool of qualified job applicants. Let's examine 2.1 what job analysis is and how it is used in recruiting and 2.2 how companies use internal **and** external recruiting to find qualified job applicants.

2.1 Job Analysis and Recruiting

job analysis
a purposeful, systematic process for collecting information on the important work-related aspects of a job

Job analysis is a "purposeful, systematic process for collecting information on the important work-related aspects of a job."[24] Typically, a job analysis collects four kinds of information:

- work activities, such as what workers do and how, when, and why they do it;
- the tools and equipment used to do the job;

- the context in which the job is performed, such as the actual working conditions or schedule; and
- the personnel requirements for performing the job, meaning the knowledge, skills, and abilities needed to do a job well.[25]

Job analysis information can be collected by having job incumbents and/or supervisors complete questionnaires about their jobs, by direct observation, by interviews, or by filming employees as they perform their jobs.

job description
a written description of the basic tasks, duties, and responsibilities required of an employee holding a particular job

job specifications
a written summary of the qualifications needed to successfully perform a particular job

Job descriptions and job specifications are two of the most important results of a job analysis. A **job description** is a written description of the basic tasks, duties, and responsibilities required of an employee holding a particular job. **Job specifications**, which are often included as a separate section of a job description, are a summary of the qualifications needed to successfully perform the job. Exhibit 12.2 shows a job description and the job specifications for a helicopter pilot for the city of Little Rock, Arkansas.

Because a job analysis clearly specifies what a job entails, as well as the knowledge, skills, and abilities that are needed to do a job well, companies must complete a job analysis *before* beginning to recruit job applicants. Exhibit 12.3 shows that job analysis, job descriptions, and job specifications are the foundation on which all critical human resource activities are built. They are used during recruiting and selection to match applicant qualifications with the requirements of the job. They are used throughout the staffing process to ensure that selection devices and the decisions based on these devices are job related. For example, the questions asked in an interview should

exhibit 12.2

Job Description and Job Specifications for a Helicopter Pilot for the City of Little Rock, Arkansas

JOB DESCRIPTION FOR HELICOPTER PILOT
To provide assistance for air searches, river rescues, high-rise building rescues, and other assignments, by providing air survey and aviation response. Pilots a rotary-wing aircraft, serving as pilot or co-pilot, to assist in air searches, river rescues, high-rise building rescues, and other assignments. Ensures that aircraft is properly outfitted for each assignment (equipment, rigging tools, supplies, etc.). Performs preflight inspection of aircraft; checks rotors, fuel, lubricants, controls, etc. Prepares written reports on assignments; maintains flight logs. Obtains weather reports; determines to proceed with assignments given forecasted weather conditions. Operates a radio to maintain contact with and to report information to airport personnel and Police Department personnel.
JOB SPECIFICATIONS FOR HELICOPTER PILOT
Must possess a valid Commercial Pilot's License for rotary-wing aircraft before employment and maintain licensure for the duration of employment in this position. Must have considerable knowledge of Federal Aviation Administration (FAA) laws and regulations, rotary-wing aircraft operating procedures, air traffic safety, flying procedures and navigational techniques, and FAA and police radio operation and procedures. Must have some knowledge of preventive maintenance methods, repair practices, safety requirements and inspection procedures. Must have skill in the operation of a rotary-wing aircraft, radio equipment, the ability to conduct safety inspections of aircraft, to maintain aircraft maintenance logs and prepare reports, to detect and identify aircraft malfunction symptoms, to detect and recognize ground conditions and characteristics (i.e., utility line breaks, river currents, etc.), to read maps and air navigation charts, and to communicate effectively, both orally and in writing. Must have completed high school; at least one-thousand hours of flight time experience in piloting rotary-wing aircraft; OR any equivalent combination of experience and training which provides the required knowledge, skills, and abilities.

Source: "Job Description: Helicopter Pilot," City of Little Rock, Arkansas, [Online] available at http://www.accesslittlerock.org/HumanResources/h000274.htm, 31 May 2003.

exhibit 12.3

Importance of Job Analysis to Human Resource Management

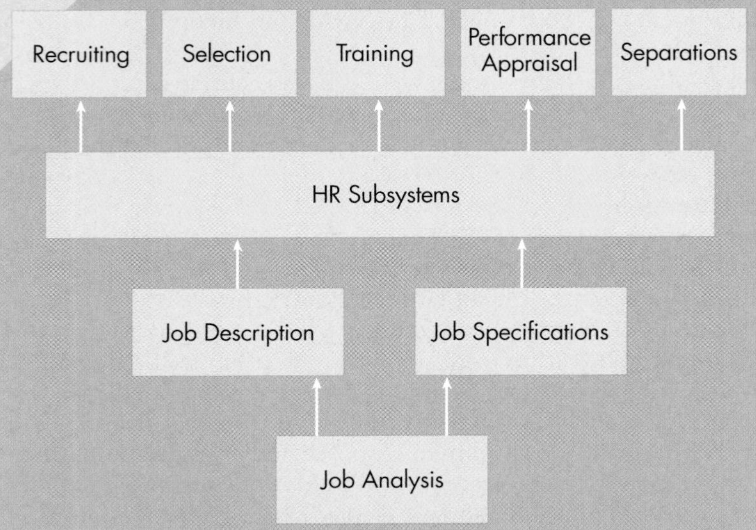

be based on the most important work activities identified by a job analysis. Likewise, during performance appraisals, employees should be evaluated in areas that a job analysis has identified as the most important in a job.

Job analyses, job descriptions, and job specifications also help companies meet the legal requirement that their human resource decisions be job related. To be judged *job related,* recruitment, selection, training, performance appraisals, and employee separations must be valid and be directly related to the important aspects of the job, as identified by a careful job analysis. In fact, in *Griggs v. Duke Power Co.* and *Albemarle Paper Co. v. Moody,* the U.S. Supreme Court ruled that companies should use job analyses to help establish the job relatedness of their human resource procedures.[26] The EEOC's *Uniform Guidelines on Employee Selection Procedures* also recommend that companies base their human resource procedures on job analysis.

2.2 Internal and External Recruiting

internal recruiting
the process of developing a pool of qualified job applicants from people who already work in the company

Internal recruiting is the process of developing a pool of qualified job applicants from people who already work in the company. Internal recruiting, sometimes called "promotion from within," improves employee commitment, morale, and motivation. Recruiting current employees also reduces recruitment startup time and costs, and because employees are already familiar with the company's culture and procedures, they are more likely to succeed in new jobs. GlaxoSmithKline, a pharmaceutical and health-care company, internally recruits 20 first-level managers each year to keep recruiting costs low and to keep talented people in the company.[27] Job posting and career paths are two methods of internal recruiting. *Job posting* is a procedure for advertising job openings within the company to existing employees. A job description and requirements are typically posted on a bulletin board, in a company newsletter, or in an internal computerized job bank that is accessible only to employees. Job posting helps organizations discover hidden talent, allows employees to take responsibility for career planning, and makes it easier for companies to retain talented workers who are dissatisfied in their current jobs and would otherwise leave the company.[28] A *career path* is a planned sequence of jobs through which employees may advance within an organization. For example, a person who starts as a sales representative may

www.experiencing management.com

You may learn more about the recruitment and selection process by interacting with this concept at our animated concept and activity site. Choose Human_Resources from the "select a topic" pull-down menu, then Recruitment and Selection Process from the "overview tab."

http://www.experiencingmanagement.com

move up to sales manager and then to district or regional sales manager. Career paths help employees focus on long-term goals and development while also helping companies do succession or replacement planning.

external recruiting
the process of developing a pool of qualified job applicants from outside the company

External recruiting is the process of developing a pool of qualified job applicants from outside the company. External recruitment methods include advertising (newspapers, magazines, direct mail, radio, or television), employee referrals (asking current employees to recommend possible job applicants), walk-ins (people who apply on their own), outside organizations (universities, technical/trade schools, professional societies), employment services (state or private employment agencies, temporary agencies, and professional search firms), special events (career conferences or job fairs), and Internet job sites. Which external recruiting method should you use? Studies show that employee referrals, walk-ins, newspaper advertisements, and state employment agencies tend to be used most frequently for office/clerical and production/service employees. By contrast, newspaper advertisements and college/university recruiting are used most frequently for professional/technical employees. When recruiting managers, organizations tend to rely most heavily on newspaper advertisements, employee referrals, and search firms.[29] In the last few years the biggest changes in external recruiting have come as a result of the Internet, which is an inexpensive way to post very detailed job openings. Companies typically receive far more responses to Internet ads than to newspaper ads, which has its advantages and disadvantages. Managers have more candidates from which to choose, but the sheer volume of responses increases the importance of proper screening and selection.

Review 2
Recruiting

Recruiting is the process of finding qualified job applicants. The first step in recruiting is to conduct a job analysis to collect information about the important work-related aspects of the job. The job analysis is then used to write a job description of basic tasks, duties, and responsibilities and to write job specifications indicating the knowledge, skills, and abilities needed to perform the job. Job analyses, descriptions, and specifications help companies meet the legal requirement that their human resource decisions be job related. Internal recruiting, or finding qualified job applicants from inside the company, can be done through job posting and career paths. External recruiting, or finding qualified job applicants from outside the company, is done through advertising, employee referrals, walk-ins, outside organizations, employment services, special events, and Internet job sites. The Internet is a particularly promising method of external recruiting because of its low cost, wide reach, and ability to communicate and receive unlimited information.

3 Selection

Once the recruitment process has produced a pool of qualified applicants, the selection process is used to determine which applicants have the best chance of performing well on the job. When the East Providence, Rhode Island Police Department has job openings, it follows a "rule of three," meaning no matter how many candidates it has for an opening, it only looks at the top three applicants, as determined by a standardized written test. Those top three applicants for every position must then pass a physical fitness test and a background check. Every applicant who makes it that far is then put on a list of official candidates for police jobs for two years. Only the best candidates on that list participate in group interviews with the city manager, police chief, deputy chief, a police captain, and the Police Department's personnel director and affirmative action officer, each of whom privately ranks the candidates after each interview. Applicants with the highest rankings from the group interviews are offered positions in the Police Academy. The remaining applicants from the group interviews may be considered two more times before being rejected.[30]

selection the process of gathering information about job applicants to decide who should be offered a job

validation the process of determining how well a selection test or procedure predicts future job performance. The better or more accurate the prediction of future job performance, the more valid a test is said to be.

As this example illustrates, **selection** is the process of gathering information about job applicants to decide who should be offered a job. To make sure that selection decisions are accurate and legally defendable, the *Uniform Guidelines on Employee Selection Procedures* recommend that all selection procedures be validated. **Validation** is the process of determining how well a selection test or procedure predicts future job performance. The better or more accurate the prediction of future job performance, the more valid a test is said to be. See the "What Really Works" section of this chapter for more on the validity of common selection tests and procedures.

Let's examine common selection procedures, such as 3.1 application forms and résumés, 3.2 references and background checks, 3.3 selection tests, and 3.4 interviews.

3.1 Application Forms and Résumés

The first selection devices that most job applicants encounter when they seek a job are application forms and résumés. Both contain similar information about job applicants, such as name, address, job and educational history, and so forth. Though an organization's application form often asks for information already provided by the applicant's résumé, most organizations prefer to collect this information in their own format for entry into a human resource information system.

Employment laws apply to application forms, as they do to all selection devices. Application forms may ask applicants for only valid, job-related information. Nonetheless, application forms commonly ask applicants for non-job-related information, such as marital status, maiden name, age, or date of high school graduation. Indeed, one study found that 73 percent of organizations have application forms that violate at least one federal or state law.[31] Exhibit 12.4 lists the kinds of information that companies may not request in application forms, during job interviews, or in any other part of the selection process. As attorney Tiberio Trimmer says, "Your objective is to hire someone qualified to perform the requirements of the job. Not asking things that are peripheral to the work itself helps you to stay on the right side of the law."[32]

Companies should also be aware that employment laws in other countries may differ from U.S. laws. For instance, in France, employers may ask for non-job-related personal information such as your age or the

DOING THE RIGHT THING

Don't Embellish Your Résumé

Your résumé is supposed to help you get the interview that can get you a job. So where do you draw the line between making yourself look attractive to a potential employer and lying? Despite the strong temptation to improve your odds of getting a job, embellishing your résumé is wrong. Moreover, the information on your résumé is legally binding. If you misrepresent information or lie on your résumé, and many do (see page 331), you're breaking the law and can be fired. But where should you draw the line? In general, if what you put on your résumé feels wrong, don't do it. More specifically, don't embellish job titles, responsibilities, employment dates, college degrees, certifications, general qualifications, or previous experience in any way. Do the right thing: Tell the truth on your résumé.[33]

exhibit 12.4

Topics That Employers Should Avoid in Application Forms, Interviews, or Other Parts of the Selection Process

1. *Children.* Don't ask applicants if they have children, plan to have them, or have or need child care. Questions about children can unintentionally single out women.
2. *Age.* Because of the Age Discrimination in Employment Act, employers cannot ask job applicants their age during the hiring process. Since most people graduate high school at the age of 18, even asking for high school graduation dates could violate the law.
3. *Disabilities.* Don't ask if applicants have physical or mental disabilities. According to the Americans with Disabilities Act, disabilities (and reasonable accommodations for them) cannot be discussed until a job offer has been made.
4. *Physical characteristics.* Don't ask for information about height, weight, or other physical characteristics. Questions about weight could be construed as leading to discrimination toward overweight people, who studies show are less likely to be hired in general.
5. *Name.* Yes, you can ask people for their name, but you cannot ask female applicants for their maiden name because it indicates marital status. Asking for a maiden name could also lead to charges that the organization was trying to establish a candidate's ethnic background.
6. *Citizenship.* Asking applicants about citizenship could lead to claims of discrimination on the basis of national origin. However, according to the Immigration Reform and Control Act, companies may ask applicants if they have a legal right to work in the United States.
7. *Lawsuits.* Applicants may not be asked if they have ever filed a lawsuit against an employer. Federal and state laws prevent this to protect whistleblowers from retaliation by future employers.
8. *Arrest records.* Applicants cannot be asked about their arrest records. Arrests don't have legal standing. However, applicants can be asked whether they have been convicted of a crime.
9. *Smoking.* Applicants cannot be asked if they smoke. Smokers might be able to claim that they weren't hired because of fears of higher absenteeism and medical costs. However, they can be asked if they are aware of company policies that restrict smoking at work.
10. *AIDS/HIV.* Applicants can't be asked about AIDS, HIV, or any other medical condition. Questions of this nature would violate the Americans with Disabilities Act, as well as federal and state civil rights laws.

Source: J. S. Pouliot, "Topics to Avoid with Applicants," Nation's Business *80, no. 7 (1992): 57.*

number of children you have. And most French employers expect you to include a picture of yourself with your curriculum vitae (i.e., résumé).[34] Consequently, companies should closely examine their application forms, interview questions, and other selection procedures for compliance with the law wherever they do business.

Résumés also pose problems for companies, but in a different way. Studies show that as many as one of every three job applicants intentionally falsifies some information on his or her résumé and that 80 percent of the information on résumés may be misleading. A study of 200,000 job applicants found that 20 percent of applicants listed college degrees they hadn't earned, 30 percent changed the dates of their employment, 40 percent reported much higher salaries, 30 percent incorrectly described their previous jobs, 27 percent falsified their references, and 25 percent reported working at nonexistent or no longer existing companies, where the fact that they never worked

PERSONAL PRODUCTIVITY T!P

Using a Reference Release Form

Employment references are often reluctant to talk. Encourage them to share information by having applicants sign a reference release form like this:

> I have applied for employment with [company name] and have listed you as a reference. Please provide answers to the following questions and return this form to [company contact] in the enclosed envelope. By this authorization, I hereby release you from any liability or action based upon the content of your answers.
>
> Thank you for your cooperation and assistance.
>
> Sincerely yours,
> [candidate signature]
> [date]

And when references talk, listen carefully to how they answer the questions (e.g., hesitancy, damning with faint praise).[37]

there couldn't be discovered.[35] Therefore, managers should verify the information collected via résumés and application forms by comparing it with additional information collected during interviews and other stages of the selection process. Another way to check résumé information is to hire a private firm to do it. Costs vary but can often be as low as $50 per person. Cynthia Myers, who runs a company that verifies résumé information, says that companies can discourage false résumés by including this warning on their application forms and recruiting literature: "All information on this form is checked by a national agency that specializes in checking credentials. If any false claims are uncovered, that applicant will no longer be considered for a position."[36]

3.2 References and Background Checks

Nearly all companies ask an applicant to provide **employment references**, such as previous employers or coworkers, that they can contact to learn more about the candidate. **Background checks** are used to verify the truthfulness and accuracy of information that applicants provide about themselves and to uncover negative, job-related background information not provided by applicants. Unfortunately, previous employers are increasingly reluctant to provide references or background check information for fear of being sued by previous employees for defamation. If former employers provide potential employers with unsubstantiated information that damages applicants' chances of being hired, applicants can (and do) sue for defamation. Many companies provide only dates of employment, positions held, and date of separation.

employment references
sources such as previous employers or coworkers who can provide job-related information about job candidates

background checks
procedures used to verify the truthfulness and accuracy of information that applicants provide about themselves and to uncover negative, job-related background information not provided by applicants

When previous employers decline to provide meaningful references or background information, they put other employers at risk of *negligent hiring* lawsuits, in which an employer is held liable for the actions of an employee who would not have been hired if the employer had conducted a thorough reference search and background check. But with previous employers generally unwilling to give full, candid references and with negligent hiring lawsuits awaiting companies that don't get such references and background information, what can companies do? Dig deeper for more information. Ask references to provide references.

Inform the applicant in writing before checking references or running a background check. This, in itself, is often enough to get applicants to share information that they previously withheld. Keep your findings confidential to minimize the chances of a defamation charge, and always document all reference and background checks, noting who was called and what information was obtained. And to reduce the likelihood that negligent hiring lawsuits will succeed, it's particularly important to document which companies and people refused to share reference check and background information.

3.3 Selection Tests

Why do some people do well in jobs while other people do poorly? If only you could know before deciding who to hire! Selection tests give organizational decision makers a chance to know who will likely do well in a job and who won't.

The basic idea behind selection testing is to have applicants take a test that measures something directly or indirectly related to doing well on the job. The selection tests discussed here are specific ability tests, cognitive ability tests, biographical data, personality tests, and work sample tests.

specific ability tests (aptitude tests)
tests that measure the extent to which an applicant possesses the particular kind of ability needed to do a job well

Specific ability tests measure the extent to which an applicant possesses the particular kind of ability needed to do a job well. Specific ability tests are also called **aptitude tests** because they measure aptitude for doing a particular task well. For example, if you took the SAT to get into college, then you've taken the aptly named Scholastic Aptitude Test, which is one of the best predictors of how well students will do in college (i.e., scholastic performance). Specific ability tests also exist for mechanical, clerical, sales, and physical work. For example, clerical workers have to be good at accurately reading and scanning numbers as they type or enter data.

cognitive ability tests
tests that measure the extent to which applicants have abilities in perceptual speed, verbal comprehension, numerical aptitude, general reasoning, and spatial aptitude

Cognitive ability tests measure the extent to which applicants have abilities in perceptual speed, verbal comprehension, numerical aptitude, general reasoning, and spatial aptitude. In other words, these tests indicate how quickly and how well people understand words, numbers, logic, and spatial dimensions. Whereas specific ability tests predict job performance in only particular types of jobs, cognitive ability tests accurately predict job performance in almost all kinds of jobs.[38] Why is this so? Because people with strong cognitive or mental abilities are usually good at learning new things, processing complex information, solving problems, and making decisions, and these abilities are important in almost all jobs. In fact, cognitive ability tests are almost always the best predictors of job performance. Consequently, if you were allowed to use just one selection test, cognitive ability tests would be the one to use. (In practice, though, companies use a battery of different tests because doing so leads to much more accurate selection decisions.)

biographical data (biodata)
extensive surveys that ask applicants questions about their personal backgrounds and life experiences

Biographical data, or **biodata**, are extensive surveys that ask applicants questions about their personal backgrounds and life experiences. The basic idea behind biodata is that past behavior (personal background and life experience) is the best predictor of future behavior. For example, during World War II, the U.S. Air Force had to quickly test tens of thousands of men without flying experience to determine who was likely to be a good pilot. Since flight training took several months and was very expensive, selecting the right people for training was important. After examining extensive biodata, it found that one of the best predictors of success in flight school was whether students had ever built model airplanes that actually flew. This one biodata item was almost as good a predictor as the entire set of selection tests that the Air Force was using at the time.[39]

Most biodata questionnaires have over 100 items that gather information about habits and attitudes, health, interpersonal relations, money, what it was like growing up in your family (parents, siblings, childhood years, teen years), personal habits, current home (spouse, children), hobbies, education and training, values, preferences, and work.[40] In general, biodata are very good predictors of future job performance, especially in entry-level jobs.

You may have noticed that some of the information requested in biodata surveys also appears in Exhibit 12.4 as topics employers should avoid in applications, interviews, or other parts of the selection process. This information can be requested in biodata questionnaires provided that the company can demonstrate that the information is job related (i.e., valid) and does not result in adverse impact against protected groups of job applicants. Biodata surveys should be validated and tested for adverse impact before using them to make selection decisions.[41]

personality tests
tests that measure the extent to which applicants possess different kinds of job-related personality dimensions

Personality is the relatively stable set of behaviors, attitudes, and emotions displayed over time that makes people different from each other. **Personality tests** measure the extent to which applicants possess different kinds of job-related personality dimensions. Research indicates that there are five major personality dimensions (the Big 5)—extraversion, emotional stability, agreeableness, conscientiousness, and openness to experience—that are related to work behavior.[42] Of these, only conscientiousness, the degree to which someone is organized, hardworking, responsible, persevering, thorough, and achievement oriented, predicts job performance across a wide variety of jobs. Conscientiousness works especially well in combination with cognitive ability tests, allowing companies to select applicants who are organized, hardworking, responsible, and smart!

work sample tests
tests that require applicants to perform tasks that are actually done on the job

Work sample tests, also called *performance tests*, require applicants to perform tasks that are actually done on the job. So, unlike specific ability, cognitive ability, biographical data, and personality tests, which are indirect predictors of job performance, work sample tests directly measure job applicants' capability to do the job. At Microtraining Plus, a company that does computer training, employee-trainers have to be able to get up in front of people they don't know and present complex information in a clear, interesting way. Therefore, CEO David Knise uses work sample tests by having job candidates make hour-long presentations to his staff on any topic *other* than computers. By asking applicants to give an hour-long presentation, "We see how applicants organize their thoughts, if they've given themselves enough time to cover the material, and if they have overall command of a classroom."[43] These work sample presentations give Microtraining direct evidence of whether job candidates can do the job if they are hired. Work sample tests generally do a very good job of predicting future job performance; however, they can be expensive to administer and can be used for only one kind of job. For example, at an auto dealership, a work sample test for mechanics could not be used as a selection test for sales representatives.

Are tests perfect predictors of job performance? No, they aren't. Some people who do well on selection tests will do poorly in their jobs. Likewise, some people who do poorly on selection tests (and therefore weren't hired) would have been very good performers. Nonetheless, valid tests will minimize these selection errors (hiring people who should not have been hired, and not hiring people who should have been hired) while maximizing correct selection decisions (hiring people who should have been hired, and not hiring people who should not have been hired). In short, tests increase the chances that you'll hire the right person for the job, that is, someone who turns out to be a good performer. So, while tests aren't perfect, almost nothing predicts future job performance as well as the selection tests discussed here. For more on how well selection tests increase the odds of hiring the right person for the job, see the "What Really Works" section of this chapter.

3.4 Interviews

interviews
a selection tool in which company representatives ask job applicants job-related questions to determine whether they are qualified for the job

In **interviews**, company representatives ask job applicants job-related questions to determine whether they are qualified for the job. Interviews are probably the most frequently used and relied on selection device. There are several basic kinds of interviews: unstructured, structured, and semistructured.

In *unstructured interviews*, interviewers are free to ask applicants anything they want, and studies show that they do. Because interviewers often disagree about which questions should be asked during interviews, different

WHAT REALLY WORKS

USING SELECTION TESTS TO HIRE GOOD WORKERS

Hiring new employees is always something of a gamble. When you say, "We'd like to offer you a job," you never know how it's going to turn out. Nonetheless, the selection tests discussed in this chapter and reviewed in this section can go a long way toward taking the gambling aspect out of the hiring process. Indeed, more than 1,000 studies based on over 100,000 study participants strongly indicate that selection tests can give employers a much better than average (50–50) chance of hiring the right workers. In fact, if you had odds like these working for you in Las Vegas, you'd make so much money the casinos wouldn't let you in the door.

Cognitive Ability Tests

There is a 76 percent chance that applicants who do well on cognitive ability tests will be much better performers in their jobs than applicants who do not do well on such tests.

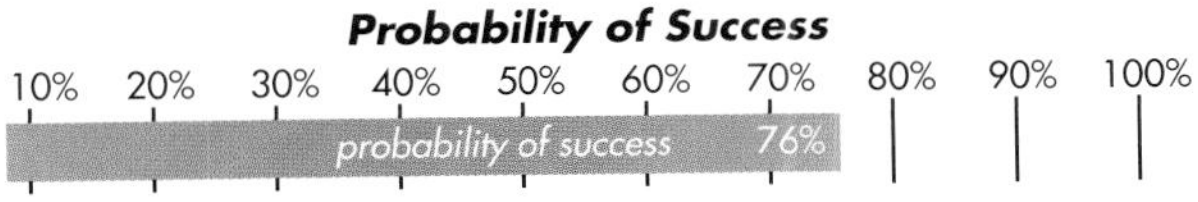

Work Sample Tests

There is a 77 percent chance that applicants who do well on work sample tests will be much better performers in their jobs than applicants who do not do well on such tests.

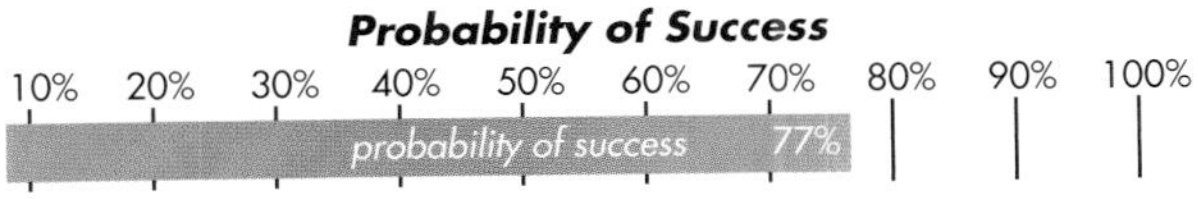

Structured Interviews

There is a 76 percent chance that applicants who do well in structured interviews will be much better performers in their jobs than applicants who do not do well in such interviews.

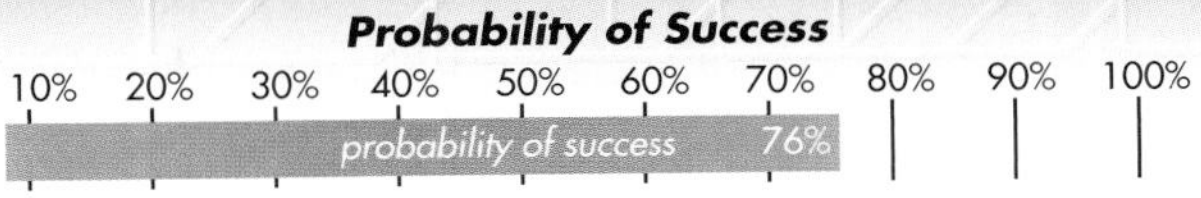

Cognitive Ability + Work Sample Tests

When deciding who to hire, most companies use a number of tests to make even more accurate selection decisions. There is an 82 percent chance that applicants who do well on a combination of cognitive ability tests and work sample tests will be much better performers in their jobs than applicants who do not do well on both tests.

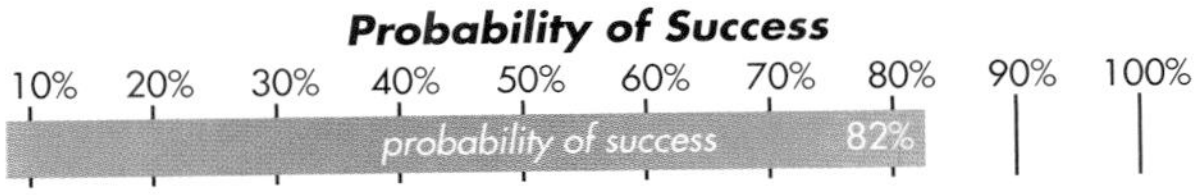

Cognitive Ability + Integrity Tests

There is an 83 percent chance that applicants who do well on a combination of cognitive ability tests and integrity tests (see Chapter 3 for a discussion of integrity tests) will be much better performers in their jobs than applicants who do not do well on both tests.

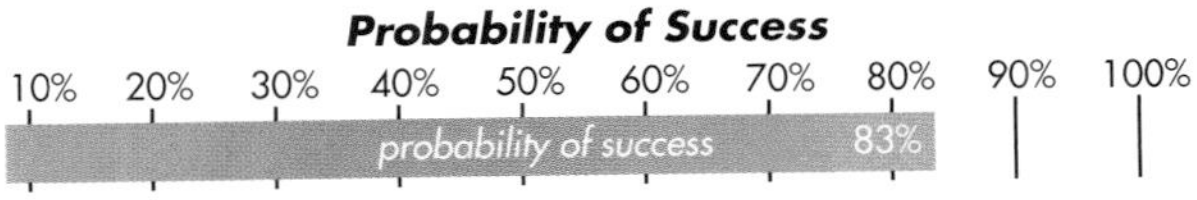

Cognitive Ability + Structured Interviews

There is an 82 percent chance that applicants who do well on a combination of cognitive ability tests and structured interviews will be much better performers in their jobs than applicants who do not do well on both tests.[44]

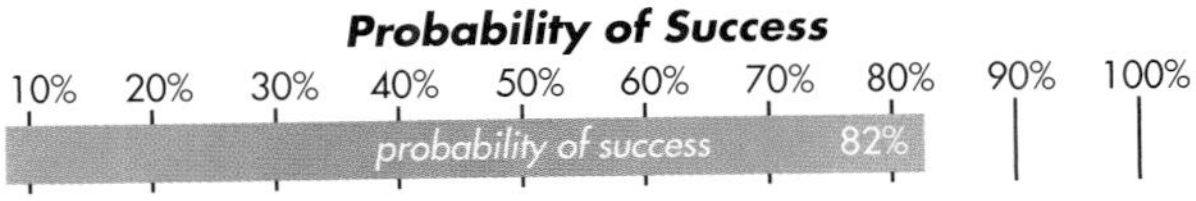

interviewers tend to ask applicants very different questions.[45] Furthermore, individual interviewers even seem to have a tough time asking the same questions from one interview to the next. This high level of inconsistency lowers the validity of unstructured interviews as a selection device because comparing applicant responses can be difficult. As a result, unstructured interviews

PERSONAL PRODUCTIVITY TIP

Preparing for Structured Interviews

Structured interviews assume that past performance predicts future performance. Therefore, structured interview questions often begin with "Tell me about a time when . . . " or "Give me an example of . . . ." Use the P-A-R (Problem-Action-Result) technique to prepare for structured interviews. Go through the job description and your résumé line by line to think up examples and stories. Then write, edit, and rehearse them in the P-A-R format. For variety, use the R-A-P approach, too. Start by describing your results. Then describe your actions. Finish by describing the problem you solved. You're less likely to be stumped by questions if you prepare in this way.[46]

are about half as accurate as structured interviews at predicting which job applicants should be hired.

By contrast, with **structured interviews**, standardized interview questions are prepared ahead of time so that all applicants are asked the same job-related questions. Four kinds of questions are typically asked in structured interviews:

- *situational questions*, which ask applicants how they would respond in a hypothetical situation (e.g., "What would you do if . . . ?").
- *behavioral questions*, which ask applicants what they did in previous jobs that were similar to the job for which they are applying (e.g., "In your previous jobs, tell me about . . . . ").
- *background questions*, which ask applicants about their work experience, education, and other qualifications (e.g., "Tell me about the training you received at . . . . ").
- *job-knowledge questions*, which ask applicants to demonstrate their job knowledge (e.g., for nurses, "Give me an example of a time when one of your patients had a severe reaction to a medication. How did you handle it?").[47]

structured interviews interviews in which all applicants are asked the same set of standardized questions, usually including situational, behavioral, background, and job-knowledge questions

The primary advantage of structured interviews is that asking all applicants the same questions makes comparing applicants much easier. Structuring interviews also ensures that interviewers ask only for important, job-related information. Not only are the accuracy, usefulness, and validity of the interview improved, but the chances that interviewers will ask questions about topics that violate employment laws are reduced.

Semistructured interviews are in between structured and unstructured interviews. A major part of the semistructured interview (perhaps as much as 80 percent) is based on structured questions, but some time is set aside for unstructured interviewing to allow the interviewer to probe into ambiguous or missing information uncovered during the structured portion of the interview.

How well do interviews predict future job performance? Contrary to what you've probably heard, recent evidence indicates that even unstructured interviews do a fairly good job.[48] When conducted properly, however, structured in-terviews can lead to much more accurate hiring decisions than unstructured interviews. In some cases, the validity of structured interviews can rival that of cognitive ability tests. But even more important, since interviews are especially good at assessing applicants' interpersonal skills, they work particularly well with cognitive ability tests. The combination (i.e., smart people who work well with others) leads to even better selection decisions than using either alone. Exhibit 12.5 provides a set of guidelines for conducting effective structured employment interviews.

Review 3
Selection

Selection is the process of gathering information about job applicants to decide who should be offered a job. Accurate selection procedures are valid, are legally defendable, and improve organizational performance. Application forms

exhibit 12.5

Guidelines for Conducting Effective Structured Interviews

INTERVIEW STAGE	WHAT TO DO
Planning the Interview	• Identify and define the knowledge, skills, abilities, and other (KSAO) characteristics needed for successful job performance.
	• For each essential KSAO, develop key behavioral questions that will elicit examples of past accomplishments, activities, and performance.
	• For each KSAO, develop a list of things to look for in the applicant's responses to key questions.
Conducting the Interview	• Create a relaxed, nonstressful interview atmosphere.
	• Review the applicant's application form, résumé, and other information.
	• Allocate enough time to complete the interview without interruption.
	• Put the applicant at ease; don't jump right into heavy questioning.
	• Tell the applicant what to expect. Explain the interview process.
	• Obtain job-related information from the applicant by asking those questions prepared for each KSAO.
	• Describe the job and the organization to the applicant. Applicants need adequate information to make a selection decision about the organization.
After the Interview	• Immediately after the interview, review your notes and make sure they are complete.
	• Evaluate the applicant on each essential KSAO.
	• Determine each applicant's probability of success and make a hiring decision.

Source: B. M. Farrell, "The Art and Science of Employment Interviews," Personnel Journal *65 (1986): 91–94.*

and résumés are the most common selection devices. Because many application forms request illegal, non-job-related information, and because as many as one-third of job applicants falsify information on résumés, these procedures are often of little value in making hiring decisions. References and background checks can also be problematic, given that previous employers are reluctant to provide such information for fear of being sued for defamation. Unfortunately, the lack of this information puts other employers at risk of negligent hiring lawsuits. Selection tests generally do the best job of predicting applicants' future job performance. In general, cognitive ability tests, biographical data, and work sample tests are the most valid tests, followed by personality tests and specific ability tests, which are still good predictors. Selection tests aren't perfect predictors of job performance, but almost nothing predicts future job performance as well as selection tests. The three kinds of job interviews are unstructured, structured, and semistructured interviews. Of these, structured interviews work best, because they ensure that all applicants are consistently asked the same situational, behavioral, background, or job-knowledge questions.

Developing Qualified Workers

Harmon Industries, which makes signaling and communications equipment for the railway and transit industries, has a new training center where its employees learn engineering, safety, teamwork, time management, and other workplace skills. Ron Breshears, Harmon's vice president of human resources and safety, says, "Training is an investment, not a cost. Once you see that, you see that you get a good return on your investment."[49] Indeed, according to the American Society for Training and Development, an investment in training increases productivity by an average of 17 percent, reduces employee turnover, and makes companies more profitable.[50]

Giving employees the knowledge and skills they need to improve their performance is just the first step in developing employees, however. The second step, and not enough companies do this, is giving employees formal feedback about their actual job performance. A CEO of a large telecommunications company hired an outside consultant to assess and coach (i.e., provide feedback) the company's top 50 managers. To the CEO's surprise, 75 percent of those managers indicated that the feedback they received from the consultant regarding their strengths and weaknesses was the only substantial feedback they had received about their performance in the last five years. On a more positive note, as a result of that feedback, two-thirds of the managers then took positive steps to improve their skills, knowledge, and job performance and expressed a clear desire for more feedback, especially from their boss, the CEO.[51] So, in today's competitive business environment, even top managers understand the importance of formal performance feedback to their growth and development.

After reading the next two sections, you should be able to

4 describe how to select the appropriate training methods.

5 discuss how to use performance appraisal to give meaningful performance feedback.

4 Training

training
developing the skills, experience, and knowledge employees need to perform their jobs or improve their performance

Training means providing opportunities for employees to develop the job-specific skills, experience, and knowledge they need to do their jobs or improve their performance. American companies spend more than $60 billion a year on training. To make sure those training dollars are well spent, companies need to 4.1 select appropriate training methods and 4.2 evaluate training.

4.1 Training Methods

Assume that you're a training director for a bank and that you're in charge of making sure that all bank employees know what to do in case of a robbery. Exhibit 12.6 lists a number of training methods you could use: films and videos, lectures, planned readings, case studies, coaching and mentoring, group discussions, on-the-job training, role-playing, simulations and games, vestibule training, and computer-based learning. Which method would be best?

To choose the best method, you should consider a number of factors, such as the number of people to be trained, the cost of training, and the objectives of the training. For instance, if the training objective is to impart information or knowledge to trainees, then you should use films and videos, lectures, and

exhibit 12.6

Training Objectives and Methods

TRAINING OBJECTIVE	TRAINING METHOD
Impart Information and Knowledge	• *Films and videos.* Films and videos share information, illustrate problems and solutions, and effectively hold trainees' attention.
	• *Lectures:* Trainees listen to instructors' oral presentations.
	• *Planned readings.* Trainees read about concepts or ideas before attending training.
Develop Analytical and Problem-Solving Skills	• *Case studies.* Cases are analyzed and discussed in small groups. The cases present a specific problem or decision, and trainees develop methods for solving the problem or making the decision.
	• *Coaching and mentoring.* Coaching and mentoring of trainees by managers involves informal advice, suggestions, and guidance. This method is helpful for reinforcing other kinds of training and for trainees who benefit from support and personal encouragement.
	• *Group discussions.* Small groups of trainees actively discuss specific topics. The instructor may perform the role of discussion leader.
Practice, Learn, or Change Job Behaviors	• *On-the-job training (OJT).* New employees are assigned to experienced employees. The trainee learns by watching the experienced employee perform the job and eventually by working alongside the experienced employee. Gradually, the trainee is left on his or her own to perform the job.
	• *Role-playing.* Trainees assume job-related roles and practice new behaviors by acting out what they would do in job-related situations.
	• *Simulations and games.* Experiential exercises place trainees in realistic job-related situations and give them the opportunity to experience a job-related condition in a relatively low-cost setting. The trainee benefits from "hands-on experience" before actually performing the job where mistakes may be more costly.
	• *Vestibule training.* Procedures and equipment similar to those used in the actual job are set up in a special area called a "vestibule." The trainee is then taught how to perform the job at his or her own pace without disrupting the actual flow of work, making costly mistakes, or exposing the trainee and others to dangerous conditions.
Impart Information or Knowledge; Develop Analytical and Problem-Solving Skills; Practice, Learn, or Change Job Behaviors	• *Computer-based learning.* Interactive videos, software, CD-ROMs, personal computers, teleconferencing, and the Internet may be combined to present multimedia-based training.

Source: A. Fowler, "How to Decide on Training Methods," People Management *25, no. 1 (1995): 36.*

planned readings. In our robbery training example, trainees would hear, see, or read about what to do in case of a robbery.

If developing analytical and problem-solving skills is the objective, then use case studies, group discussions, and coaching and mentoring. In our example, trainees would read about a real robbery, discuss what to do, and then talk to people who had been through robberies.

www.experiencing management.com

Gain additional insight about the training and development process at our animated concept and activity site. Choose Human_Resources from the "select a topic" pull-down menu, then Training and Development Process from the "overview tab."

http://www.experiencingmanagement.com

If practicing, learning, or changing job behaviors is the objective, then use on-the-job training, role-playing, simulations and games, and vestibule training. In our example, trainees would learn about robbery situations on the job, pretend that they were in a robbery situation, or participate in a highly realistic mock robbery.

If training is supposed to meet more than one of these objectives, then your best choice may be to combine one of the previous methods with computer-based training. These days, many more companies are doing just that by adopting Internet training or "e-learning." Internet training or e-learning can offer several advantages. Because employees don't need to leave their jobs, travel costs are greatly reduced. Also, because employees can take training modules when it is convenient, workplace productivity should increase and employee stress should decrease. Finally, Internet training and e-learning can be much faster than traditional training methods.

But Internet training is not always the appropriate training method. Although it can be a good way to impart information, it isn't nearly as effective for changing job behaviors or developing problem-solving and analytical skills. Plus it requires a significant investment in computers and high-speed Internet and network connections for all employees.

4.2 Evaluating Training

After selecting a training method and conducting the training, the last step is to evaluate the training. Training can be evaluated in four ways: on *reactions*, how satisfied trainees were with the program; on *learning*, how much employees improved their knowledge or skills; on *behavior*, how much employees actually changed their on-the-job behavior because of training; or on *results*, how much training improved job performance, such as increased sales or quality, or decreased costs.[52] For example, Aetna Healthcare found that its computer-based training led to higher levels of learning and saved the company $5 million a year in travel costs.[53]

Review 4
Training

Training is used to give employees the job-specific skills, experience, and knowledge they need to do their jobs or improve their job performance. To make sure training dollars are well spent, companies need to select appropriate training methods and then evaluate the training. Selection of an appropriate training method depends on a number of factors, such as the number of people to be trained, the cost of training, and the objectives of the training. If training is supposed to meet multiple objectives, then it may be best to combine one of the traditional methods with computer-based training. Training can be evaluated on reactions, learning, behavior, or results.

5 Performance Appraisal

performance appraisal
the process of assessing how well employees are doing their jobs

Performance appraisal is the process of assessing how well employees are doing their jobs. Most employees and managers intensely dislike the performance appraisal process. One manager said, "I hate annual performance reviews. I hated them when I used to get them, and I hate them now that I give them. If I had to choose between performance reviews and paper cuts, I'd take

www.experiencing management.com

Managers use performance appraisals for two purposes—development and evaluation of employees. Learn more about these uses by visiting our animated concept and activity site. Choose Human_Resources from the "select a topic" pull-down menu, then Performance Appraisal Process from the "overview tab."

http://www.experiencingmanagement.com

paper cuts every time."[54] Unfortunately, attitudes like this are all too common. In fact, 70 percent of employees are dissatisfied with the performance appraisal process in their companies. Likewise, according to the Society for Human Resource Management, 90 percent of human resource managers are dissatisfied with the performance appraisal systems used by their companies.[55]

Because performance appraisals are used for so many important purposes, companies with poor performance appraisal systems face tremendous problems. For example, performance appraisals are used as a basis for compensation, promotion, and training decisions. In human resource planning, performance appraisals are used for career planning and for making termination decisions.[56] And because of their key role in so many organizational decisions, performance appraisals are also central to many of the lawsuits that employees (or former employees) file against employers.

Let's explore how companies can avoid some of these problems with performance appraisals by 5.1 **accurately measuring job performance** and 5.2 **effectively sharing performance feedback with employees.**

5.1 Accurately Measuring Job Performance

Workers often have strong doubts about the accuracy of their performance appraisals—and they may be right. For example, it's widely known that assessors are prone to errors when rating worker performance. Three of the most common rating errors are central tendency, halo, and leniency. *Central tendency error* occurs when assessors rate all workers as average or in the middle of the scale. *Halo error* occurs when assessors rate all workers as performing at the same level (good, bad, or average) in all parts of their jobs. *Leniency error* occurs when assessors rate all workers as performing particularly well. One of the reasons that managers make these errors is that they often don't spend enough time gathering or reviewing performance data.

What can be done to minimize rating errors and improve the accuracy with which job performance is measured? In general, two approaches have been used: improving performance appraisal measures themselves and training performance raters to be more accurate.

One of the ways companies try to improve performance appraisal measures is to use as many objective performance measures as possible. **Objective performance measures** are measures of performance that are easily and directly counted or quantified. Common objective performance measures include output, scrap, waste, sales, customer complaints, or rejection rates.

objective performance measures
measures of job performance that are easily and directly counted or quantified

But when objective performance measures aren't available, and frequently they aren't, subjective performance measures have to be used instead. **Subjective performance measures** require that someone judge or assess a worker's performance. The most common kind of subjective performance measure is the trait rating scale shown in Exhibit 12.7. **Trait rating scales**, also called *graphic rating scales*, ask raters to indicate the extent to which a worker possesses a particular trait or characteristic, such as reliability or honesty. Unfortunately, trait rating scales are typically inaccurate measures of performance. Not only are managers notoriously poor judges of employee traits, but the traits are not related to job performance in any meaningful way.

subjective performance measures
measures of job performance that require someone to judge or assess a worker's performance

trait rating scales
rating scales that indicate the extent to which workers possess particular traits or characteristics

exhibit 12.7

Subjective Performance Appraisal Scales

TRAIT RATING SCALE	STRONGLY DISAGREE	1 2 3 4 5	STRONGLY AGREE
1. Employee is a hard worker.		1 2 3 4 5	
2. Employee is reliable.		1 2 3 4 5	
3. Employee is trustworthy.		1 2 3 4 5	
BEHAVIORAL OBSERVATION SCALE *Dimension: Customer Service*	ALMOST NEVER	1 2 3 4 5	ALMOST ALWAYS
1. Greets customers with a smile and a "hello."		1 2 3 4 5	
2. Calls other stores to help customers find merchandise that is not in stock.		1 2 3 4 5	
3. Promptly handles customer concerns and complaints.		1 2 3 4 5	
Dimension: Money Handling	ALMOST NEVER	1 2 3 4 5	ALMOST ALWAYS
1. Accurately makes change from customer transactions.		1 2 3 4 5	
2. Accounts balance at the end of the day, no shortages or surpluses.		1 2 3 4 5	
3. Accurately records transactions in computer system.		1 2 3 4 5	

behavioral observation scales (BOSs)
rating scales that indicate the frequency with which workers perform specific behaviors that are representative of the job dimensions critical to successful job performance

So, instead of using trait rating scales, subjective performance should be measured using behavioral observation scales. **Behavioral observation scales (BOSs)** ask raters to rate the frequency with which workers perform specific behaviors representative of the job dimensions that are critical to successful job performance. Exhibit 12.7 shows a BOS for two important job dimensions for a retail salesperson: customer service and money handling. Notice that each dimension lists several specific behaviors characteristic of a worker who excels in that dimension of job performance. (Normally, the scale would list 7 to 12 items per dimension, not 3, as in the exhibit.) Not only do BOSs work well for rating critical dimensions of performance, but studies also show that managers strongly prefer BOSs for giving performance feedback; accurately differentiating between poor, average, and good workers; identifying training needs; and accurately measuring performance.

rater training
training performance appraisal raters in how to avoid rating errors and increase rating accuracy

The second approach to improving the measurement of workers' job performance is rater training. In **rater training**, performance raters are trained to avoid rating errors (i.e., central tendency, halo, and leniency) and to improve rating accuracy. In rater training designed to minimize rating errors, trainees view videotapes of managers observing an employee performing some aspect of a job. Following each video, trainees are asked how they would have rated the worker's performance and how the manager on the tape would have rated it. Each videotape, however, is an example of the different kinds of rating errors. So trainees have a chance to observe rating errors being made (by the manager in the videotape) and then discuss how to avoid those errors.

Another common form of rater training stresses rater accuracy (rather than minimizing errors). Here, raters closely examine the key dimensions of job performance (e.g., customer service and money handling for the retail salesperson in our example) and discuss specific behaviors representative of each dimension. Trainees may then be asked to role-play examples of these behaviors or to watch videos containing behavioral examples of each dimension of job performance. Both kinds of rater training are effective.[57]

5.2 Sharing Performance Feedback

After gathering accurate performance data, the next step is to share performance feedback with employees. Unfortunately, even when performance appraisal ratings are accurate, the appraisal process often breaks down at the feedback stage. Employees become defensive and dislike hearing any negative assessments of their work, no matter how small. Managers become defensive, too, and dislike giving appraisal feedback as much as employees dislike receiving it. One manager said, "I agree that the typical annual-review process does nothing but harm. It creates divisions. It undermines morale. It makes people angry, jealous, and cynical. It unleashes a whole lot of negative energy, and the organization gets nothing in return."[58]

What can be done to overcome the inherent difficulties in performance appraisal feedback sessions? Since performance appraisal ratings have traditionally been the judgments of just one person, the boss, one approach is to use **360-degree feedback**. In this approach, feedback comes from four sources: the boss, subordinates, peers and coworkers, and the employees themselves. The data, which are obtained anonymously (except for the boss), are then compiled into a feedback report comparing the employee's self-ratings to those of the boss, subordinates, and peers and coworkers. The advantage of 360-degree programs is that negative feedback ("You don't listen.") is often more credible when it is heard from several people.

360-degree feedback
a performance appraisal process in which feedback is obtained from the boss, subordinates, peers and coworkers, and the employees themselves

A word of caution, though. About half of the companies using 360-degree feedback for performance appraisal now use the feedback only for developmental purposes. They found that sometimes with raises and promotions on the line, peers and subordinates would give high ratings in order to get high ratings from others and that they would also distort ratings to harm competitors or help people they liked. A senior manager at a New York City marketing company agrees, saying that 360-degree feedback "also allows people to vent their frustrations and anger on bosses and colleagues in an insensitive way."[59] On the other hand, studies clearly show that ratees prefer to receive feedback from multiple raters, so 360-degree feedback is likely to continue to grow in popularity.[60]

Herbert Meyer, who has been studying performance appraisal feedback for more than 30 years, makes three specific recommendations for sharing performance feedback with employees.[61] First, managers should separate developmental feedback, which is designed to improve future performance, from administrative feedback, which is used as a reward for past performance, such as for raises. When managers give developmental feedback, they're acting as coaches, but when they give administrative feedback, they're acting as judges. These roles, coaches and judges, are clearly incompatible. As coaches, managers are encouraging, pointing out opportunities for growth and improvement, and employees are typically open and receptive to feedback. But as judges, managers are evaluative, and employees are typically defensive and closed to feedback.

Second, Meyer suggests that performance appraisal feedback sessions be based on self-appraisals, in which employees carefully assess their own strengths, weaknesses, successes, and failures in writing. Because employees play an active role in the review of their performance, managers can be coaches rather than judges. Also, because the focus is on future goals and development, both employees and managers are likely to be more satisfied with the process and more committed to future plans and changes. One concern about self-appraisals is that employees will be overly positive when evaluating their performance. When the focus is on development and not administrative assessment, however, studies show that self-appraisals lead to more candid self-assessments than traditional supervisory reviews.[62]

Third, Meyer suggests eliminating the "grading" aspect of performance appraisal, in which employees are ranked on a 1 to 5 scale or are scored as below average, average, above average, or exceptional. He says that "assigning a numerical or adjectival grade, such as 'satisfactory,' 'excellent,' 'adequate,' 'outstanding,' or 'poor' to overall performance or specific performance tends to obstruct rather than facilitate constructive discussion. It treats a mature person like a school child. The administrative action taken, such as the amount of salary increase or a promotion, will communicate an overall appraisal better than will a grade."[63] See Exhibit 12.8 for a list of topics that Meyer recommends for discussion in performance appraisal feedback sessions.

exhibit 12.8

What to Discuss in a Performance Appraisal Feedback Session

1. Overall progress—an analysis of accomplishments and shortcomings.
2. Problems encountered in meeting job requirements.
3. Opportunities to improve performance.
4. Long-range plans and opportunities—for the job and for the individual's career.
5. General discussion of possible plans and goals for the coming year.

Source: H. H. Meyer, "A Solution to the Performance Appraisal Feedback Enigma," Academy of Management Executive *5, no. 1 (1991): 68–76.*

Review 5

Performance Appraisal

Most employees and managers intensely dislike the performance appraisal process. Some of the problems associated with appraisals can be avoided, however, by accurately measuring job performance and effectively sharing performance feedback with employees. Managers are prone to three kinds of rating errors: central tendency, halo, and leniency error. One way to minimize rating errors is to use better appraisal measures, such as objective measures of performance or behavioral observation scales. Another method is to directly train performance raters to minimize errors and more accurately rate the important dimensions of job performance.

After gathering accurate performance data, the next step is to share performance feedback with employees. One way to overcome the inherent difficulties in performance appraisal feedback is to provide 360-degree feedback, in which feedback is obtained from four sources: the boss, subordinates, peers and coworkers, and the employees themselves. Feedback tends to be more credible if heard from several sources. Traditional performance appraisal feedback sessions can be improved by separating developmental and administrative feedback, by basing feedback discussions on employee self-appraisals, and by eliminating the "grading" aspect.

Keeping Qualified Workers

When Toyota built a huge new truck factory in the small town of Princeton, Indiana, and began offering extensive benefits and paying workers $19 an hour, it sent a shockwave through the pay scales of employers in the area. Not surprisingly, more than 50,000 people applied for the 1,300 jobs at Toyota's plant. Of course, many of the highly skilled workers that Toyota hired used to work for other employers for much less pay. As a result, to keep workers from jumping ship to Toyota and other high-paying companies (Alcoa pays $16.50 an hour), companies throughout the Princeton area responded by increasing their pay and benefits.[64]

Gene Weisheit, director of human resources at Evansville Veneer & Lumber Company, says that increasing wages is the only way to not be left "scraping the bottom of the barrel." Accordingly, his company raised its starting pay by 50 cents to $9 an hour. His more experienced workers now earn more than $11 an hour. Other companies, like Flanders Electric Motor Service, have focused on increasing benefits to retain workers by sponsoring teams in men's and women's bowling leagues, paying for health club memberships at the local YMCA, and conducting blood pressure screening during work hours. Unfortunately, for Princeton area companies, keeping their employees will become even more difficult when Toyota hires another 1,000 well-paid workers to build a sports utility vehicle at the same manufacturing plant.

After reading the next two sections, you should be able to

6 describe basic compensation strategies and explain how they affect human resource practice.

7 discuss the three kinds of employee separations: termination, downsizing, and turnover.

6 Compensation

compensation
the financial and nonfinancial rewards that organizations give employees in exchange for their work

Compensation includes both the financial and nonfinancial rewards that organizations give employees in exchange for their work. Let's learn more about compensation by examining the 6.1 **compensation decisions that managers must** make and 6.2 **the role that employment benefits play in compensating today's employees.**

6.1 Compensation Decisions

There are four basic kinds of compensation decisions: pay level, pay variability, pay structure, and employment benefits. We'll discuss employment benefits in the next subsection.[65]

job evaluation
a process that determines the worth of each job in a company by evaluating the market value of the knowledge, skills, and requirements needed to perform it

Pay-level decisions are decisions about whether to pay workers at a level that is below, above, or at current market wages. Companies use job evaluation to set their pay structures. **Job evaluation** determines the worth of each job by determining the market value of the knowledge, skills, and requirements needed to perform it. After conducting a job evaluation, most companies try to pay the "going rate," meaning the current market wage. There are always companies, however, whose financial situation causes them to pay considerably less than current market wages. The child-care industry, for example, has chronic difficulties filling jobs because it pays well below market wages (an average of $7.86 an hour, or $16,350 a year). As a result, the applicants it attracts are increasingly less qualified.[66]

Some companies choose to pay above-average wages to attract and keep employees. *Above-market wages* can attract a larger, more qualified pool of job applicants, increase the rate of job acceptance, decrease the time it takes to fill positions, and increase how long employees stay.[67] Of course, it's very difficult to attract and keep good employees when your company has to compete with the likes of Toyota that intentionally pays above-market wages.

Pay-variability decisions concern the extent to which employees' pay varies with individual and organizational performance. Linking pay to organizational performance is intended to increase employee motivation, effort, and job performance. Piecework, sales commissions, profit sharing, employee stock ownership plans, and stock options are common pay-variability options. For instance, under **piecework** pay plans, employees are paid a set rate for each item produced up to some standard (e.g., 35 cents per item produced for output up to 100 units per day). Once productivity exceeds the standard, employees are paid a set amount for each unit of output over the standard (e.g., 45 cents for each unit above 100 units). A sales **commission** is another kind of pay variability, in which salespeople are paid a percentage of the purchase price of items they sell. The more they sell, the more they earn.

piecework
a compensation system in which employees are paid a set rate for each item they produce

commission
a compensation system in which employees earn a percentage of each sale they make

Because pay plans such as piecework and commissions are based on individual performance, they can reduce the incentive that people have to work together. Therefore, companies also use group incentives (discussed in Chapter 11) and organizational incentives, such as profit sharing, employee stock ownership plans, and stock options, to encourage teamwork and cooperation.

Profit sharing is the payment of a portion of the organization's profits to employees over and above their regular compensation. The more profitable the company, the more profit is shared. In 2000, when Ford Motor Company reported record profits, each of its automobile assembly workers received a profit-sharing check of approximately $8,000. From 2001 to 2003, however, when Ford lost money, no one got a profit-sharing check because the company did not have any profits to distribute.[68]

profit sharing
a compensation system in which a percentage of company profits is paid to employees in addition to their regular compensation

Employee stock ownership plans (ESOPs) compensate employees by awarding them shares of the company stock in addition to their regular compensation. ESOPs are different from stock options. **Stock options** give employees the right to purchase shares of stock at a set price. Options work like this. Let's say that you are awarded the right (or option) to buy 100 shares of stock from the company for $5 a share. If the company's stock price rises to $15 a share, you can exercise your options and make $1,000. When you exercise your options, you pay the company $500 (100 shares at $5 a share), but because the stock is selling for $15 in the stock market, you can sell your 100 shares for $1,500 and make $1,000. Of course, as company profits and share values increase, stock options become even more valuable to employees. Stock options have no value, however, if the company's stock falls below the option "grant price," the price at which the options have been issued to you. To learn more about ESOPs and stock options, see The National Center for Employee Ownership (**http://www.nceo.org**).

employee stock ownership plan (ESOP)
a compensation system that awards employees shares of company stock in addition to their regular compensation

stock options
a compensation system that gives employees the right to purchase shares of stock at a set price, even if the value of the stock increases above that price

Pay-structure decisions are concerned with internal pay distributions, meaning the extent to which people in the company receive very different levels of pay.[69] With *hierarchical pay structures*, there are big differences from one pay level to another. The highest pay levels are for people near the top of the pay distribution. The basic idea behind hierarchical pay structures is that large differences in pay between jobs or organizational levels should motivate people to work harder to obtain those higher-paying jobs. Many publicly owned companies have hierarchical pay structures by virtue of the huge amounts they pay their top managers and CEOs. For example, the average CEO now makes 200 times more than the average worker (down from 475 times the pay of average workers just a few years ago).[70]

By contrast, *compressed pay structures* typically have fewer pay levels and smaller differences in pay between levels. Pay is less dispersed and more similar across jobs in the company. The basic idea behind compressed pay structures is that similar pay levels should lead to higher levels of cooperation, feelings of fairness and a common purpose, and better group and team performance.

So should companies choose hierarchical or compressed pay structures? The evidence isn't straightforward, but studies seem to indicate that there are significant problems with the hierarchical approach. The most damaging is that there appears to be little link between organizational performance and the pay of top managers.[71] Furthermore, studies of professional athletes indicate that hierarchical pay structures (e.g., paying superstars 40 to 50 times more than the lowest-paid athlete on the team) hurt the performance of teams and individual players.[72] For now, it seems that hierarchical pay structures work best for independent work, where it's easy to determine the contributions of individual performers and where little coordination with others is needed to get the job done. In other words, hierarchical pay structures work best when clear links can be drawn between individual performance and individual rewards. By contrast, compressed pay structures, that is, paying everyone similar amounts of money, seem to work best for interdependent work, which requires employees to work together. Some companies are pursuing a middle ground: they are trying to balance hierarchical and compressed pay structures by giving ordinary workers the chance to earn more through ESOPs, stock options, and profit sharing.

6.2 Employment Benefits

employment benefits
a method of rewarding employees that includes virtually any kind of compensation other than wages or salaries

Employment benefits include virtually any kind of compensation other than direct wages paid to employees.[73] Three employee benefits are mandated by law: Social Security, worker's compensation, and unemployment insurance. To attract and retain a good work force, however, most organizations offer a wide variety of benefits, including retirement plans and pensions, paid holidays, paid vacations, sick leave, health insurance, life insurance, dental care, eye care, day-care facilities, paid personal days, legal assistance, physical fitness facilities, educational assistance, and discounts on company products and services. Currently, benefits cost organizations about 28 percent of their payroll, with an average cost per employee of $13,200 for a basic benefits plan.[74]

cafeteria benefit plans (flexible benefit plans)
plans that allow employees to choose which benefits they receive, up to a certain dollar value

Managers should understand that although benefits are unlikely to improve employee motivation and performance, they do affect job satisfaction, employee decisions about staying or leaving the company, and the company's attractiveness to job applicants.[75] One way that organizations make their benefit plans more attractive is by offering **cafeteria benefit plans** or **flexible benefit plans**, which allow employees to choose which benefits they receive, up to a certain dollar value.[76] Many cafeteria or flexible benefit plans start with a core of benefits, such as health insurance and life insurance, that are available to all employees. Then employees are allowed to select other benefits that best fit their needs, up to a predetermined dollar amount. Some organizations allow employees to choose from several packages of benefits. The packages are of equivalent value, but offer a different mix of benefits. For example, older employees may prefer more benefit dollars spent on retirement plans, while younger employees may prefer additional vacation days.

The drawback to flexible benefit plans has been the high cost of administering these programs. With advances in information processing technology, however, the cost of administering benefits has begun to drop in recent years.

Review 6
Compensation

Compensation includes both the financial and nonfinancial rewards that organizations give employees in exchange for their work. There are four basic kinds of compensation decisions: pay level, pay variability, pay structure, and employment benefits. Pay-level decisions determine whether workers will receive wages below, above, or at current market levels. Pay-variability decisions concern the extent to which pay varies with individual and organizational performance. Piecework, sales commission, profit sharing, employee stock ownership plans, and stock options are common pay-variability options. Pay-structure decisions concern the extent to which people in the company receive very different levels of pay. Hierarchical pay structures work best for independent work, while compressed pay structures work best for interdependent work.

Employee benefits include virtually any kind of compensation other than direct wages paid to employees. Flexible or cafeteria benefits plans offer employees a wide variety of benefits, improve job satisfaction, increase the chances that employees will stay with companies, and make organizations more attractive to job applicants. The cost of administering benefits has begun to drop in recent years.

7 Employee Separations

employee separation
the voluntary or involuntary loss of an employee

Employee separation is a broad term covering the loss of an employee for any reason. *Involuntary separation* occurs when employers decide to terminate or lay off employees. *Voluntary separation* occurs when employees decide to quit or retire. Because employee separations affect recruiting, selection, training, and compensation, organizations should forecast the number of employees they expect to lose through terminations, layoffs, turnover, or retirements when doing human resource planning.

Let's explore employee separation by examining 7.1 terminations, 7.2 downsizing, and 7.3 turnover.

7.1 Terminating Employees

Hopefully, the words "You're fired!" have never been directed at you. Lots of people hear them, however, as more than 400,000 people a year get fired from their jobs. Getting fired is a terrible thing, but many managers make it even worse by bungling the firing process, needlessly provoking the person who was fired, and unintentionally inviting lawsuits. For example, the top office manager for a professional sports team returned to the office to find his parking space taken by someone interviewing for his job. The CEO of a clothing store company gave all of his top managers a fruit basket every holiday season, except his top finance manager who was soon fired.[77] Finally, workers at a high-tech company knew that they had been fired when their security codes no longer opened the front door to their office building.[78] How would you feel if you had been fired in one of these ways? Though firing is never pleasant (and managers hate firings nearly as much as employees do), managers can do several things to minimize the problems inherent in firing employees.

First, in most situations, firing should not be the first option. Instead, employees should be given a chance to change their behavior. When problems arise, employees should have ample warning and must be specifically informed as to the nature and seriousness of the trouble they're in. After being notified, they should be given sufficient time to change. If the problems continue, the employees should again be counseled about their job performance, what could be done to improve it, and the possible consequences if things don't change (e.g., written reprimand, suspension without pay, or firing). Sometimes this is enough to solve the problem. For example, a large hospital was getting ready to fire its director of radiology because of his bad attitude and increasing rudeness to coworkers. Rather than firing him, hospital management put him on probation and hired a consultant to counsel him about working with others. Within weeks, his attitude and behavior changed, and the hospital avoided firing him and the expense of replacing him (which could have included a lawsuit).[79] If the problem isn't corrected after several rounds of warnings and discussions, however, the employee may be terminated.[80]

Second, employees should be fired only for a good reason. Employers used to hire and fire employees under the legal principle of "employment at will," which allowed them to fire employees for a good reason, a bad reason, or no reason at all. (Employees could also quit for a good reason, a bad reason, or no reason whenever they desired.) As employees began contesting their firings in court, however, the principle of wrongful discharge emerged. **Wrongful discharge** is a legal doctrine that requires employers to have a job-related reason to terminate employees. In other words, like other major human resource decisions, termination decisions should be made on the basis of job-related factors, such as violating company rules or consistently poor performance. And with former employees winning 68 percent of wrongful discharge cases, managers should record the job-related reasons for the termination, document specific instances of rule violations or continued poor performance, and keep notes and documents from the counseling sessions held with employees.[81]

wrongful discharge
a legal doctrine that requires employers to have a job-related reason to terminate employees

Finally, to reduce the chances of a wrongful discharge suit, employees should always be fired in private. State the reason for discharge, but don't go into detail or engage in a lengthy discussion with the employee. Make every attempt to be as kind and respectful as possible when informing someone that he or she is being fired. It is permissible, and sometimes a good idea, to have a witness present. This person should be from human resources or part of the employee's chain of command, such as the supervisor's boss. Company security may be nearby, but should not be in the room unless the employee has made direct threats toward others. Finally, managers should be careful not to publicly criticize the employee who has just been fired, as this can also lead to a wrongful discharge lawsuit. In general, unless someone has a "business reason to know" why an employee was fired, the reasons and details related to the firing should remain confidential.[82]

7.2 Downsizing

Downsizing is the planned elimination of jobs in a company. Whether it's because of cost cutting, declining market share, or overaggressive hiring and growth, it's estimated that companies eliminate more than 3 million jobs a year.[83] Two-thirds of companies that downsize will downsize a second time within a year.

downsizing
the planned elimination of jobs in a company

Does downsizing work? In theory, downsizing is supposed to lead to higher productivity and profits, better stock performance, and increased organizational flexibility. However, numerous studies demonstrate that it doesn't. For instance, a 15-year study of downsizing found that downsizing 10 percent of a company's work force produced only a 1.5 percent decrease in costs; that firms that downsized increased their stock price by only 4.7 percent over three years, compared to 34.3 percent for firms that didn't; and that profitability and productivity were generally not improved by downsizing.[84] These results make it clear that the best strategy is to conduct effective human resource planning and avoid downsizing altogether. Indeed, downsizing should always be a measure of last resort.

If companies do find themselves in financial or strategic situations where downsizing is required for survival, however, they should train managers in how to break the news to downsized employees, have senior managers explain in detail why downsizing is necessary, and time the announcement so that employees hear it from the company and not from other sources, such as TV or newspaper reports.[85] Exhibit 12.9 provides additional guidelines for conducting layoffs.

Finally, companies should do everything they can to help downsized employees find other jobs. One of the best ways to do this is to use **outplacement services** that provide employment-counseling services for employees faced with downsizing. Outplacement services often include advice and training in preparing résumés and getting ready for job interviews, and even identifying job opportunities in other companies. Extensive outplacement programs not only help laid-off employees, but also help the company maintain a positive image in the community affected by downsizing. Steps such as these also help employees remain productive during their final days at the company. For example, before brokerage firm Charles Schwab laid off employees, it first cut nonessential spending and executive pay and offered employees unpaid furloughs (i.e., unpaid time off). Then, when it laid off 2,000 employees, it gave them severance pay (worth up to 10 months' salary), educational allowances, and 500 to 1,000 stock options each (worth $15,000 to $30,000).[86] Schwab also offered a $7,500 bonus to any laid-off employee rehired in the next 18 months (a not uncommon occurrence). A company spokesperson said the bonus helps with "the trauma of going through a layoff. That's important not only for those who are leaving, but also for those who stay."[87]

outplacement services
employment-counseling services offered to employees who are losing their jobs because of downsizing

exhibit 12.9

Guidelines for Conducting Layoffs

1. Provide clear reasons and explanations for the layoffs.
2. To avoid laying off employees with critical or irreplaceable skills, knowledge, and expertise, get input from human resources, the legal department, and several levels of management.
3. Train managers in how to tell employees that they are being laid off (i.e., stay calm; make the meeting short; explain why, but don't be personal; and provide information about immediate concerns, such as benefits, job search, and collecting personal goods).
4. Give employees the bad news early in the day, and try to avoid laying off employees before holidays.
5. Provide outplacement services and counseling to help laid-off employees find new jobs.
6. Communicate with survivors to explain how the company and their jobs will change.

Source: M. Boyle, "The Not-So-Fine Art of the Layoff," Fortune, *19 March 2001, 209.*

Indeed, companies also need to pay attention to the "survivors," the employees remaining after layoffs have occurred, because they are the ones left running the company.[88] According to management consultant Diane Durken, "The people who are left behind start looking behind their backs and saying, 'Am I next?' They need to be rejuvenated, so they can refocus on the future. Honesty and integrity are the core of this."[89] The key to working with layoff survivors is communication, communication, and communication. Immediately following the layoffs at one company, managers met with small groups of employees to talk about how the company and their jobs would be affected.[90]

7.3 Employee Turnover

employee turnover
loss of employees who voluntarily choose to leave the company

functional turnover
loss of poor-performing employees who voluntarily choose to leave a company

dysfunctional turnover
loss of high-performing employees who voluntarily choose to leave a company

Employee turnover is the loss of employees who voluntarily choose to leave the company. In general, most companies try to keep the rate of employee turnover low to reduce recruiting, hiring, training, and replacement costs. Not all kinds of employee turnover are bad for organizations, however. In fact, some turnover can actually be good. For instance, **functional turnover** is the loss of poor-performing employees who choose to leave the organization.[91] Functional turnover gives the organization a chance to replace poor performers with better workers. In fact, one study found that simply replacing poor-performing leavers with average workers would increase the revenues produced by retail salespeople in an upscale department store by $112,000 per person per year.[92] By contrast, **dysfunctional turnover**, the loss of high performers who choose to leave, is a costly loss to the organization.

Employee turnover should be carefully analyzed to determine whether good or poor performers are choosing to leave the organization. If the company is losing too many high performers, managers should determine the reasons and find ways to reduce the loss of valuable employees. The company may have to raise salary levels, offer enhanced benefits, or improve working conditions to retain skilled workers. One of the best ways to influence functional and dysfunctional turnover is to link pay directly to performance. A study of four sales forces found that when pay was strongly linked to performance via sales commissions and bonuses, poor performers were much more likely to leave (i.e., functional turnover). By contrast, poor performers were much more likely to stay when paid large, guaranteed monthly salaries and small sales commissions and bonuses.[93]

Review 7
Employee Separations

Employee separation is the loss of an employee, which can occur voluntarily or involuntarily. Before firing or terminating employees, managers should give employees a chance to improve. If firing becomes necessary, it should be done because of job-related factors, such as violating company rules or consistently performing poorly. Downsizing is supposed to lead to higher productivity and profits, better stock performance, and increased organizational flexibility, but studies show that it doesn't. The best strategy is to downsize only as a last resort. Companies that do downsize should offer outplacement services to help employees find other jobs. Companies generally try to keep the rate of employee turnover low to reduce costs. Functional turnover can be good for organizations, however, because it offers the chance to replace poor performers with better workers. Managers should analyze employee turnover to determine who is resigning and take steps to reduce the loss of good performers.

STUDY TIP Use the chapter outline on page 318 as a study tool. After reading the whole chapter, return to the list and write a summary of each item. Check your work by reading the actual review paragraphs on pages 325, 329, 336, 340, 344, 348, and 351.

MANAGEMENT DECISION

REVERSAL OF FORTUNES

A gentle tap on your door lets you know the receptionist has the daily mail.[94] He enters your office and hands you the day's stack of correspondence, which is crowned with what looks like a personal letter from a former employee. The name takes you back four years when the person was still at the company. "Wow," you think, "Four years ago, I would never have thought I'd be in the position I am now." Back then, dotcom companies like yours were going under at the rate of one a minute, or at least so it seemed. Times were tough. To keep the company afloat and avoid massive layoffs, many of your employees agreed to take cuts in pay, which you planned to restore when business picked up. As it turned out, layoffs were unavoidable, and you had to substantially reduce your work force by cutting 50 out of 100 jobs, trim the remaining employees' benefits and make them pay for health insurance, and eliminate all executive perks—even basic ones like corporate cell phones.

Looking back now, it was those draconian measures that helped the company navigate the tidal wave that wiped out a significant part of the tech industry. And although you wouldn't characterize your current position as thriving, you have definitely pulled away from the brink of bankruptcy. This year you may even have a very modest profit of $50,000 on $5 million in revenue. You return to the letter, open it, and read:

Dear Meg,

Congratulations on your success with the company. Four years ago, the future looked bleak, but now it seems that the company is starting to recover. As you may recall, several employees agreed to take pay cuts in an attempt to avoid the layoffs that were plaguing the industry, with the proviso that the lost wages would be paid when the company turned around. Layoffs, however, inevitably came to the company—I was one of those affected—and helped it cut costs and maintain cash flow.

Now that the company has recovered to a certain extent, I would like to collect the back pay that I forfeited while I was an employee as part of the effort to keep the company afloat. According to my calculations, I voluntarily forfeited total wages amounting to $10,200. I realize that several employees are in the same situation, so perhaps it would be easier for the company to pay in scheduled installments rather than in one lump sum. I am flexible as to the schedule, but I would like to begin receiving the back pay as soon as possible. Personally, I have not recovered from the tech sector downturn as quickly as the company has.

Sincerely,
Ellen McKay

Once you finish the letter, your hands begin to automatically massage your temples. What if you get a letter like this from every employee who was laid off? There were 50 layoffs, and everyone in the company was forfeiting pay. Those who survived the layoffs are still working on reduced wages and are paying a large percentage of their health insurance premiums. But at least they still have their jobs.

Questions

1. Do you pay your former employee the wages she agreed to forfeit when the company was struggling to survive?
2. How will you handle the rest of the laid-off employees?
3. Draft a letter to the laid-off employees (Ellen McKay included) that describes your response to this situation.

360-DEGREE FEEDBACK

While most performance appraisal ratings have traditionally come from just one person, the boss, 360-degree feedback is obtained from four sources: the boss, subordinates, peers and coworkers, and the employees themselves. In this assignment, you will be gathering 360-degree feedback from people that you work with or from a team or group that you're a member of for a class.

Here are some guidelines for obtaining your 360-degree feedback:

- *Carefully select respondents.* One of the keys to good 360-degree feedback is getting feedback from the right people. In general, the people you ask for feedback should interact with you on a regular basis and should have the chance to regularly observe your behavior. Also, be sure to get a representative sample of opinions from a similar number of coworkers and subordinates (assuming you have some).
- *Get a large enough number of responses.* Except for the boss, you should have a minimum of three respondents to give you feedback in each category (peers and subordinates). Five or six respondents per category is even better.
- *Ensure confidentiality.* Respondents are much more likely to be honest if they know that their comments are confidential and anonymous. So, when you ask respondents for feedback, have them return their comments to someone other than yourself. Have this person, we'll call the person your "feedback facilitator," remove the names and any other information that would identify who made particular comments.
- *Explain how the 360-degree feedback will be used.* In this case, explain that the feedback is for a class assignment, that the results will be used for your own personal growth and development, and that the feedback they give you will not affect your grade or formal assessment at work.
- *Ask them to make their feedback as specific as possible.* For instance, writing "bad attitude" isn't very good feedback. Writing "won't listen to others' suggestions" would be much better because it would let you know how to improve your behavior. Have your respondents use the feedback form below to provide your feedback.

Here's what you need to turn in for this assignment:

1. The names and relationships (boss, peers, subordinates, classmates, teammates) of those whom you've asked for feedback.
2. The name of the person you've asked to be your feedback facilitator.
3. Copies of all written feedback that was returned to you.
4. A one-page summary of the written feedback.
5. A one-page plan in which you describe specific goals and action plans for responding to the feedback you received.

360-DEGREE FEEDBACK FORM

As part of a class assignment, I, ______________, am collecting feedback from you about my performance. What you say or write will not affect my grade. The purpose of this assignment is for me to receive honest feedback from the people I work with in order to identify the things I'm doing well and the things that I need to improve. So please be honest and direct in your evaluation.

When you have completed this feedback form, please return it to ______________. He or she has been selected as my feedback facilitator and is responsible for ensuring that your confidentiality and anonymity are maintained. After all feedback forms have been returned to ______________, he or she will make sure that your particular responses cannot be identified. Only then will the feedback be shared with me.

Please provide the following feedback.

Continue doing . . .
Describe 3 things that ______________ is doing that are a positive part of his or her performance and that you want him or her to continue doing.

1.

2.

3.

Start doing . . .
Describe 3 things that ______________ needs to start doing that would significantly improve his or her performance.

1.

2.

3.

Please make your feedback as specific and behavioral as possible. For instance, writing "needs to adjust attitude" isn't very good feedback. Writing "needs to begin listening to others' suggestions" is much better because the person now knows exactly how he or she should change his or her behavior. So please be specific. Also, please write more than one sentence per comment. This will help the feedback recipient better understand your comments.

BIZ FLIX Bowfinger

This film, which brought Steve Martin and Eddie Murphy together for the first time, offers a funny look at Hollywood film making. Bobby Bowfinger (Martin), perhaps the least successful director in films, wants to produce a low-budget film with top star Kit Ramsey (Murphy). Bowfinger's problem: recruit a crew and cast with almost no budget and trick Kit into appearing in his film.

Bowfinger interviews several candidates for the Kit Ramsey lookalike role. He rejects everyone until Jifferson (Jiff) Ramsey (also played by Murphy) auditions. This scene is an edited version of the "The Lookalike" sequence early in the film. It includes Jiff's audition, interview, and a brief look at his first day at work.

What to Watch for and Ask Yourself

1. Does Bobbie Bowfinger have a set of valid selection criteria for filling the role of a Kit Ramsey lookalike? Does Bowfinger apply the criteria uniformly to each applicant?
2. Is there a good person-job fit of Jiff Ramsey in the screen role of Kit Ramsey?
3. Do you predict that Jiff Ramsey will be successful as a Kit Ramsey substitute?

MGMT WORKPLACE Gadabout Day Spa & Salon

The Gadabout Day Spa & Salon offers its customers everything from simple haircuts and nail treatments to exotic soft-pack skin hydration and oxygen vitamin treatments. Pam McNair, the spa's founder, believes the path to satisfied clients in a service business runs through skilled and caring employees. To build self-esteem in her workers, she stresses continuous training, team play, and direct communication. She gives them respect, opportunity, competitive compensation, and a creative benefits package. The greatest benefit of working with Pam, however, is the feeling of being truly appreciated, nurtured, and supported to succeed personally as well as professionally.

What to Watch for and Ask Yourself

1. What is unique about Pam's approach to employee development?
2. What is unique about Gadabout's compensation and benefits package? How does it affect employee turnover?
3. What makes Pam a successful manager?

CHAPTER THIRTEEN

Managing Service and Manufacturing Operations

outline

WHAT WOULD YOU DO?

England, Inc., New Tazewell, Tennessee.[1] It's Sunday night and your week is about to begin. You've just finished an hour-long phone call with a good friend from college whom you hadn't heard from in years. He thought of you Sunday afternoon when he and his wife were out furniture shopping. They wanted to buy new living room furniture because a large number of family members and friends will be visiting soon when both of their children graduate on the same weekend. Unfortunately, they heard the same story at every furniture store they visited: "Sorry, we can't guarantee delivery. Normally, it takes two to six months to deliver new furniture." As he and his wife drove home in disbelief—after all, you can drive a car home the day you buy it and have appliances delivered the next day—he thought of you, remembering that you'd been in the furniture manufacturing business for years. "Why?" he said, "does it take so long to get furniture delivered?"

After getting off the phone, you had to admit that the furniture indus-

student resources

URL Explore the four levels of learning by doing the simulation module on Operations Management.

GUIDE Mini lecture reviews all the learning points in the chapter and concludes with a case on Chrysler.

VIDEO Biz Flix is a scene from *Casino*. Management Workplace is a segment on Cannondale.

PPT 12 slides with graphics provide an outline for this chapter.

FAQ Chuck tells you how to practice service recovery and turn suddenly dissatisfied customers into satisfied customers once again.

TEST 22 true/false questions, 22 multiple-choice questions, a management scenario, and 3 exhibit worksheets

try is a laggard compared to most others. In general, furniture manufacturing is a very low-tech industry. With less than $100,000 in startup money, two hardworking people using basic hand tools (scissors, heavy duty staplers, drills, hammers, saws, sanders, sewing machines, etc.) can make 10 sofas a week. Furthermore, only a handful of the large manufacturers, who account for just $1 billion of the $24 billion in furniture sales each year, use any kind of automation to speed up production and increase productivity. And when you combine slow manufacturing times with a couple of weeks for transportation (to the warehouse and then to customers), furniture delivery times are like something out of the early 1900s. At least that's the case with your company, England, Inc., a long-time furniture manufacturer.

But with competition on all sides you won't be able to continue business as usual for much longer. First, you're getting squeezed on the price front. Anyone who walks into a Wal-Mart can buy a decent quality Chinese-made leather recliner for $199. Even though customers have to settle for what's in stock, a leather recliner selling for $199 means furniture manufacturers can't increase prices as readily as in the past. Furthermore, some manufacturers are aggressively pursuing direct sales from their factories, hoping to deliver to the customer's home in just six to eight weeks. Bassett, a key retailer and manufacturer, has started a program that will allow it to deliver custom-ordered sofas to customers in just four weeks (provided the factory has the ordered fabric in stock).

So somehow you've got to find a way to improve manufacturing speed and improve productivity to get a better handle on costs. But with 85 different frames, and 550 fabrics, and thus more than 40,000 different frame-fabric combinations, it won't be easy. People order custom sofas because they want something that fits exactly into their color scheme, so you can't easily reduce their options. In short, as a build-and-deliver furniture manufacturer, you're going to have to balance customer choice and delivery speed, but how? What's the best way to optimize productivity and hold down costs? Should you invest in automation or computers, or should you find another way to get your work force to be more productive? How can you deal with the complexity of more than 40,000 different frame-fabric combinations, give customers the sofas they want, and speed production and delivery times? How can you make those different goals compatible? Finally, once you speed things up, how can you keep inventory costs under control? Most furniture manufacturers can't afford to have millions of dollars tied up in unfinished inventory (i.e., wood, fabrics, springs, etc.). If you speed up the manufacture and delivery of your sofas, won't you have to have much more inventory on hand to quickly handle customer orders? Faster delivery is great and will give you a competitive advantage, but only if you can afford to do it—and that means not tying up significant sums of cash in unfinished inventory. **If you were the manager of the England, Inc. furniture factory in New Tazewell, Tennessee, what would you do?**

The problems that England, Inc. faces in manufacturing its products are not unique to the furniture industry. Airlines, auto manufacturers, hospitals, restaurants, and many other kinds of businesses also struggle to find ways to efficiently produce quality products and services and then deliver them in a timely manner.

operations management
managing the daily production of goods and services

In this chapter, you will learn about **operations management**—managing the daily production of goods and services. You will begin by learning about the basics of operations management: productivity and quality. Next, you will read about managing operations, beginning with service operations, turning next to manufacturing operations, and finishing with an examination of the types, measures, costs, and methods for managing inventory.

Managing for Productivity and Quality

Modeled after U.S.-based Southwest Airlines, Ryanair achieves dramatically lower prices through aggressive price cutting, much higher productivity, and quality customer service. Want a frequent-flier plan? You won't find one at Ryanair. It's too expensive. Want a meal on your flight? Pack a lunch. Ryanair doesn't even serve peanuts because it takes too much time (i.e., expense) to get them out of the seat cushions. Passengers enter and exit the planes using old-fashioned, rolling stairs because Ryanair has found that they're quicker and cheaper than extendable boarding gates. As a result of this and other cost-cutting moves, Ryanair does more with less and thus has higher productivity. For example, most airlines break even on their flights when they're 75 percent full. By contrast, even with its incredibly low prices, Ryanair's productivity allows it to break even when its planes are only half full. And with this low breakeven point, Ryanair attracts plenty of customers who allow it to fill most of its seats (84 percent) and earn 20 percent net profit margins. Finally, because of its extremely low prices (and its competitors' extremely high prices), it has increased passenger traffic and profits for 15 straight years.[2]

www.experiencing management.com

Learn more about productivity and quality indicators by interacting with them at our animated concept and activity site. Choose Operations_Management from the "select a topic" pull-down menu, then Operations Management Objectives from the "overview tab."

http://www.experiencingmanagement.com

After reading the next two sections, you should be able to

1 discuss the kinds of productivity and their importance in managing operations.

2 explain the role that quality plays in managing operations.

1 Productivity

productivity
a measure of performance that indicates how many inputs it takes to produce or create an output

At their core, organizations are production systems. Companies combine inputs, such as labor, raw materials, capital, and knowledge, to produce outputs in the form of finished products or services. **Productivity** is a measure of performance that indicates how many inputs it takes to produce or create an output.

$$\text{Productivity} = \frac{\text{Outputs}}{\text{Inputs}}$$

The fewer inputs it takes to create an output (or the greater the output from one input), the higher the productivity. For example, a car's gas mileage is a common measure of productivity. A car that gets 35 miles (output) per gallon (input) is more productive and fuel efficient than a car that gets 18 miles per gallon.

Let's examine 1.1 why productivity matters and 1.2 the different kinds of productivity.

1.1 Why Productivity Matters

Why does productivity matter? For companies, higher productivity, that is, doing more with less, results in lower costs. In turn, doing more with less can lead to lower prices, faster service, higher market share, and higher profits. For example, at fast-food restaurants, every second saved in the drive-through lane increases sales by 1 percent. Furthermore, increasing the efficiency of drive-through service by 10 percent adds nearly 10 percent to a fast-food restaurant's sales. And with 65 percent of all fast-food restaurant sales coming from the drive-through window, it's no wonder that Wendy's (average drive-through time of 127.2 seconds), McDonald's (average time of 162.7 seconds), and Burger King (average time of 173.4 seconds) continue to look for ways to shorten the time it takes to process a drive-through order.[3]

For countries, productivity matters because it produces a higher standard of living. One way productivity leads to a higher standard of living is through increased wages. When companies can do more with less, they can raise employee wages without increasing prices or sacrificing normal profits. Thanks to long-term increases in business productivity, the average American family today earns 37 percent more than the average family in 1980 and 250 percent more than the average family in 1953—and that's after accounting for inflation.[4]

Rising income stemming from increased productivity creates numerous other benefits as well. For example, with productivity increases exceeding 2 percent per year during the 1990s, the U.S. economy created 20 million new jobs. Likewise, when productivity increased and incomes rose, medical coverage became more widely available. Today, more than 85 percent of Americans are covered by some form of medical insurance through their employers, compared to just 70 percent in 1960.[6]

Another way that productivity increases the standard of living is by making products more affordable or better. For example, while inflation has pushed the average cost of a car to more than $25,197 (after incentives and discounts), increases in productivity have actually made cars cheaper. In 1960, the average family needed 26 weeks of income to pay for the average car. Today, the average family needs only 19.9 weeks of income—and today's car is loaded with accessories, like air bags, power steering and brakes, power windows, cruise control, stereo/CD/DVD players, seat warmers, air conditioning, and satellite navigation, features that weren't even available in 1960.[7] So, in terms of real purchasing power, productivity gains have actually made the $25,197 car of today cheaper than the $2,000 car of 1960.

PERSONAL PRODUCTIVITY

T!P

Tracking Your Personal Productivity

Are you productive at work, or are you a time waster? Chances are, you'd be shocked at how much time you actually waste. The first step to improved personal productivity is to keep a detailed time log of your daily activities, including your time wasters. Keeping a time log can be tedious, but today computer shareware makes it easier. To download time log software, go to the ZDNet Software Library, **http://downloads-zdnet.com**, and search for the key word "time log." You'll find a number of software titles that can help you track your time and improve your personal productivity.[5]

1.2 Kinds of Productivity

partial productivity a measure of performance that indicates how much of a particular kind of input it takes to produce an output

Two common measures of productivity are partial productivity and multifactor productivity. **Partial productivity** indicates how much of a particular kind of input it takes to produce an output.

$$\text{Partial Productivity} = \frac{\text{Outputs}}{\text{Single Kind of Input}}$$

Labor is one kind of input that is frequently used when determining partial productivity. *Labor productivity* typically indicates the cost or number of hours of labor it takes to produce an output. In other words, the lower the cost of the labor to produce a unit of output, or the less time it takes to produce a unit of output, the higher the labor productivity. For example, the automobile industry often measures labor productivity by determining the average number of hours of labor it takes to completely assemble a car. The three most productive auto manufacturers can assemble a car with 32 or fewer hours of labor. Nissan assembles a car in only 29 hours of labor, Honda does it in 31.18 hours, and Toyota in 31.63 hours. These manufacturers have much higher labor productivity than General Motors, which needs 39.34 hours of labor to assemble a car, Ford, which needs 40.88 hours, and Chrysler, which needs 44.28 hours.[8] These lower labor costs give Nissan, Honda, and Toyota an average cost advantage of $350 to $450 per car.[9]

Partial productivity assesses how efficiently companies use only one input, such as labor, when creating outputs. Multifactor productivity is an overall measure of productivity that assesses how efficiently companies use all the inputs it takes to make outputs. More specifically, **multifactor productivity** indicates how much labor, capital, materials, and energy it takes to produce an output.[10]

multifactor productivity an overall measure of performance that indicates how much labor, capital, materials, and energy it takes to produce an output

$$\text{Multifactor Productivity} = \frac{\text{Outputs}}{\text{Labor} + \text{Capital} + \text{Materials} + \text{Energy}}$$

Exhibit 13.1 shows the trends in multifactor productivity across a number of U.S. industries since 1987. With a sixfold increase (from the starting point scaled at 100 in 1987 to a productivity level of 631 in 1999), the growth in multifactor productivity in the electronics components and accessories industry far exceeded the productivity growth in the railroad, cement, beverage, and paint products industries, as well as most other industries tracked by the U.S. government.

Should managers use multiple or partial productivity measures? In general, they should use both. Multifactor productivity indicates a company's overall level of productivity relative to its competitors. In the end, that's what counts most. However, multifactor productivity measures don't indicate the specific contributions that labor, capital, materials, or energy make to overall productivity. To analyze the contributions of these individual components, managers need to use partial productivity measures.

Review 1
Productivity

At their core, companies are production systems that combine inputs, such as labor, raw materials, capital, and knowledge, to produce outputs, such as finished products or services. Productivity is a measure of how many inputs it takes to produce or create an output. The greater the output from one input,

exhibit 13.1

Multifactor Productivity Growth Across Industries

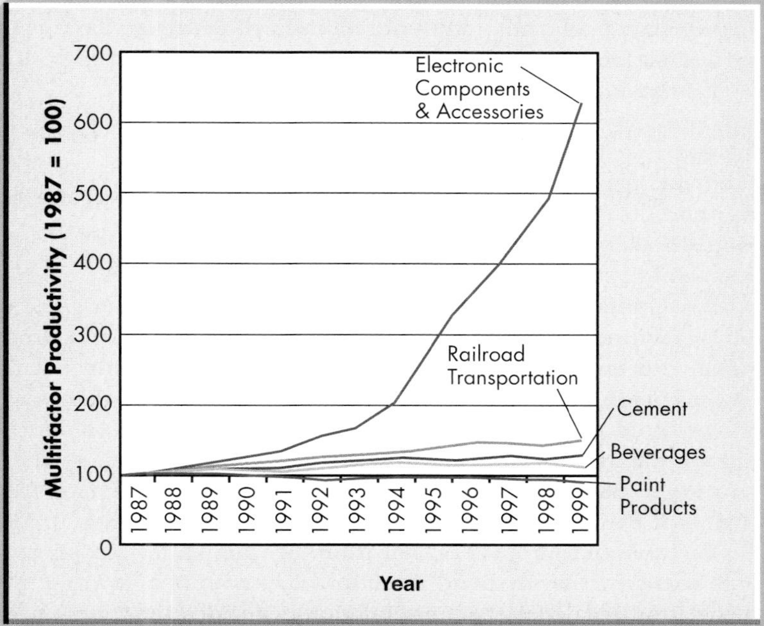

Source: "Industry Multifactor Productivity Indexes (1987=100)," Bureau of Labor Statistics, [Online] available at ftp://ftp.bls.gov/pub/special.requests/opt/dipts/indmfp2.txt, 21 February 2002.

or the fewer inputs it takes to create an output, the higher the productivity. Partial productivity measures how much of a single kind of input, such as labor, is needed to produce an output. Multifactor productivity is an overall measure of productivity that indicates how much labor, capital, materials, and energy are needed to produce an output. Increased productivity helps companies lower costs, which can lead to lower prices, higher market share, and higher profits. Increased productivity helps countries by leading to higher wages, lower product prices, and a higher standard of living.

2 Quality

With the average car costing more than $25,000, car buyers want to make sure that they're getting good quality for their money. Fortunately, as indicated by the number of problems per 100 cars (PP100), today's cars are of much higher quality than earlier models. In 1981, Japanese cars averaged 240 PP100. General Motors' cars averaged 670, Ford's averaged 740, and Chrysler's averaged 870 PP100! In other words, as measured by PP100, the quality of American cars was three to four times worse than Japanese cars. By 1992, however, U.S. carmakers had made great strides, significantly reducing the number of problems to an average of 155 PP100. Japanese vehicles had improved, too, averaging just 125 PP100. In 2003, the average improved further to just 133 PP100. American automakers, especially Cadillac (GM) with 103 PP100, continued to close the quality gap with Japanese auto companies.

quality
a product or service free of deficiencies, or the characteristics of a product or service that satisfy customer needs

The American Society for Quality gives two meanings for **quality**. It can mean a product or service free of deficiencies, such as the number of problems per 100 cars, or it can mean the characteristics of a product or service that satisfy customer needs.[11] In this sense, today's cars are of higher quality because of the additional standard features (power brakes and steering, stereo/CD player, power windows and locks, air bags, cruise control, etc.) they have compared to 20 years ago.

In this part of the chapter, you will learn about 2.1 quality-related product characteristics, 2.2 quality-related service characteristics, 2.3 ISO 9000, 2.4 the Baldrige National Quality Award, and 2.5 Total Quality Management.

2.1 Quality-Related Product Characteristics

Quality products usually possess three characteristics: reliability, serviceability, and durability.[12] A breakdown occurs when a product quits working or doesn't do what it was designed to do. The longer it takes for a product to break down, or the longer the time between breakdowns, the more reliable the product. Consequently, many companies define *product reliability* in terms of the average time between breakdowns.

Serviceability refers to how easy or difficult it is to fix a product. The easier it is to maintain a working product or fix a broken product, the more serviceable that product is. For example, though few people realize it, over the life of a car, they'll spend more for car insurance than for gas. Consequently, the Saturn division of General Motors decided that one way to lower the cost of car ownership is to make cars easier to repair after they've been in collisions.

A product breakdown assumes that a product can be repaired. However, some products don't break down—they fail. *Product failure* means products can't be repaired. They can only be replaced. Thus, durability is a quality characteristic that applies to products that can't be repaired. *Durability* is defined as the mean time to failure. A product for which durability matters is the defibrillation equipment used by emergency medical technicians, doctors, and nurses to restart patients' hearts. The mean time between failures for Medtronic Physio-Control's defibrillation units is 20 years. If a Physio-Control "LIFEPAK" does break, however, the company replaces it within 24 hours.[13]

2.2 Quality-Related Service Characteristics

Reliability, serviceability, and durability characterize high-quality products, but services are different. With services, there's no point in assessing durability. Unlike products, services don't last. Services are consumed the minute they're performed. For example, once a lawn service has mowed your lawn, the job is done until the mowers come back next week to do it again. Likewise, services don't have serviceability. You can't maintain or fix a service. If a service wasn't performed correctly, all you can do is perform the service again. Finally, the quality of service interactions often depends on how the service provider interacts with the customer. Was the service provider friendly, rude, or helpful? Consequently, five characteristics—reliability, tangibles, responsiveness, assurance, and empathy—typically distinguish a quality service.[14]

Service reliability is the ability to consistently perform a service well. Studies clearly show that reliability matters more to customers than anything else when buying services. Also, while services themselves are not tangible (you can't see or touch them), services are provided in tangible places. Thus, *tangibles* refer to the appearance of the offices, equipment, and personnel involved with the delivery of a service. *Responsiveness* is the promptness and willingness with which service providers give good service. *Assurance* is the confidence that service providers are knowledgeable, courteous, and trustworthy. *Empathy* is the extent to which service providers give individual attention and care to customers' concerns and problems.

EMC Corporation makes highly reliable computers that are used by some of the largest companies in the world. If EMC's equipment goes down for even a few minutes, its customers can lose millions from vanished sales. While its equipment is incredibly reliable, what distinguishes EMC from its competition is the level of service it provides when problems occur. In other words, EMC is a standout performer in *service reliability*, the ability to consistently perform a service well. Because of its excellent service, EMC retains an amazing 99 percent of its customers from year to year.[15]

EMC also excels in *responsiveness*, the promptness and willingness with which service providers give good service. When a Wisconsin bank lost access to its data, which were stored on an EMC machine, EMC service engineers were on the problem within minutes. In four hours EMC had created a setup identical to the bank's in a $1 billion facility designed for such purposes, where EMC engineers identified the problem and put together a software patch that had the bank up and running by the end of the day.[16]

EMC provides quality service by virtue of clear *assurance* that it can be trusted. Every customer knows that the company follows a disciplined procedure for addressing customer problems.

Finally, EMC provides quality service because of the *empathy* it has for its customers' problems. Indeed, early in the company's history, its customers' businesses were suffering because EMC could not figure out why one of its best-selling systems had unexpectedly become unreliable. Rather than make excuses or empty promises, EMC gave its customers the choice between a brand new EMC computer system or a similar system made by EMC's competitor, IBM. At the height of its problems, EMC installed more of IBM's machines than its own.[17]

2.3 ISO 9000

ISO, pronounced *ice-o*, comes from the Greek word *isos*, meaning *equal, similar, alike*, or *identical*. Thus, **ISO 9000** is a series of five international standards, from ISO 9000 to ISO 9004, for achieving consistency in quality management and quality assurance in companies throughout the world. The ISO 9000 standards were created by the International Organization for Standardization (**http://www.iso.ch**), an international agency that helps set standards for 145 countries. The purpose of this agency is to develop and publish standards that facilitate the international exchange of goods and services.[18]

ISO 9000
a series of five international standards, from ISO 9000 to ISO 9004, for achieving consistency in quality management and quality assurance in companies throughout the world

The ISO 9000 standards publications, which can be purchased from the American National Standards Institute (**http://web.ansi.org**) for about $430, are general and can be used for manufacturing any kind of product or delivering any kind of service. Importantly, the ISO 9000 standards don't describe how to make a better-quality car, computer, or widget. Instead, they describe how companies can extensively document (and thus standardize) the steps they take to create and improve the quality of their products. ISO 9000 certification is increasingly becoming a requirement for doing business with many *Fortune* 500 companies.[19] To become ISO 9000 certified, a process that can take months, companies must show an accredited third party that they are following their own procedures for improving production, updating design plans and specifications, keeping machinery in top condition, educating and training workers, and satisfactorily dealing with customer complaints.[20] Once a company has been certified as ISO 9000 compliant, the accredited third party will issue an ISO 9000 certificate that the company can use in its advertising and publications. This is the quality equivalent of the "Good Housekeeping Seal of Approval." Continued ISO 9000 certification is not guaranteed, however. Accredited third parties typically conduct periodic audits to make sure quality procedures continue to be followed. Companies that don't follow their quality systems have their certifications suspended or canceled. It's estimated that more than half of mid-sized U.S. manufacturers have achieved ISO 9000 certification.[21]

See the American National Standards Institute, the American Society for Quality (**http://www.asq.org/**), and the International Organization for Standardization for additional information on ISO 9000 guidelines and procedures.

exhibit 13.2

Criteria for the Baldrige National Quality Award

2003 CATEGORIES/ITEMS	POINT VALUES
1 LEADERSHIP	**(120)**
Organizational Leadership	70
Social Responsibility	50
2 STRATEGIC PLANNING	**(85)**
Strategy Development	40
Strategy Deployment	45
3 CUSTOMER AND MARKET FOCUS	**(85)**
Customer and Market Knowledge	40
Customer Relationships and Satisfaction	45
4 MEASUREMENT, ANALYSIS, & KNOWLEDGE MANAGEMENT	**(90)**
Measurement and Analysis of Organizational Performance	45
Information and Knowledge Management	45
5 HUMAN RESOURCE FOCUS	**(85)**
Work Systems	35
Employee Learning and Motivation	25
Employee Well-Being and Satisfaction	25
6 PROCESS MANAGEMENT	**(85)**
Value Creation Processes	50
Support Processes	35
7 BUSINESS RESULTS	**(450)**
Customer-Focused Results	75
Product and Service Results	75
Financial and Market Results	75
Human Resource Results	75
Organizational Effectiveness Results	75
Governance and Social Responsibility Results	75
TOTAL POINTS	**1,000**

Source: "Criteria for Performance Excellence," Baldrige National Quality Program 2003, *[Online] available at http://www.quality.nist.gov/PDF_files/2003_Business_Criteria.pdf, 3 June 2003.*

2.4 Baldrige National Quality Award

The Baldrige National Quality Award, which is administered by the U.S. government's National Institute for Standards and Technology, is given "to recognize U.S. companies for their achievements in quality and business performance and to raise awareness about the importance of quality and performance excellence as a competitive edge."[22] Each year, up to three awards may be given in these categories: manufacturing, service, small business, education, and health.

The cost of applying for the Baldrige Award is $5,000 for manufacturing and service companies and $2,000 for small businesses.[23] At a minimum, each company that applies receives an extensive report based on 300 hours of assessment from at least eight business and quality experts. At $6.67 an hour for small businesses and about $16.67 an hour for manufacturing and service businesses, the *Journal for Quality and Participation* called the Baldrige feedback report "the best bargain in consulting in America."[24]

Companies that apply for the Baldrige Award are judged on a 1,000-point scale based on the seven criteria shown in Exhibit 13.2.[25] With 450 out of 1,000 points, "business results" are clearly the most important. In other words, in addition to the six other criteria, companies must show that they have achieved superior quality when it comes to customers, products and services, financial performance and market share, treatment of employees, organizational effectiveness, and corporate governance and social responsibility. This emphasis on "results" is what differentiates the Baldrige Award from the ISO 9000 standards. The Baldrige Award indicates the extent to which companies have actually achieved world-class quality. The ISO 9000 standards simply indicate whether a company is following the management system it put in place to improve quality. In fact, ISO 9000 certification covers less than 10 percent of the requirements for the Baldrige Award.[26]

Most companies that apply for the Baldrige Award do so to grow, prosper, and stay competitive. Furthermore, the companies that have won the Baldrige Award have achieved superior financial returns. Since 1988, an investment in Baldrige Award winners would have outperformed the Standard & Poor's 500 stock index 90 percent of the time.[27] For additional information about the Baldrige Award, see the National Institute of Standards and Technology Web site at **http://www.quality.nist.gov**.

total quality management (TQM)
an integrated, principle-based, organization-wide strategy for improving product and service quality

customer focus
an organizational goal to concentrate on meeting customers' needs at all levels of the organization

customer satisfaction
an organizational goal to provide products or services that meet or exceed customers' expectations

continuous improvement
an organization's ongoing commitment to constantly assess and improve the processes and procedures used to create products and services

variation
a deviation in the form, condition, or appearance of a product from the quality standard for that product

2.5 Total Quality Management

Total quality management (TQM) is an integrated organization-wide strategy for improving product and service quality.[28] TQM is not a specific tool or technique. Rather, TQM is a philosophy or overall approach to management that is characterized by three principles: customer focus and satisfaction, continuous improvement, and teamwork.[29]

Contrary to most economists, accountants, and financiers who argue that companies exist to earn profits for shareholders, TQM suggests that customer focus and customer satisfaction should be a company's primary goals. **Customer focus** means that the entire organization, from top to bottom, should be focused on meeting customers' needs. **Customer satisfaction** is an organizational goal to make products or deliver services that meet or exceed customers' expectations. At companies where TQM is taken seriously, such as Enterprise Rent-a-Car, paychecks and promotions depend on keeping customers satisfied.[30] For example, Enterprise Rent-a-Car measures customer satisfaction with a detailed survey called the Enterprise Service Quality index. Enterprise not only ranks each branch office by operating profits and customer satisfaction, but it also makes promotions to higher-paying jobs contingent on above-average customer satisfaction scores.

Continuous improvement is an ongoing commitment to increase product and service quality by constantly assessing and improving the processes and procedures used to create those products and services. How do companies know whether they're achieving continuous improvement? Besides higher customer satisfaction, continuous improvement is usually associated with a reduction in variation. **Variation** is a deviation in the form, condition, or appearance of a product from the quality standard for that product. The less a product varies from the quality standard, or the more consistently a company's products meet a quality standard, the higher the quality. At Visteon Corporation, an auto parts supplier, continuous improvement means shooting for a goal of "six sigma" quality, meaning just 3.4 defective or nonstandard parts per million (PPM). Achieving this

www.experiencing management.com

Learn more about the three principles of TQM at our animated concept and activity site. Choose Operations_Management from the "select a topic" pull-down menu, then Total Quality Management from the "overview tab."

http://www.experiencingmanagement.com

goal would eliminate almost all product variation. In a recent year, Visteon made 360 million auto parts with a defect rate of 65 PPM.[31] This represents a significant improvement from several years ago when Visteon was averaging 1,000 defective PPM.

teamwork collaboration between managers and nonmanagers, across business functions, and between companies, customers, and suppliers

The third principle of TQM is teamwork. **Teamwork** means collaboration between managers and nonmanagers, across business functions, and between the company and its customers and suppliers. In short, quality improves when everyone in the company is given the incentive to work together and the responsibility and authority to make improvements and solve problems. Thanks to team members' suggestions at a Maytag plant in Cleveland, Tennessee, production has doubled, production costs have dropped by $7 million per year, and on-hand inventory of parts and finished goods has been reduced by $10 million.[32]

Together, customer focus and satisfaction, continuous improvement, and teamwork mutually reinforce each other to improve quality throughout a company. Customer-focused continuous improvement is necessary to increase customer satisfaction. However, continuous improvement depends on teamwork from different functional and hierarchical parts of the company.

Review 2
Quality

Quality can mean a product or service free of deficiencies or the characteristics of a product or service that satisfy customer needs. Quality products usually possess three characteristics: reliability, serviceability, and durability. Quality service means reliability, tangibles, responsiveness, assurance, and empathy. ISO 9000 is a series of five international standards for achieving consistency in quality management and quality assurance. The ISO 9000 standards can be used for any product or service, because they ensure that companies carefully document the steps they take to create and improve quality. ISO 9000 certification is awarded following a quality audit from an accredited third party. The Baldrige National Quality Award recognizes U.S. companies for their achievements in quality and business performance. Each year, three Baldrige Awards may be given for manufacturing, service, small business, education, and health. Companies that apply for the Baldrige Award are judged on a 1,000-point scale based on leadership; strategic planning; customer and market focus; measurement, analysis, and knowledge management; human resource focus; process management; and business results. Total quality management (TQM) is an integrated organization-wide strategy for improving product and service quality. TQM is based on three mutually reinforcing principles: customer focus and satisfaction, continuous improvement, and teamwork.

Managing Operations

At the start of this chapter, you learned that operations management means managing the daily production of goods and services. Then you learned that to manage production, you must oversee the factors that affect productivity and quality. In this half of the chapter, you will learn about managing operations in service and manufacturing businesses. The chapter ends with a discussion of inventory management, a key factor in a company's profitability.

After reading the next two sections, you should be able to

3 explain the essentials of managing a service business.

4 describe the different kinds of manufacturing operations and explain why and how companies should manage inventory levels.

3 Service Operations

Imagine that your trusty VCR breaks down as you try to record your favorite TV show. You've got two choices. You can run to Wal-Mart and spend $45 to $75 to purchase a new VCR, or you can spend about the same amount (you hope) to have it fixed at a repair shop. Either way you end up with the same thing, a working VCR. However, the first choice, getting a new VCR, involves buying a physical product (a "good"), while the second, dealing with a repair shop, involves buying a service.

Services differ from goods in several ways. First, goods are produced or made, but services are performed. In other words, services are almost always labor-intensive: Someone typically has to perform the service for you. A repair shop could give you the parts needed to repair your old VCR, but without the technician to perform the repairs, you're still going to have a broken VCR. Second, goods are tangible, but services are intangible. You can touch and see that new VCR. But you can't touch or see the service provided by the technician who fixed your old VCR. All you can "see" is that the VCR works. Third, services are perishable and unstorable. If you don't use them when they're available, they're wasted. For example, if your VCR repair shop is backlogged on repair jobs, then you'll just have to wait until next week to get your VCR repaired. You can't store an unused service and use it when you like. By contrast, you can purchase a good, such as motor oil, and store it until you're ready to use it.

Because services are different from goods, managing a service operation is different from managing a manufacturing or production operation. Let's look at 3.1 the service-profit chain and 3.2 service recovery and empowerment.

3.1 The Service-Profit Chain

One of the key assumptions in the service business is that success depends on how well employees, that is, service providers, deliver their services to customers. However, the concept of the service-profit chain, depicted in Exhibit 13.3, suggests that in service businesses, success begins with how well management treats service employees.[33]

The first step in the service-profit chain is *internal service quality*, meaning the quality of treatment that employees receive from a company's internal service providers, such as management, payroll and benefits, human resources, and so forth. For example, Southwest Airlines is legendary for its positive culture and, to the surprise of many, its excellent customer service. According to Southwest's Chairman Herb Kelleher, that's because "employees come first. If you treat them well, then they treat the customers well, and that means your customers come back and your shareholders are happy."[34]

As depicted in Exhibit 13.3, good internal service leads to employee satisfaction and service capability. *Employee satisfaction* occurs when companies treat employees in a way that meets or exceeds their expectations. In other words, the better employees are treated, the more satisfied they are, and the

exhibit 13.3

Service-Profit Chain

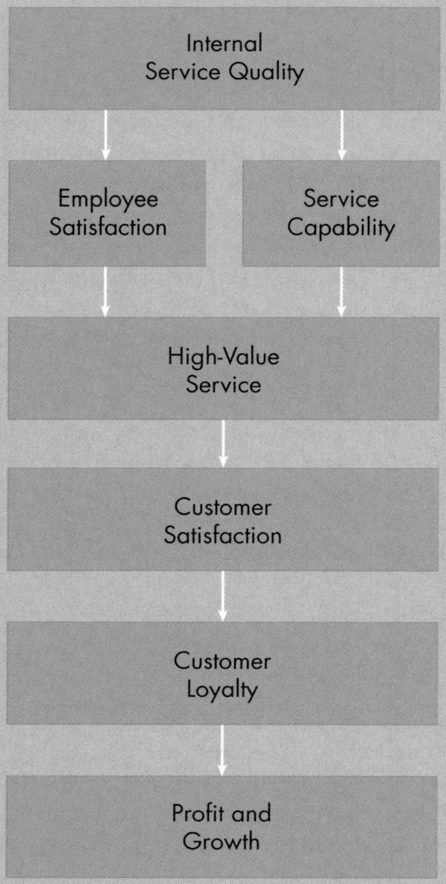

Sources: R. Hallowell, L. A. Schlesinger, & J. Zornitsky, "Internal Service Quality, Customer and Job Satisfaction: Linkages and Implications for Management," Human Resource Planning *19 (1996): 20–31; J. L. Heskett, T. O. Jones, G. W. Loveman, W. E. Sasser, Jr., & L. A. Schlesinger, "Putting the Service-Profit Chain to Work,"* Harvard Business Review, *March-April 1994, 164–174.*

more likely they are to give high-value service that satisfies customers. *Service capability* is an employee's perception of his or her ability to serve customers well. When an organization serves its employees in ways that help them to do their jobs well, employees, in turn, are more likely to believe that they can and ought to provide high-value service to customers.

Finally, according to the service-profit chain shown in Exhibit 13.3, *high-value service* leads to *customer satisfaction* and *customer loyalty*, which, in turn, lead to *long-term profits and growth.* What's the link between customer satisfaction and loyalty and profits? To start, the average business keeps only 70 to 90 percent of its existing customers each year. No big deal, you say? Just replace leaving customers with new customers. Well, there's one significant problem with that solution. It costs five times as much to find a new customer as it does to keep an existing customer. Also, new customers typically buy only 20 percent as much as established customers. In fact, keeping existing customers is so cost-effective that most businesses could double their profits by simply keeping 5 percent more customers per year![35]

3.2 Service Recovery and Empowerment

Many service businesses organize themselves like manufacturing companies. Tasks and jobs are simplified and separated, creating a clear division of labor. Equipment and technology are substituted for people whenever possible. Strict guidelines and rules take the place of employee authority and discretion. This "production-line" approach to running a service business is still widely used today in businesses that sell a high-volume, low-cost service that requires only a brief, simple transaction between customers and service providers.[36]

While the production-line model excels at efficiency and low costs, it does not work well when mistakes are made and customers become dissatisfied with the service they've received. When problems occur, service businesses must switch from the process of service delivery to the process of **service recovery**, that is, restoring customer satisfaction to strongly dissatisfied customers.[37] Sometimes, service recovery requires service employees to not only fix whatever

service recovery
restoring customer satisfaction to strongly dissatisfied customers

mistake was made, but also perform "heroic" service acts that "delight" highly dissatisfied customers by far surpassing their expectations of fair treatment. For example, Continental Airlines' Judy Dyar described what happened when the airline lost a Scottish customer's luggage containing rare Irish and Scottish books: "One of our resourceful baggage tracers called publishers and bookstores and managed to replace the books and get them to the customer in a reasonable time."[38]

Unfortunately, when mistakes occur under a "production-line" system, service employees typically don't have the discretion to resolve customer complaints. Customers who want service employees to correct or make up for poor service are frequently told, "I'm not allowed to do that," "I'm just following company rules," or "I'm sorry, only managers are allowed to make changes of any kind." In other words, the production-line system prevents them from engaging in acts of service recovery meant to turn dissatisfied customers back into satisfied customers. The result is frustration for customers and service employees and lost customers for the company.

Because production-line systems make it difficult for service employees to do service recovery, many companies are now empowering their service employees.[39] In Chapter 10, you learned that *empowering workers* means permanently passing decision-making authority and responsibility from managers to workers. With respect to service recovery, empowering workers means giving service employees the authority and responsibility to make decisions that immediately solve customer problems.[40] Empowering service workers does entail some costs, although they are usually less than the company's savings from retaining customers.

DOING THE RIGHT THING

Protect Your Front-Line Staff: The Customer Isn't Always Right

In 1909, Harry Gordon Selfridge, an American who founded London's famous Selfridge's department store, coined the phrase, "The customer is always right." Though managers and employees should do what they can to provide great service and make up for mistakes with great service recovery, the customer isn't *always* right. Companies should fire customers who use foul language, make threats against employees or other customers, lie, demand unethical or illegal service, try to bully front-line employees into granting special favors, or are just generally belligerent. Management consultant John Curtis says, "If you don't [fire these customers], you're telling your employees and your other customers that you care more about money than the safety of the people in the business." So, do the right thing. Protect your front-line staff by telling bad customers that you won't tolerate these kinds of behavior. Ask them to leave. Close their accounts. Inform them that they'll need to go elsewhere.[41]

Review 3
Service Operations

Services are different from goods. Goods are produced, tangible, and storable. Services are performed, intangible, and perishable. Likewise, managing service operations is different from managing production operations. The service-profit chain indicates that success begins with internal service quality, meaning how well management treats service employees. Internal service quality leads to employee satisfaction and service capability, which, in turn, lead to high-value service to customers, customer satisfaction, customer loyalty, and long-term profits and growth. Many service businesses are organized like manufacturers. Although this "production-line" approach is efficient and inexpensive, its strict rules and guidelines make it difficult for service workers to perform service recovery, restoring customer satisfaction to strongly dissatisfied customers. To resolve this problem, some companies are empowering service employees to perform service recovery by giving them the authority and responsibility to immediately solve customer problems. The hope is that empowered service recovery will prevent customer defections.

4 Manufacturing Operations and Inventory

Campbell's soup is the world's best-selling soup brand. In fact, Campbell's soup can be found in 93 percent of U.S. households. While Campbell's effective "hmmm-mmmm good" advertisements bring to mind images of home cooking, Campbell's obviously doesn't make its soups in small kitchens. It makes them in large factories, like its 1.4 million-square-foot facility in Maxton, North Carolina, that produces 4.9 million cans of soup per day! This factory can make over 200 different kinds of soup, as well as SpaghettiOs, pork and beans, and several kinds of gravy.[42]

www.experiencing management.com

Learn above four major issues operations managers deal with at our animated concept and activity site. Choose Operations_Management from the "select a topic" pull-down menu, then Operations Management System from the "overview tab."

http://www.experiencingmanagement.com

Like the Campbell's soup manufacturing plant described above, all *manufacturing operations* produce physical goods. To do this, they use (and create) inventory. But not all manufacturing operations or types of inventory are the same. Let's learn how various manufacturing operations differ in terms of 4.1 the amount of processing that is done to produce and assemble a product and about 4.2 the different types of inventory, 4.3 how to measure inventory levels, 4.4 the costs of maintaining an inventory, and 4.5 the different systems for managing inventory.

4.1 Amount of Processing in Manufacturing Operations

make-to-order operation
a manufacturing operation that does not start processing or assembling products until a customer order is received

As Exhibit 13.4 shows, manufacturing operations can be classified according to the amount of processing or assembly that occurs after a customer order is received. The highest degree of processing occurs in **make-to-order operations**. A make-to-order operation does not start processing or assembling products until it receives a customer order. In fact, some make-to-order operations may not even order parts until a customer order is received. Not surprisingly, make-to-order operations produce or assemble highly specialized or customized products for customers.

exhibit 13.4

Processing in Manufacturing Operations

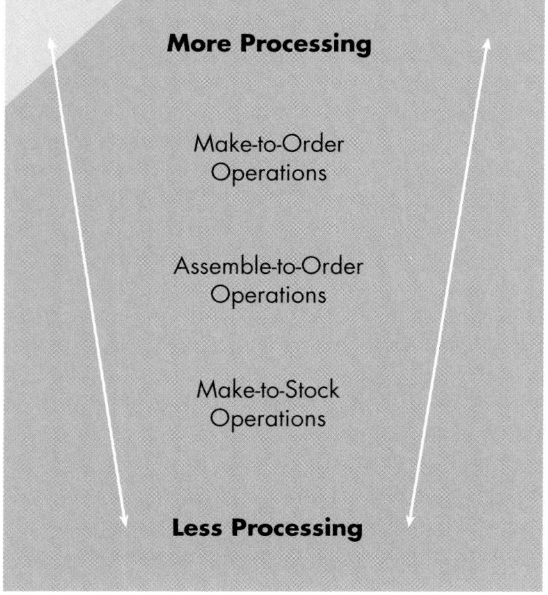

For example, Dell Computer has one of the most advanced make-to-order operations in the computer business. Because Dell has no finished goods inventory and no component parts inventory, its computers always have the latest, most advanced components, and Dell can pass on the latest price cuts to customers. Plus, Dell can customize all of its orders, big and small. For example, it took Dell just six weeks to make and ship 2,000 personal computers and 4,000 network servers for Wal-Mart. Furthermore, Dell preloaded each of these 6,000 machines with proprietary software that Wal-Mart uses in its stores and offices.[43]

A moderate degree of processing occurs in **assemble-to-order operations**. A company using an assemble-to-order operation divides its manufacturing or assembly process into separate parts or modules. The company orders parts and assembles modules ahead of customer orders. Then, based on actual customer orders or on research forecasting what customers will want, those modules are combined to create semicustomized products. For example, when a customer orders a new car,

assemble-to-order operation a manufacturing operation that divides manufacturing processes into separate parts or modules that are combined to create semicustomized products

make-to-stock operation a manufacturing operation that orders parts and assembles standardized products before receiving customer orders

General Motors may have already ordered the basic parts or modules it needs from suppliers. In other words, based on sales forecasts, GM may already have ordered enough tires, air-conditioning compressors, brake systems, and seats from suppliers to accommodate nearly all customer orders on a particular day. Special orders from customers and car dealers are then used to determine the final assembly checklist for particular cars as they move down the assembly line.

The lowest degree of processing occurs in **make-to-stock operations**. Because they produce standardized products, meaning each product is exactly the same as the next, a company using a make-to-stock operation starts ordering parts and assembling finished products before receiving customer orders. Customers then purchase these standardized products, such as Rubbermaid storage containers, microwave ovens, and vacuum cleaners, at retail stores or directly from the manufacturer. Because parts are ordered and products are assembled before customers order the products, make-to-stock operations are highly dependent on the accuracy of sales forecasts. If sales forecasts are incorrect, make-to-stock operations may end up building too many or too few products, or they may make products with the wrong features or lacking the features that customers want.

4.2 Types of Inventory

inventory the amount and number of raw materials, parts, and finished products that a company has in its possession

When auto sales dropped by 16 percent, General Motors shut down 14 of its 29 assembly plants and laid off half of its workers for periods ranging from one to five weeks to reduce inventories and cut costs. GM had a 116-day supply of new trucks and sports utility vehicles on hand, well over its goal of a 72-day supply. Paul Ballew, a general director for market and industry analysis at GM, said, "With sales moderating, the industry had to work through this inventory bubble."[44] **Inventory** is the amount and number of raw materials, parts, and finished products that a company has in its possession. General Motors made the mistake of having too much inventory on hand and had to close its plants to let existing sales draw down inventory levels to an acceptable and affordable level.

raw material inventories the basic inputs in a manufacturing process

component parts inventories the basic parts used in manufacturing that are fabricated from raw materials

work-in-process inventories partially finished goods consisting of assembled component parts

Exhibit 13.5 on the next page shows the four kinds of inventory a manufacturer stores: raw materials, component parts, work-in-process, and finished goods. The flow of inventory through a manufacturing plant begins when the purchasing department buys raw materials from vendors. **Raw material inventories** are the basic inputs in the manufacturing process. For example, to begin making a car, automobile manufacturers purchase raw materials like steel, iron, aluminum, copper, rubber, and unprocessed plastic.

Next, raw materials are fabricated or processed into **component parts inventories**, meaning the basic parts used in manufacturing a product. For example, in an automobile plant, steel is fabricated or processed into a car's body panels, and steel and iron are melted and shaped into engine parts like pistons or engine blocks. Component parts inventories are sometimes purchased directly from vendors.

The component parts are then assembled to make unfinished **work-in-process inventories**, which are also known as partially finished goods. This process is also called *initial assembly*. For example, steel body panels are welded to each other and to the frame of the car to make a "unibody," which comprises the unpainted interior frame and exterior structure of the car. Likewise, pistons, camshafts, and other engine parts are inserted into the engine block to create a working engine.

exhibit 13.5

Types of Inventory

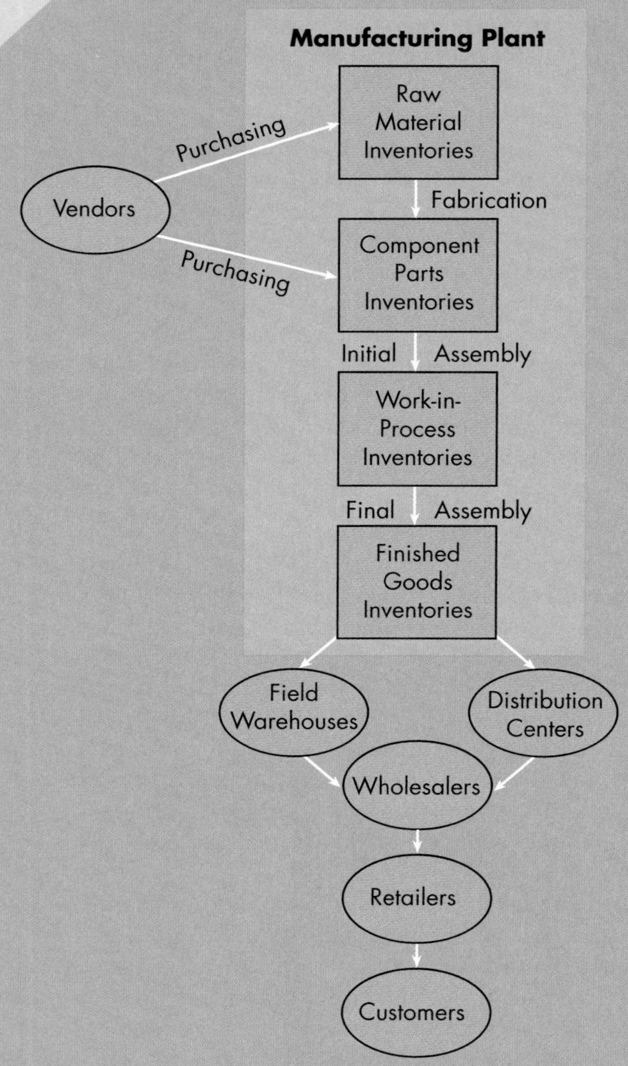

Source: R. E. Markland, S. K. Vickery, & R. A. Davis, Operations Management, *2e (Mason, OH: South-Western, 1998). Reprinted with permission.*

Next, all the work-in-process inventories are assembled to create **finished goods inventories**, which are the final outputs of the manufacturing process. This process is also called *final assembly*. For a car, the engine, wheels, brake system, suspension, interior, and electrical system are assembled into a car's painted unibody to make the working automobile, which is the factory's finished product. In the last step in the process, the finished goods are sent to field warehouses, distribution centers, or wholesalers, and then to retailers for final sale to customers.

4.3 Measuring Inventory

As you'll learn below, uncontrolled inventory can lead to huge costs for a manufacturing operation. Consequently, managers need good measures of inventory to prevent inventory costs from becoming too large. Three basic measures of inventory are average aggregate inventory, weeks of supply, and inventory turnover.

If you've ever worked in a retail store and had to "take inventory," you probably weren't too excited about the process of counting every item in the store and storeroom. It's an extensive process that is a bit easier today because of bar codes that mark items and computers that can count and track them. Nonetheless, inventories still differ depending on when in the month or week they're taken, even varying from day to day. Because of such differences, companies often measure **average aggregate inventory**, which is the average overall inventory during a particular time period. Average aggregate inventory for a month can be determined by simply averaging the inventory counts at the end of each business day for that month. One way companies know whether they're carrying too much or too little inventory is to compare their average aggregate inventory to the industry average for aggregate inventory. For example, 72 days of inventory is the average for the automobile industry.

Inventory is also measured in terms of *weeks of supply*, meaning the number of weeks it would take for a company to run out of its current supply of inventory. In general, there is an acceptable number of weeks of inventory for a

finished goods inventories
the final outputs of manufacturing operations

average aggregate inventory
average overall inventory during a particular time period

particular kind of business. Too few weeks of inventory on hand, and a company risks a **stockout**—running out of inventory. During a recent holiday season, the busiest shopping time of the year, Gateway stores quickly ran out of its best-selling \$3,000 to \$6,000 high-definition plasma TVs. The shortage was so severe that Gateway headquarters had to send posters of the flat-screen TVs so that Gateway stores could give them to customers who wouldn't receive the real TVs they had ordered until some time in February.[45] On the other hand, too many weeks of inventory on hand, and the business incurs high costs (discussed below). Excess inventory can only be reduced through price cuts or by temporarily stopping production.

stockout
the situation when a company runs out of finished product

Another common inventory measure, **inventory turnover**, is the number of times per year that a company sells or "turns over" its average inventory. For example, if a company keeps an average of 100 finished widgets in inventory each month, and it sold 1,000 widgets this year, then it "turned" its inventory 10 times this year.

inventory turnover
the number of times per year that a company sells or "turns over" its average inventory

In general, the higher the number of inventory "turns," the better. In practice, a high turnover means that a company can continue its daily operations with just a small amount of inventory on hand. For example, let's take two companies, A and B, which, over the course of a year, have identical inventory levels (520,000 widget parts and raw materials). If company A turns its inventories 26 times a year, it will completely replenish its inventory every two weeks and have an average inventory of 20,000 widget parts and raw materials. By contrast, if company B turns its inventories only two times a year, it will completely replenish its inventory every 26 weeks and have an average inventory of 260,000 widget parts and raw materials. So, by turning its inventory more often, company A has 92 percent less inventory on hand at any one time than company B.

> **www.experiencing management.com**
>
> Reinforce your understanding of inventory management concepts by interacting with them at our animated concept and activity site. Choose Operations_Management from the "select a topic" pull-down menu, then Inventory Management from the "overview tab."
>
> http://www.experiencingmanagement.com

Across all kinds of manufacturing plants, the average number of inventory turns is approximately eight per year, although the average can be higher or lower for different industries.[46] For example, the average auto company turns its entire inventory 13 times per year. Some of the best auto companies, however, more than double that rate, turning their inventory 27.8 times per year, or once every two weeks, which can cut costs by several hundred million dollars per year.[47]

4.4 Costs of Maintaining an Inventory

Maintaining an inventory incurs four kinds of costs: ordering, setup, holding, and stockout. **Ordering cost** is not the cost of the inventory itself, but the costs associated with ordering the inventory. It includes the costs of completing paperwork, manually entering data into a computer, making phone calls, getting competing bids, correcting mistakes, and simply determining when and how much new inventory should be reordered. For example, ordering costs are relatively high in the restaurant business, because 80 percent of food service orders (reordering food supplies) are processed manually. It's estimated that the food industry could save \$6.6 billion if all restaurants converted to electronic data interchange (see Chapter 5).

ordering cost
the costs associated with ordering inventory, including the cost of data entry, phone calls, obtaining bids, correcting mistakes, and determining when and how much inventory to order

Setup cost is the cost of changing or adjusting a machine so that it can produce a different kind of inventory.[48] For example, 3M uses the same production machinery to make several kinds of industrial tape, but it must adjust

setup cost
the costs of downtime and lost efficiency that occur when a machine is changed or adjusted to produce a different kind of inventory

the machines whenever it switches from one kind of tape to another. There are two kinds of setup costs, downtime and lost efficiency. *Downtime* occurs whenever a machine is not being used to process inventory. So, if it takes five hours to switch a machine from processing one kind of inventory to another, then five hours of downtime have occurred. Downtime is costly because companies earn an economic return only when machines are actively turning raw materials into parts or parts into finished products. The second setup cost is *lost efficiency*. Typically, after a switchover, it takes some time to recalibrate a machine to its optimal settings. It may take several days of fine-tuning before a machine finally produces the number of high-quality parts that it is supposed to. So, each time a machine has to be changed to handle a different kind of inventory, setup costs (downtime and lost efficiency) rise.

holding cost
the cost of keeping inventory until it is used or sold, including storage, insurance, taxes, obsolescence, and opportunity costs

stockout costs
the costs incurred when a company runs out of a product, including transaction costs to replace inventory and the loss of customers' goodwill

Holding cost, also known as *carrying* or *storage cost*, is the cost of keeping inventory until it is used or sold. Holding cost includes the cost of storage facilities, insurance to protect inventory from damage or theft, inventory taxes, the cost of obsolescence (holding inventory that is no longer useful to the company), and the opportunity cost of spending money on inventory that could have been spent elsewhere in the company. For example, it's estimated that at any one time, U.S. airlines have a total of $60 billion worth of airplane parts in stock for maintenance, repair, and overhauling their planes. The holding cost for managing, storing, and purchasing these parts is nearly $12.5 billion—or roughly one-fifth of the cost of the parts themselves.[49]

Stockout costs are the costs incurred when a company runs out of a product. There are two basic kinds of stockout costs. The first is the transaction costs of overtime work, shipping, and the like that are incurred in trying to quickly replace out-of-stock inventories with new inventories. The second and perhaps more damaging cost is the loss of customers' goodwill when a company cannot deliver the products that it promised. Marc Pritchard, vice president and general manager for Procter & Gamble, says, "Research shows the number-one complaint of mass shoppers is product availability. Twenty-five percent of shoppers walk out of the mass store without a purchase. What's worse is what you'd find in the back of stores and in manufacturers' warehouses—$1.3 billion in inventory, think of that—but we still can't keep the right product in stock."[50]

© AP PHOTO / DELANE B. ROUSE

Perhaps the best-known stockout situations occur whenever Scholastic Press releases a new Harry Potter book. Because the publisher did not print millions of copies of the third and fourth books in the Harry Potter series, the threat of a stockout loomed almost immediately after their release. For the fifth Harry Potter book, Order of the Phoenix, *Scholastic ordered a first print run of 6 million copies (subsequent print runs have pushed the total to over 9 million). After three weeks on the market, the book's sales topped 8.5 million copies worldwide, so despite such aggressive print runs, Scholastic has to stay on top of its production in order not to encounter a stockout situation.*

4.5 Managing Inventory

Inventory management has two basic goals. The first is to avoid running out of stock and angering and dissatisfying customers. Consequently, this goal seeks to increase inventory levels to a "safe" level that won't risk stockouts. The second is to efficiently reduce inventory levels and costs as much as possible without impairing daily operations. Thus, this goal seeks a minimum level of inventory. The following inventory management techniques—economic order quantity (EOQ), just-in-time inventory (JIT), and materials requirement planning (MRP)—are different ways of balancing these competing goals.

economic order quantity (EOQ)
a system of formulas that minimizes ordering and holding costs and helps determine how much and how often inventory should be ordered

Economic order quantity (EOQ) is a system of formulas that helps determine how much and how often inventory should be ordered. EOQ takes into account the overall demand (D) for a product while trying to minimize ordering costs (O) and holding costs (H). The formula for EOQ is

$$EOQ = \sqrt{\frac{2DO}{H}}$$

For example, if a factory uses 40,000 gallons of paint a year (D), ordering costs (O) are $75 per order, and holding costs (H) are $4 per gallon, then the optimal quantity to order is 1,225 gallons:

$$EOQ = \sqrt{\frac{2(40{,}000)(75)}{4}} = 1{,}225$$

And, with 40,000 gallons of paint being used per year, the factory uses approximately 110 gallons per day:

$$\left(\frac{40{,}000\ gallons}{365\ days} = 110\right)$$

Consequently, the factory would order 1,225 new gallons of paint approximately every 11 days:

$$\left(\frac{1{,}225\text{ gallons}}{110\text{ gallons per day}} = 11.1\ days\right)$$

just-in-time (JIT) inventory system
an inventory system in which component parts arrive from suppliers just as they are needed at each stage of production

While EOQ formulas try to minimize holding and ordering costs, the just-in-time (JIT) approach to inventory management attempts to eliminate holding costs by reducing inventory levels to near zero. With a **just-in-time (JIT) inventory system**, component parts arrive from suppliers just as they are needed at each stage of production. By having parts arrive "just in time," the manufacturer has little inventory on hand, and thus avoids the costs associated with holding inventory. For example, thanks to its JIT inventory system, Toyota's Georgetown, Kentucky car factory has only 2.8 hours' worth of inventory on hand at any one time. This extremely low level of inventory saves Toyota millions of dollars a year in inventory expenses.[51]

To have just the right amount of inventory arrive at just the right time requires a tremendous amount of coordination between manufacturing operations and suppliers. One way to promote tight coordination under JIT is close proximity. Most parts suppliers for Toyota's Georgetown, Kentucky plant are located within 200 miles of the plant. Furthermore, parts are picked up from suppliers and delivered to Toyota as often as 16 times a day.[52]

Another way is to have a shared information system that allows a manufacturer and its suppliers to know the quantity and kinds of parts inventory the other has in stock. One way factories and suppliers facilitate information sharing is to use the same part numbers and names. Ford's seat supplier accomplishes this by sticking a bar code on each seat, which Ford then uses to route the seat through its factory.

kanban
a ticket-based JIT system that indicates when to reorder inventory

Manufacturing operations and their parts suppliers can also facilitate close coordination by using the Japanese system of kanban. **Kanban**, which is Japanese for "sign," is a simple ticket-based system that indicates when it is time to reorder inventory. Suppliers attach kanban cards to batches of parts. Then, when an assembly-line worker uses the first part out of a batch, the kanban card is removed. The cards are then collected, sorted, and quickly returned to the supplier, who begins resupplying the factory with parts that match the order information on the kanban cards. And, because prices and batch sizes are typically agreed to ahead of time, kanban tickets greatly reduce paperwork and ordering costs.[53]

materials requirement planning (MRP)
a production and inventory system that determines the production schedule, production batch sizes, and inventory needed to complete final products

A third method for managing inventory is **materials requirement planning (MRP)**. MRP is a production and inventory system that, from beginning to end, precisely determines the production schedule, production batch sizes, and inventories needed to complete final products. The three key parts of MRP systems are the master production schedule, the bill of materials, and inventory records. The *master production schedule* is a detailed schedule that indicates the quantity of each item to be produced, the planned delivery dates for those items, and the time by which each step of the production process must be completed in order to meet those delivery dates. Based on the quantity and kind of products set forth in the master production schedule, the *bill of materials* identifies all the necessary parts and inventory, the quantity or volume of inventory to be ordered, and the order in which the parts and inventory should be assembled. *Inventory records* indicate the kind, quantity, and location of inventory that is on hand or that has been ordered. When inventory records are combined with the bill of materials, the resulting report indicates what to buy, when to buy it, and what it will cost to order. Today, nearly all MRP systems are available in the form of powerful, flexible computer software.[54]

independent demand system
an inventory system in which the level of one kind of inventory does not depend on another

dependent demand system
an inventory system in which the level of inventory depends on the number of finished units to be produced

Which inventory management system should you use? Economic order quantity (EOQ) formulas are intended for use with **independent demand systems**, in which the level of one kind of inventory does not depend on another. For example, because inventory levels for automobile tires are unrelated to the inventory levels of women's dresses, Sears could use EOQ formulas to calculate separate optimal order quantities for dresses and tires. By contrast, JIT and MRP are used with **dependent demand systems**, in which the level of inventory depends on the number of finished units to be produced. For example, if Yamaha makes 1,000 motorcycles a day, then it will need 1,000 seats, 1,000 gas tanks, and 2,000 wheels and tires each day. So, when optimal inventory levels depend on the number of products to be produced, use a JIT or MRP management system.

Review 4
Manufacturing Operations and Inventory

Manufacturing operations produce physical goods. Manufacturing operations can be classified according to the amount of processing or assembly that occurs after receiving an order from customers. Make-to-order operations, in which assembly doesn't begin until products are ordered, involve the most processing. The next-highest degree of processing occurs in assemble-to-order operations, in which preassembled modules are combined after orders are received to produce semicustomized products. The least processing occurs in make-to-stock operations, in which standard parts are ordered, on the basis of sales forecasts, and assembled before orders are received.

There are four kinds of inventory: raw materials, component parts, work-in-process, and finished goods. Because companies incur ordering, setup, holding, and stockout costs when handling inventory, inventory costs can be enormous. To control those costs, companies measure and track inventory in three ways: average aggregate inventory, weeks of supply, and turnover. Companies meet the basic goals of inventory management (avoiding stockouts and reducing inventory without hurting daily operations) through economic order quantity (EOQ) formulas, just-in-time (JIT) inventory systems, and materials requirement planning (MRP). EOQ formulas minimize holding and ordering costs by determining how much and how often inventory should be ordered. By having parts arrive just when they are needed at each stage of production, JIT systems attempt to minimize inventory levels and holding costs. JIT systems often depend on proximity, shared information, and the Japanese system of kanban. MRP precisely determines the production schedule, production batch sizes, and the ordering of inventories needed to complete final products. The three key parts of MRP systems are the master production schedule, the bill of materials, and inventory records. Use EOQ formulas when inventory levels are independent, and use JIT and MRP when inventory levels are dependent on the number of products to be produced.

STUDY TIP Close your book and write a list of the key concepts in this chapter. Or create flashcards for key concepts (concept on one side, explanation and example on the other). Flashcards are great portable study aids that you can use over and over, in a group, with a partner, or on your own.

MANAGEMENT DECISION

NO FACIAL FOR YOU!

On Friday at 9 A.M., a very tired-looking woman walks into the city location of Marshall's Day Spa. She wants to book a facial at 12:30 that day if possible. No other time will work because she has to drop off her child at preschool at 12:15 and pick up the child at 2:15. The employee at Marshall's explains that the time will not work at that location, but that the suburban location (15 minutes away) has a slot available. The bedraggled customer is elated. She will be able to have a relaxing facial and still return to the city in time to pick up her child.

At 12:30, the woman walks through the doors of the suburban location of Marshall's Day Spa. She checks in at the desk and sits down in the waiting area. An employee at the desk immediately calls her name but does not lead her back into the spa. Instead, the employee explains that there was a mistake in booking the appointment. "We have a large group of new employees going through training at the moment. You were accidentally booked for next Wednesday, not today. Will that work for you?" The very disappointed customer says no, she was really hoping to have the facial today, and explains her time constraints. "Hold on, please. Let me get my manager," the employee replies.

As the manager of the suburban location of Marshall's, you are in charge of service delivery and recovery—even in this instance, when the mistake was made by another location. The cost of the facial the customer booked is $90. With so many trainees, this will probably not be the last mistake in booking during the training period. Competition in the day spa market is fierce, so how you respond to problems that arise during the intensive training period could affect business for several months, if not longer.

Questions

1. List possible ways you can recover from the booking mistake with this customer.
2. Decide on the best service-recovery option.
3. Map out a plan to maintain service quality during the training period.

DEVELOP YOUR CAREER POTENTIAL

TAKE A FACTORY TOUR

Imagine that you arrive back at your dorm room one afternoon to find your roommate watching a Mister Rogers rerun.[55] When asked why, your roommate replies, "Management homework." Crazy? Maybe not. Fred Rogers may well hold the record for factory tours. During his long career, he broadcast footage to millions of children showing how Cheerios, plastic drinking straws, graham crackers, pasta, spoons, and a host of other familiar products are made. He was even at Crayola when the one-billionth crayon rolled off the production line.

Fred Rogers wasn't the only American who's ever been interested in manufacturing. Each year, thousands visit corporate facilities like these:

- Coca-Cola **(http://www.coke.com)** has an interactive, virtual factory tour where participants try to guess the optimal amount of sugar, water, and secret formula needed to create a batch of Coca-Cola, practice quality inspection, package Coca-Cola for shipment, and much more.
- The JCPenney Museum **(http://www.jcpenney.net/company/history/archive2.htm)** displays the history and products of James Cash Penney and the company he founded.
- Hershey's Chocolate World in Hershey, Pennsylvania **(http://www.hersheys.com)**, is the home of Hershey Food Corporation's free visitors' center with a Disney-like ride through a simulated chocolate factory. If you don't like chocolate, check out Jelly Belly at **http://jellybelly.com/Cultures/en-US/Fun/Tours/Virtual+Tour.htm**.
- The Boeing Everett Tour Center **(http://www.boeing.com/companyoffices/aboutus/tours/)** introduces visitors to how Boeing makes its 747, 767, and 777 passenger jets.
- Cereal City **(http://www.kelloggscerealcityusa.org/)** shows how Kellogg makes its best-selling cereals.

In fact, visiting factories has become so popular that there are now two books on the subject: *Watch It Made in the U.S.A.: A Visitor's Guide to the Companies That Make Your Favorite Products*, by Karen Axelrod and Bruce Brumberg (John Muir Publications), and *Inside America: The Great American Industrial Tour Guide, 1,000 Free Industrial Tours Open to the Public Covering More Than 300 Different Industries*, by Jack and Eunice Berger (Heritage Publications).

If you've never toured a factory, you might wonder what all the fuss is about. According to author Karen Axelrod, "Everyone's eyes get bigger when they see the way things work. Everyone becomes a five-year-old." Barbara Bernstein of Annapolis, Maryland, says, "I'm interested in how companies make anything, plastic bags for grocery stores, peanut butter, Formica, anything." There's just something magical about watching the manufacture of familiar products like cereal, cars, or candy.

Your assignment for this Develop Your Management Potential is to take a factory tour. Consult one of the books mentioned above, visit one of the following Web sites listing factory tours in your region (**http://www.factorytoursusa.com**, **http://www.factorytour.com**, or **http://www.bygpub.com/books/tg2rw/factory-tours.htm**), do a quick Web search using the key words "factory tour," or simply ask around about a good factory tour near you. When on your tour, gather some literature and ask the following questions:

1. What steps or procedures does the company take to ensure the quality of its products?
2. How does the company measure productivity, and how does its productivity compare to others in the industry?
3. Describe the basic steps used to make the finished products in this factory. As you do this, be sure to describe the raw materials inventories, component parts inventories, and work-in-process inventories used to create the finished products.
4. What did you find most impressive about the factory or manufacturing processes? Also, using the material from the chapter, describe one thing that the company could do differently to improve quality, increase productivity, or reduce inventory.

BIZ FLIX Casino

Martin Scorsese's lengthy, complex, and beautifully filmed *Casino* offers a close look at the gambling casinos of Las Vegas and their organized crime connections in the 1970s. It completes his trilogy that began with *Mean Streets* (1973) and continued with *Goodfellas* (1990).[56] In *Casino*, ambition, greed, drugs, and sex ultimately destroy the mob's gambling empire. The film includes strong performances by Robert De Niro, Joe Pesci, and Sharon Stone. The violence and expletive-filled dialogue give *Casino* an R rating.

This scene, which comes from the beginning of "The Truth about Las Vegas" sequence, opens the film and establishes important background about casino operations. Listen carefully to Sam Rothstein's (De Niro) voice-over. He quickly describes the casino's operation and explains how it tries to reach its goals.

What to Watch for and Ask Yourself

1. What type of operations management does this scene show—manufacturing operations management or service operations management?
2. Are the customers directly involved in this operation? If they are, in what way? What likely effects does their involvement have on the casino's operation and its management?
3. Does the casino have independent or interdependent operation processes?

MGMT WORKPLACE Cannondale

Cannondale makes a variety of bicycles that appeal to casual riders as well as professionals. Part of Cannondale's ability to serve all members of its diverse audience equally well comes from its attention to detail at the operations level. The folks at Cannondale contend that operations management begins at the point of design. After the design stage, Cannondale has several systems in place to help control and manage the fabrication, assembly, and finishing processes. Material tags, instruction sheets, bar code identification tags, small batch sizes, and computerized tracking systems keep workers organized and the production process synchronized. Rick Hinson, the plant and operations manager, estimates that the operations initiatives have reduced finished goods inventory by 50 percent.

What to Watch for and Ask Yourself

1. How are Cannondale's production control and efficiency initiatives likely to affect the quality of its products? Explain.
2. Discuss both the advantages and the disadvantages of being a make-to-order operation.
3. Discuss the importance of reducing finished goods inventory.

Leading

PART FIVE

PHOTOS: KEITH WOOD/CORBIS © AP PHOTO/SHEALAH CRAIGHEAD © AP PHOTO/AL BEHRMAN

CHAPTER FOURTEEN

Motivation

outline

WHAT WOULD YOU DO?

CDW Headquarters, Chicago, Illinois.[1] CDW (Computer Discount Warehouse) got its start 20 years ago when Michael Krasny needed cash and offered his used IBM computer for sale. When he was overwhelmed with calls from people who wanted to buy it, he realized that he had stumbled onto a business opportunity and went on to found CDW. which was one of the first companies to sell computers directly to customers. Krasny readily admits, "CDW was not a vision created from a business plan. It has been an evolution of passion—passion for technology."

Though CDW still sells directly to customers, 97 percent of its sales are to small and medium-sized businesses. Unlike most 1-800 computer retailers or Web site "e-tailers," however, CDW assigns each customer a dedicated account manager who helps find technology solutions to fit that customer's needs. Each account manager is supported by team specialists who provide expertise in bandwidth, telephony, storage, security, power, network design, technol-

student resources

URL Explore the four levels of learning by doing the simulation module on Motivation.

GUIDE Mini lecture reviews all the learning points in the chapter and concludes with a case on Sun Microsystems.

VIDEO Biz Flix is a scene from *For Love of the Game.* Management Workplace is a segment on Wahoo's Fish Tacos.

PPT 12 slides with graphics provide an outline for this chapter.

FAQ Chuck gives you suggestions on how to manage your time to meet your goals.

TEST 24 true/false questions, 25 multiple-choice questions, a management scenario, and 11 exhibit worksheets

ogy services, software licensing, and other areas. According to CDW's president, despite its Web site and 1-800 phone number, "It's an old-fashioned, feet-on-the-street model," built on one-to-one relationships. In fact, each time a customer logs onto his or her personalized Web page at CDW.com, a picture of the customer's account representative appears on the page.

One-to-one relationship selling isn't very effective, however, if employees keep quitting and those pictures keep changing—and that's the problem. In the tech industry, 75 to 90 percent of employees leave their companies within two years of being hired. While the rate is lower at CDW, between 60 and 70 percent after two years, that's still much too high, especially for a company that uses one-to-one relationships as its competitive advantage. Basically, this means that one-third of CDW's customers gets a new account representative each year. That rises to two-thirds of all customers over two years and 100 percent of customers after three. Clearly, this kind of turnover has the potential to destroy CDW's competitive advantage. And with Dell Computer breathing down CDW's neck, that couldn't happen at a worse time. With $35 billion in revenue, Dell is seven times the size of CDW. Furthermore, Dell is the market leader in sales of personal computers and network servers. And now, with Dell beginning to sell printers, large-scale storage systems, and computer networking (beyond servers), it's moving directly into CDW's key sales territory of small and medium-sized businesses. Moreover, since Dell has laid off 5,700 workers, its costs, which were already the lowest in the industry, are now brutally low from a competitive standpoint. Since high employee turnover weakens CDW's one-to-one relationship selling, those businesses could very well decide to buy from Dell instead.

So, it's imperative that you find a way to reduce turnover. The recruitment and replacement costs are enormous, and customer service is clearly being hurt. Fortunately, you don't have to reduce turnover to zero for CDW's strategy to work. Since account representatives with three years' experience typically sell three times as much as reps with one year of experience, all you have to do is get account representatives to stay longer before quitting. If account representatives stay for three or four years instead of one or two, sales will be much higher and will continue to grow. But what should you offer to motivate your employees—money, benefits, opportunities for growth, interesting work, or something else? Assuming different people are motivated by different things, how can CDW keep everyone motivated? That seems almost impossible. And, if you somehow find a variety of rewards that appeal to most of CDW's employees and account representatives, won't employee turnover take care of itself? In other words, do you have to do anything to specifically encourage people to stay longer with the company? Or would a smorgasbord of rewards be enough? Finally, with Dell on the horizon, you've not only got to get people to stay longer, you've also got to motivate them to perform better. What's the best way to do that? **If you were in charge at CDW, what would you do?**

What makes people happiest and most productive at work? Is it money, benefits, opportunities for growth, interesting work, or something else altogether? And if people desire different things, how can a company keep everyone motivated? The set of problems that CDW is experiencing illustrates that motivating workers is never easy. It takes insight and hard work to motivate workers to join the company, perform well, and then stay with the company.

This chapter begins by reviewing the basics of motivation—effort, needs, and intrinsic and extrinsic rewards. We will start with a basic model of motivation and add to it as we progress through each section in the chapter. Next, we will explore how employees' equity perceptions and reward expectations affect their motivation. If you're familiar with the phrase "perception is reality," you're off to a good start in understanding the importance of perceptions and expectations in motivation. The third part of the chapter reviews the role that rewards and goals play in motivating employees. You'll see that finding the right combination of goals and rewards is much harder in practice than it looks. The chapter finishes with a summary of practical, theory-based actions that managers can take to motivate their workers.

What Is Motivation?

Motivation is the set of forces that initiates, directs, and makes people persist in their efforts to accomplish a goal.[2] In terms of this definition, *initiation of effort* is concerned with the choices that people make about how much effort to put forth in their jobs. ("Do I really knock myself out doing these performance appraisals or just do a decent job?") *Direction of effort* is concerned with the choices that people make in deciding where to put forth effort in their jobs. ("I should be spending time on my high-dollar accounts instead of learning this new computer system!") *Persistence of effort* is concerned with the choices that people make about how long they will put forth effort in their jobs before reducing or eliminating those efforts. ("I'm only halfway through the project, and I'm exhausted. Do I plow through to the end or just call it quits?") As Exhibit 14.1 shows, initiation, direction, and persistence are at the heart of motivation.

motivation
the set of forces that initiates, directs, and makes people persist in their efforts to accomplish a goal

exhibit 14.1

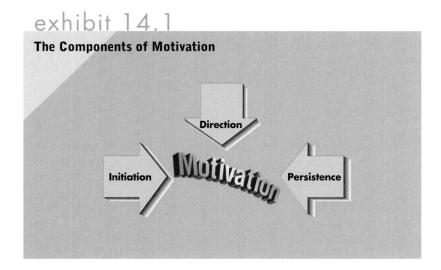

The Components of Motivation

After reading the next section, you should be able to

1 explain the basics of motivation.

1 Basics of Motivation

Take your right hand and point the palm toward your face. Keep your thumb and pinky finger straight and bend the three middle fingers so the tips are touching your palm. Now rotate your wrist back and forth. If you were in the Regent Square Tavern in Pittsburgh, Pennsylvania, that hand signal would tell waitress Marjorie Landale that you wanted a Yeungling beer. Marjorie, who isn't deaf, would not have understood that sign a few years ago. But with a state school for the deaf nearby, the tavern always has its share of deaf customers, so she decided on her own to take classes to learn how to sign. At first, deaf customers would signal for a pen and paper to write out their orders. But after Marjorie signaled that she was learning to sign, "their eyes [would] light up, and they [would] finger-spell their order."[3]

What would motivate an employee like Marjorie to voluntarily learn a new language like American Sign Language? (Sign language is every bit as much of a language as French or Spanish.) She wasn't paid to take classes in her free time. She chose to do it on her own. And while she undoubtedly makes more tip money with a full bar than with an empty one, it's highly unlikely that she began her classes with the objective of making more money. Just what is it that motivates employees like Marjorie Landale?

> **www.experiencing management.com**
>
> You may examine and learn more about how needs motivate from the dynamic model of this concept presented at our animated concept and activity site. Choose Motivation from the "select a topic" pull-down menu, then How Needs Motivate from the "overview tab."
>
> **http://www.experiencingmanagement.com**

Let's learn more about motivation by building a basic model of motivation out of 1.1 effort and performance, 1.2 need satisfaction, and 1.3 extrinsic and intrinsic rewards and then discussing 1.4 how to motivate people with this basic model of motivation.

1.1 Effort and Performance

When most people think of work motivation, they think that working hard (effort) should lead to doing a good job (performance). Exhibit 14.2 shows a basic model of work motivation and performance, displaying this process.

The first thing to notice about Exhibit 14.2 is that this is a basic model of work motivation and performance. In practice, it's almost impossible to talk about one without mentioning the other. Not surprisingly, managers often confuse the two, saying things such as "Your performance was really terrible last quarter. What's the matter? Aren't you as motivated as you used to be?" In fact, motivation is just one of three primary determinants of job performance. In industrial psychology, job performance is frequently represented by this equation:

$$\text{Job Performance} = \text{Motivation} \times \text{Ability} \times \text{Situational Constraints}$$

exhibit 14.2

A Basic Model of Work Motivation and Performance

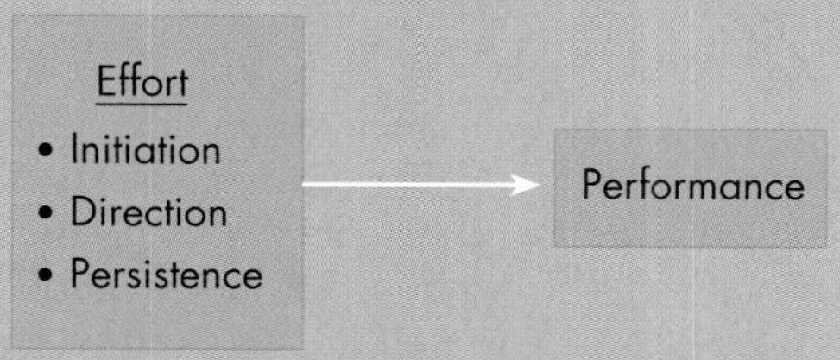

In this formula, *job performance* is how well someone performs the requirements of the job. *Motivation*, as defined above, is effort, the degree to which someone works hard to do the job well. *Ability* is the degree to which workers possess the knowledge, skills, and talent needed to do a job well. And *situational constraints* are factors beyond the control of individual employees, such as tools, policies, and resources that have an effect on job performance. Since job performance is a multiplicative function of motivation times ability times situational constraints, job performance will suffer if any one of these components is weak. Does this mean that motivation doesn't matter? No, not at all. It just means that all the motivation in the world won't translate into high performance when you have little ability and high situational constraints.

DOING THE RIGHT THING

Faking It, Not Making It

With technology these days, you may be tempted to engage in "impression management" to try to convince your boss and coworkers that you're working hard when you're really not. For instance, a tech support worker who enjoyed three-hour lunches used a program on his Palm personal computer to remotely control his office computer. He would open, close, and move files to make it look like he had just stepped away from his desk. Another trick is to leave early, but then send emails on the way home via your Blackberry device to make it look as if you are still at the office. You may be thinking that these ruses are harmless, but 59 percent of human resource managers and 53 percent of supervisors have caught employees lying about the hours they work. Furthermore, if you're using technology to fake it, you're usually leaving high-tech "tracks" and "footprints" along the way. That tech worker who controlled his office computer with his Palm PC at lunch was fired for "habitual lateness." Motivation is all about effort. So, do the right thing. Work hard for your company, your customers, and yourself.[4]

1.2 Need Satisfaction

In Exhibit 14.2, we started with a very basic model of motivation in which effort leads to job performance. However, managers want to know, "What leads to effort?" And they will try almost anything they can to find the answer. The employees at Lyon & Associates Creative Services are apparently motivated by money. At the end of the year, 20 percent of company profits are equally distributed among all full-time employees who have worked there for at least one year.[5] Money isn't everything, however. At Global Vision Strategies, which does cross-cultural training for executives, one employee preferred more vacation and $5,000 less in salary.[6] Likewise, employees at Wilton Connor Packaging, Inc. in Charlotte, North Carolina, can take their laundry to work and have it washed, dried, and folded. The company also employs a handyman, who does free minor household repairs for employees. So which of these techniques will motivate employees and lead to increased effort? The answer is all of them and none of them: It depends on employees' needs.

Needs are the physical or psychological requirements that must be met to ensure survival and well-being.[7] As shown on the left side of Exhibit 14.3, a person's unmet need creates an uncomfortable, internal state of tension that must be resolved. For example, if you normally skip breakfast, but then have to work through lunch, chances are you'll be so hungry by late afternoon that the only thing you'll be motivated to do is find something to eat. So, according to needs theories, people are motivated by unmet needs. But once a need is met, it no longer motivates. When this occurs, people become satisfied, as shown on the right side of Exhibit 14.3.

needs
the physical or psychological requirements that must be met to ensure survival and well-being

Note: Throughout the chapter, as we build on this basic model, the parts of the model that we've already discussed will appear shaded in color. For example, since we've already discussed the effort → performance part of the model, those components are shown with a colored background. When we add new parts to the model, they will have a white background. For instance, since we're adding need satisfaction to the model at this step, the need-satisfaction components of unsatisfied need, tension, energized to take action, and satisfaction are shown with a white background. This shading convention should make it easier to understand the work motivation model as we add to it in each section of the chapter.

Since people are motivated by unmet needs, managers must learn what those unmet needs are and address them. This is not always a straightforward task, however, because different needs theories suggest different needs categories. Exhibit 14.4 shows needs from three well-known needs theories. Maslow's Hierarchy of Needs suggests that people are motivated by *physiological* (food and water), *safety* (physical and economic), *belongingness* (friendship, love, social inter-

www.experiencing management.com

Examine Maslow's Hierarchy of Needs in greater detail at our animated concept and activity site. Choose Motivation from the "select a topic" pull-down menu, then Maslow's Needs Hierarchy from the "overview tab."

http://www.experiencingmanagement.com

exhibit 14.3

Adding Need Satisfaction to the Model

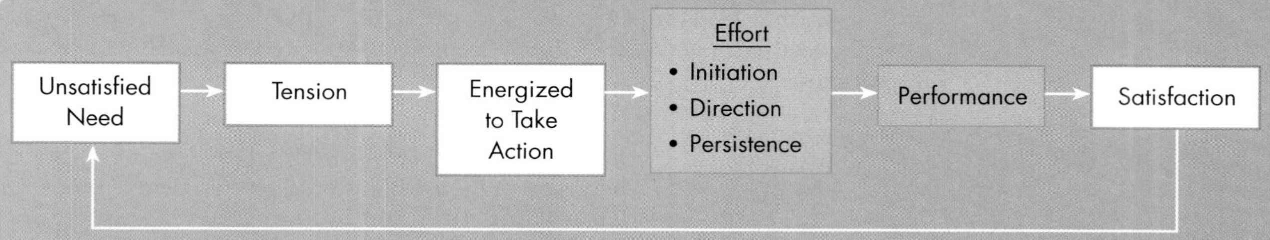

action), *esteem* (achievement and recognition), and *self-actualization* (realizing your full potential) needs.[8] Alderfer's ERG Theory collapses Maslow's five needs into three: *existence* (safety and physiological needs), *relatedness* (belongingness), and *growth* (esteem and self-actualization).[9] McClelland's Learned Needs Theory suggests that people are motivated by the need for *affiliation* (to be liked and accepted), the need for *achievement* (to accomplish challenging goals), or the need for *power* (to influence others).[10]

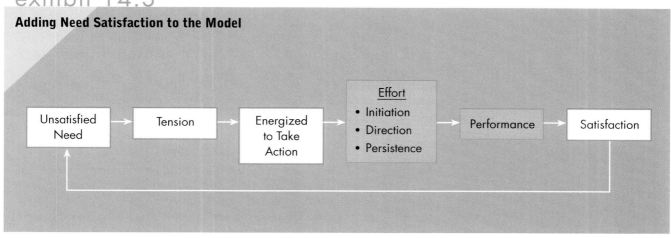

Things become even more complicated when we consider the different predictions made by these theories. According to Maslow, needs are arranged in a hierarchy from low (physiological) to high (self-actualization). Within this hierarchy, people are motivated by their lowest unsatisfied need. As each need is met, they work their way up the hierarchy from physiological to self-actualization needs. By contrast, Alderfer says that people can be motivated by more than one need at a time. Furthermore, he suggests that people are just as likely to move down the needs hierarchy as up, particularly when they are unable to achieve satisfaction at the next higher need level. McClelland, on the other hand, argues that the degree to which particular needs motivate varies tremendously from person to person, with some people being motivated primarily by achievement and others by power or affiliation. Moreover, McClelland says that needs are learned, not innate. For instance, studies show that children whose parents own a small business or hold a managerial position are much more likely to have a high need for achievement.[11]

exhibit 14.4

Needs Classification of Different Theories

	MASLOW'S HIERARCHY	ALDERFER'S ERG	McCLELLAND'S LEARNED NEEDS
Higher-Order Needs	Self-Actualization Esteem Belongingness	Growth Relatedness	Power Achievement Affiliation
Lower-Order Needs	Safety Physiological	Existence	

So, with three different sets of needs and three very different ideas about how needs motivate, how do we provide a practical answer to managers who just want to know "What leads to effort?" Fortunately, the research evidence simplifies things a bit. To start, studies indicate that there are two basic kinds of needs categories.[12] As shown in Exhibit 14.4, *lower-order needs* are concerned with safety and with physiological and existence requirements, while *higher-order needs* are concerned with relationships (belongingness, relatedness, and affiliation); challenges and accomplishments (esteem, self-actualization, growth, and achievement); and influence (power). Studies generally show that higher-order needs will not motivate people as long as lower-order needs remain unsatisfied.

So, what leads to effort? In part, needs do. Subsection 1.4 discusses how managers can use what we know from need-satisfaction theories to motivate workers.

www.experiencing management.com

Herzberg's Two-Factor Theory is a motivation concept that is related to extrinsic and intrinsic rewards. This classic concept may be examined by visiting our animated concept and activity site. Choose Motivation from the "select a topic" pull-down menu, then Herzberg's Two-Factor Theory from the "overview tab."

http://www.experiencingmanagement.com

1.3 Extrinsic and Intrinsic Rewards

No discussion of motivation would be complete without considering rewards. Let's add two kinds of rewards, extrinsic and intrinsic, to the model, as shown in Exhibit 14.5.[13]

Extrinsic rewards are tangible and visible to others and are given to employees contingent on the performance of specific tasks or behaviors.[14] External agents (managers, for example) determine and control the distribution, frequency, and amount of extrinsic rewards, such as pay, company stock, benefits, and promotions. Why do companies need extrinsic rewards? To get people to do things they wouldn't otherwise do. Companies use extrinsic rewards to motivate people to perform four basic behaviors: joining the organization, regularly attending their jobs, performing their jobs well, and staying with the organization.[15]

extrinsic reward
a reward that is tangible, visible to others, and given to employees contingent on the performance of specific tasks or behaviors

Think about it. Would you show up to work every day to do the best possible job that you could just out of the goodness of your heart? Very few people would. This is especially true in the fast-food business where employee turnover averages 200 percent a year and higher. Now, however, fast-food companies are offering significantly better external rewards to get more people

exhibit 14.5
Adding Rewards to the Model

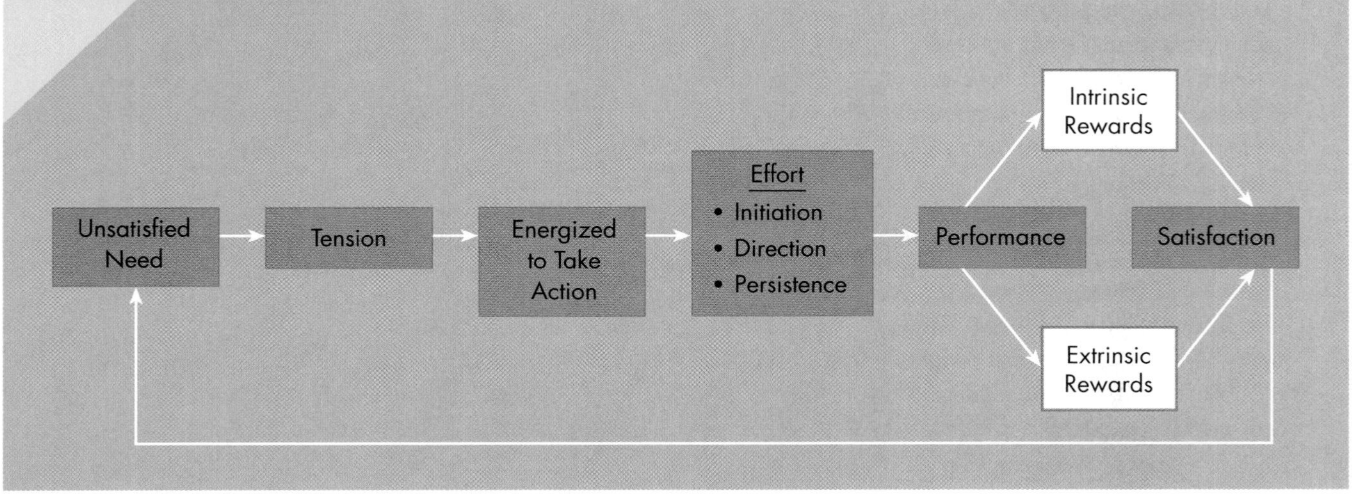

PERSONAL PRODUCTIVITY TIP

Let Employees Have Fun! Creating fun is a great way to motivate. Some companies have "treat days," when managers serve employees coffee, doughnuts, or ice cream. Others ask their managers to bring in baby pictures of themselves so that people can have fun guessing which baby was which manager. Some companies create a "stress-free zone," with a hammock, an inflatable palm tree, and a "stress-reduction dummy"—a large inflatable punching bag. One manager sends employees "stress support kits," which contain chewing gum, aspirin, a comedy cassette, wind-up toys for employees' desks, and a rubber toy for squeezing during tense moments. So, if you want to motivate employees, let them have fun.[16]

to take and keep fast-food jobs. For example, McDonald's provides its restaurant employees with medical and dental insurance, credit union memberships, discounts on home and car insurance, and money to pay for college textbooks.

By contrast, **intrinsic rewards** are the natural rewards associated with performing a task or activity for its own sake. For example, aside from the external rewards management offers for doing something well, employees often experience a sense of interest and enjoyment from the activities or tasks they perform. Examples of intrinsic rewards include a sense of accomplishment or achievement, a feeling of responsibility, the chance to learn something new or interact with others, or simply the fun that comes from performing an interesting, challenging, and engaging task.

intrinsic reward
a natural reward associated with performing a task or activity for its own sake

Which types of rewards are most important to workers in general? A number of surveys suggest that both extrinsic and intrinsic rewards are important. One survey found that the most important rewards were good benefits and health insurance, job security, a week or more of vacation (all extrinsic rewards), interesting work, the opportunity to learn new skills, and independent work situations (all intrinsic rewards). And employee preferences for intrinsic and extrinsic rewards appear to be relatively stable. Studies conducted over the last three decades have consistently found that employees are twice as likely to indicate that "important and meaningful work" matters more to them than what they are paid.[17]

1.4 Motivating with the Basics

So, given the basic model of work motivation in Exhibit 14.5, what practical things can managers do to motivate employees to increase their effort?

Start by asking people what their needs are. If managers don't know what workers' needs are, they won't be able to provide them the opportunities and rewards that can satisfy those needs. Linda Connor, vice president of corporate culture at Technology Professionals Corp (TPC) in Grand Rapids, Michigan, keeps careful notes about TPC employees' needs. She says, "I sit down at employees' 30-day reviews and ask specific questions about hobbies and interests for each member of their families."[18] Connor's notes also include ideas on how to help employees deal with stress.[19] So, if you want to meet employees' needs, do what Linda Connor does and just ask.

Next, *satisfy lower-order needs first.* Since higher-order needs will not motivate people as long as lower-order needs remain unsatisfied, companies should satisfy lower-order needs first. In practice, this means providing the equipment, training, and knowledge to create a safe workplace free of physical risks, paying employees well enough to provide financial security, and offering a benefits package that will protect employees and their families through good medical coverage and health and disability insurance. Indeed, a survey based on a representative sample of Americans found that when people choose jobs or organizations, three of the four most important factors—starting pay/salary

(62 percent), employee benefits (57 percent), and job security (47 percent)—are lower-order needs.[20]

Third, managers should *expect people's needs to change.* As some needs are satisfied or situations change, managers should expect that employees' needs will change. In other words, what motivated people before may not motivate them now. Likewise, what motivates people to accept a job may not necessarily motivate them once they have the job.

Finally, *as needs change and lower-order needs are satisfied, satisfy higher-order needs by looking for ways to allow employees to experience intrinsic rewards.* Recall that intrinsic rewards, such as accomplishment, achievement, learning something new, and interacting with others, are the natural rewards associated with performing a task or activity for its own sake. And, with the exception of influence (power), intrinsic rewards correspond very closely to higher-order needs that are concerned with relationships (belongingness, relatedness, and affiliation) and challenges and accomplishments (esteem, self-actualization, growth, and achievement). Therefore, one way for managers to meet employees' higher-order needs is to create opportunities for employees to experience intrinsic rewards by providing challenging work, encouraging employees to take greater responsibility for their work, and giving employees the freedom to pursue tasks and projects they find naturally interesting. For example, we began this section by asking, "What would motivate an employee like Marjorie Landale to voluntarily learn American Sign Language?" Marjorie wasn't paid to do this. In fact, she even spent her own money and free time to learn how to sign. The reason that Marjorie learned to sign is that doing so met her higher-order needs. It gave her a sense of accomplishment, and it allowed her to interact with deaf customers with whom she had previously been unable to interact. And Marjorie's boss was smart enough to encourage her to pursue a project that she found naturally interesting.

Review 1
Basics of Motivation

Motivation is the set of forces that initiates, directs, and makes people persist in their efforts over time to accomplish a goal. Managers often confuse motivation and performance, but job performance is a multiplicative function of motivation times ability times situational constraints. If any one of these components is weak, job performance will suffer. Needs are the physical or psychological requirements that must be met to ensure survival and well-being. When needs are not met, people experience an internal state of tension. But, once a particular need is met, it no longer motivates. When this occurs, people become satisfied and are then motivated by other unmet needs. Different motivational theories, such as Maslow's Hierarchy of Needs (physiological, safety, belongingness, esteem, and self-actualization), Alderfer's ERG Theory (existence, relatedness, and growth), and McClelland's Learned Needs Theory (affiliation, achievement, and power), specify a number of different needs. However, studies show that there are only two general kinds of needs, lower-order needs and higher-order needs, and that higher-order needs will not motivate people as long as lower-order needs remain unsatisfied. Both extrinsic and intrinsic rewards motivate people. Extrinsic rewards, which include pay, company stock, benefits, and promotions, are used to motivate people to join organizations and attend and perform their jobs. The basic model of motivation suggests that managers can motivate employees by asking them what their needs are, satisfying lower-order needs first, expecting people's needs to change, and satisfying higher-order needs through intrinsic rewards.

How Perceptions and Expectations Affect Motivation

When Jennifer Shroeger became the manager of UPS's Buffalo, New York district, employee turnover was nearly 50 percent per year. Most of those who left were part-time workers, who make up half of UPS's work force. It became Shroeger's job to get them to stay. She began by asking part-time applicants what they wanted. Many of them answered, "a full-time job." It usually takes six years of part-time work to get a full-time job driving a UPS truck, however. So Shroeger began by setting realistic expectations, telling part-time applicants that full-time work was unlikely, but that she did have good-paying part-time jobs with good benefits (health insurance and up to $23,000 in college benefits) and the flexibility to accommodate occasional days off. Next, Shroeger turned her attention to workers' expectations about the demanding work. Most new workers were shocked and overwhelmed by the hectic pace of unloading one box every three seconds, or 1,200 an hour, typically 5,000 per night. Many never came back the next night. Many more never made it past their first week. Now trainers like Carla Wass work directly with new part-timers, explaining the job, correcting their mistakes, and encouraging them. It seems to help. Since Shroeger has focused on setting realistic expectations about rewards and the demanding nature of the job itself, employee turnover has dropped from 50 percent to just 6 percent. Moreover, hiring and recruiting costs have dropped by $1 million, the number of days lost to injury is down by 20 percent, and the percentage of packages delivered on the wrong day has dropped from 4 percent to 1 percent.[21]

After reading the next two sections, you should be able to

2 use equity theory to explain how employees' perceptions of fairness affect motivation.

3 use expectancy theory to describe how workers' expectations about rewards, effort, and the link between rewards and performance influence motivation.

2 Equity Theory

Finnish businessman Jaako Rytsola was out driving in his car one evening. "The road was wide and I was feeling good. It was nice to be driving when there was no one in sight." Unfortunately for Rytsola, he wasn't really alone. A police officer pulled him over and issued him a speeding ticket for driving 43 miles per hour in a 25 mph zone. The cost of the ticket: $71,400! Janne Rajala, a college student, was also pulled over for driving 18 mph over the speed limit. However, Rajala's ticket cost him only $106. The $71,294 difference occurred because Finland bases traffic fines on the driver's income and the severity of the offense, which in this case was identical.

Is Finland's method of determining speeding fines fair or unfair? Most Americans would argue that Finland's approach is unfair, that fairness requires that fines be proportional to the offense and that everyone who breaks the law to the same degree should pay the same fine. By contrast, most Finns believe that fines proportional to income are fair. Erkki Wuouma of Finland's Ministry of the Interior says, "This is a Nordic tradition. We have progressive taxation and progressive punishments. So the more you earn, the more you pay." Rytsola pays more because he is a high-earning Internet entrepreneur. Rajala pays less because he's a low-earning college student.[22]

Equity theory is not an absolute. It is dependent on many factors, including culture. Jaako Rytsola, pictured here with his Lamborghini, was fined $71,400 for speeding because in Finland traffic fines are based on a person's income. People of other cultures may not have the same view of equity as the Finns!

Fairness, or what people perceive to be fair, is also a critical issue in organizations. **Equity theory** says that people will be motivated at work when they perceive that they are being treated fairly. In particular, equity theory stresses the importance of perceptions. So, regardless of the actual level of rewards people receive, they must also perceive that, relative to others, they are being treated fairly.

As explained below, equity theory doesn't focus on objective equity. Instead, equity theory says that equity, like beauty, is in the eye of the beholder.

Let's learn more about equity theory by examining 2.1 the components of equity theory, 2.2 how people react to perceived inequities, and 2.3 how to motivate people using equity theory.

2.1 Components of Equity Theory

equity theory
a theory that states that people will be motivated when they perceive that they are being treated fairly

inputs
in equity theory, the contributions employees make to the organization

outcomes
in equity theory, the rewards employees receive for their contributions to the organization

referents
in equity theory, others with whom people compare themselves to determine if they have been treated fairly

The basic components of equity theory are inputs, outcomes, and referents. **Inputs** are the contributions employees make to the organization. Inputs include education and training, intelligence, experience, effort, number of hours worked, and ability. **Outcomes** are the rewards employees receive in exchange for their contributions to the organization. Outcomes include pay, fringe benefits, status symbols, job titles and assignments, and even the leadership style of their superiors. And, since perceptions of equity depend on comparisons, **referents** are others with whom people compare themselves to determine if they have been treated fairly. Usually, people choose to compare themselves to referents who hold the same or similar jobs or who are otherwise similar, in gender, race, age, tenure, or other characteristics.[23]

According to the equity theory process shown in Exhibit 14.6, employees compare their outcomes, the rewards they receive from the organization, to their inputs, their contributions to the organization. This comparison of outcomes to inputs is called the **outcome/input (O/I) ratio**. After an internal comparison in which they compare their outcomes to their inputs, employees then make an external comparison in which they compare their O/I ratio with the O/I ratio of a referent.[24] When people perceive that their O/I ratio is equal to the referent's O/I ratio, they conclude that they are being treated fairly. But, when people perceive that their O/I ratio is different from their referent's O/I ratio, they conclude that they have been treated inequitably or unfairly.

Inequity can take two forms, underreward and overreward. **Underreward** occurs when a referent's O/I ratio is better than your O/I ratio. In other words, the referent you compare

exhibit 14.6

Outcome/Input Ratios

$$\frac{\text{OUTCOMES}_{\text{SELF}}}{\text{INPUTS}_{\text{SELF}}} = \frac{\text{OUTCOMES}_{\text{REFERENT}}}{\text{INPUTS}_{\text{REFERENT}}}$$

outcome/input (O/I) ratio
in equity theory, an employee's perception of how the rewards received from an organization compare with the employee's contributions to that organization

underreward
when the referent you compare yourself to is getting more outcomes relative to inputs than you are

overreward
when you are getting more outcomes relative to inputs than the referent to whom you compare yourself

yourself to is getting more outcomes relative to his or her inputs than you are. When people perceive that they have been underrewarded, they tend to experience anger or frustration. For example, when a manufacturing company received notice that some important contracts had been canceled, management cut employees' pay by 15 percent in one plant but not in another. Just as equity theory predicts, theft doubled in the plant that received the pay cut. Likewise, employee turnover increased from 5 percent to 23 percent.[25]

By contrast, **overreward** occurs when a referent's O/I ratio is worse than your O/I ratio. In this case, you are getting more outcomes relative to your inputs than your referent is. In theory, when people perceive that they have been overrewarded, they experience guilt. Not surprisingly, people have a very high tolerance for overreward. It takes a tremendous amount of overpayment before people decide that their pay or benefits are more than they deserve.

2.2 How People React to Perceived Inequity

What happens when people perceive that they have been treated inequitably at work? Exhibit 14.7 shows that perceived inequity affects satisfaction. In the case of underreward, this usually translates into frustration or anger; with overreward, the reaction is guilt. These reactions lead to tension and a strong

exhibit 14.7

Adding Equity Theory to the Model

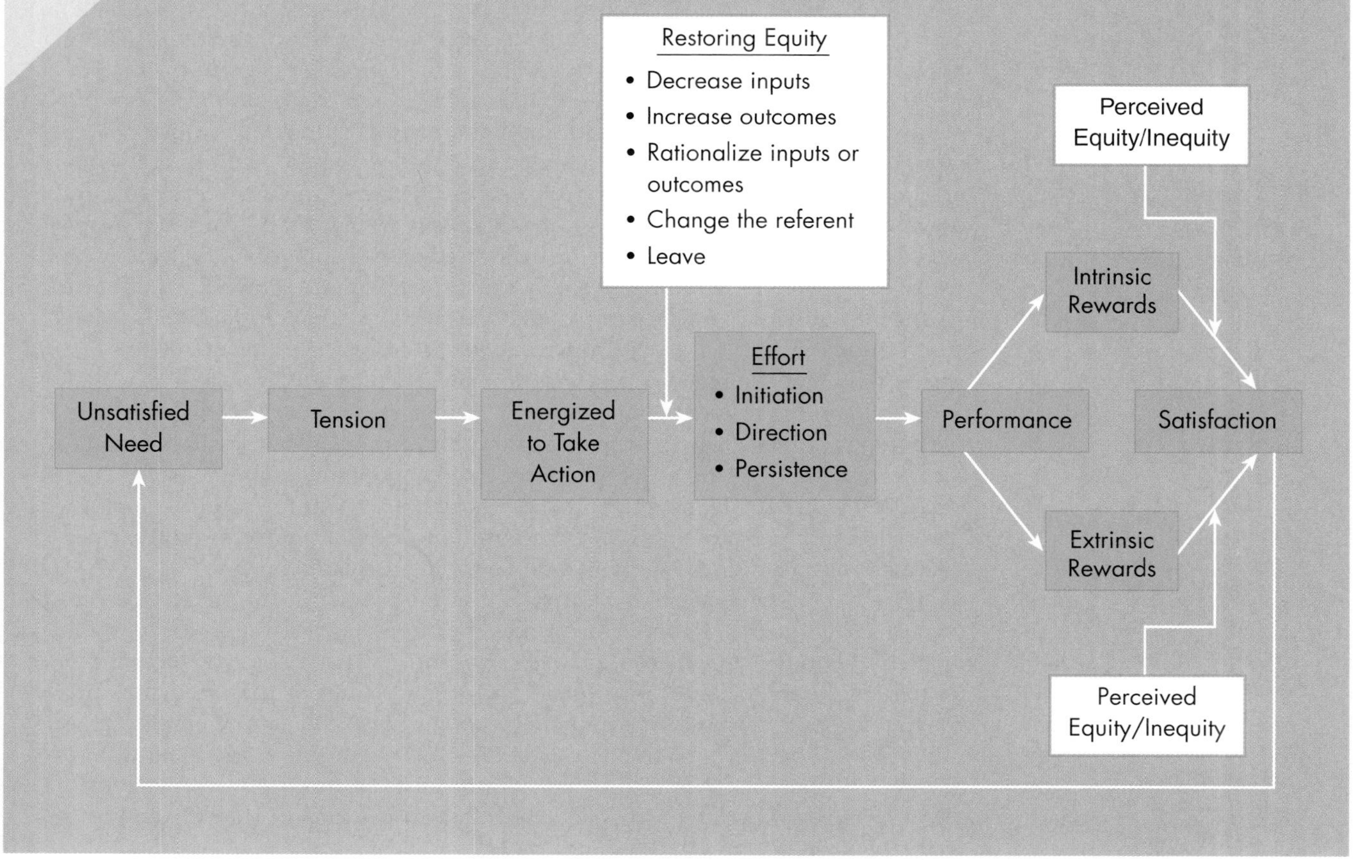

need to take action to restore equity in some way. At first, a slight inequity may not be strong enough to motivate an employee to take immediate action. If the inequity continues or there are multiple inequities, however, tension may build over time until a point of intolerance is reached, and the person is energized to take action.[26]

When people perceive that they have been treated unfairly, they may try to restore equity by reducing inputs, increasing outcomes, rationalizing inputs or outcomes, changing the referent, or simply leaving. We will discuss these possible responses in terms of the inequity associated with underreward, which is much more common than the inequity associated with overreward.

People who perceive that they have been underrewarded may try to restore equity by *decreasing or withholding their inputs (i.e., effort).* For example, when pilots of Comair, a regional U.S. airline, were negotiating higher salaries, they disrupted flight schedules by calling in sick and not showing up to work.

Increasing outcomes is another way people try to restore equity. This might include asking for a raise or pointing out the inequity to the boss and hoping that he or she takes care of it. Sometimes, however, employees may go to external organizations, such as labor unions, federal agencies, or the courts for help in increasing outcomes to restore equity. For instance, the U.S. Department of Labor estimates that 10 percent of workers are not getting the extra overtime pay they deserve when they work more than 40 hours a week.[27] For example, the managers of Waffle House restaurants sued the company because they were working an average of 89 hours a week without any overtime pay. Because Waffle House managers were required to perform and be proficient in the duties of hourly employees in addition to their managerial responsibilities, the courts ruled that managers were really employees who deserved overtime pay. As a result, they were awarded $2,868,841.50 in back overtime pay.[28]

Another method of restoring equity is to *rationalize or distort inputs or outcomes.* Instead of decreasing inputs or increasing outcomes, employees restore equity by making mental or emotional "adjustments" in their O/I ratios or the O/I ratios of their referents. For example, suppose that a company downsizes 10 percent of its work force. It's likely that the survivors, the people who still have jobs, will be angry or frustrated with company management because of the layoffs. If alternative jobs are difficult to find, however, these survivors may rationalize or distort their O/I ratios and conclude, "Well, things could be worse. At least I still have my job." Rationalizing or distorting outcomes may be used when other ways to restore equity aren't available.

Changing the referent is another way of restoring equity. In this case, people compare themselves to someone other than the referent they had been using for previous O/I ratio comparisons. Since people usually choose to compare themselves to others who hold the same or similar jobs or who are otherwise similar, they may change referents to restore equity when their personal situations change, such as a decrease in job status or pay.

Finally, when none of these methods—reducing inputs, increasing outcomes, rationalizing inputs or outcomes, or changing referents—are possible or restore equity, *employees may leave* by quitting their jobs, transferring, or increasing absenteeism.[29] Attorneys and accountants at the Securities and Exchange Commission (SEC) quit their jobs at twice the rate of employees in other federal agencies. Why? Because the SEC's attorneys and accountants are paid 40 percent less than their counterparts at other government agencies. They also leave the SEC because they can get jobs in the private sector that pay $180,000 to $250,000 per year.[30]

2.3 Motivating with Equity Theory

What practical things can managers do to use equity theory to motivate employees? They can *start by looking for and correcting major inequities.* Among other things, equity theory makes us aware that an employee's sense of fairness is based on subjective perceptions. What one employee considers grossly unfair may not affect another employee's perceptions of equity at all. Although these different perceptions make it difficult for managers to create conditions that satisfy all employees, it's critical that they do their best to take care of major inequities that can energize employees to take disruptive, costly, or harmful actions, such as decreasing inputs or leaving. So, whenever possible, managers should look for and correct major inequities.

Second, managers can *reduce employees' inputs.* Increasing outcomes is often the first and only strategy that companies use to restore equity, yet reducing employee inputs is just as viable a strategy. In fact, with dual-career couples working 50-hour weeks, more and more employees are looking for ways to reduce stress and restore a balance between work and family. Consequently, it may make sense to ask employees to do less, not more; to have them identify and eliminate the 20 percent of their jobs that don't increase productivity or add value for customers; and to eliminate company-imposed requirements that really aren't critical to the performance of managers, employees, or the company (e.g., unnecessary meetings and reports). The SAS Institute, maker of the Statistical Analysis Software used by nearly every major company in the United States, has been reducing employees' inputs with success for years. SAS closes its offices at 6 P.M. every evening. Employees receive unlimited sick days each year and are encouraged to spend time with their families. The payoff? With an employee turnover of just 3.7 percent a year (compared to 20 percent and up for most software companies), the company saves $67 million a year in unnecessary costs and expenses.[31]

Finally, managers should *make sure decision-making processes are fair.* Equity theory focuses on **distributive justice**, the degree to which outcomes and rewards are fairly distributed or allocated. However, **procedural justice**, the fairness of the process used to make reward allocation decisions, is just as important.[32] Procedural justice matters because even when employees are unhappy with their outcomes (i.e., low pay), they're much less likely to be unhappy with company management if they believe that the procedures used to allocate outcomes were fair. For example, employees who are laid off tend to be hostile toward their employer when they perceive that the procedures leading to the layoffs were unfair. By contrast, employees who perceive layoff procedures to be fair tend to continue to support and trust their employers.[33] Also, if employees perceive that their outcomes are unfair (i.e., distributive injustice), but that the decisions and procedures leading to those outcomes were fair (i.e., procedural justice), they are much more likely to seek constructive ways of restoring equity, such as discussing these matters with their manager. In contrast, if employees perceive both distributive and procedural injustice, they may resort to more destructive tactics, such as withholding effort, absenteeism, tardiness, or even sabotage and theft.[34]

distributive justice
the perceived degree to which outcomes and rewards are fairly distributed or allocated

procedural justice
the perceived fairness of the process used to make reward allocation decisions

Review 2
Equity Theory

The basic components of equity theory are inputs, outcomes, and referents. After an internal comparison in which employees compare their outcomes to their inputs, they then make an external comparison in which they compare their O/I ratio with the O/I ratio of a referent, a person who works in a similar job or is otherwise similar. When their O/I ratio is equal to the referent's O/I ratio, employees perceive that they are being treated fairly. But, when their O/I ratio is different from their referent's O/I ratio, they perceive that they have been treated inequitably or unfairly. There are two kinds of inequity, underreward and overreward. Underreward, which occurs when a referent's O/I ratio is better than the employee's O/I ratio, leads to anger or frustration. Overreward, which occurs when a referent's O/I ratio is worse than the employee's O/I ratio, can lead to guilt, but only when the level of overreward is extreme. When employees perceive that they have been treated inequitably (i.e., underreward), they may try to restore equity by reducing inputs, increasing outcomes, rationalizing inputs or outcomes, changing the referent, or simply leaving. Managers can use equity theory to motivate workers by looking for and correcting major inequities, reducing employees' inputs, and emphasizing procedural as well as distributive justice.

3 Expectancy Theory

How attractive do you find each of the following rewards? A company concierge service that will pick up your car from the mechanic and send someone to be at your house when the cable guy or repair person shows up. A "7 to 7" travel policy that stipulates that no one has to leave home for business travel before 7 A.M. on Mondays and that everyone should be home from business travel by 7 P.M. on Fridays. The opportunity to telecommute so that you can feed your kids breakfast, pick them up after school, and tuck them into bed at night.[35]

If you have kids, you might love the chance to telecommute; but if you don't, you may not be interested. If you don't travel much on business, you won't be interested in the "7 to 7" travel policy; but if you do, you'll probably love it. One of the hardest things about motivating people is that rewards that are attractive to some employees are unattractive to others. **Expectancy theory** says that people will be motivated to the extent to which they believe that their efforts will lead to good performance, that good performance will be rewarded, and that they will be offered attractive rewards.[36]

expectancy theory
a theory that states that people will be motivated to the extent to which they believe that their efforts will lead to good performance, that good performance will be rewarded, and that they will be offered attractive rewards

Let's learn more about expectancy theory by examining 3.1 the components of expectancy theory and 3.2 how to use expectancy theory as a motivational tool.

3.1 Components of Expectancy Theory

Expectancy theory holds that people make conscious choices about their motivation. The three factors that affect those choices are valence, expectancy, and instrumentality.

Valence is simply the attractiveness or desirability of various rewards or outcomes. Expectancy theory recognizes that the same reward or outcome, say, a promotion, will be highly attractive to some people, will be highly disliked by others, and will not make much difference one way or the other to still others. Accordingly, when people are deciding how much effort to put forth, expectancy theory says that they will consider the valence of all possible rewards and outcomes that they can receive from their jobs. The greater the sum of those valences, each of which can be positive, negative, or neutral, the more effort people will choose to put forth on the job.

valence
the attractiveness or desirability of a reward or outcome

Expectancy is the perceived relationship between effort and performance. When expectancies are strong, employees believe that their hard work and ef-

expectancy
the perceived relationship between effort and performance

forts will result in good performance, so they work harder. By contrast, when expectancies are weak, employees figure that no matter what they do or how hard they work, they won't be able to perform their jobs successfully, so they don't work as hard.

instrumentality the perceived relationship between performance and rewards

Instrumentality is the perceived relationship between performance and rewards. When instrumentality is strong, employees believe that improved performance will lead to better and more rewards, so they choose to work harder. When instrumentality is weak, employees don't believe that better performance will result in more or better rewards, so they choose not to work as hard.

Expectancy theory holds that for people to be highly motivated, all three variables—valence, expectancy, and instrumentality—must be high. Thus, expectancy theory can be represented by the following simple equation:

$$\text{Motivation} = \text{Valence} \times \text{Expectancy} \times \text{Instrumentality}$$

If any one of these variables (valence, expectancy, or instrumentality) declines, overall motivation will decline, too.

Exhibit 14.8 incorporates the expectancy theory variables into our motivation model. Valence and instrumentality combine to affect employees' willingness to put forth effort (i.e., the degree to which they are energized to take

exhibit 14.8

Adding Expectancy Theory to the Model

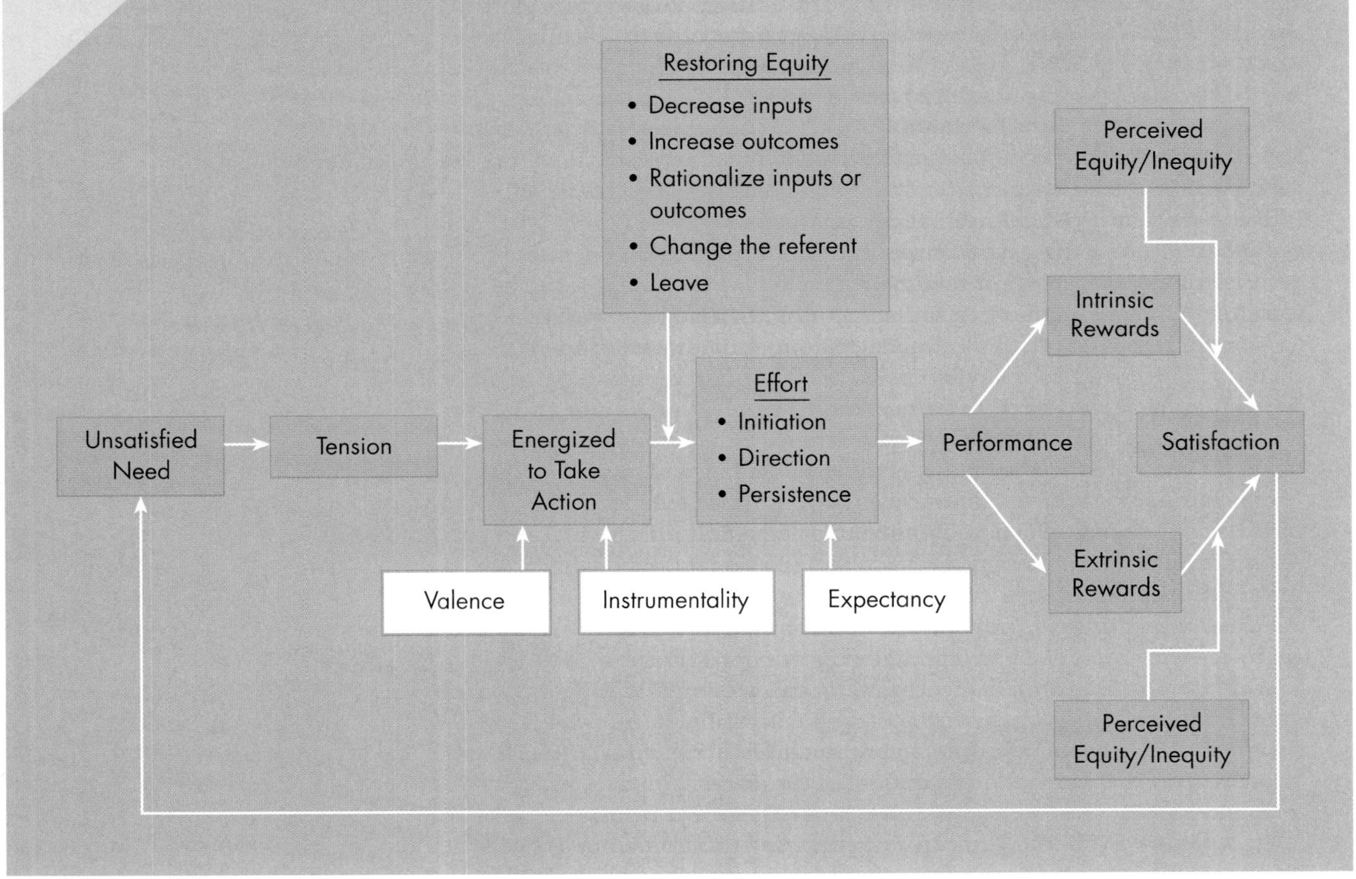

action), while expectancy transforms intended effort ("I'm really going to work hard in this job") into actual effort. If you're offered rewards that you desire and you believe that you will in fact receive these rewards for good performance, you're highly likely to be energized to take action. However, you're not likely to actually exert effort unless you also believe that you can do the job (i.e., that your efforts will lead to successful performance).

3.2 Motivating with Expectancy Theory

What practical things can managers do to use expectancy theory to motivate employees? First, they can *systematically gather information to find out what employees want from their jobs.* In addition to individual managers directly asking employees what they want from their jobs (see Subsection 2.3 "Motivating with Equity Theory"), companies need to survey their employees regularly to determine their wants, needs, and dissatisfactions. Since people consider the valence of all the possible rewards and outcomes that they can receive from their jobs, regular identification of wants, needs, and dissatisfactions gives companies the chance to turn negatively valent rewards and outcomes into positively valent rewards and outcomes, thus raising overall motivation and effort. Marc Albin, CEO of Albin Engineering, says, "My experience in managing people is, they're all different. Some people want to be recognized for their cheerful attitude and their ability to spread their cheerful attitude. Some want to be recognized for the quality of their work, some for the quantity of their work. Some like to be recognized individually; others want to be recognized in groups."[37]

> **www.experiencing management.com**
>
> Test your understanding of expectancy theory by interacting with the activities presented at our animated concept and activity site. Choose Motivation from the "select a topic" pull-down menu, then Expectancy Model from the "overview tab."
>
> **http://www.experiencingmanagement.com**

Second, managers can *take specific steps to link rewards to individual performance in a way that is clear and understandable to employees.* Unfortunately, most employees are extremely dissatisfied with the link between pay and performance in their organizations. A study based on a representative sample found that 80 percent of employees wanted to be paid according to a different kind of pay system! Moreover, only 32 percent of employees were satisfied with how their annual pay raises were determined, and only 22 percent were happy with the way the starting salaries for their jobs were determined.[38] One way to make sure that employees see the connection between pay and performance (see Chapter 12 for a discussion of compensation strategies) is for managers to publicize the way in which pay decisions are made. This is especially important given that only 41 percent of employees know how their pay increases are determined.[39] For example, at Allstate Insurance, the company compensation team wrote a pamphlet called "Tracking the Clues to Your Pay," which explained how Allstate carefully uses market value surveys and analyses to determine employee pay. Making this explanation available helped counter the widespread belief that employee pay was determined in some random way.[40]

Finally, managers should *empower employees to make decisions if management really wants them to believe that their hard work and effort will lead to good performance.* If valent rewards are linked to good performance, people should be energized to take action. However, this works only if they also believe that their efforts will lead to good performance. One of the ways that managers destroy the expectancy that hard work and effort will lead to good performance is by restricting what employees can do or by ignoring employees' ideas. In Chapter 10, you learned that *empowerment* is a feeling of intrinsic motivation, in which workers perceive their work to have meaning and perceive themselves to be competent, to have an impact, and to be capable of self-determination.[41] So, if managers want workers to have strong expectancies, they should empower them to make decisions. Doing so will motivate employees to take active rather than passive roles in their work.

Review 3

Expectancy Theory

Expectancy theory holds that three factors affect the conscious choices people make about their motivation: valence, expectancy, and instrumentality. Valence is simply the attractiveness or desirability of various rewards or outcomes. Expectancy is the perceived relationship between effort and performance. Instrumentality is the perceived relationship between performance and rewards. Expectancy theory holds that for people to be highly motivated, all three factors must be high. If any one of these factors declines, overall motivation will decline, too. Managers can use expectancy theory to motivate workers by systematically gathering information to find out what employees want from their jobs, by linking rewards to individual performance in a way that is clear and understandable to employees, and by empowering employees to make decisions, which will increase their expectancies that hard work and effort will lead to good performance.

How Rewards and Goals Affect Motivation

No matter what management tried, it couldn't find a way to improve the dismal safety record at Monsanto's Pensacola, Florida plant. Nothing it tried seemed to work. At wit's end management called in psychologists and statisticians to identify the causes and teach workers how to avoid accidents by reinforcing each other's safe behavior. After the consultants identified dozens of possible causes, workers were given "scorecards" to count the number of times they observed other employees performing safe or potentially unsafe behaviors. Using the feedback obtained from the scorecards, management set specific safety goals and recognized safe workers at weekly meetings and in quarterly reviews. When an entire division improved its safety behavior, everyone won a free lunch or a coffee mug. Plus, safety records were considered in promotion decisions. The plant's safety record improved from 6.5 injuries per 100 workers to just 1.6 injuries. Overall, injuries dropped by more than 75 percent, all without heavy-handed supervision or punishment.[42]

reinforcement theory
a theory that states that behavior is a function of its consequences, that behaviors followed by positive consequences will occur more frequently, and that behaviors followed by negative consequences, or not followed by positive consequences, will occur less frequently

After reading the next three sections, you should be able to

4 explain how reinforcement theory works and how it can be used to motivate.

5 describe the components of goal-setting theory and how managers can use them to motivate workers.

6 discuss how the entire motivation model can be used to motivate workers.

4 Reinforcement Theory

Reinforcement theory says that behavior is a function of its consequences, that behaviors followed by positive consequences (i.e., reinforced) will occur more frequently, and that behaviors followed by negative consequences, or not followed by positive consequences, will occur less frequently.[43] Therefore, to

PERSONAL PRODUCTIVITY TIP

Try Praise

Positive reinforcement doesn't have to be costly. In fact, praise and recognition are just as important to employees as financial rewards, but many managers forget to praise employees or simply don't know how. Until praising employees becomes second nature to you, here are some simple ways to make sure you're praising employees effectively

- Put praising employees on your to-do list.
- Set aside 10 minutes at the end of the day to write notes or emails to employees who deserve praise.
- If you can't be there in person, praise using the telephone, voice mail, or email.
- Finally, make sure your praise is prompt, sincere, specific, and positive.[47]

improve its safety record, Monsanto decided to reinforce safe behaviors. Chuck Davis, a safety consultant, says, "It's better to recognize a guy for success than beat him up for failure. It's amazing how little reward a guy needs so he doesn't stick his arm in a machine."[44] More specifically, **reinforcement** is the process of changing behavior by changing the consequences that follow behavior.[45]

Reinforcement has two parts: reinforcement contingencies and schedules of reinforcement. **Reinforcement contingencies** are the cause-and-effect relationships between the performance of specific behaviors and specific consequences. For example, if you get docked an hour's pay for being late to work, then a reinforcement contingency exists between a behavior, being late to work, and a consequence, losing an hour's pay. A **schedule of reinforcement** is the set of rules regarding reinforcement contingencies, such as which behaviors will be reinforced, which consequences will follow those behaviors, and the schedule by which those consequences will be delivered.[46]

Exhibit 14.9 incorporates reinforcement contingencies and reinforcement schedules into our motivation model. First, notice that extrinsic rewards and the schedules of reinforcement used to deliver them are the primary method for creating reinforcement contingencies in organizations. In turn, those reward contingencies directly affect valences (the attractiveness of rewards), instrumentality (the perceived link between rewards and performance), and effort (how hard employees will work).

reinforcement
the process of changing behavior by changing the consequences that follow behavior

reinforcement contingencies
cause-and-effect relationships between the performance of specific behaviors and specific consequences

schedule of reinforcement
rules that specify which behaviors will be reinforced, which consequences will follow those behaviors, and the schedule by which those consequences will be delivered

positive reinforcement
reinforcement that strengthens behavior by following behaviors with desirable consequences

negative reinforcement
reinforcement that strengthens behavior by withholding an unpleasant consequence when employees perform a specific behavior

Let's learn more about reinforcement theory by examining 4.1 the components of reinforcement theory, 4.2 the different schedules for delivering reinforcement, and 4.3 how to motivate with reinforcement theory.

4.1 Components of Reinforcement Theory

As just described, *reinforcement contingencies* are the cause-and-effect relationships between the performance of specific behaviors and specific consequences. There are four kinds of reinforcement contingencies: positive reinforcement, negative reinforcement, punishment, and extinction.

Positive reinforcement strengthens behavior (i.e., increases its frequency) by following behaviors with desirable consequences. **Negative reinforcement** strengthens behavior by withholding an unpleasant consequence when employees perform a specific behavior. Negative reinforcement is also called *avoidance learning* because workers perform a behavior to *avoid* a negative consequence. For example, at the Florist Network, a small business in Buffalo, New York, company management instituted a policy of requiring good attendance for employees to receive their annual bonuses. Employee attendance has improved significantly now that excessive absenteeism can result in the loss of $1,500 or more, depending on the size of the bonus.[48]

By contrast, **punishment** weakens behavior (i.e., decreases its frequency) by following behaviors with undesirable consequences. For example, the standard disciplinary or punishment process in most companies is an oral warn-

exhibit 14.9

Adding Reinforcement Theory to the Model

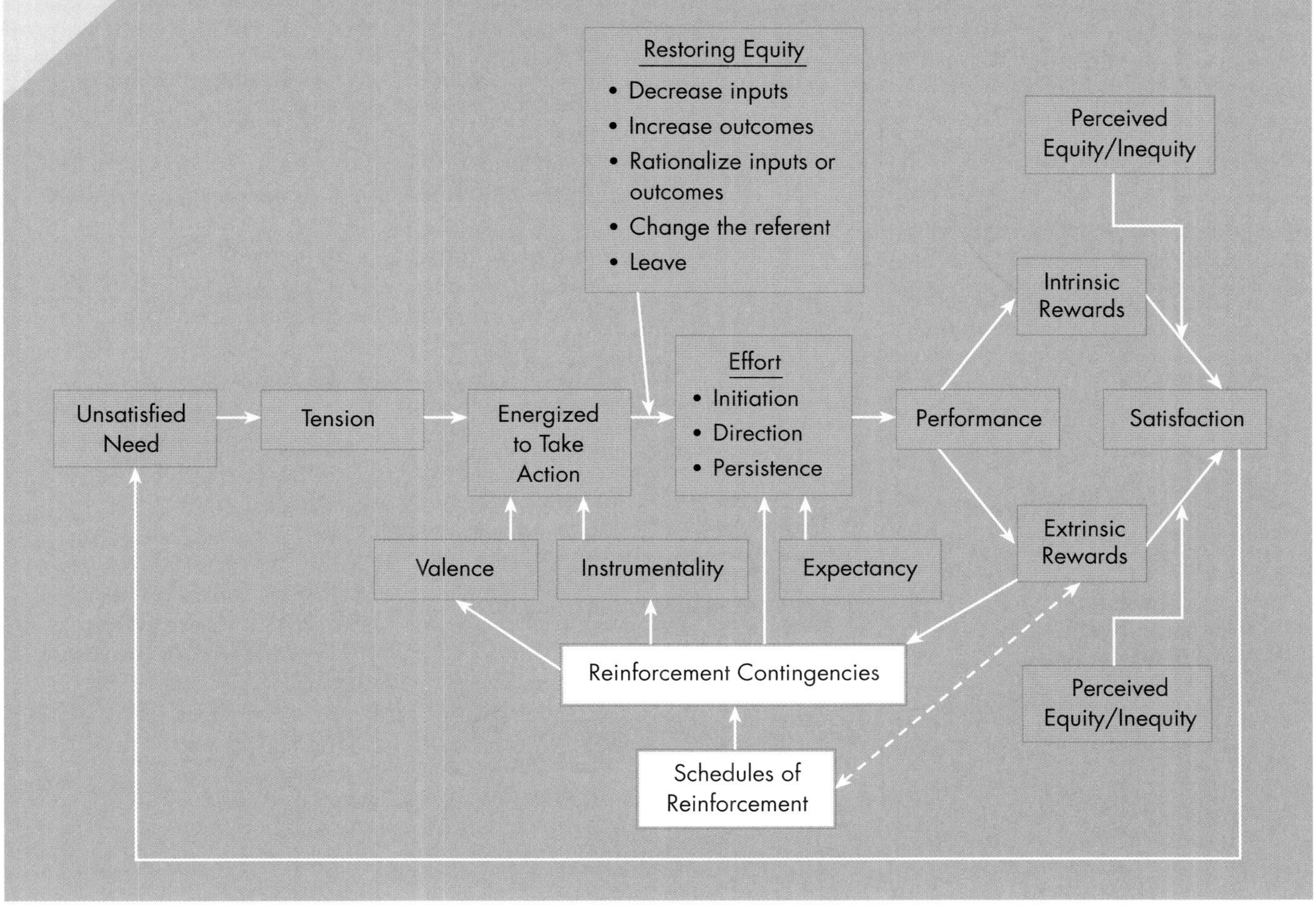

punishment reinforcement that weakens behavior by following behaviors with undesirable consequences

extinction reinforcement in which a positive consequence is no longer allowed to follow a previously reinforced behavior, thus weakening the behavior

ing ("Don't ever do that again."), followed by a written warning ("This letter is to discuss the serious problem you're having with . . . "), followed by three days off without pay ("While you're at home not being paid, we want you to think hard about . . . "), followed by being fired ("This was your last chance. You're fired."). Though punishment can weaken behavior, managers have to be careful to avoid the backlash that sometimes occurs when employees are punished at work. For example, Frito-Lay began getting complaints from customers that they were finding potato chips with obscene messages written on them. Frito-Lay eventually traced the problem to a potato chip plant where supervisors had fired 58 out of the 210 workers for disciplinary reasons over a nine-month period. The remaining employees were so angry over what they saw as unfair treatment from management that they began writing obscene phrases on potato chips with felt-tipped pens.[49]

Extinction is a reinforcement strategy in which a positive consequence is no longer allowed to follow a previously reinforced behavior. By removing the positive consequence, extinction weakens the behavior, making it less likely to occur. Based on the idea of extinction, a company would cut the financial rewards given to company leaders and managers when the company performs poorly. For example, at Sun Microsystems no one—including the CEO—receives a bonus if the company misses its targets.[50]

continuous reinforcement schedule a schedule that requires a consequence to be administered following every instance of a behavior

intermittent reinforcement schedule a schedule in which consequences are delivered after a specified or average time has elapsed or after a specified or average number of behaviors has occurred

fixed interval reinforcement schedule an intermittent schedule in which consequences follow a behavior only after a fixed time has elapsed

variable interval reinforcement schedule an intermittent schedule in which the time between a behavior and the following consequences varies around a specified average

fixed ratio reinforcement schedule an intermittent schedule in which consequences are delivered following a specific number of behaviors

4.2 Schedules for Delivering Reinforcement

A *schedule of reinforcement* is the set of rules regarding reinforcement contingencies, such as which behaviors will be reinforced, which consequences will follow those behaviors, and the schedule by which those consequences will be delivered. There are two categories of reinforcement schedules: continuous and intermittent.

With **continuous reinforcement schedules**, a consequence follows every instance of a behavior. For example, employees working on a piece-rate pay system earn money (consequence) for every part they manufacture (behavior). The more they produce, the more they earn. By contrast, with **intermittent reinforcement schedules**, consequences are delivered after a specified or average time has elapsed or after a specified or average number of behaviors has occurred. As Exhibit 14.10 shows, there are four types of intermittent reinforcement schedules. Two of these are based on time and are called *interval reinforcement schedules*, while the other two, known as *ratio schedules*, are based on behaviors.

With **fixed interval reinforcement schedules**, consequences follow a behavior only after a fixed time has elapsed. For example, most people receive their paychecks on a fixed interval schedule (e.g., once or twice per month). As long as they work (behavior) during a specified pay period (interval), they get a paycheck (consequence). With **variable interval reinforcement schedules**, consequences follow a behavior after different times, some shorter and some longer, that vary around a specified average time. On a 90-day variable interval reinforcement schedule, you might receive a bonus after 80 days or perhaps after 100 days, but the average interval between performing your job well (behavior) and receiving your bonus (consequence) would be 90 days.

With **fixed ratio reinforcement schedules**, consequences are delivered following a specific number of behaviors. For example, a car salesperson might receive a $1,000 bonus after every 10 sales. Therefore, a salesperson

exhibit 14.10

Intermittent Reinforcement Schedules

	INTERMITTENT REINFORCEMENT SCHEDULES	
	FIXED	VARIABLE
INTERVAL (TIME)	Consequences follow behavior after a fixed time has elapsed.	Consequences follow behavior after different times, some shorter and some longer, that vary around a specified average time.
RATIO (BEHAVIOR)	Consequences follow a specific number of behaviors.	Consequences follow a different number of behaviors, sometimes more and sometimes less, that vary around a specified average number of behaviors.

with only 9 sales would not receive the bonus until he or she finally sold a 10th car.

variable ratio reinforcement schedule
an intermittent schedule in which consequences are delivered following a different number of behaviors, sometimes more and sometimes less, that vary around a specified average number of behaviors

With **variable ratio reinforcement schedules**, consequences are delivered following a different number of behaviors, sometimes more and sometimes less, that vary around a specified average number of behaviors. With a 10-car variable ratio reinforcement schedule, a salesperson might receive the bonus after 7 car sales, or after 12, 11, or 9 sales, but the average number of cars sold before receiving the bonus would be 10 cars.

Which reinforcement schedules work best? In the past, the standard advice was to use continuous reinforcement when employees were learning new behaviors, since reinforcement after each success leads to faster learning. Likewise, the standard advice was to use intermittent reinforcement schedules to maintain behavior after it is learned, since intermittent rewards are supposed to make behavior much less subject to extinction.[51] However, except for interval-based systems, which usually produce weak results, the effectiveness of continuous reinforcement, fixed ratio, and variable ratio schedules differs very little.[52] In organizational settings, all three produce consistently large increases over noncontingent reward schedules. So managers should choose whichever of these three is easiest to use in their companies.

4.3 Motivating with Reinforcement Theory

What practical things can managers do to use reinforcement theory to motivate employees? Professor Fred Luthans, who has been studying the effects of reinforcement theory in organizations for more than a quarter of a century, says that there are five steps to motivating workers with reinforcement theory: *identify, measure, analyze, intervene,* and *evaluate* critical performance-related behaviors.[53]

Identify means identifying critical, observable, performance-related behaviors. These are the behaviors that are most important to successful job performance. In addition, they must also be easily observed so that they can be accurately measured. *Measure* means measuring the baseline frequencies of these behaviors. In other words, find out how often workers perform them. *Analyze* means analyzing the causes and consequences of these behaviors. Analyzing the causes helps managers create the conditions that produce these critical behaviors, and analyzing the consequences helps them determine if these behaviors produce the results that they want. *Intervene* means changing the organization by using positive and negative reinforcement to increase the frequency of these critical behaviors. *Evaluate* means evaluating the extent to which the intervention actually changed workers' behavior. This is done by comparing behavior after the intervention to the original baseline of behavior before the intervention. For more on the effectiveness of reinforcement theory, see the "What Really Works?" feature in this chapter.

In addition to these five steps, managers should remember three other things when motivating with reinforcement theory. *Don't reinforce the wrong behaviors.* Although reinforcement theory sounds simple, it's actually very difficult to put into practice. One of the most common mistakes is accidentally reinforcing the wrong behaviors. In fact, sometimes managers reinforce behaviors that they don't want! For example, the salary and bonus system was not working correctly at Discovery Communications, which runs the Discovery Channel on cable and satellite TV. Because the company's reward system did not allow managers to give large raises to people who stayed in the same

WHAT REALLY WORKS

FINANCIAL, NONFINANCIAL, AND SOCIAL REWARDS

Throughout this chapter, we have been making the point that there is more to motivating people than money. But we haven't yet examined how well financial (money or prizes), nonfinancial (performance feedback), or social (recognition and attention) rewards motivate workers by themselves or in combination. However, the results of two meta-analyses, one with 19 studies based on more than 2,800 people (study 1) and another based on 72 studies and 13,301 people (study 2), clearly indicate that rewarding and reinforcing employees greatly improve motivation and performance, especially when combined.

Financial Rewards

On average, there is an 68 percent chance that employees whose behavior is reinforced with financial rewards will outperform employees whose behavior is not reinforced. This increases to 84 percent in manufacturing organizations but drops to 61 percent in service organizations.

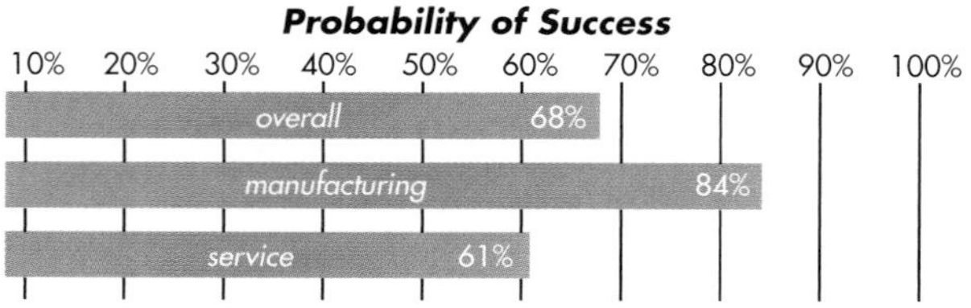

Nonfinancial Rewards

On average, there is an 58 percent chance that employees whose behavior is reinforced with nonfinancial rewards will outperform employees whose behavior is not reinforced. This increases to 87 percent in manufacturing organizations but drops to 54 percent in service organizations.

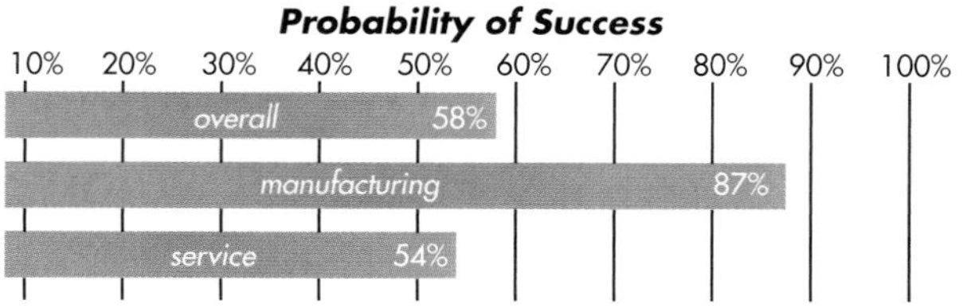

Social Rewards

On average, there is a 63 percent chance that employees whose behavior is reinforced with social rewards will outperform employees whose behavior is not reinforced.

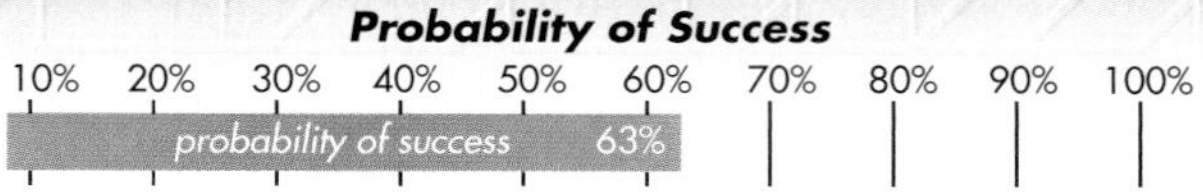

Financial and Nonfinancial Rewards

On average, there is a 62 percent chance that employees whose behavior is reinforced with a combination of financial and nonfinancial rewards will outperform employees whose behavior is not reinforced.

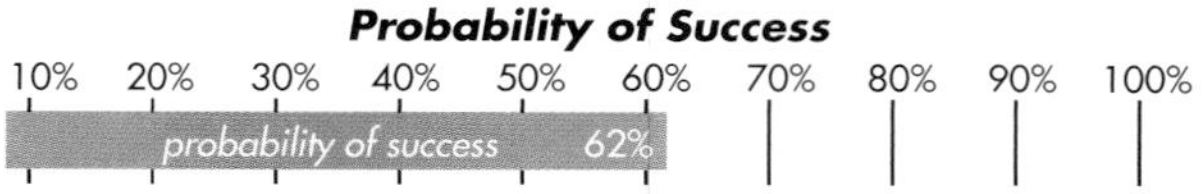

Financial and Social Rewards

On average, there is only a 52 percent chance that employees whose behavior is reinforced with a combination of financial and social rewards will outperform employees whose behavior is not reinforced.

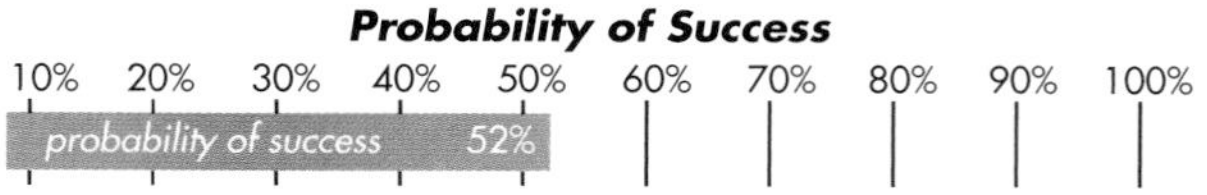

Nonfinancial and Social Rewards

On average, there is a 61 percent chance that employees whose behavior is reinforced with a combination of nonfinancial and social rewards will outperform employees whose behavior is not reinforced.

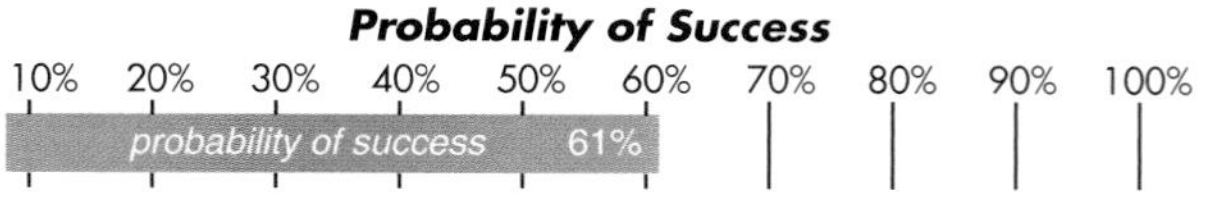

Financial, Nonfinancial, and Social Rewards

On average, there is a 90 percent chance that employees whose behavior is reinforced with a combination of financial, nonfinancial, and social rewards will outperform employees whose behavior is not reinforced.[54]

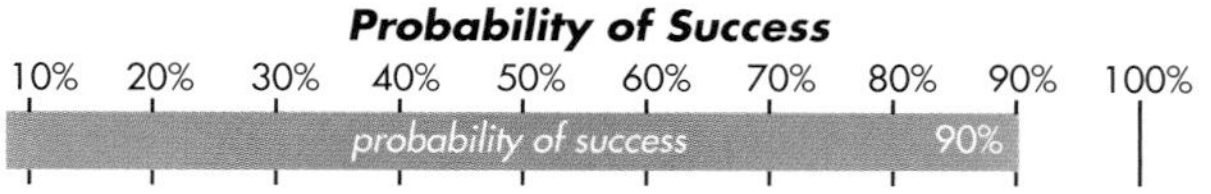

job from year to year, managers used promotions to get workers higher pay and keep them in the company. The system was so rigid, however, that they frequently promoted good workers before they were ready or promoted them into jobs for which they weren't qualified.[55]

Managers should also *correctly administer punishment at the appropriate time.* Many managers believe that punishment can change workers' behavior and help them improve their job performance. Furthermore, managers believe that fairly punishing workers also lets other workers know what is or isn't acceptable.[56] A danger of using punishment is that it can produce a backlash against managers and companies, but if administered properly, punishment can weaken the frequency of undesirable behaviors without creating a backlash.[57] To be effective, the punishment must be strong enough to stop the undesired behavior and must be administered objectively (same rules applied to everyone), impersonally (without emotion or anger), consistently and contingently (each time improper behavior occurs), and quickly (as soon as possible following the undesirable behavior). In addition, managers should clearly explain what the appropriate behavior is and why the employee is being punished. Employees typically respond well when punishment is administered this way.[58]

Finally, managers should *choose the simplest and most effective schedule of reinforcement.* When choosing a schedule of reinforcement, managers need to balance effectiveness against simplicity. In fact, the more complex the schedule of reinforcement, the more likely it is to be misunderstood and resisted by managers and employees. Since continuous reinforcement, fixed ratio, and variable ratio schedules are about equally effective, continuous reinforcement schedules may be the best choice in many instances by virtue of their simplicity.

Review 4
Reinforcement Theory

Reinforcement theory says that behavior is a function of its consequences. Reinforcement has two parts: reinforcement contingencies and schedules of reinforcement. The four kinds of reinforcement contingencies are positive reinforcement and negative reinforcement, which strengthen behavior, and punishment and extinction, which weaken behavior. There are two kinds of reinforcement schedules, continuous and intermittent; intermittent schedules, in turn, can be divided into fixed and variable interval schedules and fixed and variable ratio schedules. Managers can use reinforcement theory to motivate workers by following five steps (identify, measure, analyze, intervene, and evaluate critical performance-related behaviors); not reinforcing the wrong behaviors; correctly administering punishment at the appropriate time; and choosing a reinforcement schedule, such as continuous reinforcement, that balances simplicity and effectiveness.

goal
a target, objective, or result that someone tries to accomplish

5 Goal-Setting Theory

goal-setting theory
a theory that states that people will be motivated to the extent to which they accept specific, challenging goals and receive feedback that indicates their progress toward goal achievement

The basic model of motivation with which we began this chapter showed that individuals feel tension after becoming aware of an unfulfilled need. Once they experience tension, they search for and select courses of action that they believe will eliminate this tension. In other words, they direct their behavior toward something. This something is a goal. A **goal** is a target, objective, or result that someone tries to accomplish. **Goal-setting theory** says that people will be motivated to the extent to which they accept specific, challenging goals and receive feedback that indicates their progress toward goal achievement.

Let's learn more about goal setting by examining 5.1 the components of goal-setting theory and 5.2 how to motivate with goal-setting theory.

5.1 Components of Goal-Setting Theory

The basic components of goal-setting theory are goal specificity, goal difficulty, goal acceptance, and performance feedback.[59] **Goal specificity** is the extent to which goals are detailed, exact, and unambiguous. Specific goals, such as "I'm going to have a 3.0 average this semester," are more motivating than general goals, such as "I'm going to get better grades this semester."

goal specificity
the extent to which goals are detailed, exact, and unambiguous

Goal difficulty is the extent to which a goal is hard or challenging to accomplish. Difficult goals, such as "I'm going to have a 3.5 average and make the Dean's List this semester," are more motivating than easy goals, such as "I'm going to have a 2.0 average this semester."

goal difficulty
the extent to which a goal is hard or challenging to accomplish

Goal acceptance, which is similar to the idea of goal commitment discussed in Chapter 4, is the extent to which people consciously understand and agree to goals. Accepted goals, such as "I really want to get a 3.5 average this semester to show my parents how much I've improved," are more motivating than unaccepted goals, such as "My parents really want me to get a 3.5 this semester, but there's so much more I'd rather do on campus than study!"

goal acceptance
the extent to which people consciously understand and agree to goals

Performance feedback is information about the quality or quantity of past performance and indicates whether progress is being made toward the accomplishment of a goal. Performance feedback, such as "My prof said I need a 92 on the final to get an 'A' in that class," is more motivating than no feedback, "I have no idea what my grade is in that class." In short, goal-setting theory says that people will be motivated to the extent to which they accept specific, challenging goals and receive feedback that indicates their progress toward goal achievement.

performance feedback
information about the quality or quantity of past performance that indicates whether progress is being made toward the accomplishment of a goal

How does goal setting work? To start, challenging goals focus employees' attention (i.e., direct effort) on the critical aspects of their jobs and away from unimportant areas. Goals also energize behavior. When faced with unaccomplished goals, employees typically develop plans and strategies to reach those goals. Goals also create tension between the goal, which is the desired future state of affairs, and where the employee or company is now, meaning the current state of affairs. This tension can be satisfied only by achieving or abandoning the goal. Finally, goals influence persistence. Since goals only "go away" when they are accomplished, employees are more likely to persist in their efforts in the presence of goals. Exhibit 14.11 incorporates goals into the motivation model by showing how goals directly affect tension, effort, and the extent to which employees are energized to take action.

5.2 Motivating with Goal-Setting Theory

What practical things can managers do to use goal-setting theory to motivate employees? One of the simplest, most effective ways to motivate workers is to give them *specific, challenging goals*, yet an amazing number of managers never do this. One manager who does is Jim Schaefer. When Schaefer's top management asked him to increase profits at his oil refinery plant by $7 million, he turned around and promised them profits of $60 million. Then, with this difficult goal on the line, he met with senior managers and union leaders every 90 days to set specific goals for overall improvement in the plant. He also met with first-level supervisors every 30 days to get them to develop specific

exhibit 14.11

Adding Goal-Setting Theory to the Model

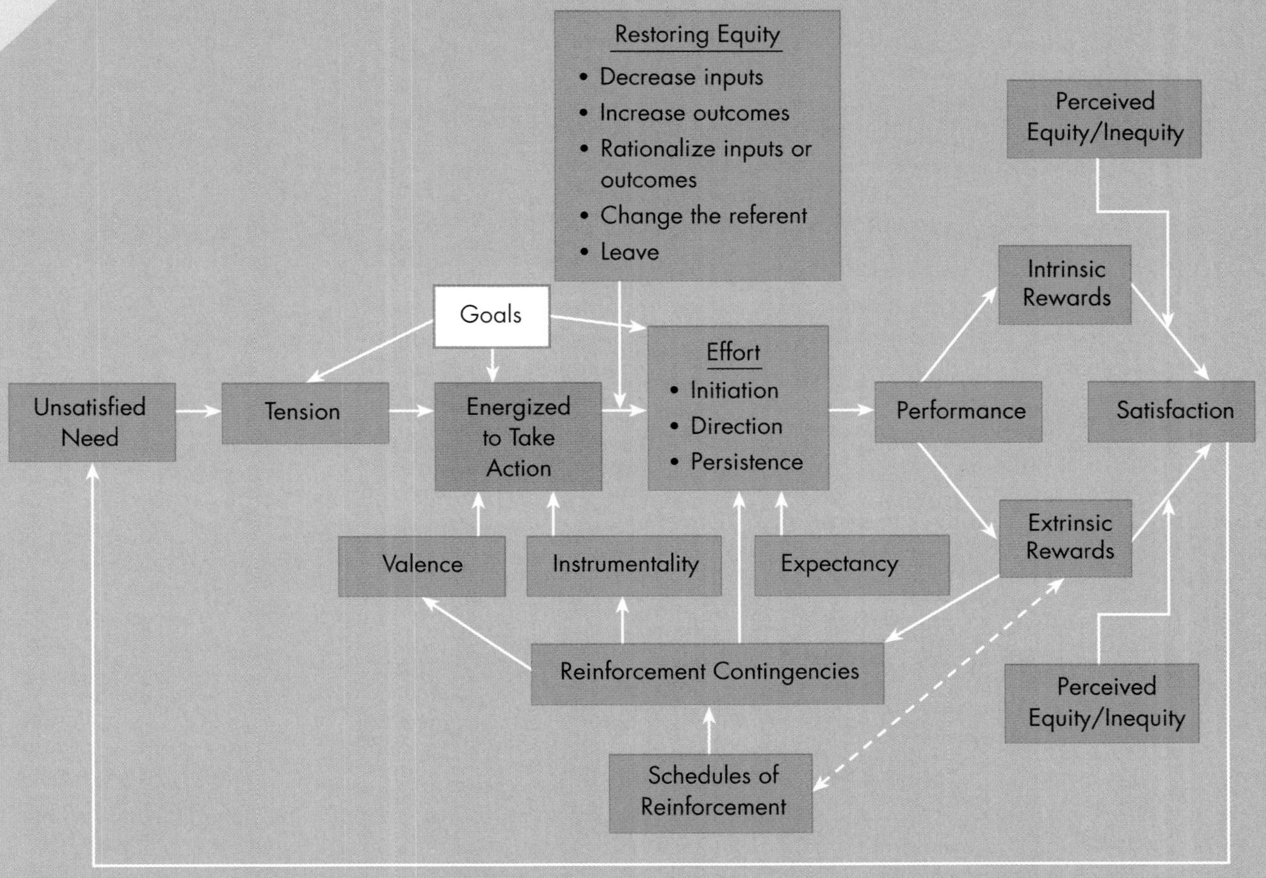

goals for improving their departments. The result? While most oil refineries scratch and claw to find ways to produce 1 percent more oil, thanks to specific, challenging goals, Schaefer's oil refinery increased its production by 20 percent.[60] For more information on assigning specific, challenging goals, see the discussion in Chapter 4 on S.M.A.R.T. goals.

Second, managers should *make sure workers truly accept organizational goals.* Specific, challenging goals won't motivate workers unless they really accept, understand, and agree to the organization's goals. For this to occur, people must see the goals as fair and reasonable. Plus, they must trust management and believe that managers are using goals to clarify what is expected from them rather than to exploit or threaten them ("If you don't achieve these goals . . . "). Participative goal setting, in which managers and employees generate goals together, can help increase trust and understanding and thus acceptance of goals. Furthermore, providing workers with training can help increase goal acceptance, particularly when workers don't believe they are capable of reaching the organization's goals.[61]

Finally, managers should *provide frequent, specific, performance-related feedback*. Once employees have accepted specific, challenging goals, they should receive frequent performance-related feedback so that they can their track progress toward goal completion. Feedback leads to stronger motivation and effort in three ways.[62] Receiving specific feedback that indicates how well they're performing can encourage employees who don't have specific, challenging goals to set goals to improve their performance. Once people meet goals, performance feedback often encourages them to set higher, more difficult goals. And feedback lets people know whether they need to increase their efforts or change strategies in order to accomplish their goals.

For example, in an effort to improve worker safety on offshore oil-drilling platforms, an oil company generated a list of dangerous work behaviors by analyzing previous accident reports, reviewing industry safety manuals, and interviewing and observing workers. Following detailed safety training, each work crew set goals to engage in safe behaviors 100 percent of the time on each shift. Management posted a weekly safety record in the galley of each rig, where workers would see it when they gathered for meals and coffee breaks. Previously, employees were engaging in safe work behaviors just 76 percent of the time. After a year of goal setting (100 percent safe behavior on each shift) and weekly performance feedback at two oil rigs, however, workers behaved safely over 90 percent of the time.[63] So, to motivate employees with goal-setting theory, make sure they receive frequent performance-related feedback so that they can track their progress toward goal completion.

Review 5
Goal-Setting Theory

A goal is a target, objective, or result that someone tries to accomplish. Goal-setting theory says that people will be motivated to the extent to which they accept specific, challenging goals and receive feedback that indicates their progress toward goal achievement. The basic components of goal-setting theory are goal specificity, goal difficulty, goal acceptance, and performance feedback. Goal specificity is the extent to which goals are detailed, exact, and unambiguous. Goal difficulty is the extent to which a goal is hard or challenging to accomplish. Goal acceptance is the extent to which people consciously understand and agree to goals. Performance feedback is information about the quality or quantity of past performance and indicates whether progress is being made toward the accomplishment of a goal. Managers can use goal-setting theory to motivate workers by assigning specific, challenging goals, making sure workers truly accept organizational goals, and providing frequent, specific, performance-related feedback.

6 Motivating with the Integrated Model

We began this chapter by defining motivation as the set of forces that initiates, directs, and makes people persist in their efforts to accomplish a goal. We also asked the basic question that managers ask when they try to figure out how to motivate their workers: "What leads to effort?" Though the answer to that question is likely to be somewhat different for each employee, Exhibit 14.12 helps you begin to answer it by consolidating the practical advice from the theories reviewed in this chapter in one convenient location. So, if you're having difficulty figuring out why people aren't motivated where you work, Exhibit 14.12 provides a useful, theory-based starting point.

exhibit 14.12

Motivating with the Integrated Model

MOTIVATING WITH	MANAGERS SHOULD . . .
THE BASICS	Ask people what their needs are.
	Satisfy lower-order needs first.
	Expect people's needs to change.
	As needs change and lower-order needs are satisfied, satisfy higher-order needs by looking for ways to allow employees to experience intrinsic rewards.
EQUITY THEORY	Look for and correct major inequities.
	Reduce employees' inputs.
	Make sure decision-making processes are fair.
EXPECTANCY THEORY	Systematically gather information to find out what employees want from their jobs.
	Take specific steps to link rewards to individual performance in a way that is clear and understandable to employees.
	Empower employees to make decisions if management really wants them to believe that their hard work and efforts will lead to good performance.
REINFORCEMENT THEORY	Identify, measure, analyze, intervene, and evaluate critical performance-related behaviors.
	Don't reinforce the wrong behaviors.
	Correctly administer punishment at the appropriate time.
	Choose the simplest and most effective schedules of reinforcement.
GOAL-SETTING THEORY	Assign specific, challenging goals.
	Make sure workers truly accept organizational goals.
	Provide frequent, specific, performance-related feedback.

STUDY TIP Don't forget to review with *Effective Management Online* (**http://www.em-online.swlearning.com**). Personalize the material by thinking about what motivates you to perform better in school, at work, or even in community groups and civic organizations. You can also use some of the earlier study tips for Chapter 14 material.

MANAGEMENT DECISION

MINING HUMAN CAPITAL

Labor is probably the single largest expense of any business.[64] According to some estimates, labor costs average about 60 percent of sales. In addition to salaries, labor costs include health insurance, paid time off, child-care benefits, tuition reimbursements, and any number of other programs designed to extrinsically motivate the work force. Many companies offer the same types of benefits across their organizations without knowing whether the benefits really motivate employees at all. In other words, companies often don't know what return they are getting on their labor investment. The same is true where you work.

As you head back to your desk from a meeting on cafeteria-style benefit plans, your boss intercepts you and asks to speak with you about cutting labor costs. As she plops into your side chair, she is already describing a new type of software that applies data-mining technology to employee information to determine what is the best motivator. "We can get rid of one-size-fits-all benefit programs and tailor the benefits to each employee. This software lets you slice and dice employee data, like age, seniority, education, commute time, residential ZIP code, even the age and condition of the person's office," she says. "We could find out if we could pay someone, say, 20 percent less if we gave a three-month sabbatical every couple of years. Or we could predict the reaction of certain employees if we cut our 401(k) match. Maybe that's not as important to everyone as we think. We could find out who'd quit based on that and who could care less. Basically, we could find out what incentives would spike productivity the most with each employee, and that way we could cut costs without sabotaging morale. It would reduce the guesswork of rewarding our employees. Here is some literature on the various programs. I'd like you to draft a recommendation to top management by next Monday. I'm really excited about this." She leaves a small stack of brochures on your desk corner and leaves your office.

All you can do is to wonder, "What will the employees think of this idea?"

Questions

1. Which motivational theory provides the biggest justification for employee data mining? Explain.
2. Does employee data mining violate any of the motivational theories? If so, which ones and how?
3. Will you recommend mining employee data, or despite your boss's enthusiasm, will you present reasons not to begin mining employee data? Explain your choice, using the motivational theories in the chapter as support for your recommendation.

CUT YOUR COSTS, NOT YOUR MORALE

Management textbooks abound with discussions of the importance of honest and open communication when disseminating negative information to employees.[65] One study suggests that the best way to ruin morale and motivation is to spring bad news on employees without explaining the reasoning or rationale. Yet, despite the need to maintain a high level of motivation and morale during a receding economy, many companies cut perks without communicating the need to their employees. During the high-tech boom at the end of the twentieth century, many companies implemented programs to increase productivity, motivation, and job satisfaction. Some of the perks provided were minor, such as free soft drinks, catered lunches, snacks, and tickets to events such as baseball games or the opera. Other free perks were more extravagant, such as concierge services to run errands for employees, service their vehicles, and pick up their laundry. Some firms even provided their employees with in-house massages and annual Caribbean cruises. Obviously, cutting these nonvalue-added expenses can save tremendous money for a struggling firm. In fact, many firms cut out both the extravagant perks and the basics as a way to conserve much-needed cash. Cutting perks, however, doesn't have to be forever. Perks can be powerful motivational tools that companies can reintegrate into their performance reward systems.

For this assignment, consider your own budget and expenses in terms of revenue and perks. Imagine that like so many companies, you experience a cash crunch. Your revenue (income) shrinks 25 percent, so you must trim some fat from your budget.

Exercises

1. First, you will need to review your expenditures. What "perks" have you built into your budget as a student? (Think pizza and beer.) Make a list of all your nonvalue-added expenses. This includes anything not directly related to your studies (like books, tuition, enrollment fees, pens, paper, etc.) or your fixed expenses (like rent, car payments, insurance, etc.).

2. If you experienced a 25 percent reduction in your income—as numerous firms did after the tech bubble burst—which perks would you eliminate? In addition, are there items that you previously considered necessities that you could cut out? An example would be selling your car (thereby eliminating car payments and related insurance) and taking public transportation or catching a ride with a friend. What about getting a roommate, moving into the dorms, or living with your parents?

3. Often employees develop a sense of entitlement about perks, and when the perks are trimmed, great dissatisfaction can result. Companies even lose employees when perks are cut. In this exercise, let's consider that cutting out your nonvalue-added (i.e., fun) expenditures may put a crimp in your social life. In fact, you may have trouble staying in the loop. What can you do to "retain" your social friends as you cut down on your personal perks? Do you think that "retention" will even be an issue for you? Why or why not?

4. Once you have taken the axe to your perks, how can you reincorporate them into your budget, this time as motivational tools? Which perks would motivate you to have perfect attendance in class? To make an "A"? Straight "A's"? Be creative. The purpose is to see if you can modify your own behavior by using your perks.

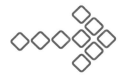

BIZ FLIX For Love of the Game

Billy Chapel (Kevin Costner), a 20-year veteran pitcher with the Detroit Tigers, learns just before the season's last game that the team's new owners want to trade him. He also learns that his partner Jane Aubrey (Kelly Preston) intends to leave him. Faced with these daunting blows, Chapel wants to pitch a perfect final game. Director Sam Raimi's love of baseball shines through in some striking visual effects.

This scene is a slightly edited version of the "Just Throw" sequence, which begins the film's exciting closing scenes in which Chapel pitches his last game. In this scene, the Tigers' catcher Gus Sinski (John C. Reilly) comes out to the pitching mound to talk to Billy.

What to Watch for and Ask Yourself

1. What is Billy Chapel's level of esteem needs at this point in the game?
2. Do you expect Gus Sinski's talk to have any effect on Chapel? If it will, what will be the effect?
3. What rewards potentially exist for Billy Chapel? Remember, this is the last baseball game of his career.

MGMT WORKPLACE Wahoo's Fish Tacos

Entrepreneurs Wing Lam, Ed Lee, and Mingo Lee built Wahoo's Fish Taco from a single meager taco stand to a 22-store, 300-employee enterprise. Wahoo's serves great tasting, very healthy, and quickly prepared food to people with an active lifestyle. As the company grew, the core management team decided that promotion from within at the store level would be critical. To make it easy for any motivated Wahoo employee to excel, top management cultivates fanatical attention to customer service. They also use rigorously standardized operating procedures and explicit training programs. They believe that building a positive internal experience for their workers will motivate employees to provide the same experience for their customers.

What to Watch for and Ask Yourself

1 What motivational theory best describes the practices at Wahoo's? Explain.

2. How do the managers at Wahoo measure performance? What effect do performance measures have on the motivation of Wahoo's employees?

CHAPTER FIFTEEN

Leadership

outline

WHAT WOULD YOU DO?

Xerox Headquarters, Stamford, Connecticut.[1] "We know it's a difficult time for the company, and a difficult decision for you, but we'd like you to be Xerox's new CEO. Think it over this weekend, and give us an answer on Monday." Your heart is still pounding as you hang up the phone, pick it back up, and call your husband and two sons to let them know what just happened. You have been with Xerox for over two decades, with most of that time in sales, but you never expected to be CEO. No one ever mentioned it in career discussions. No one said that you might be "groomed" for the job. In fact, for years you have thought about leaving Xerox to spend more time with your sons; each time you bought a new briefcase for work you told your husband, a former Xerox manager who spent 35 years with the company, that it would be the last. So you and your husband are truly surprised that the board of directors has offered you the job.

Unfortunately, there couldn't be a worse time to take over: Xerox is in

student resources

URL	GUIDE	VIDEO	PPT	FAQ	TEST
Explore the four levels of learning by doing the simulation module on Leadership.	Mini lecture reviews all the learning points in the chapter and concludes with a case on Unique Restaurants.	Biz Flix is a scene from *U-571*. Management Workplace is a segment on Buffalo Zoo.	12 slides with graphics provide an outline for this chapter.	Chuck reminds us that you don't have to be charismatic to be a good leader.	24 true/false questions, 23 multiple-choice questions, a management scenario, and 5 exhibit worksheets

the worst shape of its 70 years of existence. Outflanked by Hewlett-Packard in desktop computer printers and under attack from Canon, Minolta, and other Japanese copy machine companies, Xerox has $17.1 billion in debt and only $154 million in cash in the bank (a minuscule amount for a company of its size). Furthermore, the Securities and Exchange Commission is investigating the company for fraudulently overstating $6.4 billion in revenues over the last few years. In addition, three years of steeply declining revenues and increasing losses have caused the company's stock price to fall from $64 a share to just $4.43. You and others have even heard rumors that top-level finance and accounting executives have been pushing for Xerox to file for Chapter 11 bankruptcy to temporarily protect itself from creditors and give it time to reorganize, repay, and recover.

You and your coworkers are astounded at how far the company has fallen. After all, from the 1960s through the 1980s, Xerox was one of the premier high-tech companies. The invention of its copy machines led to astronomical growth, averaging 34 percent per year at one time. Furthermore, Xerox Parc, Xerox's research and development division, invented the first personal computers well before IBM and Apple began making them. But those advantages and innovations were frittered away over the next 15 years. The company was incredibly averse to change and earned the nickname "Burox," for its slow, stodgy, bureaucratic culture. In many locations, thanks to a confusing matrix structure, literally no one knew who was in charge. No one could answer basic questions like, "How many copiers did we sell this quarter?" "Why did we lose our top customers to Canon and Minolta?" "What are your costs?" Indeed, it was an understatement to say that Xerox was in complete disarray.

After spending the longest weekend of your life discussing the offer with your husband and sons, you wake up on Monday morning still not sure what to do. Earlier you had awakened in a cold sweat from a nightmare in which you became CEO and then failed, causing 80,000 workers to lose their jobs and 16,000 retirees to lose their retirement benefits. You just don't know if you have what it takes to be CEO. You aren't particularly charismatic or heroic. And with a degree in English and journalism, you don't feel like the "CEO type." You can't help wondering whether you are the right person for the job. Moreover, if you do take the job, you aren't sure what steps you'd need to take as a leader. You've seen numerous CEOs come and go at Xerox over the years, so you know what a new CEO should not do. But if someone were to ask, "What are the two most important things you could do as Xerox's new leader?" you aren't sure you could answer. Finally, given the depth of Xerox's problems, can the company be turned around? When all of the CEOs before you have failed, what can you do differently to transform the company? What can you do to get scared Xerox managers and employees to see beyond their own needs to those of the organization? **If you were asked to be Xerox's new CEO, what would you do?**

Do I have what it takes to lead? What are the most important things leaders do? How can I transform a poorly performing department, division, or company? Do I need to adjust my leadership depending on the situation and the employee? Why doesn't my leadership inspire people? If you've ever been "in charge," or even just thought about it, chances are you've considered similar questions. Well, you're not alone, millions of leaders in organizations across the world struggle with these fundamental leadership issues on a daily basis.

We begin this chapter by discussing what leadership is, who leaders are, meaning their traits and characteristics, and what leaders do that makes them different from people who aren't leaders. Next we examine four major contingency theories of leadership that specify which leaders are best suited for which situations or how leaders should change their behavior to lead different people in different circumstances. The chapter ends with a review of strategic leadership issues, such as charismatic and transformational leadership, which are concerned with working with others to meet long-term goals and with creating a viable future for an organization.

What Is Leadership?

When Cynthia Danaher became general manager of Hewlett-Packard's Medical Products Group, she told her 5,300 employees, "I want to do this job, but it's scary and I need your help." She also told them that they finally had a boss who "knows how to make coffee." After three years of experience as a leader, she now regrets her choice of words. If she had a chance to hold that meeting again, she says that she would emphasize goals and challenge her people to find ways to meet them. She says, "People say they want a leader to be vulnerable just like them, but deep down they want to believe you have the skill to move and fix things they can't. And while anyone who starts something new is bound to feel some anxiety, you don't need to bare your soul." Moreover, she says that for leaders, setting a direction is more important than making employees feel comfortable.[2]

leadership
the process of influencing others to achieve group or organizational goals

As H-P's Cynthia Danaher discovered, **leadership** is the process of influencing others to achieve group or organizational goals.

After reading the next two sections, you should be able to

1 explain what leadership is.

2 describe who leaders are and what effective leaders do.

1 Leadership

Southwest Airlines flies two to three times as many passengers per employee as other airlines at a cost 25 to 40 percent below its competitors' costs.[3] A key part of Southwest's performance is that it empties its planes, refills them with passengers, crews, fuel, and food (peanuts and soft drinks); and has them back on the runway in 20 minutes, compared to an hour for most airlines. This allows Southwest to keep each of its planes filled with paying passengers about three more hours a day. Why is Southwest able to achieve such incredible results? Because the people of Southwest Airlines have been successfully influenced to achieve company goals (i.e., leadership).

Let's learn more about leadership by exploring 1.1 the differences between leaders and managers.

1.1 Leaders versus Managers

In Chapter 1, we defined *management* as getting work done through others. In other words, managers don't do the work themselves. Managers help others do their jobs better. By contrast, *leadership* is the process of influencing others to achieve group or organizational goals. So what are the key differences between leadership and management?

According to Professor Warren Bennis, the primary difference, as shown in Exhibit 15.1, is that leaders are concerned with doing the right thing, while managers are concerned with doing things right.[4] In other words, leaders begin with the question, "What should we be doing?" while managers start with "How can we do what we're already doing better?" Leaders focus on vision, mission, goals, and objectives, while managers focus on productivity and efficiency. Managers see themselves as preservers of the status quo, while leaders see themselves as promoters of change and challengers of the status quo in that they encourage creativity and risk taking. Managers have a relatively short-term perspective, while leaders take a long-term view. Managers are more concerned with *means*, how to get things done, while leaders are more concerned with *ends*, what gets done. Managers are concerned with control and limiting the choices of others, while leaders are more concerned with expanding people's choices and options.[5] Finally, managers solve problems so that others can do their work, while leaders inspire and motivate others to find their own solutions.

Let's illustrate the difference between managers and leaders by taking another look at Southwest Airlines. After the federal government deregulated the airline industry, giving airlines the right to determine how many flights they would have and where those flights would go (previously, this was determined by the government), one of the first things Southwest did was reassess its strategic plan and objectives. Howard Putnam, Southwest's CEO at the time, told his top managers, "We aren't going to leave this room until we can write up on the wall, in a hundred words or less, what we are going to be when we grow up." And then, unlike other airlines, which simply tried to improve what they were already doing (i.e., management), Southwest critically examined what it was doing, why it was doing what it was doing, and whether it should continue to do what it had been doing. As a result of Putnam's leadership, Southwest mapped out a strategy that has made it highly competitive and highly profitable.[6]

exhibit 15.1

Managers versus Leaders

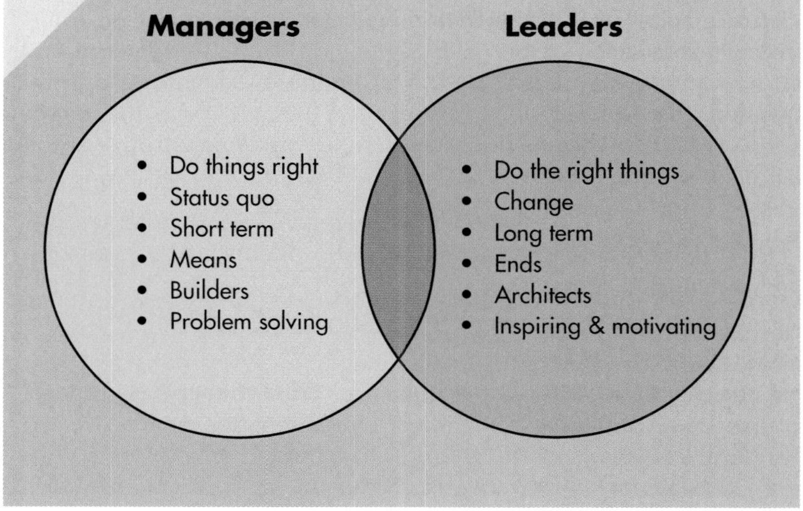

Though leaders are different from managers, in practice, organizations need them both. Managers are critical to getting out the day-to-day work, and leaders are critical to inspiring employees and setting the organization's long-term direction. The key issue is the extent to which organizations are properly led or properly managed. Warren Bennis summed up the difference between leaders and managers by noting that "American organizations (and probably those in much of the rest of the industrialized world) are under led and over managed. They do not pay enough attention to doing the right thing, while they pay too much attention to doing things right."[7]

Andrea Jung, CEO of Avon, certainly is concerned with doing the right things, with change, and with developing Avon's long-term strategy. Under Jung, Avon has developed numerous new brands and identified new ways to sell them. Jung has moved Avon out of the 1950s and made the company relevant to the twenty-first century.

Review 1
Leadership

Leadership is the process of influencing others to achieve group or organizational goals. Leaders are different from managers. The primary difference is that leaders are concerned with doing the right thing, while managers are concerned with doing things right. Furthermore, managers have a short-term focus and are concerned with the status quo, with means rather than ends, and with solving others' problems. By contrast, leaders have a long-term focus and are concerned with change, with ends rather than means, and with inspiring and motivating others to solve their own problems. Organizations need both managers and leaders. But, in general, companies are overmanaged and underled.

2 Who Leaders Are and What Leaders Do

Every year, *Fortune* magazine conducts a survey to determine corporate America's "most admired" companies. And, every few years, as part of that study, it takes a look at the leaders of those companies. Interestingly, the last time it did this, it found that the CEOs of its 10 most admired companies were surprisingly different. In fact, said *Fortune,* "Every conceivable leadership style is represented by these CEOs."[8] General Electric's then CEO was described as "combative," as someone who "tilts his head, and thrusts out his chin as if to say, 'Go ahead, take your best shot'—and is never happier than when you do." Southwest Airlines' then CEO was described as "a prankster and a kisser so unabashedly affectionate that his company's ticker symbol is LUV, so hands-on he has loaded baggage and served peanuts to passengers." In fact, Southwest's CEO admitted that he was terrible at understanding the financial side of business, something that no regular CEO would ever admit. Finally, Coca-Cola's then CEO was the mirror image of Southwest's CEO. *Fortune* described him as "undemonstrative and a 'financial wizard.'"

So, if the CEOs of *Fortune*'s "most admired" corporations are all different, just what makes a good leader? Let's learn more about who leaders are by investigating 2.1 leadership traits and behaviors.

2.1 Leadership Traits and Behaviors

trait theory
a leadership theory that holds that effective leaders possess a similar set of traits or characteristics

traits
relatively stable characteristics, such as abilities, psychological motives, or consistent patterns of behavior

Trait theory is one way to describe who leaders are. **Trait theory** says that effective leaders possess a similar set of traits or characteristics. **Traits** are relatively stable characteristics, such as abilities, psychological motives, or consistent patterns of behavior. Early versions of trait theory stated that leaders

> **www.experiencing management.com**
>
> Learn how managerial use of power affects employee behavior and productivity. Visit our animated concept and activity site. Choose Leadership from the "select a topic" pull-down menu, then Power from the "overview tab."
>
> **http://www.experiencingmanagement.com**

are born, not made. In other words, you either have the "right stuff" to be a leader, or you don't. And if you don't, there is no way to get "it."

For some time, it was thought that trait theory was wrong and that there are no consistent trait differences between leaders and nonleaders, or between effective and ineffective leaders. However, more recent evidence shows that "successful leaders are not like other people," that successful leaders are indeed different from the rest of us.[9] More specifically, as shown in Exhibit 15.2, leaders are different from nonleaders in the following traits: drive, the desire to lead, honesty/integrity, self-confidence, emotional stability, cognitive ability, and knowledge of the business.[10]

Drive refers to high levels of effort and is characterized by achievement, motivation, ambition, energy, tenacity, and initiative. Successful leaders also have a stronger *desire to lead.* They want to be in charge and think about ways to influence or convince others about what should or shouldn't be done. *Honesty/integrity* is also important to leaders. *Honesty,* being truthful with others, is a cornerstone of leadership. Without honesty, leaders won't be trusted. When leaders have it, subordinates are willing to overlook other flaws. *Integrity* is the extent to which leaders do what they said they would do. Leaders may be honest and have good intentions, but if they don't consistently deliver on what they promise, they won't be trusted.

Self-confidence, believing in one's abilities, also distinguishes leaders from nonleaders and is critical to leadership. Leaders make risky, long-term decisions and must convince others of the correctness of those decisions. Self-confident leaders are more decisive and assertive and are more likely to gain others' confidence. Moreover, self-confident leaders will admit mistakes because they view them as learning opportunities rather than a refutation of their leadership capabilities. This also means that leaders have *emotional stability.* Even when things go wrong, they remain even-tempered and consistent in their outlook and in the way they treat others. Leaders who can't control their emotions, who anger quickly or attack and blame others for mistakes, are unlikely to be trusted.

exhibit 15.2

Leadership Traits

Leaders are also smart. Leaders typically have strong *cognitive abilities.* This means that leaders have the capacity to analyze large amounts of seemingly unrelated, complex information and see patterns, opportunities, or threats where others might not see them. Finally, leaders also "know their stuff," which means they have superior technical knowledge about the businesses they run. Leaders who have a good *knowledge of the business* understand the key technological decisions and concerns facing their companies. More often than not, studies indicate that effective leaders have long, extensive experience in their industries.

Thus far, you've read about who leaders *are.* However, traits alone are not enough to make a successful leader. Traits are a precondition for success. After all, it's hard to imagine a truly successful leader who lacks all of these qualities. Leaders who have these traits (or many of them) must then take actions that encourage people to achieve

WHAT REALLY WORKS

LEADERSHIP TRAITS DO MAKE A DIFFERENCE

For decades, researchers assumed that leadership traits, such as drive, emotional stability, cognitive ability, and charisma, were not related to effective leadership. However, more recent evidence shows that there are reliable trait differences between leaders and nonleaders. In fact, 54 studies based on more than 6,000 people clearly indicate that in terms of leadership traits, "successful leaders are not like other people."

Traits and Perceptions of Leadership Effectiveness

Several leadership models argue that successful leaders will be viewed by their followers as good leaders. (This is completely different from determining whether leaders actually improve organizational performance.) Consequently, one test of trait theory is whether leaders with particular traits are viewed as more or less effective leaders by their followers.

Intelligence. On average, there is a 75 percent chance that intelligent leaders will be seen as better leaders than less intelligent leaders.

Dominance. On average, there is only a 57 percent chance that leaders with highly dominant personalities will be seen as better leaders than those with less dominant personalities.

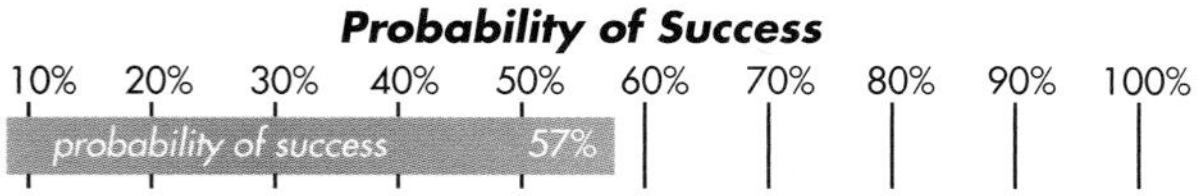

Extroversion. On average, there is a 63 percent chance that extroverts will be seen as better leaders than introverts.

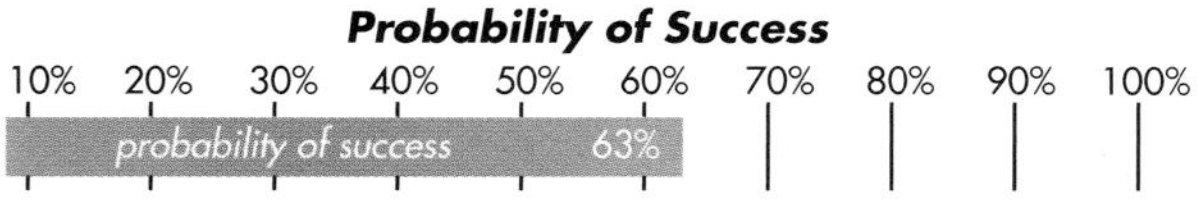

Charisma and Leadership Effectiveness

As discussed at the end of the chapter, *charismatic leadership* is the set of behavioral tendencies and personal characteristics of leaders that creates an exceptionally strong relationship between leaders and their followers. More specifically, charismatic leaders articulate a clear vision for the future that is based on strongly held values or morals; model those values by acting in a way consistent with the company's vision; communicate high performance expectations to followers; and display confidence in followers' abilities to achieve the vision.

Charisma and Performance. On average, there is a 72 percent chance that charismatic leaders will have better-performing followers and organizations than less charismatic leaders.

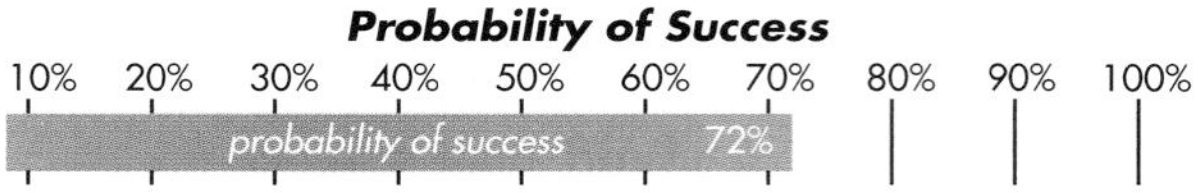

Charisma and Perceived Leader Effectiveness. On average, there is an 89 percent chance that charismatic leaders will be perceived as more effective leaders than less charismatic leaders.

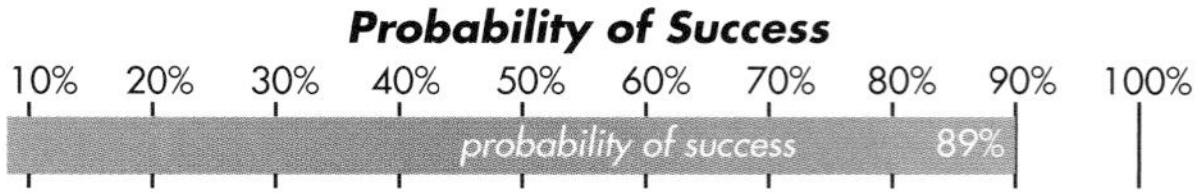

Charisma and Leader Satisfaction. On average, there is a 90 percent chance that the followers of charismatic leaders will be more satisfied with their leaders than the followers of less charismatic leaders.[11]

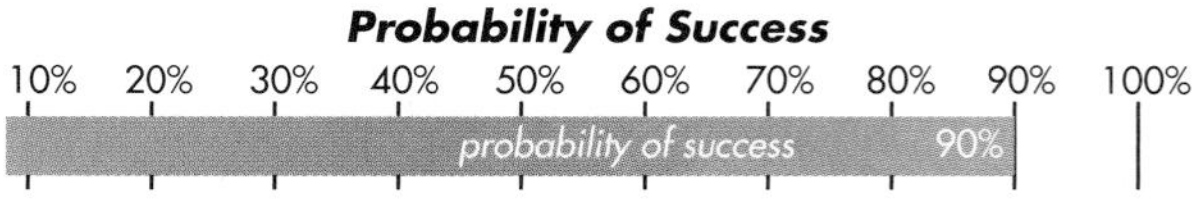

group or organizational goals.[12] Accordingly, we now examine what leaders *do*, meaning the behaviors they perform or the actions they take to influence others to achieve group or organizational goals.

Researchers at the University of Michigan, Ohio State University, and the University of Texas examined the specific behaviors that leaders use to im-

PERSONAL PRODUCTIVITY TIP

Monitor These Signs of Failing Leadership

Successful leaders seem to have a sixth sense that helps them monitor how followers feel about them and their ideas. You can develop your own "sixth sense" by monitoring these signs of failed leadership: (1) performance—not meeting your numbers and goals; (2) execution—not meeting commitments to direct reports; (3) isolation—bad news and problems aren't coming to you; (4) turnover—talented subordinates start leaving because of you or organizational problems; and (5) people problems—not having the emotional strength to confront or replace poor-performing key subordinates. So, develop your "sixth sense" and monitor these signs of failed leadership.[14]

prove subordinate satisfaction and performance. Hundreds of studies were conducted and hundreds of leader behaviors were examined. At all three universities, two basic leader behaviors emerged as central to successful leadership: initiating structure (called *job-centered leadership* at the University of Michigan and *concern for production* at the University of Texas) and considerate leader behavior (called *employee-centered leadership* at the University of Michigan and *concern for people* at the University of Texas).[13] In fact, these two leader behaviors form the basis for many of the leadership theories discussed in this chapter.

initiating structure
the degree to which a leader structures the roles of followers by setting goals, giving directions, setting deadlines, and assigning tasks

consideration
the extent to which a leader is friendly, approachable, and supportive and shows concern for employees

Initiating structure is the degree to which a leader structures the roles of followers by setting goals, giving directions, setting deadlines, and assigning tasks. A leader's ability to initiate structure primarily affects subordinates' job performance. Indeed, in an article entitled "Why CEOs Fail," *Fortune* magazine indicated that CEOs who initiate structure are likely to succeed, whereas those who don't are likely to fail and often lose their jobs.

Consideration is the extent to which a leader is friendly, approachable, and supportive and shows concern for employees. Consideration primarily affects subordinates' job satisfaction. Specific leader consideration behaviors include listening to employees' problems and concerns, consulting with employees before making decisions, and treating employees as equals. Eighty-three of the 170 people who worked at Sandler O'Neill, a small financial firm located on the 104th floor of World Trade Center Tower Two, died when the towers collapsed after the terrorist attacks on September 11, 2001. Jimmy Dunne, the principal partner of Sandler O'Neill, immediately hired grief counselors for the families, organized a center to help them go about the grisly task of recovering remains, and established a charity fund to which people could contribute to help them. Within two weeks of the tragedy, the company sent each deceased employee's family a check for the employee's salary through the end of the year. It also extended each family's health benefits for the next five years. Plus, Dunne told the families that they would also receive the sales commissions and year-end bonuses that their loved ones would have collected had they lived. In the end, the company paid the families more than 30 percent of its capital.[15]

Although researchers at all three universities generally agreed that initiating structure and consideration were basic leader behaviors, they differed on the interaction and effectiveness of these behaviors. The University of Michigan studies indicated that initiating structure and consideration were mutually exclusive behaviors on opposite ends of the same continuum. In other words, leaders who wanted to be more considerate would have to do less initiating of structure (and vice versa). The University of Michigan studies also indicated that only considerate leader behaviors (i.e., employee-centered) were associated with successful leadership. By contrast, researchers at Ohio State University and the University of Texas found that initiating structure and consideration were independent behaviors, meaning that leaders can be considerate and initiate structure at the same time. Additional evidence confirms this finding.[16] The same researchers also concluded that the most effective leaders were strong on both initiating structure and considerate leader behaviors.

This "high-high" approach can be seen in the upper right corner of the Blake/Mouton leadership grid, shown in Exhibit 15.3. Blake and Mouton used two leadership behaviors, concern for people (i.e., consideration) and concern for production (i.e., initiating structure), to categorize five different leadership styles. Both behaviors are rated on a 9-point scale with 1 representing "low" and 9 representing "high." Blake and Mouton suggest that a "high-high" or 9,9 leadership style is the best. They call this style *team management* because leaders who use it display a high concern for people (9) and a high concern for production (9). By contrast, leaders use a 9,1 *authority-compliance* leadership style when they have a high concern for production and a low concern for people. A 1,9 *country club* style occurs when leaders care about having a friendly and enjoyable work environment but don't really pay much attention to production or performance. The worst leadership style, according to the grid, is the 1,1 *impoverished* leader, who shows little concern for people or production and does the bare minimum needed to keep his or her job. Finally, the 5,5 *middle-of-the-road* style occurs when leaders show a moderate amount of concern for both people and production.

exhibit 15.3

Blake/Mouton Leadership Grid

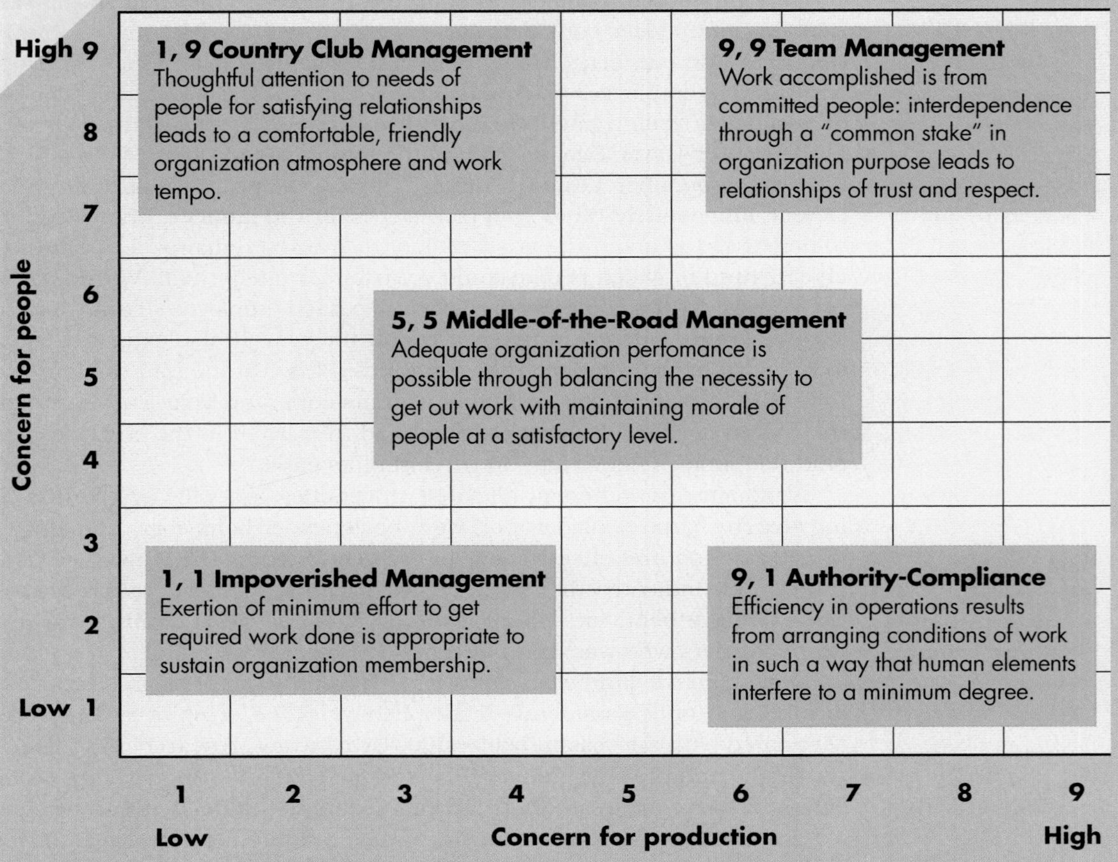

High 9
8
7
6
5
4
3
2
Low 1
Concern for people
1, 9 Country Club Management
Thoughtful attention to needs of people for satisfying relationships leads to a comfortable, friendly organization atmosphere and work tempo.
9, 9 Team Management
Work accomplished is from committed people: interdependence through a "common stake" in organization purpose leads to relationships of trust and respect.
5, 5 Middle-of-the-Road Management
Adequate organization perfomance is possible through balancing the necessity to get out work with maintaining morale of people at a satisfactory level.
1, 1 Impoverished Management
Exertion of minimum effort to get required work done is appropriate to sustain organization membership.
9, 1 Authority-Compliance
Efficiency in operations results from arranging conditions of work in such a way that human elements interfere to a minimum degree.
1 2 3 4 5 6 7 8 9
Low
Concern for production
High

Source: R. R. Blake & A. A. McCanse, "The Leadership Grid®," Leadership Dilemmas—Grid Solutions *(Houston: Gulf Publishing Company), 21. Copyright © 1991, by Scientific Methods, Inc. Reproduced by permission of the owners.*

Is the team management style, with a high concern for production and a high concern for people, the "best" leadership style? Logically, it would seem so. Why wouldn't you want to show high concern for both people and production? Nonetheless, nearly 50 years of research indicate that there isn't one "best" leadership style. The "best" leadership style depends on the situation. In other words, no one leadership behavior by itself and no one combination of leadership behaviors work well across all situations and employees.

Review 2

Who Leaders Are and What Leaders Do

Trait theory says that effective leaders possess traits or characteristics that differentiate them from nonleaders. Those traits are drive, the desire to lead, honesty/integrity, self-confidence, emotional stability, cognitive ability, and knowledge of the business. However, traits aren't enough for successful leadership. Leaders who have these traits (or many of them) must also behave in ways that encourage people to achieve group or organizational goals. Two key leader behaviors are initiating structure, which improves subordinate performance, and consideration, which improves subordinate satisfaction. There is no "best" combination of these behaviors. The "best" leadership style depends on the situation.

Situational Approaches to Leadership

After leader traits and behaviors, the situational approach to leadership is the third major method used in the study of leadership. There are four major situational approaches to leadership—Fiedler's contingency theory, path-goal theory, Hersey and Blanchard's Situational Leadership theory, and Vroom, Yetton, and Jago's normative decision model. All assume that the effectiveness of any **leadership style**, the way a leader generally behaves toward followers, depends on the situation.[17] Accordingly, there is no one "best" leadership style. Nonetheless, these theories differ in one significant way. Fiedler's contingency theory assumes that leadership styles are consistent and difficult to change. Therefore, leaders must be placed in or "matched" to a situation that fits their leadership style. In contrast, the other three situational theories all assume that leaders are capable of adapting and adjusting their leadership styles to fit the demands of different situations.

leadership style
the way a leader generally behaves toward followers

After reading the next four sections, you should be able to

3 explain Fiedler's contingency theory.
4 describe how path-goal theory works.
5 discuss Hersey and Blanchard's Situational Leadership theory.
6 explain the normative decision theory.

contingency theory
a leadership theory that states that in order to maximize work group performance, leaders must be matched to the situation that best fits their leadership style

3 Putting Leaders in the Right Situation: Fiedler's Contingency Theory

Fiedler's **contingency theory** states that in order to maximize work group performance, leaders must be matched to the right leadership situation.[18] More specifically, as shown in Exhibit 15.4, the first basic assumption of Fiedler's theory is that leaders are effective when the work groups they lead perform well. So, instead of judging leaders' effectiveness by what the leaders do (i.e., initiating structure and consideration) or who they are (i.e., trait theory), Fiedler assesses leaders by the conduct and performance of the people they supervise. Second, Fiedler assumes that leaders are generally unable to change their leadership styles and that they will be more effective when their styles are matched to the proper situation. Third, Fiedler assumes that the favorableness of a situation for a leader depends on the degree to which the situation permits the leader to influence the behavior of group members. Thus, Fiedler's third assumption is consistent with our definition of leadership, which is the process of influencing others to achieve group or organizational goals.

exhibit 15.4

Fiedler's Contingency Theory

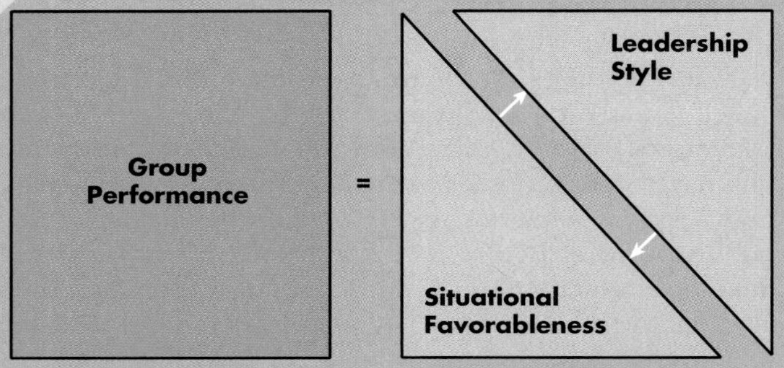

Let's learn more about Fiedler's contingency theory by examining 3.1 the least preferred coworker and leadership styles, 3.2 situational favorableness, and 3.3 how to match leadership styles to situations.

3.1 Leadership Style: Least Preferred Coworker

When Fiedler refers to *leadership style*, he means the way in which a leader generally behaves toward followers. However, Fiedler also assumes that leadership styles are tied to leaders' underlying needs and personalities. And since personality and needs are relatively stable, he assumes that leaders are generally incapable of changing their leadership styles. For example, Apple CEO Steve Jobs is renowned for his hot temper. Stories about Jobs's temper have been around for more than 20 years. In other words, over the last two decades, Jobs's leadership style and personality have been remarkably consistent.[19]

> **www.experiencingmanagement.com**
>
> Interact with Fiedler's contingency theory and test your understanding by visiting our animated concept and activity site. Choose Leadership from the "select a topic" pull-down menu, then Contingency Leadership from the "overview tab."
>
> **http://www.experiencingmanagement.com**

Fiedler uses a questionnaire called the Least Preferred Coworker scale (LPC) to measure leadership style. When completing the LPC scale, people are instructed to consider all of the people with whom they have ever worked and then to choose the one person with whom they "have worked LEAST well." Fiedler explains, "This does not have to be the person you liked least well, but should be the one person with whom you have the most trouble getting the job done."[20]

Take a second yourself to identify your LPC. It's usually someone you had a big disagreement with or, for whatever reason, couldn't work with. After identifying their LPC, people use the sample LPC scale shown in Exhibit 15.5 to "describe" their LPC.

Complete the LPC yourself. Did you describe your LPC as pleasant, friendly, accepting, relaxed, close, warm, and supportive? Or did you describe the person as unpleasant, unfriendly, rejecting, tense, distant, cold, and hostile? People who describe their LPC in a positive way (scoring 64 and above on the full LPC scale) have *relationship-oriented*

exhibit 15.5

Sample Items from the Least Preferred Coworker Scale

Pleasant	8	7	6	5	4	3	2	1	Unpleasant
Friendly	8	7	6	5	4	3	2	1	Unfriendly
Rejecting	1	2	3	4	5	6	7	8	Accepting
Tense	1	2	3	4	5	6	7	8	Relaxed
Distant	1	2	3	4	5	6	7	8	Close
Cold	1	2	3	4	5	6	7	8	Warm
Supportive	8	7	6	5	4	3	2	1	Hostile

Source: F. E. Fiedler & M. M. Chemers, Improving Leadership Effectiveness: The Leader Match Concept, *2nd Ed. (New York: John Wiley & Sons, 1984). Available at http://depts.washington.edu/psych/faculty/*cv/fiedler_cv.pdf, 23 March 2002. Reprinted by permission of authors.*

leadership styles. After all, if they can still be positive about their least preferred coworker, they must be people oriented. By contrast, people who describe their LPC in a negative way (scoring 57 or below) have *task-oriented* leadership styles. Given a choice, they'll focus first on getting the job done and second on making sure everyone gets along. Finally, a third group with moderate scores (from 58 to 63) has a more flexible leadership style and can be somewhat relationship oriented or somewhat task oriented.

3.2 Situational Favorableness

Fiedler assumes that leaders will be more effective when their leadership styles are matched to the proper situation. More specifically, Fiedler defines **situational favorableness** as the degree to which a particular situation either permits or denies a leader the chance to influence the behavior of group members.[21] In highly favorable situations, leaders find that their actions influence followers, but in highly unfavorable situations, leaders have little or no success influencing the people they are trying to lead.

Three situational factors determine the favorability of a situation: leader-member relations, task structure, and position power. The most important situational factor is **leader-member relations**, which refers to how well followers respect, trust, and like their leaders. When leader-member relations are good, followers trust the leader and there is a friendly work atmosphere. **Task structure** is the degree to which the requirements of a subordinate's tasks are clearly specified. With highly structured tasks, employees have clear job responsibilities, goals, and procedures. **Position power** is the degree to which leaders are able to hire, fire, reward, and punish workers. The more influence leaders have over hiring, firing, rewards, and punishments, the greater their power.

Leader-member relations, task structure, and position power can be combined into eight situations that differ in their favorability to leaders. In general, the most favorable leader situation occurs when followers like and trust their leaders and know what to do because their tasks are highly structured. Also, the leaders have the formal power to influence workers through hiring, firing, rewarding, and punishing them. Therefore, in this situation, it's relatively easy for a leader to influence followers. By contrast, the least favorable situation for leaders occurs when followers don't like or trust their leaders. Plus, followers are not sure what they're supposed to be doing, given that their tasks or jobs are highly unstructured. Finally, leaders find it difficult to influence followers since they don't have the ability to hire, fire, reward, or punish the people who work for them. In short, it's very difficult to influence followers under these conditions.

situational favorableness
the degree to which a particular situation either permits or denies a leader the chance to influence the behavior of group members

leader-member relations
the degree to which followers respect, trust, and like their leaders

task structure
the degree to which the requirements of a subordinate's tasks are clearly specified

position power
the degree to which leaders are able to hire, fire, reward, and punish workers

3.3 Matching Leadership Styles to Situations

After studying thousands of leaders and followers in hundreds of different situations, Fiedler found that the performance of relationship- and task-oriented leaders followed the pattern displayed in Exhibit 15.6.

Relationship-oriented leaders with high LPC scores were better leaders (i.e., their groups performed more effectively) under moderately favorable situations. In moderately favorable situations, the leader may be liked somewhat, tasks may be somewhat structured, and the leader may have some position power. In this situation, a relationship-oriented leader improves leader-member relations, which is the most important of the three situational factors. In turn, morale and performance improve. By contrast, as Exhibit 15.6 shows, task-oriented leaders with low LPC scores are better leaders in highly favorable and unfavorable situations. Task-oriented leaders do well in favorable situations where leaders are liked, tasks are structured, and the leader has the power to hire, fire, reward, and punish. In these favorable situations, task-oriented leaders effectively step on the gas of a well-tuned car that's in perfect running condition. Their focus on performance sets the goal for the group, which then charges forward to meet it. But task-oriented leaders also do well in unfavorable situations in which leaders are disliked, tasks are unstructured, and the leader doesn't have the power to hire, fire, reward, and punish. In these unfavorable situations, the task-oriented leader sets goals, which focus attention on performance, and clarifies what needs to be done, thus overcoming low task structure. This is enough to jump-start performance, even if workers don't like or trust the leader. Finally, though not shown in Exhibit 15.6, people with moderate LPC scores, who can be somewhat relationship oriented or somewhat task oriented, tend to do fairly well in all situations because they can adapt their behavior. Typically, though, they don't perform quite as well as relationship-oriented or task-oriented leaders whose leadership styles are well matched to the situation.

Recall, however, that Fiedler assumes that leaders are incapable of changing their leadership styles. Accordingly, the key to applying Fiedler's contingency theory in the workplace is to accurately measure and match leaders to situations or to teach leaders how to change situational favorableness by

exhibit 15.6

Matching Leadership Styles to Situations

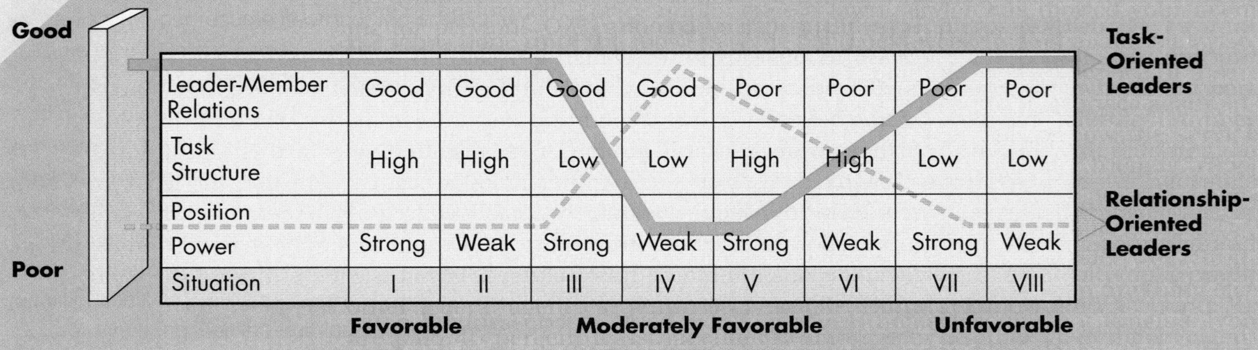
Good
Poor
Leader-Member Relations
Good
Good
Good
Good
Poor
Poor
Poor
Poor
Task Structure
High
High
Low
Low
High
High
Low
Low
Position Power
Strong
Weak
Strong
Weak
Strong
Weak
Strong
Weak
Situation
I
II
III
IV
V
VI
VII
VIII
Favorable
Moderately Favorable
Unfavorable
Task-Oriented Leaders
Relationship-Oriented Leaders

changing leader-member relations, task structure, or position power. While matching or placing leaders in appropriate situations works particularly well, practicing managers have had little luck with "reengineering situations" to fit their leadership styles. The primary problem, as you've no doubt realized, is the complexity of the theory. In a study designed to teach leaders how to reengineer their situations to fit their leadership styles, Fiedler found that most of the leaders simply did not understand what they were supposed to do to change their leadership situations. Furthermore, if they didn't like their LPC profile (perhaps they felt they were more relationship oriented than their scores indicated), they arbitrarily changed it to better suit their view of themselves. Of course, the theory won't work as well if leaders are attempting to change situational factors to fit their perceived leadership style and not their real leadership style.[22]

Review 3

Putting Leaders in the Right Situation: Fiedler's Contingency Theory

Fiedler's theory assumes that leaders are effective when their work groups perform well, that leaders are unable to change their leadership styles, that leadership styles must be matched to the proper situation, and that favorable situations permit leaders to influence group members. According to the Least Preferred Coworker (LPC) scale, there are two basic leadership styles. People who describe their LPC in a positive way have relationship-oriented leadership styles. By contrast, people who describe their LPC in a negative way have task-oriented leadership styles. Situational favorableness occurs when leaders can influence followers and is determined by leader-member relations, task structure, and position power. In general, relationship-oriented leaders with high LPC scores are better leaders under moderately favorable situations, while task-oriented leaders with low LPC scores are better leaders in highly favorable and unfavorable situations. Since Fiedler assumes that leaders are incapable of changing their leadership styles, the key is to accurately measure and match leaders to situations or to teach leaders how to change situational factors. While matching or placing leaders in appropriate situations works well, "reengineering situations" to fit leadership styles doesn't because of the complexity of the model, which makes it difficult for people to understand.

4 Adapting Leader Behavior: Path-Goal Theory

path-goal theory
a leadership theory that states that leaders can increase subordinate satisfaction and performance by clarifying and clearing the paths to goals and by increasing the number and kinds of rewards available for goal attainment

Just as its name suggests, **path-goal theory** states that leaders can increase subordinate satisfaction and performance by clarifying and clearing the paths to goals and by increasing the number and kinds of rewards available for goal attainment. Said another way, leaders need to clarify how followers can achieve organizational goals, take care of problems that prevent followers from achieving goals, and then find more and varied rewards to motivate followers who achieve those goals.[23]

For path clarification, path clearing, and rewards to increase followers' motivation and effort, however, leaders must meet two conditions. First, leader behavior must be a source of immediate or future satisfaction for followers. Therefore, the things you do as a leader must please your followers today or lead to activities or rewards that will satisfy them in the future.

Second, while providing the coaching, guidance, support, and rewards necessary for effective work performance, leader behaviors must complement and not duplicate the characteristics of followers' work environments. Thus, leader behaviors must offer something unique and valuable to followers beyond what they're already experiencing as they do their jobs or what they can already do for themselves.

In contrast to Fiedler's contingency theory, path-goal theory assumes that leaders can change and adapt their leadership styles. Exhibit 15.7 illustrates this process, showing that leaders change and adapt their leadership styles contingent on their subordinates or the environment in which those subordinates work.

exhibit 15.7

Path-Goal Theory

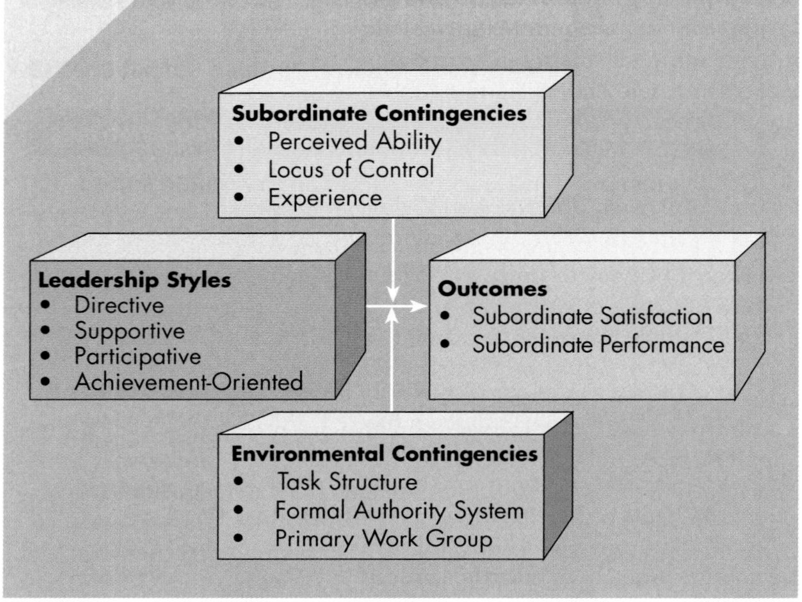

Let's learn more about path-goal theory by examining 4.1 the four kinds of leadership styles that leaders use, 4.2 the subordinate and environmental contingency factors that determine when different leader styles are effective, and 4.3 the outcomes of path-goal theory in improving employee satisfaction and performance.

4.1 Leadership Styles

As illustrated in Exhibit 15.7, the four leadership styles in path-goal theory are directive, supportive, participative, and achievement oriented.[24] **Directive leadership** involves letting employees know precisely what is expected of them, giving them specific guidelines for performing tasks, scheduling work, setting standards of performance, and making sure that people follow standard rules and regulations.

directive leadership
a leadership style in which the leader lets employees know precisely what is expected of them, gives them specific guidelines for performing tasks, schedules work, sets standards of performance, and makes sure that people follow standard rules and regulations

supportive leadership
a leadership style in which the leader is friendly to and approachable by employees, shows concern for them and their welfare, treats them as equals, and creates a friendly climate

Supportive leadership involves being friendly to and approachable by employees, showing concern for them and their welfare, treating them as equals, and creating a friendly climate. Supportive leadership is very similar to considerate leader behavior. Supportive leadership often results in employee job satisfaction and satisfaction with leaders. This leadership style may also result in improved performance when it increases employee confidence, lowers employee job stress, or improves relations and trust between employees and leaders.[25] For example, husband and wife Shane and Allison Alexander both work for Wal-Mart in Madisonville, Kentucky. Over the years, the Wal-Mart managers in their store have shown concern for them in a number of important ways. For example, since the Alexanders had only one car, Wal-Mart scheduled them for alternating shifts, which also allowed them to care for their baby.[26]

Participative leadership involves consulting employees for their suggestions and input before making decisions. Participation in decision making should help followers understand which goals are most important and clarify the paths to accomplishing them. Furthermore, when people participate in decisions, they become more committed to making them work.

Achievement-oriented leadership means setting challenging goals, having high expectations of employees, and displaying confidence that employees

One small employer that has achieved impressive results by using participative leadership is Just Born, Inc., a Bethlehem, Pennsylvania–based candy manufacturer that is probably best known for its Marshmallow Peeps, an Easter-basket favorite. Employee participation is a central value, demonstrated through project and cost-saving teams, company-sponsored community service work, training programs, and employee group meetings that give employees additional opportunities to take on new roles and responsibilities.

will assume responsibility and put forth extraordinary effort. Former U.S. Army general Norman Schwarzkopf believes that leaders generally don't ask enough of their people. Early in his career, Schwarzkopf was placed in charge of helicopter maintenance at a military base, something that he knew little about. Since readiness is always a key factor in military operations, he asked what percentage of the helicopter fleet was available for flight operations on any given day. The answer was "roughly 75 percent." Schwarzkopf recalls telling workers, "I don't know anything about helicopter maintenance, but I'm establishing a new standard—85 percent." Within a short time, 85 percent of the helicopter fleet was available for daily flight operations. The moral, according to the general, is that employees usually will not perform above your expectations, so it's important to expect a lot.[27]

4.2 Subordinate and Environmental Contingencies

As shown in Exhibit 15.7, path-goal theory specifies that leader behaviors should be fitted to subordinate characteristics. The theory identifies three kinds of subordinate contingencies: perceived ability, experience, and locus of control. *Perceived ability* is simply how much ability subordinates believe they have for doing their jobs well. Subordinates who perceive that they have a great deal of ability will be dissatisfied with directive leader behaviors. Experienced employees are likely to react in a similar way. Since they already know how to do their jobs (or perceive that they do), they don't need or want close supervision. By contrast, subordinates with little experience or little perceived ability will welcome directive leadership.

Locus of control is a personality measure that indicates the extent to which people believe that they have control over what happens to them in life. *Internals* believe that what happens to them, good or bad, is largely a result of their choices and actions. *Externals*, on the other hand, believe that what happens to them is caused by external forces beyond their control. Accordingly, externals are much more comfortable with a directive leadership style, while internals greatly prefer a participative leadership style because they like to have a say in what goes on at work.

Path-goal theory specifies that leader behaviors should complement rather than duplicate the characteristics of followers' work environments. There are three kinds of environmental contingencies: task structure, the formal authority system, and the primary work group. As in Fiedler's contingency theory, *task structure* is the degree to which the requirements of a subordinate's tasks are clearly specified. When task structure is low and tasks are unclear, directive leadership should be used because it complements the work environment. When task structure is high and tasks are clear, however, directive leadership duplicates what task structure provides and is not needed. Alternatively, when tasks are stressful, frustrating, or dissatisfying, leaders should respond with supportive leadership.

The *formal authority system* is an organization's set of procedures, rules, and policies. When the formal authority system is unclear, directive leadership

participative leadership
a leadership style in which the leader consults employees for their suggestions and input before making decisions

achievement-oriented leadership
a leadership style in which the leader sets challenging goals, has high expectations of employees, and displays confidence that employees will assume responsibility and put forth extraordinary effort

complements the situation by reducing uncertainty and increasing clarity. But, when the formal authority system is clear, directive leadership is redundant and should not be used.

Primary work group refers to the amount of work-oriented participation or emotional support that is provided by an employee's immediate work group. Participative leadership should be used when tasks are complex and there is little existing work-oriented participation in the primary work group. When tasks are stressful, frustrating, or repetitive, supportive leadership is called for.

Finally, since keeping track of all of these subordinate and environmental contingencies can get a bit confusing, Exhibit 15.8 provides a summary of when directive, supportive, participative, and achievement-oriented leadership styles should be used.

4.3 Outcomes

Does following path-goal theory improve subordinate satisfaction and performance? Preliminary evidence suggests that it does.[28] In particular, people who work for supportive leaders are much more satisfied with their jobs and their bosses. Likewise, people who work for directive leaders are more satisfied with their jobs and bosses (but not quite as much as when their bosses are supportive) and perform their jobs better, too. Does adapting one's leadership style to subordinate and environmental characteristics improve subordinate satisfaction and performance? At this point, because of the difficulty of completely testing this complex theory, it's too early to tell.[29] However, since the data clearly show that it makes sense for leaders to be both supportive *and* directive, it also makes sense that leaders could improve subordinate satisfaction and performance by adding participative and achievement-oriented leadership styles to their capabilities as leaders.

exhibit 15.8

Path-Goal Theory: When to Use Directive, Supportive, Participative, or Achievement-Oriented Leadership

DIRECTIVE LEADERSHIP	SUPPORTIVE LEADERSHIP	PARTICIPATIVE LEADERSHIP	ACHIEVEMENT-ORIENTED LEADERSHIP
Unstructured tasks	Structured, simple, repetitive tasks	Experienced workers	Unchallenging tasks
Inexperienced workers	Stressful, frustrating tasks	Workers with high perceived ability	
Workers with low perceived ability	When workers lack confidence	Workers with internal locus of control	
Workers with external locus of control	Clear formal authority system	Workers not satisfied with rewards	
Unclear formal authority system		Complex tasks	

Review 4

Adapting Leader Behavior: Path-Goal Theory

Path-goal theory states that leaders can increase subordinate satisfaction and performance by clarifying and clearing the paths to goals and by increasing the number and kinds of rewards available for goal attainment. For this to work, however, leader behavior must be a source of immediate or future satisfaction for followers and must complement and not duplicate the characteristics of followers' work environments. In contrast to Fiedler's contingency theory, path-goal theory assumes that leaders can and do change and adapt their leadership styles (directive, supportive, participative, and achievement oriented), depending on their subordinates (experience, perceived ability, internal or external) or the environment in which those subordinates work (task structure, formal authority system, or primary work group).

5 Adapting Leader Behavior: Hersey and Blanchard's Situational Leadership® Theory*

Have you ever had a new job that you didn't know how to do and your boss was not around to help you learn it? Conversely, have you ever known exactly how to do your job but your boss kept treating you like you didn't? Hersey and Blanchard's Situational Leadership theory is based on the idea of follower readiness. Hersey and Blanchard argue that employees have different levels of readiness for handling different jobs, responsibilities, and work assignments. Accordingly, Hersey and Blanchard's **situational theory** states that leaders need to adjust their leadership styles to match followers' readiness.[30]

situational theory
a leadership theory that states that leaders need to adjust their leadership styles to match their followers' readiness

Let's learn more about Hersey and Blanchard's situational theory by examining 5.1 worker readiness and 5.2 different leadership styles.

5.1 Worker Readiness

worker readiness
the ability and willingness to take responsibility for directing one's behavior at work

Worker readiness is the ability and willingness to take responsibility for directing one's behavior at work. Readiness is composed of two components. *Job readiness* consists of the amount of knowledge, skill, ability, and experience people have to perform their jobs. As you would expect, people with greater skill, ability, and experience do a better job of supervising their own work. *Psychological readiness*, on the other hand, is a feeling of self-confidence or self-respect. Likewise, confident people do a better job of guiding their own work than do insecure people. Job readiness and psychological readiness are combined to produce four different levels of readiness in Hersey and Blanchard's Situational Leadership theory. The lowest level, R1, represents insecure people who are neither willing nor able to take responsibility for guiding their own work. R2 represents people who are confident and are willing but not able to take responsibility for guiding their own work. R3 represents people who are insecure and are able but not willing to take responsibility for guiding their own work. And R4 represents people who are confident and willing and able to take responsibility for guiding their own work. It's important to note that a follower's readiness is usually task specific. For example, you may be highly confident and capable when it comes to personal computers, but know nothing about setting up budgets for planning purposes. Thus, you would possess

*Situational Leadership® is a registered trademark of the Center for Leadership Studies.

readiness (R4) with respect to computers and but not (R1) with respect to budgets.

5.2 Leadership Styles

Similar to Blake and Mouton's managerial grid, situational theory defines leadership styles in terms of task behavior (i.e., concern for production) and relationship behavior (i.e., concern for people). These two behaviors can be combined to form four different leadership styles: telling, selling, participating, and delegating. Leaders choose one of these styles depending on the readiness a follower has for a specific task.

A *telling* leadership style (high task behavior and low relationship behavior) is based on one-way communication, in which followers are told what, how, when, and where to do particular tasks. Telling is used when people are at the R1 stage. For instance, someone using a telling leadership style would identify all the steps in a project and give explicit instructions on how to execute each one.

A *selling* leadership style (high task behavior and high relationship behavior) involves two-way communication and psychological support to encourage followers to "own" or "buy into" particular ways of doing things. Selling is used most appropriately at the R2 stage. For instance, someone using a selling leadership style might say, "We're going to start a company newsletter. I really think that's a great idea, don't you? We're going to need some cost estimates from printers and some comments from each manager. But that's pretty straightforward. Oh, don't forget that we need the CEO's comments, too. She's expecting you to call. I know that you'll do a great job on this. We'll meet next Tuesday to see if you have any questions once you've dug into this. By the way, we need to have this done by next Friday."

> **www.experiencing management.com**
>
> You may learn more about Hersey & Blanchard's situational theory by examining the model and completing the activities at our animated concept and activity site. Choose Leadership from the "select a topic" pull-down menu, then Situational Leadership from the "overview tab."
>
> **http://www.experiencingmanagement.com**

A *participating* style (low task behavior and high relationship behavior) is based on two-way communication and shared decision making. Participating is used with employees at R3. Since the problem is with motivation and not ability, someone using a participating leadership style might solicit ideas from a subordinate about a project, let the subordinate get started, but ask to review progress along the way.

A *delegating* style (low task behavior and low relationship behavior) is used when leaders basically let workers "run their own show" and make their own decisions. Delegating is used for people at R4. For instance, someone using a delegating leadership style might say, "We're going to start a company newsletter. You've got 10 days to do it. Run with it. Let me know when you've got it done. I'll email you a couple of ideas, but other than that, do what you think is best. Thanks."

In general, as people become more "ready," and thus more willing and able to guide their own behavior, leaders should become less task oriented and more relationship oriented. Then, as people become even more "ready," leaders should become both less task oriented and less relationship oriented until people eventually manage their own work with little input from their leaders.

How well does Hersey and Blanchard's situational theory work? Despite its intuitive appeal (managers and consultants tend to prefer it over Fiedler's contingency theory because of its underlying logic and simplicity), most studies don't support situational theory.[31] While managers generally do a good job of judging followers' readiness levels, the theory doesn't seem to work well, except at lower levels, where a telling style is recommended for people who are insecure and neither willing nor able to take responsibility for guiding their own work.[32]

Review 5

Adapting Leader Behavior: Hersey and Blanchard's Situational Leadership Theory

According to situational theory, leaders need to adjust their leadership styles to match their followers' readiness, which is the ability (job readiness) and willingness (psychological readiness) to take responsibility for directing one's work. Job readiness and psychological readiness combine to produce four different levels of readiness (R1–R4), which vary based on people's confidence, ability, and willingness to guide their own work. Situational theory combines task and relationship behavior to create four leadership styles—telling (R1), selling (R2), participating (R3), and delegating (R4)—that are used with employees at different readiness levels.

6 Adapting Leader Behavior: Normative Decision Theory

Many people believe that making tough decisions is at the heart of leadership. Yet experienced leaders will tell you that deciding how to make decisions is just as important. The **normative decision theory** (also known as the *Vroom-Yetton-Jago model*) helps leaders decide how much employee participation (from none to letting employees make the entire decision) should be used when making decisions.[33]

normative decision theory
a theory that suggests how leaders can determine an appropriate amount of employee participation when making decisions

Let's learn more about normative decision theory by investigating 6.1 decision styles and 6.2 decision quality and acceptance.

6.1 Decision Styles

Unlike nearly all of the other leadership theories discussed in this chapter, which have specified leadership styles, that is, the way a leader generally behaves toward followers, the normative decision theory specifies five different decision styles or ways of making decisions. (See Chapter 4 for a more complete review of decision making in organizations.) As shown in Exhibit 15.9, those styles vary from *autocratic decisions* (AI or AII) on the left, in which leaders make the decisions by themselves, to *consultative decisions* (CI or CII), in which leaders share problems with subordinates but still make the decisions themselves, to *group decisions* (GII) on the right, in which leaders share the problems with subordinates and then have the group make the decisions. GE Aircraft Engines in Durham, North Carolina, uses this approach when making decisions. According to *Fast Company* magazine, "At GE/Durham, every decision is either an 'A' decision, a 'B' decision, or a 'C' decision. An 'A' decision is one that the plant manager makes herself, without consulting anyone."[34] Plant manager Paula Sims says, "I don't make very many of those, and when I do make one, everyone at the plant knows it. I make maybe 10 or 12 a year."[35] "B" decisions are also made by the plant manager, but with input from the people affected. "C" decisions, the most common type, are made by consensus, by the people directly involved, with plenty of discussion. With "C" decisions, the view of the plant manager doesn't necessarily carry more weight than the views of those affected."[36]

exhibit 15.9

Decision Styles and Levels of Employee Participation

Leader solves the problem or makes the decision

Leader is willing to accept any decision supported by the entire group

AI	AII	CI	CII	GII
Using information available at the time, the leader solves the problem or makes the decision.	The leader obtains necessary information from employees, and then selects a solution to the problem. When asked to share information, employees may or may not be told what the problem is.	The leader shares the problem and gets ideas and suggestions from relevant employees on an individual basis. Individuals are not brought together as a group. Then the leader makes the decision, which may or may not reflect their input.	The leader shares the problem with employees as a group, obtains their ideas and suggestions, and then makes the decision, which may or may not reflect their input.	The leader shares the problem with employees as a group. Together, the leader and employees generate and evaluate alternatives and try to reach an agreement on a solution. The leader acts as a facilitator and does not try to influence the group. The leader is willing to accept and implement any solution that has the support of the entire group.

Source: Adapted from V. H. Vroom & P. W. Yetton, Leadership and Decision Making *(Pittsburgh: University of Pittsburgh Press, 1973), 13.*

6.2 Decision Quality and Acceptance

According to the normative decision theory, using the right degree of employee participation improves the quality of decisions and the extent to which employees accept and are committed to decisions. Exhibit 15.10 lists the decision rules that normative decision theory uses to increase decision quality and employee acceptance and commitment. The quality, leader information, subordinate information, goal congruence, and problem structure rules are used to increase decision quality. For example, the leader information rule states that if a leader doesn't have enough information to make a decision on his or her own, then the leader should not use an autocratic decision style.

The commitment probability, subordinate conflict, and commitment requirement rules shown in Exhibit 15.10 are used to increase employee acceptance and commitment to decisions. For example, the commitment requirement rule says that if decision acceptance and commitment are important, and the subordinates share the organization's goals, then you shouldn't use an autocratic or consultative style. In other words, if followers want to do what's best for the company and you need their acceptance and commitment to make a decision work, then use a group decision style and let them make the decision.

As you can see, these decision rules help leaders improve decision quality and follower acceptance and commitment by eliminating decision styles that don't fit the decision or situation they're facing. Normative decision theory then operationalizes these decision rules in the form of yes/no questions,

exhibit 15.10

Normative Theory Decision Rules

DECISION RULES TO INCREASE DECISION QUALITY
Quality Rule. If the quality of the decision is important, then don't use an autocratic decision style.
Leader Information Rule. If the quality of the decision is important, and if the leader doesn't have enough information to make the decision on his or her own, then don't use an autocratic decision style.
Subordinate Information Rule. If the quality of the decision is important, and if the subordinates don't have enough information to make the decision themselves, then don't use a group decision style.
Goal Congruence Rule. If the quality of the decision is important, and subordinates' goals are different from the organization's goals, then don't use a group decision style.
Problem Structure Rule. If the quality of the decision is important, the leader doesn't have enough information to make the decision on his or her own, and the problem is unstructured, then don't use an autocratic decision style.
DECISION RULES TO INCREASE DECISION ACCEPTANCE
Commitment Probability Rule. If having subordinates accept and commit to the decision is important, then don't use an autocratic decision style.
Subordinate Conflict Rule. If having subordinates accept the decision is important and critical to successful implementation and subordinates are likely to disagree or end up in conflict over the decision, then don't use an autocratic or consultative decision style.
Commitment Requirement Rule. If having subordinates accept the decision is absolutely required for successful implementation and subordinates share the organization's goals, then don't use an autocratic or consultative style.

Sources: Adapted from V. H. Vroom, "Leadership," in Handbook of Industrial and Organizational Psychology, *ed. M. D. Dunnette (Chicago: Rand McNally, 1976); V. H. Vroom & A. G. Jago,* The New Leadership: Managing Participation in Organizations *(Englewood Cliffs, NJ: Prentice Hall, 1988).*

which are shown in the decision tree displayed in Exhibit 15.11. You start at the left side of the model and answer the first question, "How important is the technical quality of this decision?" by choosing "high" or "low." Then you continue by answering each question as you proceed along the decision tree until you get to a recommended decision style.

Let's use the model to make the decision of whether to change from a formal business attire policy to a casual wear policy. The problem sounds simple, but it is actually more complex than you might think. Follow the yellow line in Exhibit 15.11 as we work through the decision in the discussion below.

Problem: Change to Casual Wear?

1. *Quality requirement: How important is the technical quality of this decision?* High. This question has to do with whether there are quality differences in the alternatives and whether those quality differences matter. Although most people would assume that quality isn't an issue here, it really is, given the overall positive changes that generally accompany changes to casual wear.
2. *Commitment requirement: How important is subordinate commitment to the decision?* High. Changes in culture, like dress codes, require subordinate commitment or they fail.

exhibit 15.11

Normative Decision Theory Tree for Determining the Level of Participation in Decision Making

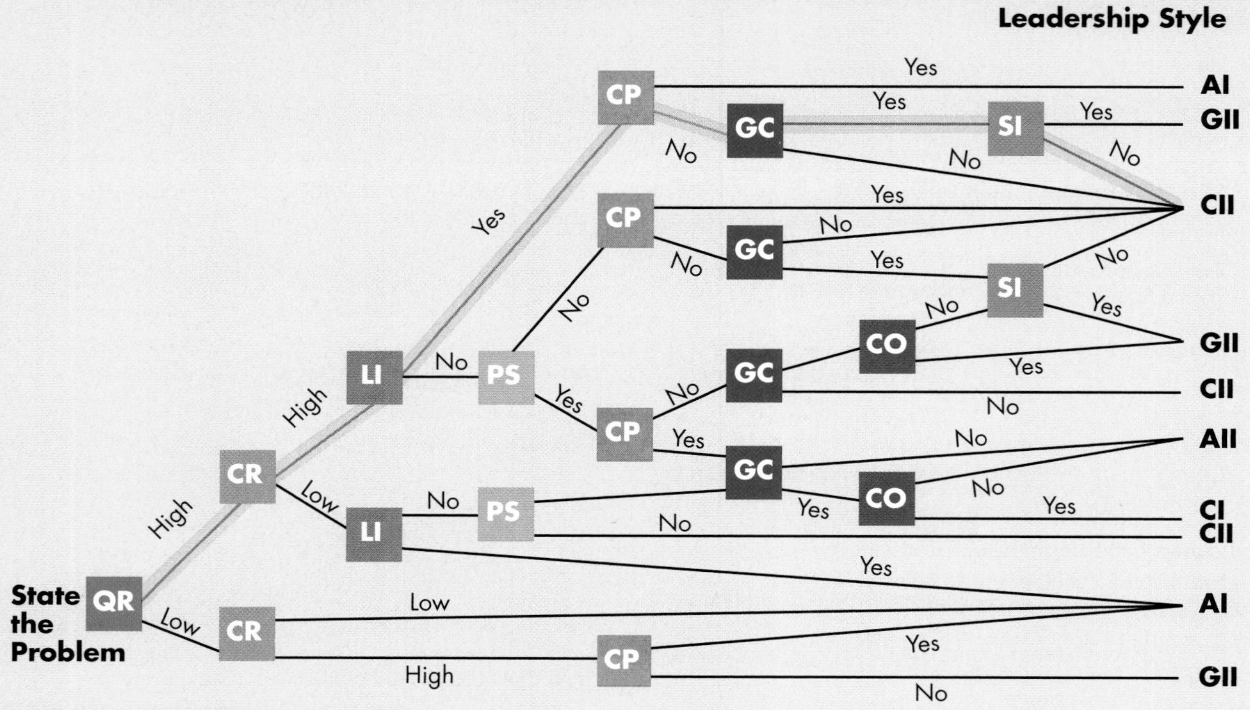

Problem Attributes

QR	Quality requirement:	How important is the technical quality of this decision?
CR	Commitment requirement:	How important is subordinate commitment to the decision?
LI	Leader's information:	Do you have sufficient information to make a high-quality decision?
PS	Problem structure:	Is the problem well structured?
CP	Commitment probability:	If you were to make the decision by yourself, is it reasonably cerain that your subordinate(s) would be committed to the decision?
GC	Goal congruence:	Do subordinates share the organizational goals to be attained in solving this problem?
CO	Subordinate conflict:	Is conflict among subordinates over preferred solutions likely?
SI	Subordinate information:	Do subordinates have sufficient information to make a high-quality decision?

Source: V. H. Vroom & P. W. Yetton, Leadership and Decision Making *(Pittsburgh, PA: University of Pittsburgh Press, 1973). Adapted and reprinted by permission of University of Pittsburgh Press.*

3. *Leader's information: Do you have sufficient information to make a high-quality decision?* Yes. Let's assume that you've done your homework. Much has been written about casual wear, from how to make the change to the effects it has in companies (almost all positive).
4. *Commitment probability: If you were to make the decision by yourself, is it reasonably certain that your subordinate(s) would be committed to the decision?* No. Studies of casual wear (see item 3, leader information) find that employees' reactions are almost uniformly positive. Nonetheless, employees are likely to be angry if you change something as personal as clothing policies without consulting them.
5. *Goal congruence: Do subordinates share the organizational goals to be attained in solving this problem?* Yes. The goals that usually accompany a change to casual dress policies are a more informal culture, better communication, and less money spent on business attire.
6. *Subordinate information: Do subordinates have sufficient information to make a high-quality decision?* No. Most employees know little about casual wear policies or even what constitutes casual wear in most companies. Consequently, most companies have to educate employees about casual wear practices and policies before making a decision.
7. *CII is the answer:* With a CII, or consultative decision process, the leader shares the problem with employees as a group, obtains their ideas and suggestions, and then makes the decision, which may or may not reflect their input. So, given the answers to these questions (remember, different managers won't necessarily answer these questions the same way), the normative decision theory recommends that leaders consult with their subordinates before deciding whether to change to a casual wear policy.

How well does the normative decision theory work? A leading leadership scholar has described it as the best supported of all leadership theories.[37] In general, the more managers violate the decision rules in Exhibit 15.10, the less effective their decisions are, especially with respect to subordinate acceptance and commitment.[38]

Review 6

Adapting Leader Behavior: Normative Decision Theory

The normative decision theory helps leaders decide how much employee participation should be used when making decisions. Using the right degree of employee participation improves the quality of decisions and the extent to which employees accept and are committed to decisions. The theory specifies five different decision styles or ways of making decisions: autocratic decisions (AI or AII), consultative decisions (CI or CII), and group decisions (GII). The theory improves decision quality via the quality, leader information, subordinate information, goal congruence, and unstructured problem decision rules. The theory improves employee commitment and acceptance via the commitment probability, subordinate conflict, and commitment requirement decision rules. These decision rules help leaders improve decision quality and follower acceptance and commitment by eliminating decision styles that don't fit the decision or situation they're facing. Normative decision theory then operationalizes these decision rules in the form of yes/no questions, as shown in the decision tree displayed in Exhibit 15.11.

Strategic Leadership

Thus far, you have read about three major leadership ideas: traits, behaviors, and situational theories. Leader *traits* are relatively stable characteristics, such as abilities or psychological motives. Traits capture who effective leaders are. Leader *behaviors* are the actions leaders take to influence others to achieve group or organizational goals. Behaviors capture what effective leaders do (i.e., initiate structure and consideration). And *situational theories* indicate that the effectiveness of a leadership style, the way a leader generally behaves toward followers, depends on the situation. Situational theories capture what leaders need to do or not do in particular situations or circumstances. This final part of the chapter introduces a fourth major leadership idea—strategic leadership—and its components: visionary, charismatic, and transformational leadership.

strategic leadership
the ability to anticipate, envision, maintain flexibility, think strategically, and work with others to initiate changes that will create a positive future for an organization

Strategic leadership is the ability to anticipate, envision, maintain flexibility, think strategically, and work with others to initiate changes that will create a positive future for an organization.[39] Over the last 25 years, every dollar invested in Walgreen's—that's right, plain old Walgreen's, the drugstore chain—would be worth twice as much as a dollar invested in Intel, five times as much as a dollar invested in General Electric, eight times as much as a dollar invested in Coca-Cola, and 15 times as much as a dollar invested in the general stock market. During that time, CEO Charles Walgreen III transformed the company by focusing Walgreen's managers and employees on the strategic objective of "providing the best drugstore service in America." While that seems rather unremarkable today given Walgreen's current success, adopting that objective completely changed the company because it led to the sale of its historic and highly profitable food service division started by his grandfather (for over 70 years, every Walgreen's had a food counter that served breakfast, lunch, and dinner). Despite objections that this would destroy the company, Walgreen sold the profitable food division precisely because it didn't fit the new strategic objective. Food service had nothing to do with drugstores and was a business in which Walgreen's could not be "the best." Furthermore, in achieving this remarkable transformation and success, "not once did Mr. Walgreen stand in front of the mirror and point to himself as a key factor, preferring instead to point out the window to credit the great people he had on his team."[40] Thus, strategic leadership captures how leaders inspire their companies to change and their followers to give extraordinary effort to accomplish organizational goals.

After reading the next section, you should be able to

7 explain how visionary leadership (i.e., charismatic and transformational leadership) helps leaders achieve strategic leadership.

7 Visionary Leadership

visionary leadership
leadership that creates a positive image of the future that motivates organizational members and provides direction for future planning and goal setting

In Chapter 4, we defined *vision* as a statement of a company's purpose or reason for existing. Similarly, **visionary leadership** creates a positive image of the future that motivates organizational members and provides direction for future planning and goal setting.[41]

Two kinds of visionary leadership are 7.1 charismatic leadership and 7.2 transformational leadership.

7.1 Charismatic Leadership

Charisma is a Greek word meaning "gift from God." The Greeks saw people with charisma as divinely inspired and capable of incredible accomplishments. German sociologist Max Weber viewed charisma as a special bond between leaders and followers.[42] Weber wrote that the special qualities of charismatic leaders enable them to strongly influence followers. Weber also noted that charismatic leaders tend to emerge in times of crisis and that the radical solutions they propose enhance the admiration that followers feel for them. Indeed, charismatic leaders tend to have incredible influence over their followers, who may become fanatically devoted to and inspired by their leaders. From this perspective, charismatic leaders are often seen as larger-than-life or uniquely special.

Charismatic leaders have strong, confident, dynamic personalities that attract followers and enable the leaders to create strong bonds with their followers. Followers trust charismatic leaders, are loyal to them, and are inspired to work toward the accomplishment of the leader's vision. Followers who become devoted to charismatic leaders may go to extraordinary lengths to please them. Therefore, we can define **charismatic leadership** as the behavioral tendencies and personal characteristics of leaders that create an exceptionally strong relationship between them and their followers. Charismatic leaders also

charismatic leadership
the behavioral tendencies and personal characteristics of leaders that create an exceptionally strong relationship between them and their followers

- articulate a clear vision for the future that is based on strongly held values or morals,
- model those values by acting in a way consistent with the vision,
- communicate high performance expectations to followers, and
- display confidence in followers' abilities to achieve the vision.[43]

As described above, followers trust charismatic leaders, are loyal to them, and are inspired to work toward the accomplishment of the leader's vision. But does charismatic leadership work? Studies indicate that it often does. In general, the followers of charismatic leaders are more committed and satisfied, are better performers, are more likely to trust their leaders, and simply work harder.[44] Nonetheless, the risks associated with charismatic leadership are at least as large as its benefits, particularly if ego-driven leaders take advantage of fanatical followers.

In general, there are two kinds of charismatic leaders, ethical charismatics and unethical charismatics.[45] **Ethical charismatics** provide developmental opportunities for followers, are open to positive and negative feedback, recognize others' contributions, share information, and have moral standards that emphasize the larger interests of the group, organization, or society. Ethical charismatics produce stronger commitment, higher satisfaction, more effort, better performance, and greater trust.

ethical charismatics
charismatic leaders who provide developmental opportunities for followers, are open to positive and negative feedback, recognize others' contributions, share information, and have moral standards that emphasize the larger interests of the group, organization, or society

By contrast, **unethical charismatics** control and manipulate followers, do what is best for themselves instead of their organizations, want to hear only positive feedback, share only information that is beneficial to themselves, and have moral standards that put their interests before everyone else's. Because followers can become just as committed to unethical charismatics as to ethical charismatics, unethical charismatics pose a tremendous risk for companies. John Thompson, a management consultant, warns, "Often what begins as a mission becomes an obsession. Leaders can cut corners on values and become driven by self-interest. Then they may abuse anyone who makes a mistake."[46]

unethical charismatics
charismatic leaders who control and manipulate followers, do what is best for themselves instead of their organizations, want to hear only positive feedback, share only information that is beneficial to themselves, and have moral standards that put their interests before everyone else's

www.experiencing management.com

Learn why transformational leaders are necessary when organizations face crises by visiting our animated concept and activity site. Choose Leadership from the "select a topic" pull-down menu, then Transformational Leadership from the "overview tab."

http://www.experiencingmanagement.com

There are stark differences between ethical and unethical charismatics on several leader behaviors: exercising power, creating the vision, communicating with followers, accepting feedback, stimulating followers intellectually, developing followers, and living by moral standards. For example, in terms of creating a vision, ethical charismatics include followers' concerns and wishes by having them participate in the development of the company vision. By contrast, unethical charismatics develop a vision by themselves solely to meet their personal agendas. One unethical charismatic said, "The key thing is that it is my idea; and I am going to win with it at all costs."[47]

So, what can companies do to reduce the risks associated with unethical charismatics?[48] To start, they need a clearly written code of conduct that is fairly and consistently enforced for all managers. Next, companies should recruit, select, and promote managers with high ethical standards. Also, companies need to train leaders how to value, seek, and use diverse points of view. Leaders and subordinates also need training regarding ethical leader behaviors so that abuses can be recognized and corrected. Finally, companies should celebrate and reward people who exhibit ethical behaviors, especially ethical leader behaviors.[49]

transformational leadership
leadership that generates awareness and acceptance of a group's purpose and mission and gets employees to see beyond their own needs and self-interests for the good of the group

7.2 Transformational Leadership

While charismatic leaders are able to articulate a clear vision, model values consistent with that vision, communicate high performance expectations, and establish very strong relationships with their followers, **transformational leadership** goes further by generating awareness and acceptance of a group's purpose and mission and by getting employees to see beyond their own needs and self-interest for the good of the group.[50] Like charismatic leaders, transformational leaders are visionary, but they transform their organizations by getting their followers to accomplish more than they intended and even more than they thought possible.

exhibit 15.12

Components of Transformational Leadership

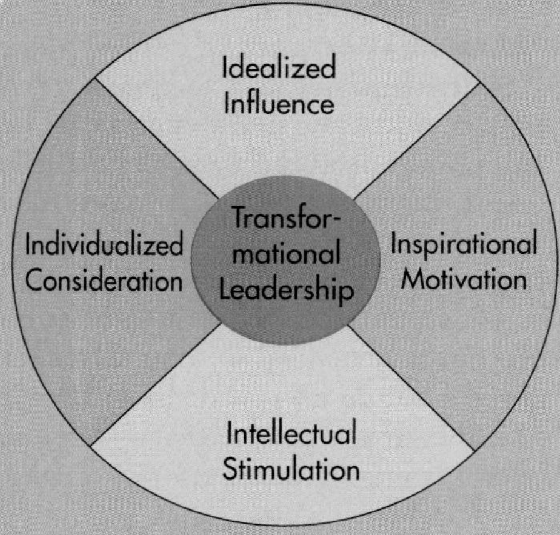

Transformational leaders are able to make their followers feel that they are a vital part of the organization and help them see how their jobs fit with the organization's vision. By linking individual and organizational interests, transformational leaders encourage followers to make sacrifices for the organization because they know that they will prosper when the organization prospers. As Exhibit 15.12 shows, transformational leadership has four components: charismatic leadership or idealized influence, inspirational motivation, intellectual stimulation, and individualized consideration.[51]

Charismatic leadership or idealized influence means that transformational leaders act as role models for their followers. Because transformational leaders put others' needs ahead of their own and share risks with their followers, they are admired, respected, and trusted, and followers want to emulate them. Thus, in contrast to purely charismatic leaders (especially unethical charismatics),

DOING THE RIGHT THING

Make Sure Leaders Are Accountable

In most organizations, very few people have the job security, confidence, or chutzpah to openly and actively question the motives, decisions, and performance of top managers. Nonetheless, for the sake of control, ethics, and checks and balances, it's critical that leaders be held accountable. One place to start is by conducting annual performance appraisals for the CEO and other top managers. Those appraisals should include 360 feedback from peers (other top managers), subordinates, and superiors (in the case of the CEO, this would be the board of directors). Most important, board members, to whom the CEO reports, need to play a much more active role in holding top management accountable. More board members need to be independent, meaning they don't do business with the firm or have personal relationships with top management. Moreover, according to CEO Barbara Franklin, the board of directors should be filled with "people who do speak up and won't back down if they don't get the answers they want." After each board meeting, outside members of the board (i.e., those not with the company) should also meet alone to hold frank discussions about top management and the company. Finally, the performance of board members themselves should be evaluated and then disclosed in public proxy statements so that shareholders can decide which board members, if any, should be replaced. So, do the right thing. Make sure leaders are accountable. If they aren't, have the courage to ask why.[53]

transformational leaders can be counted on to do the right thing and maintain high standards for ethical and personal conduct. For example, CEO Alan Lacy didn't hesitate to fire two top managers when they misled him about the revenue and profit outlook for Sears' credit business (i.e. credit cards and loans), which accounts for more than half of Sears' profits. Lacy explained his actions, saying, "There's a higher standard today. As a CEO, I've got to sign a certificate affirming that our financial reporting is not just in conformance with GAAP [Generally Accepted Accounting Principles] but that it fairly presents the business."[52]

Inspirational motivation means that transformational leaders motivate and inspire followers by providing meaning and challenge to their work. By clearly communicating expectations and demonstrating commitment to goals, transformational leaders help followers envision future states, such as the organizational vision or mission. In turn, this leads to greater enthusiasm and optimism about the future.

Intellectual stimulation means that transformational leaders encourage followers to be creative and innovative, to question assumptions, and to look at problems and situations in new ways, even if they are different from the leader's ideas. Feargal Quinn, CEO of the Irish supermarket chain Superquinn's, encourages his managers to question assumptions and look at problems in new ways by having them "jump the counter" and spend time as customers, shopping, asking questions, and waiting in line. Likewise, when store managers come up with a new idea, Quinn encourages them to implement it as long as they follow two rules. First, all new ideas or innovations must be tested in stores before they become permanent. Second, once Superquinn's has added a service-oriented practice or procedure, you can add another, but you can't take away or stop an established practice or procedure without input from others.[54]

Individualized consideration means that transformational leaders pay special attention to followers' individual needs by creating learning opportunities, accepting and tolerating individual differences, encouraging two-way communication, and being a good listener. One of the ways that Jack Welch, General Electric's incredibly successful former CEO, showed individualized consideration was through the personal, spontaneous, handwritten notes that he sent to people throughout GE.

Finally, a distinction needs to be drawn between transformational leadership and transactional leadership. While transformational leaders use visionary and inspirational appeals to influence followers, **transactional leadership** is based on an exchange process, in which followers are rewarded for good performance and punished for poor performance. When leaders administer rewards fairly and offer followers the rewards that they want, followers will often

transactional leadership
leadership based on an exchange process, in which followers are rewarded for good performance and punished for poor performance

reciprocate with effort. A problem, however, is that transactional leaders often rely too heavily on discipline or threats to bring performance up to standards. Though this may work in the short run, it's much less effective in the long run. Also, as discussed in Chapters 11 and 14, many leaders and organizations have difficulty successfully linking pay practices to individual performance. As a result, studies consistently show that transformational leadership is much more effective on average than transactional leadership. In the United States, Canada, Japan, and India, and at all organizational levels, from first-level supervisors to upper-level executives, followers view transformational leaders as much better leaders and are much more satisfied when working for them. Furthermore, companies with transformational leaders have significantly better financial performance.[55]

Review 7
Visionary Leadership

Strategic leadership requires visionary, charismatic, and transformational leadership. Visionary leadership creates a positive image of the future that motivates organizational members and provides direction for future planning and goal setting. Charismatic leaders have strong, confident, dynamic personalities that attract followers, enable them to create strong bonds, and inspire followers to accomplish the leader's vision. Followers of ethical charismatic leaders work harder, are more committed and satisfied, are better performers, and are more likely to trust their leaders. Followers can be just as supportive and committed to unethical charismatics, but these leaders can pose a tremendous risk for companies. Unethical charismatics control and manipulate followers and do what is best for themselves instead of their organizations. To reduce the risks associated with unethical charismatics, companies need to enforce a clearly written code of conduct; recruit, select, and promote managers with high ethical standards; train leaders to value, seek, and use diverse points of view; teach everyone in the company to recognize unethical leader behaviors; and celebrate and reward people who exhibit ethical behaviors. Transformational leadership goes beyond charismatic leadership by generating awareness and acceptance of a group's purpose and mission and by getting employees to see beyond their own needs and self-interest for the good of the group. The four components of transformational leadership are charisma or idealized influence, inspirational motivation, intellectual stimulation, and individualized consideration.

STUDY TIP Your professor and TA are the most valuable resources in your course. If you have questions on the fundamental concepts of leadership, go to office hours. Report back to your study partner or group.

MANAGEMENT TEAM DECISION

DESIGNING LEADERSHIP

What a terrible day.[56] Not only has your boss been indicted by the feds for obstructing justice, but the plan to fill the leadership vacuum she left behind has just collapsed. For months, the threat of an indictment has hovered over Martha Stewart like the sword of Damocles, so management had created a leadership plan in case Stewart was indicted. She would cede her position of CEO of Martha Stewart Living Omnimedia (MSLO) to the company's chief operating officer, Sharon Patrick, and Arthur Martinez, former chairman and CEO of Sears and an MSLO director, would take over as chairman. Patrick was formerly head of Rainbow Programming Holdings (a system of cable networks, including Bravo movie channel) and has been with MSLO since its initial public offering. Although she has been praised for her business acumen, she is not prepared to be the public face of MSLO. Martinez has been a key director for MSLO and brings enormous experience in merchandising and retailing to the table. Thankfully, when the ink dried on the indictment, at least you had a direction for the company and experienced leaders to take over the helm.

At least you did until 8 A.M. this morning, when Martinez changed his mind. He cited Stewart's determination to continue playing a strong role in operations and strategy as his reason for declining the chairmanship. Stewart stepped down as the chair and CEO of MSLO, but not from her post as chief creative officer. So now you need to find a person to fill the chair's slot. For years, the board of directors has urged Stewart to refresh the management of MSLO, but Stewart has been reluctant to do so, fearing the onset of a talent drain. Now, however, the company finds itself with few internal candidates who can guide the company in the absence of its namesake.

In addition, Stewart has been the galvanizing force behind everything the multibillion dollar company does. Until the insider trading scandal erupted, Stewart's face was the omnipresent icon of the company, from developing products to fronting most of its media outlets (she was on every cover of the flagship magazine, *Living*). Since being charged—and subsequently found guilty—Stewart has made every attempt to separate the personal issue of the indictment from MSLO. She no longer appears on its magazine covers, a new magazine launched during the scandal does not leverage her name, and she has resigned from most of her management positions at the company as well as from her seat on the New York Stock Exchange.

Despite efforts to keep Stewart's personal problems with the law separate from the business, MSLO's market capitalization has dropped (its stock price has fallen), subscriptions to *Living* have fallen off, and both *Living* magazine and the *Martha Stewart Living* television show have lost advertisers. To reassure stockholders, the market, suppliers, and consumers, the company needs to stabilize its leadership during this crisis. But how? Martha Stewart is MSLO, and her troubles have become MSLO's troubles.

For this exercise, your management team will map out a leadership plan for MSLO now that Martha Stewart has stepped down from key management positions.

Questions

1. In the situation described, does MSLO need a leader or a manager?
2. Do you fill the chair's position with a visionary leader, or do you focus on finding a disturbance handler who can implement a retrenchment strategy?
3. How can a company whose leadership is so closely associated with the company brand overcome a scandal that touches one of its officers but is unrelated to the business itself? Is it even possible?

DEVELOP YOUR CAREER POTENTIAL

LEADERSHIP REVISITED

You can learn a lot about leadership traits, behaviors, and styles by reading books, but until you're actually in charge, you won't be able to test those ideas for yourself. Likewise, you can learn a tremendous amount about leadership by studying and observing the people who lead you. Until you are actually in the position of leading, however, you won't know if their leadership practices and styles will work for you. In short, when learning about leadership, there is no substitute for leadership experience.

Fortunately, many people are leaders, even if they don't have the title. Many people have younger brothers or sisters, friends, or family members who look up to them and follow their lead. Many employees are respected for their wisdom, knowledge, and ability to solve difficult problems, even though they are not the formal supervisor. You may be able to think of a time when you have assumed the role of leader in a job, at school, or possibly as a member of an extracurricular club, fraternity, sorority, or social organization. As you remember that leadership experience, try to determine what type of a leader you were. Think about how you helped solve problems or worked to inspire and motivate those around you. Were you more of a leader or a manager? Did you consistently apply the same leadership style with all people and in all situations, or did you change leadership styles to fit a specific problem or situation? Did your leadership style work? Was it accepted by those around you? What was the context of the situation or job? Were the individuals self-motivated and self-directed, or did you have to provide direction and assistance every step of the way? As you think back on this experience, consider using the Internet resources listed below to deepen your understanding of your own leadership style and potential. Then answer the questions that follow.

Internet Resources

You can learn more about your personal leadership style by visiting some or all of the following Web sites:

- **http://www.nsba.org/sbot/toolkit/LeadSA.html** This is a good Web site illustrating qualities of effective leaders.
- **http://www.emode.com/emode/tests/leader.jsp** At this site, you can take a 17-question quiz that ranks your ability to lead.
- **http://www.stevesullivan.com** This site features a 10-question test that determines your knowledge about leadership and provides review material to increase your awareness regarding leadership theories and applications.

To learn more about leadership and to see current articles discussing leadership theories and techniques, visit some or all of the following Web sites:

- **http://www.nwlink.com/~donclark/leader/leader.html** Big Dog's Leadership page provides a basic background on leadership designed for new supervisors and managers.
- **http://www.articles911.com** The leadership category at this site contains free articles on leadership development, improvement, practices, and assessment styles.
- **http://www.personal-development.com/articles.htm** This Web site contains many free articles aimed at developing an individual's leadership style, teaching time management techniques, increasing self-esteem, overcoming public speaking anxiety, and much more.

Questions

After reviewing some of the informative Web sites listed above, use your knowledge of leadership, your personal leadership style, and information gleaned from previous experiences to answer the following questions:

1. Describe a situation in which you became a leader or assumed a leadership role.
2. What surprises did you discover when assuming this role?
3. Did you initially fear any aspect of being a leader that turned out to be much easier than you expected? If so, describe your experience.
4. What was the most difficult thing about being a leader?
5. After reading this chapter on leadership, what information could you use that would make you a better leader today than you were back then?

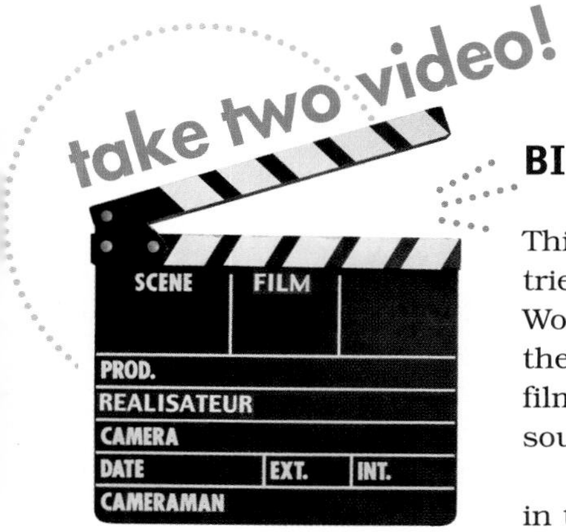

BIZ FLIX U-571

This action-packed thriller deals with a U.S. submarine crew's efforts to retrieve an Enigma encryption devise from a disabled German submarine during World War II. After the crew gets the device, the U.S. submarine sinks, and they must use the German submarine to escape from enemy destroyers. The film's almost nonstop action and extraordinary special effects will look and sound best with a home theater system.

This scene is an edited composite of the "To Be a Captain" sequence early in the film. The S33, an older U.S. submarine, is embarking on a secret mission. Before departure, the S33's officers receive a briefing on their mission from Office of Naval Intelligence representatives on board. Executive officer Lt. Andrew Tyler (Matthew McConaughey) reports on the submarine's status to Lt. Commander Mike Dahlgren (Bill Paxton). The film continues with the S33 finding the disabled German submarine.

What to Watch for and Ask Yourself

1. What aspects of leadership does Dahlgren say are important for a submarine commander?
2. Which leadership behaviors or traits does he emphasize?
3. Are these traits or behaviors right for this situation? Why or why not?

MGMT WORKPLACE Buffalo Zoo

When the board of directors at the Buffalo Zoo hired Donna Fernandes as their new CEO and president, the company desperately needed a turnaround. The zoo was plagued by operational ineptitude, dilapidated buildings, and dwindling membership, and the staff was cynical about Donna's ability to institute change. With boundless energy, faith in her support staff, commitment to her plan, and consistent follow-through, Donna has converted the mindset of the organization to one of accomplishment and optimism. Since her arrival, the board has raised more money, increased membership, and started numerous refurbishment projects. Those involved acknowledge that Donna's leadership is the force that has made it all happen.

What to Watch for and Ask Yourself

1. Identify and describe Donna's leadership traits and explain how she applies them to the job.
2. Identify and describe Donna's leadership style.
3. Explain how Donna uses strategic and visionary leadership.

CHAPTER SIXTEEN

Managing Communication

outline

WHAT WOULD YOU DO?

Procter & Gamble Headquarters, Cincinnati, Ohio.[1] Procter & Gamble, otherwise known as P&G, has been in business since 1837. P&G sells some of the world's best-known household and consumer brands including Tide detergent, Folger's coffee, Crest toothpaste, Charmin toilet paper, Bounty paper towels, Head & Shoulders shampoo, Ivory soap, and Pampers diapers. You've worked for P&G for 25 years and just became its CEO a month ago. What an intense month it's been. Your predecessor, Durk Jager, had been CEO for only 17 months, the shortest tenure for any P&G CEO.

Jager moved aggressively to change P&G, but the company struggled under his leadership. Hoping to find the next billion dollar brand (like Tide), he encouraged departments to set "stretch goals" for big improvements. But then he allowed them to base their budgets on those targets, long before the targets were reached. Consequently, overspending was rife, as costs grew much faster than revenues. Jager also tried to "globalize"

student resources

Experiencing Management
Explore the four levels of learning by doing the simulation module on Communication.

Study Guide
Mini lecture reviews all the learning points in the chapter and concludes with a case on *Christian Science Monitor.*

Take Two Video
Biz Flix is a scene from *Patch Adams*. Management Workplace is a segment on Le Meridien Hotel in Boston.

PowerPoint®
12 slides with graphics provide an outline for this chapter.

Author Insights
Chuck talks about the importance of choosing the right medium for your message, and avoiding firing off angry emails.

Self Test
24 true/false questions, 22 multiple-choice questions, a management scenario, and 6 exhibit worksheets

P&G's brands, for instance, by changing the name of P&G's dishwashing liquid in Germany from Fairy, as it was known there, to Dawn, as it was known in the United States. Since German consumers weren't familiar with the Dawn brand, sales dropped drastically. Finally, Jager, who had a reputation for being hard driving and abrasive, had trouble getting P&G's 103,000 employees and managers to fully buy into his plans. One consultant said, "Durk tried to move too fast and didn't listen to his people." In the end, P&G's stock lost a total of $70 billion in value while Jager was CEO.

Unfortunately, the "market" wasn't any happier when P&G announced that you would replace Jager. P&G's stock dropped $4 from $62 to $58 on your first day on the job and was at $53 at the end of your first month. However, the market wasn't reacting so much to you as to the serious problems facing P&G: encouraging talented managers to stay (25 percent of brand managers had left the company); calming upset brand managers in Europe (who had watched their sales dive thanks to the failed brand globalization efforts); finding ways to improve sales of P&G's leading brands; and simplifying P&G's organizational structure (which had assumed a confusing matrix structure over the last few years).

At this point, though, you feel you've got a fairly good plan to fix these problems. First, you're going to refocus P&G on its core, the 10 $1 billion brands, like Tide and Pampers, that account for most of its sales and revenues. That should simplify things for everyone. Next, globalization of brands is over. Although there will still be a focus on innovation, the company will try for smaller successes instead of trying to hit home runs by developing new blockbuster $1 billion brands. The internal focus will be on innovating with existing products, while the external focus will be on acquiring innovative ideas and brands from outside the company. Finally, in a symbolic move, you're redoing P&G's legendary 11th floor, home to the company's top executives. Two-thirds of the space is being turned into a learning center, and the rest will house those same top-level executives in open offices that, in theory, will make it easier for them to communicate with each other. Those changes should get you off to a good start and help turn around the company. The hard part, though, will be changing the pattern of communication throughout the company. People are still stinging from the hard-charging, combative approach of your predecessor, so you need to find a way to make regular P&G employees feel comfortable communicating with top management again. What's the best way to do that? And, with a history of centralized authority in which P&G management sent marching orders from headquarters, the traditional focus has been on "getting the message out." But that's only half the communication formula. These days, it's also important to "improve reception" by finding out what others feel and think. So how can P&G do a better job of hearing what people inside the company feel and think? Likewise, with an emphasis on its core brands and small-scale innovation, how can P&G do a better job of hearing what people outside the company feel and think? **If you were the new CEO of Procter & Gamble, what would you do?**

It's estimated that managers spend over 80 percent of their day communicating with others.[2] Indeed, much of the basic management process—making things happen; meeting the competition; organizing people, projects, and processes; and leading—cannot be performed without effective communication. If this weren't reason enough to study communication, consider that effective oral communication, such as listening, following instructions, conversing, and giving feedback, is the most important skill for college graduates who are entering the work force.[3] Furthermore, across all industries, poor communication skill is the single most important reason that people do not advance in their careers.[4] Finally, communication is especially important for top managers like P&G's CEO. As Mark DeMichele, president of Arizona Public Service Company, put it, "Communication is the key to success. CEOs can have good ideas, a vision, and a plan. But they also have to be able to communicate those plans to people who work for them."[5]

This chapter begins by examining the role of perception in communication and how perception can make it difficult for managers to achieve effective communication. Next, you'll read about the communication process and the various kinds of communication found in most organizations. In the last half of the chapter, the focus is on improving communication in organizations. You'll learn about one-on-one communication, how to communicate effectively organization-wide, and how to conduct conversations to initiate change throughout an organization.

What Is Communication?

Carly Fiorina, CEO of Hewlett-Packard, uses a number of methods to talk and listen to H-P's 147,000 employees. Keeping a hectic travel schedule, she often pops up unannounced in H-P offices to talk to managers and employees. When H-P's merger with Compaq Computer was finally approved, she walked the halls at Compaq headquarters in Houston with Michael Capellas, then Compaq's CEO, taking pictures and putting on hats. Fiorina also holds informal "coffee talks" with small groups of employees to discuss what's going on with the company and to hear their concerns and issues.[6]

communication
the process of transmitting information from one person or place to another

Communication is the process of transmitting information from one person or place to another. CEOs like Carly Fiorina understand that effective communication between managers and employees is essential to the success of projects like H-P's merger with Compaq.

After reading the next two sections, you should be able to

1 explain the role that perception plays in communication and communication problems.

2 describe the communication process and the various kinds of communication in organizations.

1 Perception and Communication Problems

One study found that when *employees* were asked whether their supervisor gave recognition for good work, 13 percent said their supervisor gave a pat on the back, while 14 percent said their supervisor gave sincere and thorough praise. But, when the *supervisors* of these employees were asked if they gave recognition for good work, 82 percent said they gave pats on the back, while

80 percent said that they gave sincere and thorough praise.[7] Given that these managers and employees worked closely together, how could they have had such different perceptions of something as simple as praise?

Let's learn more about perception and communication problems by examining 1.1 **the basic perception process,** 1.2 **perception problems,** 1.3 **how we perceive others,** and 1.4 **how we perceive ourselves.** We'll also consider how all of these factors make it difficult for managers to achieve effective communication.

1.1 Basic Perception Process

perception the process by which individuals attend to, organize, interpret, and retain information from their environments

perceptual filters the personality-, psychology-, or experience-based differences that influence people to ignore or pay attention to particular stimuli

As shown in Exhibit 16.1, **perception** is the process by which individuals attend to, organize, interpret, and retain information from their environments. And since communication is the process of transmitting information from one person or place to another, perception is obviously a key part of communication. However, perception can also be a key obstacle to communication.

As people perform their jobs, they are exposed to a wide variety of informational stimuli, such as emails, direct conversations with the boss or coworkers, rumors heard over lunch, stories about the company in the press, or a video broadcast of a speech from the CEO to all employees. Just being exposed to an informational stimulus, however, is no guarantee that an individual will pay attention or attend to that stimulus. People experience stimuli through their own **perceptual filters**—the personality-, psychology-, or experience-based differences that influence them to ignore or pay attention to particular stimuli. Because of filtering, people exposed to the same information will often disagree about what they saw or heard. For example, every major stadium in the National Football League has a huge TV monitor on which fans can watch replays. As the slow motion videotape is replayed on the monitor, you can often hear cheers *and* boos, as fans of both teams perceive the same replay in completely different ways. This happens because the fans' perceptual filters predispose them to attend to stimuli that support their team and not their opponents.

exhibit 16.1

Basic Perception Process

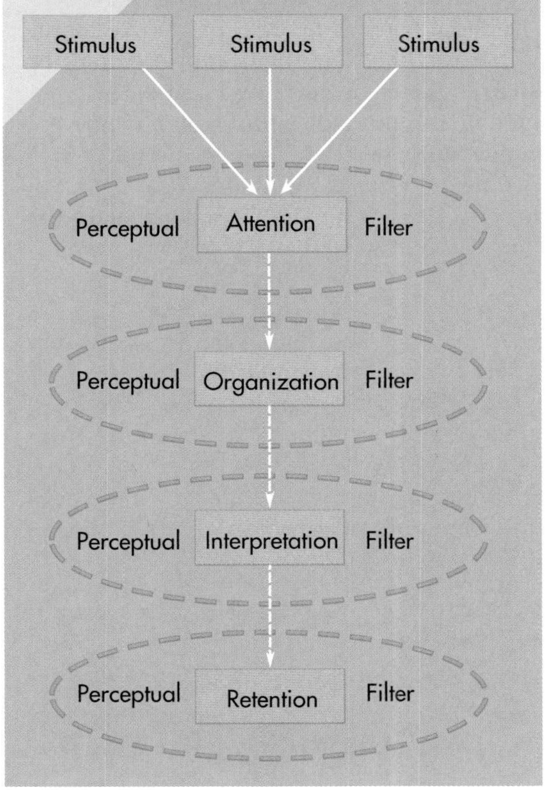

And the same perceptual filters that affect whether we believe our favorite team was "robbed" by the referees also affect communication, that is, the transmitting of information from one person or place to another. As shown in Exhibit 16.1, perceptual filters affect each part of the *perception process*: attention, organization, interpretation, and retention.

Attention is the process of noticing or becoming aware of particular stimuli. Because of perceptual filters, we attend to some stimuli and not others. *Organization* is the process of incorporating new information (from the stimuli that you notice) into your existing knowledge. Because of perceptual filters, we are more likely to incorporate new knowledge that is consistent with what we already know or believe. *Interpretation* is the process of attaching meaning to new knowledge. Because of perceptual filters, our preferences and beliefs strongly influence the meaning we attach to new information (e.g., "This must mean that top management supports our project."). Finally, *retention* is the process of remembering interpreted information. In other words, retention is what we recall and commit to memory after we have perceived something. Of course, perceptual filters also affect retention, that is, what we're likely to remember in the end.

In short, because of perception and perceptual filters, people are likely to pay attention to different things, organize and interpret what they pay attention to differently, and, finally, remember things differently. Consequently, even when people are exposed to the same communications (e.g., organizational memos, discussions with managers or customers), they can end up with very different perceptions and understandings. This is why communication can be so difficult and frustrating for managers. Let's review some of the communication problems created by perception and perceptual filters.

1.2 Perception Problems

Perception creates communication problems for organizations because people exposed to the same communication and information can end up with completely different ideas and understandings. Two of the most common perception problems in organizations are selective perception and closure.

At work, we are constantly bombarded with sensory stimuli—phones ringing, people talking in the background, computers dinging as new email arrives, people calling our names, and so forth. As limited processors of information, we cannot possibly notice, receive, and interpret all of this information. As a result, we attend to and accept some stimuli but screen out and reject others. This isn't a random process, however. **Selective perception** is the tendency to notice and accept objects and information consistent with our values, beliefs, and expectations, while ignoring or screening out inconsistent information. For example, Robert Benmosche, CEO of MetLife Insurance, could not figure out how to lower the height of the brand new chair he was sitting in at the company conference center in Long Island City, New York. Several times throughout the meeting he fiddled with the chair's controls, trying to lower it to a more comfortable position. Though he never said anything about the chair to anybody, he got a call a week later from the manager of the conference center wanting to know if he should replace all of the new chairs. Benmosche said, "Someone just saw that I couldn't lower my chair. And they said, 'Oh, he must be unhappy about that,' without ever asking me."[8]

selective perception
the tendency to notice and accept objects and information consistent with our values, beliefs, and expectations, while ignoring or screening out or not accepting inconsistent information

Once we have initial information about a person, event, or process, **closure** is the tendency to fill in the gaps where information is missing, that is, to assume that what we don't know is consistent with what we already know. If employees are told that budgets must be cut by 10 percent, they may automatically assume that 10 percent of employees will lose their jobs, too, even if that isn't the case. Not surprisingly, when closure occurs, people sometimes "fill in the gaps" with inaccurate information, and this can create problems for organizations.

closure
the tendency to fill in gaps of missing information by assuming that what we don't know is consistent with what we already know

1.3 Perceptions of Others

Attribution theory says that we all have a basic need to understand and explain the causes of other people's behavior.[9] In other words, we need to know why people do what they do. According to attribution theory, we use two gen-

attribution theory
a theory that states that we all have a basic need to understand and explain the causes of other people's behavior

eral reasons or attributions to explain people's behavior: an *internal attribution*, in which behavior is thought to be voluntary or under the control of the individual, and an *external attribution*, in which behavior is thought to be involuntary and outside of the control of the individual.

For example, have you ever seen someone changing a flat tire on the side of the road and thought to yourself, "What rotten luck—somebody's having a bad day"? If you did, you perceived the person through an external attribution known as the defensive bias. The **defensive bias** is the tendency for people to perceive themselves as personally and situationally similar to someone who is having difficulty or trouble.[10] And, when we identify with the person in a situation, we tend to use external attributions (i.e., the situation) to explain the person's behavior. For instance, since flat tires are fairly common, it's easy to perceive ourselves in that same situation and put the blame on external causes, such as running over a nail.

defensive bias
the tendency for people to perceive themselves as personally and situationally similar to someone who is having difficulty or trouble

Now, let's assume a different situation, this time in the workplace:

> A utility company worker puts a ladder on a utility pole and then climbs up to do his work. As he's doing his work, he falls from the ladder and seriously injures himself.[11]

Answer this question: Who or what caused the accident? If you thought, "It's not the worker's fault. Anybody could fall from a tall ladder," then you're still operating from a defensive bias in which you see yourself as personally and situationally similar to someone who is having difficulty or trouble. In other words, you made an external attribution by attributing the accident to an external cause, meaning the situation.

In reality, however, most accident investigations end up blaming the worker (i.e., an internal attribution) and not the situation (i.e., an external attribution). Typically, 60 to 80 percent of workplace accidents each year are blamed on "operator error," that is, the employees themselves. However, more complete investigations usually show that workers are really responsible for only 30 to 40 percent of all workplace accidents.[12] Why are accident investigators so quick to blame workers? Because they are committing the **fundamental attribution error**, which is the tendency to ignore external causes of behavior and to attribute other people's actions to internal causes.[13] In other words, when investigators examine the possible causes of an accident, they're much more likely to assume that the accident is a function of the person and not the situation.

fundamental attribution error
the tendency to ignore external causes of behavior and to attribute other people's actions to internal causes

Which attribution, the defensive bias or the fundamental attribution error, are workers likely to make when something goes wrong? In general, employees and coworkers are more likely to perceive events and explain behavior from a defensive bias. Because they do the work themselves and see themselves as similar to others who make mistakes, have accidents, or are otherwise held responsible for things that go wrong at work, employees and coworkers are likely to attribute problems to external causes, such as failed machinery, poor support, or inadequate training. By contrast, because they are typically observers (who don't do the work themselves) and see themselves as situationally and personally different from workers, managers (i.e., the boss) tend to commit the fundamental attribution error and blame mistakes, accidents, and other things that go wrong on workers (i.e., an internal attribution).

Consequently, in most workplaces, when things go wrong, workers and managers can be expected to take completely opposite views. Therefore, together, the defensive bias, which is typically used by workers, and the fundamental attribution error, which is typically made by managers, present a significant challenge to effective communication and understanding in organizations.

1.4 Self-Perception

self-serving bias
the tendency to overestimate our value by attributing successes to ourselves (internal causes) and attributing failures to others or the environment (external causes)

The **self-serving bias** is the tendency to overestimate our value by attributing successes to ourselves (internal causes) and attributing failures to others or the environment (external causes).[14] The self-serving bias can make it especially difficult for managers to talk to employees about performance problems. In general, people have a need to maintain a positive self-image. This need is so strong that when people seek feedback at work, they typically want verification of their worth (rather than information about performance deficiencies) or assurance that mistakes or problems haven't been their fault.[15] And, when managerial communication threatens people's positive self-image, they can become defensive and emotional. They quit listening, and communication becomes ineffective. In the second half of the chapter, which focuses on improving communication, we'll explain ways in which managers can minimize this self-serving bias and improve effective one-on-one communication with employees.

Review 1
Perception and Communication Problems

Perception is the process by which people attend to, organize, interpret, and retain information from their environments. Perception is not a straightforward process, however. Because of perceptual filters, such as selective perception and closure, people exposed to the same information stimuli often end up with very different perceptions and understandings. Perception-based differences can also lead to differences in the attributions (internal or external) that managers and workers make when explaining workplace behavior. In general, workers are more likely to explain behavior from a defensive bias, in which they attribute problems to external causes (i.e., the situation). Managers, on the other hand, tend to commit the fundamental attribution error, attributing problems to internal causes (i.e., the worker associated with a mistake or error). Consequently, when things go wrong, it's common for managers to blame workers and for workers to blame the situation or context in which they do their jobs. Finally, this problem is compounded by a self-serving bias that leads people to attribute successes to internal causes and failures to external causes. So, when workers receive negative feedback from managers, they may become defensive and emotional and not hear what their managers have to say. In short, perceptions and attributions represent a significant challenge to effective communication and understanding in organizations.

2 Kinds of Communication

Each year, on the anniversary of your hiring date, you receive a written assessment of your performance from your boss. This year, after receiving your performance appraisal, you gripe about it to your best friend, a coworker in a cubicle down the hall. Despite your griping, however, you appreciate that your boss cut you some slack, allowing you extra days off when you went through a divorce earlier this year. How did your boss know you were having personal prob-

www.experiencing management.com

Learn more about the basic communication process at our animated concept and activity site. Choose Communication from the "select a topic" pull-down menu, then Communication Process from the "overview tab."

http://www.experiencingmanagement.com

lems? He knew something was wrong when he noticed your rounded shoulders, the bags under your eyes, and your overall lack of energy. There are many kinds of communication—formal, informal, coaching/counseling, and nonverbal—but they all follow the same fundamental process.

Let's learn more about the different kinds of communication by examining **2.1 the communication process**, **2.2 communication channels**, **2.3 coaching and counseling, or one-on-one communication**, and **2.4 nonverbal communication**.

2.1 The Communication Process

Earlier in the chapter, we defined *communication* as the process of transmitting information from one person or place to another. Exhibit 16.2 displays a model of the communication process and its major components: the sender (message to be conveyed, encoding the message, transmitting the message); the receiver (received message, decoded message, and the message that was understood); and noise, which interferes with the communication process.

encoding
putting a message into a written, verbal, or symbolic form that can be recognized and understood by the receiver

decoding
the process by which the receiver translates the written, verbal, or symbolic form of a message into an understood message

The communication process begins when a *sender* thinks of a message he or she wants to convey to another person. This could be what the sender wants someone else to know ("The meeting has been changed to 3 P.M."), to do ("Make sure to include last quarter's financial information in the proposal."), or to not do ("Sorry, the budget is tight. You'll have to fly coach rather than business class."). The next step is to encode the message. **Encoding** means putting a message into a written, verbal, or symbolic form that can be recognized and understood by the receiver. The sender then *transmits the message* via *communication channels.* With some communication channels such as the telephone and face-to-face communication, the sender receives immediate feedback, whereas with others such as email (text messages and file attachments), fax, beepers, voice mail, memos, and letters, the sender must wait for the receiver to respond.

exhibit 16.2

The Interpersonal Communication Process

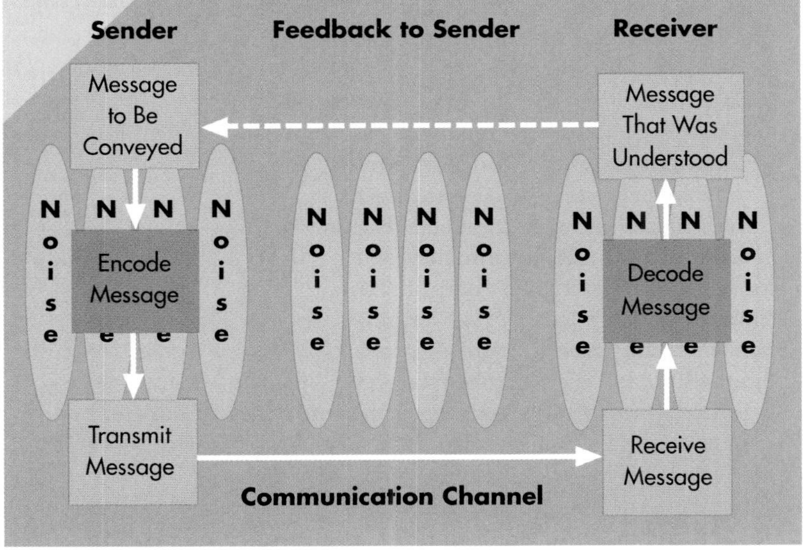

After the message is received, the next step is for the receiver to decode it. **Decoding** is the pro-cess by which the receiver translates the written, verbal, or symbolic form of the message into an understood message. However, the message, as understood by the receiver, isn't always the same message that was intended by the sender. Because of different experiences or perceptual filters, receivers may attach a completely different meaning to a message than was intended.

The last step of the communication process occurs when the receiver gives the sender feedback.

feedback to sender
in the communication process, a return message to the sender that indicates the receiver's understanding of the message

Feedback to sender is a return message to the sender that indicates the receiver's understanding of the message (of what the receiver was supposed to know, to do, or to not do). Feedback makes senders aware of possible miscommunications and enables them to continue communicating until the receiver understands the intended message.

Unfortunately, feedback doesn't always occur in the communication process. Complacency and overconfidence about the ease and simplicity of communication can lead senders and receivers to simply assume that they share a common understanding of the message and to not use feedback to improve the effectiveness of their communication. This is a serious mistake, especially since messages and feedback are always transmitted with and against a background of noise. **Noise** is anything that interferes with the transmission of the intended message. Noise can occur in any of the following situations:

noise
anything that interferes with the transmission of the intended message

1. The sender isn't sure what message to communicate.
2. The message is not clearly encoded.
3. The wrong communication channel is chosen.
4. The message is not received or decoded properly.
5. The receiver doesn't have the experience or time to understand the message.

When managers wrongly assume that communication is easy, they reduce communication to something called the "conduit metaphor."[16] Strictly speaking, a conduit is a pipe or tube that protects electrical wire. The **conduit metaphor** refers to the mistaken assumption that senders can pipe their intended messages directly into the heads of receivers with perfect clarity and without noise or perceptual filters interfering with the receivers' understanding of the message. However, this just isn't possible. Even if managers could telepathically direct their thoughts straight into receivers' heads, misunderstandings and communication problems would still occur because words and symbols typically have multiple meanings, depending on how they're used. For example, consider the extremely common word, *fine*. Depending on how you use it, *fine* can mean a penalty, a good job, that something is delicate, small, pure, flimsy, or that something is okay.

conduit metaphor
the mistaken assumption that senders can pipe their intended messages directly into the heads of receivers with perfect clarity and without noise or perceptual filters interfering with the receivers' understanding of the message

formal communication channel
the system of official channels that carry organizationally approved messages and information

In summary, the conduit metaphor causes problems in communication by making managers too complacent and confident in their ability to easily and accurately transfer messages to receivers. Managers who want to be effective communicators need to carefully choose words and symbols that will help receivers derive the intended meaning of a message. Furthermore, they need to be aware of all steps of the communication process, beginning with the sender (message to be conveyed, encoding the message, transmitting the message) and ending with the receiver (received message, decoded message, understanding the message, and using feedback to communicate what was understood).

www.experiencing management.com

Test what you have learned about communication channels by visiting our animated concept and activity site. Choose Communication from the "select a topic" pull-down menu, then Channels of Communication from the "overview tab."

http://www.experiencingmanagement.com

2.2 Communication Channels

An organization's **formal communication channel** is the system of official channels that carry organizationally approved messages and information. Organizational objectives, rules, policies, procedures, instructions, commands, and requests for information are all transmitted via the formal communication system or "channel." There are three formal communication channels: downward communication, upward communication, and horizontal communication.[17]

downward communication
communication that flows from higher to lower levels in an organization

Downward communication flows from higher to lower levels in an organization. Downward communication is used to issue orders down the organizational hierarchy, to give organizational members job-related information, to give managers and workers performance reviews from upper managers, and to clarify organizational objectives and goals.[18]

upward communication
communication that flows from lower to higher levels in an organization

Upward communication flows from lower levels to higher levels in an organization. Upward communication is used to give higher-level managers feedback about operations, issues, and problems; to help higher-level managers assess organizational performance and effectiveness; to encourage lower-level managers and employees to participate in organizational decision making; and to give those at lower levels the chance to share their concerns with higher-level authorities. Citibank Malaysia started a program called "pulse lunches," in which the top managers in each Citibank market listened to employee concerns at lunch and then addressed those concerns soon after.[19] These lunches were so successful that today Citibank uses "pulse lunches" in 102 different countries.[20]

horizontal communication
communication that flows among managers and workers who are at the same organizational level

Horizontal communication flows among managers and workers who are at the same organizational level. For instance, horizontal communication occurs when the day shift supervisor comes in at 7:30 A.M. for a half-hour discussion with the midnight shift supervisor who leaves at 8:00 A.M., or when the regional marketing director meets with the regional accounting director to discuss costs and plans for a new marketing campaign. Horizontal communication helps facilitate coordination and cooperation between different parts of a company and allows coworkers to share relevant information. It also helps people at the same level resolve conflicts and solve problems without involving high levels of management.

In general, what can managers do to improve formal communication? First, decrease reliance on downward communication. Second, increase chances for upward communication by increasing personal contact with lower-level managers and workers. Third, encourage much greater use of horizontal communication. Finally, be aware of the problems associated with downward, upward, and horizontal communication, some of which are listed on **http://em-online.swlearning.com.**

informal communication channel ("grapevine")
the transmission of messages from employee to employee outside of formal communication channels

By contrast, an organization's **informal communication channel**, sometimes called the "**grapevine**," is the transmission of messages from employee to employee outside of formal communication channels. The grapevine arises out of curiosity, that is, the need to know what is going on in an organization and how it might affect you or others. To satisfy this curiosity, employees need a consistent supply of relevant, accurate, in-depth information about "who is doing what and what changes are occurring within the organization."[21]

Grapevines arise out of informal communication networks, such as the gossip or cluster chains shown in Exhibit 16.3. In a *gossip chain*, one "highly connected" individual shares information with many other managers and workers. By contrast, in a *cluster chain*, numerous people simply tell a few of their friends. The result in both cases is that information flows freely and quickly through the organization. Some believe that grapevines are a waste of employees' time, that they promote gossip and rumors that fuel political speculation, and that they are sources of highly unreliable, inaccurate information. Yet studies clearly show that grapevines are highly accurate sources of

exhibit 16.3

Grapevine Communication Networks

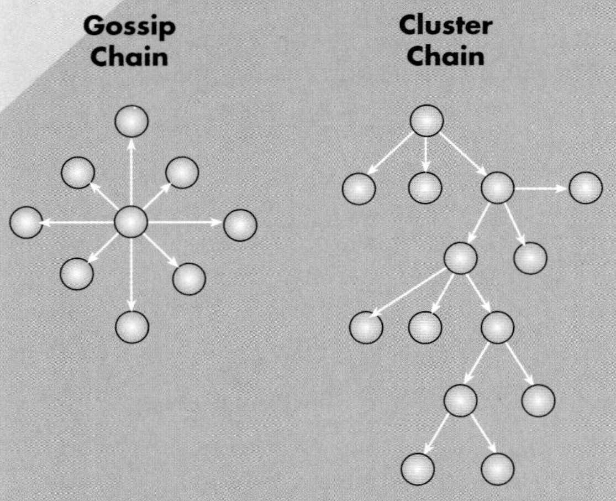

Source: K. Davis & J. W. Newstrom, Human Behavior at Work: Organizational Behavior, *8th ed. (New York: McGraw-Hill, 1989).*

information for a number of reasons.[22] First, because grapevines typically carry "juicy" information that is interesting and timely, information spreads rapidly. Second, since information is typically spread by face-to-face conversation, senders can seek feedback to make sure they understand the message that is being communicated. This reduces misunderstandings and increases accuracy. Third, since most of the information in a company moves along the grapevine, as opposed to formal communication channels, people can usually verify the accuracy of information by "checking it out" with others.

What can managers do to "manage" organizational grapevines? The very worst thing managers can do is withhold information or try to punish those who share information with others. The grapevine abhors a vacuum, and in the absence of information from company management, rumors and anxiety will flourish. A better strategy is to embrace the grapevine and keep employees informed about possible changes and strategies.

Finally, in addition to using the grapevine to communicate with others, managers should not overlook the grapevine as a tremendous source of valuable information and feedback. In fact, information flowing through organizational grapevines is estimated to be 75 to 95 percent accurate.[23]

2.3 Coaching and Counseling: One-on-One Communication

coaching
communicating with someone for the direct purpose of improving the person's on-the-job performance or behavior

Coaching and counseling are two kinds of one-on-one communication. **Coaching** is communicating with someone for the direct purpose of improving the person's on-the-job performance or behavior.[24] Managers tend to make two mistakes when coaching employees. First, they wait much too long before talking to the employee about the problem. Second, when managers finally work up the courage to confront the employee, they get angry. In Section 3, you'll learn a number of specific steps for effective one-on-one communication and coaching.

counseling
communicating with someone about non-job-related issues that may be affecting or interfering with the person's performance

By contrast, **counseling** is communicating with someone about non-job-related issues that may be affecting or interfering with the person's performance. For example, after a top-performing employee was repeatedly late and absent from work, he was asked if he had some personal problems that he needed to discuss. It turned out that he had gone through a divorce and that his teenage son, who was in trouble for truancy and stealing, was now his sole responsibility.

Today, when workers are worried, stressed, and distracted by non-job-related issues that interfere with their job performance, most managers have the option of referring them to an *employee assistance program*, or *EAP*. EAPs are typically free when provided as part of company benefit packages. EAPs provide referrals to organizations and professionals that can help employees and their family members address personal issues. EAPs can provide immediate counseling and support in emergencies or times of crisis.

DOING THE RIGHT THING

Protect Personal, Confidential Information

By virtue of their jobs, managers are privy to information that others aren't. Although much of that information will be about the company, some of it will be personal and confidential information about employees. As a manager, you have a moral and legal obligation to protect employees' privacy. Moreover, sharing others' personal, confidential information may dissuade employees from confiding in managers or seeking help from a company's employee assistance program. Does this mean that if employees confide in you that you can't tell anyone else? No, if you're a manager, sometimes you may have to inform your boss or human resources about a situation. But only inform those who have a need to know and who are also obligated to protect employee privacy. Furthermore, not all information that employees disclose to you should be protected. Information about discrimination, sexual harassment, potential workplace violence, or conflicts of interest between employees and the company may need to be shared with upper management to protect the rights and well-being of others. So, when employees disclose personal, confidential information, do the right thing. Don't discuss it with others unless it falls into one of the exceptions discussed here.

2.4 Nonverbal Communication

When people talk, they send both verbal and nonverbal messages. Verbal messages are sent and received through the words we speak. "That was a great presentation." By contrast, nonverbal messages are sent through body language, facial expressions, or tone of voice. For instance, hearing "THAT was a GREAT presentation!" is very different from hearing "ahem [clearing throat], that was, ahem, ahem, a great presentation."

More specifically, **nonverbal communication** is any communication that doesn't involve words. Nonverbal communication and messages almost always accompany verbal communication and may support and reinforce the verbal message or contradict it. The importance of nonverbal communication is well established. Researchers have estimated that as much as 93 percent of any message is transmitted nonverbally, with 55 percent coming from body language and facial expressions and 38 percent coming from the tone and pitch of the voice.[25] Since many nonverbal cues are unintentional, receivers often consider nonverbal communication to be a more accurate representation of what senders are thinking and feeling than the words they use. If you have ever asked someone out on a date and been told "yes," but realized that the real answer was "no," then you understand the importance of paying attention to nonverbal communication.

nonverbal communication
any communication that doesn't involve words

kinesics
movements of the body and face

paralanguage
the pitch, rate, tone, volume, and speaking pattern (i.e., use of silences, pauses, or hesitations) of one's voice

Kinesics and paralanguage are two kinds of nonverbal communication.[26] **Kinesics** (from the Greek word *kinesis*, meaning "movement") are movements of the body and face.[27] These movements include arm and hand gestures, facial expressions, eye contact, folding arms, crossing legs, and leaning toward or away from another person. For example, people tend to avoid eye contact when they are embarrassed or unsure of the message they are sending. Crossed arms and/or legs usually indicate defensiveness or that the person is not receptive to the message or the sender. Also, people tend to smile frequently when they are seeking someone's approval. It turns out that kinesics play an incredibly important role in communication because they provide clues about people's true feelings, over and beyond what they say (or don't say).

Paralanguage includes the pitch, rate, tone, volume, and speaking pattern (i.e., use of silences, pauses, or hesitations) of one's voice. For example, when people are unsure what to say, they tend to decrease their communication effectiveness by speaking softly. When people are nervous, they tend to talk faster and louder. These characteristics have a tremendous influence on whether listeners are receptive to what speakers are saying. Lawyers have long used the power of their voices to influence jurors. For instance, tobacco company lawyers complained about the dramatic way in which plaintiffs' attorney Stanley Rosenblatt would read secret company documents aloud to jurors. Rosenblatt, who would vary his voice from a slow whisper to a fast, loud voice that filled the entire courtroom, said that opposing attorneys always insisted that "I should read in a very flat monotone."[28]

In short, since nonverbal communication is so informative, especially when it contradicts verbal communication, managers need to learn how to monitor and control their nonverbal behavior.

Review 2
Kinds of Communication

Organizational communication depends on the communication process, formal and informal communication channels, one-on-one communication, and nonverbal communication. The major components of the communication process are the sender, the receiver, noise, and feedback. The conduit metaphor refers to the mistaken assumption that senders can pipe their intended messages directly into receivers' heads with perfect clarity. With noise, perceptual filters, and little feedback, however, this just isn't possible. Formal communication channels, such as downward, upward, and horizontal communication, carry organizationally approved messages and information. By contrast, the informal communication channel, called the "grapevine," arises out of curiosity and is carried out through gossip or cluster chains. Managers should use the grapevine to keep employees informed and to obtain better, clearer information for themselves. There are two kinds of one-on-one communication. Coaching is used to improve on-the-job performance while counseling is used to communicate about non-job-related issues affecting job performance. Nonverbal communication, such as kinesics and paralanguage, accounts for as much as 93 percent of a message's content and understanding. Since nonverbal communication is so informative, managers need to learn how to monitor and control their nonverbal behavior.

How to Improve Communication

An employee comes in late every day, takes long lunches, and leaves early. His coworkers resent his tardiness and having to do his share of the work. Another employee makes as many as 10 personal phone calls a day on company time. Still another employee's job performance has dropped significantly in the last three months. How do you communicate with these employees to begin solving these problems? Or suppose that you supervise a division of 50, 100, or even 1,000 people. How can you communicate effectively with everyone in that division? Moreover, how can top managers communicate effectively with everyone in the company when employees work in different offices, states, countries, and time zones? Turning that around, how can managers make themselves accessible so that they can hear what employees feel and think throughout the organization?

When it comes to improving communication, managers face two primary tasks, managing one-on-one communication and managing organization-wide communication.

After reading the next two sections, you should be able to

3 explain how managers can manage effective one-on-one communication.

4 describe how managers can manage effective organization-wide communication.

3 Managing One-on-One Communication

In Chapter 1, you learned that, on average, first-line managers spend 57 percent of their time with people, middle managers spend 63 percent of their time directly with people, and top managers spend as much as 78 percent of their time dealing with people.[29] These numbers make it clear that managers spend a great deal of time in one-on-one communication with others.

Learn more about managing one-on-one communication by reading how to 3.1 choose the right communication medium, 3.2 be a good listener, 3.3 give effective feedback, and 3.4 improve cross-cultural communication.

3.1 Choosing the Right Communication Medium

communication medium
the method used to deliver an oral or written message

Sometimes messages are poorly communicated simply because they are delivered using the wrong **communication medium**, which is the method used to deliver a message. For example, the wrong communication medium is being used when an employee returns from lunch, picks up the note left on her office chair, and learns she has been fired. The wrong communication medium is also being used when an employee pops into your office every 10 minutes with a simple request. (An email would be better.)

There are two general kinds of communication media: oral and written communication. *Oral communication* includes face-to-face and group meetings through telephone calls, videoconferencing, or any other means of sending and receiving spoken messages. Studies show that managers generally prefer oral communication over written because it provides the opportunity to ask questions about parts of the message that they don't understand. Oral communication is also a rich communication medium because it allows managers to receive and assess the nonverbal communication that accompanies spoken messages (i.e., body language, facial expressions, and the voice characteristics associated with paralanguage). Furthermore, you don't need a personal computer and an Internet connection to conduct oral communication. Simply schedule an appointment, track someone down in the hall, or catch someone on the phone. Oral communication should not be used for all communication, however. In general, when messages are simple, such as a quick request or a presentation of straightforward information, memos or email are often the better communication medium.

Written communication includes letters, email, and memos. Although most managers still like and use oral communication, email in particular is changing how they communicate with workers, customers, and each other. Email is the fastest-growing form of communication in organizations primarily because of its convenience and speed. For instance, because people read six times faster than they can listen, they usually can read 30 email messages in 10 to 15 minutes.[30] By contrast, dealing with voice messages can take a considerable amount of time. Fred DeLuca, founder of the Subway sandwich shop franchise, says, "I get about 60 messages a day from employees and franchisees, and I listen to all of them. For my sanity, I set a time limit of 75 seconds, because people can be long-winded when they're excited. When I hear, 'You have 30 messages,' I know right away that I'll spend 60 minutes on voice mail. I take two minutes per message, listening and returning or forwarding."[31]

Written communication, such as email, is well suited for delivering straightforward messages and information. Furthermore, with email accessible at the

PERSONAL PRODUCTIVITY TIP

Writing Memos

Memos often create misperceptions and send unintended messages. Yet they are sometimes necessary to create a record of decisions or responsibilities. To write good memos:

- Don't use accusatory or autocratic language, such as "I am appalled by your decision" or "I don't like your attitude."
- Avoid absolutes, such as "never," "cannot," and "must not."
- Keep them short and to the point—use bullet points for structure.
- Never write anything in a memo that you don't want everyone else to see.
- Always consider whether a phone call or personal conversation would be more effective than a memo.[33]

office, at home, and on the road (by laptop computer or Web-based email), managers can use email to stay in touch from anywhere at almost any time. And, since email and other written communications don't have to be sent and received simultaneously, messages can be sent and stored for reading at any time. This allows managers to send and receive many more messages using email than using oral communication, which requires people to get together in person or by phone or videoconference. But, warns management consultant Tom Durel, "Don't assume that you did your part just because you sent out a bunch of memos. If you really want to communicate, you need to take the time to get real-time feedback."[32]

Although written communication is well suited for delivering straightforward messages and information, it is not well suited to complex, ambiguous, or emotionally laden messages, which are better delivered through oral communication.

3.2 Listening

Are you a good listener? You probably think so. But, in fact, most people, including managers, are terrible listeners, retaining only about 25 percent of what they hear.[34] You qualify as a poor listener if you frequently interrupt others, jump to conclusions about what people will say before they've said it, hurry the speaker to finish his or her point, are a passive listener (not actively working at your listening), or simply don't pay attention to what people are saying.[35] On this last point, attentiveness, college students were periodically asked to record their thoughts during a psychology course. On average, 20 percent of the students were paying attention (only 12 percent were actively working at being good listeners), 20 percent were thinking about sex, 20 percent were thinking about things they had done before, and the remaining 40 percent were thinking about a number of things (worries, religion, lunch, daydreaming, etc.), none of which were related to class.[36]

How important is it to be a good listener? In general, about 45 percent of the total time you spend communicating with others is spent listening. Furthermore, listening is important for managerial and business success, even for those at the top of an organization. In fact, managers with better listening skills are rated as better managers by their employees and are much more likely to be promoted.[37]

So, what can you do to improve your listening ability? First, understand the difference between hearing and listening. According to *Webster's New World Dictionary*, **hearing** is the "act or process of perceiving sounds," whereas **listening** is "making a conscious effort to hear." In other words, we react to sounds, such as bottles breaking or music being played too loud, because hearing is an involuntary physiological process. By contrast, listening is a voluntary behavior. So, if you want to be a good listener, you have to choose to be a good listener. Typically, that means choosing to be an active, empathetic listener.[38]

Active listening means assuming half the responsibility for successful communication by actively giving the speaker nonjudgmental feedback that

hearing
the act or process of perceiving sounds

listening
making a conscious effort to hear

active listening
assuming half the responsibility for successful communication by actively giving the speaker nonjudgmental feedback that shows you've accurately heard what he or she said

shows you've accurately heard what he or she said. Active listeners make it clear from their behavior that they are listening carefully to what the speaker has to say. Active listeners put the speaker at ease, maintain eye contact, and show the speaker that they are attentively listening by nodding and making short statements.

Several specific strategies can help you be a better active listener. First, *clarify responses* by asking the speaker to explain confusing or ambiguous statements. Second, when there are natural breaks in the speaker's delivery, use this time to paraphrase or summarize what has been said. *Paraphrasing* is restating what has been said in your own words. *Summarizing* is reviewing the speaker's main points or emotions. Paraphrasing and summarizing give the speaker the chance to correct the message if the active listener has attached the wrong meaning to it. Paraphrasing and summarizing also show the speaker that the active listener is interested in the speaker's message. Exhibit 16.4 lists specific statements that listeners can use to clarify responses, paraphrase, or summarize what has been said.

Active listeners also avoid evaluating the message or being critical until the message is complete. They recognize that their only responsibility during the transmission of a message is to receive it accurately and derive the intended meaning from it. Evaluation and criticism can take place after the message is accurately received. Finally, active listeners also recognize that a large portion of any message is transmitted nonverbally and thus pay very careful attention to the nonverbal cues transmitted by the speaker.

empathetic listening
understanding the speaker's perspective and personal frame of reference and giving feedback that conveys that understanding to the speaker

Empathetic listening means understanding the speaker's perspective and personal frame of reference and giving feedback that conveys that understanding to the speaker. Empathetic listening goes beyond active listening because it depends on our ability to set aside our own attitudes or relationships to be able to see and understand things through someone else's eyes. Empathetic listening is just as important as active listening, especially for managers, because it helps build rapport and trust with others.

The key to being a more empathetic listener is to show your desire to understand and to reflect people's feelings. You can *show your desire to understand* by listening, that is, asking people to talk about what's most important

exhibit 16.4

Clarifying, Paraphrasing, and Summarizing Responses for Active Listeners

CLARIFYING RESPONSES	PARAPHRASING RESPONSES	SUMMARIZING RESPONSES
Could you explain that again?	What you're really saying is	Let me summarize . . . .
I don't understand what you mean.	If I understand you correctly	Okay, your main concerns are . . . .
I'm confused. Would you run through that again?	So your perspective is that	Thus far, you've discussed . . . .
I'm not sure how	In other words	To recap what you've said . . . .
	Tell me if I'm wrong, but what you're saying is	

Source: E. Atwater, I Hear You, *revised ed. (New York: Walker, 1992).*

to them and then by giving them sufficient time to talk before responding or interrupting. Management consultant Neil Grammer tells this story about being an empathetic listener:

> One of the best sales meetings I've ever had taught me a valuable lesson about the importance of listening. The meeting was with an investment bank's managing director. The appointment lasted 30 minutes—28 of those minutes were spent by the director telling me everything about his business and personnel. I told him nothing more about my company and its services than I had in our initial phone conversation. As the meeting concluded, he enthusiastically shook my hand and proclaimed how much he was looking forward to working with me—someone who understood his business.[39]

Reflecting feelings is also an important part of empathetic listening because it demonstrates that you understand the speaker's emotions. Unlike active listening, in which you restate or summarize the informational content of what has been said, the focus is on the affective part of the message. As an empathetic listener, you can use the following statements to reflect the speaker's emotions:

→ So, right now you're feeling . . . .
→ You seem as if you're . . . .
→ Do you feel a bit . . . ?
→ I could be wrong, but I'm sensing that you're feeling . . . .

3.3 Giving Feedback

In Chapter 12, you learned that performance appraisal feedback (i.e., judging) should be separated from developmental feedback (i.e., coaching).[40] At this point, we now focus on the steps needed to communicate feedback one-on-one to employees.

To start, managers need to recognize that feedback can be constructive or destructive. **Destructive feedback** is disapproving without any intention of being helpful and almost always causes a negative or defensive reaction in the recipient. In fact, one study found that 98 percent of employees responded to destructive feedback from their bosses with either verbal aggression (two-thirds) or physical aggression (one-third).[41]

destructive feedback feedback that disapproves without any intention of being helpful and almost always causes a negative or defensive reaction in the recipient

constructive feedback feedback intended to be helpful, corrective, and/or encouraging

By contrast, **constructive feedback** is intended to be helpful, corrective, and/or encouraging. It is aimed at correcting performance deficiencies and motivating employees. When providing constructive feedback, Jenet Noriega Schwind, vice president and chief people officer of Zantaz.com, an e-business archiving company, tells employees, "What I'm going to tell you may be upsetting to you—but it's important to your success." She says, "When you are telling people things they don't necessarily want to hear, you have to deliver your message in a way that gets their attention and acceptance."[42]

For feedback to be constructive rather than destructive, it must be immediate, focused on specific behaviors, and problem oriented. *Immediate feedback* is much more effective than delayed feedback because manager and worker can recall the mistake or incident more accurately and discuss it in greater detail. For example, if a worker is rude to a customer and the customer immediately reports the incident to management, and the manager, in turn, immediately discusses the incident with the employee, there should be little disagreement over what was said or done. By contrast, if the manager waits several weeks to discuss the incident, it's unlikely that either the manager or the worker will be able to accurately remember the specifics of what occurred. When that happens, it's usually too late to have a meaningful conversation.

Specific feedback focuses on particular acts or incidents that are clearly under the control of the employee. For instance, instead of telling an employee that he or she is "always late for work," it's much more constructive to say, "In the last three weeks, you have been 30 minutes late on four occasions and more than an hour late on two others." Furthermore, specific feedback isn't very helpful unless employees have control over the problems that the feedback addresses. Indeed, giving negative feedback about behaviors beyond someone's control is likely to be seen as unfair. Similarly, giving positive feedback about behaviors beyond someone's control may be viewed as insincere.

Last, *problem-oriented feedback* focuses on the problems or incidents associated with the poor performance rather than on the worker or the worker's personality. Giving feedback does not give managers the right to personally attack workers. While managers may be frustrated by a worker's poor performance, the point of problem-oriented feedback is to draw attention to the problem in a nonjudgmental way so that the employee has enough information to correct it. So, rather than telling people that they're "idiots," focus on the problem. For instance, a shipping clerk at A&S Restaurant had a bad case of body odor. Rather than telling him "You stink" or "You're doing a lousy job because you stink," the manager explained the specific ways in which the clerk's body odor was "getting in the way of doing his job." Because the manager's feedback was specific and problem oriented and didn't attack or blame the employee, the employee didn't get defensive and took steps to take care of his body odor.[43]

3.4 Improving Cross-Cultural Communication

cross-cultural communication transmitting information from a person in one country or culture to a person from another country or culture

As you know by now, effective communication is very difficult to accomplish. **Cross-cultural communication**, which involves transmitting information from a person in one country or culture to a person from another country or culture, is even more difficult. But you can do a number of things to increase your chances for successful cross-cultural communication: familiarize yourself with a culture's general work norms; determine whether a culture is emotionally affective or neutral; develop respect for other cultures; and understand how address terms and attitudes toward time (polychronic versus monochronic time, and appointment, schedule, discussion, and acquaintance time) differ from culture to culture.

In Chapter 7, you learned that expatriates who receive predeparture language and cross-cultural training make faster adjustments to foreign cultures and perform better on their international assignments.[44] Therefore, *familiarizing yourself with a culture's general work norms*, that is, the shared values, beliefs, and perceptions toward work and how it should be done, is the first step for successful cross-cultural communication. (See Chapter 7 for a more complete discussion of international cultures.)

Mercedes-Benz wisely took the time to familiarize itself with U.S. culture and work norms when it built a manufacturing plant in Vance, Alabama. The management team, consisting primarily of Germans and Americans, spent six months deciding how Mercedes would blend German and American management philosophies and work practices. The biggest disagreements were over

© AP PHOTO/DAVE MARTIN

When Mercedes built a manufacturing plant in Vance, Alabama, the company went to great lengths to familiarize itself with American (and Alabaman) cultural and work norms. Management successfully blended elements of German and American cultures at the Vance facility. The result: After only one year in operation, employees at the plant produced the 50,000th M-Class all-activity vehicle.

image and decorum. Consistent with their hierarchical work norms, the Germans preferred private offices along narrow hallways, whereas the Americans, who were generally more egalitarian, preferred open offices where people of all ranks could easily find and talk to each other. Likewise, the German managers preferred formal business attire because it emphasized status differences (i.e., hierarchy), whereas the Americans pushed for casual wear, such as dress slacks with polo shirts and sweaters bearing the Mercedes logo. Because the plant is in Alabama, the team eventually opted for open offices and casual dress.[45]

Determining whether a culture is emotionally affective or neutral is also important to cross-cultural communication. People in **affective cultures** tend to display their emotions and feelings openly when communicating, whereas people in **neutral cultures** do not.[46] For example, while Italians are prone to strong bursts of emotion (positive and negative), Chinese don't show strong emotions because doing so is thought to disrupt harmony and lead to conflict. Likewise, while a smiling American is displaying happiness, a smiling Japanese may be trying to hide another emotion or avoid answering a question.[47] The mistake most managers make is misunderstanding the differences between affective and neutral cultures. People from neutral cultures aren't by definition cold and unfeeling. They just don't show their emotions in the same way or with the same intensity as people from affective cultures. The key is to recognize the differences and then make sure your judgments are not based on the lack or presence of emotional reactions. Exhibit 16.5 provides a more detailed explanation of the differences between affective and neutral cultures.

affective cultures
cultures in which people display emotions and feelings when communicating

neutral cultures
cultures in which people do not display emotions and feelings when communicating

Respecting other cultures is also an important part of improving cross-cultural communication. Because we use our own culture as the standard of comparison, it's very easy to make the common mistake of assuming that "different" means "inferior."[48] According to Professor Nancy J. Adler, "Evaluating others' behavior rarely helps in trying to understand, communicate with, or conduct business with people from another culture."[49] The key, she says, is taking a step back and realizing that you don't know or understand everything that is going on and that your assumptions and interpretations of others' behavior and motives may be wrong. So, instead of judging or evaluating your international business colleagues, observe what they do. Also, delay your judgments until you have more experience with your colleagues and their culture. Lastly, treat any judgments or conclusions you do make as guesses, and then double-check those judgments or conclusions with others.[50] The more patient you are in forming opinions and drawing conclusions, the better you'll be at cross-cultural communication.

address terms
cultural norms that establish whether you should address businesspeople by their first names, family names, or titles

Next, you can improve cross-cultural communication by *knowing the address terms* that different cultures use to address each other in the workplace.[51] **Address terms** are the cultural norms that establish whether you address businesspeople by their first names, family names, or titles. When

exhibit 16.5

Affective and Neutral Cultures

IN AFFECTIVE CULTURES, PEOPLE	IN NEUTRAL CULTURES, PEOPLE
1. reveal thoughts and feelings through verbal and nonverbal communication.	1. don't reveal what they are thinking or feeling.
2. express and show feelings of tension.	2. hide tension and only show it accidentally in face or posture.
3. let their emotions flow easily, intensely, and without inhibition.	3. suppress emotions, leading to occasional "explosions."
4. admire heated, animated, and intense expression of emotion.	4. admire remaining cool, calm, and relaxed.
5. are used to touching, gesturing, and showing strong emotions through facial expressions (all are common).	5. resist touching, gesturing, and showing strong emotions through facial expressions.
6. make statements with emotion.	6. often make statements in an unexpressive manner.

Source: F. Trompenaars, Riding the Waves of Culture: Understanding Diversity in Global Business *(London: Economist Books, 1994).*

meeting for the first time, Americans and Australians tend to be informal and address each other by first names, even nicknames. Such immediate informality is not accepted in many cultures, however. For instance, an American manager working in one of his company's British subsidiaries introduced himself as "Chuck" to his British employees and coworkers. Nonetheless, even after six months on the job, his British counterparts still referred to him as Charles. And the more he insisted they call him "Chuck," the more they seemed to dig in their heels and call him "Charles."[52] So, to decrease defensiveness, know your address terms before addressing your international business counterparts.

Understanding different cultural attitudes toward time is another major consideration for effective cross-cultural communication. Cultures tend to be either monochronic or polychronic in their orientation toward time.[53] In **monochronic cultures**, people tend to do one thing at a time and view time as linear, meaning that time is the passage of sequential events. You may have heard the saying, "There are three stages in people's lives: when they believe in Santa Claus, when they don't believe in Santa Claus, and when they are Santa Claus." The progression from childhood, to young adulthood, to parenthood (when they are Santa Claus) reflects a linear view of time. Schedules are important in monochronic cultures because you schedule time to get a particular thing done.

monochronic cultures
cultures in which people tend to do one thing at a time and view time as linear

By contrast, in **polychronic cultures**, people tend to do more than one thing at a time and view time as circular, meaning that time is a combination of the past, present, and future.

polychronic cultures
cultures in which people tend to do more than one thing at a time and view time as circular

As you can easily imagine, businesspeople from monochronic cultures are driven to distraction by what they perceive as the laxness of polychronic cultures, while people from polychronic cultures chafe under what they perceive

appointment time
a cultural norm for how punctual you must be when showing up for scheduled appointments or meetings

schedule time
a cultural norm for the time by which scheduled projects or jobs should actually be completed

discussion time
a cultural norm for how much time should be spent in discussion with others

acquaintance time
a cultural norm for how much time you must spend getting to know someone before the person is prepared to do business with you

as the strict regimentation of monochronic cultures. Conflicts between these two views of times occur rather easily. Exhibit 16.6 provides a more detailed explanation of the differences between monochronic and polychronic cultures.

Differences in monochronic and polychronic time show up in four important temporal concepts that affect cross-cultural communication: appointment time, schedule time, discussion time, and acquaintance time.[54] **Appointment time** refers to how punctual you must be when showing up for scheduled appointments or meetings. In the United States, you are considered "late" if you arrive more than five minutes after the appointed time. Swedes don't even allow five minutes, expecting others to arrive "on the dot." By contrast, in Latin countries, people can arrive 20 to 30 minutes after a scheduled appointment and still not be considered late.

Schedule time is the time by which scheduled projects or jobs should actually be completed. In the United States and other Anglo cultures, a premium is placed on completing things on time. By contrast, more relaxed attitudes toward schedule time can be found throughout Asia and Latin America.

Discussion time concerns how much time should be spent in discussion with others. In the United States, we carefully manage discussion time to avoid "wasting" time on nonbusiness topics. In Brazil, though, because of the emphasis on building relationships, as much as two hours of general discussion on nonbusiness topics can take place before moving on to business issues.

Finally, **acquaintance time** is how much time you must spend getting to know someone before the person is prepared to do business with you. Again,

exhibit 16.6

Monochronic versus Polychronic Cultures

PEOPLE IN MONOCHRONIC CULTURES	PEOPLE IN POLYCHRONIC CULTURES
• Do one thing at a time	• Do many things at once
• Concentrate on the job	• Are highly distractible and subject to interruptions
• Take time commitments (deadlines, schedules) seriously	• Meet time commitments only if possible without extreme measures
• Are committed to the job	• Are committed to people
• Adhere religiously to plans	• Change plans easily and often
• Are concerned about not disturbing others (privacy is to be respected)	• Are more concerned with relationships (family, friends, business associates) than with privacy
• Show respect for private property (rarely lend or borrow things)	• Frequently borrow and lend things
• Emphasize promptness	• Vary their promptness by the relationship
• Are accustomed to short-term relationships	• Tend to build lifetime relationships

Source: E. T. Hall & M. R. Hall, Understanding Cultural Differences *(Yarmouth, ME: Intercultural Press, 1990).*

in the United States, people quickly get down to business and are willing to strike a deal on the same day if the terms are good and initial impressions are positive. In the Middle East, however, it may take two or three weeks of meetings before reaching this comfort level. The French also have a different attitude toward acquaintance time. Polly Platt, author of *French or Foe*, a book that explains French culture and people for travelers and businesspeople, says, "Know that things are going to take longer and don't resent it. Realize that the time system is different. Time is not a quantity for them. We save time, we spend time, we waste time; all this comes from money. The French don't. They pass time. It's a totally different concept."[55]

Review 3

Managing One-on-One Communication

One-on-one communication can be managed by choosing the right communication medium, being a good listener, giving effective feedback, and understanding cross-cultural communication. Managers generally prefer oral communication because it provides the opportunity to ask questions and assess nonverbal communication. Oral communication is best suited to complex, ambiguous, or emotionally laden topics. Written communication is best suited for delivering straightforward messages and information. Listening is important for managerial success, but most people are terrible listeners. To improve your listening skills, choose to be an active listener (clarify responses, paraphrase, and summarize) and an empathetic listener (show your desire to understand, reflect feelings). Feedback can be constructive or destructive. To be constructive, feedback must be immediate, focused on specific behaviors, and problem oriented. Finally, to increase the chances for successful cross-cultural communication, determine whether a culture is emotionally affective or neutral, familiarize yourself with a culture's general work norms, develop respect for other cultures, and understand how address terms and attitudes toward time (polychronic versus monochronic time, and appointment, schedule, discussion, and acquaintance time) differ from culture to culture.

4 Managing Organization-Wide Communication

While managing one-on-one communication is important, managers must also know how to communicate effectively with a larger number of people throughout an organization. When Bill Zollars became CEO of Yellow Corporation (now Yellow-Roadway), a trucking company, he decided that he needed to communicate directly with all 25,000 of the company's employees, most of whom did not work at company headquarters in Overland Park, Kansas. For a year and a half, he traveled all across the country conducting small, "town-hall" meetings. Zollars said, "There were days when I gave the same speech 10 times at 10 different locations. I'd start at 6:30 AM with the drivers, then I'd talk to the dockworkers, the people in the office, and the sales staff. At night, I'd meet with customers. I wanted as many employees and customers as possible to hear it from me face-to-face."[56] Effective leaders, however, don't just communicate to others; they also make themselves accessible so that they can hear what employees throughout their organizations are feeling and thinking.

www.experiencing management.com

Gain additional insight about communication in our high-tech world at our animated concept and activity site. Choose Communication from the "select a topic" pull-down menu, then Information Technology from the "overview tab."

http://www.experiencingmanagement.com

Learn more about organization-wide communication by reading the following sections about 4.1 improving transmission by getting the message out and 4.2 improving reception by finding ways to hear what others feel and think.

4.1 Improving Transmission: Getting the Message Out

Several methods of electronic communication—email, online discussion forums, televised/videotaped speeches and conferences, corporate talk shows, and broadcast voice mail—now make it easier for managers to communicate with people throughout the organization and "get the message out."

online discussion forums the in-house equivalent of Internet newsgroups; Web- or software-based discussion tools available across the company to permit employees to easily ask questions and share knowledge with each other

Although we normally think of *email*, the transmission of messages via computers, as a means of one-on-one communication, it also plays an important role in organization-wide communication. With the click of a button, managers can send email to everyone in the company via email distribution lists. Many CEOs now use this capability regularly to keep employees up-to-date on changes and developments. In fact many CEOs and top executives make their email addresses public and encourage employees to contact them directly. For example, Hewlett-Packard managers and employees can go to H-P's Web site and use a Web page (**http://www.hp.com/hpinfo/execteam/email/fiorina/**) called "email carly" to email CEO Carly Fiorina with their thoughts and suggestions.

PERSONAL PRODUCTIVITY TIP

The Dangers of Corporate Email

Email is fast and convenient, but it also presents some potential dangers. It can easily be saved, duplicated, forwarded, and printed. The original sender has no control over who sees it. And while senders delete email on their machines, most likely other copies can be found on the company's mail server or backup tapes, which most companies run every night. Email also allows disgruntled employees to easily send out sensitive or fraudulent information to competitors or outsiders. Finally, many employees use easily guessed passwords or don't log off their computers, making it easy for an outsider to gain access to email while posing as a member of your company.[57]

Discussion forums are another means of electronically promoting organization-wide communication. **Online discussion forums**, which are the in-house equivalent of Internet newsgroups, are Web- or software-based discussion tools that are available across the company to permit employees to easily ask questions and share knowledge with each other. The point is to share expertise and not duplicate solutions already "discovered" by others in the company. Furthermore, because online discussion forums remain online, they provide a historical database for people who are dealing with particular problems for the first time. For ease of use, online discussion forums are typically organized by topic. For example, BP Amoco has created "Connect," which is essentially a company Yellow Pages where more than 12,000 managers and workers have entered their contact information and listed their expertise to make it easier for others to find expert help for their problems.[58]

televised/videotaped speeches and meetings speeches and meetings originally made to a smaller audience that are either simultaneously broadcast to other locations in the company or videotaped for subsequent distribution and viewing

Televised/videotaped speeches and meetings are a third electronic method of organization-wide communication. **Televised/videotaped speeches and meetings** are simply speeches and meetings originally made to a smaller audience that are either simultaneously broadcast to other locations in the company or videotaped for subsequent distribution and viewing. After leaving Compaq Computer to become CEO of WorldCom (now MCI), Michael Capellas explained his 100-day plan for turning around the company after a $9 billion accounting scandal. To get his message out, Capellas chose a one-hour internal broadcast to the company's 60,000 employees.[59]

Corporate talk shows are a variant on televised/videotaped speeches and meetings. But instead of simply being watched, **corporate talk shows** allow

corporate talk shows
televised company meetings that allow remote audiences (employees) to pose questions to the show's host and guests

remote audience members, all of whom are typically workers or managers, to pose questions to the show's host and guests. For example, once a month, Emma Carrasco, vice president of marketing and communication, and Dan Hunt, president of Caribbean and Latin American operations, host the Virtual Leadership Academy, which is a corporate talk show for Nortel Networks. A typical broadcast is seen live by 2,000 employees in 46 countries, who call in with questions about Nortel and its competitors. Why a corporate talk show? Carrasco says, "We're always looking for ways to break down barriers in the company, and people are comfortable with the talk-show format. People watch talk shows in every country in the region, and they've learned that it's okay to say what's on their mind. In fact, it's expected."[60]

Voice messaging, or "voice mail," is a telephone answering system that records audio messages. Eighty-nine percent of respondents believe that voice messaging is critical to business communication, 78 percent believe that it improves productivity, and 58 percent would rather leave a message on a voice messaging system than with a receptionist.[61] Nonetheless, most people are unfamiliar with the ability to *broadcast voice mail* by sending a recorded message to everyone in the company. Broadcast voice mail gives top managers a quick, convenient way to address their work forces via oral communication. At Ernst & Young, the company-wide, broadcast voice mails of Chairman Phil Laskawy were so well known and well liked that E & Y employees called them "Travels with Phil." No matter where he was traveling on business for the company—and he traveled all over the world—Phil would begin his voice mails, most of which lasted 5 to 10 minutes, with a weather report, a couple of bad jokes, and an update on his beloved New York Yankees baseball team; then came the core part of his message.[62]

4.2 Improving Reception: Hearing What Others Feel and Think

When people think of "organization-wide" communication, they think of the CEO and top managers getting their message out to people in the company. But organization-wide communication also means finding ways to hear what people throughout the organization are feeling and thinking.

Surprisingly, most employees and managers are reluctant to share their thoughts and feelings with top managers. Surveys indicate that only 29 percent of first-level managers felt that their companies encouraged employees to express their opinions openly. Another study of 22 companies found that 70 percent of the people surveyed were afraid to speak up about problems they knew existed at work.

organizational silence
when employees withhold information about organizational problems or issues

Withholding information about organizational problems or issues is called **organizational silence**. Organizational silence occurs when employees believe that telling management about problems won't make a difference or that they'll be punished or hurt in some way for sharing such information.[63] For example, Bill Fowler, who is one of the most accurate machinists of industrial pumps at Blackmer/Dover Resources, said, "If I gave away my tricks, management could use [them] against me to speed things up and keep me at a flat-out pace all day long."[64] Fortunately, though, company hotlines, survey feedback, frequent informal meetings, and surprise visits are ways of overcoming organizational silence.

company hotlines
phone numbers that anyone in the company can call anonymously to leave information for upper management

Company hotlines are phone numbers that anyone in the company can call anonymously to leave information for upper management. Some companies hire outside firms to run their hotlines to maintain the complete anonymity of callers. For example, Pillsbury's hotline, which is run by In-

Touch Corporation, doesn't even reveal callers' gender. Toyota's employee handbook says, "Don't spend time worrying about something. Speak up!" The Toyota hotline is anonymous and available 24 hours a day, seven days a week. Every message is reviewed and fully investigated by Toyota's top human resources manager. Moreover, if the questions or statements left on the hotline would be of interest to others in the company, they are posted on company bulletin boards (without sacrificing callers' anonymity).[65]

survey feedback
information collected by surveys from organizational members that is then compiled, disseminated, and used to develop action plans for improvement

Survey feedback is information collected by survey from organization members that is then compiled, disseminated, and used to develop action plans for improvement. Many organizations make use of survey feedback by surveying their managers and employees several times a year.

Frequent, *informal meetings* between top managers and lower-level employees are one of the best ways for top managers to hear what others feel and think. Many people assume that top managers are at the center of everything that goes on in organizations, but top managers commonly feel isolated from most of their lower-level managers and employees. Consequently, more and more top managers are scheduling frequent, informal meetings with people throughout their companies. CEO John Chambers described how this works at Cisco Systems:

> "The birthday breakfasts are probably the most valuable sessions I do with employees. Once a month, anybody who has a birthday in that month can come and quiz [me] for about an hour and a half, and anything is fair game. We deliberately asked directors and VPs not to participate so that people who I don't get a chance normally to listen to can participate. And every single time I learn two or three things that either I need to do differently, or things that I thought were working one way weren't."[66]

Have you ever been around when a supervisor learns that upper management is going to be paying a visit? First, there's shock. Next, there's anxiety. And then there's panic, as everyone is told to drop what he or she is doing to polish, shine, and spruce up the workplace so that it looks perfect for the visit. Of course, when visits are conducted under these conditions, top managers don't get a realistic look at what's going on in the company. Consequently, one of the ways to get an accurate picture is to pay *surprise visits* to various parts of the organization. These visits should not be surprise inspections, but should be used as an opportunity to encourage meaningful upward communication from those who normally don't get a chance to work with upper management. Such surprise visits are part of the culture at Enterprise Rent-a-Car. Enterprise's former CEO Andy Taylor tells a story of one surprise visit: "We were visiting an office in Berkeley and it was mobbed, so I started cleaning cars. As it was happening, I wondered if it was a good use of my time, but the effect on morale was tremendous."[67]

Review 4
Managing Organization-Wide Communication

Managers need methods for managing organization-wide communication and for making themselves accessible so that they can hear what employees throughout their organizations are feeling and thinking. Email, online discussion forums, televised/videotaped speeches and conferences, corporate talk shows, and broadcast voice mail make it much easier for managers to improve message transmission and "get the message out." By contrast, anonymous company hotlines, survey feedback, frequent informal meetings, and surprise visits help managers avoid organizational silence and improve reception by hearing what others in the organization feel and think.

STUDY TIP Studying for comprehensive exams doesn't have to be a chore. Form a study group. Photocopy the glossary at the end of this text, and cut the copies into strips, one term per strip. Put all strips into a large bowl. Divide into two teams and have one team at a time draw out a strip. Quiz the opposing team and then read the correct answer. You can do the same with the chapter outlines at the beginning of each chapter. You can tabulate points, but you'll all win!

MANAGEMENT DECISION

READING THE SIGNALS

You are beaming with confidence as you walk down the hall to your supervisor's office.[68] In just a few hours, you are presenting the company's new advertising campaign and strategy to the board of directors. At this meeting, the board will decide to either adopt the entire proposal or subcontract all of the marketing activities to an outside firm. Therefore, it is imperative to you and your staff that this presentation be a success. John, your supervisor, delegated the marketing campaign to you because of your educational background and previous work experience in the marketing field. The proposed ad campaign is the culmination of six months' work and countless hours spent by you and your staff devising the future direction of advertising and marketing for the company. As a result, you are thoroughly pleased with what you believe is a true work of art.

As you approach John's office, you notice that he is busily typing away at his computer. John has an open-door policy and always encourages his staff to approach him with any issue, big or small. You knock lightly and John glances up to acknowledge your arrival. You inform him that you want to brief him on your upcoming presentation to the board. You also ask if now is a bad time and suggest that you can come back later if that would be more convenient. John turns back to his computer screen, but says that now is as good a time as any. Seeing that he is busy, you give him a quick rundown of the proposal and your intended presentation. You leave many of the specifics out since John has either seen or participated in a majority of the advertising plans and is aware of the strategy's direction and overall theme.

As you launch into a discussion of your presentation, you notice that John is nodding in agreement, but he has not stopped typing or looked up at you since you entered his office. Feeling that your discussion is purely one-sided, you ask if there is anything else that you should consider or include in your presentation that would make it more appealing or understandable to the board. John looks up from his computer and replies, "No, it sounds good to me. I can't think of anything else." He then turns back to his computer and resumes typing.

As you leave John's office, you realize that your confidence is not as strong as it was just a few moments ago. In fact, you are now beginning to doubt that the board will accept your proposal. Throughout John's career, he has made many presentations to the board and seems to know exactly what they want to hear. You were really counting on his experience and input to increase the effectiveness of your presentation and help you make a perfect delivery. You glance at your watch realizing that you only have two hours until your big debut.

Questions

1. What would you do in this situation? Would you go back and bluntly ask John to listen to your presentation and provide his expert advice, or would you deliver the presentation as you had previously planned? Explain your answer.
2. What could John have done differently in this situation?

DEVELOP YOUR CAREER POTENTIAL

I DON'T AGREE, BUT I'M LISTENING

Being a good listener is a critical part of effective communication. Without it, you're unlikely to be a good manager. Therefore, the purpose of this assignment is to help you develop your listening skills. And there's no better way to do that than to talk to someone whose views are quite different from yours. In the best of situations, being a good listener is difficult. Because of perceptual filters, distractions, or daydreams, we retain only about 25 percent of what we hear. When we're talking with people who have very different views and opinions, it can be almost impossible to be good listeners. We tend to interrupt, jump to conclusions about what they'll say, and hurry them to finish their points (which we don't want to listen to anyway) so that we can "correct" their thinking with our own opinions.

To complete this assignment, you'll have to find someone who has different views or opinions on some topic (handgun control, abortion, capital punishment, and euthanasia are just some of the topics on which you can always find someone with a different viewpoint). Once you've found someone, conduct a 10-minute listening session, following this simple rule: Before stating your opinion, you must first accurately reflect or paraphrase the statement that your listening partner just made (be sure to reread Subsection 3.2 on listening). For example, suppose that your listening partner says, "Women shouldn't have to ask anyone for permission for what they do to their bodies. If they decide they want an abortion, they should go ahead and have it." Before making your point or disagreeing with your partner's, you will have to accurately paraphrase that statement in your own words. If you don't paraphrase it correctly, your listening partner will tell you. If you or your partner has difficulty accurately paraphrasing a statement, ask the other person to repeat the statement, and try again. Also, don't parrot the statement by repeating it word for word. Good listening isn't mimicry. It's capturing the essence of what others have said in your own words. And, before your listening partner responds, he or she, too, has to accurately paraphrase what you say. Continue this listening-based discussion for 10 minutes.

Questions

1. Was this discussion different from the way you normally discuss contentious topics with other people? Why or why not?
2. Was it difficult to reflect or paraphrase your listening partner's perspectives? Explain and give an example.
3. Did active listening techniques or empathetic listening techniques lead to more effective listening for you? Explain.

BIZ FLIX Patch Adams

Hunter "Patch" Adams (Robin Williams), a maverick medical student, believes that laughter is the best medicine. The rest of the medical community believes that medicine is the best medicine. Unlike traditional doctors who remain aloof, Patch Adams wants to be close to his patients. Williams's wackiness comes through clearly in this film, which is based on a true story.

This scene comes from the film's early sequence "The Experiment," which takes place after the students' medical school orientation. Patch Adams and fellow medical student Truman Schiff (Daniel London) leave the University Diner. They begin Patch's experiment for changing the programmed responses of people they meet on the street. Along the way, they stumble upon a meat packers convention where this scene occurs.

What to Watch for and Ask Yourself

1. What parts of the communication process appear in this scene? Note each part of the process that you see in the scene.
2. What type of communication does this scene show? Small group, large audience, persuasive?
3. Do you think Patch Adams is an effective communicator? Why or why not?

MGMT WORKPLACE Le Meridien Hotel

Bob van den Oord, the general manager of Le Meridien Hotel in Boston, insists that being a good communicator is the central function of his job. Le Meridien is an upscale, full-service urban hotel that serves both the business and leisure markets. Communication, van den Oord says, sells the organization's vision, motivates the staff to perform well, and creates team spirit. Moreover, timely and relevant communication empowers the staff to provide consistent responses to the hotel guests at all touch points; when that happens, customer satisfaction improves. To keep his staff well informed, van den Oord holds an operations meeting for all managers every morning, and each day he posts daily briefing sheets with notes on that day's special activities, promotions, group bookings, and VIP guests.

What to Watch for and Ask Yourself

1. What are the most difficult and important obstacles that Bob van den Oord tries to overcome with communication? Explain.
2. Why do you think van den Oord prefers face-to-face communication? What are the advantages and drawbacks of that approach?
3. How does good listening positively affect other components in the communication process?

ENDNOTES

CHAPTER 1

[1] C. Terhune & D. Morse, "Refinishing Home Depot—Former GE Exec Bob Nardelli Trims Retailer's Expansion As Pace, Economy Take Toll," *The Wall Street Journal*, 25 June 2002, B1; D. Foust, "Home Depot's 'Big Disappointment': Sales; CEO Robert Nardelli talks about the changes he's instituting, employee morale, and what repairs still remain to be made," *BusinessWeek Online*, [Online] available at http://www.businessweek.com/ bwdaily/ dnflash/jan2003/nf20030117_1318.htm, 17 January 2003; B. Liu, "Inside Track—Men's Playgrounds Plug into Girl Power to Grow," *Financial Times*, 30 December 2002, 9; M. Lloyd, "Home Depot Chmn: To Spend $250M in 2003 on Store Remodels," *Dow Jones News Service*, 27 January 2003; D. Morse, "Under Renovation: A Hardware Chain Struggles to Adjust to a New Blueprint—Home Depot Chief Nardelli Tightens Central Control, and Employees Squawk—Today, He Reveals More Plans," *The Wall Street Journal*, 17 January 2003, A1; A. Pascual, "Tidying Up at Home Depot: Bob Nardelli Is Bringing GE's Discipline to a Retail Giant," *BusinessWeek*, 26 November 2001, 102; K. Pate, "Analyst Sees Cracks Growing in Home Depot's Sales, Customer Service," *The Denver Post*, 12 January 2003; Readers Report, "Putting Managers in Their Rightful Place," *BusinessWeek*, 3 February 2003, 21.

[2] K. Voigt, "Top Dogs," *The Wall Street Journal*, 15 March 2002, W1.

[3] T. Carvell, A. Horowitz, & T. Mucha, "The 101 Dumbest Moments in Business," *Business 2.0*, April 2002, 64.

[4] N. Byrnes & J. Merritt, "Professional Services: The Help Needs Help," *BusinessWeek*, 13 January 2003, 129.

[5] T. Peters, "The Leadership Alliance" (Pat Carrigan excerpt), *In Search of Excellence* (Northbrook, IL: Video Arts distributor, 1985), videocassette.

[6] Pate, "Analyst Sees Cracks Growing in Home Depot's Sales."

[7] C. Terhune, "Retail Giant Aims to Spur Sales with Less-Cluttered Stores, Increased Customer Service," *The Wall Street Journal*, 8 March 2001, B1.

[8] R. Stagner, "Corporate Decision Making," *Journal of Applied Psychology* 53 (1969): 1–13.

[9] D. W. Bray, R. J. Campbell, & D. L. Grant, *Formative Years in Business: A Long-Term AT&T Study of Managerial Lives* (New York: Wiley, 1993).

[10] H. Fayol, *Administration industrielle et generale* (Paris: Dunod, 1916); English translation, *General and Industrial Administration* (London: Pelman, 1949); P. Drucker, "Management's New Paradigms," *Forbes*, 5 October 1998, 152; H. Mintzberg, "Rounding Out the Manager's Job," *Sloan Management Review* 36 (1994): 11–25.

[11] B. Dumaine, "The New Non-Manager Managers," *Fortune*, 22 February 1993, 80–84.

[12] Sources: N. Shirouzu, "Gadget Inspector: Why Toyota Wins Such High Marks on Quality Surveys—Hajime Oba Is a Key Coach As Japanese Auto Maker Steps Up U.S. Production—Striving to Reach Heijunka," *The Wall Street Journal*, 15 March 2001, A1; G. Harris, "The Cure: With Big Drugs Dying, Merck Didn't Merge—It Found New Ones—Some Inspired Research, Aided by a Bit of Luck, Saves Company's Independence—The Path to a Novel Painkiller," *The Wall Street Journal*, 1 January 2001, A1.

[13] Dumaine, "The New Non-Manager Managers."

[14] R. J. Grisson, "Probability of the Superior Outcome of One Treatment over Another," *Journal of Applied Psychology* 79 (1994): 314–316; J. E. Hunter & F. L. Schmidt, *Methods of Meta-Analysis: Correcting Error and Bias in Research Findings* (Beverly Hills, CA: Sage, 1990).

[15] K. Brooker, "I Built This Company, I Can Save It," *Fortune*, 30 April 2001, 94.

[16] J. Simons, "Has Palm Lost Its Grip?" *Fortune*, 28 May 2001, 105.

[17] J. Creswell, "Would You Give This Man Your Company?" *Fortune*, 28 May 2001, 127.

[18] Staff Reporter, "Entrepreneur Mary Kay Ash: Unflagging Faith Lifted Her to Top of Cosmetics World," *Investor's Business Daily*, 5 May 1998, A1.

[19] A. Farnham, "Mary Kay's Lessons in Leadership," *Fortune*, 20 September 1993, 68–77.

[20] G. Colvin. "The Changing Art of Becoming Unbeatable" *Fortune*, 24 November 1997, 299–300.

[21] K. Brooker, "The Chairman of the Board Looks Back," *Fortune*, 28 May 2001, 63; K. Labich, "Is Herb Kelleher America's Best CEO?" *Fortune*, 2 May 1994, 44–52.

[22] H. S. Jonas III, R. E. Fry, & S. Srivastva, "The Office of the CEO: Understanding the Executive Experience," *Academy of Management Executive* 4 (1990): 36–47.

[23] D. Woodruff, "Europe Shows More CEOs the Door," *The Wall Street Journal*, 1 July 2002.

[24] S. Carey, "Carrier Makes Deeper Cuts As It Seeks Federal Backing Needed to Exit Chapter 11," *The Wall Street Journal*, 27 November 2002, A3; S. Carey, "UAL Will Lay Off 1,500 Workers As Part of Cost-Cutting Strategy," *The Wall Street Journal*, 6 January 2003, A3; D. Carty, "Oral Testimony of Mr. Donald J. Carty, Chairman and CEO, American Airlines: United States Senate, Committee on Commerce, Science, and Transportation," [Online] available at http://www.amrcorp.com/speeches/ 010903_senate.htm, 9 January 2003; S. McCartney, M. Trottman, & S. Carey, "Northwest, Continental, America West Post Losses As Delta Cuts Jobs," *The Wall Street Journal*, 18 November 2002, B4.

[25] Jonas III, Fry, & Srivastva, "The Office of the CEO."

[26] Q. Huy, "In Praise of Middle Managers," *Harvard Business Review*, September 2001, 72–79.

[27] J. Bailey, "Entrepreneurs Share Their Tips to Boost a Firm's Productivity," *The Wall Street Journal*, 9 July 2002, B4.

[28] S. Warren, "The Transient Workers," *The Wall Street Journal*, 28 October 2002, R4.

[29] Ibid.

[30] Tully, "What Team Leaders Need to Know," *Fortune*, 20 February 1995, 93.

[31] Tully, "What Team Leaders Need to Know."

[32] Ibid.

[33] K. Hultman, "The 10 Commandments of Team Leadership," *Training & Development*, 1 February 1998, 12–13.

[34] "What Makes Teams Work?" *Fast Company*, 1 November 2000, 109.

[35] "What Makes Teams Work?"

[36] J. S. Case, "What the Experts Forgot to Mention," *Inc.*, 1 September 1993, 66.

[37] Tully, "What Team Leaders Need to Know."

[38] H. Mintzberg, *The Nature of Managerial Work* (New York: Harper & Row, 1973).

[39] C. P. Hales, "What Do Managers Do? A Critical Review of the Evidence," *Journal of Management Studies* 23, no. 1 (1986): 88–115.

[40] "Grand Opening of Kikkoman Foods Europe," Kikkoman Corporation, [Online] available at http://www.kikkoman.com/contents/news/news15.html, 26 January 2003.

[41] "CDW Named One of the Best Companies to Work for in America for Fourth Consecutive Year," CDW Corporation, [Online] available at http://www.cdw.com/webcontent/inside/press/2002/press0123.asp, 26 January 2003.

[42] M. Murray, "As Huge Firms Keep Growing, CEOs Struggle to Keep Pace," *The Wall Street Journal*, 8 February 2001, A1.

[43] K. Hutchison, "Sears Sets Initiatives to Boost Bottom Line," *Retailing Today*, 21 May 2001, 1.

[44] M. Rose, "Cost Cuts, Other Shocks Lift Profits but Sap Morale at *Reader's Digest*," *The Wall Street Journal*, 18 April 2000.

[45] P. Sellers, "Who's In Charge Here?" *Fortune*, 24 December 2001, 76.

[46] N. Shirouzu, "Ford CEO Promises Faster Cuts in Costs, Results above Forecasts," *The Wall Street Journal*, 13 January 2003, C7.

[47] L. A. Hill, *Becoming a Manager: Mastery of a New Identity* (Boston: Harvard Business School Press, 1992).

[48] R. L. Katz, "Skills of an Effective Administrator," *Harvard Business Review*, September–October 1974, 90–102.

[49] B. Schlender, "The Beast Is Back," *Fortune*, 11 June 2001, 75.

[50] C. A. Bartlett & S. Ghoshal, "Changing the Role of Top Management: Beyond Systems to People," *Harvard Business Review*, May–June 1995, 132–142.

[51] F. L. Schmidt & J. E. Hunter, "Development of a Causal Model of Process Determining Job Performance," *Current Directions in Psychological Science* 1 (1992): 89–92.

[52] J. B. Miner, "Sentence Completion Measures in Personnel Research: The Development and Validation of the Miner Sentence Completion Scales," in *Personality Assessment in Organizations*, ed. H. J. Bernardin & D. A. Bownas (New York: Praeger, 1986), 147–146.

[53] M. W. McCall, Jr. & M. M. Lombardo, "What Makes a Top Executive?" *Psychology Today*, February 1983, 26–31; E. van Velsor & J. Brittain, "Why Executives Derail: Perspectives across Time and Cultures," *Academy of Management Executive*, November 1995, 62–72.

[54] McCall, Jr. & Lombardo, "What Makes a Top Executive?"

[55] S. Stecklow, "Chief Prerequisite for College President's Job: Stamina," *The Wall Street Journal*, 1 December 1994, B1.

[56] J. Pfeffer, *The Human Equation: Building Profits by Putting People First* (Boston: Harvard Business School Press, 1996); *Competitive Advantage through People: Unleashing the Power of the Work Force* (Boston: Harvard Business School Press, 1994).

[57] M. A. Huselid, "The Impact of Human Resource Management Practices on Turnover, Productivity, and Corporate Financial Performance," *Academy of Management Journal* 38 (1995): 635–672.

[58] D. McDonald & A. Smith, "A Proven Connection: Performance Management and Business Results," *Compensation & Benefits Review* 27, no. 6 (1 January 1995): 59.

[59] B. Schneider & D. E. Bowen, "Employee and Customer Perceptions of Service in Banks: Replication and Extension," *Journal of Applied Psychology* 70 (1985): 423–433; B. Schneider, J. J. Parkington, & V. M. Buxton, "Employee and Customer Perceptions of Service in Banks," *Administrative Science Quarterly* 25 (1980): 252–267.

[60] A. Fisher, "From Stud to Dud—In Just One Promotion," *Fortune*, 2 April 2000, 188.

[61] Hill, *Becoming a Manager.*

CHAPTER 2

[1] S. Leung, "Jaded by Fatty Burgers, Fries, Diners Are Spurning Chains: A Big Yawn for Price Cuts," *The Wall Street Journal*, 11 November 2002; S. Leung, "McHaute Cuisine: Armchairs, TVs, and Espresso—Is It McDonald's?—Burger Giant's Makeover in France Boosts Sales; Big Change for Fast Food—Some Franchisees Have a Beef," *The Wall Street Journal*, 30 August 2002, A1; S. Leung & K. Helliker, "As McDonald's Braces for Loss, CEO Has a Plan," *The Wall Street Journal*, 20 January 2003, B1; S. Leung & S. Vranica, "Happy Meals Are No Longer Bringing Smiles at McDonald's—Sales Have Fallen for Three Years; Chain Mulls Adding Mom's Meal, Carrot Sticks, Higher Quality Toys," *The Wall Street Journal*, 31 January 2003, B1; S. Leung & R. Lieber, "The New Menu Option at McDonald's: Plastic—Fast-Food Giant Will Allow Customers to Use Credit Cards; Earning Miles with Your Fries," *The Wall Street Journal*, 26 November 2002, D1; R. Morais, "The Bigger Easy; Stelios Haji-Ioannou Wants You to Surf the Web at McDonald's," *Forbes*, 23 December 2002, 28; R. Parloff, "Is Fat the Next Tobacco?" *Fortune*, 3 February 2003, 50; P. Raeburn, J. Forster, D. Foust, & D. Brady, "Why We're So Fat: Fast Food at School, Huge Portions, and Relentless TV Ads Make It Easy," *BusinessWeek*, 21 October 2002, 112; D. Stires, "Fast Food, Slow Service," *Fortune*, 30 September 2002, 38.

[2] E. Souder, "German Floods Prompt Longer Shop Hrs but Lines Are Short," *Dow Jones News Wires*, 4 September 2002.

[3] J. Apperson, "Liquor Retailer Protests Md. Law Store, Says Banning Bulk-Discount Buys Is Antitrust Violation," *Baltimore Sun*, 3 July 2000, 1A.

[4] E. Romanelli & M. L. Tushman, "Organizational Transformation as Punctuated Equilibrium: An Empirical Test," *Academy of Management Journal* 37 (1994): 1141–1166.

[5] H. Banks, "A Sixties Industry in a Nineties Economy," *Forbes*, 9 May 1994, 107–112.

[6] L. Cowan, "Cheap Fuel Should Carry Many Airlines to More Record Profits for 1st Quarter," *The Wall Street Journal*, 4 April 1998, B17A.

[7] S. Carey, "Carrier Makes Deeper Cuts As It Seeks Federal Backing Needed to Exit Chapter 11," *The Wall Street Journal*, 27 November 2002, A3; S. Carey, "UAL Will Lay Off 1,500 Workers As Part of Cost-Cutting Strategy," *The Wall Street Journal*, 6 January 2003, A3; D. Carty, "Oral Testimony of Mr. Donald J. Carty, Chairman and CEO, American Airlines: United States Senate, Committee on Commerce, Science, and Transportation," [Online] available at http://www.amrcorp.com/speeches/010903_senate.htm, 9 January 2003; S. McCartney, M. Trottman, & S. Carey, "Northwest, Continental,

America West Post Losses As Delta Cuts Jobs," *The Wall Street Journal*, 18 November 2002, B4.

[8] N. Deogun & J. Eig, "Kellogg Sets Deal to Buy Keebler for $3.7 Billion in Cash Plus Debt," *Dow Jones Business News*, 26 October 2000.

[9] G. Pacyniak, "Segmentation Hits Ever-Expanding Category (Snack Bars), *Candy Industry*, 1 November 2002, 41.

[10] J. Mason, "Healthy Food Is Eaten on the Run," *Financial Times*, 19 September 2001.

[11] J. B. White & J. S. Lublin, "Some Concerns Try to Rebuild Loyalty among Employees," *The Wall Street Journal Interactive Edition*, 27 September 1996.

[12] K. A. Dolan, "Help Wanted: Urgent!" *Forbes*, 7 October 1996, 18–20.

[13] J. Hilsenrath, "Job Market Slump Is Expected to Remain Grim in Near Term," *The Wall Street Journal Online*, [Online] available at http://online.wsj.com/article/0,,SB1042205234359553224,00.html, 13 January 2003.

[14] "We Know Where Your Friends Are," Cisco. [Online] available at http://www.cisco.com/jobs/friends/, 6 February 2003; M. Conlin, M. Mandel, M. Ardnt, & W. Zeller, "Suddenly, It's the Big Freeze: As the Economy Cools, the Hiring Door Slams Shut on Job Seekers," *BusinessWeek*, 16 April 2001, 38.

[15] B. Powell & C. Kano, "Monster Problems: Japan Is Getting Pretty Scary. So Is the U.S. in for a Fright?" *Fortune*, 2 April 2001, 82.

[16] S. Moffett, "Asian Economic Outlook—Japan: Steady Decline," *Far Eastern Economic Review*, 13 February 2003.

[17] R. Norton, "Where Is This Economy Really Heading?" *Fortune*, 7 August 1995, 54–56.

[18] "First, By the Numbers, the CFO Poll," *Fortune*, 17 February 2003, 30.

[19] J. Hearn & D. Lewis, "Keyboarding Course Work and Employment, Earnings, and Educational Attainment," *Journal of Education for Business* 68 (1993): 147; C. Meares & J. Sargent, Jr., "The Digital Work Force: Building Infotech Skills at the Speed of Innovation," U.S. Department of Commerce, Technology Administration, Office of Technology Policy, [Online] available at http://www.ta.doc.gov/reports/itsw/Digital.pdf, 23 June 2001.

[20] C. Mann, "The Year the Music Dies," *Wired*, February 2003, [Online] available at http://www.wired.com/wired/archive/11.02/ dirge_pr.html, 8 February 2003; T. Woody, "The Race to Kill Kazaa," *Wired*, February 2003, [Online] available at http://www.wired.com/wired/archive/11.02/ kazaa_pr.html, 8 February 2003.

[21] "CDW Ranks on Best Places to Work List for Fifth Straight Year," *PR Newswire*, 7 January 2003.

[22] M. Perotin, "Dallas-Based Baylor Health Care Offers Concierge Perk to Employees," *Fort Worth Star-Telegram*, 8 December 2002.

[23] R. Sharpe, "Nannies on Speed Dial: There Is Growing Army of Domestic Help Out There, and More and More Families Are Picking Up the Phone," *BusinessWeek*, 18 September 2000, 108.

[24] "The Civil Rights Act of 1991," U.S. Equal Employment Opportunity Commission, [Online] available at http://www.eeoc.gov/laws/cra91.html, 8 February 2003.

[25] "Compliance Assistance—Family and Medical Leave Act (FMLA)," U.S. Department of Labor: Employment Standards Administration Wage and Hour Division, [Online] available at http://www.dol.gov/esa/whd/fmla/, 8 February 2003.

[26] A. Caffrey, "Bay State's Enforcement of 'Rideshare' Draws Fire," *The Wall Street Journal*, 18 March 1998, NE1.

[27] R. J. Bies & T. R. Tyler, "The Litigation Mentality in Organizations: A Test of Alternative Psychological Explanations," *Organization Science* 4 (1993): 352–366.

[28] D. Jones, "Fired Workers Fight Back . . . and Win: Laws, Juries Shift Protection to Terminated Employees," *USA Today*, 2 April 1998, B1.

[29] S. Gardner, G. Gomes, & J. Morgan, "Wrongful Termination and the Expanding Public Policy Exception: Implications and Advice," *SAM Advanced Management Journal* 65 (2000): 38.

[30] Jones, "Fired Workers Fight Back."

[31] D. Smart & C. Martin, "Manufacturer Responsiveness to Consumer Correspondence: An Empirical Investigation of Consumer Perceptions," *Journal of Consumer Affairs* 26 (1992): 104.

[32] "What's New in Cotton," *Lifestyle Monitor, Cotton Inc.*, [Online] available at http://www.cottoninc.com/lifemon2a.htm, 4 October 1996.

[33] "Forever in Blue Jeans," *Lifestyle Monitor, Cotton Inc.*, [Online] available at http://www.cottoninc.com/wwd/homepage.cfm?PAGE=2677, 22 February 2001.

[34] S. G. Maycumber, "Cotton Inc.'s Lifestyle Monitor Puts Together a Year's Data; Price Looms Large in Apparel Purchases," *Daily News Record*, 4 January 1996, 11.

[35] L. Fuld, "Chapter 1: Understanding Intelligence," *CI Strategies & Tools: The New Competitor Intelligence*, [Online] available at http://www.fuld.com/chap1.html, 15 February 2003.

[36] S. A. Zahra & S. S. Chaples, "Blind Spots in Competitive Analysis," *Academy of Management Executive* 7 (1993): 7–28.

[37] Bianco & P. Moore, "Downfall: The Inside Story of the Management Fiasco at Xerox," *Business Week*, 5 March 2001, 82.

[38] J. M. Moran, "Getting Closer Together—Videophones Don't Deliver TV Quality Sound, Visuals, but They're Improving," *Seattle Times*, 15 March 1998.

[39] F. McCarthy, "The Shape of Phones to Come: Report: Telecommunications: Starting as a Hobbyist Movement Five Years Ago, 'Voice over Internet Protocol' Is Quietly Remaking the Telephone System Worldwide," *The Economist*, 23 March 2001, [Online].

[40] J. Fowler, "Long-Distance Calls Via Internet Shakeup Global Industry," *Associated Press Newswires*, 6 March 2001.

[41] T. Shurley, "Internet Phone System Could Revolutionize Long Distance," *Springfield Business Journal*, 29 May 1995.

[42] K. G. Provan, "Embeddedness, Interdependence, and Opportunism in Organizational Supplier-Buyer Networks," *Journal of Management* 19 (1993): 841–856.

[43] N. Gaouette, "Israel's Diamond Dealers Tremble: Diamond Colossus Debeers Today Launches Fundamental Changes to $56 Billion Retail Market," *Christian Science Monitor*, 1 June 2001, [Online].

[44] L. Kroll, "Tough Guy; How Leonardo Del Vecchio Built and Bullied His Way to Total Domination in the Eyeglasses Business," *Forbes*, 4 February 2002, 60.

[45] D. Birch, "Staying on Good Terms," *Supply Management*, 12 April 2001, 36.

[46] B. K. Pilling, L. A. Crosby, & D. W. Jackson, "Relational Bonds in Industrial Exchange: An Experimental Test of the Transaction Cost Economic Framework," *Journal of Business Research* 30 (1994): 237–251.

[47] "Seafood HACCP," U.S. Food and Drug Administration Center for Food Safety & Applied Nutrition, [Online] available at http://www.cfsan.fda.gov/~comm/haccpsea.html, 11 February 2003.

[48] S. Dudley, "The Coming Shift in Regulation," *Regulation*, 1 October 2002.

[49] H. Morley, "Bush Orders Cut in Regulations—Change Will Cut Red Tape for Small Businesses," *Knight-Ridder Tribune*, 17 August 2002.

[50] "Sports Stars Team Up to Defeat Tobacco Use and Secondhand Smoke," *PR Newswire*, 22 May 2001.

[51] B. Sizemore, "Peta: Lean and Mean Norfolk-Based Group's Zeal Pushes the Envelope Too Far for Some," *The Virginian-Pilot*, 3 December 2000, A1.

[52] "Staples Victory!" Ecopledge.com, [Online] available at http://ecopledge.com/ecotargets.asp?id2=8455&id3=ecotargets&id4=ECCT&, 11 February 2003.

[53] L. Holson, "In California, Blackouts Spur a Search for Home Remedies," *New York Times*, 31 May 2001, 1.

[54] D. F. Jennings & J. R. Lumpkin, "Insights between Environmental Scanning Activities and Porter's Generic Strategies: An Empirical Analysis," *Journal of Management* 4 (1992): 791–803.

[55] B. Ettore, "Managing Competitive Intelligence," *Management Review*, October 1995, 15–19.

[56] S. E. Jackson & J. E. Dutton, "Discerning Threats and Opportunities," *Administrative Science Quarterly* 33 (1988): 370–387.

[57] B. Thomas, S. M. Clark, & D. A. Gioia, "Strategic Sensemaking and Organizational Performance: Linkages among Scanning, Interpretation, Action, and Outcomes," *Academy of Management Journal* 36 (1993): 239–270.

[58] R. Daft, J. Sormunen, & D. Parks, "Chief Executive Scanning, Environmental Characteristics, and Company Performance: An Empirical Study," *Strategic Management Journal* 9 (1988): 123–139; D. Miller & P. H. Friesen, "Strategy-Making and Environment: The Third Link," *Strategic Management Journal* 4 (1983): 221–235.

[59] S. Kraft, "Tradition under Siege Supermarkets? Sacre Bleu! A Shopping Revolution Imperils French Merchants," *Los Angeles Times*, 5 May 1996, D10.

[60] S. Branch & E. Beck, "For Unilever, It's Sweetness and Light—Company Buys Ben & Jerry's, Famed Ice-Cream Maker, And Slim-Fast on Same Day," *The Wall Street Journal*, 13 April 2000, B1.

[61] C. Fishman, "Sanity Inc.: SAS Institute Inc. Is the Most Important Software Company You've Never Heard Of. It's Also the Sanest Company in America—A Place Where Employees Can Eat Lunch with Their Kids, Everyone Gets Unlimited Sick Days, and the Gate Clangs Shut at 6 P.M.," *Fast Company*, 1 January 1999, 84.

[62] Fishman, "Sanity, Inc."

[63] D. M. Boje, "The Storytelling Organization: A Study of Story Performance in an Office-Supply Firm," *Administrative Science Quarterly* 36 (1991): 106–126.

[64] S. Walton & J. Huey, *Sam Walton: Made in America* (New York: Doubleday, 1992).

[65] D. Rushe, "Wal-martians," *Sunday Times–London*, 10 June 2001, 5.

[66] L. McCauley, "How May I Help You? Unit of One," *Fast Company*, 1 March 2000, 93.

[67] D. R. Denison & A. K. Mishra, "Toward a Theory of Organizational Culture and Effectiveness," *Organization Science* 6 (1995): 204–223.

[68] Fishman, "Sanity, Inc."

[69] "Company Profile," F. H. Faulding & Company, [Online] available at http://www.faulding.com.au/home/comp_profile/mission/mission.html, 21 June 2001.

[70] S. Yearout, G. Miles, & R. Koonce, "Multi-Level Visioning," *Training & Development*, 1 March 2001, 31.

[71] T. Brown, "A Vision from Scratch," *Across the Board*, 1 May 2001, 77.

[72] E. Schein, *Organizational Culture and Leadership*, 2nd ed. (San Francisco: Jossey-Bass, 1992).

[73] S. Albert & D. A. Whetten, "Organizational Identity," *Research in Organizational Behavior* 7 (1985): 263–295; C. M. Fiol, "Managing Culture as a Competitive Resource: An Identity-Based View of Sustainable Competitive Advantage," *Journal of Management* 17 (1991): 191–211.

[74] "Continental Airlines Reports Operational Performance for 2002 and December 2002," YahooFinance, [Online] available at http://biz.yahoo.com/prnews/030102/dath018_1.html, 3 January 2002.

[75] J. Huey (with G. Bethune and H. Kelleher), "Outlaw Flyboy CEOs: Two Texas Mavericks Rant about the Wreckage of the U.S. Aviation Industry—And Reveal How They've Managed to Keep Their Companies above the Miserable Average," *Fortune*, 13 November 2000, 237.

[76] C. Daniels, "Does This Man Need a Shrink? Companies Are Using Psychological Testing to Screen Candidates for Top Jobs. But Should a Shrink Determine Your Professional Future?" *Fortune*, 5 February 2001, 205.

[77] S. Chakravarty, "Hit 'Em Hardest with the Mostest. (Southwest Airlines' Management)," *Forbes*, 16 September 1991, 48.

[78] R. Suskind, "Humor Has Returned to Southwest Airlines After 9/11 Hiatus—Flight Attendants Try Hard to Amuse the Passengers; Ms. LeMaster's Shtick," *The Wall Street Journal*, 13 January 2003, A1.

[79] Ibid.

[80] K. Godsey, "Slow Climb to New Heights; Combine Strict Discipline with Goofy Antics and Make Billions," *Success*, 1 October 1996, 20.

[81] A. Welch Bill, "Changes in Store: Developers Are Looking to Revitalize Malls That Have Been Leapfrogged by Development and Retail Trends," *Florida Trend*, November 2002, 30; L. Flynn, "Retail Village: Developers Combine Elements of Enclosed and Open-Air Malls to Form Hybrid Centers That Fit Customer Lifestyles," *Building Design & Construction*, February 2002, 22; "Seven New Restaurants and Retailers Open at Hollywood & Highland," *PR Newswire*, 8 August 2002; J. T. Slania, "Revived Malls Play New Role," *Crain's Chicago Business*, 23 September 2002, SR5; D. Starkman, "Retail Riddle: Is Shopping Entertainment?" *The Wall Street Journal*, 22 January 2003, B1+; A. York, "Staying in Style: Once the Best-Dressed Mall in Town, Kenwood Could Be In for a Makeover," *Cincinnati Business Courier*, 31 January 2003, 1.

[82] P. Flanagan, "Ten Public Relations Pitfalls," *Management Review*, October 1995, 45–48; D. Gellene, "Sears Drops Car Repair Incentives: The Company Says 'Mistakes Have Been Made' in Its Aggressive Commission Program," *Los Angeles Times*, 23 June 1992, 1; P. Hertneky, "Mastering the Media: Press Handling for Restaurant Managers," *Restaurant Hospitality*, June 1995, 59–69; B. Horowitz, "Intel Needs Damage Control," *USA Today*, 13 December 1994; L. Koss-Feder, "Crisis Brings Media Scrutiny," *Hotel & Motel Management*, 14 August 1995, 5; "How to Get Your CEO in Print or in Front of TV Cameras in the Right Light," *PR News*, 21 April 1997.

[83] C. Crowell, "Seeing the Big Picture through Software (Manufacturing Resource Planning Computer Programs)," *American Metal Market*, 22 July 1997, 12.

CHAPTER 3

[1] "History" and "Our Company," Rite Aid, [Online] available at http://www.riteaid.com/company_info/history.php, 25 March 2003; R. Berner & M. Maremont, "Lost Heir: As Rite Aid Grew, CEO Seemed Unable to Manage His Empire—Downfall Is a Complex Tale of a Family, a Board and, Finally, the Bankers," *The Wall Street Journal*, 20 October 1999, A1; J. Distefano, "Rite Aid Ex-Chief Charged in Fraud," *Philadelphia Inquirer*, 22 June 2002, A1; P. Dwyer, D. Carney, A. Borrus, L. Woellert, & C. Palmeri, "Year of the Whistleblower: The Personal Costs Are High, but a New Law Protects Truth-Tellers As Never Before," *BusinessWeek*, 16 December 2002, 106; M. Maremont, "Lawsuit Details Rite Aid's Accounting Woes," *The Wall Street Journal*, 8 February 2001, C1.

[2] A. Losciale, "Survey Finds More Than 75% of Workers Say They Have Seen Unethical Conduct," *Salt Lake Tribune*, 27 May 2000, C2.

[3] C. Smith, "The Ethical Workplace," *Association Management* 52 (2000): 70–73.

[4] D. Jones, "More Workers Do Now Than Before Recent Big Scandals," *USA Today*, 12 February 2003, B7.

[5] K. Kranhold & M. Schroeder, "Enron's Directors Knew of Problems, Senate Report Says," *The Wall Street Journal*, 8 July 2002, A3.

[6] M. Maremont, "Blind Ambition: How the Pursuit of Results Got Out of Hand at Bausch & Lomb," *BusinessWeek*, 23 October 1995.

[7] M. Bordwin, "Don't Ask Employees to Do Your Dirty Work," *Management Review*, 1 October 1995.

[8] M. Schweitzer & L. Ordonez, "The Dark Side of Goal Setting: The Role of Goals in Motivating Unethical Decision Making," *Academy of Management Proceedings* (2002), B1; Y. Dreazen, "Pressure for Sales Fostered Abuses at WorldCom," *The Wall Street Journal*, 16 May 2002, B1.

[9] D. Palmer & A. Zakhem, "Bridging the Gap between Theory and Practice: Using the 1991 Federal Sentencing Guidelines as a Paradigm for Ethics Training," *Journal of Business Ethics* 29, no. 1/2 (2001): 77–84.

[10] D. R. Dalton, M. B. Metzger, & J. W. Hill, "The 'New' U.S. Sentencing Commission Guidelines: A Wake-Up Call for Corporate America," *Academy of Management Executive* 8 (1994): 7–16.

[11] B. Ettore, "Crime and Punishment: A Hard Look at White-Collar Crime," *Management Review* 83 (1994): 10–16.

[12] F. Robinson & C. C. Pauze, "What Is a Board's Liability for Not Adopting a Compliance Program?" *Healthcare Financial Management* 51, no. 9 (1997): 64.

[13] D. Murphy, "The Federal Sentencing Guidelines for Organizations: A Decade of Promoting Compliance and Ethics," *Iowa Law Review* 87 (2002): 697–719.

[14] Robinson & Pauze, "What Is a Board's Liability?"

[15] L. A. Hays, "A Matter of Time: Widow Sues IBM over Death Benefits," *The Wall Street Journal*, 6 July 1995.

[16] T. M. Jones, "Ethical Decision Making by Individuals in Organizations: An Issue-Contingent Model," *Academy of Management Review* 16 (1991): 366–395.

[17] S. Sparks, "Federal Agents Seize Computers in 27 Cities As Part of Crackdown on Software Piracy," *The Wall Street Journal*, 12 December 2001, B4.

[18] L. Kohlberg, "Stage and Sequence: The Cognitive-Developmental Approach to Socialization," in *Handbook of Socialization Theory and Research*, ed. D. A. Goslin (Chicago: Rand McNally, 1969); L. Trevino, "Moral Reasoning and Business Ethics: Implications for Research, Education, and Management," *Journal of Business Ethics* 11 (1992): 445–459.

[19] J. L. Badaracco, Jr. & A. P. Webb, "Business Ethics: A View from the Trenches," *California Management Review* 37 (1995): 8–28.

[20] M. R. Cunningham, D. T. Wong, & A. P. Barbee, "Self-Presentation Dynamics on Overt Integrity Tests: Experimental Studies of the Reid Report," *Journal of Applied Psychology* 79 (1994): 643–658.

[21] H. J. Bernardin, "Validity of an Honest Test in Predicting Theft among Convenience Store Employees," *Academy of Management Journal* 36 (1993): 1097–1108.

[22] J. M. Collins & F. L. Schmidt, "Personality, Integrity, and White Collar Crime: A Construct Validity Study," *Personnel Psychology* (1993): 295–311.

[23] W. C. Borman, M. A. Hanson, & J. W. Hedge, "Personnel Selection," *Annual Review of Psychology* 48 (1997).

[24] G. Weaver, L. Trevino, & P. Cochran, "Corporate Ethics Programs as Control Systems: Influences of Executive Commitment and Environmental Factors," *Academy of Management Journal* 42 (1999): 41–57.

[25] P. E. Murphy, "Corporate Ethics Statements: Current Status and Future Prospects," *Journal of Business Ethics* 14 (1995): 727–740.

[26] G. Alliger & S. Dwight, "A Meta-Analytic Investigation of the Susceptibility of Integrity Tests to Faking and Coaching," *Educational and Psychological Measurement* 60 (2000): 59–72; D. S. Ones, C. Viswesvaran, & F. L. Schmidt, "Comprehensive Meta-Analysis of Integrity Test Validities: Findings and Implications for Personnel Selection and Theories of Job Performance," *Journal of Applied Psychology* 78 (1993): 679–703.

[27] S. J. Harrington, "What Corporate America Is Teaching about Ethics," *Academy of Management Executive* 5 (1991): 21–30.

[28] L. A. Berger, "Train All Employees to Solve Ethical Dilemmas," *Best's Review—Life-Health Insurance Edition* 95 (1995): 70–80.

[29] L. Trevino, G. Weaver, D. Gibson, & B. Toffler, "Managing Ethics and Legal Compliance: What Works and What Hurts," *California Management Review* 41, no. 2 (1999): 131–151.

[30] "Business Ethics Training: Teaching Right from Wrong," *Salt Lake Tribune*, 11 June 2000, E5.

[31] Trevino, Weaver, Gibson, & Toffler, "Managing Ethics."

[32] "Dilemma Database: Right vs. Right," Institute for Global Ethics, [Online] available at http://www.globalethics.org/dilemmas/default.tmpl, 23 March 2003.

[33] G. Weaver & L. Trevino, "Integrated and Decoupled Corporate Social Performance: Management Commitments, External Pressures, and Corporate Ethics Practices," *Academy of Management Journal* 42 (1999): 539–552; Weaver, Trevino, & Cochran, "Corporate Ethics Programs as Control Systems."

[34] J. Salopek, "Do the Right Thing," *Training & Development* 55 (July 2001): 38–44.

[35] M. Gundlach, S. Douglas, & M. Martinko, "The Decision to Blow the Whistle: A Social Information Processing Framework," *Academy of Management Executive* 17 (2003): 107–123.

[36] M. Schwartz, "Business Ethics: Time to Blow the Whistle?" *Globe and Mail*, 5 March 1998, B2.

[37] M. P. Miceli & J. P. Near, "Whistleblowing: Reaping the Benefits," *Academy of Management Executive* 8 (1994): 65–72.

[38] H. R. Bower, *Social Responsibilities of the Businessman* (New York: Harper & Row, 1953).

[39] "Product Safety Testing and P&G," Proctor & Gamble, [Online] available at http://www.pg.com/about_pg/science_tech/animal_alternatives/prod_safety.jhtml;jsessionid=ZXIHT3MEB0JR1QFIAJ1CZOWAVABHOLHC, 22 March 2003.

[40] Ibid.

[41] B. Carton, "Animal Instincts: Gillette Faces Wrath of Children in Testing on Rats and Rabbits," *The Wall Street Journal,* 5 September 1995.

[42] "What Others Say," Proctor & Gamble, [Online] available at http://www.pg.com/about_pg/science_tech/animal_alternatives/ what_others_say.jhtml;jsessionid=11IIMBZOJSKDJQ FIAJ1CZOWAVABHOLHC, 21 March 2003.

[43] S. L. Wartick & P. L. Cochran, "The Evolution of the Corporate Social Performance Model," *Academy of Management Review* 10 (1985): 758–769.

[44] S. Waddock, C. Bodwell, & S. Graves. "Responsibility: The New Business Imperative," *Academy of Management Executive* 16 (2002): 132–148.

[45] T. Donaldson & L. E. Preston, "The Stakeholder Theory of the Corporation: Concepts, Evidence, and Implications," *Academy of Management Review* 20 (1995): 65–91.

[46] M. B. E. Clarkson, "A Stakeholder Framework for Analyzing and Evaluating Corporate Social Performance," *Academy of Management Review* 20 (1995): 92–117.

[47] B. Agle, R. Mitchell, & J. Sonnenfeld, "Who Matters to CEOs? An Investigation of Stakeholder Attributes and Salience, Corporate Performance, and CEO Values," *Academy of Management Journal* 42 (1999): 507–525.

[48] J. Carlton, "Home Builders Centex and Kaufman Agree Not to Buy Endangered Wood," *The Wall Street Journal,* 31 March 2000, A4.

[49] L. E. Preston, "Stakeholder Management and Corporate Performance," *Journal of Behavioral Economics* 19 (1990): 361–375.

[50] E. W. Orts, "Beyond Shareholders: Interpreting Corporate Constituency Statutes," *George Washington Law Review* 61 (1992): 14–135.

[51] A. B. Carroll, "A Three-Dimensional Conceptual Model of Corporate Performance," *Academy of Management Review* 4 (1979): 497–505.

[52] Ibid.

[53] J. Lublin & M. Murrary, "CEOs Leave Faster Than Ever Before as Boards, Investors Lose Patience," *The Wall Street Journal Interactive,* 27 October 2000.

[54] D. Woodruff, "Europe Shows More CEOs the Door," *The Wall Street Journal,* 1 July 2002.

[55] C. Bowman, "Success of Capital Area's War on Smog Challenged," *Sacramento Bee,* 7 February 1998, A1.

[56] B. Robertson, "Bakery Aromas Create Smog in Sacramento, Calif., EPA Says," *Sacramento Bee,* 22 February 2000.

[57] "Daily Results: Why Your Support Matters," The Hunger Site, [Online] available at http://www.thehungersite.com/cgi-bin/WebObjects/CTDSites.woa/234/wo/QW6000rC200Sh6003/1.39.0.1.0.9.0.CustomContentLinkDisplayComponent.0.0, 22 March 2003.

[58] S. Power & N. Shirouzu, "Bridgestone Position Angers Lawmakers—Firm Balks at Wider Recall of Tires, Setting Stage for House Showdown," *The Wall Street Journal,* 5 September 2000, A3.

[59] K. Kranhold & E. White, "The Perils and Potential Rewards of Crisis Managing for Firestone," *The Wall Street Journal,* 8 September 2000, B1.

[60] P. Romeo, "McDonald's Battles Critics with $160M Recycling Plan," *Nation's Restaurant News,* 30 April 1990, 18–19; S. Shundich, "Green in Green: Beyond the Three Rs: There's a Whole New Set of Expectations When Food Service Operations Talk about Profiting from Environmental Initiatives," *Restaurants & Institutions,* 15 September 1995.

[61] "McDonald's USA Earth Effort," McDonald's, [Online] available at http://www.mcdonalds.com/countries/usa/community/environ/index.html, 22 March 2003.

[62] A. McWilliams & D. Siegel, "Corporate Social Responsibility: A Theory of the Firm Perspective," *Academy of Management Review* 26, no.1 (2001): 117–127.

[63] H. Haines, "Noah Joins Ranks of Socially Responsible Funds," *Dow Jones News Service,* 13 October 1995.

[64] J. Seglin, "The Right Thing: When Good Ethics Aren't Good Business," *New York Times,* 18 March 2001, available online.

[65] B. Finley, "Critics of Starbucks: Gifts Don't Amount to a Hill of Beans," *Denver Post,* 17 April 1998, A23; M. Scott, "An Interview with Howard Schultz, CEO of Starbucks Coffee," *Business Ethics Magazine,* November/December 1995.

[66] M. Alexander, "Charity Begins at the Coffee Cup," *Sunday Star-Times,* 17 June 2001, E4; "The Rent-a-Car Jocks Who Made Enterprise #1," *Fortune,* 28 October 1996, 125.

[67] D. Kadlec & B. Van Voorst, "The New World of Giving: Companies Are Doing More Good, and Demanding More Back," *Time,* 5 May 1997, 62.

[68] P. Carlin, "Will Rapid Growth Stunt Corporate Do-Gooders?" *Business and Society Review,* Spring 1995, 36–43.

CHAPTER 4

[1] B. Elgin, J. Kerstetter, & L. Himelstein, "Why They're Agog over Google," *BusinessWeek,* 24 September 2001, 83–84; K. Hammonds, "Growth Search," *Fast Company,* April 2003, 74–81; A. Salkever, "Google's Gaggle of Problems," *BusinessWeek Online,* [Online] available at www.businessweek.com/technology/content/jan2003/tc20030114_2858.htm, 6 April 2003; K. Swisher, "Boom Town: Beneath Google's Dot-Com Shell, a Serious Player—Sure, There Are Lava Lamps, but Also a Growing Business in Selling Web-Search Services," *The Wall Street Journal,* 21 January 2002, B1; E. Welles, "All the Right Moves," *Fortune Small Business,* September 2002, 24–33.

[2] L. A. Hill, *Becoming a Manager: Master of a New Identity* (Boston: Harvard Business School Press, 1992).

[3] "Nissan's 1st-Half Profit Is Record Amid Cost Cutting, New Models," *Dow Jones Newswires,* 20 November 2002.

[4] N. Shirouzu, J. White, & T. Zaun, "U-Turn: A Revival at Nissan Shows There's Hope for Ailing Japan Inc.—Carlos Ghosn Is Overhauling Culture by Challenging Suppliers and Assumptions—Bringing Back the 'Z' Car," *The Wall Street Journal,* 16 November 2000, A1.

[5] E. A. Locke & G. P. Latham, *A Theory of Goal Setting & Task Performance* (Englewood Cliffs, NJ: Prentice Hall, 1990).

[6] M. E. Tubbs, "Goal-Setting: A Meta-Analytic Examination of the Empirical Evidence," *Journal of Applied Psychology* 71 (1986): 474–483.

[7] J. Bavelas & E. S. Lee, "Effect of Goal Level on Performance: A Trade-Off of Quantity and Quality," *Canadian Journal of Psychology* 32 (1978): 219–240.

[8] Harvard Management Update, "Learn by 'Failing Forward,'" *The Globe and Mail,* 31 October 2000, B17.

[9] C. C. Miller, "Strategic Planning and Firm Performance: A Synthesis of More Than Two Decades of Research," *Academy of Management Performance* 37 (1994): 1649–1665.

[10] H. Mintzberg, "Rethinking Strategic Planning," Part I: Pitfalls and Fallacies, *Long Range Planning* 27 (1994): 12–21; Part II: New Roles for Planners: 22–30; H. Mintzberg, "The Pitfalls of Strategic Planning," *California Management Review* 36 (1993): 32–47.

[11] Mintzberg, "The Pitfalls of Strategic Planning."

[12] W. Tam, "Pixar Posts 30% Rise in Profit; Disney Turning Point Looms," *The Wall Street Journal*, 7 February 2003, B3.

[13] Locke & Latham, *A Theory of Goal Setting & Task Performance.*

[14] A. King, B. Oliver, B. Sloop, & K. Vaverek, *Planning and Goal Setting for Improved Performance, Participant's Guide* (Cincinnati, OH: Thomson Executive Press, 1995).

[15] H. Klein & M. Wesson, "Goal and Commitment and the Goal-Setting Process: Conceptual Clarification and Empirical Synthesis," *Journal of Applied Psychology* 84 (1999): 885–896.

[16] Locke & Latham, *A Theory of Goal Setting & Task Performance.*

[17] P. Guthrie, R. A. Ash, & V. Bendapudi, "Additional Evidence for a Measure of Morning," *Journal of Applied Psychology* 80 (1995): 186–190.

[18] J. R. Hollenbeck, C. R. Williams, & H. J. Klein, "An Empirical Examination of the Antecedents of Commitment to Difficult Goals," *Journal of Applied Psychology* 74 (1989): 18–23.

[19] "Severn Sound Cleanup Cheered: Environmental Recovery of Vacationland 'Hot Spot' Emerged from Co-Operative Effort," *The Globe and Mail*, 16 August 2002, D11.

[20] A. Bandura & D. H. Schunk, "Cultivating Competence, Self-Efficacy, and Intrinsic Interest through Proximal Self-Motivation," *Journal of Personality and Social Psychology* 41 (1981): 586–598.

[21] Locke & Latham, *A Theory of Goal Setting & Task Performance.*

[22] M. J. Neubert, "The Value of Feedback and Goal Setting over Goal Setting Alone and Potential Moderators of This Effect: A Meta-Analysis," *Human Performance* 11 (1998): 321–335.

[23] E. H. Bowman & D. Hurry, "Strategy through the Option Lens: An Integrated View of Resource Investments and the Incremental-Choice Process," *Academy of Management Review* 18 (1993): 760–782.

[24] M. Lawson, "In Praise of Slack: Time Is of the Essence," *Academy of Management Executive* 15 (2000): 125–135.

[25] N. A. Wishart, J. J. Elam, & D. Robey, "Redrawing the Portrait of a Learning Organization: Inside Knight-Ridder, Inc.," *Academy of Management Executive* 10 (1996): 7–20.

[26] P. Callahan & K. Helliker, "Knight Ridder Loses Readers but Raises Rates for Advertisers—As Publisher's Profits Rise, Some Ad Buyers Fume or Switch to Other Media," *The Wall Street Journal*, 18 June 2001, A1.

[27] J. Madore, "If You're 18 to 34 and Reading This, Your Secret's Safe with Us. Many Young Adults Are Rejecting the Traditional," *Newsday*, 3 February 2003, A27.

[28] J. C. Collins & J. I. Porras, "Organizational Vision and Visionary Organizations," *California Management Review* (Fall 1991): 30–52.

[29] Ibid.

[30] Ibid.

[31] "NASA 2002 Vision & Mission," NASA, [Online] available at http://www.policy.nasa.gov/plmission.html, 1 April 2003.

[32] P. Prada, "Euro Disney's Net Income Climbs 64%," *The Wall Street Journal*, 17 November 2000, A17; P. Prada, "Ja, Ja, Americana's Fabulosa—In Europe, Theme Parks Draw Crowds with Thrill Rides, Burgers and Bugs Bunny," *The Wall Street Journal*, 21 June 2001, B1; S. Kraft, "Disney Magic Is Finally Starting to Work at French Theme Park," *Los Angeles Times*, 4 February 1996, Business 1.

[33] L. Iococca, with W. Novak, *Iococca* (New York: Bantam, 1984).

[34] E. Marlow & R. Schilhavy, "Expectation Issues in Management by Objectives Programs," *Industrial Management* 33, no. 4 (1991): 29.

[35] "WebMBO Teams with Deloitte & Touche to Deliver Innovative Web-Based 'Management-by-Objectives and Performance Management' Solutions," *PRNewswire*, 19 June 2001.

[36] "PlanetRx to Pare Staff, Move Headquarters to Reduce Expenses," *The Wall Street Journal*, 30 August 2000, B2.

[37] D. Morse, "A Policy Change at Gap Will Test Brotherly Ties," *The Wall Street Journal*, 11 April 2001, B1.

[38] L. Aron, "Cutting Corporate Travel Costs," *Across the Board* 37, no. 3 (2000): 28–31.

[39] N. Humphrey, "References a Tricky Issue for Both Sides," *Nashville Business Journal* 11 (8 May 1995): 1A.

[40] K. R. MacCrimmon, R. N. Taylor, & E. A. Locke, "Decision Making and Problem Solving," in *Handbook of Industrial and Organizational Psychology*, ed. M. D. Dunnette (Chicago: Rand McNally, 1976), 1397–1453.

[41] "Annual Earnings for AMAZON.COM INC.," *The Wall Street Journal*, [Online] available at http://online.wsj.com/tafkam/auth/ mds/companyresearch.cgi?route=BOEH&template=company- research&profile-name=Portfolio1&profile-version=3.0&profile-type=Portfolio&profile-format-action=include&profile-read-action= skip-read&profile-write-action=skip-write&p-sym=amzn&p-type= usstock&p-name=&section=annual-earnings&bb-fov-start-period=5&bb-fov-end-period=1&profile-end=Portfolio, 25 April 2003.

[42] MacCrimmon, Taylor, & Locke, "Decision Making and Problem Solving."

[43] G. Kress, "The Role of Interpretation in the Decision Process," *Industrial Management* 37 (1995): 10–14.

[44] D. Milbrank, "We Feel Your Pain, Congress Is Saying, with Real Empathy," *The Wall Street Journal*, 1 April 1996; S. Nelson, "Shays, Moran: Defend CAA," *Roll Call*, 30 September 2002.

[45] C. Metz, "The PC Buyer's Guide: Corporate PCs," *PC Magazine*, 3 December 2002, 126.

[46] J. Koblenz, "How a Car Earns a Best Buy," *Consumer's Digest*, 1 January 1993, 54.

[47] P. Djang, "Selecting Personal Computers," *Journal of Research on Computing in Education*, 25 (1993): 327.

[48] "European Cities Monitor," Cushman & Wakefield Healy & Baker, [Online] available at http://www.frankfurt.de/sixcms_upload/media/928/euroean_cities_monitor_cwhb_2002.pdf, 26 April 2003.

[49] B. Dumaine, "The Trouble with Teams," *Fortune*, 5 September 1994, 86–92.

[50] L. Pelled, K. Eisenhardt, & K. Xin, "Exploring the Black Box: An Analysis of Work Group Diversity, Conflict, and Performance," *Administrative Science Quarterly* 44, no. 1 (March 1, 1999): 1.

[51] D. Hunter, "How to Hire Great People at Web Speed," *Fast Company*, 1 January 2001.

[52] I. L. Janis, *Groupthink* (Boston: Houghton Mifflin, 1983).

[53] C. P. Neck & C. C. Manz, "From Groupthink to Teamthink: Toward the Creation of Constructive Thought Patterns in Self-Managing Work Teams," *Human Relations* 47 (1994): 929–952.

[54] G. Moorhead, R. Ference, & C. P. Neck, "Group Decision Fiascoes Continue: Space Shuttle Challenger and a Revised Framework," *Human Relations* 44 (1991): 539–550; J. Schwartz & M. L. Wald, "'Groupthink' Is 30 Years Old, and Still Going Strong," *New York Times*, 9 March 2003, 5.

[55] A. Mason, W. A. Hochwarter, & K. R. Thompson, "Conflict: An Important Dimension in Successful Management Teams," *Organizational Dynamics* 24 (1995): 20.

[56] S. Sherman, "Secrets of HP's 'Muddled' Team," *Fortune*, 18 March 1996, 116–120.

[57] C. Olofson, "So Many Decisions, So Little Time: What's Your Problem?" *Fast Company*, 1 October 1999, 62.

[58] R. Cosier & C. R. Schwenk, "Agreement and Thinking Alike: Ingredients for Poor Decisions," *Academy of Management Executive* 4 (1990): 69–74.

[59] Ibid.

[60] B. Breen, "BMW: Driven by Design," *Fast Company*, 1 September 2002, 123.

[61] K. Jenn & E. Mannix, "The Dynamic Nature of Conflict: A Longitudinal Study of Intragroup Conflict and Group Performance," *Academy of Management Journal*, 44, no. 2 (2001): 238–251; R. L. Priem, D. A. Harrison, & N. K. Muir, "Structured Conflict and Consensus Outcomes in Group Decision Making," *Journal of Management* 21 (1995): 691–710.

[62] A. Van De Ven & A. L. Delbecq, "Nominal versus Interacting Group Processes for Committee Decision Making Effectiveness," *Academy of Management Journal* 14 (1971): 203–212.

[63] A. R. Dennis & J. S. Valicich, "Group, Sub-Group, and Nominal Group Idea Generation: New Rules for a New Media?" *Journal of Management* 20 (1994): 723–736.

[64] C. R. Schwenk, "Effects of Devil's Advocacy and Dialectical Inquiry on Decision Making: A Meta-Analysis," *Organizational Behavior and Human Decision Performance* 47 (1990): 161–176; M. Orlitzky & R. Hirokawa, "TO ERR IS HUMAN, TO CORRECT FOR IT DIVINE: A Meta-Analysis of Research Testing the Functional Theory of Group Decision-Making Effectiveness, *Small Group Research* 32, no. 3 (June 2001): 313–341.

[65] S. G. Robelberg, J. L. Barnes-Farrell, & C. A. Lowe, "The Stepladder Technique: An Alternative Group Structure Facilitating Effective Group Decision Making," *Journal of Applied Psychology* 77 (1992): 730–737; S. G. Rogelberg & M. S. O'Connor, "Extending the Stepladder Technique: An Examination of the Self-Paced Stepladder Groups," *Group Dynamics: Theory, Research, and Practice* 2 (1998): 82–91.

[66] R. B. Gallupe, W. H. Cooper, M. L. Grise, & L. M. Bastianutti, "Blocking Electronic Brainstorms," *Journal of Applied Psychology* 79 (1994): 77–86.

[67] R. B. Gallupe & W. H. Cooper, "Brainstorming Electronically," *Sloan Management Review*, Fall 1993, 27–36.

[68] Ibid.

[69] G. Kay, "Effective Meetings through Electronic Brainstorming," *Management Quarterly* 35 (1995): 15.

[70] A. LaPlante, "90s Style Brainstorming," *Forbes ASAP*, 25 October 1993, 44.

[71] S. Shellenbarger, "Should Employers Set Limits on Cell Phone Use in Vehicles?" *The Wall Street Journal*, 18 July 2001, B1; "Survey Shows about 3 Percent of Drivers Are Using Cell Phones at Any Time," *The Wall Street Journal*, 24 July 2001, B1.

[72] Dwayne Hal Dean, "Associating the Corporation with a Charitable Event through Sponsorship: Measuring the Effects on Corporate Community Relations," *Journal of Advertising*, Winter 2002, 77; Dave Nelson, "Sponsorship or Selling Out?" *Fund Raising Management*, June 1998, 32; Amy Taylor, "Poverty: Lack of Income Kills Off Low Pay Unit," *Community Care*, February 20, 2003, 9.

[73] "20 Hot Job Tracks," *U.S. News & World Report*, 30 October 1995, 98–104; C. Boivie, "Planning for the Future . . . Your Future," *Journal of Systems Management* 44 (1993): 25–27; J. Connelly, "How to Choose Your Next Career," *Fortune*, 6 February 1995, 145–146; P. Sherrid, "A 12-Hour Test of My Personality," *U.S. News & World Report*, 31 October 1994, 109.

CHAPTER 5

[1] B. Briggs, "Fighting Medical Errors on a Binary Battlefield," *Health Data Management*, 30 September 2002, 64; "Cerner Client Wins Prestigious Enterprise Value Award," *PRNewswire*, 3 February 2003; C. Koch, "Off the Charts," *CIO*, 1 February 2003, 46; L. Landro, "Health Care Goes Digital: Doctors and Hospitals Find They Can't Stay Offline Any Longer," *The Wall Street Journal*, 10 June 2002, R6; L. Landro, "Who Leads the Online Race: A Look at the Hospitals That Are Out in Front in the Drive to Bring Information Technology to Health Care," *The Wall Street Journal*, 10 June 2002, R7; "Fact Sheet: Computer Physician Order Entry," The LeapFrog Group, [Online] available at http://www.leapfroggroup.org/FactSheets/CPOE_FactSheet.pdf, 24 April 2003.

[2] R. Lenzner, "The Reluctant Entrepreneur," *Forbes*, 11 September 1995, 162–166.

[3] "Telecommunications Reports," *Telecommunications Reports International, Inc.*, 1 April 2003; N. Wingfield, "The Best Way to Surf at Top Speed—Rival Internet Services Step Up Broadband Deals; Does Cable Beat DSL?" *The Wall Street Journal*, 1 April 2003.

[4] J. Laing, "Get Wired: Why Cable Will Beat the Bells in the Race to Wire Your Home," *Barron's*, 20 August 2001, 23.

[5] R. D. Buzzell & B. T. Gale, *The PIMS Principles: Linking Strategy to Performance* (New York: Free Press, 1987); M. Lambkin, "Order of Entry and Performance in New Markets," *Strategic Management Journal* 9 (1988): 127–140.

[6] G. L. Urban, T. Carter, S. Gaskin, & Z. Mucha, "Market Share Rewards to Pioneering Brands: An Empirical Analysis and Strategic Implications," *Management Science* 32 (1986): 645–659.

[7] M. Garry & S. Mulholland, "Master of Its Supply Chain: To Keep Its Inventory Costs Low and Its Shelves Fully Stocked, Wal-Mart Has Always Invested Extensively—and First—in Technology for the Supply Chain," *Supermarket News*, 2 December 2002, 55.

[8] N. Buckley & S. Voyle, "Can Wal-Mart Conquer Markets outside the US?" *Financial Times*, 8 January 2003.

[9] Garry & Mulholland, "Master of Its Supply Chain."

[10] S. Lubar, *Infoculture: The Smithsonian Book of Information Age Inventions* (Boston: Houghton, Mifflin, 1993).

[11] Ibid.

[12] B. Worthen, "Bar Codes on Steroids," *CIO*, 15 December 2002, 53.

[13] J. Edwards, "Tag, You're It," *CIO*, 15 February 2003, 84.

[14] N. Rubenking, "Hidden Messages," *PC Magazine*, 22 May 2001, 86.

[15] D. Franklin, "Data Miners: New Software Instantly Connects Key Bits of Data That Once Eluded Teams of Researchers," *Time*, 23 December 2002, A4.

[16] D. LaGesse, "News You Can Use: Personal Tech—This Software Can Bring Back Sanity to a Crazed PC," *U.S. News & World Report*, 30 April 2001, 69.

[17] Rubenking, "Hidden Messages."

[18] G. Saitz, "Naked Truth—Data Miners, Who Taught Retailers to Stock Beer Near Diapers, Find Hidden Sales Trends, a Science That's Becoming Big Business," *The Star-Ledger*, 1 August 2002, 041.

[19] P. Klebnikov, "The Resurrection of NCR: Forget about Cash Registers—NCR's Future Is in Data Warehouses," *Forbes*, 9 July 2001, 70.

[20] B. Saporita, W. Boston, N. Gough, & R. Healy, "Can Wal-Mart Get Any Bigger? (Yes, a Lot Bigger . . . Here's How)," *Time,* 19 January 2003, 38.

[21] F. J. Derfler, Jr., "Secure Your Network," *PC Magazine,* 27 June 2000, 183–200.

[22] "Authentication," Webopedia.com, [Online] available at http://www.webopedia.com/TERM/a/authentication.html, 20 April 2003.

[23] "Authorization," Webopedia.com, [Online] available at http://www.webopedia.com/TERM/a/authorization.html, 20 April 2003.

[24] L. Seltzer, "Password Crackers," *PC Magazine,* 12 February 2002, 68.

[25] B. Grimes, "Biometric Security," *PC Magazine,* 22 April 2003, 74.

[26] "Virus Attack: Protect Your PC," Cnet.com Web Site, [Online] available at http://home.cnet.com/software/0-3746.html, 1 October 2000.

[27] G. Alwang & J. Munro, "Viruses: New Threats, New Defenses," *PC Magazine,* 22 April 2003, 112.

[28] K. Karagiannis, "Security Watch: Don't Make It Easy," *PC Magazine,* 8 April 2003, 72; M. Steinhart, "Password Dos and Don'ts," *PC Magazine,* 12 February 2002, 69.

[29] S. Patton, "Simply Secure Communications," *CIO,* 15 January 2003, 100.

[30] J. van den Hoven, "Executive Support Systems & Decision Making," *Journal of Systems Management* 47, no. 8 (March-April 1996): 48.

[31] A. O'Donnell, "Get Smart: Insurance Companies Know How to Collect Data. The Challenge Is Doing Something Meaningful, Something Intelligent, with It. In the End, Only the Smart Will Survive," *Insurance & Technology,* 1 April 2001, 30.

[32] "Intranet," Webopedia.com, [Online] available at http://www.webopedia.com/TERM/i/intranet.html, 26 August 2001.

[33] J. Barlow, "Intranet Replaces Office Grapevine," *Houston Chronicle,* 7 May 2000, Business 1.

[34] V. S. Pasher, "Employee Benefits Info within a Few Clicks," *National Underwriter Life & Health—Financial Services Edition,* 14 April 1997, S4.

[35] Barlow, "Intranet Replaces Office Grapevine."

[36] E. Varon, "Portals (Finally) Get Down," *CIO,* 1 December 2002, 70.

[37] "Web Services," Webopedia.com, [Online] available at http://www.webopedia.com/TERM/W/Web_services.html, 22 April 2003.

[38] S. Overby, "This Could Be the Start of Something Small," *CIO,* 15 February 2003, 54.

[39] "Extranet," Webopedia.com, [Online] available at http://www.webopedia.com/TERM/E/extranet.html, 22 April 2003.

[40] S. Hamm, D. Welch, W. Zellner, F. Keenan, & P. Engardio, "Down but Hardly Out: Downturn Be Damned. Companies Are Still Anxious to Expand Online Because the Net Is a Way to Boost Sales and Shrink Costs," *BusinessWeek,* 26 March 2001, 126.

[41] S. Overby, "JetBlue Skies Ahead," *CIO,* [Online] available at http://www.cio.com/archive/070102/jetblue.html, 1 July 2002.

[42] Hamm, Welch, Zellner, Keenan, & Engardio, "Down but Hardly Out."

[43] K. C. Laudon & J. P. Laudon, *Management Information Systems: Organization and Technology* (Upper Saddle River, NJ: Prentice-Hall, 1996).

[44] C. Wagner, "End Users as Expert System Developers? (Industry Trend or Event)," *Journal of End User Computing,* 1 July 2000, 3.

[45] J. Adamy, "Safeway Introduces 'Smart' Cart for Shoppers," *Contra Costa Times,* 20 November 2002, available at http://www.wsj.com; J. Black, "How Grocery Stores Are Feeding Fears: Supermarket Chains Say Their Loyalty Cards Reward Faithful Shoppers. Privacy Advocates Say They're No Bargain at All," *Business Week Online,* 20 June 2002; J. Karolefski, "Is Loyalty in the Cards? Retailers Need to Invest in Their Frequent Shopper Programs to Achieve the Benefits of Targeted Marketing," *Supermarket News,* 7 October 2002, 19; K. McLaughlin, "The Discount Grocery Cards That Don't Save You Money," *The Wall Street Journal,* 21 January 2003, B1; R. Turcsik, "What Price Loyalty? The Best Frequent Shopper Programs Go beyond Merchandise Discounts," *Progressive Grocer,* 1 April 2003, 43; "Winn-Dixie Challenges Rival Chattanooga Grocery Stores with New Bonus Card," *Knight Ridder Tribune Business News,* 27 June 2002.

[46] "Web Form Can Be Used by Consumers to Protect Privacy," *The Wall Street Journal,* 25 May 2001; P. Davidson, "Capitol Hill Support Brews for Internet Privacy Laws," *USA Today,* 12 July 2001; H. Green, "Your Right to Privacy: Going . . . Going . . .," *BusinessWeek,* 23 April 2001.

CHAPTER 6

[1] K. Allers, "A New Banking Model: Washington Mutual Is Using a Creative Retail Approach to Turn the Banking World Upside Down," *Fortune,* 31 March 2003, 102; S. Cocheo, "Kerry Killinger Builds His Dream Bank," *ABA Banking Journal,* 1 August 2001, 22; C. Coleman, "Banks Cozy Up to Customers—To Push Products, Services, Branches Add Concierges, Emulate Aura of The Gap," *The Wall Street Journal,* 26 April 2001, B1; T. Fredrickson, "Chase Expands Elsewhere While It Trims in New York: Seeking Growth in Middle Market," *Crain's New York Business,* 21 April 2003, 31; S. Holmes, "The Wal-Mart of Consumer Finance? Kerry Killinger Is Trying to Make Washington Mutual the "Category Killer" of Retail Banking. The Competition, However, Is Heating Up," *Business Week Online,* [Online] available at http://www.businessweek.com/investor/content/mar2003/pi20030321_3352_pi001.htm, 21 March 2003; H. Timmons, "Has WaMu Been Buying Trouble? Washington Mutual Is Facing a Pair of Class Actions," *BusinessWeek,* 31 December 2001, 54; L. Tischler, "Bank of (Middle) America," *Fast Company,* March 2003, 104.

[2] R. Leifer & P. K. Mills, "An Information Processing Approach for Deciding upon Control Strategies and Reducing Control Loss in Emerging Organizations," *Journal of Management* 22 (1996): 113–137.

[3] "Say Baa-Baa to Bad Driving," *London Times,* 28 July 1996.

[4] J. Spencer, "The Point of No Return—Stores from Gap to Target Tighten Refund Rules; a 15% 'Restocking Fee,'" *The Wall Street Journal,* 14 May 2002, D1.

[5] J. Martin & J. E. Davis, "Are You As Good As You Think You Are? There's Only One Way to Know for Sure," *Fortune,* 30 September 1996, 142; R.Schultz & R. Levey, "Family Values," *Direct,* 15 May 2001, 44.

[6] M. Langley, "Wall Street's Toughest Boss," *The Wall Street Journal,* 18 February 2003, C1.

[7] H. Koontz & R. W. Bradspies, "Managing through Feedforward Control: A Future-Directed View," *Business Horizons,* June 1972, 25–36.

[8] B. Canton, "Acrobatic Squirrels Give New Meaning to Term 'Brownout'—Pole Guards, Noise, Fake Owls—Nothing Utilities Try Thwarts High-Wire Act," *The Wall Street Journal,* 4 February 2002, A1.

[9] R. Leifer & P. K. Mills, "An Information Processing Approach for Deciding upon Control Strategies and Reducing Control Loss in Emerging Organizations," *Journal of Management* 22 (1996): 113–137.

[10] C. Binkley, "Mississippi Gamble: Finest Casino That Could Be Built Was the Goal," *The Wall Street Journal*, 2 February 2000, A1.

[11] S. G. Green & M. A. Welsh, "Cybernetics and Dependence: Reframing the Control Concept," *Academy of Management Review* 13 (1988): 287–301.

[12] N. Stein, "Son of a Chicken Man," *Fortune*, 13 May 2002, 136. "Our Chicken Processes," Tyson Foods, [Online] available at http://www.tysonfoodsinc.com/corporate/processes/chicken.asp, 4 May 2003.

[13] Stein, "Son of a Chicken Man"; "The IBP Story," Tyson's IBP Fresh Meats Group, [Online] available at http:// www.ibpinc.com/about/IBPNewHistory.stm#Thomas%20E%20Wilson, 4 May 2003.

[14] Senator Bill Frist, "Letters to the Editor: Alarming Shortage of Eight Vaccines," *The Wall Street Journal*, 30 August 2002, A9; Editorial, "A Needless Vaccine Shortage," *The Wall Street Journal*, 21 May 2002, A18.

[15] N. Watson, "What's Wrong with This Printer? Believe It Or Not, It's Too Solid," *Fortune*, 17 February 2003, 120.

[16] M. Boyle, "Expensing It: Guilty As Charged When Times Are Tough, Employees Become Even More Devoted to Mastering the Art of Self-Perking," *Fortune*, 9 July 2001, 179; R. Grugal, "Be Honest and Dependable. Integrity—The Must-Have," *Investor's Business Daily*, 11 April 2003.

[17] G. Johnson, "Boeing Shelves 747X to Focus on 'Sonic Cruiser,'" *Associated Press*, 30 March 2001.

[18] B. Sandilands, "Flights Of Fantasy—The Sorry Saga of the Supersonic Jetliner," *Australian Financial Review*, 4 January 2003, 45.

[19] J. Lunsford, "Navigating Change: Boeing, Losing Ground to Airbus, Faces Key Choice—Amid Downturn, Firm Ponders Spending on Innovation or Diversifying Defensively—Debate over All-New Plane," *The Wall Street Journal*, 21 April 2003, A1.

[20] S. Carey, "Frustrated Firms Buy Planes to Streamline Travel Plans," *The Wall Street Journal Interactive Edition*, 11 October 1996.

[21] S. Shellenbarger, "Is the Awful Behavior of Some Bad Bosses Rooted in Their Past?" *The Wall Street Journal*, 17 May 2000, B1.

[22] M. Weber, *The Protestant Ethic and the Spirit of Capitalism* (New York: Scribner's, 1958).

[23] A. C. Greenberg, "Memos from the Chairman," *Fortune*, 29 April 1996, 173–175.

[24] L. Lavelle & F. J. Jespersen, "While the CEO Gravy Train May Be Slowing Down, It Hasn't Jumped the Rails. In 2000, Despite Weakening Returns, U.S. Company Chieftains Bagged on Average a Princely $13.1 Million," *BusinessWeek*, 16 April 2001, 76.

[25] S. Williford, "Nordstrom Sets the Standard for Customer Service," *Memphis Business Journal*, 1 July 1996, 21.

[26] R. T. Pascale, "Nordstrom: Respond to Unreasonable Customer Requests!" *Planning Review* 2 (May–June 1994): 17.

[27] Ibid.

[28] Ibid.

[29] J. R. Barker, "Tightening the Iron Cage: Concertive Control in Self-Managing Teams," *Administrative Science Quarterly* 38 (1993): 408–437.

[30] Ibid.

[31] R. Keenan, "Women Urging Others to 'Just Say No,' Don't Enjoy Just Saying 'Yes,'" *Detroit News*, 23 August 2000, 1.

[32] Barker, "Tightening the Iron Cage."

[33] C. Manz & H. Sims, "Leading Workers to Lead Themselves: The External Leadership of Self-Managed Work Teams," *Administrative Science Quarterly* 32 (1987): 106–128.

[34] J. Slocum & H. A. Sims, "Typology for Integrating Technology, Organization and Job Design," *Human Relations* 33 (1980): 193–212.

[35] C. C. Manz & H. P. Sims, Jr., "Self-Management as a Substitute for Leadership: A Social Learning Perspective," *Academy of Management Review* 5 (1980): 361–367.

[36] S. Levy, "Strip Mining the Corporate Life," *Newsweek*, 12 August 1996, 54–55.

[37] R. S. Kaplan & D. P. Norton, "Using the Balanced Scorecard as a Strategic Management System," *Harvard Business Review*, January–February 1996, 75–85; R. S. Kaplan & D. P. Norton, "The Balanced Scorecard: Measures That Drive Performance," *Harvard Business Review*, January–February 1992, 71–79.

[38] J. Meliones, "Saving Money, Saving Lives," *Harvard Business Review*, November–December 2000, 57–65.

[39] M. H. Stocks & A. Harrell, "The Impact of an Increase in Accounting Information Level on the Judgment Quality of Individuals and Groups," *Accounting, Organizations and Society*, October–November 1995, 685–700.

[40] G. Colvin, "America's Best & Worst Wealth Creators: The Real Champions Aren't Always Who You Think. Here's an Eye-Opening Look at Which Companies Produce and Destroy the Most Money for Investors—Plus a New Tool for Spotting Future Winners," *Fortune*, 18 December 2000, 207.

[41] B. Morris, "Roberto Goizueta and Jack Welch: The Wealth Builders," *Fortune*, 11 December 1995, 80–94.

[42] B. Birchard, "Metrics for the Masses," *CFO*, May 1999, 75.

[43] S. Tully, "The Real Key to Creating Wealth," *Fortune*, 20 September 1993, 38–50.

[44] "Handling Complaints," Office of Consumer and Business Affairs, [Online] available at http://www.ocba.sa.gov.au/ba_complaints.htm, 2 September 2001; F. F. Reichheld, "Learning from Customer Defections," *Harvard Business Review*, March–April 1996, 56–69.

[45] C. B. Furlong, "12 Rules for Customer Retention," *Bank Marketing* 5 (January 1993): 14.

[46] Hepworth, "Connecting Customer Loyalty."

[47] F. F. Reichheld, "Lead for Loyalty," *Harvard Business Review* 79 (July–August 2001): 76.

[48] A. Orr, "After the Order . . . (Customer Retention Strategies)," *Target Marketing* 3 (July 1996): 20.

[49] C. A. Reeves & D. A. Bednar, "Defining Quality: Alternatives and Implications," *Academy of Management Review* 19 (1994): 419–445.

[50] D. R. May & B. L. Flannery, "Cutting Waste with Employee Involvement Teams," *Business Horizons*, September–October 1995, 28–38.

[51] A. Gynn, "Sears, WMI Continue Recycling Program," *Waste News*, 5 March 2001, 2.

[52] J. Szekely & G. Trapaga, "From Villain to Hero (Materials Industry's Waste Recovery Efforts)," *Technology Review*, 1 January 1995, 30.

[53] "Hardware Recycling Services—US," Hewlett-Packard, [Online] available at https://warp1.external.hp.com/recycle/, 6 May 2003.

[54] Reeves & Bednar, "Defining Quality."

[55] R. Buckman, "Microsoft Offers Prizes to Identify Orders of PCs without Windows," *The Wall Street Journal*, 2 May 2001; B. Kruger, "High-Tech Firms Get Piracy Alert," *Electronic News*, 7 February 2000; J. Stevenson, "Piracy Plague," *Business Mexico*, November 2000; Z. Thomas, "High Tech's Dirty Little Software Piracy Secret," *Electronic Business*, November 2000; F. Gallegos, "Software Piracy: Some Facts, Figures, and Issues," *Information System Security*, Winter 2000.

[56] S. Caulkin, "If You Want to Stay a Winner, Learn from Your Mistakes," *The Observer*, 3 March 1996, 7; J. Hyatt, "Failure 101," *Inc.*, January 1989, 18; B. McMenamin, "The Virtue of Making Mistakes," *Forbes*, 9 May 1994, 192–194; P. Sellers, "So You Fail," *Fortune*, 1 May 1995, 48–66; P. Sellers, "Where Failures Get Fixed," *Fortune*, 1 May 1995, 64; B. Weiner, I. Freize, A. Kukla, L. Reed, S. Rest, & R. M. Rosenbaum, "Perceiving the Causes of Success and Failure," in *Attribution: Perceiving the Causes of Behavior*, ed. E. Jones, D. Kanouse, H. Kelley, R. Nesbitt, S. Valins, & B. Weiner (Morristown, NJ: General Learning Press, 1971), 45–61.

CHAPTER 7

[1] S. Kirsner, "Recipe for Reinvention: The British Are Coming! The British Are Coming!" *Fast Company*, 2 April 2002, 38; G. Lindsey & C. Fleming, "Taste makers: These six visionaries have created chain menus that lead the pack with focus, flair—and fiscal success. Just who are they? Winners of our annual menu strategist awards: Pret á Management," *Restaurant Business*, 15 January 2003, 24; S. Leung, "Upper Crust: Fast-Food Chains Vie to Carve Out Empire in Pricey Sandwiches," *The Wall Street Journal*, 5 February 2002, A1; D. Sanai, "The Man Who Ate the Great British Lunch Hour," *The Independent—London*, 14 March 2001, 1; J. Simms, "Gone to Lunch," *Director*, 1 May 2002, 46.

[2] A. Bernstein, & E. Malkin, "Backlash," *BusinessWeek*, 24 April 2000, 38; J. Calmes, "American Opinion (A Special Report): Despite Buoyant Economic Times Americans Don't Buy Free Trade," *The Wall Street Journal*, 10 December 1998, A10; *USA Today*, 25 February 1992; Lou Harris Survey, March 1990, March 1992.

[3] Bernstein & Malking, "Backlash"; Lou Harris Survey, 1990, 1992; "International Trade: The Gallup Poll, May 5–7, 2000," Polling Report.com, [Online] available at http://www.pollingreport.com/trade.htm, 8 May 2003.

[4] Calmes, "American Opinion (A Special Report)."

[5] A. Hahn, "German M&A Heats Up in Q1," *Investment Dealers' Digest*, 31 March 2003, 15; D. Henry & F. Jespersen, "Mergers: Why Most Big Deals Don't Pay Off," *BusinessWeek*, 14 October 2002, 60.

[6] "Recent Media Mergers," *Chicago Sun-Times*, 8 September 1999, 63; P. Colford, "1998: A Very Big Deal: Mergers Make Giants and Shrink Competition," *Newsday*, 23 December 1998.

[7] "Global Foreign Direct Investment to Exceed $1 Trillion, UNCTAD Predicts," United Nations Conference on Trade and Development, [Online] available at http://www.unctad.org/Templates/Webflyer.asp?docID=2714&intItemID=2068&lang=1, 8 May 2003; International Accounts Data, Bureau of Economic Analysis, [Online] available at www.bea.doc.gov/bea/di1.htm, 8 May 2003.

[8] "Global Foreign Direct Investment to Exceed $1 Trillion."

[9] "Chapter 7: Industry, Technology, and the Global Marketplace—U.S. Technology in the Marketplace," Science and Engineering Indicators 2000, [Online] available at http://www.nsf.gov/sbe/srs/seind00/access/c7/c7s1.htm#c7s1l2, 8 May 2003.

[10] Ibid.

[11] "Fact Sheet: U.N. Regular Budget Scale of Assessment," United States Mission to the United Nations, [Online] available at http://www.un.int/usa/fact6.htm, 8 September 2001.

[12] "Global GDP," *CIBC Observations*, June–July 2001, 1.

[13] "What Is the G20?" G8 Information Centre, [Online] available at http://www.g7.utoronto.ca/g7/g20/g20whatisit.html, 8 May 2003.

[14] "Country Fact Sheet: United States, Number of Parent Corporations and Foreign Affiliates, Latest Available Year," World Investment Report 2000: Cross-border Mergers and Acquisitions and Development, [Online] available at http://www.unctad.org/en/pub/ps4wir00fs.en.htm, 8 May 2003.

[15] K. Granzin, "Motivational Influences on 'Buy Domestic' Purchasing: Marketing Management Implications from a Study of Two Nations," *Journal of International Marketing* 9 (2001): 73–96.

[16] G. Knight, "Consumer Preferences for Foreign and Domestic Products," *Journal of Consumer Marketing* 16, no. 2 (1998): 151–162.

[17] J. White, G. White, & N. Shirouzu, "Passing Era: Soon, the Big Three Won't Be, As Foreigners Make Inroads in U.S.—Toyota Draws Near Chrysler As Investments Pay Off; Dealers Shift Loyalties—'A Life-Threatening Disease,'" *The Wall Street Journal*, 13 August 2001, A1.

[18] B. Thevenot, "Clawing for Survival, Louisiana's Crab Processors Are Being Pinched by Low Prices and Foreign Competition," *New Orleans Times-Picayune*, 6 October 1999, A1.

[19] D. Luhnow, "Crossover Success: How NAFTA Helped Wal-Mart Reshape the Mexican Market—Lower Tariffs, Retail Muscle Translate into Big Sales; Middlemen Are Squeezed—'Like Shopping in the U.S.,'" *The Wall Street Journal*, 31 August 2001, A1.

[20] E. Ruzul & S. Ramos, "No Assurance of EU 'Yes' Vote on Tuna," *Manila Standard*, 26 April 2003.

[21] N. King, Jr., "Trade Imbalance: Why Uncle Sam Wrote a Big Check to a Sparkler Maker," *The Wall Street Journal*, 5 December 2002, A1.

[22] A. Startseva, "Quotas a Matter of 'National Security,'" *Moscow Times*, 29 January 2003.

[23] C. Hale, "HortFACT—Why Fireblight Shouldn't Be a Market Access Problem," Hortnet, [Online] available at http://www.hortnet.co.nz/publications/hortfacts/hf205010.htm, 9 May 2003; "USTR Lists Barriers to U.S. Trade, Focusing on Agriculture—Annual Report Also Emphasizes Intellectual Property, Transparency," U.S. State Department Press Releases and Documents, 1 April 2003.

[24] "Rocky Receives Customs Clarification on Imported Boots," *FN*, 31 March 2003.

[25] G. Smith, E. Malkin, J. Wheatley, P. Magnusson, & M. Arndt, "Betting on Free Trade: George Bush Wants to Turn North and South America into the World's Biggest Single Market. Is It for Real or Just a Dream?" *BusinessWeek*, 23 April 2001, 32.

[26] "ASEAN Trade with United States of America by Product Chapter (1993–2001)," ASEAN, [Online] available at http://www.aseansec.org/Trade/Files/AN_US_PC.htm, 8 May 2003.

[27] "Member Economies' Websites," Asia-Pacific Economic Cooperation, [Online] available at http://www.apecsec.org.sg/member/memb_websites.html, 10 September 2001.

[28] D. Luhnow, "Crossover Success: How NAFTA Helped Wal-Mart Reshape the Mexican Market," *The Wall Street Journal*, 31 August 2000, A1.

[29] "Workplace Code of Conduct," Fair Labor Association, [Online] available at http://www.fairlabor.org/all/code/index.html, 12 May 2003; A. Bernstein, M. Shari, & E. Malkin, "A World of Sweatshops," *BusinessWeek*, 6 November 2000, 84.

[30] R. Tomlinson, "Who's Afraid of Wal-Mart? Not Carrefour. The World's Second-Largest Retailer Is Bounding Ahead of the Bentonville Behemoth in Most Markets outside North America. But Can the French Titan Hold Its Lead?" *Fortune*, 26 June 2000, 186.

[31] A. Sundaram & J. S. Black, "The Environment and Internal-Organization of Multinational Enterprises," *Academy of Management Review* 17 (1992): 729–757.

[32] H. S. James, Jr., & M. Weidenbaum, *When Businesses Cross International Borders: Strategic Alliances and Their Alternatives* (Westport, CT: Praeger Publishers, 1993).

[33] R. Badam, "India Hooked on 'Millionaire' Show," *Associated Press*, 4 September 2000.

[34] "Frequently Asked Questions about Acquiring a McDonald's Franchise," McDonald's, [Online] available at http://www.mcdonalds.com/corporate/franchise/faq/index.html, 10 May 2003.

[35] A. E. Serwer, "Trouble in Franchise Nation," *Fortune*, 6 March 1995, 115.

[36] "Introduction to the Global Center," Yum! Brands, Inc., [Online] available at http://www.yum.com/international/default.htm, 10 May 2003.

[37] "Company Profile," Fuji Xerox, [Online] available at http://www.fujixerox.co.jp/eng/company/profile.html, 10 May 2003.

[38] D. P. Hamilton, "Fuji Xerox Is a Rarity in World Business: A Joint Venture That Works," *The Wall Street Journal*, 26 September 1996, R19; E. Terazono & C. Lorenz, "Fuji Xerox Marriage Successful: Growing Pains with Parent Easing," *The Financial Post*, 24 September 1994, 55.

[39] D. Sparks, "Partners," *BusinessWeek*, 25 October 1999, 106; B. A. Walters, S. Peters, & G. G. Dess, "Strategic Alliances and Joint Ventures: Making Them Work," *Business Horizons*, July–August 1994, 5–10.

[40] C. Webb, "Micron to Pay $250 Million in Cash for Dominion; Layoffs Uncertain in Acquisition of Manassas Chipmaker," *Washington Post*, 20 January 2002, T5.

[41] M. W. Hordes, J. A. Clancy, & J. Baddaley, "A Primer for Global Start-Ups." *Academy of Management Executive*, May 1995, 7–11.

[42] D. Pavlos, J. Johnson, J. Slow, & S. Young, "Micromultinationals: New Types of Firms for the Global Competitive Landscape," *European Management Journal* 21, issue 2 (April 2003): 164; B. M. Oviatt & P. P. McDougall, "Toward a Theory of International New Ventures," *Journal of International Business Studies*, Spring 1994, 45–64.

[43] "Bitfone Secures US$19 Mln Series B Funding AsiaPulse News," *Asia Pulse*, 16 September 2002, 4797.

[44] "Operations Review: Selected Market Results: Estimated 2002 Volume by Operating Segment," *The Coca-Cola Company 2002 Annual Report*, [Online] available at http://www.annualreport.coca-cola.com/, 11 May 2003.

[45] J. Huey, "The World's Best Brand," *Fortune*, 31 May 1993, 44.

[46] "Operations Review: Selected Market Results," *The Coca-Cola Company 2002 Annual Report;* R. Tomkins, "Coca-Cola Strives to Rival Tap Water: Despite 48% of Global Market, Coke Chafes at Fact It Supplies only 3% of Every Human's Required Daily Liquid Intake," *Financial Post*, 30 October 1997, 77; Huey, "The World's Best Brand."

[47] P. Prada, "Ja, Ja, Americana's Fabulosa—In Europe, Theme Parks Draw Crowds with Thrill Rides, Burgers and Bugs Bunny," *The Wall Street Journal*, 21 June 2001, B1.

[48] "Fact Sheet, Call Center Solutions: How Call Centers Can Work for You," The Netherlands Foreign Investment Agency, [Online] available at http://www.nfia.com/html/solution/fact.html, 15 September 2001.

[49] J. Oetzel, R. Bettis, & M. Zenner, "How Risky Are They?" *Journal of World Business* 36, no. 2 (Summer 2001): 128–145.

[50] K. D. Miller, "A Framework for Integrated Risk Management in International Business," *Journal of International Business Studies*, 2nd Quarter 1992, 311.

[51] V. Fuhrmans & G. Naik, "Drug Makers Fight to Fend Off Cuts in European Prices," *The Wall Street Journal*, 7 June 2002, A1.

[52] P. Waldman, "Your Lingerie in Iran, Even If It's for Sale: Censors Decide Many Topics Are Unmentionable in Ads," *The Wall Street Journal*, 21 June 1995, A1.

[53] G. Hofstede, "The Cultural Relativity of the Quality of Life Concept," *Academy of Management Review* 9 (1984): 389–398; G. Hofstede, "The Cultural Relativity of Organizational Practices and Theories," *Journal of International Business Studies*, Fall 1983, 75–89; G. Hofstede, "The Interaction between National and Organizational Value Systems," *Journal of Management Studies*, July 1985, 347–357.

[54] R. Hodgetts, "A Conversation with Geert Hofstede," *Organizational Dynamics*, Spring 1993, 53–61.

[55] M. Janssens, J. M. Brett, & F. J. Smith, "Confirmatory Cross-Cultural Research: Testing the Viability of a Corporation-Wide Safety Policy," *Academy of Management Journal* 38 (1995): 364–382.

[56] R. G. Linowes, "The Japanese Manager's Traumatic Entry into the United States: Understanding the American-Japanese Cultural Divide," *Academy of Management Executive* 7 (1993): 21–40.

[57] J. S. Black, M. Mendenhall, & G. Oddou, "Toward a Comprehensive Model of International Adjustment: An Integration of Multiple Theoretical Perspectives," *Academy of Management Journal* 16 (1991): 291–317; R. L. Tung, "American Expatriates Abroad: From Neophytes to Cosmopolitans," *Columbia Journal of World Business*, 22 June 1998, 125; A. Harzing, "The Persistent Myth of High Expatriate Failure Rates," *International Journal of Human Resource Management* 6 (1995): 457–475; A. Harzing, "Are Our Referencing Errors Undermining Our Scholarship and Credibility? The Case of Expatriate Failure Rates," *Journal of Organizational Behavior* 23 (2002): 127–148; N. Forster, "The Persistent Myth of High Expatriate Failure Rates: A Reappraisal," *International Journal of Human Resource Management* 8 (1997): 414–433.

[58] J. Black, "The Right Way to Manage Expats," *Harvard Business Review* 77 (March–April 1999): 52; C. Joinson, "No Returns," *HR Magazine*, 1 November 2002, 70.

[59] R. A. Swaak, "Expatriate Failures: Too Many, Too Much Cost, Too Little Planning," *Compensation and Benefits Review* 27, no. 6 (21 November 1995): 47.

[60] J. S. Black & M. Mendenhall, "Cross-Cultural Training Effectiveness: A Review and Theoretical Framework for Future Research," *Academy of Management Review* 15 (1990): 113–136.

[61] W. Arthur, Jr., & W. Bennett, Jr., "The International Assignee: The Relative Importance of Factors Perceived to Contribute to Success," *Personnel Psychology* 48 (1995): 99–114; B. Cheng, "Home Truths about Foreign Postings; To Make an Overseas Assignment Work, Employers Need More Than an Eager Exec with a Suitcase. They Must Also Motivate the Staffer's Spouse," *BusinessWeek Online*, [Online] available at http://www.businessweek.com/careers/content/jul2002/ca20020715_9110.htm, 16 July 2002.

[62] S. P. Deshpande & C. Viswesvaran, "Is Cross-Cultural Training of Expatriate Managers Effective: A Meta-Analysis," *International Journal of Intercultural Relations* 16, no. 3 (1992): 295–310.

[63] R. Donkin, "Recruitment: Overseas Gravy Train May Be Running Out of Steam—Preparing Expatriate Packages Is Challenging the Expertise of Human Resource Management," *The Financial Times*, 30 November 1994, 10.

[64] D. Eschbach, G. Parker, & P. Stoeberl, "American Repatriate Employees' Retrospective Assessments of the Effects of Cross-Cultural Training on their Adaptation to International Assignments," *International Journal of Human Resource Management* 12 (2001): 270–287.

[65] Cho Mee-young, "Starbucks Likely to Expand Asia Plan," *Reuters English News Service*, 23 August 2001, available online; "Starbucks Coffee Japan, Ltd.," *The Food Institute Report*, 19 March 2001, 6; "Starbucks Expansion Continues," *The Food Institute Report*, 19 February 2001, 3; "Starbucks," *Chain Store Age Executive Fax*, 1 November 2002, 5; Starbucks Annual Report, 2002, 16; "Starbucks Launches Café, Looks Towards International Expansion," *The Food Institute Report*, 14 September 1998; S. Theodore, "Expanding the Coffee Experience: Starbucks Keep Sales Brewing with New Products, Innovation, and Global Expansion," *Beverage Industry*, October 2002, 57; "Trouble Brewing: To Perk up Sales, Starbucks Has Big Plans to Expand on the Internet and Overseas," *Newsweek*, 19 June 1999, 40; Dori Jones Yang, "An American (Coffee) in Paris—and Rome," *U.S. News & World Report*, 19 February 2001, 47.

[66] R. W. Boatler, "Study Abroad: Impact on Student Worldmindedness," *Journal of Teaching in International Business* 2, no. 2 (1990): 13–17; R. W. Boatler, "Worldminded Attitude Change in a Study Abroad Program: Contact and Content Issues," *Journal of Teaching in International Business* 3, no. 4 (1992): 59–68; H. Lancaster, "Learning to Manage in a Global Workplace (You're on Your Own)," *The Wall Street Journal*, 2 June 1998, B1; D. L. Sampson & H. P. Smith, "A Scale to Measure Worldminded Attitudes," *Journal of Social Psychology* 45 (1957): 99–106.

CHAPTER 8

[1] "About IKEA—the Timeline—the Full Story," IKEA, [Online] available at http://www.ikea-usa.com/about_ikea/timeline/fullstory.asp, 17 May 2003; "Ikea Brings Back Scandinavian Design," *Nikkei Weekly*, 22 July 2002; "Ikea Remains King of Hearts and Purses," *Cabinet Maker*, 27 December 2002, 5; E. Beck, "Ikea Sees Quirkiness as Selling Point in U.K.," *The Wall Street Journal*, 4 January 2001, B12; D. Haffenreffer, "IKEA's Unique Four Part Strategy Spells Global Success," *CNNfn*, 15 October 2002, 11:00; L. Margonelli, "How Ikea Designs Its Sexy Price Tags," *Business 2.0*, [Online] available at http://www.business2.com/articles/mag/0,1640,43529,00.html, October 2002; H. Marsh, "Ikea's Improvement Challenge," *Marketing*, 25 April 2002, 22.

[2] "Stock Charting for AOL Time Warner, Inc." *The Wall Street Journal*, [Online] available at http://interactive.wsj.com/, 13 May 2003.

[3] J. Angwin & R. Buckman, "In Internet Access, AOL Begins to Feel Microsoft's Breath," *The Wall Street Journal*, 14 October 2002, A1; J. Borland, "Earthlink Looks to Speed Dial-Up Net," *CNET News.com*, [Online] available at http://news.com.com/2100-1032-993893.html, 24 March 2003; A. Cha, "Making the Web Pay in Small Ways; Local Internet Providers Thrive in Shadows of Giants," *Washington Post*, 22 February 2000, A1.

[4] J. Barney, "Firm Resources and Sustained Competitive Advantage," *Journal of Management* 17 (1991): 99–120; J. Barney, "Looking Inside for Competitive Advantage," *Academy of Management Executive* 9 (1995): 49–61.

[5] G. Keizer, "The Best and Worst ISPs: We Survey 2000 PC-World.com Visitors, Conduct Performance Tests, and Compare Features," *PC World*, [Online] available at http://www.pcworld.com/resource/printable/article/0,aid,18624,00.asp, 23 September 2001.

[6] Ibid.

[7] P. Boyle, "Editor's Choice: America Online," *PC Magazine*, 11 June 1996.

[8] Cha, "Making the Web Pay in Small Ways."

[9] S. Hart & C. Banbury, "How Strategy-Making Processes Can Make a Difference," *Strategic Management Journal* 15 (1994): 251–269.

[10] R. A. Burgelman, "Fading Memories: A Process Theory of Strategic Business Exit in Dynamic Environments," *Administrative Science Quarterly* 39 (1994): 24–56; R. A. Burgelman & A. S. Grove, "Strategic Dissonance," *California Management Review* 38 (1996): 8–28.

[11] L. Guerrero, "Dishes Gain on Cable TV: Cost, Features Nudge Viewers to Satellites," *Chicago Sun-Times*, 9 January 2001, 12; J. Schaeffler, "September Starts with Sizzling Satellite Sales," *Satellite News*, 16 September 2002, 35.

[12] Hart & Banbury, "How Strategy-Making Processes Can Make a Difference;" C. C. Miller & L. B. Cardinal, "Strategic Planning and Firm Performance: A Synthesis of More Than Two Decades of Research," *Academy of Management Journal* 37 (1994): 1649–1665; C. R. Schwenk, "Effects of Formal Strategic Planning on Financial Performance in Small Firms: A Meta-Analysis," *Entrepreneurship Theory and Practice*, Spring 1993, 53–64.

[13] A. Fiegenbaum, S. Hart, & D. Schendel, "Strategic Reference Point Theory," *Strategic Management Journal* 17 (1996): 219–235.

[14] Daniel Golden, "Kodak to Buy Assets, Including Process to Convert Film to CD," *The Wall Street Journal*, 12 May 2003, B3.

[15] J. Bandler, "Kodak Names Rival from Japan in Digital Bid," *The Wall Street Journal*, 16 April 2003, B3.

[16] "Reliability by Category (New Models)," ConsumerReports.org, [Online] available at http://www.consumerreports.org/main/detailv2.jsp?CONTENT%3C%3Ecnt_id=27883&FOLDER%3C%3Efolder_id=26995&bmUID=1052859363335, 13 May 2003.

[17] B. Howard, "Reader's Choice: Service & Reliability, Desktops," *PC Magazine*, August 2002, 99.

[18] D. J. Collis, "Research Note: How Valuable Are Organizational Capabilities?" *Strategic Management Journal* 15 (1994): 143–152.

[19] K. Freiberg & J. Freiberg, *Nuts! Southwest Airlines' Crazy Recipe for Business and Personal Success* (Austin, TX: Bard Press, 1996).

[20] A. Fiegenbaum & H. Thomas, "Strategic Groups as Reference Groups: Theory, Modeling and Empirical Examination of Industry and Competitive Strategy," *Strategic Management Journal* 16 (1995): 461–476.

[21] "About Gannett: Company Profile," Gannett Company, [Online] available at http://www.gannett.com/map/gan007.htm, 13 May 2003.

[22] R. K. Reger & A. S. Huff, "Strategic Groups: A Cognitive Perspective," *Strategic Management Journal* 14 (1993): 103–124.

[23] "Tribune Company 2002 Annual Report," Tribune Company, [Online] available at http://www.tribune.com/media/pdf/annual_02.pdf, 13 May 2003; "Knight Ridder Newspapers," Knight Ridder, [Online] available at http://www.kri.com/papers/ index.html, 13 May 2003.

[24] "The New York Times: Our Company," The New York Times Company, [Online] available at http://www.nytco.com/company/, 13 May 2003.

[25] "Tribune Company 2002 Annual Report"; "Knight Ridder Newspapers."

[26] "Menard, Inc.," *Hoover's Company Profiles*, 8 May 2003.

[27] J. Samuelson, "Tough Guy Billionaire," *Forbes*, 24 February 1997, 64–66.

[28] "Menards vs. Home Depot," WCCO Channel 4000, [Online] available at http://www.channel4000.com/news/dimension/news-dimension-19991117-205633.html, 25 September 2001.

[29] Ibid.

[30] H. Murphy, "Menard's Tool in Retail Battle: Gigantic Stores: Seven Towns to Get New Stores or Replacements," *Crain's Chicago Business*, 12 August 2002, 3.

[31] Ibid.

[32] M. Williams, "Intel, Chastened by Missteps, Alters Strategy to Concentrate on Chips—Folding Some Services Ventures and Cutting Costs, It Keeps Budget Big for Core Product," *The Wall Street Journal*, 16 March 2001, B1.

[33] M. Lubatkin, "Value-Creating Mergers: Fact or Folklore?" *Academy of Management Executive* 2 (1988): 295–302; M. Lubatkin & S. Chatterjee, "Extending Modern Portfolio Theory into the Domain of Corporate Diversification: Does It Apply?" *Academy of Management Journal* 37 (1994): 109–136; M. H. Lubatkin & P. J. Lane, "Psst . . . The Merger Mavens Still Have It Wrong!" *Academy of Management Executive* 10 (1996): 21–39.

[34] M. Maremont, J. Hechinger, J. Markon, & G. Zuckerman, "Tainted Chief: Kozlowski Quits under a Cloud, Worsening Worries about Tyco," *The Wall Street Journal*, 4 June 2002, A1; R. Charan & J. Useem, "Why Companies Fail," *Fortune*, 27 May 2002, 50.

[35] "About Samsung," Samsung, [Online] available at http://www.samsung.com/AboutSAMSUNG/index.htm, 14 May 2003.

[36] J. Baglole, "War of the Doughnuts—Krispy Kreme, Tim Horton's of Canada to Square Off in Each Other's Territory," *The Wall Street Journal*, 23 August 2001, B1; "Mmm, Doughnuts—The Motley Fool," *Star-Ledger, Newark*, 10 April 2003.

[37] J. A. Pearce, II, "Selecting among Alternative Grand Strategies," *California Management Review*, Spring 1982, 23–31.

[38] "Walgreen Co.," *Hoover's Company Profiles*, 6 May 2003; A. Tsao, "Why CVS May Be the Pick of the Pack; While Walgreen Is Considered the Drugstore Sector's Blue Chip, CVS Has a Much Cheaper P-E And Plenty of Upside Potential," *Business Week Online*, [Online] available at http://www.businessweek.com/bwdaily/dnflash/may2003/nf20030512_9097_db014.htm, 13 May 2003.

[39] T. Zaun, "For Subaru, Imitation Is the Most Irksome Form of Flattery—Popularity in the U.S. of Crossover Vehicles Leads to Competition," *The Wall Street Journal*, 31 January 2001, A18.

[40] J. A. Pearce II, "Retrenchment Remains the Foundation of Business Turnaround," *Strategic Management Journal* 15 (1994): 407–417.

[41] M. Pacelle, "Salvage Operation: Behind Kmart Exit from Chapter 11: Investor's Big Bet—As Debt He Held Lost Value, Mr. Lampert Forced Out CEO, Pushed Up Timetable—Still Facing Wal-Mart, Target," *The Wall Street Journal*, 6 May 2003, A1.

[42] E. Lee, "Changes at PeopleSoft Pump Up Company's Bottom Line, " *Knight-Ridder Tribune*, 6 May 2001.

[43] R. Winslow & B. Martinez, "Efforts to Switch Patients to Generic Prozac Advance—Pharmacy-Benefit Managers Launch Aggressive Bids to Lower Drug Costs," *The Wall Street Journal*, 20 August 2001, A3.

[44] M. Veverka, "Bigger and Better: Costco's Costly Expansion Is About to Pay Off—For Shoppers and Shareholders," *Barron's*, 12 May 2003, 28.

[45] R. E. Miles & C. C. Snow, *Organizational Strategy, Structure, and Process* (New York: McGraw Hill, 1978); S. Zahra & J. A. Pearce, "Research Evidence on the Miles-Snow Typology," *Journal of Management* 16 (1990): 751–768; W. L. James & K. J. Hatten, "Further Evidence on the Validity of the Self Typing Paragraph Approach: Miles and Snow Strategic Archetypes in Banking," *Strategic Management Journal* 16 (1995): 161–168.

[46] "U.S. Innovation Stories," *3M*. [Online] available at http://www.3m.com/frontindex_us.jhtml, 30 June 2003.

[47] G. Harris & J. Slater, "Bitter Pills: Drug Makers See 'Branded Generics' Eating into Profits," *The Wall Street Journal*, 17 April 2003, A1.

[48] M. Chen, "Competitor Analysis and Interfirm Rivalry: Toward a Theoretical Integration," *Academy of Management Review* 21 (1996): 100–134; J. C. Baum & H. J. Korn, "Competitive Dynamics of Interfirm Rivalry," *Academy of Management Journal* 39 (1996): 255–291.

[49] Ibid.

[50] S. Leung, "Wendy's Sees Green in Salad Offerings—More Sophistication, Ethnic Flavors Appeal to Women, Crucial to Building Market Share," *The Wall Street Journal*, 24 April 2003, B2.

[51] L. Lavelle, "The Chickens Come Home to Roost, and Boston Market Is Prepared to Expand," *The Record*, 6 October 1996.

[52] N. Shirouzu, "Though Japan Nears Saturation, Burger King Turns Up the Heat," *The Wall Street Journal Interactive Edition*, 31 January 1997.

[53] B. Upbin and D. Kruger, "Flipping Burgers; Will Burger King's New Owner Make It Sizzle?" *Forbes*, 22 July 2002, 62.

[54] G. Marcial, "How Wendy's Stayed Out of the Fire," *BusinessWeek*, 9 December 2002, 138.

[55] S. Kilman, "Leading the News: Diageo Says Industry Price War Is Crimping Its Burger King Sale," *The Wall Street Journal*, 8 November 2002, A3.

[56] J. Frontier, "Spies Like Us: You Don't Need to Be James Bond or IBM to Use Competitive Intelligence. Here's How It Works," *BusinessWeek*, 12 June 2000, F24.

[57] S. Matthews, "Financial: Salads Help McD Post First U.S. Sales Gain in 14 Months," *Chicago Sun-Times*, 14 May 2003, 69.

[58] "Bush Forms Presidential Commission to Overhaul USPS," *Catalog Age*, 1 February 2003; A. Greiling Keane, "Rx for USPS: Change," *Traffic World*, 3 March 2003, 9; K. Kraus, "Coulda Been Worse: USPS Celebrating Despite $676 Million Loss As It Refines Role in Competitive Marketplace," *Traffic World*, 16 December 2002, 30.

[59] P. Buhler, "Managing Your Career: No Longer Your Company's Responsibility," *Supervision*, May 1997.

CHAPTER 9

[1] "Corning Begins Implementation of Global Cost-Reduction Efforts," *Business Wire*, 4 June 2002, 15:01; C. Fishman, "Creative Tension: Corning Inc.'s Sullivan Park Research Facility Is One of the Most Creative Places in the World—A Place Where Brilliant (and Unruly) Scientists Literally Invent the Future," *Fast Company*, 1 November 2000, 359; C. Hymowitz, "In the Lead: Corning Manager Prods Her Researchers to Get 'in the Zone' on the Job," *The Wall Street Journal*, 20 November 2001, B1; M. Gurewitsch, "The Art and Science of Glass," *The Wall Street Journal*, 31 May 2000, A24; S. Mehta, "Can Corning Find Its Optic Nerve?" *Fortune*, 19 March 2001, 148; A. Velshi, P. Kiernan, & C. Huntington, "Stock of the Day: Corning CEO—

Jim Flaws," *CNNfn: The Money Gang*, 16 May 2003, 12:00; S. Young, "Corning to Tout Shift Out of Cookware," *The Wall Street Journal*, 5 December 2000, B8.

[2] T. M. Amabile, R. Conti, H. Coon, J. Lazenby, & M. Herron, "Assessing the Work Environment for Creativity," *Academy of Management Journal* 39 (1996): 1154–1184.

[3] Ibid.

[4] A. H. Van de Ven & M. S. Poole, "Explaining Development and Change in Organizations," *Academy of Management Review* 20 (1995): 510–540.

[5] G. Naik & T. Kamm, "Bold Stroke: Olivetti Reinvents Itself Once More, This Time as a Telecom Giant—Chief Colannino's Brash Move on Telecom Italia Portends New Greatness, If It Works—'The Italians Love to Talk,'" *The Wall Street Journal*, 22 February 1999, A1.

[6] G. Auman, "View from Above Provides Best Seat for Game," *St. Petersberg Times*, 25 January 2003, 10x; J. Krasner, "Blimp Management 101: Find a Crew with a Firm Grasp of the Bottom Line," *The Wall Street Journal*, 25 October 2000, NE4.

[7] Amabile, Conti, Coon, Lazenby, & Herron, "Assessing the Work Environment for Creativity."

[8] P. Anderson & M. L. Tushman, "Managing through Cycles of Technological Change," *Research/Technology Management*, May–June 1991, 26–31.

[9] R. N. Foster, *Innovation: The Attacker's Advantage* (New York: Summitt, 1986).

[10] iComp Index 2.0. Intel Corporation Web site, [Online] available at http://www.intel.com/procs/performance/icomp/index.htm, 5 December 1997.

[11] J. Burke, *The Day the Universe Changed* (Boston: Little, Brown, 1985).

[12] M. L. Tushman, P. C. Anderson, & C. O'Reilly, "Technology Cycles, Innovation Streams, and Ambidextrous Organizations: Organization Renewal through Innovation Streams and Strategic Change," in *Managing Strategic Innovation and Change*, ed. M. L. Tushman & P. Anderson (New York: Oxford Press, 1997), 3–23.

[13] G. Cowley & A. Underwood, "Surgeon, Drop That Scalpel," *Newsweek Special Issue: The Power of Invention*, Winter 1997–1998, 77–78.

[14] "Pony Express," *Encyclopædia Britannica Online*, [Online] available at http://www.eb.com:180/bol/topic?eu=62367&sctn=1, 6 March 1999.

[15] W. Abernathy & J. Utterback, "Patterns of Industrial Innovation," *Technology Review* 2 (1978): 40–47.

[16] H. Bolande, "Satellite Industry Looks to Web Access for Credibility in Telecommunications," *The Wall Street Journal*, 8 December 2000, B6.

[17] A. Moore, "Torture Testing Manufacturers Pound, Punish, and Even Destroy Products to Test Them to and beyond Their Limits. New Techniques Make Lab Tests Much Better, but Field Testing Is Still Critical," *Fortune*, 2 October 2000, 244.

[18] Amabile, Conti, Coon, Lazenby, & Herron, "Assessing the Work Environment for Creativity."

[19] Ibid.

[20] M. Csikszentmihalyi, *Flow: The Psychology of Optimal Experience* (New York: Harper & Row, 1990).

[21] D. Murphy, "Ways That Managers Can Help Workers—Or Hinder Them," *San Francisco Chronicle*, 26 November 2000, J1; M. Schrage, "Your Idea Is Brilliant; Glad I Thought of It," *Fortune*, 16 October 2000, 412.

[22] J. Pereira, "The 'Big' Idea: Itz Toys Flipped When 2 Kids Invented a New Game—Justin and Matthew, 11 and 12, Are Standouts; Linsay, Age 9, Is Scoring with Rapunzel," *The Wall Street Journal*, 12 February 2001, A1.

[23] K. M. Eisenhardt, "Accelerating Adaptive Processes: Product Innovation in the Global Computer Industry," *Administrative Science Quarterly* 40 (1995): 84–110.

[24] Ibid.

[25] "Rapid Prototyping = Rapid Time to Market," *Appliance Manufacturer*, 1 October 2001, 40.

[26] R. Winslow, "Atomic Speed: Utility Cuts Red Tape, Builds Nuclear Plant Almost on Schedule," *The Wall Street Journal Interactive*, 22 February 1984.

[27] A. Taylor III, "Kellogg Cranks Up Its Idea Machine: To Grow, the Company Needs New Products. but Will Fiber-Enriched Potato Chips Be a Hit?" *Fortune*, 5 July 1999, 181.

[28] L. Kraar, "25 Who Help the U.S. Win: Innovators Everywhere Are Generating Ideas to Make America a Stronger Competitor. They Range from a Boss Who Demands the Impossible to a Mathematician with a Mop," *Fortune*, 22 March 1991.

[29] M. W. Lawless & P. C. Anderson, "Generational Technological Change: Effects of Innovation and Local Rivalry on Performance," *Academy of Management Journal* 39 (1996): 1185–1217.

[30] S. Anderson & M. Uzumeri, "Managing Product Families: The Case of the Sony Walkman," *Research Policy* 24 (1995): 761–782.

[31] J. Muller, "Chrysler Redesigns the Way It Designs: Karenann Terrell's High-Tech Quest for Change," *BusinessWeek*, 2 September 2002, 26B.

[32] T. Zaun, "Micromanaging: In Japan, Tiny Cars Offer a Laboratory for Very Big Ideas—A Brutal Home Market Is Key to Success for Auto Makers," *The Wall Street Journal*, 5 August 2002, A1.

[33] J. O'Brien, "Accelerating the Process from Big Idea to Burning Rubber Foot on the Gas: High-Speed Approach to Car Production," *Birmingham Post*, 4 April 2001, 21.

[34] "End of the Road for MARS," *Music Trades*, 1 December 2002, 58.

[35] B. Herzog, "Lessons in Enterprise—Trouble in the Tower—Atwaters General Manager Stephan Earnhart Learns the Importance of Considering," *Portland Oregonian*, 1 October 2000, E1.

[36] K. Lewin, *Field Theory in Social Science: Selected Theoretical Papers* (New York: Harper & Brothers, 1951).

[37] A. B. Fisher, "Making Change Stick," *Fortune*, 17 April 1995, 121.

[38] J. P. Kotter & L. A. Schlesinger, "Choosing Strategies for Change," *Harvard Business Review*, March-April 1979, 106–114.

[39] M. Johne, "The Human Factor: Integrating People and Cultures after a Merger," *CMA Management*, 1 April 2000, 30.

[40] J. Sweatman, "Propaganda . . . It Simply Won't Work." *Corporate Trends*, [Online] available at http://www.corporatetrends.com.au/sweat1.html, 21 October 2001.

[41] R. H. Schaffer & H. A. Thomson, J. D, "Successful Change Programs Begin with Results," *Harvard Business Review on Change* (Boston: Harvard Business School Press, 1998), 189–213.

[42] T. Petzinger, Jr., "Forget Empowerment, This Job Requires Constant Brainpower," *The Wall Street Journal Interactive Edition*, 17 October 1997.

[43] R. N. Ashkenas & T. D. Jick, "From Dialogue to Action in GE WorkOut: Developmental Learning in a Change Process," in *Research in Organizational Change and Development*, vol. 6, ed.

W. A. Pasmore & R. W. Woodman (Greenwich, CT: JAI Press, 1992), 267–287.

44 T. Stewart, "GE Keeps Those Ideas Coming," *Fortune*, 12 August 1991, 40.

45 J. D. Duck, "Managing Change: The Art of Balancing," *Harvard Business Review on Change* (Boston: Harvard Business School Press, 1998), 55–81.

46 W. J. Rothwell, R. Sullivan, & G. M. McLean, *Practicing Organizational Development: A Guide for Consultants* (San Diego, CA: Pfeiffer & Co., 1995).

47 N. Shirouzu, "Gadget Inspector: Why Toyota Wins Such High Marks on Quality Surveys—Hajime Oba Is a Key Coach as Japanese Auto Maker Steps Up U.S. Production—Striving to Reach Heijunka," *The Wall Street Journal*, 15 March 2001, A1.

48 Ibid.

49 Rothwell, Sullivan, & McLean, *Practicing Organizational Development.*

50 W. Weitzel & E. Jonsson, "Reversing the Downward Spiral: Lessons from W.T. Grant and Sears Roebuck," *Academy of Management Executive* 5 (1991): 7–22.

51 J. P. Kotter, "Leading Change: Why Transformation Efforts Fail," *Harvard Business Review* 73, no. 2 (March-April 1995): 59.

52 W. Zellner, "The Right Place, The Right Time: CEO Bethune Has Continental Climbing," *BusinessWeek*, 27 May 1996, 74.

53 G. Bailey, "Manager's Journal: Fear Is Nothing to Be Afraid Of," *The Wall Street Journal Interactive Edition*, 27 January 1997.

54 P. J. Robertson, D. R. Roberts, & J. I. Porras, "Dynamics of Planned Organizational Change: Assessing Empirical Support for a Theoretical Model," *Academy of Management Journal* 36 (1993): 619–634.

55 G. Bethune, "From Worst to First: Continental Airlines Has Achieved One of the Most Dramatic Business Turnarounds of the Nineties," *Fortune*, 25 May 1998, 185–190.

56 "Air Travel Consumer Report," *U.S. Department of Transportation*, February 2003. [Online] available at http://airconsumer.ost.dot.gov/reports/2003/0302atcr.doc, 19 May 2003.

57 M. Brelis, "I've Got the Trust for CEO Bethune: The Key to Continental's Turnaround Is an Empowered Work Force, Not Slash-and-Burn," *Boston Globe*, 3 June 2001, E1.

58 Bethune, "From Worst to First."

59 Brelis, "I've Got the Trust for CEO Bethune."

60 Ibid.

61 Ibid.

62 "Get Your Fix at the Toll House Café," *Professional Candy Buyer*, January-February 2002, 62; "New Opportunities Taking Shape: Nestlé's Toll House Refrigerated Cookie Dough Keeps Raising the Bar on Innovation," *Refrigerated & Frozen Foods*, September 2002, 30; Stephanie Thompson, "Nestlé's New Line Breaks with Toll House Tradition: Big Dough Backs Break & Bake," *Advertising Age*, 27 September 1999, 8; "Vision Quest: A 10-Year Strategic Growth Plan Has Nestlé FoodServices Growing Inside and Out," *Refrigerated & Frozen Foods*, September 2002, 26.

63 J. Craddock, ed. *VideoHound's Golden Movie Retriever* (Farmington Hills, MI: The Gale Group, Inc., 2000).

CHAPTER 10

1 "Full Text of 11/13 Ballmer Memo; Memo from Microsoft CEO Steve Ballmer to Customers Focuses on How the Company's Role in the Industry Will Change Now That the Antitrust Suit Has Been Settled," *eWeek*, 13 November 2002; D. Bank, "How Steve Ballmer Is Already Remaking Microsoft," *The Wall Street Journal*, 17 January 2000, B1; B. Dudley, "Microsoft CEO Wants Company to Broaden Its Reach, Burnish Its Reputation," *Seattle Times*, 24 February 2003; J. Greene, S. Hamm, & J. Kerstetter, "Ballmer's Microsoft: How CEO Steve Ballmer Is Remaking the Company That Bill Gates Built," *BusinessWeek*, 17 June 2002, 66; K. Rebello & J. Greene, "Bill, On Switching Jobs with Steve," *BusinessWeek*, 17 June 2002, 75; B. Schlender, "Gates—The Grand Geek Steps Back," *The Business*, 7 July 2002.

2 B. Schlender, "Microsoft: The Beast Is Back," *Fortune*, 11 June 2001, 75.

3 M. Hammer & J. Champy, *Reengineering the Corporation: A Manifesto for Business Revolution* (New York: Harper & Row, 1993).

4 "About Borders Group," Borders Group, [Online] available at http://www.bordersgroupinc.com/about/index.html, 21 May 2003.

5 Marketing & Media, "Borders Will Reorganize Its Structure to Focus on Product Categories," *The Wall Street Journal*, 29 January 2001, B9.

6 J. G. March & H. A. Simon, *Organizations* (New York: John Wiley & Sons, 1958).

7 "Outline of Principal Operations," Sony Corporation, [Online] available at http://www.sony.com/SCA/outline.shtml, 21 May 2003.

8 "Names Figures Facts," Bayer, [Online] available at http://www.bayer.com/en/bayer/pdf/Names_Figures_Facts.pdf, 21 May 2003.

9 "Management's Discussion of Operations: Segment Operations, Summary of Operating Segments," *General Electric Annual Report 2002*, [Online] available at http://www.ge.com/ar2002/financial/md_and_a/summary. jsp, 21 May 2003.

10 "02 Annual Report," American Express, [Online] available at http://www.onlineproxy.com/amex/2003/ar/, 22 May 2003.

11 "Our Company: The Best Brands in the World," Coca-Cola Enterprises, [Online] available at http://www.cokecce.com/srclib/1.1.1.html, 21 May 2003.

12 L. R. Burns, "Adoption and Abandonment of Matrix Management Programs: Effects of Organizational Characteristics and Interorganizational Networks," *Academy of Management Journal* 36 (1993): 106–138.

13 H. Fayol, *General and Industrial Management*, transl. Constance Storrs (London: Pitman Publishing, 1949).

14 M. Weber, *The Theory of Social and Economic Organization*, transl. and ed. A. M. Henderson & T. Parsons (New York: Free Press, 1947).

15 Fayol, *General and Industrial Management.*

16 J. Rutledge, "Management by Belly Button," *Forbes*, 4 November 1996, 64.

17 E. E. Lawler, S. A. Mohrman, and G. E. Ledford, *Creating High Performance Organizations: Practices and Results of Employee Involvement and Quality Management in Fortune 1000 Companies* (San Francisco: Jossey-Bass, 1995).

18 C. Quintanilla, "Food: Come and Get It! Drive-Throughs Upgrade Services," *The Wall Street Journal Interactive*, 5 May 1994.

19 R. W. Griffin, *Task Design* (Glenview, IL: Scott, Foresman, 1982).

20 F. Herzberg, *Work and the Nature of Man* (Cleveland, OH: World Press, 1966).

21 A. Markels, "Team Approach: A Power Producer Is Intent on Giving Power to Its People—Groups of AES Employees Do Complex Tasks Ranging from Hiring to Investing—Making Sure Work Is 'Fun,'" *The Wall Street Journal*, 3 July 1995, A1.

[22] J. R. Hackman & G. R. Oldham, *Work Redesign* (Reading, MA: Addison-Wesley, 1980).

[23] Y. Fried & G. R. Ferris, "The Validity of the Job Characteristics Model: A Review and Meta-Analysis," *Personnel Psychology* 40 (1987): 287–322; B. T. Loher, R. A. Noe, N. L. Moeller, & M. P. Fitzgerald, "A Meta-Analysis of the Relation of Job Characteristics to Job Satisfaction," *Journal of Applied Psychology* 70 (1985): 280–289.

[24] T. Burns & G. M. Stalker, *The Management of Innovation* (London: Tavistock, 1961).

[25] M. Hammer & J. Champy, *Reengineering the Corporation: A Manifesto for Business Revolution* (New York: HarperBusiness, 1993).

[26] Ibid.

[27] J. D. Thompson, *Organizations in Action* (New York: McGraw-Hill, 1967).

[28] D. Pink, "Who Has the Next Big Idea?" *Fast Company*, 1 September 2001, 108.

[29] J. B. White, "'Next Big Thing': Re-Engineering Gurus Take Steps to Remodel Their Stalling Vehicles," *The Wall Street Journal Interactive Edition*, 26 November 1996.

[30] Ibid.

[31] G. M. Spreitzer, "Individual Empowerment in the Workplace: Dimensions, Measurement, and Validation," *Academy of Management Journal* 38 (1995): 1442–1465.

[32] K. W. Thomas & B. A. Velthouse, "Cognitive Elements of Empowerment," *Academy of Management Review* 15 (1990): 666–681.

[33] C. Daniels, "On the Job—Wall Street, Unbuttoned: The Man in the Tan Khaki Pants," *Fortune*, 1 May 2003.

[34] L. Munoz, "The Suit Is Back—Or Is It? As Dot-Coms Die, So Should Business Casual. But the Numbers Don't Lie," *Fortune*, 25 June 2001, 202; F. Swoboda, "Casual Dress Becomes the Rule," *The Las Vegas Review-Journal*, 3 March 1996.

[35] A. Merrick, "Tailors Spin a Yarn: Men's Suit Is Back! But Story Unravels—Stores Say 'Serious' Is In, Sales Keep Slacking Off; An Overstretched Theory," *The Wall Street Journal*, 27 December 2002, A1; Munoz, "The Suit Is Back."

[36] K. McCullough, "Analysis: More Companies Allowing Employees to Dress Down, Which Makes Productivity Go Up," *The Money Club*, 26 March 1996.

[37] "SHRM Online Poll Results," Society for Human Resource Management, [Online] available at http://www.shrm.org/poll/results.asp?Question=89, 21 May 2003.

[38] McCullough, "Analysis."

[39] W. Bounds, "Phone Calls Are Public Affairs for Open-Plan Office Dwellers," *The Wall Street Journal*, 10 July 2002, B1.

[40] "Designing the Ever-Changing Workplace," *Architectural Record*, September 1995, 32–37.

[41] F. Andrews, "Book Value: Learning to Celebrate Water-Cooler Gossip," *The New York Times*, 25 February 2001, L6.

[42] S. Hwang, "Cubicle Culture: Office Vultures Circle Still-Warm Desks Left Empty by Layoffs," *The Wall Street Journal*, 14 August 2002, B1.

[43] M. Rich, "Shut Up So We Can Do Our Jobs!—Fed Up Workers Try to Muffle Chitchat, Conference Calls and Other Open-Office Din," *The Wall Street Journal*, 29 August 2001, B1.

[44] Ibid.

[45] A. Camuffo, P. Romano, & A. Vinelli, "Back to the Future: Benetton Transforms Its Global Network," *Sloan Management Review* 46 (2001): 46–52.

[46] G. G. Dess, A. M. A. Rasheed, K. J. McLaughlin, & R. L. Priem, "The New Corporate Architecture," *Academy of Management Executive* 9 (1995): 7–18.

[47] B. Einhorn, "Laptop King: In a Year That's Decimated High Tech, Taiwan's Unstoppable Quanta Is Posting Double-Digit Sales Growth," *BusinessWeek*, 11 May 2001, 48.

[48] "Overview: Collaborative Business Network Solutions," *G5 Technologies: Agile Web*, [Online] available at http://www.agileweb.com/overview/index.html, 23 May 2003.

[49] J. H. Sheridan, "The Agile Web: A Model for the Future?" *Industry Week*, 4 March 1996, 31.

[50] Ibid.

[51] C. C. Snow, R. E. Miles, & H. J. Coleman, Jr., "Managing 21st Century Network Organizations," *Organizational Dynamics*, Winter 1992, 5–20.

[52] Sheridan, "The Agile Web: A Model for the Future?"

[53] M. Budman, "The Persistence of Perks," *Across the Board*, 1 February 1994; L. Fleeson, "In Today's Efficient, Egalitarian Offices, Plush Perks Are Passe," *The News Tribune*, 10 July 1994; S. Lohr, "Cubicle or Cavern? Egalitarian Work Space Duels with Need for Privacy among Brainy Folks in High-Tech Firms," *Rocky Mountain News*, 7 September 1997; T. Schellhardt, "Executive Pay (A Special Report)—Passing of Perks: Company Cars, Country Club Memberships, Executive Dining Rooms; Where Have All the Goodies Gone?" *The Wall Street Journal*, 13 April 1994.

[54] K. Freiberg & J. Freiberg, *Nuts! Southwest Airlines' Crazy Recipe for Business and Personal Success* (Austin, TX: Bard Press, 1996).

CHAPTER 11

[1] "Cessna Skyhawk," Learn to Fly.com, [Online] available at http://learntofly.com/howto/skyhawk.chtml, 29 May 2003; T. Greenwood, M. Bradford, & B. Greene, "Becoming a Lean Enterprise: A Tale of Two Firms," *Strategic Finance*, 1 November 2002, 32; B. Milligan, "Cessna Uses Baldrige Process to Identify Best Suppliers," *Purchasing*, 6 April 2000, 75; J. Morgan, "Cessna Charts a Supply Chain Flight Strategy," *Purchasing*, 7 September 2000, 42; J. Morgan, "Cross-Functional Buying: Why Teams Are Hot," *Purchasing*, 5 April 2001, 27; J. Morgan, "Cessna Aims to Drive SCM to Its Very Core: Here Are 21 Steps and Tools It's Using to Make This Happen," *Purchasing*, 6 June 2002, 31; P. Siekman, "Cessna Tackles Lean Manufacturing," *Fortune*, 1 May 2000, I222 B+; P. Siekman, "The Snap-Together Business Jet; Bombardier's New Recipe: A Dozen Big Pieces, Four Days to Assemble Them, and It's Ready to Fly," *Fortune*, 21 January 2002, 104A.

[2] B. Dumaine, "The Trouble with Teams," *Fortune*, 5 September 1994, 86–92.

[3] J. R. Katzenback & D. K. Smith, *The Wisdom of Teams* (Boston: Harvard Business School Press, 1993).

[4] S. G. Cohen & D. E. Bailey, "What Makes Teams Work: Group Effectiveness Research from the Shop Floor to the Executive Suite," *Journal of Management* 23, no. 3 (1997): 239–290.

[5] W. Zellner, "Team Player: No More 'Same-Ol'–Same-Ol,'" *BusinessWeek*, 17 October 1994, 95.

[6] S. E. Gross, *Compensation for Teams* (New York: American Management Association, 1995); B. L. Kirkman & B. Rosen, "Beyond Self-Management: Antecedents and Consequences of Team Empowerment," *Academy of Management Journal* 42 (1999): 58–74; G. Stalk & T. M. Hout, *Competing against Time: How Time-Based Competition Is Reshaping Global Markets* (New York: Free Press, 1990); S. C. Wheelwright & K. B. Clark, *Revolutionizing New Product Development* (New York: Free Press, 1992).

7 R. S. Wellins, W. C. Byham, & G. R. Dixon, *Inside Teams* (San Francisco: Jossey-Bass, 1994).

8 D. Kiley, "Crafty Basket Makers Cut Downtime, Waste. So Far, Changes Saving $3 Million a Year," *USA Today*, 10 May 2001, B3.

9 R. D. Banker, J. M. Field, R.G. Schroeder, & K. K. Sinha, "Impact of Work Teams on Manufacturing Performance: A Longitudinal Field Study," *Academy of Management Journal* 39 (1996): 867–890.

10 "Beating the Joneses (Learning What the Competition Is Doing)," *Industry Week* 1 (7 December 1998): 27.

11 Stalk & Hout, *Competing against Time*.

12 H. K Bowen, K. B. Clark, C. A. Holloway, & S. C. Wheelwright, *The Perpetual Enterprise Machine* (New York: Oxford Press, 1994).

13 Dahle, "Xtreme Teams," *Fast Company*, 1 November 1999, 310.

14 Ibid.

15 J. L. Cordery, W. S. Mueller, & L. M. Smith, "Attitudinal and Behavioral Effects of Autonomous Group Working: A Longitudinal Field Study," *Academy of Management Journal* 34 (1991): 464–476; T. D. Wall, N. J. Kemp, P. R. Jackson, & C. W. Clegg, "Outcomes of Autonomous Workgroups: A Long-Term Field Experiment," *Academy of Management Journal* 29 (1986): 280–304.

16 "Declaration of Interdependence," Whole Foods Market, [Online] available at http://www.wholefoodsmarket.com/company/declaration.html, 15 January 2002.

17 "Whole Foods Had Fresh Approach," *Work & Family Newsbrief*, January 2001, 4.

18 Wellins, Byham, & Dixon, *Inside Teams*.

19 A. Erez, J. Lepine, & H. Elms, "Effects of Rotated Leadership and Peer Evaluation on the Functioning and Effectiveness of Self-Managed Teams: A Quasi-Experiment," *Personnel Psychology* 55, issue 4 (2002): 929.

20 J. Hoerr, "The Payoff from Teamwork: The Gains in Quality Are Substantial—So Why Isn't It Spreading Faster?" *BusinessWeek*, 10 July 1989, 56.

21 T. Aeppel, "Missing the Boss: Not All Workers Find Idea of Empowerment As Neat As It Sounds—Some Hate Fixing Machines, Apologizing for Errors, Disciplining Teammates—Rah-Rah Types Do the Best," *The Wall Street Journal*, 8 September 1997, A1.

22 J. George, "Extrinsic and Intrinsic Origins of Perceived Social Loafing in Organizations," *Academy of Management Journal* 35 (1992): 191–202.

23 T. T. Baldwin, M. D. Bedell, & J. L. Johnson, "The Social Fabric of a Team-Based M.B.A. Program: Network Effects on Student Satisfaction and Performance," *Academy of Management Journal* 40 (1997): 1369–1397.

24 Hoerr, "The Payoff from Teamwork: The Gains in Quality Are Substantial—So Why Isn't It Spreading Faster?"

25 C. Joinson, "Teams at Work," *HRMagazine*, 1 May 1999, 30.

26 R. Wageman, "Critical Success Factors for Creating Superb Self-Managing Teams," *Organizational Dynamics* 26, no. 1 (1997): 49–61.

27 A. Taylor III, "Can the Germans Rescue Chrysler?" *Fortune*, 30 April 2001, 106.

28 R. T. King, Jr., "Jeans Therapy: Levi's Factory Workers Are Assigned to Teams, and Morale Takes a Hit—Infighting Rises, Productivity Falls as Employees Miss the Piecework System—'It's Not the Same Company,'" *The Wall Street Journal*, 20 May 1998, A1.

29 Ibid.

30 King, Jr., "Jeans Therapy."

31 Kirkman & Rosen, "Beyond Self-Management: Antecedents and Consequences of Team Empowerment."

32 M. Curtius, "There Is No 'I' in 'Team'—And Maybe No Point, Either: The Trend Continues but Doesn't Always Succeed. Finding the Proper Structure, Motivating Employees and Getting Managers out of the Way Can Sometimes Help," *Los Angeles Times*, 24 February 1997. D25.

33 G. Harris, "The Cure: With Big Drugs Dying, Merck Didn't Merge—It Found New Ones," *The Wall Street Journal*, 10 January 2001, A1.

34 G. Bylinsky, "Heroes of U.S. Manufacturing," *Fortune*, 19 March 2001, 177.

35 Kirkman & Rosen, "Beyond Self-Management: Antecedents and Consequences of Team Empowerment."

36 S. Easton & G. Porter, "Selecting the Right Team Structure to Work in Your Organization," in *Handbook of Best Practices for Teams*, Vol. 1, ed. G. M. Parker (Amherst, MA: Irwin, 1996).

37 "Labor-Employee Participation Committees Receive NLRB's Approval," *Personnel Manager's Legal Letter*, 1 October 2001.

38 C. Fishman, "Engines of Democracy: The General Electric Plant in Durham, North Carolina Builds Some of the World's Most Powerful Jet Engines. But the Plant's Real Power Lies in the Lessons That It Teaches about the Future of Work and about Workplace Democracy," *Fast Company*, 1 October 1999, 174.

39 R. J. Recardo, D. Wade, C. A. Mention, & J. Jolly, *Teams* (Houston: Gulf Publishing Co., 1996).

40 D. R. Denison, S. L. Hart, & J. A. Kahn, "From Chimneys to Cross-Functional Teams: Developing and Validating a Diagnostic Model," *Academy of Management Journal* 39, no. 4 (1996): 1005–1023.

41 A. M. Townsend, S. M. DeMarie, & A. R. Hendrickson, "Virtual Teams: Technology and the Workplace of the Future," *Academy of Management Executive* 13, no. 3 (1998): 17–29.

42 A. M. Townsend, S. M. DeMarie, & A. R. Henfrickson, "Are You Ready for Virtual Teams?" *HRMagazine* 41, no. 9 (1996): 122–126.

43 "The Boeing 777," Selah School District Web site, [Online] available at http://www.selah.wednet.edu, 9 September 1998.

44 Wellins, Byham, & Dixon, *Inside Teams*.

45 Townsend, DeMarie, & Hendrickson, "Virtual Teams: Technology and the Workplace of the Future."

46 W. F. Cascio, "Managing a Virtual Workplace," *Academy of Management Executive* 14 (2000): 81–90.

47 L. Miller, "What's New?" *HRMagazine*, 1 March 1999, 140.

48 R. Katz, "The Effects of Group Longevity on Project Communication and Performance," *Administrative Science Quarterly* 27 (1982): 245–282.

49 D. Mankin, S. G. Cohen, & T. K. Bikson, *Teams and Technology: Fulfilling the Promise of the New Organization* (Boston: Harvard Business School Press, 1996).

50 K. Lovelace, D. Shapiro, & L. Weingart. "Maximizing Cross-Functional New Product Teams' Innovativeness and Constraint Adherence: A Conflict Communications Perspective," *Academy of Management Journal* 44 (2001): 779–793.

51 G. Anthes, "Think Globally, Act Locally: Running Global IT Operations Effectively Often Means Creating Standard Systems and Processes That Have to Be Tweaked to Meet Local Requirements," *Computer World*, 28 May 2001, 36.

[52] L. Holpp & H. P. Phillips, "When Is a Team Its Own Worst Enemy?" *Training,* 1 September 1995, 71.

[53] S. Asche, "Opinions and Social Pressure," *Scientific America* 193 (1995): 31–35.

[54] G. Smith, "How Nucor Steel Rewards Performance and Productivity," *Business Know How,* [Online] available at http://www.businessknowhow.com/manage/nucor.htm, 26 May 2003.

[55] S. G. Cohen, G. E. Ledford, & G. M. Spreitzer, "A Predictive Model of Self-Managing Work Team Effectiveness," *Human Relations* 49, no. 5 (1996): 643–676.

[56] K. Bettenhausen & J. K. Murnighan, "The Emergence of Norms in Competitive Decision-Making Groups," *Administrative Science Quarterly* 30 (1985): 350–372.

[57] M. E. Shaw, *Group Dynamics* (New York: McGraw Hill, 1981).

[58] S. E. Jackson, "The Consequences of Diversity in Multidisciplinary Work Teams," in *Handbook of Work Group Psychology,* ed. M. A. West (Chichester, UK: Wiley, 1996).

[59] A. M. Isen & R. A. Baron, "Positive Affect as a Factor in Organizational Behavior," in *Research in Organizational Behavior* 13, ed. L. L. Cummings & B. M. Staw (Greenwich, CT: JAI Press, 1991), 1–53.

[60] C. R. Evans & K. L. Dion, "Group Cohesion and Performance: A Meta Analysis," *Small Group Research* 22, no. 2 (1991): 175–186.

[61] S. M. Gully, D. S. Devine, and D. J. Whitney, "A Meta-Analysis of Cohesion and Performance: Effects of Level of Analysis and Task Interdependence," *Small Group Research* 26, no. 4 (1995): 497–520.

[62] R. Stankiewicsz, "The Effectiveness of Research Groups in Six Countries," in *Scientific Productivity,* ed. F. M. Andrews (Cambridge: Cambridge University Press, 1979), 191–221.

[63] F. Rees, *Teamwork from Start to Finish* (San Francisco: Jossey-Bass, 1997).

[64] Gully, Devine, & Whitney, "A Meta-Analysis of Cohesion and Performance."

[65] E. Matson, "Four Rules for Fast Teams," *Fast Company,* August 1996, 87.

[66] F. Tschan & M. V. Cranach, "Group Task Structure, Processes and Outcomes," in *Handbook of Work Group Psychology,* ed. M. A. West (Chichester, UK: Wiley, 1996).

[67] D. E. Yeatts & C. Hyten, *High Performance Self Managed Teams* (Thousand Oaks, CA: Sage Publications, 1998).

[68] Ibid; J. Colquitt, R. Noe, & C. Jackson, "Justice in Teams: Antecedents and Consequences of Procedural Justice Climate," *Personnel Psychology,* 1 April 2002, 83.

[69] D. S. Kezsbom, "Re-Opening Pandora's Box: Sources of Project Team Conflict in the '90s," *Industrial Engineering* 24, no. 5 (1992): 54–59.

[70] A. C. Amason, W. A. Hochwarter, K. R. Thompson, "Conflict: An Important Dimension in Successful Management Teams," *Organizational Dynamics* 24 (1995): 20.

[71] A. C. Amason, "Distinguishing the Effects of Functional and Dysfunctional Conflict on Strategic Decision Making: Resolving a Paradox for Top Management Teams," *Academy of Management Journal* 39, no. 1 (1996): 123–148.

[72] K. M. Eisenhardt, J. L. Kahwajy, & L. J. Bourgeois III, "How Management Teams Can Have a Good Fight," *Harvard Business Review* 75, no. 4 (July-August 1997): 77–85.

[73] Eisenhardt, Kahwajy, & Bourgeois, "How Management Teams Can Have a Good Fight."

[74] C. Nemeth & P. Owens, "Making Work Groups More Effective: The Value of Minority Dissent," in *Handbook of Work Group Psychology,* ed. M. A. West (Chichester, UK: Wiley, 1996).

[75] J. M. Levin & R. L. Moreland, "Progress in Small Group Research," *Annual Review of Psychology* 9 (1990): 72–78; S. E. Jackson, "Team Composition in Organizational Settings: Issues in Managing a Diverse Work Force," in *Group Processes and Productivity,* ed. S. Worchel, W. Wood, & J. Simpson (Beverly Hills, CA: Sage, 1992).

[76] Eisenhardt, Kahwajy, & Bourgeois, "How Management Teams Can Have a Good Fight."

[77] B. W. Tuckman, "Development Sequence in Small Groups," *Psychological Bulletin* 63, no. 6 (1965): 384–399.

[78] Gross, *Compensation for Teams.*

[79] J. F. McGrew, J. G. Bilotta, & J. M. Deeney, "Software Team Formation and Decay: Extending the Standard Model for Small Groups," *Small Group Research* 30, no. 2 (1999): 209–234.

[80] Ibid.

[81] J. Case, "What the Experts Forgot to Mention: Management Teams Create New Difficulties, but Succeed for Xel Communication," *Inc.,* 1 September 1993, 66.

[82] J. R. Hackman, "The Psychology of Self-Management in Organizations," in *Psychology and Work: Productivity, Change, and Employment,* ed. M. S. Pallak & R. Perloff (Washington DC: American Psychological Association, 1986), 85–136.

[83] A. O Leary-Kelly, J. J. Martocchio, & D. D. Frink, "A Review of the Influence of Group Goals on Group Performance," *Academy of Management Journal* 37, no. 5 (1994): 1285–1301.

[84] G. Smith, "How Nucor Steel Rewards Performance and Productivity," *Business Know How,* [Online] available at http://www.businessknowhow.com/manage/nucor.htm, 26 May 2003.

[85] A. Zander, "The Origins and Consequences of Group Goals," in *Retrospections on Social Psychology,* ed. L. Festinger (New York: Oxford University Press, 1980), 205–235.

[86] M. Erez & A. Somech, "Is Group Productivity Loss the Rule or the Exception? Effects of Culture and Group-Based Motivation," *Academy of Management Journal* 39, no. 6 (1996): 1513–1537.

[87] S. Sherman, "Stretch Goals: The Dark Side of Asking for Miracles," *Fortune,* 13 November 1995, 231.

[88] K. R. Thompson, W. A. Hochwarter, & N. J. Mathys, "Stretch Targets: What Makes Them Effective?" *Academy of Management Executive* 11, no. 3 (1997): 48–60.

[89] Sherman, "Stretch Goals: The Dark Side of Asking for Miracles."

[90] G. Mazurkiewicz, "Let Your Techs Manage Themselves," *Air Conditioning, Heating & Refrigeration News,* 25 December 2000, 10.

[91] Dumaine, "The Trouble with Teams."

[92] G. A. Neuman, S. H. Wagner, & N. D. Christiansen, "The Relationship between Work-Team Personality Composition and the Job Performance of Teams," *Group & Organization Management* 24, no. 1 (1999): 28–45.

[93] M. A. Campion, G. J. Medsker, & A. C. Higgs, "Relations between Work Group Characteristics and Effectiveness: Implications for Designing Effective Work Groups," *Personnel Psychology* 46, no. 4 (1993): 823–850.

[94] B. L. Kirkman & D. L. Shapiro, "The Impact of Cultural Values on Employee Resistance to Teams: Toward a Model of Globalized Self-Managing Work Team Effectiveness," *Academy of Management Review* 22, no. 3 (1997): 730–757.

[95] Fishman, "Engines of Democracy."

[96] J. Bunderson & K. Sutcliffe, "Comparing Alternative Conceptualizations of Functional Diversity in Management Teams: Process and Performance Effects," *Academy of Management Journal* 45 (2002): 875–893.

[97] J. Hackman, "New Rules for Team Building—The Times Are Changing—And So Are the Guidelines for Maximizing Team Performance," *Optimize*, 1 July 2002, 50.

[98] M. A. Verespej, "Super Sack," *Industry Week*, 16 October 1995, 53.

[99] Joinson, "Teams at Work."

[100] Wellins, Byham, & Dixon, *Inside Teams*.

[101] S. Caudron, "Tie Individual Pay to Team Success," *Personnel Journal* 73, no. 10 (October 1994): 40.

[102] Ibid.

[103] Gross, *Compensation for Teams*.

[104] J. R. Schuster & P. K. Zingheim, *The New Pay: Linking Employee and Organizational Performance* (New York: Lexington Books, 1992).

[105] G. Shives & K. Scott, "Gainsharing and EVA: The U.S. Postal Service Experience," *WorldatWork Journal*, 1 January 2003, 21.

[106] Cohen & Bailey, "What Makes Teams Work."

[107] R. Allen & R. Kilmann, "Aligning Reward Practices in Support of Total Quality Management," *Business Horizons* 44 (May 2001): 77–85.

[108] J. H. Sheridan, "'Yes' to Team Incentives," *Industry Week*, 4 March 1996, 63.

[109] R. Fazio Maruca, "What Makes Teams Work?" *Fast Company*, November 2000; R. Rivenburg, "Extreme Management," *Los Angeles Times*, 20 November 2001.

[110] M. A. West, ed., *Handbook of Work Group Psychology* (Chichester, UK: Wiley, 1996).

CHAPTER 12

[1] "Electronic Arts Los Angeles—EALA—Hires Acclaimed Creative Talent from Film and Video Game Industries," *Business Wire*, 8 April 2003; B. Berkowitz, "Electronic Arts Readies Hollywood Production Push," *Reuters News*, 30 January 2003, 19:45; A. Muoio, "Man with a (Talent) Plan: Electronic Arts Makes Some of the World's Most Popular Computer Games. It's Rusty Rueff's Job to Fill the Company with Some of the World's Best Gamers and Software Programmers," *Fast Company*, 1 January 2001, 83; C. Salter, "Playing to Win," *Fast Company*, 2 December 2002, 80; W. Stueck, "Electronic Arts Builds Workplace Wonder High-Tech Playground: How Do You Keep Workaholic Computer Game Designers Happy? Give Them an Office That's Both Fun and Functional," *Globe & Mail*, 21 September 1998, B13; K. Tran, "Now Hot in Games: A Job—Videogame Industry Booms in Downturn, and Employers Get Picky with Their Hires," *The Asian Wall Street Journal*, 14 August 2002, A5.

[2] S. Bing, "The Feds Make a Pass at Hooters," *Fortune*, 15 January 1996, 82.

[3] C. Roush & J. Cummings, "Hooters Wins EEOC Skirmish in Sexual Bias Battle," *Atlanta Constitution*, 2 May 1996, F1; J. Malone & C. Roush, "Restaurant Chain Goes to Battle," *Atlanta Constitution*, 16 November 1995, Section F, p. 3; D. Cardinal, "Hooters Girls on Endangered Species List," *Business Record* (Des Moines, Iowa), 11 December 1995, 19; K. D. Grimsley, "Hooters Plays Hardball with the EEOC," *Washington Post*, 12 December 1995, Section H, p. 1; "EEOC's Politically Correct Crusade against Hooters a Wasted Effort," *Nation's Restaurant News*, 4 December 1995, 19; S. Keating, "Feds Press Equal-Opportunity Ogling: Hooters Says EEOC Effort to Force Male Waiters Is Absurd," *Denver Post*, 16 November 1995, Section C, p. 1; J. Hayes, "Hooters Comes Out against EEOC Sex-Bias Suit," *Nation's Restaurant News*, 27 November 1995, 3; A. Samuels, "Pushing Hot Buttons and Wings," *St. Petersburg Times*, 10 March 2003, 1A.

[4] P. S. Greenlaw & J. P. Kohl, "Employer 'Business' and 'Job' Defenses in Civil Rights Actions," *Public Personnel Management* 23, no. 4 (1994): 573.

[5] Associated Press, "Hooters Settles Suit, Won't Hire Waiters," *Denver Post*, 1 October 1997, A11.

[6] N. Shirouzu, "Nine Ford Workers File Bias Suit Saying Ratings Curb Older Staff," *The Wall Street Journal*, 15 February 2001; "Ford Reaches Tentative Settlement in Suits," *The Wall Street Journal*, 19 December 2001, B12.

[7] J. L. Ledvinka, *Federal Regulation of Personnel and Human Resource Management* (Boston: Kent Publishing Co., 1982), 137–198.

[8] "Pueblo, Colo., Steel Mill Gets Fine Reduced by OSHA to $300,000," *Knight Ridder Tribune Business News*, 17 May 2001.

[9] E. Emery, "U.S. Fines Steel Mill $487,000: OSHA Inspection Finds 107 Safety Violations in Plant," *Denver Post*, 23 August 2000, C1.

[10] Greenlaw & Kohl, "Employer 'Business' and 'Job' Defenses in Civil Rights Actions."

[11] "Judge Approves Settlement of Coca-Cola Bias Lawsuit," *The Wall Street Journal*, 30 May 2001, B7.

[12] "Rent-A-Center Settles Gender-Bias Lawsuit, Will Pay $12.3 Million," *The Wall Street Journal*, 2 November 2001.

[13] W. Peirce, C. A. Smolinski, & B. Rosen, "Why Sexual Harassment Complaints Fall on Deaf Ears," *Academy of Management Executive* 12, no. 3 (1998): 41–54.

[14] A. Levin, "Prudential Hit with 10 Discrimination Suits," *National Underwriter* 103, no. 4 (1999): 2.

[15] Peirce, Smolinski, & Rosen, "Why Sexual Harassment Complaints Fall on Deaf Ears."

[16] Ibid.

[17] "Facts about Sexual Harassment." U.S. Equal Employment Opportunity Commission, [Online] available at http://www.eeoc.gov/facts/fs-sex.html, 23 May 1999.

[18] Peirce, Smolinski, & Rosen, "Why Sexual Harassment Complaints Fall on Deaf Ears."

[19] Ibid.

[20] E. Larson, "The Economic Costs of Sexual Harassment," *Liberty Haven*, [Online] available at http://www.libertyhaven.com/personalfreedomissues/consensualcrimesorsexualissues/ecosexual.html, 27 January 2002.

[21] K. Dunham & G. Ip, "Slow Economy Takes Unusually Heavy Toll on White-Collar Jobs," *The Wall Street Journal*, 5 November 2001, A1.

[22] C. Prystay , "U.S. Solution Is Philippine Dilemma—As Recruiters Snap Up More Nurses, Hospitals in Manila Are Scrambling," *The Wall Street Journal*, 18 July 2002, A8.

[23] C. Hymowitz, "Shrewd New Tactics Help Two Companies Snare the Top Talent," *The Wall Street Journal*, 29 February 2000, B1; P. Nakache, "Cisco's Recruiting Edge—Find 'Em, Lure 'Em, Keep 'Em Happy: Devising New Ways to Steal Top Talent from Competitors Has Given This Silicon Valley Standout an Important Advantage," *Fortune*, 29 September 1997, 275.

[24] R. D. Gatewood & H. S. Field, *Human Resource Selection* (Fort Worth, TX: Dryden Press, 1998).

[25] Ibid.

[26] *Griggs v. Duke Power Co.*, 401 U.S. 424, 436 (1971); *Albemarle Paper Co. v. Moody*, 422 U.S. 405 (1975).

[27] P. R. Chowdhury, "Human Resources: Beyond Downsizing, Growing the TCM Manager," *Business Today*, 7 January 1999, 172.

[28] J. A. Breaugh, *Recruitment: Science and Practice* (Boston: PWS-Kent, 1992).

[29] J. Breaugh & M. Starke, "Research on Employee Recruitment: So Many Studies, So Many Remaining Questions" *Journal of Management* 26 (2000): 405–434.

[30] A. Milkovits, "Survey Shows Methods Vary for Selecting Police Recruits," *Providence Journal*, 19 May 2003, B-01.

[31] C. Camden & B. Wallace, "Job Application Forms: A Hazardous Employment Practice," *Personnel Administrator* 28 (1983): 31–32.

[32] J. S. Pouliot, "Topics to Avoid with Applicants," *Nation's Business* 80, no. 7 (1992): 57.

[33] J. Kennedy, "Europeans Expect Different Type of Résumé," *Chicago Sun-Times*, 3 June 1999, 73.

[34] K. Maher, "Career Journal: The Jungle," *The Wall Street Journal*, 6 May 2003, B8.

[35] J. Tamen, "Job Applicants' Résumés Are Often Riddled with Misinformation," *South Floridan Sun-Sentinel*, 24 February 2003.

[36] M. Mandell, "The High Cost of Hiring Fakers," *World Trade* 11, no. 3 (1998): 56.

[37] B. Weinstein, "Tips for Getting References to Talk," *Career. WSJ.Com.* [Online] available at http://www.careerjournal.com/jobhunting/resumes/19980909weinstein.html.

[38] J. Hunter, "Cognitive Ability, Cognitive Aptitudes, Job Knowledge, and Job Performance," *Journal of Vocational Behavior* 29 (1986): 340–362.

[39] E. E. Cureton, "Comment," in E. R. Henry, *Research Conference on the Use of Autobiographical Data as Psychological Predictors* (Greensboro, NC: The Richardson Foundation, 1965), 13.

[40] J. R. Glennon, L. E. Albright, & W. A. Owens, *A Catalog of Life History Items* (Greensboro, NC: The Richardson Foundation, 1966).

[41] Gatewood & Field, *Human Resource Selection*.

[42] J. M. Digman, "Personality Structure: Emergence of the Five-Factor Model," *Annual Review of Psychology* 41 (1990): 417–440; M. R. Barrick & M. K. Mount, "The Big Five Personality Dimensions and Job Performance: A Meta-Analysis," *Personnel Psychology* 44 (1991): 1–26.

[43] D. Fenn, "Hiring: Employee Auditions," *Inc.*, June 1996, 116.

[44] M. S. Taylor & J. A. Sniezek, "The College Recruitment Interview: Topical Content and Applicant Reactions," *Journal of Occupational Psychology* 57 (1984): 157–168.

[45] J. Cortina, N. Goldstein, S. Payne, K. Davison, & S. Gilliland, "The Incremental Validity of Interview Scores Over and Above Cognitive Ability and Conscientiousness Scores," *Personnel Psychology* 53, issue 2 (2000): 325–351; F. L. Schmidt & J. E. Hunter, "The Validity and Utility of Selection Methods in Personnel Psychology: Practical and Theoretical Implications of 85 Years of Research Findings," *Psychological Bulletin* 124, no. 2 (1998): 262–274.

[46] A. Hirsh, "Tricky Questions Reign in Behavioral Interviews," *National Business Employment Weekly* (posted on Careers. WSJ.com), [Online] available at http://www.careerjournal.com/ jobhunting/interviewing/19990420-hirsch.html, 5 February 2002.

[47] M. A. Campion, D. K. Palmer, & J. E. Campion, "A Review of Structure in the Selection Interview," *Personnel Psychology* 50, no. 3 (1997): 655–702.

[48] T. Judge, "The Employment Interview: A Review of Recent Research and Recommendations for Future Research," *Human Resource Management Review* 10, issue 4 (2000): 383–406.

[49] D. Stafford, "Workers Train, Companies Gain: Harmon Industries, Sprint, Others Make a Big Commitment," *Kansas City Star*, 16 February 1999, D1.

[50] S. Livingston, T. W. Gerdel, M. Hill, B. Yerak, C. Melvin, & B. Lubinger, "Ohio's Strongest Companies All Agree That Training Is Vital to Their Success," *Cleveland Plain Dealer*, 21 May 1997, 30S.

[51] G. Kesler, "Why the Leadership Bench Never Gets Deeper: Ten Insights about Executive Talent Development," *Human Resource Planning*, 1 January 2002, 32.

[52] D. L. Kirkpatrick, "Four Steps to Measuring Training Effectiveness," *Personnel Administrator* 28 (1983): 19–25.

[53] U. Gupta, "TV Seminars and CD-ROMs Train Workers," *The Wall Street Journal*, 3 January 1996, B1.

[54] J. Stack, "The Curse of the Annual Performance Review," *Inc.*, 1 March 1997, 39.

[55] D. Murphy, "Are Performance Appraisals Worse Than a Waste of Time? Book Derides Unintended Consequences," *San Francisco Chronicle*, 9 September 2001, W1.

[56] J. Yankovic, "Are the Reviews In?" *Pittsburgh Business Times* 16 (28 October 1996): 7.

[57] D. J. Woehr & A. I. Huffcutt, "Rater Training for Performance Appraisal: A Quantitative Review," *Journal of Occupational and Organizational Psychology* 67, no. 3 (1994): 189–205.

[58] Stack, "The Curse of the Annual Performance Review."

[59] C. Hymowitz, "Do '360' Job Reviews by Colleagues Promote Honesty or Insults?" *The Wall Street Journal*, 12 December 2000, B1.

[60] D. A. Waldman, L. E. Atwater, & D. Antonioni, "Has 360 Feedback Gone Amok?" *Academy of Management Executive* 12, no. 2 (1998): 86–94.

[61] H. H. Meyer, "A Solution to the Performance Appraisal Feedback Enigma," *Academy of Management Executive* 5, no. 1 (1991): 68–76.

[62] G. C. Thornton, "Psychometric Properties of Self-Appraisals of Job Performance," *Personnel Psychology* 33 (1980): 263–271.

[63] Meyer, "A Solution to the Performance Appraisal Feedback Enigma."

[64] T. Aeppel, "Toyota Plant Roils the Hiring Hierarchy of an Indiana Town," *The Wall Street Journal*, 6 April 1999, A1.

[65] G. T. Milkovich & J. M. Newman, *Compensation*, 4th ed. (Homewood. IL: Irwin,1993).

[66] E. Rasmusson, "Ten Things Your Child Care Provider Won't Tell You," *SmartMoney*, 1 May 2003, 69.

[67] M. L. Williams & G. F. Dreher, "Compensation System Attributes and Applicant Pool Characteristics," *Academy of Management Journal* 35, no. 3 (1992): 571–595.

[68] Business Brief, "Profit-Sharing Checks Hit Record for Hourly Workers," *The Wall Street Journal Interactive*, 28 January 2000.

[69] M. Bloom, "The Performance Effects of Pay Dispersion on Individuals and Organizations," *Academy of Management Journal* 42, no. 1 (1999): 25–40.

[70] L. Lavelle, F. Jespersen, S. Ante, & J. Kerstetter, "Executive Pay: The Days of the Fantasyland CEO Pay Package Appear to Be in the Past. A 33% Decline in Compensation Has Returned America's Bosses to the Year 1996," *BusinessWeek*, 21 April 2003, 86.

[71] W. Grossman & R. E. Hoskisson, "CEO Pay at the Crossroads of Wall Street and Main: Toward the Strategic Design of Executive Compensation," *Academy of Management Executive* 12, no. 1 (1998): 43–57.

[72] Bloom, "The Performance Effects of Pay Dispersion on Individuals and Organizations."

[73] J. S. Rosenbloom, "The Environment of Employee Benefit Plans," in *The Handbook of Employee Benefits*, ed. J. S. Rosenbloom (Chicago: Irwin, 1996), 3–13.

[74] "Employer Costs for Employee Compensation Summary," Bureau of Labor Statistics, [Online] available at http://www.bls.gov/ news.release/ecec.nr0.htm, 1 June 2003.

[75] A. E. Barber, R. B. Dunham, & R. A. Formisano, "The Impact of Flexible Benefits on Employee Satisfaction: A Field Study," *Personnel Psychology* 45 (1992): 55–75; B. Heshizer, "The Impact of Flexible Benefits on Job Satisfaction and Turnover Intentions," *Benefits Quarterly* 4 (1994): 84–90; D. M. Cable & T. A. Judge, "Pay Preferences and Job Search Decisions: A Person-Organization Fit Perspective," *Personnel Psychology* 47 (1994): 317–348.

[76] B. T. Beam & J. J. McFadden, *Employee Benefits* (Chicago: Dearborn Financial Publishing, 1996).

[77] J. Lublin, "Left Out of a Meeting? Parking Space Taken? Worry about Your Job," *The Wall Street Journal*, 3 April 2001, B1.

[78] K. Labich & E. M. Davies, "How to Fire People and Still Sleep at Night. Shedding Employees Is Something Almost Every Manager Dreads. But If You Don't Think Hard about the Process, You and Your Company Could Be Headed Straight for a World of Woes," *Fortune*, 10 June 1996, 64.

[79] Ibid.

[80] P. Michal-Johnson, *Saying Good-Bye: A Manager's Guide to Employee Dismissal* (Glenview, IL: Scott, Foresman & Co., 1985).

[81] M. Bordwin, "Employment Law: Beware of Time Bombs and Shark-Infested Waters," *HR Focus*, 1 April 1995, 19.

[82] T. Bland, "Fire at Will, Repent at Leisure," *Security Management* 44 (May 2000), 64.

[83] J. R. Morris, W. F. Cascio, & C. E. Young, "Downsizing after All These Years: Questions and Answers about Who Did It, How Many Did It, and Who Benefited from It," *Organizational Dynamics* 27, no. 3 (1999): 78–87.

[84] Ibid.

[85] K. E. Mishra, G. M. Spreitzer, & A. K. Mishra, "Preserving Employee Morale during Downsizing," *Sloan Management Review* 39, no. 2 (1998): 83–95.

[86] B. Morris & M. Borden, "White Collar Blues; Free Agency Is Over. Layoffs Are Back. Many of the People Losing Their Jobs Are White-Collar and College Educated. You Could Be Next," *Fortune*, 23 July 2001, 98.

[87] K. Frieswick, "Until We Meet Again?" *CFO*, 1 October 2001, 41.

[88] J. Ackerman, "Helping Layoff Survivors Cope: Companies Strive to Keep Morale High," *Boston Globe*, 30 December 2001, H1.

[89] Ibid.

[90] Ibid.

[91] D. R. Dalton, W. D. Todor, & D. M. Krackhardt, "Turnover Overstated: The Functional Taxonomy," *Academy of Management Review* 7 (1982): 117–123.

[92] J. R. Hollenbeck & C. R. Williams, "Turnover Functionality versus Turnover Frequency: A Note on Work Attitudes and Organizational Effectiveness," *Journal of Applied Psychology* 71 (1986): 606–611.

[93] C. R. Williams, "Reward Contingency, Unemployment, and Functional Turnover," *Human Resource Management Review* 9 (1999): 549–576.

[94] A. Fisher, "I Want to Join Another Firm's Board, but My Boss Says No," *Fortune*, 14 April 2003, 398.

CHAPTER 13

[1] S. Collins, "Waiting for the Sofa—Furniture Sales Are Back Up, but So Are Delivery Times; Five Months—and Counting," *The Wall Street Journal*, 26 April 2002, W14; J. Hagerty & R. Berner, "On the Couch: Ever Wondered Why Furniture Shopping Can Be Such a Pain?—Clues: Splintered Industry, Old-Time Technologies and Dubious Marketing—The Spring Table Falls Flat," *The Wall Street Journal*, 2 November 1998, A1; K. Kunkel, "Bassett Unveils Custom Sofa Program," *HFN The Weekly Newspaper for the Home Furnishing Network*, 5 April 1999; D. Morse, "Tennessee Producer Tries New Tactic in Sofas: Speed," *The Wall Street Journal*, 19 November, 2002, A1; J. Pierpoint, "Furniture Makers Cut Lines in Bid to Speed Delivery," *Reuters News*, 15 April 1999, 17:18.

[2] "Ryanair Profits Soar," *Daily Telegraph*, [Online] available at http://www.telegraph.co.uk/news/main.jhtml?xml=/news/2003/06/03/uryan.xml&sSheet=/portal/2003/06/03/ixportaltop.html, 3 June 2003.

[3] L. Tutor, "Navigating the Loop: The Best Drive-Through in America, 2002," *Quick Service Restaurant*, [Online] available at http://www.qsrmagazine.com/drive-thru/2002/2002_QSR_Drivethru_Study.pdf, 3 May 2003.

[4] "Historical Income Tables—Families," U.S. Census Bureau, [Online] available at http://www.census.gov/hhes/income/histinc/f06.html, 3 June 2003.

[5] S. Vaught, "Time Savers Are Lifesaver for Harried Workers," *Los Angeles Times*, 1 April 2001, W1.

[6] R. Rundle & Murray, "Health & Medicine (A Special Report)—The Have-Nots: Can the Problem of the Uninsured Be Solved? Here Are Some of the Proposed Solutions—And Their Prospects," *The Wall Street Journal*, 21 February 2001, R7.

[7] "Auto Affordability Steady in First Quarter 2003," Comerica. [Online] available at http://www.comerica.com/cma/cda/main/0,00,1_A_1299,00.html, 3 June 2003.

[8] J. Ball, "The Economy: GM Bests Ford in Efficiency, but Both Trail Japanese Firms," *The Wall Street Journal*, 14 June 2002, A2.

[9] Ibid.

[10] "Multifactor Productivity: Frequently Asked Questions," Bureau of Labor Statistics, [Online] available at http://stats.bls.gov/mprfaq.htm, 7 March 1998.

[11] "ASQ Glossary of Terms Search," American Society for Quality, [Online] available at http://www.asq.org/info/glossary/q.html, 3 June 2003.

[12] R. E. Markland, S. K. Vickery, & R. A. Davis, "Managing Quality" (Chapter 7), *Operations Management: Concepts in Manufacturing and Services* (Cincinnati, OH: South-Western College Publishing, 1998).

[13] J. H. Sheridan, "At a Glance: Physio-Control Corp," *Industry Week*, 21 October 1996, 46.

[14] L. L. Berry & A. Parasuraman, *Marketing Services* (New York: Free Press, 1991).

[15] P. Judge, "When a Customer Believes in You . . . They'll Stick with You Almost No Matter What," *Fast Company* 47 (June 2001): 138.

[16] Ibid.

[17] Ibid.

[18] "ASQ and the Standards," American Society for Quality, [Online] available at http://www.asq.org/stand/faq/faq2.html, 3 June 2003.

[19] R. Henkoff, "The Not New Seal of Quality (ISO 9000 Standard of Quality Management)," *Fortune*, 28 June 1993, 116.

[20] Ibid.

[21] P. Sebastian, "Business Bulletin: A Special Background Report on Trends in Industry and Finance," *The Wall Street Journal*, 14 November 1996, A1.

[22] "Frequently Asked Questions about the Malcolm Baldrige National Quality Award," National Institute for Standards and Technology, [Online] available at http://www.nist.gov/public_affairs/factsheet/baldfaqs.htm, 6 June 2003.

[23] "Fees for the 2002 Award Cycle," Baldrige National Quality Program 2002, [Online] available at http://www.quality.nist.gov/Fees.htm, 3 June 2003.

[24] "Frequently Asked Questions and Answers about the Malcolm Baldrige National Quality Award."

[25] "Criteria for Performance Excellence," Baldrige National Quality Program 2003, [Online] available at http://www.quality.nist.gov/PDF_files/2003_Business_Criteria.pdf, 3 June 2003.

[26] Ibid.

[27] "NIST Stock Studies Show Quality Pays (Baldrige National Quality Award)," National Institute for Standards and Technology, [Online] available at http://www.quality.nist.gov/Stock_Studies.htm, 3 June 2003.

[28] J. W. Dean, Jr. & J. Evans, *Total Quality: Management, Organization, and Strategy* (St. Paul, MN: West Publishing Co., 1994).

[29] J. W. Dean, Jr & D. E. Bowen, "Management Theory and Total Quality: Improving Research and Practice through Theory Development," *Academy of Management Review* 19 (1994): 392–418.

[30] R. Allen & R. Kilmann, "Aligning Reward Practices in Support of Total Quality Management," *Business Horizons*, 1 May 2001, 77.

[31] T. Murphy & R. Schreffler, "Life after Spin-off," *Ward's Auto World*, 1 August 2001, 34.

[32] G. Bylinsky, "Heroes of U.S. Manufacturing," *Fortune*, 19 March 2001, 178B.

[33] R. Hallowell, L. A. Schlesinger, & J. Zornitsky, "Internal Service Quality, Customer and Job Satisfaction: Linkages and Implications for Management," *Human Resource Planning* 19 (1996): 20–31; J. L. Heskett, T. O. Jones, G. W. Loveman, W. E. Sasser, Jr., & L. A. Schlesinger, "Putting the Service-Profit Chain to Work," *Harvard Business Review*, March-April 1994, 164–174.

[34] J. Huey, G. Bethune, & H. Kelleher, "Two Texas Mavericks Rant about the Wreckage of the U.S. Aviation Industry—And Reveal How They've Managed to Keep Their Companies above the Miserable Average," *Fortune*, 13 November 2000, 237.

[35] G. Brewer, "The Ultimate Guide to Winning Customers: The Customer Stops Here," *Sales & Marketing Management* 150 (March 1998): 30.

[36] T. Levitt, "Production-Line Approach to Service," *Harvard Business Review*, September-October 1972, 41–52; T. Levitt, "Industrialization of Service," *Harvard Business Review*, September-October 1976, 63–74.

[37] L. L. Berry & A. Parasuraman, "Listening to the Customer—The Concept of a Service-Quality Information System," *Sloan Management Review* 38, no. 3 (Spring 1997): 65; C. W. L. Hart, J. L. Heskett, & W. E. Sasser, Jr., "The Profitable Art of Service Recovery," *Harvard Business Review*, July-August 1990, 148–156.

[38] M. Adams, "When Something Is Wrong, Those Who Care Make It Right: Give Employees the Power to Help Customers, Experts," *USA Today*, 12 September 2000, 11E.

[39] D. E. Bowen & E. E. Lawler III, "The Empowerment of Service Workers: What, Why, How, and When," *Sloan Management Review* 33 (Spring 1992): 31–39; D. E. Bowen & E. E. Lawler III, "Empowering Service Employees," *Sloan Management Review* 36 (Summer 1995): 73–84.

[40] Bowen & Lawler III, "The Empowerment of Service Workers: What, Why, How, and When."

[41] S. Hale, "The Customer Is Always Right—Usually—Some Are Just Annoying, but Others Deserve the Boot," *Orlando Sentinel*, 15 April 2002, § 54.

[42] S. Berne, "Five Fabulous Food Plants," *Prepared Foods*, 1 June 1996, 80.

[43] G. McWilliams, "How Dell Fine-Tunes Its PC Pricing to Gain Edge in a Slow Market: Working with Suppliers, It Quickly Passes Changes in Costs to Customers, Three Prices for One Product," *The Wall Street Journal*, 8 June 2001, A1.

[44] E. Eldridge, "Signs Indicate Auto Industry Needs Tune-up: Automakers Cut Production as Inventory Swells," *USA Today*, 26 February 2001, 7B.

[45] G. McWilliams, "Under Gateway's Tree, Another Shake-Up," *The Wall Street Journal*, 6 January 2003, A13.

[46] D. Drickhamer, "Reality Check," *Industry Week*, November 2001, 29.

[47] D. Drickhamer, "Zeroing In on World-Class," *Industry Week*, November 2001, 36.

[48] J. R. Henry, "Minimized Setup Will Make Your Packaging Line S.M.I.L.E.," *Packaging Technology & Engineering*, 1 February 1998, 24.

[49] J. Donoghue, "The Future Is Now," *Air Transport World*, 1 April 2001, 78.

[50] F. Brookman, "Managing Inventory (EDI)," *Women's Wear*, 19 September 1997, 20.

[51] T. Minahan, "JIT: A Process with Many Faces," *Purchasing*, 4 September 1997, 42.

[52] N. Shirouzu, "Why Toyota Wins Such High Marks on Quality Surveys," *The Wall Street Journal*, 15 March 2001, A1.

[53] Ibid.

[54] C. Crowell, "Seeing the Big Picture through Software (Manufacturing Resource Planning Computer Programs)," *American Metal Market*, 22 July 1997, 12.

[55] E. Gehrman, "Factory Facts Show Heart, Soul of America," *Boston Herald*, 29 January 1998; E. Perkins, "Factory Tour Can Be Fun, Not to Mention Real Cheap," *Orlando Sentinel*, 1 February, 1998, L6; L. Singhania (Associated Press), "Breakfast for Battle Creek's New Cereal City," *Grand Rapids Press*, 24 May 1998, F2; C. Quintanilla, "Planning a Vacation? Give Some Thought to Spamtown USA," *The Wall Street Journal*, 30 April 1998, A1.

[56] J. Craddock, ed. *VideoHound's Golden Movie Retriever* (Farmington Hills, MI: The Gale Group, Inc., 2000).

CHAPTER 14

[1] "CDW History," CDW, [Online] available at http://www.cdw.com/webcontent/inside/history/historypg.asp, 9 June 2003; "Company Overview," CDW, [Online] available at http://www.cdw.com/webcontent/inside/companyoverview.asp, 9 June 2003; K. Jones, B. Caulfield, L. Gilman, I. Mount, E. Schonfeld, & O. Thomas, "The Dell Way," *Business 2.0*, February 2003, 61; G. McWilliams, "Little CDW Stays Robust Amid Tech Crisis," *The Wall Street Journal*, 6 February 2003, B4; P. Sloan, "Dell's Man on Deck," *Business 2.0*, February 2003, 65; M. Tatge, "Baby Dell CDW Has Become the Number One Reseller of Computer Products by Peddling the Old-Fashioned Way—Person-to-Person," *Forbes*, 27 November 2000, 92.

[2] J. P. Campbell & R. D. Pritchard, "Motivation Theory in Industrial and Organizational Psychology," in *Handbook of Industrial and Organizational Psychology*, ed. M. D. Dunnette (Chicago: Rand McNally, 1976).

[3] P. Thomas, "Waitress Makes the Difference in Bringing Deaf to Pittsburgh," *The Wall Street Journal Interactive Edition*, 2 March 1999.

[4] J. Spencer, "Shirk Ethic: How to Fake a Hard Day at the Office—White-Collar Slackers Get Help from New Gadgets; The Faux 4 A.M. E-Mail," *The Wall Street Journal*, 15 May 2003, D1.

[5] N. Mangi, "It's Payback Time: Freedom, Perks, and Parties Aren't Enough Anymore. What Top People Want Now from Small Employers Is a Raise—A Big One," *BusinessWeek*, 9 October 2000, F24.

[6] Ibid.

[7] E. A. Locke, "The Nature and Causes of Job Satisfaction," in *Handbook of Industrial and Organizational Psychology*, ed. M. D. Dunnette (Chicago: Rand McNally, 1976).

[8] A. H. Maslow, "A Theory of Human Motivation," *Psychological Review* 50 (1943): 370–396.

[9] C. P. Alderfer, *Existence, Relatedness, and Growth: Human Needs in Organizational Settings* (New York: Free Press, 1972).

[10] D. C. McClelland, "Toward a Theory of Motive Acquisition," *American Psychologist* 20 (1965): 321–333; D.C. McClelland & D. H. Burnham, "Power Is the Great Motivator," *Harvard Business Review* 54, no. 2 (1976): 100–110.

[11] J. H. Turner, "Entrepreneurial Environments and the Emergence of Achievement Motivation in Adolescent Males," *Sociometry* 33 (1970): 147–165.

[12] L. W. Porter, E. E. Lawler III, & J. R. Hackman, *Behavior in Organizations* (New York: McGraw-Hill, 1975).

[13] E. E. Lawler III & L. W. Porter, "The Effect of Performance on Job Satisfaction," *Industrial Relations* 7 (1967): 20–28.

[14] Porter, Lawler III, & Hackman, *Behavior in Organizations.*

[15] Porter, Lawler III, & Hackman, *Behavior in Organizations.*

[16] P. Brotherton, "The Company That Plays Together . . . ," *HR Magazine* 41 (December 1996): 76–82; K. Johnson, "Companies Try New Perks to Keep Stressed Workers Happy," *Lawrence Eagle-Tribune*, 26 September 1995, A1; D. Selinsky, "Happy Campers," *Success*, 1 April 2001, 54.

[17] C. Caggiano, "What Do Workers Want?" *Inc.*, November 1992, 101–104; "National Study of the Changing Workforce," Families and Work Institute, [Online] available at http://www.familiesandwork.org/summary/nscw.pdf, 6 June 2003.

[18] L. Buchanan, "Managing One-to-One," *Inc.*, 1 October 2001, 82.

[19] Ibid.

[20] "America@Work: A Focus on Benefits and Compensation," Aon Consulting, [Online] available at http://www.aon.com/pdf/america/awork2.pdf, 12 June 1999.

[21] K. Hammonds, "Handle with Care: How UPS Handles Packages Starts with How It Handles Its People," *Fast Company*, 1 August 2002, 102.

[22] S. Stecklow, "Fast Finns' Fines Fit Their Finances—Traffic Penalties Are Assessed According to Driver Income," *The Wall Street Journal*, 2 January 2001, A1.

[23] C. T. Kulik & M. L. Ambrose, "Personal and Situational Determinants of Referent Choice," *Academy of Management Review* 17 (1992): 212–237.

[24] J. S. Adams, "Toward an Understanding of Inequity," *Journal of Abnormal Social Psychology* 67 (1963): 422–436.

[25] J. Greenberg, "Employee Theft as a Reaction to Underpayment Inequity: The Hidden Costs of Pay Cuts," *Journal of Applied Psychology* 75 (1990): 561–568.

[26] R. A. Cosier & D. R. Dalton, "Equity Theory and Time: A Reformulation," *Academy of Management Review* 8 (1983): 311–319; M. R. Carrell & J. E. Dittrich, "Equity Theory: The Recent Literature, Methodological Considerations, and New Directions," *Academy of Management Review* 3 (1978): 202–209.

[27] J. Bendich, "When Is a Temp Not a Temp?" *Trial Magazine*, 1 October 2001, 42.

[28] J. Pollack, "Exemption under the Fair Labor Standards Act: The Cost of Misclassifying Employees," *Cornell Hotel & Restaurant Administration Quarterly* 42 (2001): 16.

[29] K. Aquino, R. W. Griffeth, D. G. Allen, & P. W. Hom, "Integrating Justice Constructs into the Turnover Process: A Test of a Referent Cognitions Model," *Academy of Management Journal* 40, no. 5 (1997): 1208–1227.

[30] S. Barr, "While the SEC Watches the Markets, the Job Market Is Draining the SEC," *Washington Post*, 10 March 2002, C3.

[31] C. Fishman, "Sanity, Inc.," *Fast Company*, January 1999, 85–96.

[32] R. Folger & M. A. Konovsky, "Effects of Procedural and Distributive Justice on Reactions to Pay Raise Decisions," *Academy of Management Journal* 32 (1989): 115–130; M. A. Konovsky, "Understanding Procedural Justice and Its Impact on Business Organizations," *Journal of Management* 26 (2000): 489–512.

[33] E. Barret-Howard & T. R. Tyler, "Procedural Justice as a Criterion in Allocation Decisions," *Journal of Personality and Social Psychology* 50 (1986): 296–305; Folger & Konovsky, "Effect of Procedural and Distributive Justice on Reactions to Pay Raise Decisions."

[34] R. Folger & J. Greenberg, "Procedural Justice: An Interpretive Analysis of Personnel Systems," in *Research in Personnel and Human Resources Management*, Vol. 3, ed. K. Rowland & G. Ferris (Greenwich, CT: JAI Press, 1985); R. Folger, D. Rosenfield, J. Grove, & L. Corkran, "Effects of 'Voice' and Peer Opinions on Responses to Inequity," *Journal of Personality and Social Psychology* 37 (1979): 2253–2261; E. A. Lind & T. R. Tyler, *The Social Psychology of Procedural Justice* (New York: Plenum Press, 1988); Konovsky, "Understanding Procedural Justice and Its Impact on Business Organizations."

[35] K. A. Dolan, "When Money Isn't Enough," *Forbes*, 18 November 1996, 164–170.

[36] V. H. Vroom, *Work and Motivation* (New York: John Wiley & Sons, 1964); L. W. Porter & E. E. Lawler III, *Managerial Attitudes and Performance* (Homewood, IL: Dorsey Press & Richard D. Irwin, 1968).

[37] Buchanan, "Managing One-to-One."

[38] P. V. LeBlanc & P. W. Mulvey, "How American Workers See the Rewards of Work," *Compensation & Benefits Review* 30 (February 1998): 24–28.

[39] A. Fox, "Companies Can Benefit When They Disclose Pay Processes to Employees," *HR Magazine* 47 (July 2002): 25.

[40] S. Scholl, "Allstate Pay for Performance Methodology Rewards Excellence," *ACANEWS 41*, no. 8 (1998): 24.

[41] K. W. Thomas & B. A. Velthouse, "Cognitive Elements of Empowerment," *Academy of Management Review* 15 (1990): 666–681.

[42] D. Milbank, "Workplace: Companies Turn to Peer Pressure to Cut Injuries as Psychologists Join the Battle," *The Wall Street Journal*, 29 March 1991, B1.

[43] E. L. Thorndike, *Animal Intelligence* (New York: Macmillan, 1911).

[44] Milbank, "Workplace: Companies Turn to Peer Pressure to Cut Injuries as Psychologists Join the Battle."

[45] B. F. Skinner, *Science and Human Behavior* (New York: Macmillan, 1954); B. F. Skinner, *Beyond Freedom and Dignity* (New York: Bantam Books, 1971); B. F. Skinner, *A Matter of Consequences* (New York: New York University Press, 1984).

[46] A. M. Dickinson & A. D. Poling, "Schedules of Monetary Reinforcement in Organizational Behavior Management: Latham and Huber Revisited," *Journal of Organizational Behavior Management* 16, no. 1 (1992): 71–91.

[47] P. Kitchen, "Appreciation Builds a Better Workplace," *Newsday,* 11 February 2001, F11.

[48] R. Ho, "Attending to Attendance," *The Wall Street Journal Interactive,* 7 December 1998.

[49] D. Grote, "Manager's Journal: Discipline without Punishment," *The Wall Street Journal,* 23 May 1994, A14.

[50] J. Drucker, "Performance Bonus Out of Reach? Move the Target," *The Wall Street Journal,* 29 April 2003, B1.

[51] J. B. Miner, *Theories of Organizational Behavior* (Hinsdale, IL: Dryden, 1980).

[52] Dickinson & Poling, "Schedules of Monetary Reinforcement in Organizational Behavior Management."

[53] F. Luthans & A. D. Stajkovic, "Reinforce for Performance: The Need to Go beyond Pay and Even Rewards," *Academy of Management Executive* 13, no. 2 (1999): 49–57.

[54] A. D. Stajkovic & F. Luthans, "A Meta-Analysis of the Effects of Organizational Behavior Modification on Task Performance, 1975–95," *Academy of Management Journal* 40, no. 5 (1997): 1122–1149; A. D. Stajkovic & F. Luthans, "Behavioral Management and Task Performance in Organizations: Conceptual Background, Meta-analysis, and Test of Alternative Models," *Personnel Psychology* 56, issue 1 (2003): 155–194.

[55] J. Glater, "Management: Seasoning Compensation Helps TV Operation Improve Morale," *New York Times,* [Online] available at http://query.nytimes.com/search/abstract?res=F60717F93A5F0C748CDDAA0894D9404482, 7 March 2001.

[56] K. D. Butterfield, L. K. Trevino, & G. A. Ball, "Punishment from the Manager's Perspective: A Grounded Investigation and Inductive Model," *Academy of Management Journal* 39 (1996): 1479–1512.

[57] R. D. Arvey & J. M. Ivancevich, "Punishment in Organizations: A Review, Propositions, and Research Suggestions," *Academy of Management Review* 5 (1980): 123–132.

[58] R. D. Arvey, G. A. Davis, & S. M. Nelson, "Use of Discipline in an Organization: A Field Study," *Journal of Applied Psychology* 69 (1984): 448–460; M. E. Schnake, "Vicarious Punishment in a Work Setting," *Journal of Applied Psychology* 71 (1986): 343–345.

[59] E. A. Locke & G. P. Latham, *Goal Setting: A Motivational Technique That Works* (Englewood Cliffs, NJ: Prentice-Hall, 1984); E. A. Locke & G. P. Latham, *A Theory of Goal Setting and Task Performance* (Englewood Cliffs, NJ: Prentice-Hall, 1990).

[60] T. Petzinger, Jr., "Competent Workers and a Complex Leader Keep Big Oil in Check," *The Wall Street Journal,* 4 December 1998, B1.

[61] G. P. Latham & E. A. Locke, "Goal Setting—A Motivational Technique That Works," *Organizational Dynamics* 8, no. 2 (1979): 68.

[62] Ibid.

[63] Z. Zhiwei, J. A. Wallin, & R. A. Reber, "Safety Improvements: An Application of Behaviour Modification Techniques," *Journal of Applied Management Studies* 15 (2000): 135–140.

[64] M. Conlin, "Compensation Is Getting Personal: Companies Are Mining Employee Data to Identify the Perks That Spur Productivity," *BusinessWeek Online,* 6 December 2002.

[65] M. Boyle, "How to Cut Perks without Killing Morale," *Fortune,* 19 February 2001; T. Pollock, "Managing for Better Morale," *Automotive Manufacturing & Production,* February 2001.

CHAPTER 15

[1] "Xerox's Chief Copies Good Practice Not Past Mistakes," *Irish Times,* 21 March 2003; D. Fuscaldo, "In the Pipeline: Loyalty Pays Off for Xerox Veteran," *Dow Jones News Service,* 27 August 2002, 10:00; B. Morris, "The Accidental CEO; She Was Never Groomed to Be the Boss. But Anne Mulcahy Is Bringing Xerox Back from the Dead," *Fortune,* 23 June 2003, 58; O. Kharif, "Anne Mulcahy Has Xerox by the Horns: The CEO Launched the Ailing Copier Giant's Turnaround by Cutting Costs, Emphasizing Clients, and Boosting Morale," *Business Week Online,* 29 May 2003, [Online] available at http://asia.businessweek.com/technology/content/may2003/tc20030529_1642_tc111.htm, 14 June 2003; S. Roth, "Xerox CEO Proud of Company's Recovery," *Gannett News Service,* 2 April 2003; D. Rushe, "Some Blondes Have No Time to Have Fun—Interview—Anne Mulcahy," *The Sunday Times,* 20 October 2002.

[2] C. Hymowitz, "In the Lead: How Cynthia Danaher Learned to Stop Sharing and Start Leading," *The Wall Street Journal,* 16 March 1999, B1.

[3] G. Colvin, "The Changing Art of Becoming Unbeatable," *Fortune,* 24 November 1997, 299–300.

[4] W. Bennis, "Why Leaders Can't Lead," *Training & Development Journal* 43, no. 4 (1989).

[5] A. Zaleznik, "Managers and Leaders: Are They Different?" *Harvard Business Review* 55 (1977): 76–78; A. Zaleznik, "The Leadership Gap," *The Washington Quarterly* 6 (1983): 32–39.

[6] K. Freiberg & J. Freiberg, *Nuts! Southwest Airlines' Crazy Recipe for Business and Personal Success* (Austin, TX: Bard Press, 1996).

[7] Bennis, "Why Leaders Can't Lead."

[8] T. A. Stewart, A. Harrington, & M. G. Solovar, "America's Most Admired Companies: Why Leadership Matters," *Fortune,* 2 March 1998, 70.

[9] R. J. House & R.M Aditya, "The Social Scientific Study of Leadership: Quo Vadis?" *Journal of Management* 23 (1997): 409–473; S. A. Kirkpatrick & E. A. Locke, "Leadership: Do Traits Matter?" *Academy of Management Executive* 5, no. 2 (1991): 48–60.

[10] House & Aditya, "The Social Scientific Study of Leadership"; Kirkpatrick & Locke, "Leadership: Do Traits Matter?"

[11] J. B. Fuller, C. E. P. Patterson, K. Hester, & D. Stringer, "A Quantitative Review of Research on Charismatic Leadership," *Psychological Reports* 78 (1996): 271–287; R. G. Lord, C. L. De Vader, & G. M. Alliger, "A Meta-Analysis of the Relation between Personality Traits and Leadership Perceptions: An Application of Validity Generalization Procedures," *Journal of Applied Psychology* 71, no. 3 (1986): 402–410.

[12] Kirkpatrick & Locke, "Leadership: Do Traits Matter?"

[13] E. A. Fleishman, "The Description of Supervisory Behavior," *Personnel Psychology* 37 (1953): 1–6; L. R. Katz, *New Patterns of Management* (New York: McGraw-Hill, 1961).

[14] R. Charan & G. Colvin, "Why CEOs Fail: It's Rarely for Lack of Smarts or Vision. Most Unsuccessful CEOs Stumble Because of One Simple, Fatal Shortcoming," *Fortune,* 21 June 1999, 68.

[15] K. Brooker, "Starting Over," *Fortune,* 21 January 2002, 50.

[16] P. Weissenberg & M. H. Kavanagh, "The Independence of Initiating Structure and Consideration: A Review of the Evidence," *Personnel Psychology* 25 (1972): 119–130.

[17] R. J. House & T. R. Mitchell, "Path-Goal Theory of Leadership," *Journal of Contemporary Business* 3 (1974): 81–97; F. E. Fiedler, "A Contingency Model of Leadership Effectiveness," in *Advances in Experimental Social Psychology,* ed L. Berkowitz (New York: Academic Press, 1964); V. H. Vroom & P. W. Yetton, *Leadership and Decision Making* (Pittsburgh: University of Pittsburgh Press, 1973); P. Hersey & K. H. Blanchard, *The Management of Organizational Behavior,* 4th ed. (Englewood Cliffs, NJ: Prentice Hall, 1984); S. Kerr & J. M. Jermier, "Substitutes for Leadership: Their Meaning and Measurement," *Organizational Behavior and Human Performance* 22 (1978): 375–402.

[18] F. E. Fiedler & M. M. Chemers, *Leadership and Effective Management* (Glenview, IL: Scott, Foresman, 1974); F. E. Fiedler & M. M. Chemers, *Improving Leadership Effectiveness: The Leader Match Concept,* 2d ed. (New York: John Wiley & Sons, 1984).

[19] J. Carlton, "Thinking Different: At Apple, a Fiery Jobs Often Makes Headway and Sometimes a Mess—He Knows How to Market but Clashes with Cloners and Belittles His Foes—Skewered on the Gil-O-Meter," *The Wall Street Journal,* 14 April 1998, A1.

[20] Fiedler & Chemers, *Improving Leadership Effectiveness: The Leader Match Concept.*

[21] F. E. Fiedler, "The Effects of Leadership Training and Experience: A Contingency Model Interpretation," *Administrative Science Quarterly* 17, no. 4 (1972): 455; F. E. Fiedler, *A Theory of Leadership Effectiveness* (New York: McGraw-Hill, 1967).

[22] L. S. Csoka & F. E. Fiedler, "The Effect of Military Leadership Training: A Test of the Contingency Model," *Organizational Behavior and Human Performance* 8 (1972): 395–407.

[23] House & Mitchell, "Path-Goal Theory of Leadership."

[24] House & Mitchell, "Path-Goal Theory of Leadership."

[25] B. M. Fisher & J. E. Edwards, "Consideration and Initiating Structure and Their Relationships with Leader Effectiveness: A Meta-Analysis," *Proceedings of the Academy of Management,* August 1988, 201–205.

[26] M. Gimein, "Wal-Mart's Founder Made a Pact with Employees: He Would Be Fair to Them, and They Would Work Hard for Him. It Was a Good Deal, But Can It Survive in the 24-Hour Service Economy?" *Fortune,* 18 March 2002, 120.

[27] G. Gendron, "Schwarzkopf on Leadership," *Inc.,* January 1992, 11.

[28] J. C. Wofford & L. Z. Liska, "Path-Goal Theories of Leadership: A Meta-Analysis," *Journal of Management* 19 (1993): 857–876.

[29] House & Aditya, "The Social Scientific Study of Leadership."

[30] P. Hersey & K. Blanchard, *Management of Organizational Behavior: Leading Human Resources,* 8th ed. (Escondido, CA: Center for Leadership Studies, 2001).

[31] W. Blank, J. R. Weitzel, & S. G. Green, "A Test of the Situational Leadership Theory," *Personnel Psychology* 43, no. 3 (1990): 579–597; W. R. Norris & R. P. Vecchio, "Situational Leadership Theory: A Replication," *Group & Organization Management* 17, no. 3 (1992): 331–342.

[32] Ibid.

[33] V. H. Vroom & A. G. Jago, *The New Theory of Leadership: Managing Participation in Organizations* (Englewood Cliffs, NJ: Prentice Hall, 1988).

[34] C. Fishman, "How Teamwork Took Flight: This Team Built a Commercial Engine—and Self-Managing GE Plant—from Scratch," *Fast Company,* 1 October 1999, 188.

[35] Ibid.

[36] Ibid.

[37] G. A. Yukl, *Leadership in Organizations,* 3d ed. (Englewood Cliffs, NJ: Prentice Hall, 1995).

[38] B. M. Bass, *Bass & Stogdill's Handbook of Leadership: Theory, Research, and Managerial Applications* (New York: Free Press, 1990).

[39] R. D. Ireland & M. A. Hitt, "Achieving and Maintaining Strategic Competitiveness in the 21st Century: The Role of Strategic Leadership," *Academy of Management Executive* 13, no. 1 (1999): 43–57.

[40] J. Collins, "The Secret Life of the CEO: Is the Economy Just Built to Flip?: Here's the Truth: The Problem Isn't the Market's Rise or Fall. The Problem Is People Who React to Events, Rather Than Seek to Create Something Great," *Fast Company,* 1 October 2002, 88.

[41] P. Thoms & D. B. Greenberger, "Training Business Leaders to Create Positive Organizational Visions of the Future: Is It Successful?" *Academy of Management Journal* [Best Papers & Proceedings], 1995, 212–216.

[42] M. Weber, *The Theory of Social and Economic Organizations,* trans. R. A. Henderson & T. Parsons (New York: Free Press, 1947).

[43] D. A. Waldman & F. J. Yammarino, "CEO Charismatic Leadership: Levels-of-Management and Levels-of-Analysis Effects," *Academy of Management Review* 24, no. 2 (1999): 266–285.

[44] K. B. Lowe, K. G. Kroeck, & N. Sivasubramaniam, "Effectiveness Correlates of Transformational and Transactional Leadership: A Meta-Analytic Review of the MLQ Literature," *Leadership Quarterly* 7 (1996): 385–425.

[45] J. M. Howell & B. J. Avolio, "The Ethics of Charismatic Leadership: Submission or Liberation?" *Academy of Management Executive* 6, no. 2 (1992): 43–54.

[46] P. Sellers, "What Exactly Is Charisma?" *Fortune,* 15 January 1996, 68; W. Parker, "Developing Your Charisma," Work Star Net, [Online] available at http://workstar.net/library/charisma.htm, 24 March 2002.

[47] Howell & Avolio, "The Ethics of Charismatic Leadership."

[48] Howell & Avolio, "The Ethics of Charismatic Leadership."

[49] J. M. Burns, *Leadership* (New York: Harper & Row, 1978); B. M. Bass, "From Transactional to Transformational Leadership: Learning to Share the Vision," *Organizational Dynamics* 18 (1990): 19–36.

[50] B. M. Bass, *A New Paradigm of Leadership: An Inquiry into Transformational Leadership* (Alexandra, VA: U.S. Army Research Institute for the Behavioral and Social Sciences, 1996).

[51] Bass, "From Transactional to Transformational Leadership."

[52] P. Sellers, "The New Breed: The Latest Crop of CEOs Is Disciplined, Deferential, Even a Bit Dull. What a Relief," *Fortune,* 18 November 2002, 66.

[53] J. Lublin, "Corporate Governance (A Special Report)—What's Your Solution? We Asked Some Experts, and Here's What They Said," *The Wall Street Journal,* 24 February 2003, R8.

[54] P. LaBaree, "Leader—Feargal Quinn: Ireland's 'Pope of Customer Service' Dominates His Market—and Continues to Beat Bigger and Better-Financed Rivals—with a Leadership Philosophy That Is At Once Folksy and Radical. Behind All His Success Is One Big Question: How Do We Convince Our Customers to Come Back?" *Fast Company,* 1 November 2001, 88.

[55] Bass, "From Transactional to Transformational Leadership."

[56] D. Brady, "Why Martha Is Risking All," *Business Week Online,* 12 June 2003; J. D. Heyman, "Pressure Cooker: Facing Possi-

ble Jail Time, Martha Stewart Gives Up the Helm of the Company She Built, but Rallies Her Fans and Keeps Her Trademark Cool," *People Weekly*, 23 June 2003, 56; D. Hughes, "Early Signs Indicate Martha Stewart's Company Cannot Do without Maven Herself," *Knight Ridder Tribune Business News*, 8 June 2003; "Martha Gears Up to Fight Feds," *Knight Ridder Tribune Business News*, 19 June 2003; J. Madore, "Martha Stewart's Company Should Move Away from Namesake, Experts Say," *Knight Ridder Tribune Business News*, 19 June 2003; P. Sellers, "Designing Her Defense: Martha Stewart, One Tough Cookie, Tries to Hold Her Ground in Court and at Her Company," *Fortune*, 23 June 2003, 27.

CHAPTER 16

[1] K. Brooker & J. Schlosser, "The Un-CEO; A. G. Lafley Doesn't Overpromise. He Doesn't Believe in the Vision Thing. All He's Done Is Turn Around P&G in 27 Months," *Fortune*, 16 September 2002, 88; B. Belton, "CEO Q&A: Procter & Gamble's Renovator-in-Chief," *Business Week Online*, 11 December 2002, [Online] available at http://www.businessweek.com/bwdaily/dnflash/dec2002/nf20021211_7599.htm, 16 June 2003; D. Eisenberg & D. Fonda, "A Healthy Gamble; How Did A. G. Lafley Turn Procter & Gamble's Old Brands into Hot Items? Here's the Beauty of It," *Time*, 16 September 2002, 46; S. Ellison, "P&G Lays Out Wella Strategy—After $5.75 Billion Deal, CEO Vows to Tread Lightly in Salons," *The Wall Street Journal*, 19 March 2003, B3; G. Farrell, "Impatient P&G Ousts Jager—Board Loses Confidence in CEO after 18 Months," *USA Today*, 9 June 2000, 01B; J. Neff, "P&G Inks Deal with PlanetFeedback for Pampers and Tide," *Advertising Age*, 15 July 2002, 11; E. Nelson, "Rallying the Troops at P&G—New CEO Lafley Aims to End Upheaval by Revamping Program of Globalization," *The Wall Street Journal*, 31 August 2000, B1; E. Nelson & N. Deogun, "Course Correction: Reformer Jager Was Too Much for P&G; So What Will Work?—Under New Boss Lafley, Firm Still Has a Need to Get Its Sales Growth Moving—Another Earnings Warning," *The Wall Street Journal*, 9 June 2000, A1.

[2] E. E. Lawler III, L. W. Porter, & A. Tannenbaum, "Manager's Attitudes toward Interaction Episodes," *Journal of Applied Psychology* 52 (1968): 423–439; H. Mintzberg, *The Nature of Managerial Work* (New York: Harper & Row, 1973).

[3] J. D. Maes, T. G. Weldy, & M. L. Icenogle, "A Managerial Perspective: Oral Communication Competency Is Most Important for Business Students in the Workplace," *Journal of Business Communication* 34 (1997): 67–80.

[4] R. Lepsinger & A. D. Lucia, *The Art and Science of 360 Degree Feedback* (San Francisco: Pfeiffer, 1997).

[5] I. M. Botero, "Good Communication Skills Needed Today," *The Business Journal: Serving Phoenix and the Valley of the Sun*, 21 October 1996.

[6] A. Lashinsky, "Now for the Hard Part," *Fortune*, 18 November 2002, 94.

[7] E. E. Jones & K. E. Davis, "From Acts to Dispositions: The Attribution Process in Person Perception," in *Advances in Experimental and Social Psychology*, Vol. 2, ed. L. Berkowitz (New York: Academic Press, 1965), 219–266; R. G. Lord & J. E. Smith, "Theoretical, Information-Processing, and Situational Factors Affecting Attribution Theory Models of Organizational Behavior," *Academy of Management Review* 8 (1983): 50–60.

[8] L. Spiro, "The CEO Trap," *Chief Executive* (U.S.), 1 April 2003, 24.

[9] H. H. Kelly, *Attribution in Social Interaction* (Morristown, NJ: General Learning Press, 1971).

[10] J. M. Burger, "Motivational Biases in the Attribution of Responsibility for an Accident: A Meta-Analysis of the Defensive-Attribution Hypothesis," *Psychological Bulletin* 90 (1981): 496–512.

[11] D. A. Hofmann & A. Stetzer, "The Role of Safety Climate and Communication in Accident Interpretation: Implications for Learning from Negative Events," *Academy of Management Journal* 41, no. 6 (1998): 644–657.

[12] C. Perrow, *Normal Accidents: Living with High-Risk Technologies* (New York: Basic Books, 1984).

[13] A. G. Miller & T. Lawson, "The Effect of an Informational Opinion on the Fundamental Attribution Error," *Journal of Personality and Social Psychology* 47 (1989): 873–896; J. M. Burger, "Changes in Attribution Errors over Time: The Ephemeral Fundamental Attribution Error," *Social Cognition* 9 (1991): 182–193.

[14] F. Heider, *The Psychology of Interpersonal Relations* (New York: Wiley, 1958); D. T. Miller & M. Ross, "Self-Serving Biases in Attribution of Causality: Fact or Fiction?" *Psychological Bulletin* 82 (1975): 213–225.

[15] J. R. Larson, Jr., "The Dynamic Interplay between Employees' Feedback-Seeking Strategies and Supervisors' Delivery of Performance Feedback," *Academy of Management Review* 14, no. 3 (1989): 408–422.

[16] M. Reddy, "The Conduit Metaphor—A Case of Frame Conflict in Our Language about Our Language," in *Metaphor and Thought*, ed. A. Ortony (Cambridge, England: Cambridge University Press, 1979), 284–324.

[17] G. L. Kreps, *Organizational Communication: Theory and Practice* (New York: Longman, 1990).

[18] Ibid.

[19] S. Luh, "'Pulse Lunches at Asian Citibanks Feed Workers' Morale, Lower Job Turnover," *The Wall Street Journal*, 22 May 2001, B11.

[20] Ibid.

[21] Kreps, *Organizational Communication: Theory and Practice.*

[22] W. Davis & J. R. O'Connor, "Serial Transmission of Information: A Study of the Grapevine," *Journal of Applied Communication Research* 5 (1977): 61–72.

[23] Davis & O'Connor, "Serial Transmission of Information: A Study of the Grapevine"; C. Hymowitz, "Managing: Spread the Word, Gossip Is Good," *The Wall Street Journal Interactive*, 4 October 1988.

[24] D. T. Hall, K. L. Otazo, & G. P. Hollenbeck, "Behind Closed Doors: What Really Happens in Executive Coaching," *Organizational Dynamics* 27, no. 3 (1999): 39–53.

[25] A. Mehrabian, "Communication without Words," *Psychology Today* 3 (1968): 53; A. Mehrabian, *Silent Messages* (Belmont, CA: Wadsworth, 1971); R. Harrison, *Beyond Words: An Introduction to Nonverbal Communication* (1974); A. Mehrabian, *Non-Verbal Communication* (Chicago: Aldine, 1972).

[26] M. L. Knapp, *Nonverbal Communication in Human Interaction*, 2d ed. (New York: Holt, Rinehart & Winston, 1978).

[27] H. M. Rosenfeld, "Instrumental Affiliative Functions of Facial and Gestural Expressions," *Journal of Personality and Social Psychology* 24 (1966): 65–72; P. Ekman, "Differential Communication of Affect by Head and Body Cues," *Journal of Personality and Social Psychology* 2 (1965): 726–735; A. Mehrabian, "Significance of Posture and Position in the Communication of Attitude and Status Relationships," *Psychological Bulletin* 71 (1969): 359–372.

[28] R. B. Schmitt, "Judges Try Curbing Lawyers' Body-Language Antics," *The Wall Street Journal*, 9 September 1997, B1.

[29] C. A. Bartlett & S. Ghoshal, "Changing the Role of Top Management: Beyond Systems to People," *Harvard Business Review*, May-June 1995, 132–142.

[30] T. Andrews, "E-Mail Empowers, Voice-Mail Enslaves," *PC Week*, 10 April 1995, E11.

[31] "The Joys of Voice Mail," *Inc.*, November 1995, 102.

[32] P. Roberts, "Homestyle Talkshows," *Fast Company*, October 1999, 162.

[33] R. Davidhizar and S. Erdel, "Send Me a Memo on It, or Better Yet, Don't," *Health Care Supervisor* 15 (1997): 42–47; J. Gannon, "Clear Writing Leads to Better Business," *Star-Ledger (Pittsburgh Post-Gazette)*, 30 April 2002, 52.

[34] R. G. Nichols, "Do We Know How to Listen? Practical Helps in a Modern Age," in *Communication Concepts and Processes*, ed. J. DeVitor (Englewood Cliffs, NJ: Prentice Hall, 1971); P. V. Lewis, *Organizational Communication: The Essence of Effective Management* (Columbus, OH: Grid Publishing Company, 1975).

[35] E. Atwater, *I Hear You*, revised ed. (New York: Walker, 1992).

[36] R. Adler & N. Towne, *Looking Out/Looking In* (San Francisco: Rinehart Press, 1975).

[37] B. D. Seyber, R. N. Bostrom, & J. H. Seibert, "Listening, Communication Abilities, and Success at Work," *Journal of Business Communication* 26 (1989): 293–303.

[38] Atwater, *I Hear You.*

[39] N. Grammer, "The Art—and Importance—of Listening," *Toronto Globe & Mail*, 25 June 1999, B11.

[40] H. H. Meyer, "A Solution to the Performance Appraisal Feedback Enigma," *Academy of Management Executive* 5, no. 1 (1991): 68–76.

[41] T. D. Schellhardt, "Annual Agony: It's Time to Evaluate Your Work, and All Involved Are Groaning—Employees Dislike Reviews, Even If Favorable; Bosses Wonder How to Do Them—Some Prefer Frequent Talks," *The Wall Street Journal*, 19 November 1996, A1.

[42] C. Hymowitz, "How to Tell Employees All the Things They Don't Want to Hear," *The Wall Street Journal*, 22 August 2000, B1.

[43] L. Reibstein, "What to Do When an Employee Is Talented and a Pain in the Neck," *The Wall Street Journal Interactive*, 8 August 1986.

[44] J. S. Black & M. Mendenhall, "Cross-Cultural Training Effectiveness: A Review and Theoretical Framework for Future Research," *Academy of Management Review* 15 (1990): 113–136.

[45] D. A. Blackmon, "A Factory in Alabama Is the Merger in Microcosm," *The Wall Street Journal*, 8 May 1998, B1.

[46] F. Trompenaars, *Riding the Waves of Culture: Understanding Diversity in Global Business* (London: Economist Books, 1994).

[47] N. Forster, "Expatriates and the Impact of Cross-Cultural Training," *Human Resource Management* 10 (2000): 63–78.

[48] N. J. Adler, *From Boston to Beijing: Managing with a World View* (Mason, OH: South-Western, 2002).

[49] Ibid.

[50] Ibid.

[51] R. Mead, *Cross-Cultural Management* (New York: Wiley, 1990).

[52] Ibid.

[53] Edward T. Hall, *The Dance of Life* (New York: Doubleday, 1983).

[54] E. T. Hall & W. F. Whyte, "Intercultural Communication: A Guide to Men of Action," *Human Organization* 19, no. 1 (1961): 5–12.

[55] N. Libman, "French Tip: Just Walk the Walk and Talk the Talk, but Not Too Loud," *Chicago Tribune Online*, 17 March 1996.

[56] C. Salter, "Fresh Start 2002: On the Road Again," *Fast Company*, 1 January 2002, 50.

[57] M. Coles, "Warning Note over E-Mail Legal Danger: Firms Face Big Damages for Careless Chat," *Sunday Mail*, 20 August 2000, 41.

[58] T. A. Stewart, "Telling Tales at BP Amoco: Knowledge Management at Work," *Fortune*, 7 June 1999, 220.

[59] Associated Press, "Worldcom CEO Tells Workers 'We Have the Will to Win,'" *Chicago Sun-Times*, 15 January 2003.

[60] C. Olofson, "Global Reach, Virtual Leadership," *Fast Company*, [Online] available at http://www.fastcompany.com/online/27/minm.html, 15 June 2003.

[61] M. Campanelli & N. Friedman, "Welcome to Voice Mail Hell: The New Technology Has Become a Barrier between Salespeople and Customers. Here's How Smart Sellers Are Breaking Through," *Sales & Marketing Management* 147 (May 1995): 98–101.

[62] E. Florian & W. Henderson, "Class of '01: Ellen Florian Spotlights Four Retirees—Their Legacies, Their Plans, and What They've Learned That Can Help You Work Better," *Fortune*, 13 August 2001, 185.

[63] E. W. Morrison, "Organizational Silence: A Barrier to Change and Development in a Pluralistic World," *Academy of Management Review* 25 (2000): 706–725.

[64] T. Aeppel, "Tricks of the Trade: On Factory Floors, Top Workers Hide Secrets to Success," *The Wall Street Journal*, 1 July 2002, A1.

[65] Toyota Motor Manufacturing, USA, *Team Member Handbook*, February 1988, 52–53; G. Dessler, "How to Earn Your Employees' Commitment," *Academy of Management Review* 13, no. 2 (1999): 58–67.

[66] S. Thurm, "At Fast-Moving Cisco, CEO Says: Put Customers First, View Rivals As 'Good Guys,'" *The Wall Street Journal*, 1 June 2000, B1.

[67] B. O'Reilly, "Forget Hertz and Avis: Enterprise's Quiet Invasion of Small-Town America—Along with Quirky Hiring Practices and a Generous Supply of Doughnuts—Has Made It the Nation's Biggest Rental Car," *Fortune*, 28 October 1996, 125.

[68] J. Cole, "Spotting Communication Problems," *Getting Results—For the Hands-On Manager*, May 1997, 8; A. Warfield, "Do You Speak Body Language?" *Training & Development*, April 2001, 60–61.

GLOSSARY

360-degree feedback a performance appraisal process in which feedback is obtained from the boss, subordinates, peers and coworkers, and the employees themselves

a-type conflict (affective conflict) disagreement that focuses on individuals or personal issues

absolute comparisons a process in which each criterion is compared to a standard or ranked on its own merits

accommodative strategy a social responsiveness strategy in which a company chooses to accept responsibility for a problem and to do all that society expects to solve that problem

achievement-oriented leadership a leadership style in which the leader sets challenging goals, has high expectations of employees, and displays confidence that employees will assume responsibility and put forth extraordinary effort

acquaintance time a cultural norm for how much time you must spend getting to know someone before the person is prepared to do business with you

acquisition the purchase of a company by another company

action plan the specific steps, people, and resources needed to accomplish a goal

active listening assuming half the responsibility for successful communication by actively giving the speaker nonjudgmental feedback that shows you've accurately heard what he or she said

address terms cultural norms that establish whether you should address businesspeople by their first names, family names, or titles

adverse impact unintentional discrimination in which there is a substantially different rate of selection in hiring, promotion, or other employment decisions that works to the disadvantage of members of a particular race, gender, age, ethnicity, or protected group

advocacy groups groups of concerned citizens who band together to try to influence the business practices of specific industries, businesses, and professions

affective cultures cultures in which people display emotions and feelings when communicating

affectivity the stable tendency to experience positive or negative moods and to react to things in a generally positive or negative way

affirmative action purposeful steps taken by an organization to create employment opportunities for minorities and women

age discrimination treating people differently (e.g., in hiring and firing, promotion, and compensation decisions) because of their age

agreeableness the degree to which someone is cooperative, polite, flexible, forgiving, good-natured, tolerant, and trusting

analyzers an adaptive strategy that seeks to minimize risk and maximize profits by following or imitating the proven successes of prospectors

appointment time a cultural norm for how punctual you must be when showing up for scheduled appointments or meetings

assemble-to-order operation a manufacturing operation that divides manufacturing processes into separate parts or modules that are combined to create semicustomized products

assessment centers a series of managerial simulations, graded by trained observers, that are used to determine applicants' capability for managerial work

association or affinity patterns when two or more database elements tend to occur together in a significant way

attack a competitive move designed to reduce a rival's market share or profits

attribution theory a theory that states that we all have a basic need to understand and explain the causes of other people's behavior

authentication making sure potential users are who they claim to be

authoritarianism the extent to which an individual believes that there should be power and status differences within organizations

authority the right to give commands, take action, and make decisions to achieve organizational objectives

authorization granting authenticated users approved access to data, software, and systems

autonomous work groups groups that operate without managers and are completely responsible for controlling work group processes, outputs, and behavior

autonomy the degree to which a job gives workers the discretion, freedom, and independence to decide how and when to accomplish the job

average aggregate inventory average overall inventory during a particular time period

awareness training training that is designed to raise employees' awareness of diversity issues and to challenge the underlying assumptions or stereotypes they may have about others

BCG matrix a portfolio strategy, developed by the Boston Consulting Group, that managers use to categorize the corporation's businesses by growth rate and relative market share, helping them decide how to invest corporate funds

background checks procedures used to verify the truthfulness and accuracy of information that applicants provide about themselves and to uncover negative, job-related background information not provided by applicants

balanced scorecard measurement of organizational performance in four equally important areas: finances, customers, internal operations, and innovation and learning

bar code a visual pattern that represents numerical data by varying the thickness and pattern of vertical bars

bargaining power of buyers a measure of the influence that customers have on a firm's prices

bargaining power of suppliers a measure of the influence that suppliers of parts, materials, and services to firms in an industry have on the prices of these inputs

behavior control the regulation of the behaviors and actions that workers perform on the job

behavioral addition the process of having managers and employees perform new behaviors that are central to and symbolic of the new organizational culture that a company wants to create

behavioral formality a workplace atmosphere characterized by routine and regimen, specific rules about how to behave, and interpersonal detachment

behavioral informality a workplace atmosphere characterized by spontaneity, casualness, and interpersonal familiarity

behavioral observation scales (BOSs) rating scales that indicate the frequency with which workers perform specific behaviors that are representative of the job dimensions critical to successful job performance

behavioral substitution the process of having managers and employees perform new behaviors central to the "new" organizational culture in place of behaviors that were central to the "old" organizational culture

benchmarking the process of identifying outstanding practices, processes, and standards in other companies and adapting them to your company

biographical data (biodata) extensive surveys that ask applicants questions about their personal backgrounds and life experiences

biometrics identifying users by unique, measurable body features, such as fingerprint recognition or iris scanning

bona fide occupational qualification (BFOQ) an exception in employment law that permits gender, age, religion, and the like, to be used when making employment decisions, but only if they are "reasonably necessary to the normal operation of that particular business." BFOQs are strictly monitored by the Equal Employment Opportunity Commission.

bounded rationality a decision-making process restricted in the real world by limited resources, incomplete and imperfect information, and managers' limited decision-making capabilities

brainstorming a decision-making method in which group members build on each others' ideas to generate as many alternative solutions as possible

budgeting quantitative planning through which managers decide how to allocate available money to best accomplish company goals

bureaucratic control the use of hierarchical authority to influence employee behavior by rewarding or punishing employees for compliance or noncompliance with organizational policies, rules, and procedures

bureaucratic immunity the ability to make changes without first getting approval from managers or other parts of an organization

business confidence indices indices that show managers' level of confidence about future business growth

buyer dependence the degree to which a supplier relies on a buyer because of the importance of that buyer to the supplier and the difficulty of selling its products to other buyers

c-type conflict (cognitive conflict) disagreement that focuses on problem- and issue-related differences of opinion

cafeteria benefit plans (flexible benefit plans) plans that allow employees to choose which benefits they receive, up to a certain dollar value

cash cow a company with a large share of a slow-growing market

centralization of authority the location of most authority at the upper levels of the organization

chain of command the vertical line of authority that clarifies who reports to whom throughout the organization

change agent the person formally in charge of guiding a change effort

change forces forces that produce differences in the form, quality, or condition of an organization over time

change intervention the process used to get workers and managers to change their behavior and work practices

character of the rivalry a measure of the intensity of competitive behavior between companies in an industry

charismatic leadership the behavioral tendencies and personal characteristics of leaders that create an exceptionally strong relationship between them and their followers

closure the tendency to fill in gaps of missing information by assuming that what we don't know is consistent with what we already know

coaching communicating with someone for the direct purpose of improving the person's on-the-job performance or behavior

coercion using formal power and authority to force others to change

cognitive ability tests tests that measure the extent to which applicants have abilities in perceptual speed, verbal comprehension, numerical aptitude, general reasoning, and spatial aptitude

cognitive maps graphic depictions of how managers believe environmental factors relate to possible organizational actions

cohesiveness the extent to which team members are attracted to a team and motivated to remain in it

commission a compensation system in which employees earn a percentage of each sale they make

communication the process of transmitting information from one person or place to another

communication medium the method used to deliver an oral or written message

company hotlines phone numbers that anyone in the company can call anonymously to leave information for upper management

company vision a company's purpose or reason for existing

compensation the financial and nonfinancial rewards that organizations give employees in exchange for their work

competitive advantage providing greater value for customers than competitors can

competitive analysis a process for monitoring competitors that involves identifying competitors, anticipating their moves, and determining their strengths and weaknesses

competitive inertia a reluctance to change strategies or competitive practices that have been successful in the past

competitors companies in the same industry that sell similar products or services to customers

complex environment an environment with many environmental factors

complex matrix a form of matrix departmentalization in which project and functional managers report to matrix managers, who help them sort out conflicts and problems

component parts inventories the basic parts used in manufacturing that are fabricated from raw materials

compression approach to innovation an approach to innovation that assumes that incremental innovation can be planned using a series of steps, and that compressing those steps can speed innovation

concentration of effect the total harm or benefit that an act produces on the average person

conceptual skill the ability to see the organization as a whole, how the different parts affect each other, and how the company fits into or is affected by its environment

concertive control the regulation of workers' behavior and decisions through work group values and beliefs

concurrent control a mechanism for gathering information about performance deficiencies as they occur, eliminating or shortening the delay between performance and feedback

conduit metaphor the mistaken assumption that senders can pipe their intended messages directly into the heads of receivers with perfect clarity and without noise or perceptual filters interfering with the receivers' understanding of the message

conscientiousness the degree to which someone is organized, hardworking, responsible, persevering, thorough, and achievement oriented

consideration the extent to which a leader is friendly, approachable, and supportive and shows concern for employees

consistent organizational cultures when a company actively defines and teaches organizational values, beliefs, and attitudes

constructive feedback feedback intended to be helpful, corrective, and/or encouraging

contingency theory a leadership theory that states that in order to maximize work group performance, leaders must be matched to the situation that best fits their leadership style

continuous improvement an organization's ongoing commitment to constantly assess and improve the processes and procedures used to create products and services

continuous reinforcement schedule a schedule that requires a consequence to be administered following every instance of a behavior

control a regulatory process of establishing standards to achieve organizational goals, comparing actual performance against the standards, and taking corrective action, when necessary

control loss the situation in which behavior and work procedures do not conform to standards

controlling monitoring progress toward goal achievement and taking corrective action when needed

conventional level of moral development the second level of moral development in which people make decisions that conform to societal expectations

cooperative contract an agreement in which a foreign business owner pays a company a fee for the right to conduct that business in his or her country

core capabilities the internal decision-making routines, problem-solving processes, and organizational cultures that determine how efficiently inputs can be turned into outputs

core firms the central companies in a strategic group

corporate portals allow managers and employees to use a Web browser to gain access to customized company information and to complete specialized transactions

corporate talk shows televised company meetings that allow remote audiences (employees) to pose questions to the show's host and guests

corporate-level strategy the overall organizational strategy that addresses the question "What business or businesses are we in or should we be in?"

cost leadership the positioning strategy of producing a product or service of acceptable quality at consistently lower production costs than competitors can, so that the firm can offer the product or service at the lowest price in the industry

counseling communicating with someone about non-job-related issues that may be affecting or interfering with the person's performance

country of manufacture the country where a product is made and assembled

country of origin the home country for a company, where its headquarters is located

creative work environments workplace cultures in which workers perceive that new ideas are welcomed, valued, and encouraged

creativity the production of novel and useful ideas

cross-cultural communication transmitting information from a person in one country or culture to a person from another country or culture

cross-functional team a team composed of employees from different functional areas of the organization

cross training training team members to do all or most of the jobs performed by the other team members

customer defections a performance assessment in which companies identify which customers are leaving and measure the rate at which they are leaving

customer departmentalization organizing work and workers into separate units responsible for particular kinds of customers

customer focus an organizational goal to concentrate on meeting customers' needs at all levels of the organization

customer satisfaction an organizational goal to provide products or services that meet or exceed customers' expectations

customs classification a classification assigned by government officials that affects the size of the tariff and imposition of import quotas

cybernetic the process of steering or keeping on course

cybernetic feasibility the extent to which it is possible to implement each step in the control process

data clusters when three or more database elements

occur together (i.e., cluster) in a significant way

data encryption transforms data into complex, scrambled digital codes that can only be unencrypted by authorized users who possess unique decryption keys

data mining the process of discovering unknown patterns and relationships in large amounts of data

data warehouse stores huge amounts of data that have been prepared for data mining analysis by being cleaned of errors and redundancy

decentralization the location of a significant amount of authority in the lower levels of the organization

decision criteria the standards used to guide judgments and decisions

decision making the process of choosing a solution from available alternatives

decision support system (DSS) an information system that helps managers to understand specific kinds of problems and potential solutions and to analyze the impact of different decision options using "what if" scenarios

decoding the process by which the receiver translates the written, verbal, or symbolic form of a message into an understood message

deep-level diversity differences such as personality and attitudes that are communicated through verbal and nonverbal behaviors and are learned only through extended interaction with others

defenders an adaptive strategy aimed at defending strategic positions by seeking moderate, steady growth and by offering a limited range of high-quality products and services to a well-defined set of customers

defensive bias the tendency for people to perceive themselves as personally and situationally similar to someone who is having difficulty or trouble

defensive strategy a social responsiveness strategy in which a company chooses to admit responsibility for a problem but to do the least required to meet societal expectations

de-forming a reversal of the forming stage, in which team members position themselves to control pieces of the team, avoid each other, and isolate themselves from team leaders

degree of dependence the extent to which a company needs a particular resource to accomplish its goals

delegation of authority the assignment of direct authority and responsibility to a subordinate to complete tasks for which the manager is normally responsible

Delphi technique a decision-making method in which a panel of experts responds to questions and to each other until reaching agreement on an issue

de-norming a reversal of the norming stage, in which team performance begins to decline as the size, scope, goal, or members of the team change

departmentalization subdividing work and workers into separate organizational units responsible for completing particular tasks

dependent demand systems an inventory system in which the level of inventory depends on the number of finished units to be produced

design competition competition between old and new technologies to establish a new technological standard or dominant design

design iteration a cycle of repetition in which a company tests a prototype of a new product or service, improves on that design, and then builds and tests the improved prototype

de-storming a reversal of the storming phase, in which the team's comfort level decreases, team cohesion weakens, and angry emotions and conflict may flare

destructive feedback feedback that disapproves without any intention of being helpful and almost always causes a negative or defensive reaction in the recipient

devil's advocacy a decision-making method in which an individual or a subgroup is assigned the role of a critic

dialectical inquiry a decision-making method in which decision makers state the assumptions of a proposed solution (a thesis) and generate a solution that is the opposite (antithesis) of that solution

differentiation the positioning strategy of providing a product or service that is sufficiently different from competitors' offerings such that customers are willing to pay a premium price for it

direct competition the rivalry between two companies that offer similar products and services, acknowledge each other as rivals, and act and react to each other's strategic actions

direct foreign investment a method of investment in which a company builds a new business or buys an existing business in a foreign county

directive leadership a leadership style in which the leader lets employees know precisely what is expected of them, gives them specific guidelines for performing tasks, schedules work, sets standards of performance, and makes sure that people follow standard rules and regulations

disability a mental or physical impairment that substantially limits one or more major life activities

disability discrimination treating people differently because of their disabilities

discretionary responsibilities the expectation that a company will voluntarily serve a social role beyond its economic, legal, and ethical responsibilities

discussion time a cultural norm for how much time should be spent in discussion with others

disparate treatment intentional discrimination that occurs when people are purposely not given the same hiring, promotion, or membership opportunities because of their race, gender, age, ethnic group, national origin, or religious beliefs

disposition the tendency to respond to situations and events in a predetermined manner

disseminator role the informational role managers play when they share information with others in their departments or companies

distal goals long-term or primary goals

distinctive competence what a company can make, do, or perform better than its competitors

distributive justice the perceived degree to which outcomes and rewards are fairly distributed or allocated

disturbance handler role the decisional role managers play when they respond to severe problems that demand immediate action

diversification a strategy for reducing risk by buying a variety of items (stocks or, in the case of a corporation, types of businesses), so that the failure of one stock or one business does not doom the entire portfolio

diversity a variety of demographic, cultural, and personal differences among an organization's employees and customers

diversity audits formal assessments that measure employee and management attitudes, investigate the extent to which people are advantaged or disadvantaged with respect to hiring and promotions, and review companies' diversity-related policies and procedures

diversity pairing a mentoring program in which people of different cultural backgrounds, genders, or races/ethnicities are paired together to get to know each other and change stereotypical beliefs and attitudes

dog a company with a small share of a slow-growing market

dominant design a new technological design or process that becomes the accepted market standard

downsizing the planned elimination of jobs in a company

downward communication communication that flows from higher to lower levels in an organization

dynamic environment an environment in which the rate of change is fast

dysfunctional turnover loss of high-performing employees who voluntarily choose to leave a company

economic order quantity (EOQ) a system of formulas that minimizes ordering and holding costs and helps determine how much and how often inventory should be ordered

economic responsibility the expectation that a company will make a profit by producing a valued product or service

economic value added (EVA) the amount by which company profits (revenues, minus expenses, minus taxes) exceed the cost of capital in a given year

effectiveness accomplishing tasks that help fulfill organizational objectives

efficiency getting work done with a minimum of effort, expense, or waste

electronic brainstorming a decision-making method in which group members use computers to build on each others' ideas and generate many alternative solutions

electronic data interchange (EDI) when two companies convert their purchase and ordering information to a standardized format to enable the direct electronic transmission of that information from one company's computer system to the other company's computer system

electronic scanner an electronic device that converts printed text and pictures into digital images

emotional stability the degree to which someone is angry, depressed, anxious, emotional, insecure, and excitable

empathetic listening understanding the speaker's perspective and personal frame of reference and giving feedback that conveys that understanding to the speaker

employee involvement team a team that provides advice or makes suggestions to management concerning specific issues

employee separation the voluntary or involuntary loss of an employee

employee stock ownership plan (ESOP) a compensation system that awards employees shares of company stock in addition to their regular compensation

employee turnover loss of employees who voluntarily choose to leave the company

employment benefits a method of rewarding employees that includes virtually any kind of compensation other than wages or salaries

employment references sources such as previous employers or coworkers who can provide job-related information about job candidates

empowering workers permanently passing decision-making authority and responsibility from managers to workers by giving them the information and resources they need to make and carry out good decisions

empowerment feelings of intrinsic motivation, in which workers perceive their work to have impact and meaning and perceive themselves to be competent and capable of self-determination

encoding putting a message into a written, verbal, or symbolic form that can be recognized and understood by the receiver

entrepreneur role the decisional role managers play when they adapt themselves, their subordinates, and their units to incremental change

entrepreneurial orientation the set of processes, practices, and decision-making activities that lead to new entry, characterized by five dimensions: autonomy, innovativeness, risk taking, proactiveness, and competitive aggressiveness

entrepreneurship the process of entering new or established markets with new goods or services

environmental change the rate at which a company's general and specific environments change

environmental complexity the number of external factors in the environment that affect organizations

environmental scanning searching the environment for important events or issues that might affect an organization

equity theory a theory that states that people will be motivated when they perceive that they are being treated fairly

era of ferment the phase of a technology cycle characterized by technological substitution and design competition

ethical behavior behavior that conforms to a society's accepted principles of right and wrong

ethical charismatics charismatic leaders who provide developmental opportunities for followers, are open to positive and negative feedback, recognize others' contributions, share information, and have moral standards that emphasize the larger interests of the group, organization, or society

ethical intensity the degree of concern people have about an ethical issue

ethical responsibility the expectation that a company will not violate accepted principles of right and wrong when conducting its business

ethics the set of moral principles or values that defines right and wrong for a person or group

evaluation apprehension fear of what others will think of your ideas

executive information system (EIS) a data processing system that uses internal and external data sources to provide the information needed to monitor and analyze organizational performance

expatriate someone who lives and works outside his or her native country

expectancy the perceived relationship between effort and performance

expectancy theory a theory that states that people will be motivated to the extent to which they believe that their efforts will lead to good performance, that good performance will be rewarded, and that they will be offered attractive rewards

experiential approach to innovation an approach to innovation that assumes a highly uncertain environment and uses intuition, flexible options, and hands-on experience to reduce uncertainty and accelerate learning and understanding

expert system an information system that contains the specialized knowledge and decision rules used by experts and experienced decision makers so that nonexperts can draw on this knowledge base to make decisions

exporting selling domestically produced products to customers in foreign countries

external environments all events outside a company that have the potential to influence or affect it

external locus of control the belief that what happens to you is largely the result of factors beyond your control

external recruiting the process of developing a pool of qualified job applicants from outside the company

extinction reinforcement in which a positive consequence is no longer allowed to follow a previously reinforced behavior, thus weakening the behavior

extranet allows companies to exchange information and conduct transactions with outsiders by providing them direct, Web-based access to authorized parts of a company's intranet or information system

extraversion the degree to which someone is active, assertive, gregarious, sociable, talkative, and energized by others

extrinsic reward a reward that is tangible, visible to others, and given to employees contingent on the performance of specific tasks or behaviors

feedback the amount of information the job provides to workers about their work performance

feedback control a mechanism for gathering information about performance deficiencies after they occur

feedback to sender in the communication process, a return message to the sender that indicates the receiver's understanding of the message

feedforward control a mechanism for monitoring performance inputs rather than outputs to prevent or minimize performance deficiencies before they occur

figurehead role the interpersonal role managers play when they perform ceremonial duties

finished goods inventories the final outputs of manufacturing operations

firewall a hardware or software device that sits between the computers in an internal organizational network and outside networks, such as the Internet

firm-level strategy a corporate strategy that addresses the question "How should we compete against a particular firm?"

first-line managers managers who train nonmanagerial employees and supervise their performance and who are directly responsible for producing the company's products or services

first-mover advantage the strategic advantage that companies earn by being the first to use new information technology to substantially lower costs or to make a product or service different from that of competitors

fixed interval reinforcement schedule an intermittent schedule in which consequences follow a behavior only after a fixed time has elapsed

fixed ratio reinforcement schedule an intermittent schedule in which consequences are delivered following a specific number of behaviors

flow a psychological state of effortlessness, in which you become completely absorbed in what you're doing and time seems to pass quickly

focus strategy the positioning strategy of using cost leadership or differentiation to produce a specialized product or service for a limited, specially targeted group of customers in a particular geographic region or market segment

formal communication channel the system of official channels that carry organizationally approved messages and information

forming the first stage of team development in which team members meet each other, form initial impressions, and begin to establish team norms

four-fifths (or 80 percent) rule a rule of thumb used by the courts and the EEOC to determine whether there is evidence of disparate impact. A violation of this rule occurs when the selection rate for a protected group is less than 80 percent or four-fifths of the selection rate for a nonprotected group.

franchise a collection of networked firms in which the manufacturer or marketer of a product or service, the franchisor, licenses the entire business to another person or organization, the franchisee

functional departmentalization organizing work and workers into separate units responsible for particular business functions or areas of expertise

functional turnover loss of poor-performing employees who voluntarily choose to leave a company

fundamental attribution error the tendency to ignore external causes of behavior and to attribute other people's actions to internal causes

gainsharing a compensation system in which companies share the financial value of performance gains, such as productivity, cost savings, or quality, with their workers

gender discrimination treating people differently because of their gender

General Agreement on Tariffs and Trade (GATT) a worldwide trade agreement that reduced and eliminated tariffs, limited government subsidies, and established protection for intellectual property

General Electric workout a three-day meeting in which managers and employees from different levels and parts of an organization quickly generate and act on solutions to specific business problems

general environment the economic, technological, sociocultural, and political trends that indirectly affect all organizations

generational change change based on incremental improvements to a dominant technological design such that the improved technology is fully backward compatible with the older technology

geographic departmentalization organizing work and workers into separate units responsible for doing business in particular geographic areas

glass ceiling the invisible barrier that prevents women and minorities from advancing to the top jobs in organizations

global business the buying and selling of goods and services by people from different countries

global consistency when a multinational company has offices, manufacturing plants, and distribution facilities in different countries and runs them all using the same rules, guidelines, policies, and procedures

global new ventures new companies with sales, employees, and financing in different countries that are founded with an active global strategy

goal a target, objective, or result that someone tries to accomplish

goal acceptance the extent to which people consciously understand and agree to goals

goal commitment the determination to achieve a goal

goal difficulty the extent to which a goal is hard or challenging to accomplish

goal-setting theory a theory that states that people will be motivated to the extent to which they accept specific, challenging goals and receive feedback that indicates their progress toward goal achievement

goal specificity the extent to which goals are detailed, exact, and unambiguous

government import standard a standard specified to protect the health and safety of citizens

grand strategy a broad corporate-level strategic plan used to achieve strategic goals and guide the strategic alternatives that managers of individual businesses or subunits may use

groupthink a barrier to good decision making caused by pressure within the group for members to agree with each other

growth strategy a strategy that focuses on increasing profits, revenues, market share, or the number of places in which the company does business

hearing the act or process of perceiving sounds

holding cost the cost of keeping inventory until it is used or sold, including storage, insurance, taxes, obsolescence, and opportunity costs

horizontal communication communication that flows among managers and workers who are at the same organizational level

hostile work environment a form of sexual harassment in which unwelcome and demeaning sexually related behavior creates an intimidating and offensive work environment

human resource management (HRM) the process of finding, developing, and keeping the right people to form a qualified work force

human skill the ability to work well with others

ISO 9000 a series of five international standards, from ISO 9000 to ISO 9004, for achieving consistency in quality management and quality assurance in companies throughout the world

imperfectly imitable resource a resource that is impossible or extremely costly or difficult for other firms to duplicate

incremental change the phase of a technology cycle in which companies innovate by lowering costs and improving the functioning and performance of the dominant technological design

independent demand system an inventory system in which the level of one kind of inventory does not depend on another

individualism-collectivism the degree to which a person believes that people should be self-sufficient and that loyalty to one's self is more important than loyalty to team or company

industry regulation regulations and rules that govern the business practices and procedures of specific industries, businesses, and professions

industry-level strategy a corporate strategy that addresses the question "How should we compete in this industry?"

informal communication channel ("grapevine") the transmission of messages from employee to employee outside of formal communication channels

information useful data that can influence people's choices and behavior

information overload a situation in which decision makers have too much information to attend to

initiating structure the degree to which a leader structures the roles of followers by setting goals, giving directions, setting deadlines, and assigning tasks

innovation streams patterns of innovation over time that can create sustainable competitive advantage

inputs in equity theory, the contributions employees make to the organization

instrumentality the perceived relationship between performance and rewards

intermittent reinforcement schedule a schedule in which consequences are delivered after a specified or average time has elapsed or after a specified or average number of behaviors has occurred

internal environment the events and trends inside an organization that affect management, employees, and organizational culture

internal locus of control the belief that what happens to you is largely the result of your own actions

internal motivation motivation that comes from the job itself rather than from outside rewards

internal recruiting the process of developing a pool of qualified job applicants from people who already work in the company

interorganizational process a collection of activities that take place among companies to transform inputs into outputs that customers value

interpersonal skills skills, such as listening, communicating, questioning, and providing feedback, that enable people to have effective working relationships with others

interviews a selection tool in which company representatives ask job applicants job-related questions to determine whether they are qualified for the job

intranets private company networks that allow employees to easily access, share, and publish information using Internet software

intraorganizational process the collection of activities that take place within an organization to transform inputs into outputs that customers value

intrapreneurship entrepreneurship within an existing organization

intrinsic reward a natural reward associated with performing a task or activity for its own sake

inventory the amount and number of raw materials, parts, and finished products that a company has in its possession

inventory turnover the number of times per year that a company sells or "turns over" its average inventory

job analysis a purposeful, systematic process for collecting information on the important work-related aspects of a job

job characteristics model (JCM) an approach to job redesign that seeks to formulate jobs in ways that motivate workers and lead to positive work outcomes

job description a written description of the basic tasks, duties, and responsibilities required of an employee holding a particular job

job design the number, kind, and variety of tasks that individual workers perform in doing their jobs

job enlargement increasing the number of different tasks that a worker performs within one particular job

job enrichment increasing the number of tasks in a particular job and giving workers the authority and control to make meaningful decisions about their work

job evaluation a process that determines the worth of each job in a company by evaluating the market value of the knowledge, skills, and requirements needed to perform it

job rotation periodically moving workers from one specialized job to another to give them more variety and the opportunity to use different skills

job specialization a job composed of a small part of a larger task or process

job specifications a written summary of the qualifications needed to successfully perform a particular job

joint venture a strategic alliance in which two existing companies collaborate to form a third, independent company

just-in-time (JIT) inventory system an inventory system in which component parts arrive from suppliers just as they are needed at each stage of production

kanban a ticket-based JIT system that indicates when to reorder inventory

kinesics movements of the body and face

knowledge the understanding that one gains from information

leader role the interpersonal role managers play when they motivate and encourage workers to accomplish organizational objectives

leader-member relations the degree to which followers respect, trust, and like their leaders

leadership the process of influencing others to achieve group or organizational goals

leadership style the way a leader generally behaves toward followers

leading inspiring and motivating workers to work hard to achieve organizational goals

learning-based planning learning better ways of achieving goals by continually testing, changing, and improving plans and strategies

legal responsibility the expectation that a company will obey society's laws and regulations

liaison role the interpersonal role managers play when they deal with people outside their units

licensing an agreement in which a domestic company, the licensor, receives royalty payments for allowing another company, the licensee, to produce its product, sell its service, or use its brand name in a specified foreign market

line authority the right to command immediate subordinates in the chain of command

line function an activity that contributes directly to creating or selling the company's products

listening making a conscious effort to hear

local adaptation when a multinational company modifies its rules, guidelines, policies, and procedures to adapt to differences in foreign customers, governments, and regulatory agencies

locus of control the degree to which individuals believe that their actions can influence what happens to them

Machiavellian the extent to which individuals believe that virtually any type of behavior is acceptable in trying to satisfy their needs or meet their goals

magnitude of consequences the total harm or benefit derived from an ethical decision

make-to-order operation a manufacturing operation that does not start processing or assembling products until a customer order is received

make-to-stock operation a manufacturing operation that orders parts and assembles standardized products before receiving customer orders

management getting work done through others

management by objectives (MBO) a four-step process in which managers and employees discuss and select goals, develop tactical plans, and meet regularly to review progress toward goal accomplishment

market commonality the degree to which two companies have overlapping products, services, or customers in multiple markets

materials requirement planning (MRP) a production and inventory system that determines the production schedule, production batch sizes, and inventory needed to complete final products

matrix departmentalization a hybrid organizational structure in which two or more forms of departmentalization, most often product and functional, are used together

maximizing choosing the best alternative

mechanistic organization an organization characterized by specialized jobs and responsibilities, precisely defined, unchanging roles, and a rigid chain of command based on centralized authority and vertical communication

media advocacy an advocacy group tactic of framing issues as public issues, exposing questionable, exploitative, or unethical practices, and forcing media coverage by buying media time or creating controversy that is likely to receive extensive news coverage

meta-analysis a study of studies, a statistical approach that provides one of the best scientific estimates of how well management theories and practices work

middle managers managers responsible for setting objectives consistent with top management's goals and for planning and implementing subunit strategies for achieving these objectives

milestones formal project review points used to assess progress and performance

mission a statement of a company's overall goal that unifies company-wide efforts toward its vision, stretches and challenges the organization, and possesses a finish line and a time-frame

modular organization an organization that outsources noncore business activities to outside companies, suppliers, specialists, or consultants

monitor role the informational role managers play

when they scan their environment for information

monochronic cultures cultures in which people tend to do one thing at a time and view time as linear

mood linkage a phenomenon in which one worker's negative affectivity and bad moods can spread to others

Moore's law the prediction that every 18 months, the cost of computing will drop by 50 percent as computer-processing power doubles

motivation the set of forces that initiates, directs, and makes people persist in their efforts to accomplish a goal

motivation to manage an assessment of how enthusiastic employees are about managing the work of others

multifactor productivity an overall measure of performance that indicates how much labor, capital, materials, and energy it takes to produce an output

multifunctional teams work teams composed of people from different departments

multinational corporation a corporation that owns businesses in two or more countries

national culture the set of shared values and beliefs that affects the perceptions, decisions, and behavior of the people from a particular country

needs the physical or psychological requirements that must be met to ensure survival and well-being

negative affectivity a personality trait in which individuals tend to notice and focus on the negative aspects of themselves and their environments

negative reinforcement reinforcement that strengthens behavior by withholding an unpleasant consequence when employees perform a specific behavior

negotiator role the decisional role managers play when they negotiate schedules, projects, goals, outcomes, resources, and employee raises

neutral cultures cultures in which people do not display emotions and feelings when communicating

noise anything that interferes with the transmission of the intended message

nominal group technique a decision-making method that begins and ends by having group members quietly write down and evaluate ideas to be shared with the group

nonsubstitutable resource a resource, without equivalent substitutes or replacements, that produces value or competitive advantage

nontariff barriers nontax methods of increasing the cost or reducing the volume of imported goods

nonverbal communication any communication that doesn't involve words

normative control the regulation of workers' behavior and decisions through widely shared organizational values and beliefs

normative decision theory a theory that suggests how leaders can determine an appropriate amount of employee participation when making decisions

norming the third stage of team development, in which team members begin to settle into their roles, group cohesion grows, and positive team norms develop

norms informally agreed-on standards that regulate team behavior

objective control the use of observable measures of worker behavior or outputs to assess performance and influence behavior

objective performance measures measures of job performance that are easily and directly counted or quantified

online discussion forums the in-house equivalent of Internet newsgroups; Web- or software-based discussion tools available across the company to permit employees to easily ask questions and share knowledge with each other

open office systems offices in which the physical barriers that separate workers have been removed in order to increase communication and interaction

openness to experience the degree to which someone is curious, broad-minded, and open to new ideas, things, and experiences; is spontaneous; and has a high tolerance for ambiguity

operational plans day-to-day plans, developed and implemented by lower-level managers, for producing or delivering the organization's products and services over a 30-day to six-month period

operations management managing the daily production of goods and services

opportunistic behavior a transaction in which one party in the relationship benefits at the expense of the other

optical character recognition software to convert digitized documents into ASCII text (American Standard Code for Information Interchange) that can be searched, read, and edited by word processing and other kinds of software

options-based planning maintaining planning flexibility by making small, simultaneous investments in many alternative plans

ordering cost the costs associated with ordering inventory, including the cost of data entry, phone calls, obtaining bids, correcting mistakes, and determining when and how much inventory to order

organic organization an organization characterized by broadly defined jobs and responsibility, loosely defined, frequently changing roles, and decentralized authority and horizontal communication based on task knowledge

organizational change a difference in the form, quality, or condition of an organization over time

organizational culture the values, beliefs, and attitudes shared by organizational members

organization decline a large decrease in organizational performance that occurs when companies don't anticipate, recognize, neutralize, or adapt to the internal or external pressures that threaten their survival

organizational development a philosophy and collection of planned change interventions designed to improve an organization's long-term health and performance

organizational heroes people celebrated for their qualities and achievements within an organization

organizational innovation the successful implementation of creative ideas in organizations

organizational plurality a work environment where (1) each member is empowered to contribute in a way that maximizes the benefits to the organization, customers, and themselves, and (2) the individuality of each member is respected by not segmenting or polarizing people on the basis of their membership in a particular group

organizational process the collection of activities that transform inputs into outputs that customers value

organizational silence when employees withhold information about organizational problems or issues

organizational stories stories told by organizational members to make sense of organizational events and changes and to emphasize culturally consistent assumptions, decisions, and actions

organizational structure the vertical and horizontal configuration of departments, authority, and jobs within a company

organizing deciding where decisions will be made, who will do what jobs and tasks, and who will work for whom

outcome/input (O/I) ratio in equity theory, an employee's perception of how the rewards received from an organization compare with the employee's contributions to that organization

outcomes in equity theory the rewards employees receive for their contributions to the organization

outplacement services employment-counseling services offered to employees who are losing their jobs because of downsizing

output control the regulation of worker results or outputs through rewards and incentives

overreward when you are getting more outcomes relative to inputs than the referent to whom you compare yourself

overt integrity test a written test that estimates employee honesty by directly asking job applicants what they think or feel about theft or about punishment of unethical behaviors

paralanguage the pitch, rate, tone, volume, and speaking pattern (i.e., use of silences, pauses, or hesitations) of one's voice

partial productivity a measure of performance that indicates how much of a particular kind of input it takes to produce an output

participative leadership a leadership style in which the leader consults employees for their suggestions and input before making decisions

path-goal theory a leadership theory that states that leaders can increase subordinate satisfaction and performance by clarifying and clearing the paths to goals and by increasing the number and kinds of rewards available for goal attainment

perception the process by which individuals attend to, organize, interpret, and retain information from their environments

perceptual filters the personality-, psychology-, or experience-based differences that influence people to ignore or pay attention to particular stimuli

performance appraisal the process of assessing how well employees are doing their jobs

performance feedback information about the quality or quantity of past performance that indicates whether progress is being made toward the accomplishment of a goal

performing the fourth and final stage of team development, in which performance improves because the team has matured into an effective, fully functioning team

personality the relatively stable set of behaviors, attitudes, and emotions displayed over time that makes people different from each other

personality-based integrity test a written test that indirectly estimates employee honesty by measuring psychological traits, such as dependability and conscientiousness

personality tests tests that measure the extent to which applicants possess different kinds of job-related personality dimensions

piecework a compensation system in which employees are paid a set rate for each item they produce

planning (management functions) determining organizational goals and a means for achieving them

planning choosing a goal and developing a strategy to achieve that goal

policy a standing plan that indicates the general course of action that should be taken in response to a particular event or situation

policy uncertainty the risk associated with changes in laws and government policies that directly affect the way foreign companies conduct business

political uncertainty the risk of major changes in political regimes that can result from war, revolution, death of political leaders, social unrest, or other influential events

polychronic cultures cultures in which people tend to do more than one thing at a time and view times as circular

pooled interdependence work completed by having each job or department independently contribute to the whole

portfolio strategy a corporate-level strategy that minimizes risk by diversifying investment among various businesses or product lines

position power the degree to which leaders are able to hire, fire, reward, and punish workers

positive affectivity a personality trait in which individuals tend to notice and focus on the positive aspects of themselves and their environments

positive reinforcement reinforcement that strengthens behavior by following behaviors with desirable consequences

postconventional level of moral development the third level of moral development in which people make decisions based on internalized principles

preconventional level of moral development the first level of moral development in which people make decisions based on selfish reasons

predictive patterns help identify database elements that are different

primary stakeholder any group on which an organization relies for its long-term survival

private spaces spaces used by and open to just one employee

proactive strategy a social responsiveness strategy in which a company anticipates responsibility for a problem before it occurs and would do more than society expects to address the problem

probability of effect the chance that something will happen and then harm others

problem a gap between a desired state and an existing state

procedural justice the perceived fairness of the process used to make reward allocation decisions

procedure a standing plan that indicates the specific steps that should be taken in response to a particular event

processing information transforming raw data into meaningful information

product boycott an advocacy group tactic of protesting a company's actions by convincing consumers not to purchase its product or service

product departmentalization organizing work and

workers into separate units responsible for producing particular products or services

production blocking a disadvantage of face-to-face brainstorming in which a group member must wait to share an idea because another member is presenting an idea

productivity a measure of performance that indicates how many inputs it takes to produce or create an output

profit sharing a compensation system in which a percentage of company profits is paid to employees in addition to their regular compensation

project team a team created to complete specific, one-time projects or tasks within a limited time

prospectors an adaptive strategy that seeks fast growth by searching for new market opportunities, encouraging risk taking, and being the first to bring innovative new products to market

protecting information the process of ensuring that data are reliably and consistently retrievable in a usable format for authorized users, but no one else

protectionism a government's use of trade barriers to shield domestic companies and their workers from foreign competition

proximal goals short-term goals or subgoals

proximity of effect the social, psychological, cultural, or physical distance between a decision maker and those affected by his or her decisions

public communications an advocacy group tactic that relies on voluntary participation by the news media and the advertising industry to get the advocacy group's message out

punctuated equilibrium theory a theory that holds that companies go through long, simple periods of stability (equilibrium), followed by short periods of dynamic, fundamental change (revolution), and ending with a return to stability (new equilibrium)

punishment reinforcement that weakens behavior by following behaviors with undesirable consequences

purchasing power a comparison of the relative cost of a standard set of goods and services in different countries

quality a product or service free of deficiencies, or the characteristics of a product or service that satisfy customer needs

quasi-control reducing dependence or restructuring dependence when control is necessary but not possible

question mark a company with a small share of a fast-growing market

quid pro quo sexual harassment a form of sexual harassment in which employment outcomes, such as hiring, promotion, or simply keeping one's job, depend on whether an individual submits to sexual harassment

quota a limit on the number or volume of imported products

racial and ethnic discrimination treating people differently because of their race or ethnicity

radio frequency identification (RFID) tags minuscule microchips that transmit information via radio waves and can be used to track the number and location of the objects into which the tags have been inserted

rare resource a resource that is not controlled or possessed by many competing firms

rater training training performance appraisal raters in how to avoid rating errors and increase rating accuracy

rational decision making a systematic process of defining problems, evaluating alternatives, and choosing optimal solutions

raw data facts and figures

raw material inventories the basic inputs in a manufacturing process

reactive strategy a social responsiveness strategy in which a company chooses to do less than society expects

reactors an adaptive strategy of not following a consistent strategy, but instead reacting to changes in the external environment after they occur

reciprocal interdependence work completed by different jobs or groups working together in a back-and-forth manner

recovery the strategic actions taken after retrenchment to return to a growth strategy

recruiting the process of developing a pool of qualified job applicants

reducing dependence abandoning or changing organizational goals to reduce dependence on critical resources

reengineering fundamental rethinking and radical redesign of business processes to achieve dramatic improvements in critical measures of performance, such as cost, quality, service, and speed

referents in equity theory, others with whom people compare themselves to determine if they have been treated fairly

refreezing supporting and reinforcing the new changes so they "stick"

regional trading zones areas in which tariff and nontariff barriers on trade between countries are reduced or eliminated

regulation costs the costs associated with implementing or maintaining control

reinforcement the process of changing behavior by changing the consequences that follow behavior

reinforcement contingencies cause-and-effect relationships between the performance of specific behaviors and specific consequences

reinforcement theory a theory that states that behavior is a function of its consequences, that behaviors followed by positive consequences will occur more frequently, and that behaviors followed by negative consequences, or not followed by positive consequences, will occur less frequently

related diversification creating or acquiring companies that share similar products, manufacturing, marketing, technology, or cultures

relationship behavior mutually beneficial, long-term exchanges between buyers and suppliers

relative comparisons a process in which each decision criterion is compared directly to every other criterion

resistance forces forces that support the existing state of conditions in organizations

resistance to change opposition to change resulting from self-interest, misunderstanding and distrust, or a general intolerance for change

resource allocator role the decisional role managers play when they decide who gets what resources

resource flow the extent to which companies have access to critical resources

resource scarcity the degree to which an organization's external environment has an abundance or scarcity of critical organizational resources

resource similarity the extent to which a competitor has similar amounts and kinds of resources

resources the assets, capabilities, processes, information, and knowledge that an organization uses to improve its effectiveness and efficiency, create and sustain competitive advantage, and fulfill a need or solve a problem

response a competitive countermove, prompted by a rival's attack, to defend or improve a company's market share or profit

restructuring dependence exchanging dependence on one critical resource for dependence on another

results-driven change change created quickly by focusing on the measurement and improvement of results

retrenchment strategy a strategy that focuses on turning around very poor company performance by shrinking the size or scope of the business

rules and regulations standing plans that describe how a particular action should be performed, or what must happen or not happen in response to a particular event

S.M.A.R.T. goals goals that are specific, measurable, attainable, realistic, and timely

satisficing choosing a "good enough" alternative

schedule of reinforcement rules that specify which behaviors will be reinforced, which consequences will follow those behaviors, and the schedule by which those consequences will be delivered

schedule time a cultural norm for the time by which scheduled projects or jobs should actually be completed

S-curve pattern of innovation a pattern of technological innovation characterized by slow initial progress, then rapid progress, and then again by slow progress as a technology matures and reaches its limits

secondary firms the firms in a strategic group that follow related, but somewhat different, strategies than do the core firms

secondary stakeholder any group that can influence or be influenced by a company and can affect public perceptions about its socially responsible behavior

secure sockets layer (SSL) encryption Internet browser–based form of encryption that provides secure off-site Web access to some data and programs

selection the process of gathering information about job applicants to decide who should be offered a job

selective perception the tendency to notice and accept objects and information consistent with our values, beliefs, and expectations, while ignoring or screening out or not accepting inconsistent information

self-control (self-management) a control system in which managers and workers control their own behavior by setting their own goals, monitoring their own progress, and rewarding themselves for goal achievement

self-designing team a team that has the characteristics of self-managing teams but also controls team design, work tasks, and team membership

self-managing team a team that manages and controls all of the major tasks of producing a product or service

self-serving bias the tendency to overestimate our value by attributing successes to ourselves (internal causes) and attributing failures to others or the environment (external causes)

semi-autonomous work group a group that has the authority to make decisions and solve problems related to the major tasks of producing a product or service

sequence patterns when two or more database elements occur together in a significant pattern, but one of the elements precedes the other

sequential interdependence work completed in succession, with one group's or job's outputs becoming the inputs for the next group or job

service recovery restoring customer satisfaction to strongly dissatisfied customers

setup cost the costs of downtime and lost efficiency that occur when a machine is changed or adjusted to produce a different kind of inventory

sexual harassment a form of discrimination in which unwelcome sexual advances, requests for sexual favors, or other verbal or physical conduct of a sexual nature occurs while performing one's job

shadow-strategy task force a committee within the company that analyzes the company's own weaknesses to determine how competitors could exploit them for competitive advantage

shared spaces spaces used by and open to all employees

shareholder model a view of social responsibility that holds that an organization's overriding goal should be profit maximization for the benefit of shareholders

simple environment an environment with few environmental factors

simple matrix a form of matrix departmentalization in which project and functional managers negotiate conflicts and resources

single-use plans plans that cover unique, one-time-only events

situational (SWOT) analysis is an assessment of the strengths and weaknesses in an organization's internal environment and the opportunities and threats in its external environment

situational favorableness the degree to which a particular situation either permits or denies a leader the chance to influence the behavior of group members

situational theory a leadership theory that states that leaders need to adjust their leadership styles to match their followers' readiness

skills-based diversity training training that teaches employees the practical skills they need for managing a diverse work force, such as flexibility and adaptability, negotiation, problem solving, and conflict resolution

skill-based pay a compensation system that pays employees for learning additional skills or knowledge

skill variety the number of different activities performed in a job

slack resources a cushion of extra resources that can be used with options-based planning to adapt to unanticipated changes, problems, or opportunities

social consensus agreement on whether behavior is bad or good

social integration the degree to which group members are psychologically attracted to working with each other to accomplish a common objective

social loafing behavior in which team members withhold their efforts and fail to perform their share of the work

social responsibility a business's obligation to pursue policies, make decisions, and take actions that benefit society

social responsiveness the strategy chosen by a company to respond to stakeholders' economic, legal, ethical, or discretionary expectations concerning social responsibility

specific ability tests (aptitude tests) tests that measure the extent to which an applicant possesses the particular kind of ability needed to do a job well

specific environment the customers, competitors, suppliers, industry regulations, and advocacy groups that are unique to an industry and that directly affect how a company does business

spokesperson role the informational role managers play when they share information with people outside their departments or companies

stability strategy a strategy that focuses on improving the way in which the company sells the same products or services to the same customers

stable environment an environment in which the rate of change is slow

staff authority the right to advise, but not command, others who are not subordinates in the chain of command

staff function an activity that does not contribute directly to creating or selling the company's products, but instead supports line activities

stakeholder model a theory of corporate responsibility that holds that management's most important responsibility, long-term survival, is achieved by satisfying the interests of multiple corporate stakeholders

stakeholders persons or groups with a "stake" or legitimate interest in a company's actions

standardization solving problems by consistently applying the same rules, procedures, and processes

standards a basis of comparison when measuring the extent to which various kinds of organizational performance are satisfactory or unsatisfactory

standing plans plans used repeatedly to handle frequently recurring events

star a company with a large share of a fast-growing market

stepladder technique when group members are added to a group discussion one at a time (i.e., like a stepladder), the existing group members first take the time to listen to each new member's thoughts, ideas, and recommendations, and then the group, in turn, shares the ideas and suggestions that it had already considered, discusses the new and old ideas, and then makes a decision

stock options a compensation system that gives employees the right to purchase shares of stock at a set price, even if the value of the stock increases above that price

stockout the situation when a company runs out of finished product

stockout costs the costs incurred when a company runs out of a product, including transaction costs to replace inventory and the loss of customers' goodwill

storming the second stage of development, characterized by conflict and disagreement, in which team members disagree over what the team should do and how it should do it

strategic alliance an agreement in which companies combine key resources, costs, risk, technology, and people

strategic dissonance a discrepancy between upper management's intended strategy and the strategy actually implemented by lower levels of management

strategic group a group of companies within an industry that top managers choose to compare, evaluate, and benchmark strategic threats and opportunities

strategic leadership the ability to anticipate, envision, maintain flexibility, think strategically, and work with others to initiate changes that will create a positive future for an organization

strategic plans overall company plans that clarify how the company will serve customers and position itself against competitors over the next two to five years

strategic reference points the strategic targets managers use to measure whether a firm has developed the core competencies it needs to achieve a sustainable competitive advantage

stretch goals extremely ambitious goals that, initially, employees don't know how to accomplish

structural accommodation the ability to change organizational structures, policies, and practices in order to meet stretch goals

structured interviews interviews in which all applicants are asked the same set of standardized questions, usually including situational, behavioral, background, and job-knowledge questions

subjective performance measures measures of job performance that require someone to judge or assess a worker's performance

suboptimization performance improvement in one part of an organization but only at the expense of decreased performance in another part

subsidies government loans, grants, and tax deferments given to domestic companies to protect them from foreign competition

supervised data mining user tells the data mining software to look and test for specific patterns and relationships in a data set

supplier dependence the degree to which a company relies on a supplier because of the importance of the supplier's product to the company and the difficulty of finding other sources of that product

suppliers companies that provide material, human, financial, and informational resources to other companies

supportive leadership a leadership style in which the leader is friendly to and approachable by employees, shows concern for them and their welfare, treats them as equals, and creates a friendly climate

surface-level diversity differences such as age, gender, race/ethnicity, and physical disabilities that are observable, typically unchangeable, and easy to measure

survey feedback information collected by surveys from organizational members that is then compiled, disseminated, and used to develop action plans for improvement

sustainable competitive advantage a competitive advantage that other companies have tried unsuccessfully to duplicate and have, for the moment, stopped trying to duplicate

tactical plans plans created and implemented by middle managers that specify how the company will use resources, budgets, and people over the next six months to two years to accomplish specific goals within its mission

tariff a direct tax on imported goods

task identity the degree to which a job requires, from beginning to end, the completion of a whole and identifiable piece of work

task interdependence the extent to which collective action is required to complete an entire piece of work

task significance the degree to which a job is perceived to have a substantial impact on others inside or outside the organization

task structure the degree to which the requirements of a subordinate's tasks are clearly specified

team diversity the variances or differences in ability, experience, personality, or any other factor on a team

team leaders managers responsible for facilitating team activities toward goal accomplishment

team level the average level of ability, experience, personality, or any other factor on a team

teamwork collaboration between managers and nonmanagers, across business functions, and between companies, customers, and suppliers

technical skills the ability to apply the specialized procedures, techniques, and knowledge required to get the job done

technological discontinuity a scientific advance or unique combination of existing technologies that creates a significant breakthrough in performance or function

technological substitution the purchase of new technologies to replace older ones

technology the knowledge, tools, and techniques used to transform input into output

technology cycle a cycle that begins with the "birth" of a new technology and ends when that technology reaches its limits and is replaced by a newer, substantially better technology

televised/videotaped speeches and meetings speeches and meetings originally made to a smaller audience that are either simultaneously broadcast to other locations in the company or videotaped for subsequent distribution and viewing

temporal immediacy the time between an act and the consequences the act produces

testing the systematic comparison of different product designs or design iterations

threat of new entrants a measure of the degree to which barriers to entry make it easy or difficult for new companies to get started in an industry

threat of substitute products or services a measure of the ease with which customers can find substitutes for an industry's products or services

top managers executives responsible for the overall direction of the organization

total quality management (TQM) an integrated, principle-based, organization-wide strategy for improving product and service quality

trade barriers government-imposed regulations that increase the cost and restrict the number of imported goods

traditional work group a group composed of two or more people who work together to achieve a shared goal

training developing the skills, experience, and knowledge employees need to perform their jobs or improve their performance

trait rating scales rating scales that indicate the extent to which workers possess particular traits or characteristics

trait theory a leadership theory that holds that effective leaders possess a similar set of traits or characteristics

traits relatively stable characteristics, such as abilities, psychological motives, or consistent patterns of behavior

transactional leadership leadership based on an exchange process, in which followers are rewarded for good performance and punished for poor performance

transformational leadership leadership that generates awareness and acceptance of a group's purpose and mission and gets employees to see beyond their own needs and self-interests for the good of the group

transient firms the firms in a strategic group whose strategies are changing from one strategic position to another

transition management team (TMT) a team of 8 to 12 people whose full-time job is to completely manage and coordinate a company's change process

Type A personality a person who tries to complete as many tasks as possible in the shortest possible time and is hard driving, competitive, impatient, perfectionistic, angry, and unable to relax

Type A/B personality dimension the extent to which people tend toward impatience, hurriedness, competitiveness, and hostility

Type B personality a person who is relaxed, easygoing, and able to engage in leisure activities without worrying about work

uncertainty the extent to which managers can understand or predict which environmental changes and trends will affect their businesses

underreward when the referent you compare yourself to is getting more outcomes relative to inputs than you are

unethical charismatics charismatic leaders who control and manipulate followers, do what is best for themselves instead of their organizations, want to hear only positive feedback, share only information that is beneficial to themselves, and have moral standards that put their interests before everyone else's

unfreezing getting the people affected by change to believe that change is needed

unity of command a management principle that workers should report to just one boss

unrelated diversification creating or acquiring companies in completely unrelated businesses

unsupervised data mining user simply tells the data mining software to uncover whatever patterns and relationships it can find in a data set

upward communication communication that flows from lower to higher levels in an organization

valence the attractiveness or desirability of a reward or outcome

validation the process of determining how well a selection test or procedure predicts future job performance. The better or more accurate the prediction of future job performance, the more valid a test is said to be.

valuable resource a resource that allows companies to improve efficiency and effectiveness

value customer perception that the product quality is excellent for the price offered

variable interval reinforcement schedule an intermittent schedule in which the time between a behavior and the following consequences varies around a specified average

variable ratio reinforcement schedule an intermittent schedule in which consequences are delivered following a different number of behaviors, sometimes more and sometimes less, that vary around a specified average number of behaviors

variation a deviation in the form, condition, or appearance of a product from the quality standard for that product

virtual organization an organization that is part of a network in which many companies share skills, costs, capabilities, markets, and customers to collectively solve customer problems or provide specific products or services

virtual private network (VPN) securely encrypts data sent by employees outside the company network, decrypts the data when they arrive within the company computer network, and does the same when data are sent back to employees outside the network

virtual team a team composed of geographically and/or organizationally dispersed coworkers who use telecommunication and information technologies to accomplish an organizational task

virus a program or piece of code that, against your wishes, attaches itself to other programs on your computer and can trigger anything from a harmless flashing message to the reformatting of your hard drive to a systemwide network shutdown

visible artifacts visible signs of an organization's culture, such as the office design and layout, company dress code, and company benefits and perks, like stock options, personal parking spaces, or the private company dining room

vision an inspirational statement of an organization's enduring purpose

visionary leadership leadership that creates a positive image of the future that motivates organizational members and provides direction for future planning and goal setting

voluntary export restraints voluntarily imposed limits on the number or volume of products exported to a particular country

Web services using standardized protocols to describe data from one company in such a way that those data can automatically be read, understood, transcribed, and processed by different computer systems in another company

whistleblowing reporting others' ethics violations to management or legal authorities

wholly owned affiliates foreign offices, facilities, and manufacturing plants that are 100 percent owned by the parent company

work sample tests tests that require applicants to perform tasks that are actually done on the job

work team a small number of people with complementary skills who hold themselves mutually accountable for pursuing a common purpose, achieving performance goals, and improving interdependent work processes

worker readiness the ability and willingness to take responsibility for directing one's behavior at work

work-in-process inventories partially finished goods consisting of assembled component parts

world gross national product the value of all the goods and services produced annually worldwide

World Trade Organization (WTO) the only international organization dealing with the global rules of trade between nations. Its main function is to ensure that trade flows as smoothly, predictably, and freely as possible.

wrongful discharge a legal doctrine that requires employers to have a job-related reason to terminate employees

NAME AND ORGANIZATION INDEX

SUBJECT INDEX